# Server-Based Java Programming

# Server-Based Java Programming

TED NEWARD

MANNING

Greenwich
(74° w. long.)

For online information and ordering of this and other Manning books,
go to www.manning.com. The publisher offers discounts on this book
when ordered in quantity. For more information, please contact:

Special Sales Department
Manning Publications Co.
32 Lafayette Place                   Fax: (203) 661-9018
Greenwich, CT 06830                  email: orders@manning.com

Manning Publications Co.          Copyeditor:  Elizabeth R. Martin
32 Lafayette Place                 Typesetter:  Denis Dalinnik
Greenwich, CT 06830           Cover designer:  Leslie Haimes

Printed in the United States of America
1 2 3 4 5 6 7 8 9 10 – CM – 03 02 01 00

*"To you, the reader—yes, you. A book without a reader is a pretty pointless exercise. Thank you."*

# brief contents

# contents

# foreword

As you probably have noticed, Java has arrived. My bookstore's shelves sag under the weight of hundreds of books about the wonders of Java. Even given my full-time commitment to educating people about server-side Java development, there's no way I can read everything published on the subject.

You may feel the time pressure too, but you will be glad you made time for Ted Neward's *Server-Based Java Programming* and its fresh approach. Instead of presenting Java as a language, he begins at the true beginning: with Java as a *platform*. This is *not* a book about the new J2EE APIs; it *is* a book on the correct use of the platform features that make these APIs possible and valuable. Whether you plan to pay top dollar for a Java server product or dream of rolling your own, this is a good place to learn the right questions to ask.

The underlying theme of the book is the three zeroes goal for server-development—zero development, zero administration, and zero deployment. This is laudable, because very few software developers (and fewer authors) like to talk about administration or deployment. As a result, these aspects of products are frequently built last, and designed never. Ted also starts you on the right path for writing those first lines of code, by demonstrating how to use oft-misunderstood platform features such as ClassLoaders, Serialization, threads, and JNI.

I can't tell you this is the only book you'll ever need to develop server-side code in Java. I can tell you that very few software books surprise me, very few bring a new perspective, and very few feel different from the others. This one did.

*Stuart Halloway*
DevelopMentor

# preface

In September1999, Sun Microsystems Inc. released the first draft of the Java2 Enterprise Edition specification, and Java changed forever.

Since 1997, developers and vendors have increasingly pushed Java toward the server side of the client/server architecture map. Where its original focus was in applets and web pages, Java is now more at home on the web server or database server. Chances are, if you're a professional Java programmer, and your work environment is doing anything with Java, you're in a position to consider, if not write, Java-on-the-server.

By this point, the ubiquitous story about James Gosling and an oak tree, cable set-top boxes, and the HotJava web browser are pretty much standard fare for Java programmers. For our purposes, Java's life on the server is what's important, not what came before that.

Java's emphasis toward the server began in 1997 with the release of the 1.1 version of the Java Developer's Kit (hereafter referred to as the JDK). In JDK 1.1, Sun introduced us to JDBC, JNI, and RMI. Many vendors, such as NetDynamics, had already begun pushing Java on the server side, using home-grown proprietary connections to RDBMSs, and so forth, but the 1.1 release finally solidified access to these critical server-side resources. RMI gave us the ability to look to other JVMs, JDBC let us peek inside the RDBMS, and JNI gave us the ability to call into native code for anything that wasn't covered in the first two.

A few other technologies, of lesser hype but equal importance, also made their debut in 1.1. (It must've been a busy couple of months at Sun!) The Object Serialization specification was released as part of 1.1, but was buried along with Reflection in the JavaBeans specification and API. Granted, Serialization was also a key part of RMI, but most Java enthusiasts saw Serialization as a part of the JavaBeans specification, and not much more. Java archives, or JAR files, also came along with the 1.1 release. Unfortunately, 1.1 JARs were nothing more than a convenience for shipping plural files around—no compression support was available until the Java 2/JDK 1.2 release.

Some linguistic changes came with 1.1, as well. Inner classes, anonymous classes, and a definition for the reserved word "transient" finally came into being, partly in response to the change in the AWT event-handling mechanism. Adapter classes (whose only role is to provide an accessibility layer from one interface to another) became trivial to code using anonymous nested classes, where before, it was monotonous and error-prone.

In short, the 1.1 release did far more to establish Java on the server than any subsequent release to date. So why is all the current excitement about server-side Java centered on the Java 2/ JDK 1.2 platform?

## Java2 (a.k.a. JDK 1.2 and beyond)

When JDK 1.2 was released in early 1999, Sun renamed it Java2 release. Initially, it didn't sport too much in the way of new features—instead, it offered enhancements to the existing featureset, and sneaked in a few new tidbits of technology when people weren't looking. Predominant in this release was the bundling of Swing, a.k.a. Java Foundation Class (JFC), into the core Java run-time libraries. Beyond that, however, and the introduction of a standard Collections library similar in concept to the C++ Standard Template library, most of JDK 1.2 was one enhancement after another regarding the technologies introduced in the prior version.

Realistically, JDK 1.2 was something of an iterative release of JDK 1.1. Instead of introducing radical new technology, as 1.1 did, the 1.2 release focuses on enhancing the existing APIs to make them more reliable, robust, and secure. In a sense, the Java teams simply took another iteration on the features that came with 1.2, making them more useful, ironing out the bugs, and adding the necessary parts that were missing from 1.1.

A few other technologies that began to redefine the Java2 platform came out during the year. First and foremost was the Enterprise Java Beans specification, providing a black-box component model for the Java platform. EJB introduced an entirely new set of terminology into the market-place, all of which centered around the somewhat radical idea that a vendor could create a software framework,[1] into which I could plug my server-side application's logic and components, and it would all run seamlessly. This holds two interesting premises: one, that I don't have to code some of the more generic functionality common to all servers, and two, that these "application servers" can provide additional value-added behavior that I may not otherwise code into my application, such as load-balancing, clustering, or fault-tolerance.

Other technologies came along, as well. The Servlet specification, released in 1998, describes a standard API for writing Java code that is executed upon HTTP request. The Java Naming and Directory Interface, (JNDI), provides a single API layer on top of different directory and/or nam-ing services, such as LDAP, CORBA Naming Services, the RMI Registry, even the file system on your hard drive. The Java Transaction Service and Java Transaction API provide support similar to that found within conventional RDBMS systems.

What wasn't apparent initially was Sun's intention, over the course of 1999, to release three separate versions of Java:

- *Java2 Standard Edition*
  This is the JDK we all know and love—all the java.* packages, the Swing and AWT APIs for GUI interaction, and so on. If you're a Java programmer, this is the version with which you're familiar and comfortable.

---

[1]  In the sense of a series of services available at run time from an opaque system.

- *Java2 Micro Edition*

  This is Java-for-the-embedded-device. PDAs, cellular phones, control systems mounted on heavy machinery, even the ubiquitous Java Ring from JavaOne a few years back, all would now fall under the J2ME specification. In many ways, this is where Java was originally intended to live—on embedded CPUs and hardware, using the JVM as an insulation layer to permit portability between embedded systems. This book will cover nothing of the J2ME specification or details.

- *Java2 Enterprise Edition*

  This is, from the server-developer's point of view, the most exciting thing to take place since the "invention" of the Internet. At the time of this writing, J2EE was still in beta, undergoing specification review and editing, but if J2EE's promise holds true, server-side development may take on a whole new dimension.

These three editions of Java pretty much run the gamut—from microdevices through high-end server systems. Sun's promise of "Write Once, Run Anywhere" seems ripe for the harvest.

Unfortunately, the promise is something of a misleading marketing ploy. There are aspects of the Java environment in which your code runs that will have an effect on how well your code executes, or whether it even executes. Issues such as the JVM's actual threading model, the ClassLoader partitioning used within the application server, or the JNI support within the system will all trip you up if you're not aware of them and aware of what they mean.

That's where this book comes in.

# acknowledgments

Many authors will tell you that they couldn't have written their book by themselves, and that there are far too many people to thank to list on an acknowledgments page. No truer words have ever been penned. A work such as this cannot be accomplished by one person working alone; to even attempt such a task would be the utmost folly.

A variety of people contributed to the creation and polishing of this manuscript, and to try to thank them all would take half of my allotted pages. This isn't to say I shouldn't try, only that it's nearly impossible to accomplish the goal.

To begin, I again wish to thank the folks at Manning Publications Co. for their patience and faith in me as an author. It's flattering to have a publisher approach you to do a book—it's doubly so to have them do it again. Marjan Bace, Denis Dalinnik, Syd Brown, Mary Piergies, and Elizabeth Martin are some of the best folks in the industry with which to work. Thanks too to Ted Kennedy for coordinating the technical reviews of this book. The entire staff demonstrated a wonderful willingness to bend over backward to deal with an exacting author and meet the often-conflicting goals of producing the book, and getting it right.

Of course, no author in his right mind ever attempts a book alone, and the reviewers for this book were invaluable in their comments and criticisms: Adam Smith, Bruce Arbuckle, Chandra Sekhar, Chris Pratt, Curt Powell, David Williams, Jim Graham, Kito D. Mann, Robert Lynch, Shawn Echols, Stephane Trouche, Thomas Kuehne, and Tim Leist.

In addition, I need to thank my fellow DM instructors, for their awesome contributions, simply by standing still long enough for all of us to "talk Java": Stu Halloway, Brian Maso, Brad Needham, Kevin Jones, Owen Tallman, Tim Ewald, Keith Brown and, of course, the often-imitated, never-duplicated Don Box. My appreciation of Java (and COM, XML, and just about anything else in the industry) is so much deeper, thanks to their insights.

I also wish to thank the people with whom I've worked during the development of this book, most notably the folks at Dorado Software, in El Dorado Hills, California. Many of my ideas, originally bounced off them, grew into whole segments in this book. The same goes to the folks at EdFund, in Rancho Cordova, California, where many of the principles of this book were put into place, with their blessing and encouragement.

Every author who's ever written an acknowledgments section has also thanked his parents, and I'm no exception. A more loving, supportive, wonderful couple simply doesn't exist on this planet. Mom, Dad, all that I am, I am because you taught me to be this way.

I must thank my own family: Michael, who surrendered too many nights of Nintendo with Dad, so that I could work; Matthew, whose birth firmly reminded me of what's *really* important; and most of all, Charlotte, who understood what writing another book meant, and gave me her blessing, despite expecting our second child just a month before the book's manuscript was due. Other authors may claim it, but *my* wife is the most supportive, loving, *wonderful* woman in the world. Without her, I would be lost.

Now, if you'll excuse me, I have some Nintendo to catch up on.

# about this book

With a book like this, there are bound to be a few questions the reader has before beginning. This segment will explain what each chapter covers and attempt to answer questions that I think the hypothetical reader might ask.

## The ideal "three zeroes"?

There is an ancient (perhaps misattributed) Indian proverb that states, "If you aim your arrow at the sun, you will not reach it. But your arrow will climb higher and go farther than the arrow aimed at the ground." In this book, I aim for three potentially unreachable goals:

- Zero Development—the idea that we can develop new features or additions without requiring any additional programming,
- Zero Deployment—the idea that we can make those changes available to clients in an entirely invisible fashion, and
- Zero Administration—the idea that systems can run automatically without human intervention.

These are obviously lofty goals, perhaps worthy of ridicule. But examine any network administration system, ask any system administrator, talk to any application developer, and you'll find that these are the very goals we work toward in our software. Object-oriented programming (and before it, modular decomposition) posited the idea of "Tinkertoy software," and still does. Web applications aim squarely at the zero deployment arena—the only client-side piece the client needs is a web browser. And SNMP, DMTF, and a host of other acronyms are all about making the network easier to administer. So why not try to fold these concepts in at the beginning of the project, instead of shoehorning them in at the end?

## What does this book cover?

Chapter 1 focuses on enterprise Java, using Java to develop applications for the corporate enterprise—that is, software that's not intended to be sold as shrink-wrapped off-the-shelf software, but custom-developed for in-house use. To understand Java's applicability in enterprise development, I first have to explain what I mean by that term; then I can talk about zero development, zero deployment, and zero administration.

ClassLoaders, which play a significant role toward meeting zero deployment, are covered in chapter 2. We examine the basic nature of ClassLoaders, and how they can be used to update code on the fly within a running server.

With the background and understanding of ClassLoaders, in chapter 3 we investigate how far we can go with them. We go so far as to introduce ClassLoaders that can build code at run time for execution within the same JVM.

The Java 2 extension mechanism provides golden opportunities for the three zeroes. Extensions, covered in chapter 4, can be written to pull code from other locations when requested (zero deployment). Extensions are also the fundamental reusable code-library component (zero development), and are trivial to install within a user's Java run-time environment (zero administration).

Chapter 5 covers threads, which provide an important part of the server architecture, because of their concurrency capabilities as well as performance benefits. While they may not inherently contribute to the three zeroes, many of the techniques described in this book would be nearly impossible without threads.

Chapter 6 helps the reader through the pitfalls of using threads. The Java developer who doesn't understand those issues runs serious risks of thread starvation, deadlock, or worse.

Creation of a generic server framework requires a consistent generic server control mechanism. A generic control mechanism, explained in chapter 7, provides both zero development and zero administrative benefits.

Control of an application (or application server) isn't always about being able to administer the application directly from the machine on which it sits. Too often, developers and administrators make mistakes that cost the corporate data center valuable up time, when those mistakes could be prevented by accessing and controlling the application remotely, the subject of chapter 8.

Chapter 9 shows you how to configure an application on the fly without bringing it down, and how to deal with setting or tuning parameters during the lifetime of the application.

In chapter 10, we discuss the ubiquitous TCP/IP socket framework, and Java's excellent support for it. We start by implementing simple services, then pursue zero development by factoring out common code and building a generic multithreaded ConnectionService to handle any and all socket communication. As proof, we build an HTTPConnection service. In pursuit of zero deployment, we build a SocketClassService and corresponding SocketClassLoader, to serve as server and client (respectively) for loading classes over a network.

Chapter 11 focuses on servlets, which represent an easy replacement for CGI scripts and serve as the fundamental heart of the JSP technology.

Chapter 12 covers Serialization and JDBC. Serialization can play an important role on the server, not only as a means by which objects can be stored, but as a means by which objects can be exchanged between processes. In addition, we look at how we can use Serialization to provide both remote storage and remote object construction facilities. JDBC plays a key role in the development of server applications, since most corporations and companies currently store their data inside of an RDBMS. Here, we discuss how to use the RDBMS to pursue zero deployment, as well as some of the new features of JDBC 2.0.

In chapter 13, we pursue zero development by creating a well-encapsulated, cleanly defined object model on top of enterprise systems. We set up a running example for the next several chapters by implementing a Business Object Interface layer representing a corporate employee-tracking system. Because the actual implementation is hidden from clients, applications can be written without needing to know the details of where or how data are stored, making it easier for developers to modify, enhance, or even completely replace the underlying data-storage layer(s). Two such applications are demonstrated.

Once we've built the Business Object layer, we need implementation to back it. In chapter 14, I present two such possibilities—one using an in-memory collection of Hashtables to store the objects, the other using the ubiquitous RDBMS. We discuss the particular "quirks" of each, and demonstrate how those quirks can be resolved without invalidating the *n*-tier approach in general.

Building object models that live entirely on one machine is not enough. Objects need to be accessible from other workstations and systems across the network. In chapter 15, we examine the various ways of making our EmployeeModel business object system distributed, using plain sockets, RMI (both RMI/JRMP and RMI/IIOP), CORBA, JMS, JSDT, and even mobile objects and Microsoft's DCOM. We discuss the advantages and drawbacks of each, and build two implementations as examples.

Chapter 16 looks at Java's unique properties allowing it to call—and be called by—native C/C++ code. This in turn offers opportunities for not only code, but entire system reuse. Why tear down an existing system and rebuild it from scratch, when Java classes can directly access and call the system in its native form?

Server applications don't exist within a vacuum; people are interested in the details of their execution, ranging from the most basic of "Is it still running?" to more complex "How well is it working?" statistics. In chapter 17, we build a generic HeartbeatService to allow interested parties to know when the associated Service goes down.

### Aren't some topics ignored?

Yes, specifically, EJB and Java's Security model. We talk briefly about CORBA and RMI in the chapter on middleware, but it is not intended as a tutorial. I don't cover servlets except in conceptual discussions. (For a thorough discussion of servlets, I recommend Alan Williamson's *Java Servlets By Example* from Manning Publications Co., or Jason Hunter's *Java Servlet Programming* from O'Reilly.)

### Why isn't this a book on EJB?

Because we, as an industry, don't know enough about EJB's usefulness to write about it.

EJB, as a technology, has only been available as a standard since the middle of 1998; most vendor implementations have been out for a year or so, at the time of this writing. So what is there to write about other than the specification itself? Remember, it took us no less than three years of using Java to determine that its greatest application was not applets.

### Why isn't this a book on CORBA or RMI?

Because there's more to server-side development than just distributed systems.

Not all systems require distributed objects. In fact, I've seen a couple of systems that might have performed better had they *not* been designed with distribution as a core concept. Any time a system starts strewing objects across the network, performance takes a hit—why introduce that latency if it's not necessary?

Don't misunderstand—I love distributed objects. But it's also true that a number of server-side applications never have to leave the server for any reason. In many cases, it is certainly possible to design a distributed object system to do the same thing, but would anything concrete be gained by it? Naturally, it depends on the actual application and its need to interact with the "outside world" (that is, anything not on the box in which it lives). But it's also possible to build distributed object systems that have nothing to do with RMI or CORBA; these technologies (along with DCOM, for that matter) simply make it easier to do distributed objects.

### Why isn't this a book on security?

There simply isn't room in one book to talk about the wide and deep implications opened up by security. Security in an enterprise application can range from the ubiquitous Username/Password dialog at the start of every application, through SSL sockets to send digitally encrypted information from client to server, to a full-blown government-secure system with widely varying user roles, authentication tokens, and access control lists. What's more, I don't consider myself any kind of security expert. We will discuss security in the context of enterprise applications. For a detailed discussion of the Java 2 security model, or Java cryptography extensions, or even digital signatures in applets, I recommend Li Gong's *Inside Java2 Platform Security* from Addison-Wesley.

### What do I need to know to read this?

You need to know Java, obviously.

Specifically, you need to be comfortable with the technologies found in the Java2 Standard Edition. This is not an entry-level text. I presume that you, the reader, are familiar with Java and its corresponding introductory topics. This book is about using Java to write server-oriented applications—I have to assume you "know" Java.

This also assumes that you have a rudimentary understanding of some of the basic concepts of the technologies Java encompasses—sockets, SQL, RMI/CORBA/some-other-connectivity-tool, and so on. You should have an understanding of how sockets work in Java, how SQL is written, as well as the basic concept of RMI programming. If those concepts are a mystery to you, the chapters on those topics won't help you much. I am not suggesting that you put the book back or take it back for a refund—it just means the concepts may not sink in as quickly.

### Why is this book on ClassLoaders, Threads, Sockets?

Another way to phrase this is, "Why do I need to learn about ClassLoaders, Threads, or Sockets instead of EJB?" The answer is in the form of an analogy: not all server applications will require an EJB server; not all server applications will require servlets, or RMI, or even a relational database. To use such technologies would be overkill, and would require far more work than actually necessary—think of how comfortable you'd feel if the carpenter you've hired to build an add-on to the garage showed up with dynamite and a blueprint for rebuilding your entire street.

By focusing on ClassLoaders, Threads, Sockets, and so on—as well as other technologies, such as RMI or CORBA, I'm trying to show how Java works to solve server-side problems at all levels: from the small-scale simple distributed application (did you know you can do dynamic code download without RMI?) to the enterprise-wide *n*-tier system based on CORBA or EJB.

### Why is all the code written for Java 2 (JDK 1.2)?

Around early 1999, Sun released JDK 1.2, which the company referred to as the Java 2 platform. Despite Sun's best efforts, there are some marked differences between JDK 1.1 and JDK 1.2, which I felt necessitated a conscious decision to target this book at one or the other. Granted, 99 percent of the book is applicable to both platforms. However, understanding the differences between them, the problems that will arise when porting code from JDK 1.1 to JDK 1.2, will be an issue for many Java developers over the next year.

The code for all samples and applications was developed using the Windows release of JDK 1.2 (and later minor-version upgrades) from Sun, using nothing more sophisticated as an IDE than a text editor and a makefile. None of the code, except where specifically mentioned, was tested for JDK 1.1 or 1.0.

It's my belief that, in time, more and more JDK 1.1 code will be brought over to Java 2. As a result, this book spends little time as possible on JDK 1.1-specific code, concepts, or discussion.[2]

### Why the constant reference to "patterns"?

I believe that design patterns (the concept) are becoming critical to design discussions and literature. In a study of heavy patterns usage by four corporations, James O. Coplien of AT&T found that one of the major benefits of the patterns groups is a common vocabulary for design discussions and architectural sessions.

I use the patterns from *Design Patterns* in much the same way—within the text, I will point out how "X is a classic Singleton pattern," or that "this design is a slight variation on the Decorator pattern," and so on. In this manner, I'm using the shared vocabulary of the design pattern to communicate not just the static class hierarchy one can expect, but also the run-time behavior and consequences and implications of this design. I can communicate an entire aspect about a design by saying, "Z behaves as an Abstract Factory" that would otherwise take up entire pages.

If you're not familiar with patterns, a good place to start is the "Gang Of Four" book (*Design Patterns*, by Gamma et al, from Addison-Wesley), or visit Brad Appleton's introduction to patterns, available at http://www.enteract.com/~bradapp/docs/patterns-intro.html. Ideally, both should be read, but either one gives a good background on the patterns concept, and provides working knowledge of the patterns described within this book.

### What code conventions are used in this book?

This book uses some conventions to bring important messages to the reader's attention or hammer home a certain point.

Command line examples, sample output, and code listings are set in a fixed-pitch font. Filenames, new words, and emphasized words are italicized.

---

[2]  With the release of the JDK 1.3 in May, this will only heighten the move over to the Java 2 platform.

In the code comments, the "/**" and "*/" pairs are javadoc comments; "//" comments are "implementation" comments.

While not exactly a convention, much of the code in this book is presented incrementally and in accordance with changing needs and/or requirements. In other words, the code is presented initially and a section or a chapter later, it may be changed to demonstrate how most server development takes place. This ripple effect will show how this modification affects the rest of the system.

### Source code downloads, extensions, and errata

The source code for all of the examples presented in this book is available from both the publisher's website (www.manning.com/neward3) and my own website (www.javageeks.com). I encourage you to send me your comments, opinions and (sigh) bug reports by email to tneward@manning.com or tneward@javageeks.com. I will certainly do my best to respond to as many comments as reasonable and possible. What's more, I'd like for the book to continue its development as the Java platform continues to change and mature, initially by posting white papers and/or corrections/errata on both the publisher's website (www.manning.com/Neward3), as well as my own (www.javageeks.com/SBJP).

# *goals of this book*

By the end of this book, you should be able to write an application server, complete with every feature you could possibly want out of a commercial application server system.

I have four goals for you:

- *Understand some of the basic concepts that go into an application server.*
  Application servers aren't just about new technologies. Java is built on solid foundations, and understanding those foundations and how they're used inside an application server will give you a solid background for understanding what an application server can—and can't—do for you.

- *Be able to incorporate some of those concepts into your own code.*
  Not everyone is going to use an application server for the code. In some cases, corporations won't want to pay what application server vendors are asking. In other cases, the project may be simply a proof of concept, with an emphasis on keeping costs low in case the proof fails. In still other cases, the application system simply may want to incorporate only a few of the features of a commercial application server.

- *Use the code that comes with the book in your own systems.*
  The code in this book is a simple example of how these concepts can fit within your own systems. Most of the code is good enough to act as a starting point for developing code that best fits your own needs. Many of the examples and code samples are contrived to better highlight my point. Feel free to rip out the parts of the sample code you don't need, or add the parts you do.

- *Prepare you for the coming changes in server development.*
  The release of the J2EE specification changes some of the rules. Understanding the new rules, the reasons for them, and what it all means is important if you want to remain sharp as a Java developer.

This book isn't the answer to all of your questions, but by the end of it, you should at least have a good idea of what questions to ask, if not how to answer them.

# *about the author*

I've been a software developer, in the loosest sense of the term, since our family purchased its first computer, an Apple II+, with a whopping 48K of RAM (which we soon upgraded to the flat-out maximum of 64K) back in 1978. I've written code in Applesoft BASIC, Apple 65C02 Assembler, and even a few Logo programs, just for kicks. I think my parents still have that old machine, gathering dust somewhere in the basement but just too full of memories to simply throw away.

More recently, however, I've been a software architect, first in C++, then in Java, working in the Sacramento area for the past five years or so. I've worked for firms such as Intuit, makers of the Quicken personal finance software package, and large corporations like Pacific Bell. I've seen development teams of all sizes, shapes, and methodologies (or lack thereof), using both Java and C++, building software ranging from consumer applications such as Quicken to development systems built in 100 percent pure Java to enterprise systems rolled out across the state.

I am an independent software consultant/contractor in the Sacramento, California, area. I am also an instructor with DevelopMentor, teaching Java and RMI to anyone who'll listen. When not teaching classes, or writing books, I enjoy spending time with my wife, Charlotte, and our two sons, Michael (age 6) and Matthew (age 8 months).

Readers often express an interest in the actual environment and hardware/software in use by an author when developing the text, code, or both, of a book. This text was written on a Compaq Presario 1810 laptop using Microsoft Word 97 as the word-processing program, and Adobe's Acrobat PDFWriter print driver to prepare drafts for reviewer perusal. Code was developed using a text editor, the command-line, and Sun's Java Development Kit 1.2 (and later, 1.2.1 and 1.2.2) on both the aforementioned laptop running Microsoft Windows98 as well as on a home-built PentiumII-350 workstation running Microsoft WindowsNT4.0 Service Pack 5. Portions of the code were also tested on a Pentium-90 RedHat 5.2 Linux server, running the Blackdown.org Linux port of Java 1.2 (prerelease 2).

# *about the cover illustration*

The cover illustration of this book is from the 1805 edition of Sylvain Maréchal's four-volume compendium of regional dress customs. This book was first published in Paris in 1788, one year before the French Revolution. Its title alone required no fewer than 30 words.

> *Costumes Civils actuels de tous les peuples connus dessinés d'après nature gravés et coloriés, accompagnés d'une notice historique sur leurs coutumes, moeurs, religions, etc., etc., redigés par M. Sylvain Maréchal*

The four volumes include an annotation on the illustrations: "gravé à manière noire par Mixelle d'après Desrais et colorié." Clearly, the engraver and illustrator deserved no more than to be listed by their last names—after all they were mere technicians. The workers who colored each illustration by hand remain nameless.

The colorful variety of this collection reminds us vividly of how culturally apart the world's towns and regions were just 200 years ago. Dress codes have changed everywhere and the diversity by region, so rich at the time, has faded away. It is now hard to tell the inhabitant of one continent from another. Perhaps we have traded cultural diversity for a more varied personal life—certainly a more varied and exciting technological environment. At a time when it is hard to tell one computer book from another, Manning celebrates the inventiveness and initiative of the computer business with book covers based on the rich diversity of regional life of two centuries ago, brought back to life by Maréchal's pictures. Just think, Maréchal's was a world so different from ours people would take the time to read a book title 30 words long.

**C H A P T E R   1**

# Enterprise Java

Java is ready for prime-time in the enterprise development arena. Before we can dive into reams and reams of code, concepts, ideas, and explanations, we need to establish a common lexicon, defining what I mean by enterprise development and the three zeroes. Next, we'll briefly cover Sun's perspective on what Java as an enterprise development language (and platform) means, and what alternatives exist. Last, I'll jump on the soapbox and talk about the features of Java that make it ideal for the enterprise.

## 1.1   ENTERPRISE DEVELOPMENT

When an organization, from the largest corporation to the smallest church or school, decides to acquire a software system to do *X*, it makes that decision because it has a need. That need might be to make products available to customers who might not otherwise know about them, to make data available to its internal employees in a logical, consistent manner, or to be able to perform analysis on the organization's past history and attempt to predict the future by that analysis. The need itself is unimportant—but the fact that the organization has decided it wants to use some combination of computer hardware and software is pertinent.

### 1.1.1   What is enterprise development?

Enterprise development (ED) is any application, set of applications, utility, set of utilities, or systems and/or infrastructure developed for use by a particular company, corporation, or collection of users. Enterprise applications can take many shapes and forms, and can span different, and sometimes divergent, technologies. Relational databases, legacy systems, the internal web server, even individual Microsoft Access databases sitting on users' desktops, are all part of the back-end of the enterprise development arena.

ED is different from other forms of development (such as commercial product development), in that:

- *ED applications are able to make better assumptions.*
  If the application is for internal use, then we have a better idea of not only the end user's desktop computers and attached equipment, but also the average technical level of the end users themselves. Because of this, we can tailor the application to better adjust for our users' particular needs. If the application is for traveling salesmen using the Internet to access our inventory warehouse then we write the application knowing that bandwidth is a critical concern. If the application is for users sitting in four separate locations in three different time zones, then we know already that time synchronization ("If we use a time stamp, whose time zone do we use?") will be an issue. If the application is a help-desk-ticket-management type, then we can assume the users have a certain level of technical sophistication.

- *ED applications are typically internal.*
  Most often, enterprise applications are executed on the inside of a corporate firewall; issues common to Internet applications, such as line-security (necessitating the need for secured sockets and signed certificates), are less of a concern here, because it can be assumed that the users are known to the company and are authorized to use the application. This doesn't remove a need for a certain measure of security within the application, but at least we no longer have to worry about hackers sniffing the packets between the servers and the clients. This has a number of related sub points.

  - *ED users are typically close by.*
    When the target users for the application are internal to the corporation, often the actual users are within close physical proximity. Even if the application is destined for a user group two continents and an ocean away, because the corporation typically doesn't restrict communications between its departments, the end user of the application is just a phone call, email, or fax away. This means users can be pinged directly for feedback on the application, to ensure that the application is, in fact, what they need to solve their problem. Unfortunately, this is a two-edged sword—closer proximity can often mean more interference if this is not managed properly. It can also mean greater changes in the application's functionality and user interface.

  - *ED applications are typically shorter-cycled.*
    Because of the closer proximity of the users, which fuels greater feedback than commercial developers see, ED applications will typically undergo several

revisions in the same period that a commercial application undergoes a single release. This is often referred to as taking an iterative approach during the project's development.

- *ED applications often get less QA time.*
  When applications are written for internal use only, there seems to be a greater willingness to release without doing a full test cycle. This means developers need to be more cognizant of the fact that they're flying without a parachute, and need to code accordingly.

- *ED applications cannot assume end-user responsibility.*
  Within the average corporation, the end users are not responsible for the installation and maintenance of their desktop computers; instead, that responsibility falls upon the information technology group, typically the system administrator or help desk section. In some cases, this means that every new release of an enterprise application requires an IT technician to physically walk around to each and every user's machine, install the application (either via the internal network or SneakerNet), and verify the installation was successful.

- *ED applications must be more user reactive.*
  If the end user has a problem, the call goes to the internal help desk, or sometimes to the developers directly. Under no circumstances can the corporation's developers get away with taking the user's name and number, and offering to call back later. Such behavior will typically get escalated to whatever corporate officer needs to hear it to get the problem fixed. Instead, developers must jump onto every bug and determine what the problem is. Commercial vendors have more of an insulating layer between them and the users, thus offering a bit more of a cushion regarding immediate bug fixes.[1]

- *ED applications typically require some degree of expert administration.*
  Enterprise applications, unlike commercial applications, don't stand by themselves. Typically, the enterprise application has a degree of administration that accompanies it, even if that administration is limited to user-security management (adding users, removing users, and so forth). Who does that administration, is, for purposes of this discussion, irrelevant.

- *ED applications must work within the existing architecture.*
  After the corporation has sunk major money into an infrastructure is *not* the time for developers to be approaching the boss with suggestions about doing the next application in "<insert-the-latest-technology-here>." The same is true of introducing new tools into the administrative arena—systems administrators (also referred to as system administrators) will not be happy if developers continue to throw new tools and/or servers at them with each new enterprise application.

---

[1] This is not to say that commercial software developers aren't, or shouldn't be, responsive to users. An acceptable 1-day turnaround for commercial help-desk responses is *never* acceptable inside the corporation.

Each new tool or system represents not only another step on the learning curve, but an additional point-of-failure within the corporation's infrastructure.

All of these items are pros and cons. Each provides its own unique challenges that must be met and mastered by the corporation's developers, or disaster awaits. Fortunately, Java's strengths can be leveraged, through the use of commercial application servers as well as through the techniques described in this book, to solve many of these problems.

## 1.1.2 Developing the enterprise application

Once the decision is made to develop the application, the organization next has another choice: whether to construct the software from scratch using in-house or contracted software development professionals, or to purchase an off-the-shelf system or suite of tools to solve the need. This is commonly referred to as the buy-versus-build decision, and can, depending on the size of the proposed project, be made in fleeting seconds or over a course of months.

I bring this decision to the forefront of the reader's awareness because this book, by its very nature, partly assumes that the decision being made is to build, as opposed to buy. I say partly, because learning this information serves two distinct purposes:

- *Not all applications require a full-fledged application server.*
  Some may be small-scale systems that are intended for low-end systems—running a full application server would be overkill and consume far too much in the way of resources. Some may be systems targeted for embedded systems,[2] and trying to run a full application server would simply tax the embedded device's JVM to the limits. By learning the techniques and technologies described herein, you can build your own miniapplication servers that provide much of the same functionality at half the cost.

- *Understand the application server's environment.*
  Even if your application does make full use of the J2EE model, understanding what's happening under the hood can be critical to understanding why your application behaves as it does. Without that knowledge, many of the restrictions and requirements of the J2EE model (such as the restrictions within the EJB or Servlet API specifications) will simply make no sense. Restrictions that make no sense in turn cause developers to start looking for ways to code around the restriction. This in turn can cause huge problems down the road as the application is deployed, and performs poorly—or worse, simply fails entirely. Understanding what's happening in the scaffolding around your application is a huge bonus for J2EE application developers.

---

[2] Sun has also released the "Java2 Micro Edition," targeting small systems like hand-held PDAs and cellular phones; there is no reason to believe that J2ME won't migrate over to embedded systems on larger machinery.

Building enterprise software offers the advantages of control, knowledge, and domain familiarity.

## Control

No off-the-shelf product will ever do everything an organization wants because vendors want to remain as generic as possible, in order to remain appealing to a broader range of potential customers, and organizations are demanding more and more domain-specific tasks of software and software systems.

The response time of the average vendor-to-customer demands drives a large portion of this. If a customer finds a bug within a system, and reports it, it can be up to six months before a new version is released correcting the bug. In some cases, a vendor will make a patch available to the customer to correct the immediate flaw, but that in turn offers up versioning issues for the vendor. When the customer calls the next time, with another problem, how can the vendor's technical support staff know what version the customer is using? Is this bug due to the patch, or is it something else? This leads to heartache on both sides of the relationship; the customer becomes angry at the vendor's lack of concern for the customer's needs, and the vendor grows frustrated with the incessant demands from its customer base.

As if that weren't enough, customers' needs change as time and the business cycle move forward. Vendors are flooded with feature requests and enhancement proposals. Good capitalism demands that the vendor move immediately on those features or enhancements that are demanded by many customers. However, no vendor will be able to respond to *all* feature or enhancement requests, if only because it makes no business sense to spend $100,000 to develop a feature for a customer paying $495 (or $5,000) for the next product version. This is scant comfort to the business that *needs* that feature in order to move forward with its plan to capture the entire market.

By building the software within the corporate boundaries, bugs can be fixed immediately and new features or enhancement requests can be implemented at the desire of the organization's IT management staff. As with most software development vendors, no IT staff is so large or well-staffed as to be able to handle all feature requests; however, this time, it is the organization's management that is making the need-versus-want decisions, and not an outside party with a different agenda.

The Open Source movement makes tremendous strides along these lines—in theory. Since you have full access to the source, you can simply jump into the code, make the change, and move forward. If your organization is a real supporter of the Open Source movement, you'll even make your change(s) available back to the community. Unfortunately, this model fails on a few points:

- *You must understand the source.*
  Few corporate enterprise developers have the time to fully comprehend the software they're maintaining, much less an entirely new system that's outside the corporate domain. To tell your boss that you need six months to dive into the Open

Source project's source base just to understand where to make your feature enhancement is not going to make you popular.

- *You must have a certain level of skill to understand the source.*
  Unfortunately, not everyone on the corporate development team is of a skill level to even be able to dive into the Open Source project's source base. Certainly, with enough time, the most energetic newbie could do it—but does the corporation have the time to spare?

- *Open Source projects are noncorporate entities.*
  Bluntly put, you can't throw corporate weight around when dealing with an Open Source project group. Because there's no contract, no monetary exchange, there's no leverage for the corporation to use when the Open Source project fails in some manner. With a corporate product, the corporation can take the vendor to court, if necessary, to obtain the support it needs. No such mechanism exists for corporations to use against Open Source projects.

- *Open Source projects aren't customer-centric; they're developer-centric.*
  Eric Raymond, in his online work "From a Cathedral to a Bazaar," states it best— Open Source projects are created because "the developer has an itch." Open Source projects aren't done for the benefit of the customer, they're created for the benefit of the programmers. In each and every case, a developer saw a need and began work on it. If a feature request came in from outside the project, it gets implemented only if a developer on the project feels like doing it; otherwise, it's left for someone else to pick up. Unfortunately, that goes for documentation, as well.

Open Source projects are most definitely a useful resource from which we as developers can draw.

### Knowledge

Software development is possibly the most complex act of creation mankind has yet attempted. Building bridges and vehicles is a relatively straightforward science: the laws of physics are immutable. Even the most sophisticated combat aircraft has only 70,000 or so moving parts. A software project, on the other hand, can contain up to several million executable lines of code, all of which can affect one another. As developers build the software, they learn lessons about the nature of software development, which in turn makes them more efficient and effective for the next project. Experience remains the best teacher.

### Domain familiarity

No one better understands the organization's needs than the organization. No one better understands the organization's process and practices than the organization. While software technologists may be able to describe how their software technology can solve some of the organization's needs or problems, only the organization's members can know the unique business rules and logic the organization applies to its data. The organization's IT staff may be able to adapt the vendor-built systems to the organization's needs, but it will always remain that—a system adapted to the organization's needs, and not one grown from within the organization, with the organization's processes and business logic understood from the beginning.

### Disadvantages

Unfortunately, building software within the organization carries with it three major disadvantages, which are typically the points on which a vendor will focus when marketing a product:

- *Time*
  To develop software takes time, no matter how many people or resources are thrown at the project. Analysis must be performed, design must be created, code must be written, the system must be tested, and the administrators must install it when finished. For an organization that wishes to implement its project immediately, this sort of delay can be unacceptable.
- *Money*
  To develop software also takes money, either through contracting the project out to a third-party development house, or through hiring to build the project on-site. Either way, for nontrivial projects, this can represent thousands, if not millions, of dollars the organization may not be able to afford. This also doesn't include the costs of the resources the developers will need, such as computer systems, software tools, office space, and so on.
- *Expertise*
  Building software itself is hard, but building software with advanced features such as scalability, fault-tolerance, or automated failover support can be like attempting to scale Mount Everest wearing only shorts, sandals, and sunscreen. Vendors have had years to perfect their performance-tuned software; in-house developers will often be lucky if they get a full month to test the software before it ships to the rest of the organization.

Therefore, the goal of the organization driven to build enterprise software is to minimize these three costs of custom software development.

### 1.1.3    Reinventing the wheel

I am not advocating that developers reinvent the wheel for each enterprise application. I'm an avid advocate of reusability wherever and whenever possible. Buying off-the-shelf software, including application servers, is one of the best forms of reuse and is certainly cost effective. Unfortunately, as with all other things in this industry, the buy decision comes with its own costs and consequences.

Does that mean that this book is useless to you if your company decides to buy the application server, rather than build some of the application server's functionality into the custom-developed enterprise application? Of course not.

This book offers you several advantages in working with commercial (or Open Source) application servers or engines:

- *Greater familiarity with the concepts.*
Application servers have a number of areas within which they're going to need to work, and these are discussed within these pages. ClassLoaders, for example, constitute an area that every application server will need to consider—and such decision is one that could easily affect the way your application, or the administration of your application, behaves.

- *Gain the ability to provide the features not provided by the app server.*
Suppose you are working on developing servlets for your corporate data center, which aspires to the five-nines concept, but the servlet engine you use requires the servlet engine to come down in order to reload a new servlet. Your system administrators are not going to be happy about accepting a fixed overhead of down time—even a few seconds—each time a new release is sent to them. Instead, use what you'll learn in chapters two and three to build your servlet to load code into individual ClassLoaders on each servlet request, and automatically pick up changes in code without restarting the servlet engine. It's a win-win: the system administrators are able to preserve the precious seconds lost during the servlet-engine cycling, and you get to release new code as necessary to keep the users happy.

- *Gain the ability to work around vendor defects.*
Once I was working for a company using a major vendor's EJB product. We discovered, after many late nights of debugging and code disassembly, that the vendor failed to implement the new ClassLoader relationship introduced in Java2. We eventually had to code around it. Without a good understanding of how ClassLoaders worked in Java2, we'd have been at it for much, much longer.

- *Gain the ability (within Open Source projects) to understand the internals.*
Understanding these concepts is even more critical for those developers tasked with the responsibility for the maintenance of the corporation's adopted Open Source projects. In some cases, some of the code within this book will help enhance the Open Source project directly, providing for features not already present.

## 1.2 THREE ZEROES

IT administrators and data-center directors often speak of five-nines when talking about server availability; in that, they mean that the servers (and the data they serve to the enterprise) are up and running 99.999 percent of the time. Computed out, that means those servers are down a total of about five minutes per *year*.[3] It's an ambitious goal, and any IT organization that achieves it should be justifiably proud.

---

[3] 31,536,000 seconds/year * .00001 = 315.36000, or about five minutes per year.

However, as with most goals of this nature, even that's not the ideal; the ideal, of course, is 100 percent up-time. And although 100 percent up-time (that is, servers are never down for maintenance, fault-correction, or upgrade) may be an impossible goal, the mere act of pursuing an impossible goal brings seekers closer to it than they could be without it.

Which brings me to my proposal of a new standard for enterprise software developers: three zeroes.

### 1.2.1　Zero development

Zero development, taken literally, is an oxymoron—how can you develop something without spending any time developing it? Within this book, however, I use it to refer to reusable code and/or components; it means that it costs nothing to make changes or add features to software or systems, either as upgrades to existing systems, as feature requests by users, or as new code for new systems. By this, I mean that it costs developers nothing, not that no time is spent. Consider this example: before the commercial product called Crystal Reports was available on the market, reports on the data within the corporate database had to be coded, tested, released, and maintained by developers. With the advent of the ad hoc query/reporting tool market, users could now create their own reports, run them, view the results, and modify the reports as necessary, without requiring developer time or assistance.[4]

Of course, if you believe the marketing hype splashed across the industry trade magazines, there are tools on the market to do this for you—cut your development costs to zero, or five minutes, or a few wizard-driven screens, or whatever. Unfortunately, there's usually a hidden cost to this sort of Tinkertoy software construction—the inability to extend the software beyond what the tool developers conceived, or the inability to call down to native OS APIs, and so on. Rapid application development (RAD) tools are useful to do the things for which they were designed; it's when the users want to do that extra something that the RAD tools demonstrate their inability to be flexible. With power, comes complexity. With complexity, comes power. Remove the complexity, and you remove power.

This book isn't about creating magical solutions; this book is about building software. As I will be saying over and over again throughout the book, software development (in fact, all of computer science) is about trade-offs: size against speed, power against simplicity, development time against execution time. Software developers need to understand the context of their problem before they can apply a solution, whether that solution is a prepackaged RAD product or painstaking from-the-ground-up software construction.

---

[4] Some may argue that this is still development time, only it's development time by nondevelopers (or by less-skilled developers). This may be true, but it's a philosophical discussion at this point. If a user uses the macro language of a tool to create a macro, is that programming?

If all of this sounds familiar, it's because you've been reading up on the patterns movement. Patterns, as defined by Brad Appleton's introduction to them,[5] are not a solution to just a problem, but to a problem within a predefined context. Because patterns offer so much in the way of prepared expertise, and because they offer a useful vocabulary by which we can discuss design solutions, I use patterns as part of the book's vocabulary. Patterns are a form of design reuse, and any tool we can use to speed up the development of software, even if it's just the ability to refer to the organization of common-purpose objects, brings us closer to zero development.

Zero development is not just about design reuse. It's also about building reusable software that can be used as black-box components. Java builds on this component concept from its very roots, choosing to favor shallow, broad-based inheritance hierarchies instead of the deeply nested hierarchies built with C++ in the late 1980s and early 1990s. This approach was hailed as the ultimate in software design, allowing developers to create applications out of objects. Problem was, it never happened.

Fundamentally, the problem with the deeply nested hierarchy is its dependence on inheritance as a reuse mechanism. The problem with inheritance as a reuse mechanism is simple: classes inheriting another must know details about the base class, and effective reuse dictates that objects using one another do not need to understand the details of the object being used. Inheritance also led to the fragile base class problem in which changes to a base class ripple throughout the rest of the system, wreaking havoc everywhere that classes extended the base class and made assumptions regarding its parent's behavior.

Recently, the notion of reusable objects has undergone a revolution. Led partly by the development of the Java run-time libraries, but also by a growing recognition within the C++ and other object-language communities, object developers have realized that inheritance on its own doesn't provide reuse. Instead, the emphasis on reuse is coming from componentry and Open Source advocates.

Componentry, as a reuse mechanism, first gained prominence within the software development community through the overwhelming success of Microsoft's Visual Basic. Regardless of object-oriented purists' opinions of the language and development ideology, Visual Basic's approach to reusable components, building black-box dynamic-link libraries (DLLs) (first called VBXs, later migrated to 32-bit Windows and COM as ActiveX controls) spawned an entire industry of components.

One of the key components was binary compatibility. Because VB ran only on Microsoft operating systems, multiplatform capability was not a factor, as opposed to C++, where portability could only be achieved at the source level, and poorly even then. Differences in compiler capabilities, differences in platforms underneath the

---

[5] Available at http://www.enteract.com/~bradapp/docs/patterns-intro.html

compiled code, even differences in the fundamental size of intrinsic types,[6] all led to break source code developed for one platform but compiled on another. Java, with its portability, has no such concerns, at either the source or the binary level.

The Open Source movement has also contributed tremendously to the reuse of components. With more and more individuals and companies making the source for their components available, less and less time needs to be spent on a project. Now organizations can have the best of both worlds—control of the source in the event of a bug or problem that requires an immediate fix, but without having to develop the source independently.

Zero development, by its definition, is an unattainable goal; developing software without incurring any development costs is a contradiction in terms. The closer we can approach that goal, however, the lower development costs will be, and the less time we have to spend on development of components that could otherwise be reused. Consequently, we can spend more time on what our users want. And that, above all else, is what we're here for.

### 1.2.2 Zero deployment

Software is not only developed, it must be deployed. This is the act of installing the software on the target system, whether it is a stand-alone data-center server machine, or end-user machines all across the organization. In consumer software, this is driven by an installation application, either purchased from a vendor or home-grown. In enterprise development, however, despite how capable the user of an installation application may be, the individuals installing the application are typically on their own, with minimal support from the developers. Deployment to a centralized server is far less costly than deployment to end users systems. However, if the software in question is for end users, that deployment would seem to be inherently necessary and unavoidable.

In fact, the attempt to avoid this cost is the entire driving force behind the thin client architecture, where a web browser is used to view HTML pages or interact with Java applets as their contact with the system. Because HTML is loaded from a central HTTP server, and stores nothing on the end-users' systems, deploying a new version of an application to the organization merely requires modification of the HTML pages or Java applet code on the server. Thin client systems aren't limited to just HTML/HTTP systems, however. Within the last two years, books, papers, and articles have been released describing stand-alone applications making use of distributed objects and a thin presentation layer on the end-users' machine. It's just that HTML/HTTP systems are more convenient, since almost everybody has a web browser installed on their system.

Part of the reason for this move toward zero deployment approaches is the recognition of some simple facts:

---

[6] C++ guarantees nothing about the size of an int within the C++ language, except that it will always be less than or equal to the size of a long, and greater than or equal to the size of a short. This sort of ambiguity is what led James Gosling to decide, up front, that Java's intrinsic types would be fixed, regardless of platform.

- *Users don't want to install software themselves.*
  Some will not be qualified to do so, most simply won't want to.

- *Software systems aren't completely independent anymore.*
  They're built from preexisting components and libraries, which have their own deployment costs. Connecting to a database using JDBC, for example, may require the installation of additional drivers on the end-user's system, to handle the actual low-level communications between the client and the server. In the case of Java, the Java interpreter and environment (the JRE) must be installed on the end-user's system in order to run Java code. What's worse, these collateral deployment costs aren't one-time costs; each time an upgrade or patch is made available, it must be installed on the end-user's machine all over again. This takes time (IT staff man-hours) and money (licensing fees).

- *It takes time to push these developments out.*
  Assuming an install is flawless and takes five minutes, an IT staff member can perform about ten installs an hour. For a 150-seat call center, that means two IT staff members must spend an entire day *each* performing these installations, assuming no problems along the way. Additionally, from the moment the first install takes place until the last install is finished, the entire call center will be in a state of flux—half the users will be on system 1.1, the others on 1.2 or 2.0, or whatever is being installed. This could present serious problems to the production database behind it, since what is perfectly and correctly formatted data in one version could seem corrupted to the other. Ideally, all work could stop within the call center until the install was complete, but this isn't likely, especially for a 24-by-7 call center or corporation. The situation only gets worse if the organization is worldwide. On top of this, there is always the possibility that the software will need to be recalled due to serious flaw, bug, or simple user resistance.

For these reasons, and more, software architects and developers can't ignore the costs of deploying their software. This doesn't mean trying to reduce the third-party components used or creating nifty installation scripts; this means reducing the need for frequent updates, and designing for change from the moment the system is conceived.

## 1.2.3 Zero administration

The server application's relevance to the development department doesn't end once it's been deployed to the server. Making the application easy to administer—to monitor, to control, to adapt, or to use—makes those who have to do that more administration friendly toward accepting the responsibility of keeping the server up. This is key for development staff, since it is the client's or customer's—not the developers'—opinion of the software that ultimately decides its acceptability. The most elegant software ever written is no good if the users won't touch it. More importantly, there is no need for development staff that produces software that's unusable, unstable or difficult to administer.

To developers who are accustomed to being the crown jewels within product-development companies, the move to enterprise development will come as quite a shock. Within the enterprise, the developers are no longer the *raison d'être* for the corporation's existence, but simply support staff to allow the corporation's core employees to better accomplish their job. Within some corporations, this is the system administrators, because the corporation is all about shuffling data; within others, this will be the corporation's call center, or their field representatives, or their salespeople, and the system administrators will be in the same support role as the developers. Either way, the development staff cannot afford to alienate or otherwise estrange the system administrators. Moreover, it is in the development staff's best interest to make the system administrators' jobs as easy as possible, for a variety of reasons:

- *System administrators will often be the deciding factor as to the deployability of software.* If the system administrators don't think the software is worth deploying, whatever the reason, they won't deploy it. Projects have died right at that point.

- *System administrators will often be the first-line help support for the application being developed.*
  The more the system administrators are in line with the application and supporting the development group, the less often the developers will be called to support the application after its delivery. If, however, the system administrators have no faith in the application, or in the development group that created it, users may be told about each and every place the application fails. This does nothing to improve the development group's reputation within the corporation.

- *Developers and system administrators are, from the very beginning, in an antagonistic relationship.*
  System administrators must support what developers create. If the application fails, it's the system administrators who get called. Developers typically chafe at the restrictions system administrators place on network resources, while system administrators resent the constant barrage of requests developers bring to them. Developers desire complete access to the systems on which they are doing development, while system administrators are reluctant to grant that complete access, since they will be called upon to support that system when something goes wrong. Developers must understand the system administrators' concerns, and meet them as best they can. Attempting to reduce the cost of administration of applications developed for the server goes a long way toward that.

- *System administrators and developers are part of the same IT division, which sometimes has a credibility problem.*
  Approximately half of all IT projects are canceled, and over three-fourths run over schedule, budget, or both. IT credibility suffers every time a system goes down, or an application fails. Neither side wants to be blamed for the other's mistakes, so the IT department as a whole looks fractious and divided. By working with system administrators to make their job as smooth as possible, developers not

only earn loyalty points from the system administration group, they also earn credibility points with the rest of the corporation.

Zero administration means making the applications easier to administer by providing clear GUIs instead of cryptic text files, by allowing configuration of the application to occur while it is running instead of requiring the application to be taken down and restarted, or by allowing system administrators to configure the application from any machine throughout the corporation, with security restrictions still in place. It also means that system administrators can be assured that, in the event of a failure of an application, they will be notified. Lastly, zero administration means having, at their fingertips, statistics regarding the application's performance, load on the current machine, and/or resources consumed.

We will be pursuing zero administration in a variety of ways: by building remote-enabled GUI configuration of running applications, by building configuration security into the application automatically, and by providing application-specific statistics to system administrators at any given moment in a generic manner. It's a tall order, but giving system administrators these capabilities will go a long way toward making peace between developers and system administrators.

## 1.3 JAVA IN THE ENTERPRISE

There are two views of Java in the enterprise—one from Sun, and one from me. Although they conflict somewhat, it's good to know what they are before we launch too deeply into them.

### 1.3.1 Sun's view

Sun's view of Java's role is rather clearly stated within the Java 2 Enterprise Edition overview document. Java, through its enterprise-centric APIs, such as EJB, provides the usual buzzwords: robust, mission-critical support for *n*-tier applications using thin clients. At the same time, Java provides an elegant client platform, superior in every way to anything else on the market today.

Sun sees the enterprise system as a fundamentally distributed one, with clients using thin clients, either straight web browsers over HTTP or perhaps applets, to access servlets or Java Server Pages (JSPs) running on a web server. The web server, actually a J2EE application server in disguise, in turn provides access to EJBs over RMI/IIOP (which in turn allows for CORBA access, both to and from the EJB components) for the actual business logic. The Beans themselves know how to access relational databases, in which the data is actually stored.

All the world is a Java world, and Sun is content.

### 1.3.2 Alternate views

Unfortunately, not all applications support this fundamental model.

To start with, not all applications within an enterprise system are, at heart, client/server systems like the prototypical Sun J2EE application. Some will be workflow applications, routing information between users, and requiring work to be done in between users as data packets enter and leave various stations. Other applications will be stand-alone daemon processes, polling over relational database tables as rows are inserted, and acting upon the newly introduced entities. Other applications will be triggered by calls inside the database (using Oracle 8*i*, for example, or using JNI/native code attached to the database to be called from within a database trigger), to route data through a sequence of filters and steps before storing it someplace else.

Under other situations, the heart will be a legacy mainframe system, requiring some sort of terminal session to the mainframe to carry out the necessary data-feeds. Numerous third-party toolkits and source codes have appeared, allowing Java to access 3270-emulation sessions, but these are all proprietary and nonstandard thus far. J2EE makes no representation of this within it, except to make vague references about access to legacy systems.

Worse, a number of enterprise systems are already partially (or completely) implemented in C++ or C, and Java developers are asked to integrate new changes into the existing system. JNI is about the only way to go with this, yet the J2EE specification makes no mention of this scenario except to say that it's possible. Readers are left to their own devices to figure out where the native code should live, and what implication that has for the model as a whole.

On the whole, Sun's J2EE view of the world is a sin of omission, rather than of incorrection. Most systems will, to some degree, follow the classic client-needs-data/server-feeds-data model, which the J2EE specification excels at providing. And granted, one can extend the notion of "client" to mean many things, but some of the things mentioned above would be difficult to do within J2EE.

## 1.4   WHY JAVA?

This isn't about Java's applicability as a programming language. It's about Java's applicability as an enterprise development programming language.

I want to highlight those aspects of Java that I believe directly affect our lives as enterprise developers.

### General purpose

Java is not restricted to any one medium, domain, or technology. This comes as a great surprise to some, since Java's hype is so closely tied to the Internet, web pages, and applets. Java can be used to create applications, including those on the server side, just as C++, C, or Pascal can. In fact, as the title of this book implies, Java excels at development of stand-alone server applications that have nothing to do whatsoever with the Internet, web pages, or applets.

### Concurrent

Java is the only popular[7] language that contains direct, linguistic support for concurrent (multithreaded) application development. Rather than leaving the notion of thread support to the platform upon which the language code is executed, as C++ does, Java contains direct support for threads via its `synchronized` keyword and its run-time library (namely, the Thread, Runnable, ThreadGroup, and other classes from the `java.lang` package).

This inherent support for threads suddenly makes developing reusable components for the Java environment much simpler—rather than having to try to second-guess all the platforms and environments in which a component could be run (as with C++), Java component creators can always assume that threads will be present, and must code (and architect) accordingly. For example, the creators of the JFC Swing toolkit could handle all GUI event management inside of a separate thread, rather than the C++ approach, where users had to extend a particular class (usually called TApplication or CApp) which contains the event loop code. While this approach carries its own consequences, the ability to assume threads will be present when developing code is a valuable asset. Throughout this book, we will be making use of Java's concurrent nature in a variety of ways, both to obtain better performance as well as to heighten the application's robustness and security.

### Class-based, object-oriented

I could launch into a lecture about the benefits of object-oriented programming technology here, but you're already on the OOP bandwagon if you're a Java developer.

### Strongly typed

Because Java is a strongly typed language, we can put into place safeguards within the code that prevent abuse and potential maintenance headaches. Java goes the extra distance in this via its use of interfaces, as well—it's trivial to introduce a new, purely contractual interface into the system that guarantees certain behavior, therefore making it easier to strongly type our own code. Want a particular collection to contain only objects that can be streamed out? Write the collection to take Serializable types instead of Object. Want to provide an event-based notification system? Define an interface that clients must implement in order to receive those callbacks, and have the clients register themselves with you. The strong typing allows the compiler to help us keep order imposed on the system, and that's always a bonus.

---

[7] Well-known outside of research circles, as opposed to languages unknown to programmers outside of the academic world.

### Automatic storage management

Most C++ programmers have a hard time buying the garbage collection argument. Their loss. Java's garbage collection mechanism frees us from one of the most onerous parts of development—*ownership semantics*.

Within C++, or any other language in which I must explicitly manage memory, ownership semantics take on a huge life of their own. I have to decide, either explicitly or implicitly, who owns the object. If, for example, I place a stack-allocated object into a container that assumes ownership of, and therefore responsibility for, destruction of objects placed within it, then I'm destined for disaster at worst, memory leaks at best. Java's management of memory removes the need for ownership semantic discussions. Now, I can just drop the Object into the ArrayList, and leave it at that—the ArrayList doesn't need to worry about whether or not it needs to destroy the objects contained within it. If the objects are referenced elsewhere after the ArrayList is destroyed, then they stay alive. If not, they die. Straightforward, simple, elegant.

This isn't to say that explicit memory management doesn't offer advantages. C++ offers some powerful mechanisms for low-level control of memory-management, but most enterprise applications have no need for that level of sophistication. Why use an artist's paintbrush to paint your house?

### Bytecode compilation

This is, of course, where Java finds the happy middle-ground between interpretation and full compilation. Its bytecode-compiled nature keeps us from having to fully source-interpret the code each and every time the code is run. It's a nice middle-of-the-road solution between C++ (native-code compilation) and Smalltalk (source-level interpretation).

While we're on this subject, however, let me heap praise upon the individual at Sun who conceived the notion of Java's ClassLoaders. Brilliance. Sheer, unadulterated, brilliance. By granting us, the developers, the ability to create custom ClassLoaders, we have more control over how our system functions than most developers really imagine. This, more than anything else within the language or the platform, is what gives us real power.

### 1.4.1  Criticisms of Java as a server-side language

The principal language of choice for developing server-side applications is currently C++; therefore, if Java is to compete with C++ as a server-side development language, it must answer the criticisms leveled at it by C++. It does so to some degree above, but server-side application developers have their own concerns.

### Too slow

This is, without a doubt, the most-often-used accusation against Java. Because Java is an interpreted language, so the argument goes, it can't possibly ever hope to compete on the same scale as code compiled into natively executed code. Unfortunately, this is also the hardest argument to disprove, as C++ compiler manufacturers vie with Java compiler/virtual-machine manufacturers, producing one benchmark after another that proves one side or the other is right. In truth, the only thing these incessant benchmark studies prove, is that marketing materials can skew benchmarks to say anything.

Java is an interpreted language. However, it is interpreted in the same manner that a natively compiled application is interpreted—integer opcodes and operands are executed by a CPU, branching and calling down to the hardware through driver layers when necessary. In C++ code, the executing CPU is the actual hardware CPU itself, while in Java, it's a software-driven CPU emulator. Whereas a C++ compiler compiles to the x86 or Sparc instruction set, a Java compiler compiles to the Java instruction set. This means that Java does not suffer from the same speed penalties of other interpreted languages (such as Basic or Lisp); it doesn't need to tokenize, parse, or symbolically link the source code. Instead, it only needs to find the compiled .class file, load and link it from its binary form, and execute it from there. This reduces Java's interpretation penalty significantly.

What also aids Java's case against its speed deficiencies is the recent release of a number of just-in-time (JIT) compilers, which examine (at run time) the most commonly called methods, and compile them into native code. Operating on the 80-20 rule,[8] the JIT will, in theory, transform the interpreted bytecode into actual native code, therefore reducing even further the interpretation penalty. JIT manufacturers, naturally, claim performance equivalent to that of C++ code in their benchmarks, but such announcements must be taken with a grain of salt. Sun has finally released its own JIT, the Hotspot engine, free for download from the Javasoft website. Hotspot does a good job of improving the Sun JVM engine's execution speed, not, perhaps, to comparable levels to C++ code, but good enough for many (if not most) tasks.

Java promoters can also point to the realities of the computer hardware industry, in which CPU speeds double every eighteen months, and average core memory levels follow similar exponential paths. It wasn't much more than six years ago, that the average desktop PC was an 80386/33 with 4 MB of RAM; the average desktop PC of 1998 was a Pentium-II/266 with either 32 MB or 64 MB of RAM. Server machines have undergone a similar exponential climb in processing power and speed. The argument, then, is that execution speed is less critical, since hardware will continue to climb for the forseeable future. Even should current average levels of hardware on the server be inadequate for acceptable Java performance, upgrading the server hardware is usually a far more cost-effective solution than attempting the man-hours necessary to perform accurate measurement and optimization efforts. Consider the math: $10,000 for a new multi-CPU, high-RAM level server machine, or $50/hour per man to perform the

---

[8] The 80-20 rule states that 80 percent of the time spent in an application is spent in 20 percent of the code, and vice versa. Therefore, optimization strategies focus on identifying that critical 20 percent of the code, and making it as fast as possible, through in-line assembler code (C++) or JNI code (Java).

optimization effort, including regression testing to ensure that optimization didn't alter the actual behavior or introduce bugs. If the optimization effort takes more than 200 hours, it's a complete wash—more than 200 hours (five people spending a full week), and it would have been more cost-effective to upgrade the hardware.

The truth is that Java's execution speed doesn't matter. It's the development speed that decides Java's final acceptance as a language. This may seem an odd argument to make, but about five years ago the same arguments were leveled at C++ regarding its execution speed. Instead of these concerns weighing down C++'s eventual acceptance, hardware simply got faster, and C++'s execution overhead[9] became less and less relevant. The same will become true for Java. As the hardware improves, and available memory on servers grows, Java's execution overhead will become a moot point.

Bear in mind, too, that it's because of Java's interpreted nature that we can do some of the meta-level things we're going to discuss in chapters 2 and 3—at run time, we can examine any arbitrary Java class, and know just about every programmatic detail we'd ever need about that class. No additional information, no additional type library, is required. Natively compiled code can't do that, because it needs to work for more than just OO languages; trying to run Reflection on code compiled from C or Pascal would require some very interesting fudging.

Alternatively, tell those C++ critics that if they're really concerned about performance, they'd code the thing in Assembler. In the meantime, we've got work to do.

### Too high-level

This has never been true; even beginning with Java 1.0, Java has supported the native keyword, allowing Java developers to declare methods in a Java class that are implemented in C/C++ code. For most operating systems, C or C++ is as down to the metal as anybody wants to get. Still, even for those who want to get down to the bare-bones assembler level, most C/C++ compilers allow for inline assembly code.

Java 1.0's native method integration, however, was a royal pain; it was awkward to use, it was nonportable between Java compilers, and chances were good it wouldn't work outside of the JVM compiler the vendor provided. For example, Sun's native-method approach for its JVM was radically different from Microsoft's, which in turn was radically different from the approach Netscape used. This was the impetus and drive behind the release of the JNI specification when JDK 1.1 was released.

JNI in 1.1 (and later, Java 2) radically changed all this, for the first time making it standard to be able to call down to native C/C++ code. Currently, JNI only contains bindings to allow Java to call to C/C++ functions, but there's been literally no discussion of ever allowing JNI to call into anything else. Microsoft further extended its native-integration mechanism by allowing Java code to call into COM components

---

[9] Which turned out to be far lower than most people believed. The same, I believe, will hold for Java.

quickly and easily, but the Sun-Microsoft lawsuit brings the long-term viability of Microsoft's Java implementation into question.

Regardless of your feeling on Sun's and/or Microsoft's position on their native-integration features for their respective JVMs (and whether it's breaking "standard" Java to do so), the basic fact remains that Java has the hooks necessary to get to the metal. Typically, this argument is raised in conjunction with the follow-up comment of, "We need to use 'library X' to get our work done." For example, a large body of C/C++ code exists to read data over a serial port from scientific or other monitoring equipment; for years, Java had no capabilities to read or write to the PC's serial or parallel ports from within Java code. One such situation arose in my own experience. The company for whom I was working at the time wanted to produce reports via the Crystal Reports report-generation engine, but at that time Crystal Reports had programmatic API only for C, C++ and Visual Basic.

The answer, of course, was to create a Java class API that wrappered the C++ API somewhat closely, using native methods to create, call into, and destroy a corresponding C++ object within the Java object used from the Java code. Thanks to the shallow nature of the Java classes (they provided almost no behavior on their own, passing all arguments on to the C++ object they wrapped around), the total development time for this Java-wrapper library was about four days. Java can get down to the metal when necessary, and we'll see this demonstrated in a later chapter.

### Doesn't have feature X that C++ does

Java's linguistic history very obviously comes from C++; as a result, it is constantly held up against the extremely rich linguistic featureset of C++ and comes out on the short end of the stick. A brief, cursory examination reveals several C++ features that Java lacks: default parameter values, overloaded operators, and templates. C++ programmers, especially those accustomed to these features, feel as if they're trying to code with one hand bound behind their backs when moving to Java.

Remember, however, that Java never billed itself as a complete replacement for C++, and that James Gosling deliberately left out some of these features from C++ because he felt they were too complex and confusing for developers. Bjarne Stroustrup and Gosling have different philosophies regarding the nature of user-defined objects within the language: Stroustrup, in C++, wants C++ classes to act, feel, and behave like built-in types as much as possible;[10] Gosling makes a clear differentiation from built-in types and user-defined ones.

Remember, too, that C++ lacked all of these features when it first broke onto the programming scene a decade ago. C++ 2.1 lacked templates, exception handling, RTTI, and namespaces. C++ has evolved into what it is today; Java is moving through that process now. As a result, the language is quickly becoming a different beast than

---

[10] *Design and Evolution of C++*

what Gosling introduced five years ago. Does this reduce its usefulness for program-mers today? Not at all; default parameters can always be silently supported by providing additional overloaded method calls of the same name:

```
// C++ class with default parameters on method
class Foo
{
public:
    void Bar(int x1, int x2=12, int x3=24);
};

// Means I can call it like this:
Foo f;
f.Bar(6);
f.Bar(6, 66);
f.Bar(6, 66, 666);

/**
 * Java version of the above C++ class
 */
public class Foo
{
    public void Bar(int x1)
    { Bar(x1, 12, 24); }

    public void Bar(int x1, int x2)
    { Bar(x1, x2, 24); }

    public void Bar(int x1, int x2, int x3)
    {
        // Do something with x1, x2, and x3
    }

    /**
     * Duplication of the above call syntax:
     */
    public static void main(String[] args)
    {
        Foo f = new Foo();
        f.Bar(6);
        f.Bar(6, 66);
        f.Bar(6, 66, 666);
    }
}
```

It's not quite as convenient as the C++ version, but the workaround is there, if neces-sary, until Sun adds default parameters to the Java language. What's more, default parameters are somewhat overrated, even within C++; I never used them that much in my C++ code. I found it cleaner and more understandable to use the multiple-overloaded methods approach.

Overloaded operators are definitely more of a problem within Java, especially in mathematical code. Whereas in C++, a class can overload its + and/or += implementation to support the addition of two mathematical object types, such as this:

```
Matrix m1;
Matrix m2;

GUI_interface.getUserInput(m1, m2);
Matrix m3 = m1 + m2;
```

Java has no such facility, requiring developers to use the more ungainly form:

```
Matrix m1 = new Matrix();
Matrix m2 = new Matrix();

GUI_interface.getUserInput(m1, m2);
Matrix m3 = Matrix.add(m1, m2);
    // or could use something like:
    // Matrix m3 = new Matrix(m1);
    // m3.add(m2);
```

This is awkward, overly verbose, and makes formulaic expressions in Java unnecessarily long compared to C++ equivalents. There's certainly no argument that operator overloading was a great source of language abuse in C++ code, and there's no argument that trying to read C++ code that makes heavy use of operator overloading can be difficult when the reader doesn't realize the addition taking place is actually an overloaded operator. This is more of a developer issue than it is a language issue; as Ian Malcolm says in Michael Crichton's *Jurassic Park*, "You went out and *did* it long before you wondered if you *should*." Fortunately Java appears to recognize the usefulness of operator overloading within the language—Sun is currently evaluating a proposal[11] for adding it to the next release of Java.

Finally, there's the matter of templates (generic types). In the interest of fairness, I'll make my biases clear: I really miss templates from C++. Templates in C++ have gained some new popularity for generic componentization, as evidenced by the standard template library's ability to vary not only the type the container holds, but also the method by which it allocates memory for that container, sorts the container, and so on. Templates provide some very powerful abstraction and reuse mechanism capability that Java simply cannot match at the moment.

Java's new Collection classes, introduced as part of the JDK 1.2 release, offer some of this same flexibility, but the fundamental problem (the same one that plagued C++ until templates were widely implemented in C++ compilers) is still the same: lack of type-safety. Consider the following code:

```
// C++
// This vector must contain *only* Foo types!
std::vector<Foo*> fooVector;
```

---

[11] From James Gosling himself.

```
fooVector.insert(new Foo());
    // This is acceptable--fooVector stores "Foo" instances

fooVector.insert(new Bar());
    // The above line fails to compile, since fooVector's insert()
    // method, by virtue of the template, *only* takes Foo
    // instances, and a Bar isn't a Foo

/**
 * Java version
 */
// This Vector must contain *only* Foo types!
java.util.Vector fooVector = new java.util.Vector();

fooVector.addElement(new Foo());
    // Perfectly acceptable

fooVector.addElement(new Bar());
    // Unfortunately, *also* perfectly acceptable, since Vector's
    // addElement() method takes an Object
```

As you can see, there is no programmatic way for Vector to screen out anything other than a Foo instance being placed within it. This in turn can cause problems down the road, when fooVector returns an Enumeration, and each element is cast to a Foo instance, since the programmer explicitly stated that fooVector should contain only Foo instances. Unfortunately, the new guy on the team didn't read that part, added a Bar, and caused a ClassCastException in front of the big boss on the day of the demo. Type-safety *is* your friend; use it whenever possible.

There are certainly ways around this, to gain this sort of type-safety in Java, but none of them are particularly elegant. The first is to create your own derived-from-Vector type that provides type-safe methods to add and remove the elements in question; however, this still contains several holes. First, the generic Object-parameter methods on Vector are still present on your derived class, so unless you explicitly redefine those methods to screen out illegal types, you can't prevent a programmer from adding the wrong type. This can be worked around by not extending Vector, and instead containing a Vector within the type-safe container class and delegating all work to the inner Vector:

```
public class StringVector
{
    // . . .

    public void addElement(String elem)
    {
        vector.addElement(elem);
    }

    private Vector vector = new Vector();
}
```

Unfortunately, this means that because StringVector no longer extends Vector, it cannot be passed in wherever a standard Vector is expected. While this may not present a serious difficulty, it's awkward enough to cause problems in those Java frameworks that pass collections-of-*things* around as parameters to method calls. This, too, can be worked around by providing a method to return the contained Vector, but this then opens up the possibility that anybody wishing access to the guts can get them; this violates all the rules of encapsulation.

Several experimental Java compilers, such as Pizza or GJ (Generic Java), provide extensions to the Java language that provide this sort of templatelike facility. This approach too has its drawbacks, most notably using one of these compilers wipes out the possibility of using any of the major IDEs or debuggers, since the debugger can't understand the source to provide inline source-level debugging support. Some of these compilers can produce standard Java source as output (instead of compiled bytecode), but even this sort of preprocessing has its problems. Not only is the code you write with one of these tools nonstandard, so any incoming Java developers will be somewhat at a loss, but obtaining management support for using the tool can be an uphill struggle. Since most of these utilities come from research institutions and come without corporate facilities for support, IS and IT managers won't want to touch them.

The recent Sun Community Source Licensing policy has opened up the idea of introducing generic types into Java, and I'm fervently hoping Sun gives it a serious look. As with operator overloading, templates turned out to be an easily abused feature of C++, and so scared many developers away from using them; hopefully the same story won't repeat itself within Java. Until the time that generic types become available within Java, however, we'll just have to limp along without them, using Object to hold generic-objects in non-type-safe fashion.

### Lacks the tool support of C++

This may have been true in the days of Java 1.0 in 1995; it certainly cannot be said of the Java 2 in 1999. No less than a half-dozen Java development environments are on the open market from the same companies that make C++ development environments: Borland-now-Inprise, IBM, Symantec, Metrowerks, even Microsoft, all have useful IDEs for the Java developer. Rational Software's UML CASE tool, Rational Rose, supports both C++ and Java code generation and reverse-engineering. And just as many database vendors have JDBC drivers as have ODBC drivers. It's pure rubbish to assert that Java lacks tool support.

Given that, it's an almost certainty that a follow-up comment from the critic will be something along the lines of "Well, vendor *X* doesn't have a Java version of the library or tool that I need, and they do have a C++ version." Java still isn't left out, however—through JNI, or CORBA, C++ libraries and/or tools can be used within the Java environment. Chances are more than likely that vendor *X* is already at work on a Java port of its library or tool, if for no other reason than to try to capitalize on the Java hype-wave that's sweeping the IT industry.

### *Too new; too unproven*

The same was said of C++ a decade ago; that didn't stop C++ from becoming the overwhelming language of choice for system- and business-level development. This argument is losing credibility every day, as Java gains acceptance in more and more corporate development shops and organizations with every passing hour. While Java may not command the same kinds of numbers of developers that C++ does today, it's getting closer and closer with every survey.

In addition, it doesn't take much in the way of research to find a number of firms, including some very large Fortune 500 companies, using Java as the development platform/language. In fact, the whole Y2K problem contributed to this—the Javasoft website recently posted a transcript of an interview at JavaOne with a number of Sun personalities, including Gosling. During this interview, Gosling stated a "number of people came up to me and said, 'Since we had to fix the Y2K thing, we just rewrote the whole thing in Java.'"

I believe this argument is simply corporate inertia at work: "We don't use it now, we've standardized on language 'Z', we'll have to train new people on it," and so on and so forth. These points all have merit. Standardization is good—it helps centralize the corporation's training and development efforts. Simply because a new technology is there doesn't mean a company should rush to embrace it—new tools/languages/environments can carry hidden and unknown costs that can come back and haunt a firm later. But, while all of these points hold merit, without a conscious drive to make use of new technologies where appropriate,[12] corporations would still be using Z80 Assembler for *n*-tier distributed object development.

## 1.5   SUMMARY

Java is an ideal language for development on the server. Its garbage collection support removes the tiresome need for developers to concern themselves with ownership semantics for objects, at the cost of some performance. Its simplistic syntax reduces the learning curve for developers new to Java, and its similiarity to C++ allows for easy migration of C++ developers to Java, at the cost of some of C++'s advanced (and extremely powerful) features, such as templates.

Enterprise development has its own unique forces and context, different from that of other types of development such as "vertical market" consumer products, such as word processors or personal-accounting applications. Enterprise developers must try to reduce the costs at the same time they maximize the benefits of building custom software. Toward that end, we will work for the idealized three zeroes: zero development, zero deployment, and zero administration. As part of that, we will build reusable software components and a sample generic application system.

Welcome to *Server-Based Java*. I hope you enjoy the ride.

---

[12] I cannot stress this enough. Java is not, nor ever will be, the silver bullet solution to any and all problems. For it to succeed, it must be applied to problems it is capable of solving.

## 1.6 ADDITIONAL READING

- Erich Gamma, Richard Helm, Richard Johnson, and John Vlissides, *Design Patterns: Elements of Reusable Object Design* (Addison-Wesley, 1995).

This canonical patterns book, is also known as the "Gang of Four" or "GOF" book in pattern circles. Just about every patterns book written builds off of these twenty-three. Readers are highly encouraged to at least have a passing familiarity with this book, as Java itself makes use of most, if not all, of these patterns throughout its run-time library and core object model.

# C H A P T E R   2

# *ClassLoaders*

Java's dynamic class loading mechanism is "unusual in supporting all of the following features: *laziness, type-safe linkage, user-defined extensibility,* and *multiple communicating name spaces.*"[1] In this chapter, we will examine that mechanism and discover not only how it provides us with some powerful capabilities, but how they can be used to achieve one Holy Grail of enterprise development: the ability to upgrade code on a running server without taking the server down.

If you're not familiar with the basics of Java's dynamic linking capabilities (for example, why your CLASSPATH needs to be set during both compilation *and* execution of your Java code), then I recommend *Inside the Java Virtual Machine* by Bill Venner. If you prefer, you can obtain much of the same material from the Java Language specification and/or the Java Virtual Machine specification.

---

[1]   Sheng Liang and Gilad Bracha, "Dynamic Class Loading in the Java Virtual Machine," from the 13th Annual ACM SIGPLAN Conference on Object-Oriented Programming Systems, Languages and Applications (OOPSLA '98), Vancouver, BC, Canada, October 1998.

## 2.1 DYNAMIC LINKING

Java is a dynamically linked system. This means all code is linked into the executing JVM at run time, instead of at compile time, as with C++.[2] The means by which this dynamic linking takes place is through Java's ClassLoader system, which is wrapped up in the java.lang.ClassLoader class, and works along with support within the JVM. There is no exception to this rule—all code loaded into the JVM must come through a ClassLoader, even the standard Java run-time library. Upon JVM startup, a bootstrap ClassLoader subtype is created (within the JVM—no Java code is present yet), and the first class—Object—is loaded into the system from its corresponding .class representation.

This dynamic linking carries with it implicit assumptions. Because the JVM knows nothing about the code at the time of JVM startup, it has to be able to examine each and every loaded class and verify its methods, parameters, fields, and inheritance relationships in order to verify that the code isn't malicious or dangerous. Without this, it would be possible to accidentally mismatch versions of .class files, and potentially trash the VM, which would *not* look good in front of a client or executive vice president. Without this, type-safety within the VM would also be impossible.

Because the JVM already has to do this rather deep run-time introspection of the code, Sun chose (as of JDK 1.1) to make this introspection capability available to the users of the system. This is known as Java Reflection, and offers us unique, *run-time dynamic loading* capabilities.

### 2.1.1 Run-time dynamic loading

Run-time dynamic loading, as I choose to call it, is different from load-time dynamic loading. The latter is the usual form of coding familiar to most Java programmers:

```java
public class Hello
{
    public static void main(String[] args)
    {
        System.out.println("Hello, world!");
    }
}
```

In the above, when the JVM loads the Hello class, it notices that the compiler has flagged Hello as using the System class. If System (more accurately, java.lang.System) hasn't been loaded by this point, the JVM must run off and load System in before it can finish loading Hello. The same is true of String and Object (which Hello implicitly extends, remember), and any classes used in turn by those two classes.

---

[2] Excluding, of course, dynamic linking with C++. Even then, however, the linker brings in stubs that are capable of performing the actual dynamic linking step; from a purely technical perspective, C++ does not support dynamic linking implicitly.

Run-time dynamic linking, however, looks and feels different from standard compile-time dynamic linking. In this approach, we defer until run time the name of the class to load, instead of coding it directly into the source code.

```java
public class DynamicCode
{
    public static void main(String[] args)
        throws Exception// a lazy way to not deal with Exceptions
    {
        // Get the name of the class to load and execute off the command
        // line's first argument (after "java DynamicCode")
        if (args.length < 1)
        {
            System.out.println("Usage: java DynamicCode <class to run>");
            System.exit(-1);
        }

        Class cls = Class.forName(args[0]); // ***
        Object obj = cls.newInstance();     // ***
```

The above two lines are the interesting ones—we are constructing an object without knowing (or, for that matter, caring) what its actual type is. Class.forName returns to us a java.lang.Class object, and in the next line, we ask the Class object for a new instance of an object whose type is represented by that Class.

```java
        // Cast the Object to a Runnable so we can invoke the run() method
        // on it
        Runnable r = (Runnable) obj;
        r.run();
    }
}
```

The rest of the application simply casts the returned object to a Runnable object, then executes its run method. Naturally, if the object's type doesn't implement Runnable, we'll get a ClassCastException at run time, and the application will fail. This is one of the things we surrender in doing this kind of compile-time type ignorance—compile-time type-safety is pretty much thrown out the window.

Note that the Class class represents the type of an object. In Java we can represent (at run time) the nature of the type system as actual Object instances (of type Class) within the system.

```java
Class cls = Class.forName("java.lang.String");
Object obj = cls.newInstance();
String s = (String)obj;
```

In the above code, the instance cls[3] represents the Java class String. This means that, using Java's Reflection mechanism we can examine all sorts of things about the class

---

[3]  One thing to remember when working with the Class type in Java—because "class" is a keyword, any attempt to use it as a variable name will yield all sorts of compile errors.

java.lang.String, and through the use of the `newInstance` method, create new instances of String, and so forth. The key to remember is that `cls` is not a String; `cls` is a Class. The next line, where we create an instance of the object whose type is represented by `cls`, is where we finally end up with a String object—`obj` is a String. We guarantee that by doing the cast on the next line.

If `cls` in the above case represents the String class, why can't we get String back from `newInstance`? Why does it have to return an Object, which we then have to downcast? The reason, of course, has to do with the fact that the Java compiler, at compile time, has no idea of the type you're creating when you call `newInstance`. The argument to Class.forName could be anything, even an invalid class name. Because Java lacks any sort of "parameterized" type facility (such as that found in C++ templates), we can't code the return type to do the compile-time check for type-safety later.

This is just one example where templates in Java would be really useful; for example, we could write, instead:

```
Class<String> cls = Class.forName("java.lang.String");
String str = cls.newInstance();
```

Unfortunately, doing this would break too many other Java linguistic and run-time rules, so I think we'll just have to do without templates in Java.

Going back to the original code snippet, we take the first argument given to us on the command line. We create a Class around that argument, and we create an instance of an object from that Class, all without knowing what it really is. In fact, we don't care about its actual type. We're effectively writing a statement where we are new-ing an object, without needing the object's name. To prove it, let's write more code, and try running it:

```
public class First
    implements Runnable
{
    public void run()
    {
        System.out.println("First!");
    }
}

public class Second
    implements Runnable
{
    public void run()
    {
        System.out.println("Second!");
    }
}
```

Remember, DynamicCode.java knows nothing about these two classes. Prove it to yourself by deleting the files from the working directory when you compile these, and notice how DynamicCode.java compiles without a hitch. (Remember, the Java compiler automatically compiles classes that are referenced in source code if they're not already compiled, so any dependencies between code modules are immediately resolved, unlike in C++ or C.) It'll even run (albeit with an exception if you specify an argument)—no dependency is present.

Now, if you run DynamicCode, passing in First or Second:

```
C:\projects\ssj\cd\src\chap02> java DynamicCode First
First!
C:\projects\ssj\cd\src\chap02> java DynamicCode Second
Second!
```

Notice that in each case, the appropriate string was printed. Java loaded the First.class, found its `run()` method, and executed it; the same for Second.class. All of this happened flawlessly, without knowing about either class at the time the developer compiled the DynamicCode.java code.

In fact, we've achieved something a number of C++ programmers would kill for—the ability to create code that can be loaded at run time and executed, without having to know its type at the time the project was compiled. A number of technologies have arisen from this concept: Netscape plug-ins, Microsoft ActiveX objects, CORBA (through its Dynamic Invocation and Dynamic Skeleton interfaces), and so forth. This is powerful technology at our fingertips.

Some of you may be curious to know why First and Second have to implement Runnable; others of you may be curious to know if this dynamic instantiation capability violates Java's type-safety guarantee. The answer to both questions is related. We need to have some interface to cast the Object returned from `Class.newInstance`, so we can call on it without violating type safety. Runnable happens to provide a convenient interface to do that. It doesn't have to be Runnable; it could be any interface we define, which is precisely what we'll do when we build the first cut of our Generic Java Application Server system later in the book.

It's not necessary to require that all classes implement a particular interface in order to be called through run-time dynamic linking; we can also use Java's Reflection API to accomplish the same task.

## 2.1.2    Reflection

Reflection is the ability to examine the type of an object at run time. Put in practical terms, Reflection allows us to do away with compile-time type requirements, and call any arbitrary method at any arbitrary time on any arbitrary object without having to know that object's type at compile time (listing 2.1).

**Listing 2.1   Coding DynamicCode for Reflection**

```java
public class ReflectingDynamicCode
{
    public static void main(String[] args)
        throws Exception// a lazy way to not deal with Exceptions
    {
```

```
// Get the name of the class to load and execute off the command
// line's first argument (after "java DynamicCode")
//
if (args.length < 1)
{
    System.out.println("Usage: java DynamicCode <class to run>");
    System.exit(-1);
}

Class cls = Class.forName(args[0]);
Object obj = cls.newInstance();

// Reflect on the Class; find the method named "run" that takes
// no arguments and returns no return value
//
java.lang.reflect.Method[] methods = cls.getMethods();
for (int i=0; i<methods.length; i++)
{
    System.out.println("Checking name of " + cls.getName()
        + "." + methods[i].getName());
    if (methods[i].getName().equals("run"))
    {
        if (methods[i].getReturnType().equals(java.lang.Void.TYPE) &&
            methods[i].getParameterTypes().length == 0)
        {
            // methods[i] is the Method that corresponds to the
            // method "void run()". Call it.
            //
            Object ret = methods[i].invoke(obj, null);
            if (ret != null)
                System.out.println("??? run()'s not supposed to " +
                    "return me something!");
        }
    }
}
}
}
```

Loading and running it with First and Second (this time with Runnable removed from the class declaration) yields the following results:

```
C:\Projects\SSJ\cd\src\chap2> java ReflectingDynamicCode ReflectedFirst
Checking name of ReflectedFirst.equals
Checking name of ReflectedFirst.getClass
Checking name of ReflectedFirst.hashCode
Checking name of ReflectedFirst.notify
Checking name of ReflectedFirst.notifyAll
Checking name of ReflectedFirst.toString
Checking name of ReflectedFirst.wait
Checking name of ReflectedFirst.wait
Checking name of ReflectedFirst.wait
```

```
Checking name of ReflectedFirst.run
First!

C:\Projects\SSJ\cd\src\chap2>
```

Notice that in the code for ReflectedFirst, there's no longer the Runnable interface, just to make sure we're not somehow casting it back to a Runnable to make the run call work.

What's going on in this new version is a bit interesting, so let's take it step by step. The first difference is listed below.

```
// Reflect on the Class; find the method named "run" that takes
// no arguments and returns no return value
//
java.lang.reflect.Method[] methods = cls.getMethods();
for (int i=0; i<methods.length; i++)
{
    System.out.println("Checking name of " + cls.getName()
        + "." + methods[i].getName());
    if (methods[i].getName().equals("run"))
    {
        if (methods[i].getReturnType().equals(java.lang.Void.TYPE) &&
            methods[i].getParameterTypes().length == 0)
        {
            // methods[i] is the Method that corresponds to the
            // method "void run()". Call it.
            //
            Object ret = methods[i].invoke(obj, null);
            if (ret != null)
                System.out.println("??? run()'s not supposed to " +
                    "return me something!");
        }
    }
}
```

In DynamicCode.java, the code simply cast the returned Object to a Runnable. If the cast succeeded, then it called run on it. It can do this because the Runnable type is known at the time the code is compiled. If we happen to try to run DynamicCode on a class file that doesn't implement Runnable, then we'll get a java.lang.ClassCastException at the point we make the cast. This is simple Java.

In this second version, ReflectingDynamicCode doesn't attempt the cast. Instead, it asks the Class object for all of its methods, via the Class.getMethods call. This API call returns an array of java.lang.reflect.Method objects. We could have asked this Class for a list of all the interfaces it supports (via the getInterfaces call), or even a list of all the fields of this Class (via getFields) had we desired. But since we're only interested in knowing whether or not we can call run on this class, the code just pulls back all the Methods on this Class.

Once we have the array of Methods, we simply iterate through them until we find a Method with the name "run." Because Java allows us to overload parameter types to methods with the same name, we need to make sure we have the void-return, no-args version. This is accomplished by asking the Method object what its return type is, and comparing it against the Class object java.lang.Void.TYPE. We then check to make sure that its parameter types count is zero, that is, it's not expecting any arguments, and we know we've found the right one.

Method provides a singularly powerful API call, called `invoke`. This method allows us to fill in the parameters (if there were any), hand it an Object on which to make the call (which in this case will be the Object we got from `newInstance` way back when), and then makes the call. If there's a return value, it will be handed back as an Object (which will be `null` if the return type is declared as `void`, as is the case here). C/C++ programmers can think of it as a generic function pointer—once you've got it, you just call through it without caring where it came from.

We have, without knowing anything about a type at compile time, executed a method, fulfilling all the rules of type-safety while we were at it. This is powerful stuff! This is precisely the same technology Microsoft created when it created the OLE Automation API—the ability to call methods on an object without knowing about that object ahead of time. Visual Basic (up through version 4) was built on this foundation, and was (is) wildly successful. The JavaBeans technology system uses Reflection extensively, as well, for much the same purpose. Most of your upcoming EJB servers and environments will also use it to discover what code they need to generate to support your Enterprise JavaBeans.

So why don't we make use of this in the first version, instead of limiting ourselves to the Runnable interface? Two reasons: Reflection is *slow*. Granted, you'll only have to do it once, when you first load the Class, but it will still take time to do. Second, our server needs to know precisely how to call all these methods. Yes, we can find out what parameters are expected in a method call, but we can't (not through Reflection, anyway) find out what those parameters are supposed to mean. Does that String parameter mean a person's name, or a textual representation of a number to write to disk? Is that `boolean` for indicating the object should display an OK button in the window, or for indicating that the object needs to persist itself to disk, right now? It's a far better design decision (and maintenance decision) to have a single interface that all objects subscribe to if they want to participate in your system. Still, Reflection can sometimes get you out of situations that would otherwise be untenable.

### Reflection and the metamodel

One of the most powerful features of the Reflection model is the ability to work with the *metamodel* of a class system. The metamodel is to an object system what metadata is to a database—a description of the model itself. Just as being able to influence the metadata of a database system can lead to powerful (and potentially very complex) capabilities, so too can being able to use the metamodel of an object system give you some important capabilities.

Consider the following code in listing 2.2:

```java
import java.lang.reflect.*;

public class TestSuite
{
    public TestSuite(String classname)
    {
        try
        {
            // Load the Class given by classname
            //
            Class cls = Class.forName(classname);

            // See if it exposes a "void test()" method; if so, call it
            //
            java.lang.reflect.Method[] methods = cls.getMethods();
            for (int i=0; i<methods.length; i++)
            {
                //System.out.println("Checking name of " + cls.getName()
                //     + "." + methods[i].getName());
                if (methods[i].getName().equals("test"))
                {
                    if (methods[i].getReturnType().equals(
                        java.lang.Void.TYPE) &&
                        methods[i].getParameterTypes().length == 0)
                    {
                        // methods[i] is the Method that corresponds to the
                        // method "void test()". Call it.
                        //
                        Object ret = methods[i].invoke(null, null);
                        if (ret != null)
                            System.out.println("??? test()'s
                                not supposed to " +
                                "return me something!");
                    }
                }
            }
        }
        catch (Exception ex)
        {
            ex.printStackTrace();
        }
    }

    public static void main(String[] args)
    {
        // Iterate through each arg, attempting to load that class
        // and execute its test() method
        //
        for (int i=0; i<args.length; i++)
```

```
        {
            new TestSuite(args[i]);
        }
    }

    public static void test ()
    {
        System.out.println("Running test....");

        // . . .

        System.out.println("Test complete!");
    }
}
```

The foregoing code can effectively act as your regression testing system—simply define a test method in each class you want to test, place the name of the class on the command line to TestSuite, and execute the TestSuite class. TestSuite will load the class and call its static test method. If no method is found, it just moves on to the next one.

So what? We could do the same thing, just by defining main and calling the class directly from the command line. What real advantage does this offer us? Aside from the practical advantage of having a single class to run in order to test any class in your Java system, there's the more important realization of what you can do with Reflection. You could create SQL schema based on a class's fields, in order to be able to store any Java type within an RDBMS. You could use it as JavaBeans does, to introspect a particular class and determine what operations it supports. You could generate code (as most EJB servers/containers do) to wrap an externally created class, in order to help ensure against poorly written code crashing your system. You could also use Reflection to obtain a flexibility that interfaces can't offer—simply tell your clients that they have to write methods that conform to a given signature (as we do above with the test method), and they will be able to plug into your system. This way, clients don't have to implement or extend any particular class in order to hook in to your server framework. That offers a measure of flexibility that simply can't be met in any other popular language.

### Reflection considerations

There is one drawback: Reflection carries with it the loss of compile-time error checking. Assume that I use the above TestSuite as my regression-testing mechanism, and I accidentally misspell the method test as tset. What happens? Absolutely nothing, at least at compile time. Because the compiler can't realize the intent of the call— Reflection takes place at run time, remember, not compile time, so compile-time information isn't available—it can't tell you that you've misspelled the method. Unfortunately, you won't get a run-time error, either, except that you'll never fall into the code block that calls Method.invoke to invoke the test. The same will be true if you get the name right, but accidentally give it a parameter to the call.

Reflection is a powerful feature of Java. By offering us the ability to inspect a loaded class at run time, we gain the ability to program generically and at the meta object level. In fact, several systems have been built by researchers toward that exact purpose—providing meta-object support at run time via Java's Reflection model. Here are some possibilities (some of which we'll explore later in this book):

- Using Reflection to determine if a loaded class supports a given interface (such as Runnable, to know if it can be multithreaded, or Serializable, to know if instances of it can be serialized safely).

- Using Reflection to determine if a loaded class follows a certain design paradigm (such as the Service interface built later in this chapter to support GJAS) or pattern.

- Using Reflection to build, at run time or as part of a compile-time system, Proxy classes to provide location-transparency of user code.

- Using Reflection to build metadata representations of object types.

Reflection can be a powerful mechansim; just be aware of the costs and implications of using it within your own systems.

## 2.2 CLASSLOADERS: RULES AND EXPECTATIONS

Java has specific rules regarding the use of ClassLoaders and how (and when) class files are loaded, reloaded, or unloaded from the JVM. Understanding these rules is crucial to unlocking the power of ClassLoaders, both in using them as well as in creating your own custom versions.

### 2.2.1 Java .class file format

While understanding the Java compiled bytecode format (commonly referred to as the .class file format) is not critical to understanding Java's ClassLoader mechanism, a good working knowledge of its layout is useful to have for discussion of the custom ClassLoaders we'll get into later.

In truth, this format really isn't a format for how the bytes must lay out while residing on disk; this format only describes how the bytecode making up a given compiled Java class must exist when handed to the ClassLoader `defineClass` method. This means that:

- *Java doesn't care if the bytecode comes from the local disk or from some other resource.* In fact, Java doesn't care if the bytecode didn't exist more than a second or two ago, a fact which makes technologies like JSP possible.

- *Java doesn't care in what format within a file the bytecode is stored while it is resting on disk.*
  Although it wouldn't be Sun-certifiable 100 percent pure Java, a Java interpreter could even require its bytecode to be in an entirely different format when loading from disk.

- *Java doesn't care where the bytecode came from before it was bytecode.*
  Several programming languages have already been ported to compile into the Java bytecode format, for execution in any standard Java virtual machine, such as Ada95, BASIC, and Logo.

Despite the flexibility of being able to load Java bytecode from customized formats, 99.9 percent of the Java developers in the world will make use of the standard Java .class file format, varying only in the way the code is stored or the way the code is generated/compiled.

*Java Virtual Machine Specification* by Tim Lindholm and Frank Yellin defines the Java .class file format as a single instance of the following ClassFile pseudostructure:

**Listing 2.3    A ClassFile pseudostructure**

```
ClassFile
{
  u4 magic;
  u2 minorVersion;
  u2 majorVersion;
  u2 constantPoolCount;
  constantPoolInfo
  {
    u1 tag;
    u1 info[];
  } constantPool[constantPoolCount-1];
  u2 accessFlags;
  u2 thisClass;
  u2 superClass;
  u2 interfacesCount;
  u2 interfaces[interfacesCount];

  u2 fieldsCount;
  fieldInfo
  {
    u2 accessFlags;
    u2 nameIndex;
    u2 descriptorIndex;
    u2 attributesCount;
    attributeInfo { … } attributes[];    // see below for attributeInfo
  } fields[fieldsCount];

  u2 methodsCount;
  methodInfo
  {
    u2 accessFlags;
    u2 nameIndex;
    u2 descriptorIndex;
    u2 attributesCount;
    attributeInfo { … } attributes[];    // see below for attributeInfo
  } methods[methodsCount];
```

```
  u2 attributesCount;
  attributeInfo
  {
    u2 attributeNameIndex;
    u4 attributeLength;
    u1 info[attributeLength];
  } attributes[attributesCount];
}
```

(where u1 is an unsigned single-byte type, u2 is an unsigned two-byte type, and u4 is an unsigned four-byte type).

While I won't go into deep details regarding the .class layout, the constants, values, and various specification-mandated attribute types or constant pool entry types,[4] I do want to draw attention to a peculiar quirk of the format. Notice that places where one might expect strings or character arrays to appear, name index values appear instead. This is because within the Java bytecode format, *all* constants, strings, numbers, method names and signatures (both defined within this method and calls on other classes), field names, even this class's name and its parent's name, are all stored within a single table called the *constant pool*. All name indexes, then, are offset into this constant pool, which stores both the actual type of the constant in the tag field, and the data of the constant (numeric value, UTF-8 string for names, and so forth) in the info field. Note that there are no fixed-lengths in any part of the format; this forces any code that wants to parse and pick apart the compiled bytecode to do it in a byte-by-byte fashion.

Also notice that there is no field for package within the format; this is because the class is stored in its fully qualified classname, a la com.javageeks.classloader.FileSystemClassLoader, instead of as FileSystemClassLoader, as specified within the .java file. In fact, the name stored won't be the dot-separated name at all, but in Java's unique mangling signature: Lcom/javageeks/classloader/FileSystemClassLoader; (note that the semicolon is part of the name). Any place where a class name is expected or used, the full mangled name is used instead.

A quick and easy way to identify if a particular bytecode stream is a valid .class format stream is to check the first four bytes of the stream for the value 0xCAFEBABE. This is the official magic number for Java class files, and any conformant .class format stream has to follow along if it wants to play in the JVM.

### 2.2.2 Using ClassLoader

Using a ClassLoader is actually relatively simple, from the client's point of view—instantiate a ClassLoader with the appropriate information, ask it for a Class by name, and if the ClassLoader can comply, one will be provided; if not,

---

[4] See Bill Venners' *Inside the Java Virtual Machine* (McGraw-Hill, 1998) for an excellent description, or the *Java Virtual Machine Specification* (Addison-Wesley, 1997), by Tim Lindholm and Frank Yellin.

a `ClassNotFoundException` will be thrown. Boiled down to code, it looks like this:

```
ClassLoader cl = . . .;
Class classString;

// Create an instance of the class "java.lang.String"
try
{
    classString = cl.loadClass("java.lang.String");
}
catch (ClassNotFoundException cnfEx)
{
    cnfEx.printStackTrace();
}
```

Once the Class is retrieved, typically the next step is to instantiate an object of that type. The `Class.newInstance` method creates an instance of the type represented by the Class, calling the class' default constructor as in listing 2.4:[5]

**Listing 2.4   Calling Class.newInstance**

```
Class classString; // from above
try
{
    Object obj = classString.newInstance();
}
catch (InstantiationException instEx)
{
    // Instantiation of an object of that type cannot occur; this is
    // usually due to an attempt by the programmer to instantiate a
    // nonconcrete type, like an interface, an abstract class, etc.
    instEx.printStackTrace();
}
catch (IllegalAccessException illAccEx)
{
    // The JVM cannot access the necessary constructor to initialize
    // an instance of this class; this is usually because the
    // class's default constructor is private or otherwise
    // unavailable
    illAccEx.printStackTrace();
}
catch (ExceptionInInitializerError exInInitErr)
{
    // An initializer block within the class threw an exception,
    // which terminated the initialization of the object; because
    // Java forbids objects remaining in an indeterminate state,
```

---

[5] It's impossible to invoke a constructor other than the default constructor through `Class.newInstance`. This is why, when a class is compiled, the Java compiler will synthesize a default constructor for you if the code does not provide one.

```
        // the exception killed the object and came back here
        exInInitErr.printStackTrace();
    }
    catch (SecurityException secEx)
    {
        // A Java Security policy prevents the instantiation of objects
        // from a Class in this codebase
        secEx.printStackTrace();
    }
```

The above code is functionally equivalent to

```
String str = new String();
```

"All that work, just to get a lousy String?" Don't underestimate the power of what we've done here; we've effectively created an instance of a class, without needing to know anything of that type at run time. This sort of loose coupling can do some truly amazing things.

### 2.2.3  java.lang.ClassLoader

ClassLoader's design is an almost perfect Factory Method[6] pattern: an abstract Creator (ClassLoader) defines an interface by which a Product is returned to callers (client code or the JVM itself, depending on the situation). Users are then able to subclass the Creator to create ConcreteCreator (custom ClassLoader) classes which return ConcreteProduct (again, Class objects, the only deviation from the pattern as defined by the Gang of Four) instances.

With the release of the Java 2 platform, ClassLoader's interface and semantics were redefined somewhat to make it easier for developers to extend the Java class-loading mechanism quickly and easily. As a result, some existing ClassLoader code written for 1.1 or 1.0 may not function properly within the Java 2 platform environment; unfortunately, there's no trivial way to know except to visit the code and reimplement the ClassLoader-derived class.

The most signficant change between Java 1.x and Java 2 is the relationship of ClassLoaders to one another. In Java 2, all ClassLoaders have a parent ClassLoader to whom they will give first shot at class-loading. This is known as the delegating ClassLoader model, and marks a significant change from how ClassLoaders operated in previous versions of Java.

#### ClassLoader delegation

Java has changed the way ClassLoaders were meant to be written from Java 1.0 to Java 2. As a result, much of the existing literature regarding the creation of ClassLoaders is flat-out wrong, and (hopefully) will be corrected soon. Most of this wrongness is due

---

[6] *Design Patterns*, p 107

to Java's changing the intent of the Factory Methods within the ClassLoader API; specifically, the intent of the `loadClass` method changed, and from that one change stems most (if not all) of the problems.

In Java 1.x, the approach to creating a custom ClassLoader was to override the loadClass method and provide an implementation there that located and loaded the bytecode, then called `defineClass` to return the actual Class instance. For example, this description and example come straight from the JDK 1.1.7 documentation set:

> The network class loader subclass must define the method `loadClass` to load a class from the network. Once it has downloaded the bytes that make up the class, it should use the method `defineClass` to create a class instance. A sample implementation is:
>
> ```
> class NetworkClassLoader {
>     String host;
>     int port;
>     Hashtable cache = new Hashtable();
>
>     private byte loadClassData(String name)[] {
>         // load the class data from the connection
>         . . .
>     }
>
>     public synchronized Class loadClass(String name,
>                 boolean resolve) {
>         Class c = cache.get(name);
>         if (c == null) {
>             byte data[] = loadClassData(name);
>             c = defineClass(data, 0, data.length);
>             cache.put(name, c);
>         }
>         if (resolve)
>             resolveClass(c);
>         return c;
>     }
> }
> ```

The `loadClass` method, then, serves as the Factory Method within the pattern in the JDK 1.x ClassLoader.

Note, also, that the Java 1.x ClassLoader required that derived types hold a reference to loaded Class instances. This was not to support caching of Class instances, as some surmised, but to ensure that the Class couldn't be garbage-collected until all objects using it were also released. Java already knows if a Class has been loaded into the JVM or not, so it will not ask the ClassLoader to load a class already loaded; thus, caching was wasted. Instead, because the Class instance is a normal Java object like any other, it could be garbage-collected unless a reference was held to it somewhere within the system.

The Java 1.1 ClassLoader system pictorially resembles figure 2.1.

As you can see, if a request for a new Class comes in to a particular ClassLoader, the ClassLoader must check with the system ClassLoader first, then attempt to load the Class itself.

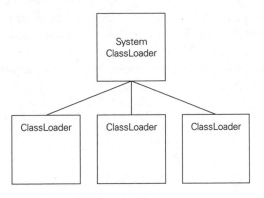

**Figure 2.1**
**Java 1.1 ClassLoader relationships**

This approach worked for single-level `ClassLoader` hierarchies (running an AppletClassLoader to download code from an HTTP server, for example). However, when Java developers began to examine more complex relationships (loading a ClassLoader from within customClassLoader, for example), it became obvious that this design would fail hideously over time—the 1.1 model couldn't track the complex Loader-within-a-Loader relationships. Consider this concept: normally, the Java bookstrap ClassLoaders are used to load Java code from disk or extension. However, for a given project, a ClassLoader is written to load Java code from a database. A second custom ClassLoader is deployed within that database, to reach across the wire to find classes running on a server. When the bootstrap ClassLoader loads the client class, the client creates an instance of the custom database ClassLoader (which, because it must be found by the primordial ClassLoaders, must reside on disk), and uses that to load a series of classes. As part of that, the socket-based ClassLoader is loaded and instantiated, and used to pull more code across the wire for execution (figure 2.2).

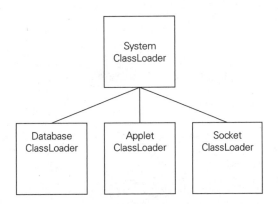

**Figure 2.2**
**Socket ClassLoader and database-ClassLoader working together**

Now, when a class, stored in the database, is requested of the socket ClassLoader, under the 1.1 rules, it will fail completely; the 1.1 ClassLoader scheme knows only about itself (the socket ClassLoader, in this case) and the bootstrap (a.k.a. the system) ClassLoader. Because the class requested comes from the database ClassLoader, both attempts, one by the socket ClassLoader, the other by the system ClassLoader, will fail.

Thus was the concept of parent ClassLoaders born: instead of automatically deferring the request to the system ClassLoader, under Java 2, a ClassLoader should instead ask the ClassLoader that loaded *it*. This allows for the mentioned sort of chaining all the way back to the root, the system ClassLoader, which, for purposes of our discussion, has no parent (figure 2.3).

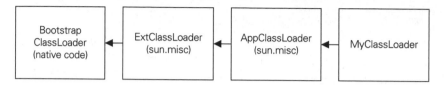

**Figure 2.3   The Java2 ClassLoader Delegation model—parents and children**

When Java 2 revamped the ClassLoader mechanism (to allow for the cool Extension system, which we'll explore in detail in chapter 4), unfortunately it had to break a few of its Java 1.x rules. To start, `loadClass` is no longer the method to override within Class-Loader; instead, that task falls to `findClass`. In the new system, `loadClass` provides the necessary delegate-to-your-parent-first behavior, so derived ClassLoader types don't have to worry about their parent ClassLoader:

```
// From src/java/lang directory in the JDK 1.2
public class ClassLoader
{
    protected synchronized Class loadClass(String name,
                                           boolean resolve)
        throws ClassNotFoundException
    {
        // First, check if the class has already been loaded
        Class c = findLoadedClass(name);
        if (c == null) {
            try {
                if (parent != null) {
                    c = parent.loadClass(name, false);
                } else {
                    c = findBootstrapClass(name);
                }
            } catch (ClassNotFoundException e) {
                // If still not found, then call findClass in order
                // to find the class.
                c = findClass(name);
            }
        }
        if (resolve) {
            resolveClass(c);
        }
        return c;
    }
}
```

As you can see, ClassLoader.loadClass is first going to check to see if the class has already been loaded. If not, it will call its parent's `loadClass` method to see if the parent knows where to find the class. This is important. It's going to have ramifications on the way GJAS (and any other dynamic-class-loading system built using Java 2) will be loaded and stored. If the parent fails to load the class, only then does the derived ClassLoader type get a crack at loading the Class via its `findClass` method.

That's the way it's supposed to work. But as you can see, comparing the JDK 1.x example with the Java 2 approach reveals a serious hole. If NetworkClassLoader, as defined by the Java 1.x documentation set, is compiled and executed, the whole delegating-ClassLoader paradigm is broken. This means that if the NetworkClassLoader is created by a class which in turn was loaded from a different ClassLoader, NetworkClassLoader will not defer loading of classes to its parent when asked to; instead, it will attempt to load the code via its own methods, fail, and throw a ClassNotFoundException.

In point of fact, it's much easier to break this parent-ClassLoader scheme than you might first imagine. Consider this ClassLoader constructor—the default one invoked if no parentClassLoader is specified as a constructor parameter:

```
// From src/java/lang directory in the JDK 1.2
protected ClassLoader()
{
    SecurityManager security = System.getSecurityManager();
    if (security != null) {
        security.checkCreateClassLoader();
    }
    this.parent = getSystemClassLoader();   // *** line 7
    initialized = true;
}
```

The relevant line is line 7 which calls `getSystemClassLoader()` to obtain the system ClassLoader as this ClassLoader's parent. This is a dangerous implementation because it makes the same fundamental assumption that the 1.1 ClassLoader scheme did, that your parent, by default, will always be the system ClassLoader.

In fact, the default assumption should be that your parent ClassLoader will be the one that loaded you, regardless of which ClassLoader it actually is (system or otherwise). JavaSoft may not call this a bug, per se, but in order to properly support ClassLoader-chaining, derived ClassLoaders must now ensure that they pass their parent to the constructor, as in:

```
public class DerivedClassLoader extends ClassLoader
{
  public DerivedClassLoader()
  {
    super(DerivedClassLoader.class.getClassLoader());

    // . . . Other initialization . . .
  }
}
```

The use of .class within the call to the ClassLoader constructor may seem awkward and unusual here; unfortunately, it's necessary, since Java disallows calling getClass on an object within its constructor, since the object may not be fully formed or initialized yet. The .class keyword, on the other hand, refers explicitly to the Class for the class DerivedClassLoader, which is statically resolvable, and so doesn't require completed initialization of this DerivedClassLoader instance. The drawback is that any class name might be accidentally used here, which makes this code sequence particularly vulnerable to cut-and-paste errors.

You might find this all a bit esoteric; after all, most Java code isn't written to use multiple custom ClassLoaders, or even to use one. Unfortunately, this concerns Java programmers more than they might expect. With the increase of generic application servers (EJB or otherwise, such as the GJAS system we're building within this book), multiple ClassLoaders are on the way. For example, most EJB servers will define their own ClassLoader to control the loading and unloading of EJBs within the server; if the Beans in turn attempt to use a custom ClassLoader, then everybody's got to play by the rules of the Java 2 system, or else things will break very quickly. Another such case is the ubiquitous applet—with the relaxation of constraints on the applet sandbox (assuming verification of the applet code, of course, on the client machine), it becomes possible for applets to do some custom ClassLoading. However, applets, as we've already discussed, are already using AppletClassLoader to pull down their Applet-derived class and any supporting code required by the applet. Toss in a RMIClass-Loader, or any other form, and if everybody's not playing by the rules, ClassNotFound-Exceptions (or ClassCastExceptions, as classes attempt to cross name space barriers) rule the day.

A few other rules changed in Java 2, as well. Java 1.x required that the loadClass method be synchronized, in case multiple Threads using the same ClassLoader asked for a class at the same time. Unfortunately, this wasn't a very well-popularized fact, and several ClassLoaders were written without the synchronized keyword, leading to the possibility of multiple Threads inside the same ClassLoader instance's loadClass. Java 2 takes care of this, since loadClass is synchronized (and will continue to hold the lock while findClass is called within it) and thus requires no explicit synchronization on the part of its derived types.

The only ClassLoader in the system without a parent ClassLoader is the bootstrap ClassLoader, which is responsible for the loading of the Java run-time classes. This (implemented entirely within the JVM, so details regarding its behavior and/or existence are not standard across JVMs) will always be the first in any ClassLoader chain, and will be responsible for the loading of all classes within the Java run-time library.[7] We'll cover the changes this made when we talk about custom ClassLoaders.

---

[7]  Basically all the classes stored in the rt.jar file in the JRE\lib directory, plus some others.

## ClassLoader API

In keeping with the Factory Method pattern, the designers of Java provide three abstract methods which subclasses of ClassLoader must implement in order to provide all ClassLoader operations. However, because not all ClassLoaders will want to provide all operations, ClassLoader also provides a no-op definition of each method. This way, if a ClassLoader doesn't want to provide class-loading, resource-loading and/or native-library-loading support, no additional code need be written to indicate that.

ClassLoader's API can be broken into the following groups:

- *The public API*
  `getParent` returns the parent ClassLoader to this one. `getResource/`
  `getResourceAsStream/getResources` returns a single resource, as an InputStream, or an Enumeration of all resources available within this instance. "Resources" is a deliberately vague term, and can include such things as image files (.GIF or .JPEG, for example), audio or other multimedia files, or even plain text or other data. One such type resource could be Serialized data of initial data values within the class. `getSystemClassLoader/getSystemResource/get-`
  `SystemResourceAsStream/getSystemResources` return the system versions of the above: the system (or bootstrap, or root) ClassLoader, or the resources loadable from within the system ClassLoader. Finally, `loadClass` is the API used to load, link, and initialize Java classes.

- *The FactoryMethod APIs*
  `findClass`, `findLibrary`, `findResource`, and `findResources` are the factory methods as described by the Factory Method pattern. These will be the APIs overridden in derived classes, and as such, will be covered later. `findSystem-`
  `Class` is effectively a wrapper around `getSystemClassLoader().find-`
  `Class()`, and will not need to be overridden by derived ClassLoaders, despite its seemingly related name.

- *The base APIs*
  `defineClass` provides a convenience method for translating a bytecode array to a Class object, performing all the loading, linking, and initialization necessary on the class. Internally, `defineClass` defaults to the use of a native method, `defineClass0`, so the actual work necessary to define a class within the JVM remains hidden from prying eyes unless you have the Java 2 Source Release. `definePackage` provides the ability to define a new Package instance (which represents all packages loaded by this ClassLoader) within this ClassLoader; frankly, unless your ClassLoader is dealing explicitly with signed/sealed .jar files,[8] this method won't be of much use. The same goes for `getPackage` and/or

---

[8] This sort of security is more intended toward relaxing some of the restrictions on the applet sandbox, and more than likely won't be applicable within a server application. This may change, however, as the Java Security model changes to accommodate more server-side idioms and needs.

`getPackages`; in fact, I'm not entirely sure of the reason for these methods to be here, marked protected. That sort of information would seem to be of more use to external clients than to derived ClassLoader types. `loadClass` comes in two versions, one for public view (described earlier), and one for internal use. Both provide the delegating behavior of the new JDK 1.2 ClassLoader model, so avoid overriding them unless you have a *very* good idea of what you're doing. `resolveClass` is used to resolve all symbolic representations, as described earlier; fortunately, custom ClassLoaders never need to call this method, since `defineClass` and native JVM behavior take care of all the details once the bytecode has been obtained. Lastly, `setSigners` is used to establish the signers of a class, again, in relation to the relaxation of the applet sandbox.

More details on the methods' parameters and exception-declarations can be found in the Java documentation set. Later in chapter 3, we'll go over the details of creating a custom ClassLoader to be fully Java 2-compliant.

A Class always remembers the ClassLoader that loaded it,[9] and any classes referenced by that Class that haven't been loaded will be loaded (if possible) by that same ClassLoader. This is how, in fact, AppletClassLoader manages to know to load Classes from the web server's loaded page instead of trying to load it from the web browser's Java libraries. Thus, when the applet is first loaded into the client web browser, as it executes, any classes it uses will also be loaded by the AppletClassLoader that loaded the applet in the first place. The same will hold true for any ClassLoader, not just AppletClassLoader.

## 2.2.4 Java name spaces

In Java, a class's name is not just its class name, or its package name plus class name. When identifying classes already loaded by a JVM, a particular bytecode image is identified by its package name, its class name, and the instance of the ClassLoader used to define it. That is, for any Class ($c$) in a package ($p$) loaded by a ClassLoader instance ($cl$), the JVM class name key for that Class is

```
(c, p, cl)
```

In this manner, each ClassLoader forms a unique name space. Everything related directly to classes, including static data, is contained within it. This means that if a class with static data is loaded into two separate name spaces, then two sets of static data are maintained for that class, one within each name space.

Classes are also unrecognizable across name spaces. While a class is permitted to extend a class from another name space, two classes of the same package name/class name are *not* identical if loaded within separate name spaces, and any attempt to cast

---

[9]  Specifically, the `ClassLoader` instance that called `ClassLoader.defineClass` to turn the array of bytes into a verified, executable `Class`.

from one to the other will generate ClassCastExceptions. We'll see an example of this concept in action when we start examining custom ClassLoaders in chapter 3.

## 2.3 JAVA'S BUILT-IN CLASSLOADERS

As mentioned, Java comes with several ClassLoaders within the standard Java JDK run-time library. Some of these are openly available (those within the `java.*` packages), while others aren't visible unless a Java decompiler is used on the rt.jar file in the Java 2 jre/lib directory, or the Java 2 source download is examined. Regardless, all of the listed ClassLoaders that follow are available with any Java 2-compliant installation.

### 2.3.1 java.security.SecureClassLoader

SecureClassLoader is new to Java, coming as part of the Java 2 platform's revamped security emphasis. Its primary purpose is to provide secure control over the loading and using of compiled bytecode within the JVM. As such, its intent is not to provide a secure means by which class code can be loaded, as you might expect, but to provide a base class which other ClassLoader types can extend and use to hook into Java's security system. As such, it is the base class to a number of the other ClassLoaders within the Java run-time library, most notably URLClassLoader.

Because it is intended as an abstract base class, and not to be used directly, Secure-ClassLoader's two constructor methods are both marked protected, making it impossible for developers to instantiate one directly. Full details on using the SecureClassLoader is beyond the scope of this book, since getting into that leads directly into discussion of Java's Security system.

### 2.3.2 java.net.URLClassLoader

The URLClassLoader is, in fact, just about the only implemented ClassLoader within the Java 1.2 run-time library. All other ClassLoaders extend this class in some form or another, providing additional functionality around the URLClassLoader class in the form of the Decorator pattern.[10] If readers understand the URLClassLoader and its capabilities, and nothing else, they will already be ahead of the game.

#### Using URLClassLoader to load from disk

The most common type of URL used with URLClassLoader (within the JDK source code, if not user code) is to load classes from local disk. The code below looks in the subdirectory "subdir" under the current directory for a "Hello.class" class file. It then uses the `loadClass` method of URLClassLoader to retrieve the Class object for "Hello", and in the same line calls the `newInstance` method of Class to create a new instance of the Hello class. Because the Hello class (in this example) contains a

---

[10] *Design Patterns*, p. 175

`System.out.println` call to write "Hello!", we can visually see that the class was loaded, verified, and linked.

The code is as follows:

```
public class FileURLClient
{
    /**
     * Attempt to instantiate an instance of the class
     * Hello, found in the subdirectory "subdir" from the
     * chap02 directory
     */
    public static void main(String[] args)
        throws Exception
    {
        URL[] urlArray =
        {
            new java.io.File("subdir/").toURL()
        };

        URLClassLoader ucl = new URLClassLoader(urlArray);
        Object obj =
            ucl.loadClass("Hello").newInstance();

        // Hello should print "Hello" to the System.out stream
    }
}
```

In this example, I use the `File.toURL` method to create a URL from an existing File object, so as to be able to deal with operating-system-specific path issues (such as path separator characters, or absolute versus relative path names, and so forth) generically.[11] I strongly suggest to anyone looking to use, build, or work with file URLs to do the immediate work using java.io.File objects, then use the `toURL` method of File to obtain the actual URL, rather than trying to build the URL using the java.net.URL constructors.

URLClassLoader also silently deals with Java libraries, .jar and .zip files, as well:

```
import java.net.URL;
import java.net.URLClassLoader;

public class FileURLClient
{
    /**
     * Attempt to instantiate an instance of the class
     * Hello, found in the subdirectory "subdir" from the
     * chap02 directory
     */
```

---

[11] The whole file name/path name issue is probably one of Java's weakest areas in terms of its portability. Because different operating systems use differing characters and syntax to represent files and directories, trying to represent a file in an absolute path is nearly impossible to do in a generic way. For example, a subdirectory "temp" off of the root directory is "/temp" in UNIX, "C:\temp" in Windows, and "Hard Drive:temp" in the MacOS; things get even more convoluted when dealing with multiple drives.

```
        public static void main(String[] args)
            throws Exception
        {
            URL[] urlArray =
            {
                new java.io.File("subdir.jar").toURL()
            };

            URLClassLoader ucl = new URLClassLoader(urlArray);
            Object obj =
                ucl.loadClass("Hello").newInstance();

            // Hello should print "Hello" to the System.out stream
        }
    }
```

By simply adding .jar to the end of the URL, the URL will look to open the .jar file and extract the classes (and resources) from there, instead of via the file system. In the example above, using .jar told URLClassLoader to look for Hello.class within the .jar file, instead of looking for "Hello.class" as a file within the subdirectory "subdir". This holds true for any use of URLClassLoader, including using it to retrieve classes via an HTTP server and/or FTP server.

### Using URLClassLoader to load from a HTTP server

Using URLClassLoader to pull class code from an HTTP server is usually of far more interest to most Java developers. It is, in fact, the basic means by which applets exist—the applet code (which must extend Applet, of course) is pulled down from the HTTP server into the browser's process space, started, and stopped when the user moves on to another page. If we can harness this mechanism for use in our own applications, we can gain a tremendous amount of flexibility and make a significant step toward zero deployment.

First, let's examine how to use URLClassLoader to load a class from an HTTP server:

```
// imports not shown

public class HTTPURLClient
{
    /**
     * Attempt to instantiate an instance of the class
     * com.javageeks.util.Hello, found only on the javageeks.com
     * HTTP server in the "/SSJ/examples" directory.
     */
    public static void main(String[] args)
        throws Exception
    {
        URL[] urlArray =
        {
            new URL("http", "www.javageeks.com",
                    "/SSJ/examples/")
        };
```

```
        URLClassLoader ucl = new URLClassLoader(urlArray);
        Object obj =
            ucl.loadClass("chap02.Hello").newInstance();

        // Hello should print "Hello from JavaGeeks.com!" to the
        // System.out stream
    }
}
```

The example creates a URL representing the URL http://www.javageeks.com/SSJ/ examples, hands it into a URLClassLoader instance, just as the prior file example did, and asks URLClassLoader to instantiate an instance of the class "com.java-geeks.util.Hello". That class, whose code is not shown here, in turn writes a message to the System.out stream from its constructor. This application has one distinctive difference, however, from the earlier file://-based version; if this class is executed on a machine without a working connection to the Internet, a ClassNotFoundException will be thrown. Any attempt to look for the source code to "Hello.java" in the download bundle from the web site will fail; this compiled class file exists only on the java-geeks.com server, to prove that the code cannot be loaded from local disk by accident. The class file can only come from the web site.

The zero deployment advantages to using URLClassLoader are myriad. Assume, for a moment, that we have a department that performs routine report-analysis on a corporate database or data warehouse. New reports are constantly being requested, existing reports are being modified, and old reports are being removed as the business needs change. The development team could attempt to build a complex menu that allows users to select the reports from within the application. Unfortunately, this would require recoding each time the list of reports changed, eating into productive development time, and would require the application to be redistributed to all the department's users, eating into productive system administrator time.

Instead, if the code can be centralized to load from a single source (the department's internal HTTP server, for example), then a thin bootstrap client can be distributed (once) to the department's users. This thin boostrap client then uses the HTTP server to load the actual client code and its supporting classes, from which the users select the report they'd like to run. Or, if the bootstrap client is slightly more intelligent, it can open the URL as a standard URL and walk across the .class files it finds there, looking for those that meet a particular mask and displaying those to the user. Regardless, we've now reduced the deployment costs of these constantly changing reports to almost nothing, since developers now only need focus on the development of the reports themselves, and not the front-end GUIs to support them.

### Using URLClassLoader to load from an FTP server

Having demonstrated that we can easily load code from an HTTP server, which seems to be all the rage these days, it might seem curious that the next demonstration centers on loading code from an FTP server. Let's first demonstrate that it can be done, then discuss why we might care about it.

The actual act of using an FTP server to access the code is remarkably similar to that code using an HTTP server, except that the URLs used to access the FTP server are more complex:

```
// imports not shown

public class FTPURLClient
{
    /**
     * Attempt to instantiate an instance of the class
     * com.javageeks.util.Hello, found only on the javageeks.com
     * FTP server in the "examples" directory.
     */
    public static void main(String[] args)
        throws Exception
    {
        URL[] urlArray =
        {
            new URL("ftp", "reader:password@www.javageeks.com:",
                    "/")    // using 'reader' account
        };

        URLClassLoader ucl = new URLClassLoader(urlArray);
        Object obj =
            ucl.loadClass("Hello").newInstance();

        // Hello should print "Hello from JavaGeeks.com!" to the
        // System.out stream
    }
}
```

This code is almost identical to the HTTPURLClient code from earlier, except that the URL specified in the `urlArray` array is different; in fact, it's downright strange. The first argument, `"ftp"`, is understandable, indicating the URL is to use the "ftp://" prefix to the URL, and the third argument, `"/SSJ/examples/"` indicates the sub-directory to which the URL refers. The second argument, however, makes almost no sense, unless the reader is intimately familiar with the URL specification.

Normally, an FTP URL looks like ftp://www.javageeks.com/SomeDir, indicating the FTP protocol, on the server www.javageeks.com, in the directory SomeDir. However, FTP isn't a user-less protocol like HTTP; in order to utilize an FTP connection, a username and password must be given to the FTP server for authentication. This is what the reader:password@ in front of the server name is for, to pass the username (reader) and password (password) to the FTP server as login information. The trailing colon on the URL is to work around a bug in the Java run-time libraries (specifically, in the URLConnection class) which assumes that any colon in the URL will be a port designator, and so uses `String.lastIndexOf(":")` to find it. Unfortunately, if the trailing colon isn't there, it assumes that reader is the full server name and password@ftp.javageeks.com is the port number to use, which generates an `InvalidPortRangeException`.

Once the strangeness of the FTP URL is hurdled, the rest of FTPURLClient is straightforward—pass the URL array into an instance of URLClassLoader, then ask the URLClassLoader to instantiate an instance of "Hello". As with the HTTPURL-Client, when this class is executed on a machine with a connection to the Internet (the code is coming from the JavaGeeks site), the Hello constructor displays its welcoming message.

Principally, there are two reasons to go through the exercise of showing how over-the-wire ClassLoading can be done with an FTP server. First, because FTP is an acceptable URL protocol, we should at least verify that it can be done. Secondly, if it can be done, there's likely to be some organization or development team looking to do it. For example, an FTP server provides enhanced security (requiring a user account and password on the FTP server, if anonymous access isn't allowed), thus preventing unauthorized use of the classes, or perhaps providing per-user code access.

This second reason contains more merit than might be immediately obvious. The notion of user roles is ubiquitous within server-side applications, so much so that numerous patterns have been written describing it.[12] It's not uncommon within a variety of enterprise systems to see code such as the following, which displays different dialogs based on whether or not the user is an "Administrator":

```
if (getUser().getRole().equals("Administrator"))
    new AdministratorDialog().execute();
else
    new UserDialog().execute();
```

Or worse, the developer will try to save a few lines of code and do these `if-else` statements within the dialog itself, to determine if certain fields should be editable versus read-only, visible versus hidden, or even labeled differently or containing different data, based on these sorts of decisions.

What's wrong with that? Everything. Principally, you are now encoding business rules into the dialog presentation code; your dialog now needs to worry about user roles, and how to obtain the current user ID, and so forth. The more of these rules that make it into your presentation-layer code, the more difficult that code is to maintain, enhance, and support.

Worse yet, adding a new role into the system requires changes across the entire system—every place this sort of "can a user role do *X*?" is made, a new branch to the if/else logic must be added to accommodate the new role. This is time-consuming, tedious, and very bug-prone. If, instead, user roles can be restricted as a group from certain classes, it simplifies the addition (removal, or modification) of those roles.

---

[12] See "Additional reading" for a list of pattern resources.

Using the FTPClassLoader allows the developer to make use of the security measures built into the FTP server (which, on UNIX systems, in turn relies on the security measures built into the UNIX operating system on which the FTP server is running) to discriminate between users, and, implicitly, their roles within the system by specifying the URL by just its username and password. Then, the preceding dialog-execution can be written as:

```
public static void main(String[] args)
{
    String username;
    String password;

    // obtain username/password from user
    new LoginDialog(username, password).execute();

    URL ftpURL = new URL("ftp", username + ":" + password +
                        "@ftp.javageeks.com", "/Classes/");
    urlClassLoader = new URLClassLoader(ftpURL);
        // urlClassLoader is stored within this class instance

    // . . .
}

public void displayDialog()
{
    SomeRoleSensitiveDialog srsd =
        (SomeRoleSensitiveDialog)urlClassLoader.loadClass(
            "Dialog").newInstance();
    srsd.execute();

        // Note that this assumes that the bytecode itself thinks its name
        // is "Dialog.class" (that is, it was compiled from a file called
        // "Dialog.java"); if it was compiled from any other .java filename,
        // the bytecode will fail verification by the JVM!
}
```

What's the advantage? The fact that the dialog now knows nothing about user roles; that knowledge is now incorporated into the FTP system itself,[13] and is broken out into separate dialogs. More importantly, changes to one user-role's dialog won't affect the other, so testing will be easier and more isolated. Development might be trickier, because developers will be forced to maintain separate directory trees for each user-role set of classes (one for admins, one for users, and so on), since the class names on the local disk will all be identical, but this is usually fairly manageable and in some cases, it is preferable.

In many cases, however, the majority of code that best belongs in a centralized fashion like this (either through the FTP server, HTTP server or even SQL database)

---

[13] This presumes that the FTP system will drop users into different directories based on user IDs, which may not be standard features on all FTP systems. It's far more likely that different departments will maintain their own FTP servers.

encompasses the various business rules and objects for a given system, since these are the ones that typically change the most from version to version.

Placing this code into the centralized server means that these rules can be differentiated from one client to another, even within the same system, substituting the client name in place of user-role, as in the foregoing example.[14] A sample of this would be a data-entry system for customer information—different departments within the enterprise will have different "rules" for which fields are required and which are optional. Marketing, for example, may insist on obtaining some market-segment data (such as age group), while technical/product support will insist on having detailed records about the product in the system's database. By placing this code on separate FTP servers, based on department name, we can silently differentiate between departments without requiring any modification to the client code. This is a significant step toward both zero development (client code need not be rewritten for different departments) and zero deployment (since changed code needs only be copied up to the appropriate place on the FTP server). It even aids in zero administration, since now a new security system specific to the application needn't be maintained by the system administrators; once users are added to the UNIX (or whatever hosts the FTP server) user database, they are automatically (again, assuming the FTP server uses the underlying operating system's user database for authentication, which most do) added to the list of authorized users of the client code. This in turn helps the system administrator—the fewer passwords users have to memorize to get their work done, the more likely they are to use nontrivial passwords that are harder to break using password-generating tools.

### Using URLClassLoader for custom URL types

URLClassLoader isn't restricted to just file, http or ftp URL types. In fact, just as the URL syntax is intended to be open and flexible to new protocol types, so too is URLClassLoader intended to be open and flexible for loading classes from any supported URL type.

While the details are too long to get into here, the basic idea is simple: URLClassLoader obtains its URL objects (from which it in turn obtains objects to open and read the URL resource) from a `URLStreamHandlerFactory`. `URLStreamHandlerFactory` is a simple interface, sporting a single method, `createURLStreamHandler`. By creating a custom class that implements `URLStreamHandlerFactory` that in turn creates URLStreamHandler-derived classes (as appropriate to the protocol passed in), you can create a custom protocol to support loading classes and/or other resources from any other source imaginable.

---

[14] The Strategy or Façade patterns fit in well here.

### 2.3.3 sun.applet.AppletClassLoader

The AppletClassLoader, as its name implies, is the ClassLoader intended for use by web browsers to download and start execution of Applet bytecode on a web page. Because each web browser may provide its own implementation of a ClassLoader that downloads the bytecode, this ClassLoader may not be the one used within your favorite web browser. Moreover, its use would only be of interest to those who are seeking to exactly duplicate applet-download semantics, including the full security restrictions placed on applets.

AppletClassLoader extends URLClassLoader, as might be expected. As a result, any web browser written to use AppletClassLoader automatically picks up its ability to load code via more than one .jar file or subdirectory, via the HTML <CODEBASE> directive. In fact, it's fairly easy to discover which Web browsers use this version of Sun's AppletClassLoader, and which don't, because several popular Web browsers won't accept more than one .jar file as a source for an applet. As a result, if developers create nontrivial applets, test their execution under more than just the Sun applet viewer or HotJava Web browser, they may be unpleasantly surprised.

Aside from its support for Java's security model, `AppletClassLoader` doesn't hold any surprises but there is a bit of trivia involved. Applets can share static data across applet instances, and so can use that as an inter-applet communication mechanism. Once you realize that, at least historically, a new AppletClassLoader is started for each web page loaded, and is then used to load the applet code into the client browser, you understand how applets can share static data across instances, since static data is on a per-ClassLoader basis. This is neither mandated, nor required, and can, in fact, represent a security hole.

### 2.3.4 java.rmi.server.RMIClassLoader

RMIClassLoader, contrary to what you might believe, isn't a ClassLoader, but a wrapper class around the marshaling and loading of classes in the RMI run-time system. In fact, RMIClassLoader is a simple bridge around the sun.rmi.server.LoaderHandler class, which in turn maintains a map of inner Loader classes, which are the actual classes extending URLClassLoader.

Given URLClassLoader's ability to download code from an HTTP or FTP server, as well as the customized ClassLoaders we'll be developing throughout the rest of the book, the usefulness of RMIClassLoader wanes somewhat, except for RMI itself. Even then, RMIClassLoader isn't the interesting part of the mechanism, since it defers all behavior to its concrete implementation, LoaderHandler, which in turn provides the support for the `java.rmi.server.codebase` property and other RMI-classloading functionality.

RMI plays a key role in the pursuit of zero deployment; however, we'll get more into the capabilities of RMI later.

### 2.3.5 Bootstrap ClassLoader

This is technically not a ClassLoader, either, since it exists solely within the native code boundaries of the JVM, and is used to load the key core Java classes (like Object) into the virtual machine. It relies on the `sun.boot.class.path` property to find the Java run-time library (rt.jar, in JDK 1.2, under the jre/lib directory), meaning that it is possible for us to change this value to point to another location, although it's certainly not recommended for the faint of heart.

### 2.3.6 sun.misc.Launcher$ExtClassLoader

The ExtClassLoader, also referred to as the extensions ClassLoader, is responsible for the loading of Java Extensions classes, which we cover in more detail in chapter 4. For now, it's enough to state that ExtClassLoader, which extends URLClassLoader, stores the .jar files in the directories specified in the `java.ext.dirs` property as separate URLs, each of which is passed into its URLClassLoader base-class constructor.

### *sun.misc.Launcher$AppClassLoader*

The AppClassLoader, also referred to as the system or application ClassLoader, is another URLClassLoader-derivative class that handles the loading of code specified in the `java.class.path` property. Each directory or .jar file found along the CLASS-PATH is transformed into a URL, which is passed to the URLClassLoader base-class constructor on construction of the AppClassLoader.

This ClassLoader is also the returned instance when ClassLoader.getSystemClass-Loader is called; as a result, this will typically (unless your code runs under its own ClassLoader, as do applets or servlets) be the ClassLoader that loads your code. As a result, it's fairly easy to see why your code has access to all installed Java Extensions—because AppClassLoader uses the Extensions ClassLoader as its delegating parent; everything in the Extensions directory or directories is now available to your code.

The implication here is that your code is not loaded by the same ClassLoader that loads the Java run-time classes. This won't have serious effects on most normal application code, but advanced use of ClassLoaders can lead to problems. For example, any code stored as an extension, attempting to load code off of the CLASSPATH, will run into problems related to the Java ClassLoader name space separation.

## 2.4 SUMMARY

ClassLoaders are, without a doubt, one of the most powerful technologies within Java; by allowing us, as developers, to control from where code can be loaded, we can now distribute applications in ways that we couldn't dream about five years ago. This concept extends to more than just zero deployment.

Consider a system in which customized behavior needs to be developed for a series of clients, varying not only on a per-client basis, but on a per-entity basis within the client. For example, an insurance company may want to perform different tasks on the call-center representative's PC during an insurance sales call, depending on what data is entered. Some sample ideas might be:

- Pop up a message box reminding the rep to suggestive-sell life-insurance policies to callers over the age of 30

- Introduce new specials on various policies, but only if the candidate fits a particular criteria

- Remind the call-center rep of the month's current internal promotional program, reminding him/her to undertake particular actions based on the rep's proximity to the promotional target

Realistically, these sorts of monthly changes could drive a developer mad—a new release, every month? Recoding, retesting, everything, every month?

Instead of coding these sorts of mutable rules directly within the application code, set up a custom ClassLoader. Create the custom ClassLoader at a particular point during the call and load code associated with this call directly from the database, or from a socket, so long as the code is coming from a code source separate from the application's. This allows the developers to change code associated with the databse without having to modify the existing code base.

Of course, this is dependent on knowing how to create your own ClassLoaders. Unfortunately, creating them seems to be something of a mystic art—even in late 1999, books and articles are being published that get it wrong. In the next chapter, I'll show you how Sun wants you to build ClassLoaders, so that they'll fit flawlessly within the Java ClassLoader hierarchy.

## 2.5   ADDITIONAL READING

- *Java Virtual Machine Specification* (2nd Edition) (Addison-Wesley).

   This is the new-and-improved version of the *Java Virtual Machine Specification* with the latest enhancements and changes made for JDK 1.2. Chapter 5 describes the ClassLoader mechanism in detail. If you plan to do any work with custom ClassLoaders, you will want to read this text; ditto for anyone working with the ClassFile API, as you'll need some knowledge of Java's assembly language opcodes and operands. It's also good to know, just in general, since this forms the reference for those wishing to provide compliant JVM implementations. If it's not in here, the JVM doesn't have to provide it. The JVMS is also available online, at http://java.sun.com/docs/books.

- *Java Language Specification* (2nd Edition) (Addison-Wesley).

   This, like the *Java Virtual Machine Specification*, is the definition of the Java language and all that it offers. In particular, it contains a description of how the ClassLoader mechanism works from the perspective of the language itself.

- Sheng Liang and Gilad Bracha, *"Dynamic Class Loading in the Java Virtual Machine"* (presented at 13th Annual ACM SIGPLAN Conference on Object-

Oriented Programming Systems, Languages, and Applications (OOPSLA '98), Vancouver, BC, Canada, October, 1998).

Sheng Liang presented this paper to the OOPSLA '98 conference on the new JDK 1.2 ClassLoader mechanism, and it remains the finest description of the ClassLoader mechanism to date.

**C H A P T E R   3**

# Custom ClassLoaders

If the Internet has taught the world anything about information, it's that it can come from a variety of places, in a variety of formats, accessible in a variety of ways. Nobody had any concept of the e-zine before the web craze. They make sense, now—same concept as a printed magazine with authors writing articles for readers to read, but a different delivery system. The same holds true for e-newspaper sites offered by Yahoo or Pointcast. We can apply that precept to our Java bytecode, as well—same concept, finding bytecode for execution by the JVM, just different delivery systems.

## 3.1   EXTENDING CLASSLOADER

A Java 2 ClassLoader needs to override one of three of the `find` methods:

- `findClass`: This method is expected to obtain the bytecode for the fully qualified class name given in its sole parameter. Once the bytecode is found, a derived ClassLoader must call defineClass, passing in the name of the class, the bytecode array, the offset at which to start, and the length of the array. The reason for the offset and length as parameters is an attempt to allow for optimization on the part of derived ClassLoaders. Instead of loading bytecode one class at a time, a ClassLoader can load/download/compile a set of classes, an entire package, or perhaps the entire .jar file (or more) once. Then, when asked, it provides the same bytecode array over and over again, using different offsets and lengths to indicate the position of each class within the master array.

- findResource: This method is expected to obtain the bytes for a given arbitrary name. Although most common usage has this name being a filename, nothing within the ClassLoader specification requires that this be the case. Instead, ClassLoader implementations are free to use the "/"-separated names as any sort of naming convention protocol they deem practical. As with find-Class, findResource is called from the ClassLoader's public method, getResource, which also delegates the first attempt at finding the resource to its parent ClassLoader. If you implement this method, be sure to provide similar semantics for the findResources method, as well.

- findLibrary: This method will likely be the least-often overridden method, because only developers who use JNI to write native-code libraries for Java need worry about it. This method is called when a ClassLoader is told to load a class which uses a native library. Unlike the findClass or findResource methods, findLibrary need only return an absolute pathname to the native library in question, rather than the actual binary data itself.

Note that every class holds a reference back to the ClassLoader that loaded it, so any class code that requires the use of an external resource shouldn't reference it (for loading, playing, unloading, whatever) any other way than by calling

```
URL urlToResource = this.getClass().getClassLoader().getResource(. . .);
```

Why? If the class is ever moved from being loaded from disk to being loaded from a customized ClassLoader, then any references to load anything from disk will fail. The foregoing code sequence works in all cases, presuming that the same ClassLoader that loaded the class also knows how to retrieve the needed resource. This in turn leads to the suggestion that if you create a custom ClassLoader, at least provide implementations for findClass and findResource.

Having said all that, let's examine some custom ClassLoaders in a more practical fashion.

### 3.1.1 FileSystemClassLoader

Let's start by duplicating existing functionality by building a ClassLoader that picks up class bytecode from the local file system. (Listing 3.1) We're not going to try anything tricky here, so we'll not worry about .jar/.zip files or resources. The code can be found on the publisher's web site (as part of the com.javageeks.classloader package, in the Lib subdirectory), reproduced here for convenience:

**Listing 3.1  Code for a FileSystemClassLoader**

```
import java.io.*;
import java.net.*;
import java.util.*;
```

```java
public class FileSystemClassLoader extends ClassLoader
{
    /**
     * Default constructor uses the home directory of the JDK as its
     * root in the file system.
     */
    public FileSystemClassLoader()
        throws FileNotFoundException
    {
        this(System.getProperties().getProperty("java.home"));
    }
    /**
     * Constructor taking a String indicating the point on the local
     * file system to take as the root in the file system.
     */
    public FileSystemClassLoader(String root)
        throws FileNotFoundException
    {
        super(FileSystemClassLoader.class.getClassLoader());

        // Test to make sure root is a legitimate directory on the
        // local file system
        //
        File f = new File(root);
        if (f.isDirectory())
            m_root = root;
        else
            throw new FileNotFoundException();
    }

    /**
     * Attempt to find the bytecode given for the class <code>name</code>
     * from a file on disk. Will not look along CLASSPATH, nor in .jar
     * files
     */
    public Class findClass(String name)
        throws ClassNotFoundException
    {
        try
        {
            // Assume that 'name' follows standard Java package-to-directory
            // naming conventions, where each "." represents a directory
            // separator character (backslash on Windows, slash on Unix,
            // colon on MacOS).
            //
            String pathName = m_root + File.separatorChar +
                name.replace('.', File.separatorChar) + ".class";

            // Try to open the file and read in its contents
            //
            FileInputStream inFile =
                new FileInputStream(pathName);
            byte[] classBytes = new byte[inFile.available()];
```

```
            inFile.read(classBytes);

            // Now we've got the bytecode, but we still need to turn it
            // into a verified class; that's what the method
            // ClassLoader.defineClass is for.
            //
            return defineClass(name, classBytes, 0, classBytes.length);
        }
        catch (java.io.IOException ioEx)
        {
            ioEx.printStackTrace();
            throw new ClassNotFoundException();
        }
    }

    private String m_root = null;

    // Test driver
    //
    public static void main(String[] args)
        throws Exception
    {
        String userDir = System.getProperties().getProperty("user.dir");
        FileSystemClassLoader fscl = new FileSystemClassLoader(userDir);

        // Test the ClassLoader by trying to load itself! (I first found
        // the idea in "Java Virtual Machine", by Troy Downing and Jon
        // Meyer (O'Reilly), who in turn credit
        // http://magma.Mines.edu/students/d/drferrin/Cool_Beans.)
        //
        Class c = fscl.loadClass("FileSystemClassLoader");

        // Instantiate an instance of the FileSystemClassLoader as an
        // Object; leave it like this for the moment
        //
        Object o = c.newInstance();

        // Verify that it is, in fact, a FileSystemClassLoader
        //
        System.out.println(o.getClass().getName());

        // Note--because of the Java name space's mechanism, this cast will
        // fail! This is because FileSystemClassLoader was first loaded by
        // the primordial ClassLoader, and the attempt to cast the new
        // Object (which was returned by the FileSystemClassLoader we
        // created a few lines ago) will fail, because you cannot cast
        // across ClassLoader lines.
        //
        FileSystemClassLoader fscl2 = (FileSystemClassLoader)c.newInstance();
    }
}
```

This isn't all that tricky—two constructors, one which takes a String, the other which takes nothing, define the root of our FileSystemClassLoader's search path. The meat of the action occurs in `findClass`. This method is the one responsible for attempting to locate the bytecode represented by the passed-in name (given in the parameter name). We convert the package name to a path, the class name to a file name, tack .class on the end, and attempt to load it in. If it succeeds, we use the base class' `defineClass` method to turn the bytes into verified class bytecode, and a Class instance results. If it fails, we throw a `java.lang.ClassNotFoundException`, as per the standard ClassLoader documentation. It's all pretty simple—we even provide a `main` method, so we can test the component.

So why do we get a `java.lang.ClassCastException` on the last line of `main`?

```
C:\Projects\SSJ\cd\src\chap2>java FileSystemClassLoader
FileSystemClassLoader
Exception in thread "main" java.lang.ClassCastException:
    FileSystemClassLoader
        at FileSystemClassLoader.main(FileSystemClassLoader.java:105)

C:\Projects\SSJ\cd\src\chap2>
```

The answer brings us back to Java's name space concept, and the notion that classes loaded into separate name spaces are independent and unrelated types. This is probably the trickiest part of Java's classloading scheme, and the hardest one to track down when an error occurs.

When we first started up the FileSystemClassLoader, the Application Class-Loader (the one used by the JVM to load the classes necessary to even execute a Java class) loads in the FileSystemClassLoader image. That is, given the discussion of classes being unique on class name/package name/classloader instance.

```
"FileSystemClassLoader" = ("FileSystemClassLoader", "", "AppClassLoader #1")
```

Later, however, we use the FileSystemClassLoader to load a new Class into the JVM:

```
"FileSystemClassLoader" = ("FileSystemClassLoader", "",
                    "FileSystemClassLoader #1")
```

The JVM sees these two as separate, distinct class types, both of which extend `java.lang.Object` (loaded by the Application ClassLoader, of course). When we ask the Object `obj` to return its Class, it hands back a Class that identifies itself as "FileSystemClassLoader", which is right. However, it's the version loaded by FileSystemClassLoader #1, not bootstrap ClassLoader #1; that is,

```
o.getClass().getClassLoader() != fscl.getClass().getClassLoader();
```

Thus, when we try to cast obj ("FileSystemClassLoader", "", "FileSystemClassLoader #1") from Object to FileSystemClassLoader ("FileSystemClassLoader", "", "AppClassLoader #1"), the JVM is not going to see any relationship between these two classes, and throws a ClassCastException in protest.

Although this may seem like an overly restrictive arrangement on the surface, it has its benefits. Because each ClassLoader forms a unique name space, any static member data for a given class must be partitioned within a name space; that is, if a class having a static member is loaded via two separate ClassLoaders, the JVM has two separate instances of the static data for that class. This in turns leads us to completely partition classes away from one another, even to the point of loading different versions of the same class into the JVM. This will in turn form the core of our ability to load new code into a running server without affecting existing clients.

## 3.1.2 HashtableClassLoader

Another simple ClassLoader is the HashtableClassLoader (listing 3.2), which simply returns class instances from a Map of class names to byte arrays. It doesn't attempt to find the class bytecode from any other location other than its stored Map instance, making it extremely fast in lookup:

### Listing 3.2 Code for a HashtableClassLoader

```
import java.io.*;
import java.net.*;
import java.util.*;

class ByteArray
    implements java.io.Serializable
{
    public ByteArray(byte[] bytes)
    {
        m_bytes = bytes;
    }

    public byte[] getBytes()
    {
        return m_bytes;
    }

    private byte[] m_bytes;
}

public class HashtableClassLoader extends java.lang.ClassLoader
{
    public HashtableClassLoader()
    {
        this(new HashMap());
    }
    public HashtableClassLoader(Map table)
    {
        super(HashtableClassLoader.class.getClassLoader());
        m_classtable = table;
    }

    public void putClass(String className, byte[] bytes)
    {
```

```
            m_classtable.put(className, new ByteArray(bytes));
    }

    public Class findClass(String className)
        throws ClassNotFoundException
    {
        try
        {
            ByteArray byteArray = (ByteArray)m_classtable.get(className);
            byte[] bytes = byteArray.getBytes();
            return defineClass(className, bytes, 0, bytes.length);
        }
        catch (Exception ex)
        {
            throw new ClassNotFoundException(className, ex);
        }
    }

    // Internal members
    //
    private Map m_classtable;

    // Driver
    //
    public static void main(String[] args)
        throws Exception
    {
        // Try the HashtableClassLoader
        HashtableClassLoader hcl = new HashtableClassLoader();

        // Load "Hello.class" from root dir into the Hashtable
        FileInputStream fis = new FileInputStream("/Hello.class");
        int ct = fis.available();
        byte[] Hello_bytes = new byte[ct];
        fis.read(Hello_bytes);

        hcl.putClass("Hello", Hello_bytes);

        // Try the loadClass
        Object obj = hcl.loadClass("Hello").newInstance();
    }
}
```

As you can see, HashtableClassLoader does nothing other than call `defineClass`
on the byte array stored within the Map instance. Because HashtableClassLoader is
Serializable, and most Map-implementing classes are likewise (most notably, Hash-
Map and Hashtable), HashtableClassLoader offers interesting possibilities as a traveling ClassLoader when serialized and sent to another JVM.

### 3.1.3　CompilerClassLoader

Now that we've examined the basics of customized ClassLoaders, let's try something
trickier. Instead of simply loading a bytecode image from disk, we will generate the

bytecode at run time via a CompilerClassLoader. This is only possible because several Java compilers, including the JDK "jcvcc" compiler, are themselves written in Java and are available as Java packages for use, as opposed to native executables.

The CompilerClassLoader offers a number of advantages, not the least of which is that the compilation step can now be removed from development, another move toward both zero deployment and zero administration. Additionally, Java can now be embedded within user objects, perhaps as a macro language and compiled on the fly for use within user applications. In fact, this idea has proven to be popular already— it forms the basis for the JSP specification.

Listing 3.3 shows the code for CompilerClassLoader. Note that in order for this to run successfully, the classes underneath the sun.tools package hierarchy must be available at run time. Technically, this is a violation of the JDK's licensing scheme, so be sure to check with JavaSoft or Sun representatives if you plan to use this approach to develop software for commercial resale. In the meantime, in order to run this code, ensure that the tools.jar from the JDK 1.2 lib directory is somewhere on the CLASS-PATH or is installed as an Extension on the target system.

**Listing 3.3    Code for a CompilerClassLoader**

```java
import java.io.*;
import java.net.*;
import java.util.*;

public class CompilerClassLoader extends java.lang.ClassLoader
{
    /**
     * Uses "user.home" as root dir to work from
     */
    public CompilerClassLoader()
    {
        try
        {
            m_sourceDirRoot = new File(System.getProperty("user.home"));
        }
        catch (Exception ex)
        {
            ex.printStackTrace();
            m_sourceDirRoot = null;
        }
    }
    /**
     *
     */
    public CompilerClassLoader(File sourceDirRoot)
    {
        m_sourceDirRoot = sourceDirRoot;
    }

    public String getClasspath()
    {
```

```
        return m_classpath;
    }
    public void setClasspath(String classpath)
    {
        m_classpath = classpath;
    }

    /**
     * Retrieve compiled code
     */
    protected Class findClass(String name)
        throws ClassNotFoundException
    {
```

As with any ClassLoader-extending class, the heart is in its `findClass` method. Here, we go through an *x*-step process to find (that is, compile) the class bytecode in question:

```
    if (m_sourceDirRoot == null)
        throw new ClassNotFoundException("No root dir specified!");
```

This is a simple sanity-check to make certain CompilerClassLoader has a directory from which to load.

```
    // Translate the Java-canonical name into an equivalent
    // file name; anything after a "$" is removed, since "$"
    // only shows up in anonymous/inner classes, which are
    // from the "$"-prefixed file. Tack a .java on it, and
    // look for the file
    String javaName = name;
    if (javaName.indexOf("$") > 0)
        javaName = javaName.substring(0, javaName.indexOf("$"));
    // Replace "." with File.fileSeparatorChar's
    javaName = javaName.replace('.', File.separatorChar);
    javaName += ".java";

    File javaFile = new File(m_sourceDirRoot, javaName);
    System.out.println("Looking for " + javaFile.toString());
```

The first step is to find the .java file we need to compile. This is more difficult than it might seem. Under normal circumstances, a .java file will translate directly into a .class file; for example, "Hello.java" will become "Hello.class". Three exceptions kick in almost immediately, however. Anonymous classes and inner classes will both compile with a "$" embedded after the .java file name, so an inner class Foo inside of the class Hello in Hello.java will compile to Hello$Foo.class, and an anonymous class will put a number in place of the inner-class name (Hello-$1.class). Each of these situations can be dealt with, since the .java file name that produced them is available (strip off everything to the right of "$" in the class name). What really kills this implementation is the fact that a .java file can contain more than one distinct class; in fact, the HashtableClassLoader implementation in listing 3.2 does precisely this, defining a package-access class ByteArray in the HashtableClassLoader.java file. This in turn produces the ByteArray.class file, which contains no hint that it is actually available through another .java file. Unfortunately, aside from trying to perform some kind of caching mechanism for those classes already compiled, there is no way around this, and it represents a hole in this implementation.

```
// Attempt to compile it down to bytecode
String[] javacArgs = new String[]
{
    //"-classpath",
    //m_classpath,
    "-deprecation",
    javaFile.getPath()
};
ByteArrayOutputStream javacOut = new ByteArrayOutputStream();
sun.tools.javac.Main javaCompiler =
    new sun.tools.javac.Main(
        new PrintStream(javacOut, true), "javac");
```

Next, we create an instance of the sun.tools.javac.Main class, passing into the constructor the PrintStream instance to use for output messages (which, in this case, we want written to a ByteArrayOutputStream, since we don't necessarily know where these messages will ultimately go. It could easily be a GUI application that exercises this ClassLoader). We also need the name to use for the application's name; here, we use "javac" for consistency. No other initialization is necessary.

```
if(!javaCompiler.compile(javacArgs))
{
    throw new ClassNotFoundException(javacOut.toString());
}
```

Next, we need to do the actual compilation. This is as simple as calling compile with the array of Strings containing the normal command-line arguments to javac; we specify the "-classpath" and "-deprecation" options, hand the name of the .java file to compile, and if compile returns true, the .class files produced by that .java file now reside on disk. A more sophisticated CompilerClassLoader might control the directory to which the .class files are written, or provide more in the way of the command-line options (optimization, dependency-tracking, and so forth), but this implementation doesn't for sake of simplicity.

```
// If we got here, the file compiled just fine; load its
// bytecode into the byte array
String className = null;
if (name.lastIndexOf("$") > -1)
{
    className = name.replace('.', File.separatorChar)
        + ".class";
}
else
{
    className = javaName.substring(0,
        javaName.lastIndexOf(".")) + ".class";
```

```
        }

        try
        {
            File inFile =
                new File(m_sourceDirRoot, className);
            FileInputStream in =
                new FileInputStream(inFile);

            byte[] bytecode = new byte[(int)inFile.length()];
            in.read(bytecode, 0, (int)inFile.length());

            // Hand the bytecode to ClassLoader.defineClass
            // and return
            return defineClass(name, bytecode, 0, bytecode.length);
```

Lastly, we need to get the compiled bytecode into the JVM. This part is the simplest of the steps—simply find the .class file on the disk (corresponding to the class name requested), call defineClass on it, and hand it back.

```
        }
        catch (java.io.IOException ioEx)
        {
            throw new ClassNotFoundException(ioEx.toString());
        }
    }

    // Internal members
    private File m_sourceDirRoot;
    private String m_classpath;

    // Test driver
    public static void main(String[] args)
        throws Exception
    {
        PCClassLoader cl = new PCClassLoader(new File("C:\\"));
        cl.loadClass("Test.PkgHello").newInstance();
    }
}
```

One drawback to this implementation is the fact that it produces .class files on disk that must then be loaded by CompilerClassLoader; for a large number of Java files, this could get costly in terms of performance and disk space. Ideally, the Javac class interface would be written to accept any sort of stream as the source code input, and produce ByteArrayOutputStream instances as output, but the Javac interface doesn't provide this. While it might be possible to create classes that fit in with the Javac framework that provided this stream-based behavior, it would require an intimate knowledge of the source code. The same, unfortunately, is also true of Pizza, GJ, and other Java compilers.

### 3.1.4     StrategyClassLoader and ClassLoaderStrategy

The Strategy pattern allows you to "Define a family of algorithms, encapsulate each one, and make them interchangeable. Strategy lets the algorithm vary independently from the clients that use it."[1] This is precisely what we want out of the ClassLoader scheme—vary the implementation without changing the scaffolding around it. Unfortunately, the ClassLoader implementation, as it stands, provides a severe impediment to effective reuse and encapsulation of ClassLoaders.

The ClassLoader API, despite its redesign to delegate all class-bytecode loading to the `findClass` method, still expects `findClass` to call `defineClass` with the loaded bytecode, because it requires `findClass` to return a Class instance. Had `findClass` been required to return only the bytecode (as a `byte[]` return value, instead of a Class), then derived classes could use the Decorator or Strategy pattern to enhance, modify, or provide alternative means of loading bytecode. For example, consider the (very real) desire of silently adding debugging messages to compiled bytecode when running the server in debug mode; instead of having to extend URLClassLoader and reimplement its `findClass` method with our particular extended behavior thrown in, we could take a ClassLoader instance as a parameter, call its `findClass` method to find the bytecode (without caring how the ClassLoader loaded or generated it), and instrument the bytecode before passing it back to ClassLoader for definition.

StrategyClassLoader is an attempt to work around this limitation; it extends `ClassLoader`, but expects the guts of the loading behavior to come in the form of a ClassLoaderStrategy-implementing instance. ClassLoaderStrategy is an interface that factors out the heart of the ClassLoader interface for derived classes:

```
public interface ClassLoaderStrategy
{
    public byte[] findClassBytes(String className);

    public URL findResourceURL(String resourceName);
    public Enumeration findResourcesEnum(String resourceName);

    public String findLibraryPath(String libraryName);
}
```

As you can see, it's not a particularly large interface. However, it does provide the basic change to the ClassLoader interface that I complained about earlier—it requires implementors to only return the bytecode for the Class, and not to have to call `defineClass` to obtain a Class instance. That behavior in turn falls to the Strategy-ClassLoader class.

StrategyClassLoader uses the ClassLoaderStrategy instance only to obtain the bytecode, resource, or native library; it otherwise provides all the standard behavior a good Java 2 ClassLoader should. The abbreviated code looks like this:

```
public class StrategyClassLoader extends ClassLoader
{
    public StrategyClassLoader(ClassLoaderStrategy strategy)
    {
```

---

[1] *Design Patterns*, p. 315

```
        this(strategy, StrategyClassLoader.class.getClassLoader());
    }
    public StrategyClassLoader(ClassLoaderStrategy strategy,
                               ClassLoader parent)
    {
        super(parent);

        m_strategy = strategy;
    }

    protected Class findClass(String name)
        throws ClassNotFoundException
    {
        byte[] classBytes = m_strategy.findClassBytes(name);

        if (classBytes == null)
        {
            throw new ClassNotFoundException();
        }

        return defineClass(name, classBytes, 0, classBytes.length);
    }

    // . . . Other methods omitted for brevity . . .

    // Internal members
    //
    private ClassLoaderStrategy m_strategy;
}
```

Check the full code listing for the complete version; this snippet is only intended to demonstrate StrategyClassLoader's implementation for classes.

With judicious use of the ClassLoaderStrategy interface, StrategyClassLoader could become the last ClassLoader you ever have to write (listing 3.4). Because it implements all the necessary rules for extending ClassLoader, while at the same time allowing flexibility in the actual loading of code, we get precisely the right combination of flexibility and reuse for which we are looking.

**Listing 3.4    Code for the StrategyClassLoader**

```
    public static void main(String[] args)
        throws Exception
    {
        // Create an anonymous Strategy to use for this
        // test alone
        ClassLoaderStrategy strat = new ClassLoaderStrategy()
        {
            public byte[] findClassBytes(String className)
            {
                // Load "Hello.class" from root dir
                try
                {
                    java.io.FileInputStream fis =
```

```
                        new java.io.FileInputStream("/Hello.class");
                    int ct = fis.available();
                    byte[] Hello_bytes = new byte[ct];
                    fis.read(Hello_bytes);

                    return Hello_bytes;
                }
                catch (Exception ex)
                {
                    return null;
                }
            }

            public java.net.URL
                findResourceURL(String resourceName)
            {
                return null;
            }
            public java.util.Enumeration
                findResourcesEnum(String resName)
            {
                return null;
            }

            public String findLibraryPath(String libraryName)
            {
                return "";
            }
        };

        StrategyClassLoader scl = new StrategyClassLoader(strat);

        Object obj = scl.loadClass("Hello").newInstance();
    }
```

This is obviously a contrived example, but shows the kind of flexibility we have in the ClassLoaderStrategy interface. In this case, the anonymous ClassLoaderStrategy class will look for "Hello.class" in the root directory of the current drive, load it, and hand it back as the compiled code; it works for this example, but nothing else.

When reading the source code for the custom ClassLoaders, readers will note that each ClassLoader class is also a ClassLoaderStrategy-implementing class.[2] This is so that each ClassLoader can participate in either scheme (Java's standard ClassLoader system or the StrategyClassLoader system). This helps improve the system's overall flexibility; where possible, my code makes use of the StrategyClassLoader and appropriate Class-

---

[2] This is also the reason for the peculiar names of the ClassLoaderStrategy interface. Because Java disallows methods to overload based solely on return type, the only way to differentiate between the interface method and the ClassLoader-inherited method is to change the name from `findClass` to `findClassBytes` in my interface.

LoaderStrategy-implementing classes, but where necessary, I can always fall back on the standard ClassLoader-implementing approach.

For those still stuck in the Java 1.1 environment, we can make use of the Class-LoaderStrategy approach by providing a slightly modified version of StrategyClass-Loader; the code is part of the `com.javageeks.classloader` package. The only real variation between this class and the StrategyClassLoader for Java 2 is that it does the delegation to the Strategy instance inside `loadClass` instead of in Java 2's `find-Class`. In fact, the StrategyClassLoader becomes even more important to the JDK 1.1 environment because of its ability to load classes from multiple sources. Because JDK 1.1 lacks the delegating-parent concept, there is simply no way to define a multitiered array of ClassLoaders, as in 1.2.

### 3.1.5    CompositeClassLoader

Recall that one of the rules regarding the ClassLoader mechanism is that a given class can be associated with only a single given ClassLoader. What's more, the parental relationship of the delegating ClassLoader system means that ClassLoaders cannot work as peers—that is, a group of ClassLoaders working together to find a class from a variety of sources, each with equal opportunity to find the class requested.

Because all CLASSPATH entries are referenced from a single ClassLoader, it will attempt to look in all CLASSPATH-entry locations for a referenced class. Think about what happens if a separate ClassLoader were to be created for each entry in the CLASS-PATH. When a class ("A"), loaded from the first entry in the CLASSPATH references a second class ("B") found only in the second entry on the CLASSPATH, "B" will never get loaded. "A" will look to its own ClassLoader, not find it, then look to its parent ClassLoader, which will be the ExtClassLoader (which knows nothing about CLASS-PATHs), and also won't find it. Therefore, "B" doesn't exist, according to the Class-Loader hierarchy. Unfortunately, we don't want a hierarchy here; we want a flat linear list of ClassLoaders to test before giving up.

When a class is requested, the AppClassLoader, as it checks the CLASSPATH, looks at each directory or .jar file in order, until one is found or it runs out of entries. Were each of these entries in the CLASSPATH a separate ClassLoader, only that Class-Loader and its immediate parent would be checked. This means that if class Foo was originally found in the first entry of the CLASSPATH, then any class Foo used would be checked using that same ClassLoader or its parent. So if Bar were referenced by Foo, but existed in the second entry in the CLASSPATH, it would never be loaded.

Unfortunately, CLASSPATH has two drawbacks: it can only be used for classes stored on disk, and, because it's an environment setting, any end user can inadvertently corrupt, destroy, or modify it. Even worse, automated installers can modify the CLASSPATH, setting their code before yours, giving their code precedence over yours when classes of the same name are loaded.

It can be advantageous to distribute code for Java servers in multiple places, even though they might all be part of the same conceptual unit. For example, a standard reporting system may store the framework for the reporting engine (which changes infrequently, at best) in a .jar file on an HTTP server, but the ever-changing reports themselves in the same database as the data on which they're reporting. A security system may store insecure code in the open on disk, but wish to pull code under security restrictions from a centralized security server via a socket.

Listing 3.5 is the code for the CompositeClassLoader class, which takes any number of ClassLoaderStrategy-implementing objects and defers the retrieval of bytecode to those Strategy objects.

**Listing 3.5   Code for CompositeClassLoader**

```
public class CompositeClassLoader extends ClassLoader
    implements ClassLoaderStrategy
{
    public CompositeClassLoader()
    {
        this(CompositeClassLoader.class.getClassLoader(), null);
    }
    public CompositeClassLoader(ClassLoaderStrategy[] loaders)
    {
        this(CompositeClassLoader.class.getClassLoader(), loaders);
    }
    public CompositeClassLoader(ClassLoader parent)
    {
        this(parent, null);
    }
    public CompositeClassLoader(ClassLoader parent,
                                ClassLoaderStrategy[] loaders)
    {
        // Establish parent ClassLoader relationship
        //
        super(CompositeClassLoader.class.getClassLoader());

        // Copy over ClassLoaderStrategy instances (if any)
        //
        if (loaders != null && loaders.length > 0)
        {
            for (int i=0; i<loaders.length; i++)
            {
                m_loaders.addElement(loaders[i]);
            }
        }
    }

    public void addLoader(ClassLoaderStrategy cls)
    {
        m_loaders.addElement(cls);
    }
    public Enumeration enumLoaders()
    {
        return m_loaders.elements();
```

*CHAPTER  3   CUSTOM CLASSLOADERS*

```
        }
        public void removeLoader(ClassLoaderStrategy cls)
        {
            m_loaders.remove(cls);
        }

        public byte[] findClassBytes(String className)
        {
            byte[] bytecode = null;

            for (Enumeration enum = enumLoaders();
                 enum.hasMoreElements(); )
            {
                ClassLoaderStrategy strat =
                    (ClassLoaderStrategy)enum.nextElement();
                bytecode = strat.findClassBytes(className);

                if (bytecode != null)
                {
                    return bytecode;
                }
            }

            return bytecode;
        }
        public URL findResourceURL(String resourceName)
        {
            URL resource = null;

            for (Enumeration enum = enumLoaders();
                 enum.hasMoreElements(); )
            {
                ClassLoaderStrategy strat =
                    (ClassLoaderStrategy)enum.nextElement();
                resource = strat.findResourceURL(resourceName);

                if (resource != null)
                {
                    return resource;
                }
            }

            return resource;
        }
        public Enumeration findResourcesEnum(String resourceName)
        {
            Enumeration resourceEnum = null;

            for (Enumeration enum = enumLoaders();
                 enum.hasMoreElements(); )
            {
                ClassLoaderStrategy strat =
                    (ClassLoaderStrategy)enum.nextElement();
                resourceEnum = strat.findResourcesEnum(resourceName);

                if (resourceEnum != null)
```

```
                {
                    return resourceEnum;
                }
            }

            return resourceEnum;
        }
        public String findLibraryPath(String libraryName)
        {
            String libPath = null;

            for (Enumeration enum = enumLoaders();
                  enum.hasMoreElements(); )
            {
                ClassLoaderStrategy strat =
                    (ClassLoaderStrategy)enum.nextElement();
                libPath = strat.findLibraryPath(libraryName);

                if (libPath != null)
                {
                    return libPath;
                }
            }

            return libPath;
        }

        protected Class findClass(String name)
            throws ClassNotFoundException
        {
            byte[] classBytes = findClassBytes(name);

            if (classBytes == null)
            {
                throw new ClassNotFoundException();
            }

            return defineClass(name, classBytes, 0, classBytes.length);
        }

        // Internal members
        //
        private Vector m_loaders = new Vector();
}
```

The test driver (see the source code for details) creates two ClassLoaderStrategy objects, one a FileSystemClassLoader, and the other a HashtableClassLoader, and demonstrates how classes can be loaded from either ClassLoader with equanimity. This is where the idea of using Strategy objects, to vary the implementation, really pays off—the CompositeClassLoader doesn't care where any of the ClassLoaderStrategy instances actually find the code, only that one of them can. And because CompositeClassLoader is, in and of itself, both a standard ClassLoader and a ClassLoaderStrategy-implementing class, it can be used as either with equal efficacy.

## 3.1.6   Other ClassLoader tricks

In addition to providing ways by which bytecode can be loaded, a ClassLoader-extending class can perform surgery and/or modification of the bytecode loaded from some source, or even generate the bytecode directly from scratch, as mentioned earlier. We've already demonstrated how a CompilerClassLoader can compile .java files into .class code each time a class is requested, but under certain circumstances we will want to generate the .class code directly from bytecode assembler directives. More often, we will want to instrument, modify, or enhance bytecode to provide certain behaviors.

### Dynamically generating bytecode

Dynamically creating code, at run time, provides the ultimate in flexibility—if you don't have the behavior you want, create it!

The code demonstrating this concept can be found as part of the chapter 2 sample applications; it's too long to list here. The concept is simple: in the DynamicGen.java file, a StrategyClassLoader is created, passing in an instance that uses the ClassFile API (the source code can be found on the publisher's web site at www.manning.com/ neward3; please make sure to copy it to your Java installation's Extensions directory, or put it on the CLASSPATH before running the sample) to dynamically build the code to print "Hello, world!" on the console when constructed. Again, it's a trivial example, but it demonstrates how we can have total control over what we can do at run time.

### Modifying bytecode on the way in

After the bytecode has been loaded from disk, but before the Class instance has been defined (by a call to `defineClass`), a ClassLoader is free to modify the bytecode as desired. Consider, for a moment, a hypothetical LogClassLoader, which extends URLClassLoader to load classes from any URL, but then modifies the method byte-code to write a message to a log file indicating method-entry and method-exit. Although it greatly slows execution, this can be very useful for debugging purposes, especially in environments where conventional debugging isn't feasible, practical, or easy (such as servlet debugging). Alternatively, as another example, we could use this filtering behavior to silently provide RMI stubs/skeletons when users request an RMI object or class.

This idea of modifying bytecode during the loading process isn't new; in fact, some very interesting research, led by Shigeru Chiba of the University of Tsukuba, into Java's capacity for metaprogramming is taking place. Metaprogramming is a new concept, represented only in its most primitive form by generic class mechanisms like C++ templates; metaprogramming offers powerful abstraction capabilities not possible with a noninterpreted system like C++. This research has led to the development of the OpenJava and Javassist compilers, which read a form of meta-Java code, and in turn modify the generated Java code on the way into the JVM. In addition, Kestrel, the JDK version 1.3, defines a new technology called dynamic proxies, which makes the previous ClassLoaders almost trivial to create.

### 3.1.7  Other ClassLoaders

As we move through this book and visit other subjects, we'll come back to the idea of ClassLoaders and all the different ways we can get bytecode served up to us, so don't think we're completely done with this subject. There's a lot of potential here; it's my opinion that it's not Java's portability, simplistic syntax, or even its built-in thread support, but its classloading capabilities that far outstrip any other language for server-side application development.

## 3.2  ON-THE-FLY CODE UPGRADES

One of the givens in enterprise development is that evolution is inevitable—as code is released into production, users will find bugs, come up with new ideas, or have new requirements. It's inevitable. The problem is, once a server goes into production, the system administrators are loathe to take the system down just to upgrade the code. Remember, they're looking to keep the system up and running as long as possible—downtime translates into direct loss of money for most IT organizations. So you're stuck with fixed, monthly upgrade dates, which leads your customers to believe that you're not supporting them as quickly as you should be.

For years, developers have been searching for ways to upgrade code without bringing the server (or any clients using the code at the time of the upgrade) completely down. It could be done, under strict conditions, but most of the time the conditions imposed were unacceptable to developers. For example, certain development systems could allow for it, but they were usually interpreted, proprietary systems that lacked language features, speed, or acceptance outside of that vendor's product.

Java gives us the ability to do this sort of dynamic, on-the-fly upgrade without:

- taking the server down
- interrupting service to other unrelated clients
- interrupting service to clients currently using the code to be replaced.

Remember what we said about class uniqueness within the Java classloading scheme? Within the JVM, a unique class is a tuple of the class's fully qualified package-and-class name and the instance of the ClassLoader that loaded it. In Java terms, a ClassLoader holds a reference to each and every class it loads. Each class, in turn, holds a reference back to the ClassLoader that loaded it. So long as either one of these are referenced from anywhere else in the JVM, that code will be used for new instances of that type. For example, when we say

```
FileSystemClassLoader fscl = new FileSystemClassLoader("D:\\");
for (int i=0; i<10; i++)
```

```
{
    Class c = fscl.loadClass("com.neward.MyClient");
    Object o = c.newInstance();
}
```

even if the .class file is modified during the middle of this loop, the old code is used. This is because when we call `Class.newInstance`, we reference back to the Class-Loader that loaded the Class, and find it has already loaded that class. No new load is necessary. However, if we write

```
for (int i=0; i<10; i++)
{
    FileSystemClassLoader fscl = new FileSystemClassLoader("D:\\");
    Class c = fscl.loadClass("com.blah.MyClient");
    Object o = c.newInstance();
}
```

then if the .class file for MyClient changes in the middle of the loop, we will pick up those changes.

Don't believe me? Let's test it. You'll find the following code on the publisher's web site:

**Listing 3.6    Code for ClassLoadTest**

```
import com.javageeks.classloader.FileSystemClassLoader;

public class ClassLoadTest
{
    public static void main(String[] args)
        throws Exception     // cheap way to avoid catch()ing Exceptions
    {
        // The idea is simple: load a .class and run() it, then pause for
        // 10 seconds before doing it again. If you modify the .class file
        // during the pause, then the new ClassLoader should pick up the
        // modification and execute the new file instead of the old one
        //
        System.out.println(args.length);

        if (args.length > 0)
        {
            if (args[0].startsWith("-unique"))
            {
                // We want to use a unique ClassLoader isntance on each
                // loop
                //
                while (true)
                {
                    FileSystemClassLoader fscl =
                        new FileSystemClassLoader("./TestDir");
                    Class c = fscl.loadClass(args[1]);
                    Object o = c.newInstance();
                    System.out.println(o.toString());
```

```
                System.out.println("Sleeping for 15 seconds....");
                Thread.sleep(15*1000);
            }
        }
        else
        {
            // We want to use the same ClassLoader instance on each
            // loop
            //
            FileSystemClassLoader fscl =
                new FileSystemClassLoader("./TestDir");
            while (true)
            {
                Class c = fscl.loadClass(args[0]);
                Object o = c.newInstance();
                System.out.println(o.toString());

                System.out.println("Sleeping for 15 seconds....");
                Thread.sleep(15*1000);
            }
        }
    }
    else
    {

        System.out.println(
            "Usage: java ClassLoadTest [-unique] classname");
        System.out.println("\tWhile the code is running,
            open a new command");
        System.out.println("\tshell and execute TestDir's SWITCH.BAT.");
        System.out.println(
            "\tThis will switch Hello.class from one version");
        System.out.println("\tto the other.");
        return;
    }
  }
}
```

The point of this code should be fairly obvious: based on whether the -unique
command-line option is present, either use a single FileSystemClassLoader
instance to load the class, or else use the same instance repeatedly. Within the
TestDir subdirectory under Chap02, you'll find a LoadTest.java file, which has
been compiled into two different versions:

```
public class LoadTest
{
    public LoadTest()
    {
        Thread t = new Thread(new Runnable()
        {
            public void run()
```

*CHAPTER 3  CUSTOM CLASSLOADERS*

```
        {
            try
            {
                while (true)
                {
                    System.out.println("Hello, " +
                    //"from the first LoadTest!"); // ***
                    "from the second LoadTest!");
                    Thread.sleep(5*1000);
                }
            }
            catch (Exception ex)
            {
            }
        }
    });
    t.setDaemon(true);
    t.start();
    }
}
```

Within that directory, two sets of .class files exist for LoadTest; the first (Load-Test1.class and LoadTest1$1.class) uses the "from the first LoadTest" line, the second (LoadTest2.class and LoadTest2$1.class) uses the "from the second LoadTest" line. Remember, Java checks the compiled class name within the .class file against the name given on the command line, so we can't just issue

```
java ClassLoadTest LoadTest1
```

and expect it to load the LoadTest1.class and execute it; we want the two different versions of the .class files to have the same name, to pretend as if LoadTest is getting a new version that needs to be deployed.

To make this work, issue the following commands from a Win32 Command shell[3] in the Chap02 directory:

```
start java ClassLoadTest LoadTest
```

A new shell should appear, and the following output (or something very similar) should appear:

```
1
LoadTest@eb9de113
Sleeping for 15 seconds....
Hello, from the first LoadTest!
Hello, from the first LoadTest!
```

---

[3] Again, this example assumes you're running in a Win32 (Windows NT, Windows 95/98) environment. From within a UNIX environment, however, it shouldn't be too difficult to adapt the switch.bat file to a standard shell-script file. Where I tell you to type "start java …", instead use the Unix "run-in-the-background" switch, "&": "java …. &", and everything should work out just fine.

```
Hello, from the first LoadTest!
LoadTest@d5a1e113
Sleeping for 15 seconds....
Hello, from the first LoadTest!
Hello, from the first LoadTest!
Hello, from the first LoadTest!
Hello, from the first LoadTest!
Hello, from the first LoadTest!
Hello, from the first LoadTest!
LoadTest@d7f1e113
Sleeping for 15 seconds....
Hello, from the first LoadTest!
Hello, from the first LoadTest!
Hello, from the first LoadTest!
Hello, from the first LoadTest!
Hello, from the first LoadTest!
Hello, from the first LoadTest!
```

As you can see, ClassLoadTest, every fifteen seconds, is creating an instance of LoadTest from the TestDir subdirectory. Now, if we go back to the original Command prompt, change directories into TestDir, and call the switch batch file, nothing changes. Because we started ClassLoadTest without the -unique option, it's reusing the same FileSystemClassLoader instance over and over again to load the LoadTest class and newInstance it. Since that instance of FileSystemClassLoader has already loaded the LoadTest class (with the first version), it won't go back to the disk.

Now, however, if we close everything and start again with an instance of Class-LoadTest run this time with the -unique option, we get a very different result. In this case, from within the Command shell in the Chap02 directory, issue the following command, followed by the second command a few seconds later:

```
start java ClassLoadTest -unique LoadTest
```

(Wait a few seconds)

```
cd TestDir
switch
```

Look what shows up in the console window:

```
2
LoadTest@d58ce277
Sleeping for 15 seconds....
Hello, from the first LoadTest!
Hello, from the first LoadTest!
Hello, from the first LoadTest!
LoadTest@d064e277
Sleeping for 15 seconds....
Hello, from the first LoadTest!
Hello, from the second LoadTest!
Hello, from the first LoadTest!
Hello, from the second LoadTest!
```

*CHAPTER 3 CUSTOM CLASSLOADERS*

```
Hello, from the first LoadTest!
Hello, from the second LoadTest!
```

When told to use a new ClassLoader instance each time to load a class, if the new class on disk is different from the version loaded by a different ClassLoader, the new version gets picked up, even if the old version is still being executed.

This is going to provide a substantial payoff later, in chapter 5, when we begin the implementation of the Generic Java Application Server (GJAS).

## 3.3 GJAS: FIRST STEPS

So where does all this discussion leave us? How does this talk of classloading and run time linking affect us in the server environment?

Remember that one of our goals in this book is to create a flexible, generic, extensible server framework and system that you can use in your own server-based environment. A frequently asked question is: how do we avoid writing the same code over and over again? We could, for example, write a simple Java class that is intended to be fired up off the command line when the user logs in, executes, and terminates. This solution, however, will be acceptable only for the most simplistic of services. Once we start talking about writing TCP/IP socket servers, as well as servers that need to restart as soon as the machine restarts (in the event of a power failure or controlled shutdown, for example), repeatedly rewriting that complexity does nothing except see how careful (or careless) we are with our ability to cut and paste.

We can do better.

### 3.3.1 Goals

The GJAS needs to have the following qualities, at least to start:

- *Extensible*
  We should be able to plug in additional services and/or servers without requiring any code change to the server itself.
- *Generic*
  We shouldn't be excluded from including a particular server or service from within this system due to the system's approach or limitations.
- *Dynamic*
  We should be able to vary which servers or services are started from run to run (that is, the first time we run it, we should be able to run three servers that say, "Hello, world!"; the next run, two Hello servers and one that executes a command line) without necessitating a code change.
- *Independence*
  No server or service should be able to bring down the JVM (and therefore other executing servers/services in the system).

We're not going to delve into implementation code quite yet; we need to address a few other issues first, such as scalability and robustness. However, we can at least take a first pass at the design and the interfaces required.

Meeting these requirements requires Java's ClassLoading mechanism as well as careful interface design. Extensibility can be met by defining a simple Service interface which clients must implement, which we load and construct at run time. Genericness can be met both through this run-time construction and careful design. Dynamicness can be met by creating an API that our system exposes, allowing users to vary how the servers/services are loaded. Independence can be met by making certain that any Java exception thrown from within a user service can be thrown out of the system itself, bringing down the JVM.

The code for the following classes can be found in the CustomClassLoader directory on the publisher's web site. There will be other versions in other directories that won't match what we're building thus far, so make sure you're looking in the right place. Figure 3.1 shows the UML diagram of the system so far:

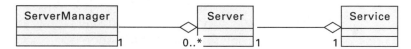

**Figure 3.1   Simplified UML diagram of GJAS so far**

### 3.3.2   Service

We'll start with the basic interface that any service wanting to be a part of the GJAS framework/system must implement (listing 3.7).

**Listing 3.7   Code for Service.java**

```
/**
 * Note: Service's Serializable interface should be honored,
 * because Serialization is the basic means of exchange between
 * JVMs in RMI calls, and if a Service is not Serializable then it
 * cannot be transferred across JVMs.
 *
 * If a Service needs to maintain "interim" data that should not
 * be Serialized, then remember to mark the data members as
 * transient. Also, remember that a given Serializable
 * class can control what happens when it is serialized and
 * deserialized by means of the writeObject and readObject methods.
 * This would allow, for example, those Services that make use of
 * JDBC Connections (as an example) to close down and reopen the
 * Connection upon serialization and subsequent deserialization.
 */
public interface Service
    implements java.io.Serializable
{
    /**
     * Start the Service. All but the most simplistic Services
```

```java
 * should fire off their own thread from here.
 */
public void start()
    throws Exception;
/**
 * Stop the Service.
 */
public void stop()
    throws Exception;
/**
 * Pause the Service.
 */
public void pause()
    throws Exception;
/**
 * Resume the Service.
 */
public void resume()
    throws Exception;

/**
 * Get the current state of the Service; must be one of the
 * following types: STOPPED, STARTING, RUNNING, STOPPING,
 * PAUSING, PAUSED, or RESUMING.
 */
public String getState();
public static final String STOPPED = "STOPPED";
public static final String STARTING = "STARTING";
public static final String RUNNING = "RUNNING";
public static final String STOPPING = "STOPPING";
public static final String PAUSING = "PAUSING";
public static final String PAUSED = "PAUSED";
public static final String RESUMING = "RESUMING";

/**
 * Return a String uniquely identifying this instance of the
 * Service; this String must be unique not just to the Service
 * class, but to the Service instance itself. Suggested return
 * format is something like:
 *
 * String instanceID = this.getClass().getName() + ":" +
 * getClassVersion() + ":" + getMillisecondCount();
 *
 * Note that maintaining an "instance count" of the number of
 * instances of this class will fail, since all instances will
 * be maintained within their own ClassLoader, and static
 * members are stored on a per-ClassLoader basis.
 */
public String getInstanceID()
    throws Exception;
}
```

The first question might very well be why we choose to force all GJAS-compliant servers to have to implement Service, instead of simply requiring a compliant class to make public certain methods of a particular signature, and use Reflection to call them? After all, wouldn't using Reflection offer a measure of flexibility that went beyond most other programming languages?

The answer isn't clear-cut, and stems mostly from personal choice. It's my preference to accept the limitations of an interface-based API in exchange for the additional compile-time checking that the compiler gives me, both as the server developer, as well as the client developer (the one who's developing the services that will be plugged into the system). It's also easier for me as a server developer to manage, specifically from a code perspective. Not only are methods on the client service easier to call, but they are also easier to read and understand.

It would also be a simple matter to combine the two approaches—in the Server-Manager implementation (which we cover in a later chapter), we could add code to use Reflection within the system if the class loaded didn't implement Service. It's a bit of overkill—only one approach or the other should be used—but it can be a useful trick under other circumstances.

### 3.3.3    Server

Given that we already have a basic interface we want any user of our system to have to implement in order to be hooked in, why create another layer between the server manager (IServerManager), and the actual Service? At the moment, the need for it is fairly light—we probably could, in fact, just call the Service methods directly and be happy with it. As we move on, though, we'll find that we have to do various things around each call to the Service methods. For example, we'll eventually want code in place that spins off a Thread to make the call to the Service method, and waits for a few seconds to see if the call comes back, just in case Service is stuck in an infinite loop or otherwise blocked. That way, we won't lock up the entire system. So Server will become our handle to a Service, with each Service instance having a wrapper Server around it. Server, in essence, will isolate us from Service being able to bring the entire system down.

This is a classic example of the Proxy pattern, in which we're defining another object instance to act as the gateway to another object. In this case, the Server instance will act as the Proxy to the actual Service instance. This nets us absolutely zero advantage (and an additional function-call indirection for our trouble, which means we're actually worse off than calling the Service instance directly, at least for right now) at the moment, but becomes more critical later.

The code for Server is, at this point, rudimentary and straightforward. Note that we first specify Server as an interface (IServer), in order to preserve Server's intent as a location-transparent class—we don't want to know precisely how ServerManager is hiding the `Service` from us (listing 3.8).

**Listing 3.8   Code for IServer**

```
 **
 * The "public" interface for Servers; note that the Server instance
 * type will vary directly with the ServerManager used, in order to
 * best support the location transparency concept. IServer serves as
 * the Proxy to the Service instances loaded into the ServerManager;
 * any control of the Services must come through the Server, since
 * the client, if it tries to hold a Service instance within its own
 * JVM for "faster" access, may be holding a stale or otherwise
 * unstable reference.
 */
public interface IServer
    extends java.io.Serializable
{
    /**
     * Starts the wrapped Service instance. Services have 15 seconds in
     * which to either initialize, or else start a thread to perform the
     * necessary initialization and return. If a Service fails to respond
     * within 15 seconds of the start of its start call, the Server
     * and/or ServerManager are free to destroy it.
     */
    public boolean start();
    /**
     * Stops the wrapped Service instance; as with start, the
     * Service gets 15 seconds to stop itself before the ServerManager is
     * free to take more drastic steps.
     */
    public boolean stop();
    /**
     * Pauses the wrapped Service. The Service should respond within 15
     * seconds of the start of this call; however, failure to do so is not
     * sufficient grounds for the ServerManager or Server to destroy it.
     */
    public boolean pause();
    /**
     * Resumes the wrapped Service. The Service should respond within 15
     * seconds of the start of this call; however, failure to do so is not
     * sufficient grounds for the ServerManager or Server to destroy it.
     */
    public boolean resume();
    /**
     * Kills the wrapped Service.
     */
    public void kill();

    /**
     * Returns the state of the wrapped Service.
     */
    public String getState();

    /**
```

```
    * Returns the instance ID of the wrapped Service.
    */
   public String getInstanceID();

   /**
    * Returns the last Exception thrown, if any, by the wrapped Service.
    */
   public Exception getLastError();
}
```

As you can see, IServer isn't much more than a small shell around the Service methods. Notice also how IServer extends the Serializable interface; this is so that (in later chapters) we can send IServer instances across RMI connections, sockets, or even serialize it out to disk. By making IServer Serializable, we add a tremendous amount of flexibility to how IServer can interact with the ServerManager.

### 3.3.4    ServerManager

The core GJAS is the ServerManager class, which is the shell in which user-defined Service-derived classes will execute. ServerManager, more than any other class in the GJAS system, is the heart and soul of its application server. It holds the Services added to it, hands out references to Services as requested by clients, and provides the basic backplane for the GJAS system. However, in order to provide the maximum amount of location transparency, we don't necessarily want the ServerManager class itself doing the actual work—we'd like to be able to connect with ServerManagers in other virtual machines, and so forth. We'll get to that later, but we'll lay the groundwork now.

We create ServerManager in a separated fashion. First, we'll create the basic ServerManager interface, called IServerManager, that any class wishing to provide ServerManager-like behavior must implement. Next, we'll create a class, ServerManager, that provides static-level access to the IServerManager instance. We want only one ServerManager instance in a given JVM (the classic Singleton pattern), but we don't know ahead of time which we want. The reason we go to all this trouble is that we want to provide a single way of interacting with the ServerManager, but we want to vary the actual ServerManager implementation used. We write the ServerManager class to check to ensure that only one IServerManager instance is ever set as *the* instance, and require any IServerManager-implementing class to set itself as the ServerManager instance.

A ServerManager needs to provide, at a minimum, the following interface:

```
public interface IServerManager
{
    public void shutdown();

    public IServer loadService(Service svc);
    public IServer addService(Service svc);
    public void removeService(String instanceID);
    public void killService(String instanceID);
```

```
public String[] getServices();
public IServer getService(String instanceID);

public void log(String msg);
public void log(Exception ex);
public void error(String msg);
public void error(Exception ex);
}
```

ServerManager's API can be broken down into three sections: control of the Server-Manager itself, Service management, and diagnostic/logging support.

Controlling the ServerManager itself consists of one method: `shutdown`. The method prepares the ServerManager to go down, and is required to take all the Services down in as clean a manner as it can before terminating. Shutdown is an unvetoable action, so if any Service tries to resist or simply takes too long, the ServerManager is free to terminate it.

The next set of methods deals with adding, removing, and enumerating the Services running within the ServerManager. As might be expected, `addService` adds the Service instance to the ServerManager and calls `start` on the Service as it does. The `loadService` method adds the Service instance, but doesn't call `start`; this means that `addService` is the same as `loadService(Service).start()`. Notice that both return the `IServer` instance we discussed above. The `removeService` method removes the Service specified by the `instanceID` parameter, calling `stop` on the Service first. The `killService` method removes the Service altogether from the ServerManager—theoretically, when the `Service` is no longer referenced by the ServerManager, it will be garbage-collected, but don't depend on this behavior. The `getServices` method returns the array of Strings given by calling each Service's `getInstanceID` method, and `getService` returns the `IServer` instance wrapping the Service in question.

The `log` and `error` methods provide a single unified logging/error-reporting facility. You may be wondering why, if we're trying so hard to keep Services separate from ServerManager, we would turn around and place the logging and error-reporting facilities inside of ServerManager. For now, it makes the most sense to put them there. If you have a real problem with that, feel free to create a Service (call it LogService and/or ErrorService) that exposes the same APIs. In any event, accessing the APIs in ServerManager is as simple as calling

```
ServerManager.log("Started the FooBotz Service");
```

Because ServerManager is a Singleton, we have no concerns about `log` or `error` output being fragmented across multiple locations, which could very easily be a problem if the logging and error-reporting services are standard services.

## 3.4 SUMMARY

ClassLoaders offer powerful functionality for our server framework and system. We've moved from the traditional bundle-up-all-the-code, get-the-system-administrators-to-install-it-on-all-the-users'-machines approach to a more distributed, zero-deployment system. We can drop our code in a single centralized point, be that a shared filesystem, FTP server, or HTTP server, and any new clients will pick up the new code, even as any old clients continue to finish their interaction using the old code. As the last of the old clients disappears, so does the loaded bytecode for the old instances. We've also seen how we can modify the class bytecode as it is loaded into the JVM, thanks to the class filters concept, or even build entirely new bytecode on the fly.

# CHAPTER 4

# *Extensions*

JDK 1.2 offers a new mechanism for updating code: the Java extension mechanism. From the JDK 1.2 documentation, (jdk1.2/docs/guide/extensions/index.html):

> Extensions are packages of Java classes (and any associated native code) that application developers can use to extend the functionality of the core platform. The extension mechanism allows the Java virtual machine (VM) to use the extension classes in much the same way as the VM uses the system classes. The extension mechanism also provides a way for needed extensions to be retrieved from specified URLs when they are not already installed in the JDK or JRE.

That last sentence should strike a nerve—"provides a way for needed extensions to be retrieved from specified URLs when they are not already installed in the JDK or JRE." That would seem to imply that if a class isn't present within the CLASSPATH or local file system we can grab it from someplace else. That's precisely what it means.

## 4.1    TYPES OF EXTENSIONS

The Java extension mechanism divides the world of Java extensions into two camps: installed and download. Each carries its own advantages and drawbacks.

### 4.1.1    Installed extensions

An installed extension is code that resides within the JRE's extension directory, which within the Sun JRE distribution, is the JRE\1.2\lib\ext directory. Any compiled Java code, whether in .class or .jar form, will be silently added to the JVM's CLASSPATH if it resides within this directory.

In this respect, the JRE's extension directory now mimics the same semantics as most modern operating systems and shared libraries. For example, under Win32, a DLL will be found by a `LoadLibrary()` call regardless of the directory in which the application is executing if the DLL resides in the Windows directory or Windows system directory. Most UNIX OSs have something similar using the `LD_LIBRARY_PATH` environment variable.

This makes distribution of Java applications much, much easier. Formerly, installing a Java application to a client's machine required not only the installation of the .class or .jar file to the local file system, but also modification of the user's CLASS-PATH environment variable to include the new directory or directories or the .jar file itself. While not a monumental task, users can (and quite frequently do) change their environment variable settings, making Java applications particularly vulnerable. Now, install scripts can copy the code over to the extension directory, and Java will automatically find it.

Unfortunately, Java will look only in that specific directory, and not in any sub-directories underneath it. This means that this directory is likely to become cluttered and crowded as multiple applications install themselves to this one place. It also raises the ugly possibility that versioning issues will begin to appear on user systems as applications using common third-party JAR files (GNU code, or third-party GUI toolkits) which start accidentally overwriting newer versions with older versions on install. The Windows development community has been struggling with this problem for a decade, and accidental overwrites still occur despite their best efforts. Unless Sun quickly takes steps to address this, I would be very careful about how files are named when installed to this directory.

Fortunately, Java doesn't seem to care what the JAR file itself is named; for that reason, I'd suggest any JAR file to be installed to this directory follow a naming convention similar to that of Sun's package names. For example, if I create a .jar file containing the "HelloWorld.class" file, version 1, then I'd rename it "com.javageeks.HelloWorld.jar". That way, in my install scripts, I can check for an earlier version of my application, and search through the .jar file for a text file labeled "version", and read which version of my code I'm thinking about overwriting.

One undocumented[1] trick regarding extensions is the `java.ext.dirs` property. When the Java run time starts, it defaults this property to be the JRE's lib/ext directory. However, by using the -D parameter at the command line (or by specifying the equivalent option when using JNI invocation), it's possible to change or add directories to this path list.

As proof, create a simple Hello.java class and put it in the root of your file system; here I'm assuming it's a Wintel PC, on the C: drive. Now fire up the Java interpreter with the -D parameter like so:

```
java -Djava.ext.dirs=C:\ Hello
```

UNIX Java users would run:

```
java -Djava.ext.dirs=/ Hello
```

Your Hello class will be loaded and executed although it resides in the root directory instead of in the standard Extensions directory.

This in turn offers some hope for directory management. Each subdirectory (corresponding to a single application, development group, component, whatever) can be added to the `java.ext.dirs` property when the JVM is started. Naturally, this, too, could quickly become unmanageable, but until Sun changes this behavior, it's the best we can do.[2]

What would actually be very cool would be to modify the `java.ext.dirs` property, or its equivalent within the ClassLoader, to add Extension directories as the application executes. Unfortunately, URLClassLoader, which serves as the base class for Launcher$ExtClassLoader, doesn't make its `addURL` method public, so we have no hope of being able to do that. Once the Extension directories are loaded into the ExtClassLoader, they're fixed for the lifetime of the JVM.

### 4.1.2 Building an installed extension

Building an installed extension is as simple as building a normal JAR file. Begin with standard Java code, compile it, and condense it into a JAR file:

```java
// HelloWorld.java (in src/chap2)
//
public class HelloWorld
{
    public static void main(String[] args)
    {
        System.out.println("Hello, world!");
    }
}
```

---

[1] As of this writing it only shows up when every property in the JVM is displayed via `System.get-Properties`.

[2] If you hold a Sun Community Source License to Java 2, you could modify the source for the Extensions ClassLoader that manages the extensions directory (sun.misc.Launcher$ExtClassLoader). While such a modification would immediately render your environment impure Java, sometimes these sorts of localized source changes are necessary and beneficial in the long run.

```
/*
From the command line, do:

javac HelloWorld.java
jar cvf com.javageeks.HelloWorld.jar HelloWorld.class
copy com.javageeks.HelloWorld.jar your-JRE-directory\lib\ext

or, if you use the GNU make from the CD, edit the makefile.rules
file in the 'src' directory, and do:

make clean all

*/
```

As I described, typically if I'm packaging up a JAR file for release or installation on end-user machines, I'll also include a text file labeled "version" in the JAR:

```
Major 1
Minor 0
```

Then, inside of an install script or install executable, I can look for an existing com.javageeks.HelloWorld.jar file within the Extension directory. If one exists, I can open it using the java.util.zip classes, extract the version file, parse it, and determine if I need to overwrite what's there.

Once the JAR file is created, copy it to the Extension directory, and attempt to execute it:

```
copy HelloWorld.jar C:\prg\jdk1.2\jre\lib\ext
cd \
java HelloWorld
```

That's all there is to it.

### 4.1.3 Download extensions

For all the power in the installed extension mechanism, download extensions will be the ones in which people will probably be most interested. This is the ability to download code from a URL if it is not already present on the system. However, as the JDK 1.2 extension guide tells us, (jdk1.2/docs/guide/extensions/extensions.html):

> Unlike the case of installed extensions, the location of the JAR files that serve as download extensions is irrelevant. A download extension is an extension because it is specified as the value of the Class-Path header in another JAR file's manifest, **not** because it has any particular location.
>
> Another difference between installed and download extensions is that only applets and applications bundled in a JAR file can make use of download extensions. Applets and applications not bundled in a JAR file don't have a manifest from which to reference download extensions.

The key part comes in the second paragraph: "… only applets and applications bundled in a JAR file can make use of download extensions." So, in order to make use of download extensions, we need to have our application in a JAR file, with the Manifest file indicating where else to look for code that the JVM can't find.

This offers some serious code-reuse capabilities, especially in a corporate intranet. In a sense, this is the DLL or shared library concept taken to a distributed context. Remember, the original idea of the shared library (or DLL, under Windows) was to prevent multiple copies of the same code loaded everywhere. By providing a mechanism by which code could be loaded only once across all processes using it, the shared library/DLL concept not only reduced per-process memory requirements, but also allowed for across-the-board updates of code by simply replacing the shared library.

Java now provides the same possibilities via this download extension mechanism. Suppose a team makes use of the com.javageeks.foobar component library, which happens to be in version 2.0, to do its development. Normally, before the download extension mechanism, the .jar file or .class files for the foobar library would need to be deployed with the development team's application. Should javageeks.com release a new version of foobar (version 3), the development team needs to make a new release with the new foobar .jar/.class files in it, even if no new development has taken place on the application.

Instead, with the download extension mechanism, the development team can mark the application's JAR as being dependent on the foobar library by using javageeks.com's URL to reference it:

```
Class-Path: http://www.javageeks.com/javalib/foobar.jar
```

Now, should javageeks.com release a new version of the foobar library, the development team need not do anything to take advantage of the new version; in fact, it may not even be aware of the new version. Just as DLLs could (in theory) be silently upgraded with newer versions as bug fixes and patches were released, new download extensions can also be silently upgraded without client knowledge.

This, of course, presumes that the download extension always exists at the given URL referenced within the application's .jar file. This may not be the case for commercial or freeware source sites, but on a corporate intranet developers certainly would. Just hang the shared component .jar/.class files from a known location on the corporate or departmental web server, and any application which makes use of that .jar/.class file library will automatically pick up any new updates.

Download extensions do carry some restrictions that installed extensions don't. Each and every time an application or JAR file is run that uses a download extension that resides off of a web server, the code will have to come across the wire in its entirety (jdk1.2\docs\guide\extensions\extensions.html):

> The extension mechanism will not install a download extension in the JRE or JDK directory structure. Download extensions **do not** become installed extensions after they have once been downloaded.
>
> Unlike installed extensions, download extensions cannot have any native code.

This means that each and every time the user fires up the application, it will have to download all of the application's class files over the wire. This can mean long load times, especially if your network bandwidth is tight, or you have a large number of users and/or a low-end intranet Web server.

Additionally, the restriction regarding native code may have more impact than might originally have been estimated. As seen in later chapters, JNI and native code can have some powerful applications in server-side Java applications.

### 4.1.4 Building a download extension

The Manifest file specification is given in jdk1.2\docs\guide\jar\manifest.html, and the specific headers for Java extensions are given in jdk1.2\docs\guide\extensions\extensions.html. Creating a Manifest file means you create a subdirectory (off the directory in which the JAR file will be built) called META-INF, and in that directory, create a file called MANIFEST.MF. It needs to contain, at a minimum, the following line:

```
Manifest-Version: 1.0.
```

This establishes it as a Manifest file to any JAR-reading utility that works with the JAR file. Optionally, it can also contain a line indicating the creator of the JAR file:

```
Created-By: JavaGeeks.com
```

You can establish this as an executable JAR file with the following line:

```
Main-Class: com.javageeks.ClientApp.Main.
```

This line indicates that when this JAR is specified to the Java interpreter using the -jar flag, this class (com.javageeks.ClientApp.Main, in the above example) contains the main method to execute. Specifying this line effectively allows us to create a stand-alone JAR file to execute on user machines. Effectively, saying

```
java -jar YourJar.jar
```

where YourJar.jar contains a Main-Class line of ClientApp.Main is the same as

```
set CLASSPATH=%CLASSPATH%;YourJar.jar
java ClientApp.Main
```

As a result, for the first time, Java now has the ability to ship a prepackaged single file that contains all the necessary elements for execution, without requiring modifications to the user's environment settings.

The key to download extensions is the Class-Path manifest setting, as demonstrated in this line:

```
Class-Path: servlet.jar foo.jar footoo.jar
```

Class-Path tells the JRE where else it needs to look for the additional classes that this JAR file references. This line contains the file or URL reference telling the JVM where to find additional .jar files on which this JAR depends. It will then attempt to use these JAR files to resolve any requested classes during execution of the application code.

Readers familiar with the Java applet model will undoubtedly be curious why download extensions would even be necessary, given that an applet embedded in a Java page offers the same sort of functionality. After all, the applet model allows web page designers to download code as necessary into the client JVM to execute applets. In fact, the two approaches are distinctly related. However, in an application that uses download extensions, no security restrictions are in place—the infamous applet sandbox doesn't exist in a standard Java application unless, of course, it is loaded into the application via Java's SecurityManager. This in turn means that all of those things inaccessible to Java applets is freely available to download extension code.

Additionally, the loading code doesn't come from an HTML page, so no web browser is required to execute the application. This in turn means that the loading application remains independent of web servers, HTTP, or HTML.

### Example: HelloDownload

In this particular example, because not all readers will have access to a web server with which to test, we'll create a JAR file that in turn depends on one in a nonstandard location. In this case, we'll be trying to use code from the root directory of the C:\ drive on a PC.

To start, create and compile two simple Java classes:

```
// Download.java
//
public class Download
{
    public void sayHello()
    {
        System.out.println("Hello from Download");
    }
}

// HelloDownload.java
//
public class HelloDownload
{
    public static void main(String[] args)
    {
        Download dl = new Download();
        dl.sayHello();
    }
}
```

Overly simplistic, but the classes should prove the point. The idea is simple: Hello-Download depends on the class Download to run. Therefore, HelloDownload will be either an installed extension or an executable JAR file (we need to make this front-end a JAR file, as well), and will reference the Download.jar file in its Manifest file:

```
Manifest-Version: 1.0
Created-By: JavaGeeks.com
Class-Path: C:/Download.jar[3]
```

Create the HelloDownload.jar file with the Manifest file named manifest by specifying the name of the Manifest file on the jar utility command-line:

```
jar cvfm HelloDownload.jar manifest HelloDownload.class
```

Create the Download.jar file in the normal fashion:

```
jar cvf Download.jar Download.class version
```

Copy the Download.jar file to the root directory of the C:\ drive, and the HelloDownload.jar (renaming it to com.javageeks.HelloDownload.jar, if you wish) to the Extension directory. Change directory to someplace other than the current directory, so as to make sure we're not picking up the code in the current directory, and execute:

```
java HelloDownload
```

Given a working JDK 1.2 installation, you should see the "Hello from Download" message on your console window.

The Class-Path header can be a file-relative path or a standard HTTP URL. If you have a web server, change the location of the Download.jar to be a location off your web root, change the `Class-Path` in the manifest file to be that URL, rebuild the HelloDownload.jar file, and try running it. Because ExtClassLoader extends URL-ClassLoader, any given URL type—file, http, or ftp—are all viable candidates in the Class-Path tag.

## 4.2    IMPLICATIONS OF THE EXTENSIONS MECHANISM

Using Java extensions carries implications that may or may not be immediately obvious.

### 4.2.1    Distributed libraries through download extensions

One of the problems with building applications using a dynamic linking mechanism is the inevitable necessity of upgrading the libraries which support the application. If an application uses library "X," there will undoubtedly be other applications also using it, and a subsequent version of one of these libraries may in turn require a new version of the "X" library. Getting this out to all the users of the application can be a much more difficult problem, for the same reasons as those making it difficult to distribute the application in the first place. This becomes even more of an issue when libraries in turn use other libraries. Suddenly, there's an entire tree of dependencies.

The download extension mechanism offers one practical solution to this problem. By marking the .jar files that a library or an application uses, any updates to a dependent

---

[3] Readers running the example on a UNIX installation will need to change the Class-Path line in the manifest file to read "/Download.jar" or "/~/Download.jar" instead of "C:/Download.jar". There's nothing magical about the root directory; any directory on the file system can be used.

library can be picked up automatically. Two options are now possible—if maximum performance is desired, system administrators can manually copy new versions of the library down to end-users' machines, or a stand-alone daemon process on the end-users' system can check (at startup or every twenty-four hours, or any other practical time) the current versions of its .jar files against a central repository. Alternatively, the extension can use http URLs, and pull them as necessary from the same centralized repository. (Both approaches could be used simultaneously, as best benefits each individual application.)

The one drawback to this approach is that download extensions cannot load native library code. Typically, however, on end-user systems, native code will be less attractive due to the higher administrative support necessary to make it work, especially in heterogeneous networks. In those rare situations where native code needs to be moved to each end-user's workstation, the version-checking download daemon process can pull both .jar files and native code at the same time.

### 4.2.2    Java EXEs; relation to C++ static linking

The ability of the Java 2 interpreter to execute .jar files directly also makes possible the ability to create stand-alone java executable files, .jar files, that contain all of the necessary .class files to execute a given application. Recall from the start of chapter 2 one of the disadvantages of dynamic linking: an application that uses dynamic linking will always be vulnerable to upgrades of the classes on which it depends. In the C++ environment, this can be avoided by linking all referenced code statically, as part of the compiled executable, so that the necessary dependent code travels with and is never upgraded by a dynamic library upgrade.

This sort of static linking carries another, more practical benefit, in that many popular web browsers do not support more than one .jar file in the <APPLET> tag. Because of this, attempting to keep the application's code physically separate from the support code it uses will yield unworkable results when that applet is viewed from a nonconforming browser. Instead, by packaging the entire codebase into a single .jar, that file can be placed on the HTTP server and referenced from the web page. True, it means all of the code must be downloaded each time, and that this may not be a trivial amount of data; however, in this case, only if the web browser caches the downloaded .jar file will any time savings be realized, since the necessary classes will need to be downloaded at least once. By static-linking the .jar file, only those classes used by the application, and not any extraneous code, are downloaded.

Performing this sort of static linking is not pain-free. While it may be a simple matter to identify which code written by the developer needs to be deployed as part of this stand-alone application .jar, doing the same for the Java run-time library[4] or

---

[4]  While this may seem overzealous, it actually helps when trying to deal with different Web browsers implementing different versions of the JDK. For example, most Web browsers aren't JDK 1.2-compliant, and most only supported up to about JDK 1.1.6 or so. Because JDK 1.2 introduced a number of classes not found within JDK 1.1.6, such as the CORBA org.omg.* classes, any CORBA-using applet needs to have those along for the ride.

third-party libraries used by the application can be another thing altogether. To go along with this, code and any resources (graphics, sounds, resource bundles, and so forth) used by the application need to be stored within the .jar file.

Because Java stores any classes used by a particular class within the class' compiled bytecode format, as Class entries in the class's constant pool, we could create an automated tool to scan a particular class' compiled bytecode, pick out all the Class entries found there, and perform the same scan recursively. Such tools exist already, many of which can be found within the Open Source community. This list-of-classes can then be fed into the Sun jar utility to build the .jar file directly.

## 4.3  PACKAGING EXTENSIONS

If extensions provide an easy path for reusable components and component libraries, then it's natural to make GJAS (as well as other components we develop along the way) an extension. Unfortunately, while parts of GJAS migrate very easily to the extension architecture, the nature of Java's ClassLoader architecture requires additional complexity within the GJAS codebase. Since the extensions' ClassLoader is unavailable for modification or separate instantiation, we need to make sure that any `Services` loaded by GJAS are first loaded by ClassLoaders other than the extensions' ClassLoader unless all other avenues have been played out. The ClassLoader relationship to our Services is illustrated in figure 4.1.

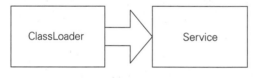

**Figure 4.1  ClassLoader-to-classes relationship**

To start, the stand-alone components can be bundled up into packages and used independently of the GJAS architecture. This includes the ClassLoader components (com.javageeks.classloader), the thread components (com.javageeks.thread), and socket clients (com.javageeks.client) developed along the way.[5] Because these components will not need to use the change-on-the-fly mechanism ClassLoaders provide and GJAS takes advantage of, we have no problems with storing them as extensions.

The same is true of the Service, Server, and ServerManager classes, the core parts of GJAS itself. Correspondingly, this means that any upgrade of GJAS will require taking down the GJAS process, updating the codebase, and restarting the process. Should developers require the ability to upgrade the GJAS components, then GJAS (or any other component that requires on-the-fly upgrading) cannot be stored in extensions, and will probably want to make use of some other mechanism for easy distribution.

---

[5]  The .jar file is created in the "Lib" directory on the publisher's web site; see the makefile there for details on the specifics of how these files are created and stored.

In the source tree on the web site, the entire "com.javageeks" is packaged into a single .jar file. This may not be desirable in large-scale Java applications, since an upgrade to any of the contained packages requires the replacement of the entire .jar file. Instead, each package could be broken out into separate .jar files, with dependencies on other .jar files labeled as download extensions, and upgraded individually as necessary. This approach offers more flexibility in terms of piecemeal upgrades, but sacrifices development ease; developers must now track each "library" separately. This also requires separate versioning of each jar, and some greater testing to verify that various versions of each "library" work together.

### 4.3.1 The build-time vs. run-time dilemma

Unfortunately, this isn't the only tension between the development and deployment environments. Because Java is both a build-time and run-time interpretive system, it makes no inherent distinction between run time and build time. This seems like double-talk, without further explanation.

One of the first things a Java developer learns is that if the CLASSPATH isn't set to include all of the classes used by an application, the code won't compile. For example, unless the JSDT classes are on the CLASSPATH,[6] any code containing even an `import` statement will not compile.

The reason is simple: the javac compiler is actually implemented in Java, and it uses the CLASSPATH to find the classes to which a particular source file refers in order to carry out its compile-time type checking. The javac compiler, in fact, is a simple wrapper around the class sun.tools.javac.Main, and can be invoked using java sun.tools.javac.Main, assuming the JDK 1.2 tools.jar file is on the CLASSPATH.

All of this doesn't seem to have any relevance, at least not until we get into the build time versus run time dilemma. There will be occasions, within development, when a developer needs to have both a build-time environment and a run-time environment on his/her machine. The classic case is with GJAS itself—even though we need the Service classes we'll be building to be available at build time, we don't want them to be stored in the Extensions directory at run time. If they're on the CLASS-PATH or in the Extensions directory, the system ClassLoader (AppClassLoader or Ext-ClassLoader) will pick up the classes instead of our new ClassLoader instance, and we won't be able to do the load-new-code-on-the-fly trick demonstrated in the last chapter. If the code is stored on the CLASSPATH or in the Extensions directory, testing may be adversely affected, as in the case of GJAS.

Fortunately, this situation arises only on developers' machines, since only developers require both the build-time and run-time environments. Neither the testing nor the production environments require the build-time classes, since they'll be picked up by the individual ClassLoader instances and not by the system loader. Fortunately, as well, most developers won't be faced with this situation, since most developers won't

---

[6] Or in the Extensions directory.

be facing this sort of situation (where classes need to be picked up by a custom Class-Loader and *not* the system Loader).

Unfortunately, when working with an application server like GJAS, developers will run into this situation head on. One solution is to use multiple JDK environments, one CLASSPATH/extensions setup for compilation, and another for testing/execution. For example, the developer can install the JDK under C:\JDK1.2, and install a stand-alone JRE under C:\JRE1.2. The developer then runs two distinct Command Prompt shells, one with PATH and CLASSPATH set to the JDK for compilation, and the other with PATH and CLASSPATH set to point to the JRE.

This is awkward for a number of reasons. First, any code compiled within the first shell must be transferred to the second shell's CLASSPATH or extension setup. This can be as simple as specifying a "-d <directory>" option to javac when compiling, but can easily be forgotten or mismatched if the build process isn't completely automated. Secondly, it's often difficult to maintain two separate clean environments, especially if the application uses files or other environment variables, some of which may need to be stored within the Win32 Registry (or other OS-specific centralized storage). This typically isn't too much of an issue since most of these supports are run-time related, not build-time. Lastly, it's not uncommon for developers to get confused, and run the tests from within the wrong shell, and get back results they don't expect.

This build-time/run-time dilemma doesn't rear its ugly head too often, since it only occurs when the multiple-code-loading mechanism needs to be in effect. Within a developer's test arena, once that mechanism has been proven, then all testing is typically geared against one Service class, and not a whole host at once within the same run. For that reason, developers can usually keep the same CLASSPATH for both compilation and testing, and simply know that the code will get picked up by the App- or ExtClassLoader, and not their own custom version.

## 4.4    *THE PLUG-IN*

One of the interesting aspects of .jar files is their growing service as the level of atomicity for black-box components. For example, EJB defines a Bean as a .jar, the Servlet 2.2 specification talks about Web-apps being bundled into .jars (with the extension .war), and the Java2 Enterprise Edition specification uses the same approach. On top of all this, as we've seen, the Sun interpreter will examine a .jar's Manifest file for the `Main-Class` attribute for the class name to execute when given a -jar argument to the JVM. If .jar files are going to become the *de facto* standard for Java deployment, certainly we can make use of it, as well.

As we'll see in a moment, allowing end users the ability to drop in new black-box components gives your code tremendous flexibility. Consider a traditional client/server reporting/data-viewing application. Under traditional development approaches, we might code each report or view as a separate class, linking them all into a single .exe (or .jar), and distributing that to the user. Each time a new report or view was required, we'd have to re-release a new .exe/.jar.

Under an extensible-system approach, however, we'd instead create a basic interface that report or view classes must implement. Instead of building the code into a single .jar file, the application would be a simple shell which in turn looked into a subdirectory (or other location) for the .jar files representing each report type. The user could then pick from a list of the reports found, and the application shell would load the code from that .jar file. If a new report were required, we'd simply code up the new .jar file, and either distribute that to the users, or have the IT staff distribute it via some other form of push to the end-user's machines. Numerous advantages abound:

- *Testing is simpler.*
  Because the existing application shell hasn't been touched, that code doesn't need to be retested before releasing the new report. Your QA department will like you better if they don't have to retest the entire application every other week and your customers will like you even better because of a faster release cycle.

- *Development can be "parallelized."*
  Individual developers (perhaps more junior than would otherwise be required) can be given tasks that involve writing the individual reports. Work can proceed in a more parallel fashion, potentially speeding up the release cycle. In addition, the junior developers won't be able to get into the application shell code where they might introduce additional bugs or violate the basic application design.

- *Promotes encapsulation.*
  If the only way the report can interact with the application is through this well-defined API, then the application knows nothing about the internals of the report, and vice-versa. This promotes encapsulation and allows later maintenance to take place without concern for what else might break.

- *Power-user flexibility.*
  If you happen to have a user who is more technically knowledgeable than his/her peers, he/she can be given the API documentation to allow creation of their own reports without having to bother the developers.

In short, by allowing this kind of drop-in flexibility in your applications, you allow the users to be better served.

## 4.4.1 The plug-in concept

A class, when loaded, registers itself with some sort of manager which is responsible for calling on the registered class instances when applicable. Usually, in order to support type-safety (and avoid having to use Reflection to discover the plug-in's methods), the plug-in class will implement a common interface that defines the basic behavior required of each plug-in class.

As an example, consider a scripting engine/interpreter. In order to maximize the interpreter's flexibility, we want to allow the engine to interpret different languages based on the script file's extension—.js for JavaScript, .vbs for VBScript, and so on. Each language-interpreter class will implement a basic LanguageInterpreter interface, which will look like this:

```
public interface LanguageInterpreter
{
    public boolean canInterpret(String filename);
    public int interpret(String filename, String[] args)
        throws Exception;
}
```

(The throws declaration is just a cheap way to allow the LanguageInterpreter-implementation class to pass exceptions back to the engine; a production-level application should define more clear-cut exception types, such as SyntaxException, ExecutionException, etc.) The first method, canInterpret, is called to see if the LanguageInterpreter-implementation class can, in fact, interpret the given script file. This allows a single LanguageInterpreter-implementation to support more than one scripting language. The second method, interpret, is where the LanguageInterpreter-implementation does the actual work of parsing and executing the script file.

Having done this, the ScriptingEngine class becomes ridiculously straightforward. When told to execute a file, it simply iterates through its list of LanguageInterpreters, asking each if it can interpret the file, and if so, orders it to do so. We define the ScriptingEngine class as:

```
public class ScriptingEngine
{
    private LanguageInterpreter[] interps;
        // How this is populated is explained later

    public int interpret(String scriptFile, String[] args)
    {
        for (int i=0; i<interps.length; i++)
        {
            if (interp[i].canInterpret(scriptFile))
                return interp[i].interpret(scriptFile, args);
        }

        return -1; // Nobody recognized it
    }

    public static void main(String[] args)
    {
        ScriptingEngine engine = new ScriptingEngine();
        engine.interpret(args[0], args);
    }
}
```

The ScriptingEngine is trivial; the only question mark comes in regard to the array of LanguageInterpreter instances, interps. How does it get initialized?

Conventional design would have each LanguageInterpreter-implementation class defined and stored within the application, and the array initialized within the ScriptingEngine code as follows:

```
public ScriptingEngine
{
    private LanguageInterpreter[] interps =
    {
        new JavaScriptInterpreter(),
        new VBScriptInterpreter(),
        new REXXInterpreter()
    };
}
```

Unfortunately, this means that ScriptingEngine now has the sum total of all languages supported by the engine, and cannot be reconfigured at run time to accommodate new languages. This means that if we need to support a new language, we have to ship out an entirely new application. Ick.

Alternatively, we could provide a properties file that the ScriptingEngine examines, parses, and executes Class.forName() on each line:

```
# languages.properties file
JavaScriptInterpreter
VBScriptInterpreter
REXXInterpreter
```

Then, the ScriptingEngine parses this languages.properties file (which, presumably, is stored on the user's hard disk) to establish which languages the engine knows about:

```
public ScriptingEngine
{
    private LanguageInterpreter[] interps;

    static
    {
        // Open languages.properties
        // For each line, call Class.forName().newInstance() and
        // store it into the returned array
    }
}
```

While attractive, this approach suffers from one critical flaw: if the languages.properties file is corrupted, deleted, or otherwise rendered unusable, the ScriptingEngine is paralyzed. Now it knows about no languages, and will fail every script file handed to it. There must be a better way.

## 4.4.2  Enter plug-ins

What we really want is for each intalled language interpreter to register itself with the scripting engine. Ideally, this registration (which takes place when we initialize the ScriptingEngine with the array of LanguageInterpreter instances) would be code-independent, so that users could add new LanguageInterpreters without having to modify code.

This approach isn't a new one. For example, Adobe Photoshop uses this notion of plug-ins extensively, and even built an industry (dominated mostly by Kai's Power Tools) around plug-ins for Photoshop. OLE began life looking to do this sort of plug-in capability, as well, by providing interfaces that allowed those objects to place themselves on the menu bar, provide context-sensitive help, and more. The Emacs text editor is perhaps the crowning glory of this concept, with plug-ins ranging from email clients to full-fledged development-and-debugger modules for just about any language. Jeff Nelson, in his book *Programming Mobile Objects in Java*, shows how even mobile objects can participate in this sort of extend-the-app process by having the extensions download themselves into a text editor.

In a C++ environment, with an operating system that supports shared libraries, we can iterate through a directory that we designate as a plug-in directory, and explicitly load each library into the process' address space. Because each OS provides a method that is called when the shared library is loaded into the process space (DllMain or DllEntryPoint under Win32, for example), the LanguageInterpreter instance can be registered with the ScriptingEngine within this method.

Within Java, however, we have a few hangups. Because Java is already a dynamic-loading system, we don't have to build a custom approach for each platform—the ClassLoading mechanism is already there and in place. Unfortunately, that's the only part that Java gives us; the rest gets tricky.

Remember that one of the Java ClassLoading buzzwords is lazy. This means that even if a .jar file or directory containing .class files is specified in the user's CLASS-PATH, the classes stored within that .jar or directory aren't loaded until the system needs the class. Recall, also, that needing a class comes when another class depends on the class in question, or the class is explicitly loaded using Class.forName or Class-Loader.loadClass.

In the case of our ScriptingEngine, we could get each LanguageInterpreter to register itself with the ScriptingEngine as follows:

```
public class ScriptingEngine
{
    // Everything else, as before

    private static List interps = new Vector();
    public static void register(LanguageInterpreter interp)
    {
        interps.add(interp);
    }

    public int interpret(String scriptFile, String[] args)
    {
        for (Iterator i = interps.iterator(); i.hasNext(); )
        {
            LanguageInterpreter interp =
```

```
                    (LanguageInterpreter)i.next();
            if (interp.canInterpret(scriptFile))
                return interp.interpret(scriptFile, args);
        }

        return -1; // Nobody recognized it
    }
}
```

Now, all we need to do is get each LanguageInterpreter to register an instance of itself with the ScriptingEngine. Usually, this means that the ScriptingEngine (or, more generically, the plug-in manager, where the LanguageInterpreter is the plug-in) is a Singleton, or else uses a static list of plug-ins, as demonstrated in the code snippet above. Within the LanguageInterpreter-derived classes, one of two approaches can be used: either register the instance in a base class,

```
public abstract class LanguageInterpreterBase
    implements LanguageInterpreter
{
    public LanguageInterpreterBase()
    {
        // ... other initialization, as necessary

        ScriptingEngine.register(this);
    }
}
```

or the derived class can register an instance of itself in a static initializer block:

```
public class PerlInterpreter
    implements LanguageInterpreter
{
    static
    {
        ScriptingEngine.register(new PerlInterpreter());
    }
}
```

I prefer the second approach, since the first approach requires that the class in question must be loaded, and then a new instance of it created, before the registration with the plug-in manager takes place. In the second approach, the registration takes place as soon as the class (PerlInterpreter, in this case) is loaded into the JVM.

Furthermore, if a single plug-in can handle more than one type of call, the plug-in's static initializer block can make as many registrations as necessary:

```
public class ShellInterpreter
    implements LanguageInterpreter
{
    static
    {
        ScriptingEngine.register(new ShellInterpreter(), ".bat");
        ScriptingEngine.register(new ShellInterpreter(), ".cmd");
```

```
        ScriptingEngine.register(new ShellInterpreter(), ".sh");
        // ... and so on
    }
}
```

In this way, we're preserving the encapsulation of the plug-in by not having to know anything about what needs to happen to register it with its manager—the plug-in does that as soon as it's loaded into the VM.

If we designate a given directory into which plug-ins must be dropped in order to be loaded, we're going to run into two problems in short order. Remember that Java .class files are stored in directories corresponding to package names, so if we want to allow plug-ins to be packaged like other Java classes, we have to recursively scan through all directories under our plug-in directory.

The greater problem is that most plug-ins of a nontrivial nature are going to use more than one .class file to implement their behavior. Unfortunately, when they're all stored in the same directory, we're not going to know which ones are the plug-in class, and which ones are the supporting class. As a result, we'll have to load each and every one of them—whether or not they'll be used—into the VM. This violates one of the basic precepts of Java's ClassLoading mechanism—if you don't use it, it never gets loaded. It also means a huge performance hit as each and every one of those classes is loaded at plug-in registration time.

If, on the other hand, we require the plug-ins to come in a .jar or .zip file, we have another option.

### 4.4.3    Marking a .jar file as a plug-in

One of the little-known facts about .jar files (or their ancestors, the .zip file) is that every class used to open, examine, retrieve, and create a .jar file is already part of the JDK run-time library. The `java.util.zip` and `java.util.jar` packages contain all of the code used by the jar utility and the java.net.URLClassLoader class. To examine the contents of a .jar's Manifest file, it's as simple as the following:

```
import java.io.*;
import java.util.*;
import java.util.jar.*;
import java.util.zip.*;

public class JarLister
{
    public static void main (String args[])
        throws Exception
    {
        JarInputStream fin =
            new JarInputStream(new FileInputStream(args[0]));
```

We need to open the .jar file, so we use the JarInputStream class, which, like all Java stream classes, decorates (as in the Decorator pattern sense) another InputStream, which in this case will be a FileInputStream.

```
Manifest manifest = fin.getManifest();
if (manifest != null)
{
```

Next, we obtain the .jar's "META-INF/MANIFEST.MF" file, if it exists. Note that not all .jar files have a Manifest file, since .zip files are technically .jar files and many, if not all, .zip files created before the release of JDK 1.1 (and many long after that) didn't have a Manifest file. Hence, we have to check for a `null` return value from `getManifest`.

```
Attributes attribs = manifest.getMainAttributes();
```

Attributes is the class representing the attributes that can be attached to either the .jar file or each of the entries within it. By calling `getMainAttributes`, we're asking for the attributes that apply to the .jar file itself (such as the Main-Class or Created-By attributes discussed earlier).

```
Set set = attribs.keySet();
for (Iterator i = set.iterator(); i.hasNext(); )
{
    Attributes.Name key = (Attributes.Name)i.next();
    System.out.println(key + ": " +
                        attribs.getValue(key));
}
}
}
}
```

And, as you might guess, the last block of code iterates through each of the entries in the Attributes object, printing each one out to the console. Note that the Iterator returned from the Set obtained from the Attributes object is not iterating over String objects, but instead over Attributes.Name objects. If you attempt to cast the returned object from the Iterator to a String, you'll get a ClassCastException.

Now that we know how to get the attributes of the .jar file's manifest, we can introduce our own custom .jar tags. We'll create a custom tag within the manifest, Plugin-Class, that contains the class name (fully qualified) of the plug-in class itself. Then the PluginClassLoader only needs to find this attribute, get the name of the class, and do a `ClassLoader.loadClass` using that value. This will load the plug-in class, which will fire off the plug-in's static initializer block(s), which will in turn register the plug-in with its manager.

### 4.4.4    PluginClassLoader

The code for PluginClassLoader, from the com.javageeks.classloader package, follows:

```
package com.javageeks.classloader;

import java.io.*;
import java.net.*;
import java.util.*;
import java.util.jar.*;
```

```
/**
 * PluginClassLoader is not an actual ClassLoader, but serves a role
 * of preloading "plugin" classes into the JVM, so that the Plugins
 * can register themselves with whatever "plugin manager" they use.
 *
 * See Chapter 4 of Server-Side Java for a detailed
 * description of how it all works together.
 */
public class PluginClassLoader
{
    /**
     * Interface to allow interested clients to be notified each
     * time a new plugin class is loaded into the JVM.
     */
    public static interface Listener
    {
        public void pluginLoaded(String pluginName);
        public void exception(Exception ex);
    }
```

Listener is simply an interface that allows interested parties, when they construct the PluginClassLoader, to be called back when a new plug-in is loaded. This allows GUIs, for example, to display a status bar that flashes "loading plugin XYZ..." to the user while starting up. The exception method is called when an exception is thrown during the load-up process.

```
    // Private data
    //
    private URLClassLoader urlClassLoader;
```

We use a URLClassLoader to load the classes from the list of .jar files we'll be building later in the code because it already has that functionality built within it. By not extending URLClassLoader, and instead containing an instance of it, we can also drop the URLClassLoader (and, implicitly, any classes loaded by it if they're not referenced elsewhere) and reload the plug-ins.

```
    /**
     *
     */
    public PluginClassLoader(String dir)
    {
        this(dir, new Listener()
        {
            public void pluginLoaded(String pluginName) { }
            public void exception(Exception ex) { }
        });
    }
    /**
     *
     */
    public PluginClassLoader(String dir, Listener listener)
    {
```

```
        File file = new File(dir);
        reload(file, listener);
    }
/**
 *
 */
public PluginClassLoader(File dir)
{
    this(dir, new Listener()
    {
        public void pluginLoaded(String pluginName) { }
        public void exception(Exception ex) { }
    });
}
/**
 *
 */
public PluginClassLoader(File dir, Listener listener)
{
    reload(dir, listener);
}
```

These four constructors are really just convenience wrappers around the `reload` method. Where no Listener is passed in, the constructor builds a NullObject[7] Listener, which does nothing when called on; that way, the actual implementation in `reload` needs never to check for a null Listener object, and can call on it without worrying.

```
/**
 * Reload the plug ins; note that the old URLClassLoader held
 * internally is released, so if the plug-in classes loaded
 * earlier aren't in use within the app, they'll get GC'ed.
 *
 * HOWEVER, if an instance of an earlier-loaded
 * plugin class is still in existence, it will remain an
 * entirely separate and distinct type from the type loaded
 * in on this plass, even if the .class files are identical!
 * This is because classes loaded into two separate (non-
 * parentally-related) ClassLoaders are considered separate
 * and unrelated types, even if their contents are identical.
 */
public void reload(String dir, Listener listener)
{
    reload(new File(dir), listener);
}
/**
 * Reload the plugins; note that the old URLClassLoader held
 * internally is released, so if the plugin classes loaded
 * earlier aren't in use within the app, they'll get GC'ed.
 *
```

---

[7]  This is called the NullObject pattern (*Pattern Languages of Program Design 3*, p. 5).

```
   * HOWEVER, if an instance of an earlier-loaded
   * plugin class is still in existence, it will remain an
   * entirely separate and distinct type from the type loaded
   * in on this plass, even if the .class files are identical!
   * This is because classes loaded into two separate (non-
   * parentally related) ClassLoaders are considered separate
   * and unrelated types, even if their contents are identical.
   */
public void reload(File dir, Listener listener)
{
```

The reload method is the heart-and-soul of the entire PluginClassLoader, so we'll take it in easy chunks.

```
      String[] contents = getPluginDirContents(dir);
```

The getPluginDirContents method simply obtains a list of all the .jar and .zip files in the directory specified by the File object dir. As we'll see later, it guarantees that it will always return a String array of some length, even if that length is zero, so no null-check is necessary.

```
      Vector urls = new Vector();
      Vector plugins = new Vector();
      for (int i=0; i<contents.length; i++)
      {
          try
          {
              File jarFile = new File(dir, contents[i]);

              Attributes attribs =
                  new JarFile(jarFile).getManifest().getMainAttributes();

              if (attribs.getValue("Plugin-Class") != null)
              {
                  String pluginClass =
                      attribs.getValue("Plugin-Class");

                  urls.add(jarFile.toURL());
                  plugins.add(pluginClass.trim());
                      // Need the trim(); getValue() has the
                      // annoying habit of leaving a trailing
                      // space on the end of the class, which will
                      // cause the loadClass() to fail later.
              }
          }
          catch (IOException ioEx)
          {
              // Just continue; ignore the file and move on
          }
          catch (NullPointerException npEx)
          {
              // No manifest, perhaps?
          }
      }
```

This seemingly complex piece of code is doing one thing: checking each .jar/.zip file for that Plugin-Class manifest entry we talked about earlier. If it's found, we add the URL of the .jar/.zip file to the Vector urls, and the value of the Plugin-Class attribute to the Vector plugins. We need the URL of the .jar/.zip file to pass into the URLClassLoader constructor, and we'll need the name of the class so that we can preload it into the JVM (which will force it to register with the rest of the system).

```
urlClassLoader =
    URLClassLoader.newInstance(
        convertUrlVectorToArray(urls),
        getClass().getClassLoader());
```

This is simply another way of calling a new URLClassLoader(...). The convert-UrlVectorToArray method is a convenience method to convert the Vector urls to an array of URL objects, which is what URLClassLoader expects. Notice also how we explicitly pass in the ClassLoader that loaded this (the PluginClassLoader) class as our delegating parent—again, this is because we want to preserve the parent-child ClassLoader relationship appropriately, as discussed in chapter 2.

```
// Preload each of the plugins, giving them the chance to
// register (in their static initializer block) with whatever
// "PluginManager" they choose to.
//
for (int i=0; i<plugins.size(); i++)
{
    String plugin = (String)plugins.elementAt(i);
    try
    {
        Class.forName(plugin, true, urlClassLoader);

        listener.pluginLoaded(plugin);
    }
    catch (Exception ex)
    {
        listener.exception(ex);
    }
}
```

Now that we've constructed the URLClassLoader around the Plugin-Class-marked .jar/.zip files, we need to load each plug-in class into the JVM, which in turn allows those classes, in a static-initializer block, to register instances of themselves with the appropriate plug-in manager. Notice, as the comment points out, that we have to call newInstance on the loaded class before it is loaded into the JVM; this requires that the plug-in has a default constructor that can be called by outside clients, or an Exception will be thrown.

```
/**
 * Releases the handle on the URLClassLoader used internally;
 * this will have the effect of allowing all the plug in classes,
 * if not referenced anywhere else within the application, to be
```

```
     * GC'ed the next time GC takes place.
     */
    public void unload()
    {
        urlClassLoader = null;
    }

    /**
     * Returns a String array of filenames in the directory which are
     * potential plug-in files.
     *
     * @param dir The File object representing the directory to iterate
     *            through
     */
    private String[] getPluginDirContents(File dir)
    {
        // sanity-check--does the directory exist?
        if ( (!dir.exists()) ||
             (!dir.isDirectory()) )
        {
            return new String[0];
        }

        String[] contents = dir.list(new FilenameFilter()
        {
            public boolean accept(File dir, String name)
            {
                if (name.endsWith(".jar") ||
                    name.endsWith(".zip"))
                {
                    return true;
                }
                else
                    return false;
            }
        });
        return contents;
    }
    /**
     * Returns a String array of filenames in the directory which are
     * .class files.
     *
     * @param dir The File object representing the directory to iterate
     *            through
     */
    private String[] getPluginDirClasses(File dir)
    {
        String[] contents = dir.list(new FilenameFilter()
        {
            public boolean accept(File dir, String name)
            {
                if (name.endsWith(".class"))
                    return true;
```

*CHAPTER 4  EXTENSIONS*

```
                else
                    return false;
            }
        });
        return contents;
    }
    /**
     * Simple helper method to convert a Vector of URL objects into an
     * array of URL objects (required by URLClassLoader)
     */
    private URL[] convertUrlVectorToArray(Vector urls)
    {
        URL[] urlArray = new URL[urls.size()];
        for (int i=0; i<urlArray.length; i++)
        {
            urlArray[i] = (URL)urls.elementAt(i);
        }
        return urlArray;
    }

    /**
     * Test suite--just load whatever plugins happen to be in the
     * current directory.
     */
    public static void main(String[] args)
        throws Exception
    {
        PluginClassLoader pcl =
            new PluginClassLoader(".", new Listener ()
            {
                public void pluginLoaded(String pluginName)
                {
                    System.out.println(pluginName + " loaded.");
                }
                public void exception(Exception ex)
                {
                    System.out.println("Exception:");
                    ex.printStackTrace();
                }
            });
    }
}
```

The remainder of the code entails the convenience methods mentioned earlier, and a main method for testing. Main simply builds a PluginClassLoader on the current directory, where presumably a collection of some plug-in .jars can be found and loaded.[8]

---

[8] The Extensions directory contains three .jar files, PluginOne.jar, PluginTwo.jar, and PluginThree.jar, all of which register themselves with the PluginManager class; they simply spit a string to the console when they're registered, just to prove that they are, in fact, loaded and registered.

## 4.4.5  Example: PluginApp

Let's demonstrate the concept by building a simple, useless GUI application that can be extended by plug-in .jars; by itself, the application does absolutely nothing—it displays a File menu and a Help menu. The File menu has two options: Exit, which is self-explanatory, and Reload, which will call the PluginClassLoader's method to reload the plug-ins found; this will allow us to test PluginClassLoader's dynamic-reload capability. The Help menu has just one option, About.

There's not much to it. The code to produce this application, complete with plug-in support, is also not very large or complicated:

```java
import java.awt.*;
import java.awt.event.*;
import java.util.Iterator;
import java.util.Vector;
import javax.swing.*;
import com.javageeks.classloader.PluginClassLoader;

/**
 *
 */
public class PluginApp
{
    // Private data
    //
    private JFrame frame;
    private static Vector plugins = new Vector();
    private transient boolean canQuit;
        // State variable used in method exit(); should be modified
        // *only* within that context and not used elsewhere.
```

These are the `private` data members of PluginApp; of these, only one is of real importance—`plugins` is the Vector of registered plug-ins that the application will use during its run. The `frame` object is the JFrame this application uses as its main window, and `canQuit` is a state variable used later.

```java
    /**
     * Plug ins must implement this interface; the app will call
     * the plug in when appropriate.
     */
    public static interface Plugin
    {
        public void addToMenuBar(JMenuBar menu);
        public boolean canQuit();
    }
```

The Plugin interface, here, is the basic interface any of our sample plug-ins should use if they want to "hook into" this application—it defines two methods, `addToMenuBar`, which gives each plug-in a chance to add a menu item or menu to the application's menu bar, and `canQuit`, which gives each plug-in a chance to cancel a user's request to quit. (This is where the traditional "File is not saved—still quit?" message would go.)

```
/**
 * Plug ins make themselves known to the App by calling this
 * method.
 */
public static void registerPlugin(PluginApp.Plugin plugin)
{
    // Just keep a reference to it for future use
    plugins.add(plugin);
}

/**
 * This is an interface to ease calling across all the plug ins
 * in the system.
 */
protected static interface PluginAction
{
    public void action(Plugin plugin);
}
/**
 * General-purpose method for calling an action across all the
 * currently registered plugins.
 */
private void doPlugins(PluginAction pluginAction)
{
    for (Iterator iter = plugins.iterator(); iter.hasNext(); )
    {
        Plugin p = (Plugin)iter.next();
        pluginAction.action(p);
    }
}
```

This is a shorthand version for iterating across all plug-ins to do something. When we want to make a call across all the registered plug-ins on this application, we create an anonymous PluginAction class/object on the spot, and pass it into doPlugins; we'll see this used in just a bit.

```
/**
 *
 */
public PluginApp()
{
}

/**
 *
 */
public PluginClassLoader.Listener getPluginListener()
{
    return new PluginClassLoader.Listener()
    {
        public void pluginLoaded(String pluginName)
        {
            System.out.println(pluginName + " loaded.");
```

```
            }
        public void exception(Exception ex)
        {
            System.out.println("Exception:");
            ex.printStackTrace();
        }
    };
}
```

This method creates the usual console-output PluginClassLoader.Listener that we've seen before. In a production-quality application, however, this is where you would update the splash screen or status bar with messages such as "Loading plug-in XYZ...."

```
/**
 * Display the application
 */
public void show()
{
    frame = new JFrame("PluginApp Example");
    frame.addWindowListener(new WindowAdapter()
    {
        public void windowClosing(WindowEvent e)
        {
            exit();
        }
    });

    JPanel contentPanel = new JPanel();
    contentPanel.add("North", createMenubar());

    frame.getContentPane().add(contentPanel);

    frame.pack();
    frame.show();
}
```

The show method is unremarkable, with one exception—the call to create-Menubar, which will iterate across all the plug-ins asking them if they wish to modify the menu bar.

```
/**
 *
 */
public void exit()
{
    canQuit = true;
    doPlugins(new PluginAction()
    {
        public void action(Plugin plugin)
        {
            if (plugin.canQuit() == false)
            {
                canQuit = false;
```

```
                }
            }
        });

        if (canQuit)
        {
            System.exit(0);
        }
    }
```

This is the first of two samples demonstrating how doPlugins works. We create an anonymous PluginAction class that calls each plug-in's canQuit method, setting the PluginApp state variable canQuit to false if any indicate that we can't quit yet. (Presumably this is the user telling us this, but perhaps we want to allow plug-ins the capability to prevent the user from quitting without performing some necessary task first.)

```
/**
 * Build the application-shell's menu bar; just "File" and "Help"
 */
private JMenuBar createMenubar()
{
    final JMenuBar mb = new JMenuBar();
    JMenu menu;
    JMenuItem mi;

    // "File"--"Reload"
    menu = new JMenu("File");
    mi = new JMenuItem("Reload");
    mi.addActionListener(new ActionListener()
    {
        public void actionPerformed(ActionEvent e)
        {
            pluginCL.reload(".",getPluginListener());
        }
    });
    menu.add(mi);

    // "File"--"Exit"
    mi = new JMenuItem("Exit");
    mi.addActionListener(new ActionListener()
    {
        public void actionPerformed(ActionEvent e)
        {
            exit();
        }
    });
    menu.add(mi);

    mb.add(menu);

    // "Help"--"About"
    menu = new JMenu("Help");
    mi = new JMenuItem("About");
    mi.addActionListener(new ActionListener()
```

```
        {
            public void actionPerformed(ActionEvent e)
            {
            }
        });
        menu.add(mi);
        mb.add(menu);

        // Allow the Plugins to register themselves
        doPlugins(new PluginAction()
        {
            public void action(Plugin plugin)
            {
                plugin.addToMenuBar(mb);
            }
        });

        return mb;
    }
```

Finally, the `createMenubar` method builds the JMenuBar instance that will be added to the application's main window. Notice, however, at the end of the method, that we iterate through each installed plug-in, calling on its `addToMenuBar` method (passing in the JMenuBar we just created). This is the mechanism by which the plug-ins can allow themselves to be invoked within this application; within other systems, plug-ins may be called with some discriminatory information to discern which plug-in to load (as in the scripting engine example above), or may simply be tried, round robin, until one is found that works.[9]

```
    /**
     *
     */
    public static void main (String args[])
    {
        // Create the basic app object
        PluginApp app = new PluginApp();

        // Display the app
        app.show();
    }
}
```

And `main`, of course, creates an instance of the application and invokes its `show` method.

Next, let's examine a simple example plug-in for this application:

```
import java.awt.*;
import java.awt.event.*;
import javax.swing.*;
```

---

[9] This is what James O. Coplien called the "exemplar idiom"; *Advanced C++ Programming Styles and Idioms* (Addison-Wesley, 1992).

The usual necessary-for-Swing imports. Nothing new here.

```
public class PluginOne
    implements PluginApp.Plugin
{

    static
    {
        PluginApp.registerPlugin(new PluginOne());
    }
```

As discussed before, when PluginOne is loaded into the JVM, it registers an instance of itself with the PluginApp class.

```
    public PluginOne()
    { }

    public void addToMenuBar(JMenuBar menuBar)
    {
        System.out.println("addToMenuBar called");
        final JMenuBar menu = menuBar;

        // Put us into the "File" menu
        for (int i=0; i<menu.getMenuCount(); i++)
        {
            JMenu m = menu.getMenu(i);

            System.out.println(m.getText());
            if ("File".equals(m.getText()))
            {
                System.out.println("Found File menu; adding self");
                JMenuItem mi = new JMenuItem("PluginOne");
                mi.addActionListener(new ActionListener()
                {
                    public void actionPerformed(ActionEvent e)
                    {
                        int result = JOptionPane.showConfirmDialog(
                            null,
                            "Do you like PluginOne?",
                            "information",
                            JOptionPane.YES_NO_CANCEL_OPTION,
                            JOptionPane.INFORMATION_MESSAGE);
                        if (result == JOptionPane.YES_OPTION)
                        {
                            JOptionPane.showMessageDialog(
                                null, "I'm glad");
                        }
                        else if (result == JOptionPane.NO_OPTION)
                        {
                            JOptionPane.showMessageDialog(
                                null, "I'm sorry to hear that");
                        }
                        else if (result == JOptionPane.CANCEL_OPTION)
                        {
                            JOptionPane.showMessageDialog(
```

```
                            null, "Operation cancelled");
                        }
                        else          .
                        {
                            // How is this possible?!? Swing is broken!
                        }
                    }
                });
                m.add(mi);
            }

            break;
        }
    }
```

This long snippet of code is an exercise in Swing mechanics; for those who aren't Swing gurus, the code simply adds a menu item to the bottom of the File menu, called "PluginOne". When the user picks "PluginOne" from the File menu, a "Yes/ No/Cancel" dialog box will be displayed, and a second dialog box will display "I'm glad," "I'm sorry to hear that," or "Operation canceled," depending on which button the user pressed. Nothing overly exciting here.

```
    public boolean canQuit()

    {
        System.out.println("PluginOne sez yes, you may quit");
        return true;
    }
}
```

Lastly, the canQuit method spits a message out to the console, informing us that PluginOne was given a chance to cancel the File-Exit command, and chose not to do so.

### 4.4.6    Uses for plug-ins

The plug-in concept can extend in many directions. As discussed earlier, a scripting language engine could use plug-ins as the interpreters of the various script languages it understands, allowing users to drop in support for new languages by simply copying in the appropriate script-language .jar file. A web server could support servlets in much the same way—instead of a Plugin-Class tag, requiring the .jar file to contain a Servlet-Class tag, indicating the Servlet class to load.[10] An application, as demonstrated above, could allow sophisticated end users to create additional functionality for the application. A graphics conversion (or any kind of file-conversion application, for that matter) can use plug-ins to manage each file format the application wants to handle, so long as there is a good interim format that can be handed between the formatters. Even games can make use of this concept. A basic card

---

[10] The Java2 Enterprise Edition specification uses XML "Deployment Descriptors" instead of attributes in the .jar file, but it's the same concept.

game shell can implement the rules of various card games (cribbage, gin rummy, and poker) as plug-ins loaded when the game shell starts up.

The plug-in concept represents a good marketing strategy, as well—customers can be given the basic application shell for free (available for download, for example), with a simple demo as their only available plug-in. Then, as customers begin using the application and demand greater functionality, more powerful plug-ins can be made available, which customers buy and copy into the application's plug-ins directory. This approach has the advantage of giving the user a free, non-timing-out version of the application that may be good for lightweight use, but requires purchase for heavier use. Customers who require support outside of the existing realm of plug-ins can contact the company for a custom plug-in, which the company can then turn around and resell to other customers, as well.

## 4.5   SUMMARY

Developers would be well-advised to think of Java's extension mechanism as under the same rules as developing reusable libraries in other languages such as C++. Many of the same concepts, and trade-offs apply. For example, development of code without using libraries means the entire code base can be assumed to be the same version. Breaking up the code into separate, modular, libraries means now that each library, as well as each application, must be versioned, tracked, and tested against the entire application suite before it can be released. Using the library concept also means that developers will be restricted from wholesale replacement of components, since other applications may be dependent on the particular structure and/or usage of components in the library, which restricts developers.[11]

For all its drawbacks, the Java extension mechanism is the first step Java has shown toward building reusable component libraries and toolkits other than those shipped as part of the JDK. It may be argued that the .jar file was the critical step, but the modification of the CLASSPATH necessary to use a given .jar file made it awkward to use .jar files, especially when large numbers were used. CLASSPATHs over 500 characters long aren't uncommon when making use of a half-dozen .jar files at once, which is not unreasonable in any moderately-sized project. The Java extension mechanism makes the modification of the CLASSPATH almost completely unnecessary now.

---

[11] In an ideal world, each component would have its `public` interface fixed and immutable, but this is an unattainable target. As needs within the development team change, use of particular components grows, and initially acceptable and elegant designs grow more and more unworkable, and wholesale replacement of the design becomes necessary.

# C H A P T E R    5

# *Threads*

The Java language is the only popular development language or environment to provide native, intrinsic support for threads and the necessary related concurrency control constructs. Not only are Java threads a built-in, inherent part of the language and execution environment, they simplify the concurrent programming model significantly from native alternatives. Consider the Win32/C++ environment. Here, threads are OS-level constructs that must be created through a Win32 API call, `CreateThread` with its associated half-dozen or so parameters. Because this is an API call, its interface is designed for a C development environment; as a result, trying to tie the notion of object in C++ to thread in Win32 is not trivial. It requires an arcane hookup using static methods of C++, thunk layers, or equally mystical manipulation of assembly code in order to get C++ objects that look, feel, and act like threads. In fact, Java's support for threads has enamored C++ developers to the point that a company, Object-Oriented Concepts (www.ooc.com), has gone so far as to create a Java-like threads library for C++ developers.

Threads, while not directly moving us toward zero development, zero deployment, or zero administration, are key building blocks toward all three goals. By building Thread constructs in a reusable manner, we reduce necessary development costs for the next project, moving toward zero development. By judiciously spinning off threads in key areas, we can make it possible to perform more than one task at once, such as configure the application during its execution (zero administration). Furthermore, threads are critical to good performance, when used properly.

But for all its simplicity, concurrent programming in Java is still overly intimidating to a number of Java developers. They feel that threads will somehow mysteriously lock up their application, or cause it to hang without warning, without reason, and without any way to debug the problem. As with most things, there is an element of truth to this belief. And if that's the case, why bother using them?

## 5.1 WHY THREADS?

Threads and concurrent design provide possibilities that simply wouldn't be available in a single-threaded environment. Threads allow you to continue execution in another portion of your code while the CPU is blocking on something, or providing service on the behalf of another, unrelated client. Threads, in fact, are to your process what multiprocessing is to a single machine—the ability to provide services to more than one client at a time, without imposing overly complex restrictions on those clients.

### 5.1.1 Concurrent processing

The use of threads permits an application to perform two actions simultaneously without having to execute them sequentially. The classic example given is the notion of printing while you work. In a user application, such as a word processor, threads can be fired off to take care of background tasks, such as checking spelling or printing, while the user continues to work in the foreground. One particularly interesting application of threads is the use of a background thread to perform compilation in development environments such as Microsoft Developer Studio or Borland C++.

The use of threads in this manner raises some interesting design questions, however. What if a user modifies a file during the middle of a compilation on that file? Should the compiler use the file as it existed when the build sequence began or should it use the most recent contents? If the compiler uses the file as it existed, then what point is there to being able to edit the file during compilation? If the compiler uses the current contents, how does it guarantee that the contents of the file at *this* second is the same as it was when it built the previous unit?

Where the use of threads in user applications has some dubious applications in certain areas, the use of threads in server applications is an essential requirement for performance and scalability. A server that can process only a single client at a given moment is unnecessarily restrictive; this means that to control two concurrent users, two machines must be purchased. This is unnecessarily wasteful, especially when the tasks being performed are identical. For example, a web server fundamentally executes the precise same sequence of steps for each and every web request it receives:

- Parse the HTTP header to determine the URL requested
- Locate the resource on the server, after appropriate validation (if any) is passed
- Return the resource to the waiting requester and prepare to receive the next request

This would almost seem to be a throwback to procedural development—execute a sequence of steps, in fixed order, starting at the top of the flow and moving through to the bottom, only to go back to the top again. In a single-threaded server, the first client to come in would be serviced in fast fashion, but other clients coming in with requests during the processing of the first request would have to queue up until the server could react to them. With web sites and internal corporate intranet sites looking to handle upward of thousands of concurrent requests, this is obviously not acceptable.

One alternative to the use of threads would be to run multiple instances of the single-threaded application, each one performing its actions independently of the others. (UNIX systems have used this approach for years, and, in fact, the Apache web server still makes use of it.) This approach carries two problems, however. The first is *resource management*; in most operating environments, only a single process may have access to certain scarce resources (such as sockets, or printers, or even disk space). Attempting to coordinate requests and contentions between independent processes can be a complex and overly arduous task. Using the web server example, a separate process must do the listening on port 80, and in turn farm out the requests to other processes listening on a range of internally known ports. The second problem is that of *process independence*: in most operating environments, processes are prevented from seeing another process space. This means that each copy of a given file, object, or resource must be loaded, stored, and used. Caching algorithms to help speed up the access of frequently accessed pages become useless across process boundaries.

Threads share the same process space, but receive their own execution stack; each thread carries its own set of registers, allowing it to execute independently of the others. Since they share the same process space, however, one thread can access a resource loaded in by another thread. Since they share the same process space, one thread can access a network resource (such as a socket) even as another thread finishes up its work with it. This means a lower footprint for the same functionality, since a given resource need only be loaded once.

## 5.1.2   Scalability per machine

Without threads, attempting to serve more than one client request concurrently requires either multiple processes, or multiple machines. The use of multiple processes carries additional run time overhead, since the entire process footprint must be duplicated multiple times. Multiple machines lead to different problems, such as the coordination of processes or avoiding the duplication of data across two machines, especially common where database environments (or any other read/write server) are used. This is painful, especially when you realize that the CPU spends about 90 percent of its available time waiting for something—disk I/O, network I/O, user input, and so forth.

The use of threads allows the server to serve the needs of a number of clients simultaneously and still preserve operating system process independence. Most importantly, the Java scheduler (or the native scheduler, depending on whether this is a green or native threads platform) can allow other threads to execute while a particular one is blocked, waiting for I/O or other time-consuming tasks to complete.

In fact, this is where much of the notion that threads improve your application performance originates. Threads inherently do not improve the performance of an application; in fact, they slow it down! If this seems ludicrous, consider the following: In order to support the independence of two threads, the entire CPU register set and execution stack must be saved off and restored each time this thread is swapped out and back in again. This is known in thread parlance as a context switch. This switch does not occur in a single-threaded application. So, in a given sequence of operations, all of which are CPU-intensive, if you break it up into multiple threads, instead of improving performance, you may actually degrade it, on a single-CPU system.

However, for most server-side development, the majority of the CPU is not spent in heavy-CPU computation, but heavy I/O operation. This means that the CPU has a tremendous amount of idle time, where it blocks on a response from a request or an operation. It is this time that threads can reclaim for you, thereby appearing to improve your application's performance. It becomes even more positive when the application can delegate all of its disk I/O requests (such as writing logging information) to a different thread, leaving the delegating thread to continue with its CPU-intensive tasks. The goal in this case is to make use of 100 percent of the CPU's available time, leaving no time spent in idleness.

About multiple-CPU machines and performance: it would seem that using a multiple-CPU machine would only improve performance. This is not necessarily true, unfortunately. Under certain circumstances, this can actually reduce performance, as most OSs do not simply map a thread to a CPU, as many threading-proponents would claim. Instead, the OS scheduler typically swaps a thread into a CPU for a time slice, then maps it back out when the time slice is finished. Considering that simply booting into NT 4.0 Workstation fires off at least seventy threads just to run Explorer and various behind-the-scenes services, I also wouldn't expect to see machines that have one CPU per thread, either.

### 5.1.3    Encapsulation

Because Java sees threads as objects, thread objects can not only encapsulate behavior, but also the data and state variables that go along with that behavior. A web request-response thread, for example, needs to store the URL which the request is trying to access, and ensure that the response sent back is specific to that URL. It also needs to store the socket on which the request came, so that it knows where to send the response. Database requests carry an SQL statement that must be executed and results returned. They need to track the state of open cursors or iterators as clients investigate the result sets returned.

Because of Java's threads-as-objects approach, it becomes trivial to associate data with a thread. Any time we can wed behavior to data and remove requirements to understand the interaction between the two from the public domain we have simplified the system. Less work will be required to maintain it, improve it, or understand it.

### 5.1.4 Design and implementation

The ability to create, use, and otherwise treat threads as objects in Java[1] leads to a number of design possibilities and approaches. Several of these are immediately intuitive—cancelable operations threads, and so forth. Several are not. Consider, for example, the Façade pattern from the *Design Patterns* book. Façade encapsulates a subsystem made up of many additional objects behind a single object interface. The example used in the book is that of a compiler. Threads can be integrated into the design in either a subtle or obvious approach—subtle, in that threads can be used within the Façade, away from the client's perceptions, to help improve the Façade's responsiveness, or obvious, in that the Façade can be treated as an asynchronous system. Either way, the use of threads within the pattern allows for additional flexibility, customization, and opportunity for reuse.

Threads can also make the implementation of other systems trivial or simpler than in sequential systems. For example, finite state machines were commonly used in single-threaded systems (such as MS-DOS or very early versions of UNIX) to allow multiple actions to take place concurrently—a task was given the chance to execute one stage of its state machine, then it returned to the central scheduler to allow other tasks to execute. The advent of thread capability within the system allows developers to unroll the finite state machines into a single-dimensional sequence of steps, which can be easily represented as simple, straightforward procedural logic.

## 5.2 JAVA THREADS

While Java's thread support is impressive in its flexibility and simplicity, the concept of suddenly having two things happening at once may be confusing for Java developers who may not have run into the concept before. Fortunately, the widespread acceptance of Java as a server-side development language reduces the mystery and myth that surrounds the subject; as more and more experience, knowledge, and skill are brought to the topic, it becomes easier and easier for developers to pick up the necessary details.

There are a number of books on programming for Java that cover the rudimentary aspects of Threads, so it would be tempting to simply tell you to check out one of those books for your basic introduction to the subject. However, I believe that threads are such an important concept to understand that I'm going to go back over the Thread

---

[1]  Or any other language that supports the notion of threads-as-objects, even C++ (once you build it yourself, of course, since C++ has no inherent support for Threads, as does Java).

API (`java.lang.Runnable`, `java.lang.Thread`, `java.lang.ThreadGroup` and the assorted Exception classes associated therewith) in some detail, to make sure we're all on the same page.

## 5.2.1 java.lang.Thread and java.lang.Runnable

The core of Java's threading API comes in these two classes; while you may be able to dodge some of the Thread classes for a while, like ThreadGroup, you can't do anything with threads without touching these two.

If you simply start at the top of `java/lang/Thread.java` and start reading down, once you get past a number of internal fields and methods (and a curious entry labeled `InheritableThreadLocalEntry`, which we'll get to later), you run across these constants:

```
public final static int MIN_PRIORITY = 1;
public final static int NORM_PRIORITY = 5;
public final static int MAX_PRIORITY = 10;
```

As you might well guess, these are the priority settings for threads. Each thread fired from within Java has a corresponding priority level, ranging from 1 to 10. These numbers are not absolutes—they don't correspond to a certain number of milliseconds for time slices, and so forth. They are only useful in how they relate to one another. Thus, if you set all of your threads to be MAX_PRIORITY, all you'll do is starve other threads in the system, such as the garbage-collection thread. Priorities are set using the Thread's `getPriority` and `setPriority` methods.

Continuing farther down, we run across a few native methods:

- `currentThread` returns the Thread object corresponding to the Thread currently executing
- `yield` surrenders control of this time slice to another Thread (determined by the JVM or OS scheduler, not you)
- `sleep` parks your thread for a number of milliseconds (or milliseconds and nanoseconds, depending on the version of `sleep` you use).

These are all well-documented and intuitive to understand, so I won't go over them in any greater detail.

Next (after skipping a `private` method), you run into a block of Thread constructor methods. Summarized, they look like:

```
public Thread()
public Thread(Runnable target)
public Thread(ThreadGroup group, Runnable target)
public Thread(String name)
public Thread(ThreadGroup group, String name)
public Thread(Runnable target, String name)
public Thread(ThreadGroup group, Runnable target, String name)
```

If you examine them as a group, you see a pattern—each constructor is one variation on the (target, group, name) tuple. Threads can be constructed with a name argument, which is nothing more than an identification tag for your own use, a target argument, which we'll discuss momentarily, or a group argument, which we'll discuss in a later section. Or you can construct a Thread with nothing at all, which is typically not very useful unless you extend Thread in a subclass, which I do not recommend. If you leave out a name argument, Thread will set a default name of "Thread-" plus an incremental thread-count, and you can retrieve or modify this name with the getName and setName methods. The group parameter indicates that this Thread is to be made part of the ThreadGroup group.

The target parameter, however, is by far the most important. Without it, when the Thread's start method is called, the created thread calls Thread.run(), which by default does nothing. If you pass in a target, however, Thread.start() will actually call the Runnable's run method. For example, these two snippets of code accomplish the same thing:

```
public class ThreadSubclass extends Thread
{
    public ThreadSubclass() { }
    public void run()
    { System.out.println("ThreadSubclass.run() called"); }
}
ThreadSubclass t = new ThreadSubclass();
t.start();

public class RunnableObject
    implements Runnable
{
    public RunnableObject() { }
    public void run()
    { System.out.println("RunnableObject.run() called"); }
}
Thread t = new Thread(new RunnableObject());
t.start();
```

While both print "<classname>.run() called!" to the console window, these are two very different approaches—one relies on the time-honored tradition of using inheritance for reuse, the other uses the more recent approach of componentry.

When object-orientation first became widespread, one of its key features was inheritance, and the reuse that could be obtained by its use. Simply write a base class, developers were told, and any class that inherits from that base class can use its behavior by default. This *implementation inheritance*, as it is now known, became commonplace and led to the deeply-nested type hierarchies that were characterized by Smalltalk and early C++ environments and libraries.

*Componentry*, on the other hand, seeks to avoid implementation inheritance wherever possible—instead of extending a type, you use the type, and plug in various other components to customize its behavior. In the example, we don't extend Thread;

instead, we plug a Runnable component, with which Thread knows how to work, into the Thread object itself.

Why two different approaches? It turns out that componentry more closely achieves the goal of black-box reuse than implementation inheritance. One problem with implementation inheritance is that of *preserving base-class semantics*. For example, if we extend Thread's run method, do we need to call the base class version in order to make sure everything still runs correctly? If so, do we need to call it before we do our custom behavior, after, or some time in between? A classic case of this comes up in the Java AWT 1.0. If we extend handleEvent in a Component, do we need to call the base class version? (Yes.) When? (Depends.) And what if we handle the event, and don't want to pass it up the chain—will that break something? (Possibly.)

As developers continued to work with implementation inheritance-based systems, they found that they needed to know a tremendous amount about the system's internals in order to make certain they didn't accidentally break something. This directly violates another precept of object-oriented development, that of encapsulation. I shouldn't have to know information about a particular class in order to use it, but in an implementation inheritance design, I often have to, both to extend its behavior as well as to simply preserve its current behavioral semantics.

Another problem arose as these libraries continued to evolve. Library coders wanted to make changes, either in response to bug reports or to improve certain classes. They found they couldn't because users of the library were counting on (in their derived class code) certain member variables to be set before they were called, or were changing the value of those member variables in order to influence the behavior of the base class, and so forth. This led to less flexibility both on the part of the library developers as well as the library users.

The last problem with this approach centers on what Peter Coad referred to as the principle of perpetual employment.[2] Each new behavior required in an implementation inheritance-based system requires an entirely new subclass to be constructed, with all of the required knowledge about the base class to go with it. For example, assume you purchased a UI library that provides a TextEditor component. The following week, you receive the requirement to create a hex-edit editor window. In an implementation-inheritance model, you subclass TextEditor, and override its behavior to put out hex numbers instead of single characters, react to keystrokes by replacing the current hex number at the cursor location with a new hex number, and so forth. The week following, you receive the requirement to create an HTMLEditor component. So, you fire up your trusty development environment, and proceed to subclass TextEditor again, this time with appropriate HTML tags and editor commands. The week after that, you're asked to create an XMLEditor component. You get the idea. Under certain circumstances, it's possible to use one of your derived classes as a base

---

[2] From *Object-Oriented Programming*, by Peter Coad and Jil Nicola (Prentice Hall/Yourdon Press 1993).

from which to start working (such as XMLEditor from HTMLEditor). You can some-times factor common code from the two into an interim base class (XMLEditor and HTMLEditor—both inherit from MarkupLanguageEditor, perhaps?). As soon as a request comes for a class that reaches across the inheritance chain (an XMLHexEditor view?), though, you're in trouble.[3]

Componentry seeks to avoid this sort of need for internal knowledge and still allows for infinite extension without requiring an unending number of corresponding subclasses. Rather than force me to extend a class (which, remember, in Java gives me access to all of its internal fields not marked `private`), a component developer creates a well-defined collection of classes that I can plug in to achieve certain specific effects. A wonderful example of this is the JFC GUI code, also known as Swing. With the JTree and JTable classes, I can plug in a Model class that tells the GUI component how to build itself—with JTree, with nodes and leaves, with JTable, with columns and rows. JTable goes even further with this concept. If I want to create the ability to edit data within the cell, I can implement the TableCellEditor interface, provide the necessary methods that JTable promises to call in well-defined ways, and I can effectively cus-tomize this JTable instance without knowing anything about JTable's internals. More importantly, those internals remain the sole knowledge of the component creator, which means the creator can continue to improve or radically change the way JTable works under the hood without concern of breaking my code.

Bringing the discussion back to Thread and Runnable: remember that the two code snippets above are *behaviorally* equivalent. However, suppose I create a new and improved Thread class. ThreadSubclass (from the example above) cannot make use of this new Thread-based class without changing its `extends` clause, which in turn breaks other parts of the code. RunnableObject, however, can be plugged into the new Thread class, since Threads interact with Runnables in a very well-defined way.

```
NewAndImprovedThread newThread =
    new NewAndImprovedThread(new RunnableObject());
newThread.start();
```

In effect, we've made use of the new behavior of NewAndImprovedThread without having to modify a single line within RunnableObject. This is one of the principal benefits of componentry.

Some may argue that this is unnecessary, since Thread is already a well-defined class with little room for improvement. I disagree. Let's examine two common usages

---

[3] It was to support this concept ("a SeaPlane IS-A Plane *and* IS-A Boat") that led Bjarne Stroustrup to introduce multiple inheritance into C++, a decision which was hotly contested for years, and has since fallen out of favor.

of Thread: to perform a particular action at a given time, and to periodically perform an action (every *n* seconds) (listing 5.1).

```
/**
 * PeriodicThread is a specific type of Thread that fires off its
 * associated Runnable evry <code>interval</code> milliseconds.
 */
public class PeriodicThread extends Thread
{
    private PeriodicThread()
    {
        // This prevents instantiation without an associated Runnable;
        // I don't want to allow the possibility of this code from
        // ever compiling:
        //
        // new PeriodicThread().start();
        //
    }

    /**
     * Constructor taking the Runnable whose run method we
     * wish to call every interval milliseconds.
     */
    public PeriodicThread(Runnable r, int interval)
    {
        super();

        m_runnable = r;
        m_interval - interval;
    }

    /**
     * The run method spins in an infinite loop, calling
     * run on the owned Runnable instance every interval
     * milliseconds (as specified in the constructor). The time spent
     * in the Runnable's run method is not taken into
     * account in the period spent sleeping.
     */
    public void run()
    {
        try
        {
            while (true)
            {
                Thread.sleep(m_interval);
                m_runnable.run();
            }
        }
        catch (InterruptedException iEx)
        {
            return;
```

```
        }
    }

    private int m_interval = 0;
    private Runnable m_runnable = null;

    /**
     * Test driver for the PeriodicThread component
     */
    public static void main(String[] args)
        throws Exception
    {

        PeriodicThread pt = new PeriodicThread(new Runnable()
        {
            public void run()
            {
                System.out.println("Fired!");
            }
        }, 10 * 1000);
        pt.start();

        PeriodicThread pt2 = new PeriodicThread(new Runnable()
        {
            public void run()
            {
                System.out.println("Hired!");
            }
        }, 15*1000);
        pt2.start();

        System.out.println("Use Ctrl-C to quit.");
        pt.join();
        pt2.join();
    }
}

/**
 * ScheduledThread
 */
public class ScheduledThread extends Thread
{
    private ScheduledThread()
    {
        // Prevent "new ScheduledThread().start()"
        //
    }

    public ScheduledThread(Runnable runnable, java.util.Date when)
    {
        m_runnable = runnable;
        m_when = when;
    }

    public void run()
    {
```

```
            try
            {
                // Make sure "when" is after now.
                //
                while (m_when.after(new java.util.Date()))
                {
                    Thread.sleep(1000);
                }

                // If the above test failed, it's time
                // to run our target
                //
                m_runnable.run();
            }
            catch (InterruptedException intEx)
            {
                return;
            }
        }

    private java.util.Date m_when;
    private Runnable m_runnable;
}
```

Now, any Runnable object can be fired off right away, fired off every *n* seconds, or fired off at a specific time. Or any combination of the three:

```
Thread t =
    new ScheduledThread(
        new PeriodicThread(
            new Runnable() { . . .}, 15 * 1000),
        new Date( /* some date here */ ) );
t.start();
```

This creates a Thread that, when the Date given occurs, will fire off a PeriodicThread to perform some action every (15 * 1000) milliseconds, or every fifteen seconds. Try to combine the two thread concepts into a single subclass, and you'd need to create a new subclass from Thread called PeriodicScheduledThread. Then, if you want to reverse the use (a PeriodicThread that fires off a new ScheduledThread every *n* seconds), you'd need a new ScheduledPeriodicThread... you get my drift.

## 5.2.2    Starting threads

The next set of methods in Thread deals with starting the thread itself. Actually, only one method really deals with starting the Thread, the `start` method. This method, when called, creates an underlying thread (either an OS native thread, or a green thread), starts it, and returns to the caller.

When the new thread is started, it does not continue execution within the `start` method, as users of UNIX's `fork` system call would expect, nor does it execute a particular function, as users of Win32's `CreateProcess` system API would expect.

Instead, the starting point for any started Thread is always the same—the Thread object's run method:

```
public void run() {
    if (target != null) {
        target.run();
    }
}
```

As you can see, if the Thread has no `target` instance within it (which it will only have if a Runnable instance were specified in a constructor), then the Thread's `run` method is effectively a no-op. Correspondingly, when the `run` method returns, the created thread dies.

The method after `start`, called `exit`, sounds intriguing, as does the comment attached to it: "This method is called by the system to give a Thread a chance to clean up before it actually exits." Unfortunately, it's `private`, meaning we can't override it, correct? Not true—the JDK 1.2 has a particularly strange hole regarding this method; despite the fact that private methods are not supposed to be dynamically bound, the `Thread.exit` method appears to be just that. The following code not only compiles, but executes in an entirely different manner than it should:

```
public class ThreadExit
{
    public static void main(String[] args)
        throws Exception
    {
        Thread t = new Thread()
        {
            private void exit()
            {
                System.out.println("Thread.exit()");
            }
        };
        t.start();
        t.join();
    }
}
```

When run, `"Thread.exit()"` appears on the console window. This might seem like an opportunity for some thread cleanup, but be *very* careful here. Because `Thread.exit()` is marked `private`, you can't call up to it from the derived class, and the implementation of `exit` yields some disturbing thoughts:

```
private void exit() {
    if (group != null) {
        group.remove(this);
        group = null;
    }
    /* Aggressively null object connected to Thread: see bug 4006245 */
    target = null;
}
```

It's that last comment that bothers me: "see bug 4006245." The bug in question was found in Java 1.0, and marked fixed in Java 1.1, and deals with the garbage collector taking a long time to collect Thread instances. In an effort to force garbage collection to occur earlier, Sun chose to aggressively null-out the references held within Thread. The fact that we're unable to call back up to the base version of exit means we can't take advantage of the fix.

If we can't make use of this information without running some risks, why bring it up at all? The fact is that per-Thread cleanup is a useful concept, especially since exit, unlike finalizers, has some well-defined context regarding its cleanup. Having this ability open to us is a useful one. Be careful if you use it, and if your JVM suddenly appears to be requiring a much larger footprint than you would expect, look to see if this is the culprit.

Having discussed how to start threads, let's talk about how to stop them.

### 5.2.3    Stopping threads

To go along, it would seem, with Thread.start is Thread.stop. This makes sense—if start creates and launches the thread, then stop must stop and destroy the thread. JavaSoft has chosen to mark stop as deprecated, subject to removal in future versions of Java (From jdk1.2/docs/api/java/lang/Thread.html):

> This method is inherently unsafe. Stopping a thread with Thread.stop causes it to unlock all of the monitors that it has locked (as a natural consequence of the unchecked ThreadDeath exception propagating up the stack). If any of the objects previously protected by these monitors were in an inconsistent state, the damaged objects become visible to other threads, potentially resulting in arbitrary behavior. Many uses of stop should be replaced by code that simply modifies some variable to indicate that the target thread should stop running. The target thread should check this variable regularly, and return from its run method in an orderly fashion if the variable indicates that it is to stop running. If the target thread waits for long periods (on a condition variable, for example), the interrupt method should be used to interrupt the wait.
>
> For more information, see "Why are Thread.stop, Thread.suspend and Thread.resume Deprecated?" (jdk1.2/docs/guide/misc/threadPrimitiveDeprecation.html).

The central problem with stop is that it is an immediate and terminable action; objects used by this thread have no opportunity to react to the termination of the thread, and as a result, may be in a damaged or inconsistent state. What the JDK documentation suggests, instead of the use of stop to shut down a thread, is to code something as follows:

```
public class StoppableThreadObject
    implements Runnable
{
    public void run()
    {
        while (!stopped)
        { do_some_work(); }
    }

    public void stop()
    { stopped = true; }

    private volatile boolean stopped = false;
}

StoppableThreadObject sto = new StoppableThreadObject();
Thread t = new Thread(sto);

// . . . later

sto.stop();
```

Code written in this manner allows objects used by StoppableThreadObject to clean themselves up before the thread completely goes away. However, this approach has one particular flaw: If the Thread gets wrapped up in an infinite loop or other similarly busy action, it can't check the stopped flag to see if it's time to quit. This approach also relies on the developer being a good citizen and checking his flag every so often to see if it's time to quit. If the developer decides to be stingy, or simply forgets to check the flag in a long sequence of code, it could be a very long time before the stop takes effect. This may not be acceptable in some situations.

The stop method comes in two versions, one which takes no arguments, the other which takes a single Exception argument. Both perform the same operation—wake up the Thread, force it to throw either (in the no-arg version of stop) a new ThreadDeath object, or the Exception argument specified. Usually, if you need to call stop, you'll call the no-arg version, because there are some special semantics associated with ThreadDeath that you won't get otherwise.[4]

One alternative approach to stop is the interrupt method. This method causes the current Thread to immediately cease its current action (under specific circumstances[5]) and throw a new InterruptedException, which then propagates back up the chain, all the way back to the run method of the Runnable or Thread that was called by this thread. User code can check to see if either throw an interrupt

---

[4] If the Thread propagates the ThreadDeath exception all the way back to the JVM's native implementation, the JVM knows to destroy the underlying thread at the OS/JVM level. Accordingly, if you *catch* the ThreadDeath exception, make sure you re-throw it, or the thread will never actually die!

[5] Specifically, the thread needs to be in a sleep or wait—a thread blocking for any other reason won't cause it to be interrupted

by calling the `isInterrupted` method.[6] We can then recode the preceding StoppableThreadObject as:

```
public class StoppableThreadObject
    implements Runnable
{
    public void run()
    {
        try
        {
            while (!Thread.currentThread().isInterrupted())
            { do_some_work(); }
        }
        catch (InterruptedException interruptedException)
        {
            // Clean up here
        }
    }
}

StoppableThreadObject sto = new StoppableThreadObject();
Thread t = new Thread(sto);

// . . . later
t.interrupt();
```

This way, we still get the semantics we desire (immediate cessation of the Thread), but also allow any owned objects to clean themselves up appropriately. An alternative implementation would use a `finally` clause to the `try` block in `run` to allow the StoppableThreadObject to clean itself up on any `Exception` thrown, not just interruptions.

You may also notice that the Thread methods `suspend` and `resume` were also deprecated starting in JDK 1.1. The reason for this was similar to the reasons given for deprecating `stop`; this sort of immediate action on the Thread can lead to situations where the Thread still holds resources that can mess up other Threads. In this case, suspending a Thread while it holds a monitor inside of a synchronization block (see below) means no other Threads can enter that block while the first one is suspended. This can lead to deadlock. (If the Thread that made the `suspend` call is itself blocked from ever calling `resume` on that same Thread, those two Threads are infinitely deadlocked.)

One other thing to note is that almost all of the Thread methods that involve manipulating a Thread's current status involve a check to the Java SecurityManager before continuing.

---

[6] Which, unfortunately, clears the interrupted flag in the Thread, so that if the first call to `isInterrupted` returns `true`, any subsequent calls will return `false`, at least until the Thread is interrupted again.

## 5.2.4    Daemon threads

One of the interesting features of Java's thread support is that an application doesn't exit the JVM until all created threads have terminated. To prove it, let's try the following code:

```
public class Wait
{
    public static void main(String[] args)
    {
        new Thread(new Runnable()
        {
            public void run()
            {
                try
                {
                    Thread.sleep(15 * 1000);
                    System.out.println("Exiting run() thread");
                }
                catch (InterruptedException iEx)
                {
                    iEx.printStackTrace();
                }
            }
        }).start();

        System.out.println("End of main()");
    }
}
```

If you run this, you'll get

```
C:\Projects\SSJ\cd\src\chap3>java Wait
End of main()
Exiting run() thread

C:\Projects\SSJ\cd\src\chap3>
```

with the `"Exiting run() thread"` text appearing on the console fifteen seconds after `"End of main()"`.

Certain tasks make better sense performed as a background task in a separate thread, such as garbage collection or spelling checker in a text editor. Unfortunately, this behavior of the JVM would seem to make these operations impossible. If the JVM isn't going to quit until all threads are terminated, then constantly spinning tasks, like garbage collection, will keep the JVM active until the user explicitly kills it (via CTRL-C in the console window, "kill" on UNIX, or the Task Manager under NT).

Fortunately, the Java Thread model offers a solution—`setDaemon` allows us to mark the thread as a *daemon thread*. In UNIX parlance, a daemon process is one that starts when the machine is first booted, and runs continuously in the background until the machine is shut down, or the process is explicitly teminated by a user. Java makes the same analogy to threads—marking a thread as a daemon thread means that it intends to run continuously in the background, and, more importantly, doesn't count against the "all Threads must die for the JVM to quit" condition. If we modified the previous code snippet to read:

```
public class Wait
{
    public static void main(String[] args)
    {
        Thread t = new Thread(new Runnable()
        {
            public void run()
            {
                try
                {
                    Thread.sleep(15 * 1000);
                    System.out.println("Exiting run() thread");
                }
                catch (InterruptedException iEx)
                {
                    iEx.printStackTrace();
                }
            }
        });
        t.setDaemon(true);
        t.start();

        System.out.println("End of main()");
    }
}
```

then we execute the code, and we see

```
C:\Projects\SSJ\cd\src\chap3>java Wait
End of main()

C:\Projects\SSJ\cd\src\chap3>
```

In other words, main exits as soon as it is finished, because all other executing Threads are daemon threads. The created Thread never gets a chance to write its output, because it's still sleeping when main quits and the JVM decides to shut down.

Note that if you try to call setDaemon after the Thread starts, Java will throw an IllegalStateException; you must set daemon status on the Thread before it starts. The method isDaemon can be used to ask a Thread if it is set to daemon status or not.

### 5.2.5 Threads and ClassLoaders

One of the quiet changes the JDK 1.2 made to the Thread API was the addition of two potentially useful methods: setContextClassLoader and getContextClassLoader. Remember, associated with each class is a reference to the ClassLoader that loaded it. The thread's context ClassLoader will be the one used to find new classes and resources for this thread. If you don't set a context ClassLoader, then it will default to the ClassLoader used to create the Thread object representing the new thread. The context ClassLoader can be loaded at any time during the Thread's lifetime, unlike the thread's daemon status.

The thread's context ClassLoader has a unique role within the Java system. When the JVM is first started, a Thread object is created, to call the main class's main method. As part of that initialization at JVM-start, the AppClassLoader is set as the primordial Thread's context ClassLoader. However, that having been said, the context ClassLoader, under normal circumstances, is never consulted as a ClassLoader in the chain. This means that if a Class can't be found by the App- or ExtClassLoaders (or any custom ClassLoaders that were called before it got to App- and ExtClassLoader), the thread's context ClassLoader is never called.

This naturally leads into the question, "Why include it then, if it's not called anywhere?" It's provided there for use by packages that wish to make use of a particular (mutable) ClassLoader, without having to hard-code knowledge about a particular ClassLoader into the package. In other words, certain packages (namely, RMI) will consult with the thread's context ClassLoader to find classes that they require, but that this must be coded for explicitly within those certain packages—if you don't call Thread.getContextClassLoader to obtain the ClassLoader from which to load a class, it will never be called.

All of the above essentially boils down to this: for the most part, unless you are doing dynamic class-loading, you don't have to worry about the Thread's context ClassLoader. Having it available, however, opens up some powerful functionality, especially in regard to the discussion of ClassLoaders and dynamically upgrading systems on the fly from the last chapter. For example, a web server providing Servlet support might create a ServletClassLoader to load the servlet class from disk, spin off a Thread in which to allow the servlet to execute, and set the ServletClassLoader as the Thread's context ClassLoader, thus ensuring that any RMI-calls within the servlet also use the ServletClassLoader (and its parent chain, as well) as part of the class-search process.

## 5.2.6    java.lang.ThreadGroup

It's not uncommon for groups of threads to work together in some fashion. A web server, for example, may wish to have a group of threads on hand to farm out socket requests; FTP or mail servers may do the same. AI systems using multiple threads to explore different paths of decision-making may want to group certain threads together to allow them to interact with one another in a neural-net approach. A diagnostic message tracer may keep one thread per diagnostic message sink (file, window, and so on). However, these groups of threads in turn have nothing to do with other groups of threads within the system (such as the garbage-collection thread(s), and so forth). It would be nice to be able to refer to a logical group of threads, without referring to the entire set within the system.

Java provides this capability with the class `java.lang.ThreadGroup`, a specialized collection class for Threads. ThreadGroup contains a variety of methods to control, access, and hierarchically group collections of threads.

Constructing a ThreadGroup can take one of several forms:

```
public ThreadGroup(String name)
public ThreadGroup(ThreadGroup parent, String name)
```

ThreadGroups have a name and a parent ThreadGroup. If you don't specify a parent, the code assumes that the ThreadGroup of the current thread is to be the parent. You can retrieve the parent of a ThreadGroup by calling `getParent`, the name by calling `getName`, the maximum priority of all threads within the ThreadGroup by calling `getMaxPriority`, and set this maximum priority with `setMaxPriority`. You can mark all threads within this ThreadGroup by calling `setDaemon` on the Thread-Group, and when the last thread or ThreadGroup owned by this ThreadGroup is destroyed, the ThreadGroup will die with it.

Threads and ThreadGroups can be added or removed via the `add` and `remove` methods. The `list` method writes out (to System.out, and nowhere else, unfortunately) a list of all Threads and ThreadGroups owned by this ThreadGroup. Of more interest are the `enumerate` and `activeCount` methods. Calling `activeCount` returns the current number of Threads executing as part of this ThreadGroup, and `enumerate` populates an array of Thread references with references to the threads owned by this ThreadGroup. Thus, to iterate across all threads in a given Thread-Group and print out their `toString` representation, the code looks like this:

```
ThreadGroup tg = . . .; // obtain ThreadGroup we want to query
int count = tg.activeCount();
Thread[] list = new Thread[count + count/2];
  // allow some padding since the count could change in
  // between the calls to activeCount() and enumerate()
tg.enumerate(list);

for (int i=0; i<list.length && list[i] != null; i++)
System.out.println(list[i].toString());
```

Because Threads could be added to the ThreadGroup in between calls to `activeCount` and `enumerate`, I artificially bump up the count returned by `activeCount` by 50 percent just to accommodate this possibility. The reason I do this is given in the ThreadGroup documentation for the `enumerate` method (Jdk1.2/doc/api/java/lang/ThreadGroup.html#enumerate()):

> An application should use the `activeCount` method to get an estimate of how big the array should be. If the array is too short to hold all the threads, the extra threads are silently ignored.

Because `enumerate` promises to silently ignore any extra Threads if room isn't provided for them in the passed-in array of Thread references, I make extra room and test for `null`, just to be safe.[7]

ThreadGroups owned by this ThreadGroup can also be retrieved, in the same way, using the `activeGroupCount` and the versions of `enumerate` that take an array of ThreadGroup references. The ThreadGroup version of `enumerate` also has one more possible parameter, `recurse`, which indicates whether the caller wishes to know all ThreadGroups owned by this or any owned-in-turn ThreadGroups. Passing `true` in for `recurse` will return a count or list of ThreadGroups from `this` on down to the very bottom of the ThreadGroup tree.

ThreadGroup, like Thread, also has a number of methods that were deprecated in JDK 1.1. The methods `stop`, `suspend` and `resume` were all deprecated in Thread-Group for the same reasons they were deprecated in Thread. If you choose to use them, however, be aware that they will in turn call the same method on every Thread and ThreadGroup owned within this ThreadGroup. ThreadGroup also has `interrupt`, which does the same thing. Note that while `destroy` within ThreadGroup will actually, in turn, call `destroy` on each Thread and ThreadGroup within it, the `destroy` method of Thread simply throws a NoSuchMethodError to indicate it is a no-op method.

## 5.3   THREAD IMPLEMENTATIONS IN JAVA

Within the Java environment, a developer never creates a thread. This may sound ludicrous, but hear me out. Within Java, the code

```
new Thread(new Runnable() {
    public void run()
    { System.out.println("Wow!"); }
}).start();
```

does not, in fact, create a thread. It constructs a java.lang.Thread object, which in turn instructs the Java virtual machine to create a thread of execution, and in that thread of execution, invokes the `run` method of the owned Runnable object.

It may seem to be splitting hairs, but this is an important distinction. In native C/C++ development, you can create threads directly via the various OS threading APIs. In Java, however, you do not create threads—the JVM does this for you. This leads to an important distinction between Java and C++ development: You cannot assume you have a native OS thread for every Thread object.

The JVM requires very little when it comes to threading support. This is done intentionally—Java was originally intended as an embedded systems development language for the development of code on cable-TV set-top boxes. It could not be assumed that the underlying chip (or OS, as it turned out) had the capability to support multiple threads.

---

[7]   Why not return a `Thread[]`, or a `Vector` containing the `Thread` references? Why force me to pass in a preallocated array? Java added the implicit .length field to arrays just to avoid this sort of "C-ism."

As a result, JVM thread implementations fall into one of two categories: "green" and "native."

### 5.3.1 Green threads

Green threads are effectively a figment of your imagination; they do not exist as OS-level constructs, but are scheduled by the JVM itself in a nonpreemptive format. Essentially, the JVM has a single thread of execution, and it manages the context-swapping by hand between Java Thread objects, the same arrangement as under 16-bit Windows. This has dangerous implications for your code. It means that one poorly constructed thread can bring down the entire JVM.

Remember, that not all Java acts remain exclusively within the JVM. Occasionally we do have to run out to the native OS to accomplish certain tasks. A classic example is file management. If you look inside of java.io.File, you'll find that actual implementation of most methods defers to a class called java.io.FileSystem, which in turn is made up of nothing but `native` methods that do the actual work of calling the various OS-level file-management calls. The problem is that most (if not all) of these calls will block when called, not returning control back to the thread that called them until they are complete.

If I create a thread to perform a long blocking I/O call, another thread to do GUI updates, and expect the GUI thread to remain responsive during the blocking I/O call, I'm in for a big disappointment. Even worse, if the garbage-collection mechanism for the JVM, which typically runs in its own thread, is poorly constructed, I could be in for a long wait at the point in my application where I suddenly need to recycle unused objects.

This is less of a problem than I make it out to be until you start making your own native calls. JVM implementors, on platforms that lack native thread support (such as Windows 3.1, MS-DOS or older versions of the MacOS), can write their native implementations of classes such as java.io.FileSystem to be friendly, yielding control back to the JVM scheduler periodically while performing large I/O operations. And because the JVM scheduler has the opportunity to switch a thread away before or after any bytecode instruction, there is no concern for yielding the CPU as there was in 16-bit Windows operations.

### 5.3.2 Native threads

Native thread JVMs, on the other hand, match OS threads to Java threads on a one-to-one basis (or fairly close to it). These implementations are by far easier to work with, since any native calls performed by the thread will block within its own thread, leaving the other threads within the process to execute normally.

### 5.3.3 Hybrids

Combinations in between green and native threads are possible. For example, Java-Soft's own Solaris Reference Implementation for JDK 1.2 uses a hybrid model, where Java threads are given to a pool of native POSIX threads for execution in scheduled fashion; while not single-threaded, as most early green JVM implementations were, it's also not single-thread-per-Java-thread, either.

### 5.3.4    Implications

This leaves Java developers in something of a predicament. Java advocates a platform independent development model, where the particulars of a given operating system or environment are shielded from you by the JVM principle: Write Once, Run Anywhere. Unfortunately, this holds less effectively in practice, especially in areas where the JVM specification is not clear, such as thread support.

In practical terms, this boils down to a complete violation of the Java write/run principle: know your targets. If you know that code you write will be run on a green-threaded platform, make certain that any native calls don't block indefinitely. At the very least, you can forewarn users before undertaking long blocking operations that will hang the JVM until they return.

As I stated before, this is less of an issue than first consideration might make it appear to be. Most JVM implementations will use native threads, where available, and environments in which threads are not available (embedded systems for microchips, for example) will typically not be environments on which Java servers (not applications) will execute. In those environments, the JVM scheduler will usually suffice for thread management. After all, embedded systems probably don't have to make much in the way of native calls, since there's no layer between them and the hardware. They are the hardware!

## 5.4    SUMMARY

If you've never done Thread coding before, you may be a bit apprehensive about jumping into this concurrent programming thing. The horror stories about developers spending entire weeks (or even months) trying to track down these subtle timing-dependent bugs in multithreaded applications are legendary. That having been said, however, I also have to point out that the horror stories about developers spending entire weeks (or even months) trying to track down a bug due to a misplaced semicolon are *also* legendary. The point is that Threads are simply too powerful a programming practice to ignore due to fear, uncertainty, and doubt. Threads are your friends—learn them, live them, love them.

## 5.5    ADDITIONAL READING

- Scott Oaks and Henry Wong, *Java Threads* (O'Reilly, 1997).

  Part of the O'Reilly Java series, this is a great introduction to Java threads. While not JDK 1.2-friendly, the book is stocked to the brim with incredibly useful information, including an appendix on how to debug multithreaded applications using the Java debugger jdb.

# C H A P T E R    6

# *Threading issues*

Firing off Threads helter-skelter is never an answer to a problem. Threads introduce a new problem into the developer's life, that of *concurrency*. Most developers see concurrency only within the context of multiple threads, but the problem itself extends much further than that. Take, for example, a collection of processes all operating simultaneously, working together as part of a single system. If two processes need access to the same file, either the processes must rely on the operating system's native support for concurrency, or they must work out a concurrent-access system of their own to ensure that the two processes aren't stepping on one another's toes.

Introducing Threads into a Java application/applet/servlet/Bean simply magnifies this problem. Now, not only does a process need to synchronize access to resources outside of the boundaries of the process, but also to resources inside it. If two Threads attempt to modify the same element or member simultaneously, there is no guarantee as to which one will ultimately succeed—if either one does.

Note that Threading and concurrency are not always hand-in-hand; under the classic definition of concurrency, no multithreaded application executing on a single CPU system is ever running concurrently. Instead, they are all executing serially, in a time-sliced fashion. True concurrent execution is only possible on multiple-CPU systems when two threads may be executing on two different CPUs at the same time. And, as stated before, it is possible to have concurrency without multiple Threads. For the most part, however, Java developers must think of Threads as being concurrent, since the JVM itself (and the vagaries of "Write Once, Run Anywhere") means we will never know if we're on a 1-CPU or a 64-CPU system.

## 6.1    SYNCHRONIZATION

If threads are executing in a concurrent fashion, there runs the risk that they can also access or modify object or type instances concurrently, as well. More dangerously, it also means that threads can be executing within the same method simultaneously. This has serious implications for how you write your code; for example, a naïve implementation of a dynamic-array class (similar in concept to Java's Vector class) could be written as:

```
public class DynamicArray

{
    // other methods omitted for clarity

    public void add(Object obj)
    {
        Object[] temp = new Object[m_data.length];  // 1
        System.arraycopy(m_data, 0, temp, 0, m_data.length); // 2

        m_data = new Object[temp.length + 1]; // 3
        System.arraycopy(temp, 0, m_data, 0, temp.length); // 4
        m_data[m_data.length] = obj; // 5
    }
}
```

Unfortunately, this code is not thread-safe. If two threads of execution happen to enter the add method at the same time, serious problems will result. Assume that we have two threads, *A* and *B*, that are attempting to both add an Object to a single DynamicArray instance, which currently holds five items. Thread *A* enters add and executes line 1. We're all right so far—temp now holds an empty array of five Object references. Thread *B* now enters add, and executes line 1. The m_data array still holds only five references, so temp in thread *B* now holds an array of five empty Object references. Thread *A* gets control, and executes lines 2 through 5. The array is copied over and back, with no problems. Unfortunately, when *B* executes line 2, m_data will hold six items, not five, and you'll get an IndexOutOfBoundsException from System.arraycopy.

There are a dozen different ways this scenario could play itself out; because the order of scheduling is nondeterministic, we have no way of knowing precisely in which order the two threads execute each line. Remember, too, that threads can be switched in or out between bytecode instructions, and each line above will compile down to more than one bytecode instruction each. This raises the possibility that the threads could be switched out and in the middle of the line, leaving even more possibilities for chaos to occur.

This problem has plagued every concurrent development environment yet invented. Entire languages have been invented, solely on the basis of concurrency synchronization, and reams of paper are sacrificed to the subject. Java, however, boils it down to a single keyword: synchronized. By marking a method as such, Java will block other threads from entering that method until the current thread within that method exits. Similarly, if a synchronized block is entered within a method, the JVM will guarantee that no other thread will enter that block until the current thread finishes it. This means that we could rewrite the add method above as:

```java
public class DynamicArray
{
    // other methods omitted for clarity

    public synchronized void add(Object obj)
    {
        Object[] temp = new Object[m_data.length];  // 1
        System.arraycopy(m_data, 0, temp, 0, m_data.length); // 2

        m_data = new Object[temp.length + 1]; // 3
        System.arraycopy(temp, 0, m_data, 0, temp.length); // 4
        m_data[m_data.length] = obj; // 5
    }

    /*
     * Or, we could write it this way:
    public void add(Object obj)
    {
        synchronized
        {
            Object[] temp = new Object[m_data.length];  // 1
            System.arraycopy(m_data, 0, temp, 0, m_data.length); // 2

            m_data = new Object[temp.length + 1]; // 3
            System.arraycopy(temp, 0, m_data, 0, temp.length); // 4
            m_data[m_data.length] = obj; // 5
        }
    }
     */
}
```

The two methods are identical in operation—thread *B* will now be prevented from entering add until thread *A* has finished executing line 5 completely.

This is probably the worst part of concurrent development. Knowing where to synchronize, why to synchronize, and when not to synchronize remains more art than science for most developers. Even worse, trying to debug synchronization problems (such as the one above) can be frustrating and elusive, since the problem may only occur under very specific circumstances. In that example, a problem would only be detected when the IndexOutOfBoundsException was thrown, and that exception would only be thrown when two threads manage to enter the same method at almost exactly the same time. With several hundred thousand method calls from which to choose, and several million clock cycles in which to choose them, getting two threads to hit the same method in the same order in a consistent manner to allow for testing and debugging is a truly aggravating experience.

Determining when to synchronize, and how to prove (or disprove) that a method is fully thread-safe is a subject that easily encompasses entire volumes on its own. It's this very subject that provides most of the rumors surrounding how difficult it is to program with threads. What's worse, there is no quick and easy way to determine if your code is thread-safe. The best advice is to err in your code on the side of caution, preferring to oversynchronize the code rather than the opposite, and that you test like crazy for long periods of time.

## 6.1.1   Thread-local storage

One way to avoid thread synchronization code is to give each thread its own copy of particular variables and objects. This is called *thread-local storage*, and comes in two forms in Java.

The first is the easier to understand, although it uses no linguistic features to enforce it. Whenever possible, associate the data required by the thread with the thread by wrapping it up into the Runnable object being executed by the thread and marking it `private`. If only one thread has access to the data in question, then no synchronization is necessary. (This assumes that a new Runnable object would be created for each new Thread fired off.) Alternatively, make the run method of the Runnable class completely stateless, with no dependencies on internal or external state, even within the class itself.

This is an overly simplistic solution, however, and doesn't cover all cases. There will be objects (particularly Singleton objects accessed from multiple threads) that have to maintain separate data per thread within themselves. For these situations, Java 1.2 offers the second alternative, the java.lang.ThreadLocal class, which wraps a generic Object, one per thread.

```
public class Whatever
{
    public ThreadLocal m_threadLocal = new java.lang.ThreadLocal() {
        protected Object initialValue() { return new Integer(5); }
    };
}
```

This creates a ThreadLocal object that wraps an Integer object, initializing its initial value to 5. If you don't override the `initialValue` method of ThreadLocal, it will contain `null`.

When thread *A* calls `Whatever.m_threadLocal.set(new String-("Five"))`, this value will only be seen by that thread. Any other thread calling `System.out.println(Whatever.m_threadLocal.get().toString())` will see the original Integer object created by the initialization block. Thread *A* cannot see thread *B*'s version of `m_threadLocal`, and vice versa.

Thread-local storage won't solve *all* your synchronization problems, but it certainly can help with some.

## 6.2  EXCEPTION-HANDLING WITH MULTIPLE THREADS

Threads raise some questions regarding standard exception-handling behavior. Within Java, when an exception is thrown and not caught within the method that threw it, it filters upward. Specifically, it propagates back to the caller of the method until either it is caught, or it is thrown back out of main. This assumes that main declares itself as throwing some (or all) Exception types, as I frequently do with examples found in this book:

```
public class Sample
{
    public static void main(String[] args)
        throws Exception      // cheap way of avoiding try/catch blocks
                              // within main()
    {
        // . . .
    }
}
```

If this is the behavior expected of the main thread's entry point (main), it might seem intuitive to expect this same behavior from any secondary threads created during the execution of your Java code—that exceptions thrown out of a Thread's or Runnable's run method would pass back out to the caller.

The problem with this idea is that it confuses the compile-time model with the actual run-time model; a thread, once started, has no relation to the physical proximity of the code that started it. A naïve approach to catching an exception might look like this:

```
try
{
    Thread t = new Thread(new Runnable()
    {
        public void run()
        {
            while (!Thread.currentThread().isInterrupted())
                doSomething();
        }
    }).start();

    // Later . . .

    t.interrupt();
}
catch (InterruptedException intEx)
{
    System.out.println("Interrupted!");
}
```

This doesn't work. Specifically, if this code does compile (which would only happen if a method declared to throw InterruptedException is called within the `try` block, since `Thread.start` doesn't itself declare `throws InterruptedException`), you will never receive the InterruptedException thrown when the Thread is interrupted. Java's threading system is nondeterministic—execution of the thread that created the secondary thread may have moved completely outside of the `try` block when the `interrupt` finally finishes. For a more exaggerated example of this, consider:

```
try
{
    Thread t = new Thread(new Runnable()
    {
        public void run()
        {
            Thread.sleep(24 * 60 * 60 * 1000);
                // sleep for one day
            doSomething();
        }
    }).start();
}
catch (Exception intEx)
{
    System.out.println("Interrupted!");
}
```

In this case, the started thread is sleeping for twenty-four hours before attempting its doSomething method. It's foolish, however, to believe that the thread that created the doSomething thread will be patiently awaiting the start of t's execution. The JVM will have long since moved beyond the `try/catch` block that enclosed the `start` call.

Instead, when an exception propagates out of `run`, the JVM finds the Thread-Group instance that parents the Thread that threw the exception, and passes the Thread and the Exception to its `uncaughtException` method. By default, if the exception object thrown is anything other than a ThreadDeath object, `uncaughtException` prints the stack trace and exits. Throwing a ThreadDeath object, however, is the normal way to terminate a thread, so `uncaughtException` does nothing.

In some cases, however, the caller (or creator) of a thread wants to know if the Thread terminated abnormally. One approach, which I call last error approach, is to have each thread store the Exception it throws within its associated Thread object, and have callers check the status of the Thread and the associated Exception when the Thread terminates:

```
public class ExceptionRunnable implements Runnable
{
    public void run()
    {
```

```
        try
        {
            // . . .
        }
        catch (Throwable t)
        {
            lastError = t;
        }
    }

    public Throwable getLastError()
    { return lastError; }

    protected Throwable lastError;
}
```

Problems with this approach are:

- *It's nonstandard Java.*
  This get-last-error idiom is not one used anywhere else within Java, and so won't seem right to developers accustomed to working with Java-like constructs.

- *It requires clients to actively check the status of the thread before checking the value of* `lastError`.
  Simply checking to see if `getLastError` returns anything other than `null` won't work, since that doesn't indicate when the thread has terminated. This could be worked around by setting `lastError` to some benign non-null value at initialization.

- *In line with the point above, it also requires clients to check this repeatedly until the Thread terminates.*
  Clients must either `join` with the Thread object until it terminates, and then check the status of `lastError`, or repeatedly poll the `getLastError` method (which is definitely unfriendly to the rest of the Threads in the JVM scheduler). Clients that `join` with the Thread are then blocked from taking further action until the thread terminates, but if these two threads are to act in this sort of serial fashion, perhaps a rethink of the design or implementation is in order.

Another approach might be to define a customized ThreadGroup class that, when `uncaughtException` is called, in turn propagates the exception to the main (or another secondary) thread, but this approach suffers from the original—no one Thread has the ability to call into another.

ThreadGroups can, however, take other approaches within `uncaughtException` (listing 6.1). One approach might be to use a callback, or event listener approach, where interested parties implement a particular interface, register themselves with the ThreadGroup, which in turn calls on them when an exception is thrown from the Thread.

**Listing 6.1   Code for ExceptionListener**

```java
public interface ExceptionListener
{
    public void exceptionThrown(Thread t, Throwable e);
}

import java.util.Enumeration;
import java.util.Vector;
public class ThreadGroupEx extends ThreadGroup
{
    public ThreadGroupEx(String name)
    {
        super(name);
    }
    public ThreadGroupEx(ThreadGroup parent, String name)
    {
        super(parent, name);
    }

    public void registerListener(ExceptionListener l)
    {
        m_listeners.add(l);
    }
    public void removeListener(ExceptionListener l)
    {
        m_listeners.remove(l);
    }

    public void uncaughtException(Thread t, Throwable e)
    {
        for (Enumeration enum = m_listeners.elements();
            enum.hasMoreElements(); )
        {
            ExceptionListener el =
                (ExceptionListener)enum.nextElement();

            el.exceptionThrown(t, e);
        }

        super.uncaughtException(t, e);
    }

    private Vector m_listeners = new Vector();
}
```

Problems with this approach come when clients must now deal with the asynchronous nature of the callback or event-notification call. The caller can't simply block on the thread using `join` or `wait`, because the exception-notification will in turn be trying to call on a blocked thread, which results in deadlock. The asynchronous call could come on a third thread, but there are other approaches to using the third thread to wait for the exception that would be more intuitive or straightforward to use.

Another version is to create a shim Runnable class that acts as an Adapter class and in turn calls a version of Runnable whose `run` method is declared to throw Exceptions (listing 6.2).

**Listing 6.2   Code for ExceptionableRunnable**

```java
public interface ExRunnable
{
    public void run()
        throws Throwable;
}

public class ExceptionableRunnable
    implements java.lang.Runnable
{
    public ExceptionableRunnable(ExRunnable target)
    {
        m_target = target;
    }

    public void run()
    {
        try
        {
            m_target.run();
        }
        catch (Throwable t)
        {
            thrown = t;
        }
    }

    public Throwable thrown = null;
    private ExRunnable m_target = null;

    public static void main(String[] args)
        throws Exception
    {
        ExceptionableRunnable er =
            new ExceptionableRunnable(
                new ExRunnable()
                {
                    public void run()
                        throws Throwable
                    {
                        Thread.sleep(5*1000);
                        throw new Exception("Generic Exception");
                    }
                });
        Thread t = new Thread(er);
        t.start();
        t.join();
```

```
        if (er.thrown != null)
        {
            System.out.println("ExceptionableRunnable threw:");
            er.thrown.printStackTrace();
        }
    }
}
```

This approach allows clients to continue execution while waiting for the running thread to exit, without having to worry about an asynchronous notification. In addition, it's a reusable component—it can be used repeatedly without modification in a variety of situations and systems. There are drawbacks: it's not a Runnable anymore and clients now have to poll the `thrown` member when the Thread is finished. This is awkward for clients to use and unfriendly to the JVM scheduler, as already noted.

## 6.3    THREAD IDIOMS AND PATTERNS

"Design patterns," writes Doug Lea,[1] "are used to help organize the wealth of techniques available for structuring concurrent programs. A pattern describes a form, usually an *object structure* (also known as a *micro-architecture*) consisting of one or more interfaces, classes, and/or objects that obey certain static and dynamic constraints and relationships."

Patterns are one of the best ways by which to examine a new and (potentially) unfamiliar territory or technology. The next section presents several patterns culled from a variety of resources, including pseudo-patterns of my own experience. Patterns specifically relating to concurrent programming can be found in Lea's book and various papers by Douglas Schmidt (at http://www.cs.wusl.edu/~schmidt/patterns-ace.html).

### 6.3.1    Client-Dispatcher-Server

"When we need to distribute software components over a network of computers, the location-transparent communication between them becomes an important aspect of their design. In the Client-Dispatcher-Server pattern, an intermediate layer between clients and servers is introduced: the dispatcher component. It provides location transparency by means of a name service and hides the details of establishing the communication connection between client components and their servers."[2]

In a Client-Dispatcher-Server system, contrary to traditional client/server systems, clients do not attempt to communicate with the server directly; instead, they first contact a Dispatcher component, which then in turn reroutes to (or internally makes the request of) the server (figure 6.1).

---

[1]  See "Additional reading."

[2]  *Pattern Langues of Program Design 2*, p. 476. The pattern itself is Copyright © 1995 Siemens AG. All Rights Reserved.

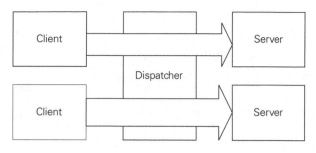

**Figure 6.1**
**Client-Dispatcher-Server diagram**

At first glance, this may not seem to be a concurrent pattern as much as a distributed one, and more suitable for chapter 11, in which we talk about sockets. However, with a bit of embellishment, it's not difficult to see how this pattern is applicable to a concurrent architecture more than a distributed one. For example, most web servers (which includes the one we will build in chapter 11) will follow this model, using a single thread to listen on port 80,[3] and farming out each actual request/connection received to a separate thread as the requests come in. The applicability of the pattern also increases when services begin to accept requests from communication mechanisms other than sockets.

Two such sources that come to mind are files or databases—a service could fire off a Polling thread to check a given directory for a file, and undertake action based on its contents. Here, the Polling thread would be the Dispatcher, and the thread which actually parses the file and performs the actions is the Server. Databases can be polled, as well, looking for particular data to come through, and particular actions taken based on the content of the data scanned. For example, a salesperson may request that an email be fired to him/her as soon as a sale is made for any customer within a particular sales territory. The Dispatcher thread is the one which scans the database, and the Server thread is the one which examines the data in detail, determining if an email is required, and performing the actual work of firing the email.

Our GJAS will be acting as the Dispatcher in the system, acting as the intermediary between client components (those attempting to use the Services hosted by GJAS) and their servers (the Services themselves). Because we've not yet gotten to sockets and networks, GJAS remains a single-machine system, but the concept holds even in that case. Once we get into more interactive services via sockets (chapter 11) or RMI (chapter 15), we'll see how GJAS fits this pattern like a glove.

### 6.3.2 Fire-and-forget

One common idiom in threading, especially with Java's first-class support for threads and anonymous classes, is the fire-and-forget model of threading. Threads are fired off, and the thread itself is not tracked afterward:

---

[3] The port for the HTTP protocol.

```
new Thread(new Runnable() {
    public void run()
    {
        // Do something here
    }
}).start();
```

The Thread object's handle isn't held because there is no further need to access it. It is "forgotten." No attempt will be made to pause, suspend, or interrupt the Thread. It is expected to either complete its assignment, or throw an exception out of run and terminate. Either way, the Thread runs to completion and dies.

### 6.3.3    ActiveObject

ActiveObject is an object instance that has its own thread of execution on its behalf. In this pattern, the creator of the object often has no knowledge of the thread created on behalf of the object:

```
public ActiveObject
    implements Runnable
{
    public ActiveObject()
    {
        new Thread(this).start();
    }

    public void run()
    {
        // . . .
    }
}
```

In pseudo-real-time simulation systems, or systems where independent objects are interacting within an environment, this can be particularly useful. Users of ActiveObject need not worry about the peculiarities of the thread-to-object relationship, or about setting priorities appropriately; the object encapsulates all of that information within itself.

The lifetime of the thread is intimately tied to that of the object; if the object ever leaves its run method (due to exception or voluntary exit), the thread dies, taking the object with it. The two are inseparable, since ActiveObject offers no way to obtain the Thread it encapsulates.

### 6.3.4    SpinLoop

In a SpinLoop thread, the thread spends most of its execution time constantly checking some condition, taking action only when (if ever) that condition changes. This is the classic busy-wait loop, often coded as:

```
while (m_flag != false)
{
    // do nothing
```

```
    }
    doSomething();
```

In most cases, this sort of loop is inefficient and a tremendous waste of the CPU—there is no attempt to give the CPU any hints about when it might be safe to leave this thread alone. Moreover, most of the time the constant checks are unnecessary—do you really need to know the precise nanosecond the m_flag variable changes? Most of the time, it's not necessary, and a 100 millisecond sleep call in between checks can drastically improve performance for other threads in the system.

## 6.3.5 Polling (PeriodicThread)

Akin to the SpinLoop is the PollingThread idiom. This is a particular type of Spin-Loop that, instead of constantly checking the value of the condition, waits a certain period of time, checks a condition, and either acts or waits again. PollingThreads are particularly useful in areas where the condition can take more than trivial amounts of time or resources, such as checking a database to see if a particular type of record has come in, or watching a directory to see if a file has been placed there or otherwise modified since the last check.

PollingThreads usually take the form:

```
public class RDBMSCheck implements Runnable
{
    public void run()
    {
        try
        {
            Thread.sleep(60 * 1000); // check every minute
            if ((ResultSet rs = get_database_records()).next())
            {
                // Take some action here
            }
        }
        catch (InterruptedException intEx)
        {
        }
    }
}
```

Because this is such a common idiom, however, it can be factored back into a component that manages the wait and action:

```
/**
 * PeriodicThread is a specific type of Thread that fires off its
 * associated Runnable evry <code>interval</code> milliseconds.
 */
public class PeriodicThread extends Thread
{
    private PeriodicThread()
    {
```

```
        // This prevents instantiation without an associated Runnable;
        // I don't want to allow the possibility of this code from
        // ever compiling:
        //
        // new PeriodicThread().start()
        //
    }

    /**
     * Constructor taking the Runnable whose run method
     * we wish to call every interval milliseconds.
     */
    public PeriodicThread(Runnable r, int interval)
    {
        super();

        m_runnable = r;
        m_interval = interval;
    }

    /**
     * The run method spins in an infinite loop, calling run on
     * the owned Runnable instance every interval milliseconds
     * (as specified in the constructor). The time spent
     * in the Runnable's run method is not taken into
     * account in the period spent sleeping.
     */
    public void run()
    {
        try
        {
            while (true)
            {
                Thread.sleep(m_interval);
                m_runnable.run();
            }
        }
        catch (InterruptedException iEx)
        {
            return;
        }
    }

    private int m_interval = 0;
    private Runnable m_runnable = null;
}
```

Another interesting aspect of the PeriodicThread class is that the no-arg default constructor is declared private. Because a PeriodicThread is useless without a target or time interval to wait, I prevent users from being able to instantiate one without those arguments.

## 6.3.6    DelayedFire (ScheduledThread)

In a DelayedFire thread, the execution of the behavior desired is delayed by some period of time, similar to the `cron` utility of UNIX or `at` in Windows NT. This is useful in situations where action needs to be taken after giving the user a window of opportunity to take action. For example, in an interactive service, users need to be notified of impending shutdown if the administrator of the service needs to take the system down. While this could be coded to simply wait the one or five minutes or so on the current thread, it can make coding easier if the shutdown implementation is coded within its own thread. This way, if the shutdown needs to be stopped, the only action required is to destroy the shutdown Thread object, instead of complicated shutdown-OK flags and state-machine logic.

Delaying a thread's execution can come in one of two forms—clients may want to delay execution for *n* seconds, or have the thread fire off at the absolute time "12:00 midnight today." Coding the first is the far simpler case (simply have the thread `sleep` for the *n* number of seconds), but the second case is not difficult, given Java's rich support for Date comparisons (listing 6.3).

### Listing 6.3    Code for ScheduledThread

```
public class ScheduledThread extends Thread
{
    private ScheduledThread()
    {
        // Prevent "new ScheduledThread().start()"
        //
    }

    public ScheduledThread(Runnable runnable, java.util.Date when)
    {
        m_runnable = runnable;
        m_when = when;
    }

    public void run()
    {
        try
        {
            // Make sure "when" is after now.
            //
            while (m_when.after(new java.util.Date()))
            {
                Thread.sleep(1000);
            }

            // If the above test failed, it's time
            // to run our target
            //
            m_runnable.run();
        }
```

```
        catch (InterruptedException intEx)
        {
            return;
        }
    }

    private java.util.Date m_when;
    private Runnable m_runnable;
}
```

Within the ScheduledThread's `run` method, the Date's `after` method is used to determine if the current time stamp (obtained from Date's default constructor) is after the time given. If it is, then the Runnable's `run` method is executed.

Again, as with PeriodicThread, the default constructor of the ScheduledThread is declared `private`. This is done to prevent users from instantiating a ScheduledThread without a Runnable, a time stamp, or delay argument.

### 6.3.7 Futures

Futures, or FutureReplies, as they're also called, allow you to call a method asynchronously, perform other tasks in the meantime, and obtain the result of the call if it's ready. For example, it's common in web browsers to download the specified text and images separately, allowing users who don't care to see the images to view the text without having to wait. Futures fit into this very nicely—as the web browser is parsing the returned HTML, each image (which must be downloaded separately, as per the HTTP specification) can be requested in a Future, and the web browser can then continue to parse the text. As each image-thread returns with the complete graphics file, the browser can then take the time (presuming it's done with the text by this time) to place the image in the browser window appropriately.

Futures are also useful within enterprise scenarios. A database query, for example, is a terrific candidate for a Future idiom—the query is carried out in the Future thread, and the user interface can continue to perform other tasks (such as preparing the GUI to display the results) until the time in which it needs the results.

Futures typically appear similar to the following:

```
// Fire off the query in a Future
FutureThread ft = new FutureThread(
    new FutureRunnable()
    {
        public Object run()
            throws java.sql.SQLException
        {
            Statement stmt = aJDBCConnection.createStatement();
            return stmt.executeQuery("SELECT * FROM . . .");
        }
    });
ft.start();
```

*CHAPTER 6   THREADING ISSUES*

```
// . . . Bring up the GUI element associated with the query

ResultSet rs = (ResultSet)ft.getResult();
    // If the query isn't finished yet, we block here waiting for
    // it to return

while (rs.next())
{
    // . . .
}
```

This approach also allows users to cancel the query at any time if they so desire. Notice that in the foregoing, the FutureThread class takes a different type Runnable class as its parameter—FutureThread could easily take a standard Runnable as its target, but would then need to have some way within the Runnable object of setting the results object so that the user could obtain it via FutureThread.

One possible FutureThread implementation looks like that in listing 6.4.

**Listing 6.4   Code for a FutureThread implementation**

```
public interface FutureRunnable
{
    public Object run();
}

public class FutureThread extends Thread
{
    public FutureThread(FutureRunnable run)
    {
        m_target = run;
        start();
    }

    public void run()
    {
        m_result = m_target.run();
    }

    public Object getResult()
        throws InterruptedException
    {
        if (Thread.currentThread() != this)
            this.join();

        return m_result;
    }
    public Object getResult(long timeout)
        throws InterruptedException
    {
        if (Thread.currentThread() != this)
            this.join(timeout);

        return m_result;
    }
}
```

```java
    private Object m_result;
    private FutureRunnable m_target;

    public static void main(String[] args)
        throws Exception
    {

    FutureThread ft = new FutureThread(
        new FutureRunnable()
        {
            public Object run()
            {
                try
                {
                    Thread.sleep(5*1000);
                    return new String("Finished!");
                }
                catch (InterruptedException intEx)
                {
                    return null;
                }
            }
        });

    System.out.println("OK, we're waiting now....");
    String result = (String)ft.getResult(10 * 1000);
    if (result != null)
        System.out.println("Result: " + result);
    else
        System.out.println("We didn't finish in 10 seconds.");
    }
}
```

One curiosity about this implementation is that if the FutureThread fails to come back within the timeout specified in the getResult method, no attempt is made to terminate the thread via stop. This means that if you change the timeout parameter in the supplied main to be one second, instead of ten, the JVM won't exit immediately after printing "We didn't finish in 10 seconds....". Instead, because the JVM must wait until all user threads are finished, it will wait until the FutureThread is finished before exiting. Fixing this behavior is as easy as calling setDaemon(true) in the FutureThread constructor.

## 6.4  GJAS

Talking about thread support for GJAS at this point falls into the category of a philosophical discussion, because as of yet GJAS doesn't exist as a system. However, we want to at least think about how we're going to use multiple Threads (if at all) within the GJAS code, and a little jaunt down Abstract lane will give us a better sense of precisely what we need to do once we get to the point of writing code.

Adding thread support to GJAS could be a matter of requiring Services to, when `start` is called, fire off a Thread for their own use and return immediately thereafter. In fact, this would be a workable system and function adequately for some time. However, this is not a robust, or stable, mechanism. At some point a developer will create a Service that fails to adhere to this rule, perform behavior that blocks in `start`, and wonder why the entire system hangs.

We could, therefore, remove Service as the base from which clients derive, and make it the point to which all user code must extend, with base functionality dealing with the creation of Threads. This fails on two points. First, any method in a class can be overridden, and users will just as easily forget to call `super.start()` or `super.stop()` in their derived-class as they would to fire off the thread from `Service.start` in the first place. Second, this imposes large restrictions on what can now be plugged into our system; because Java is a single-inheritance language, we have now arbitrarily imposed the base class on users of our system. Using Service allowed us to give users the flexibility to hook in third-party products and code into our system without huge overhead.

We can't, it would seem, enforce the requirement that Services fire off a thread, and we can't do it for the user. What's left?

Actually, we don't have to require that Services fire off a thread in order to remain robust and stable. In fact, some Services may not require an additional thread at all, as we'll see in the chapter on Threads, when we start writing some actual Services, `ExecService`, a Service that executes an arbitrary command-line, is one such case. `ExecService` fires off a command-line when `start` is invoked, and does nothing for the remainder of its lifetime.[4] If a Service needs to fire off a thread to do its work, then it must do it within `start`. ServerManager still needs to ensure that a rogue Service doesn't bring the entire JVM to a halt, however.

## 6.4.1  Adding thread support to GJAS

One of the first things we'll do to improve on GJAS's current configuration is prevent a single rogue Service from bringing down the entire system. Consider this: we start a Service to bring up your favorite text editor, and another Service line after that to print "We're back!" to the screen. If we were to run the system without such antirogue Service protection, then the system will hang when the text editor comes up, and refuse to continue until the text editor is closed. The reason, of course, is that our first Service is blocking, waiting on the text editor to complete its execution before returning.

Fixing this is a matter of applying the Future pattern to the various Service calls. We'll use a Future to call the Service's `start` method, for example, and wait for fifteen seconds; if the call to `start` hasn't returned by then, we'll assume the Service

---

[4] We could add code to the end of the `ExecService.start()` method to remove itself from the ServerManager when its created process completes, so as to remove its overhead from the system once it completes its required task.

has either hung itself or is still working, and return to our caller. We have, however, two places where we can apply this improvement. We could do it inside of Server-Manager, or inside of the corresponding Server instance.

Here again is a decision based largely on personal choice; I choose to make the improvement in Server, since it is intended to be my wrapper around a Service. I'm also thinking down the road, where I may wish to expose Server objects to controllers other than ServerManager. If I place this Future code inside of Server, then others can simply call on Server's versions of these methods without needing to understand (or worry) about what to do if the Service simply runs away with the call and never returns.

One other note before we dive into the next chapter: you may well be surprised to notice that rather than use the classes I demonstrated for you previously, I choose to use Lea's concurrent library. His library is far more extensive and well-written than anything I could write on my own and this is one place where a buy decision carries no risk. Lea has released his code into the public domain (making it freely available to anyone who want to download it), and he has released the source for the library at the same time, meaning that the other risk of buy decisions is now reduced. If I find a bug, I can correct it on my own, assuming Lea cannot get it fixed before I need it.

You are, of course, free to use whichever approach (buy or build) works best for you in your system. Remember, GJAS is not intended to be a production-quality system out of the box, but a proof of concept system that in turn leads to something stronger, more robust, and more tailored to your (and your company's) needs.

Given that, we'll modify the `Server.start` method (listing 6.5):

---
### Listing 6.5   Code of a modified Server.start
---

```
/**
 * Start the wrapped Service instance. Services have 15 seconds in
 * which to either initialize, or else start a thread to perform
 * the necessary initialization and return. If a Service fails to
 * respond within 15 seconds of the start of its start
 * call, the Server and/or ServerManager are free to destroy it.
 */
public boolean start()
{
    // We want to fire off a Thread to make the start() call, and wait
    // up to 15 seconds to see if we return. If we don't by the time
    // the 15 seconds are up, we assume the Service has run off into
    // Limbo and needs to be killed. (Most Services of any complexity
    // will need to fire off their own Thread to do their work, so
    // their start() methods should come back pretty quickly.)
    //
    try
    {
        FutureResult futureResult = new FutureResult();
        Runnable cmd = futureResult.setter(new Callable()
        {
            public Object call()
```

```
                {
                    try
                    {
                        m_service.start();
                    }
                    catch (Exception ex)
                    {
                        m_exception = ex;
                        ServerManager.instance().log(ex);
                    }
                    return null;
                }
            });
            new ThreadedExecutor().execute(cmd);
            futureResult.timedGet(15*1000);
                // we want to wait 15 seconds, no more.

            return true;
        }
        catch (TimeoutException tEx)
        {
            m_exception = tEx;

            // The Service ran out of time starting up; kill it, note the
            // failure to start, and return
            //
            ServerManager.instance().log(tEx);
        }
        catch (InterruptedException iEx)
        {
            m_exception = iEx;

            // For some reason, the thread doing the call failed; note the
            // failure to start, and return
            //
            ServerManager.instance().log(iEx);
        }
        catch (InvocationTargetException itEx)
        {
            m_exception = itEx;

            // Java Reflection failed; note the failure, and return
            //
            ServerManager.instance().log(itEx);
        }
        catch (Exception ex)
        {
            m_exception = ex;
            ServerManager.instance().log(ex);
        }
        return false;
    }
```

What seems to be a tremendous increase in complexity turns out to be mostly `catch` handlers. The core of what we want to do occurs in the first third of the listing:

```java
FutureResult futureResult = new FutureResult();
Runnable cmd = futureResult.setter(new Callable()
{
    public Object call()
    {
        try
        {
            m_service.start(args);
        }
        catch (Exception ex)
        {
            m_exception = ex;
            ServerManager.instance().log(ex);
        }
        return null;
    }
});
new ThreadedExecutor().execute(cmd);
futureResult.timedGet(15*1000);
    // we want to wait 15 seconds, no more.

return true;
```

We create a FutureResult (imported from `EDU.oswego.cs.dl.util.concurrent`), and set it to hold an anonymous Callable instance, one which, in its `call` routine, creates a `try` block, makes the call to `Service.start`, and catches all Exceptions thrown out of there.

This looks a bit different than expected, given the code I listed above for Futures. The reason is simple—Lea's code is much more flexible and componentized than mine. Listing 6.6 is FutureResult.

---

**Listing 6.6   Code for FutureResult(Lea)**

```java
/*

  File: FutureResult.java

  Originally written by Doug Lea and released into the public domain.
  This may be used for any purposes whatsoever without acknowledgment.
  Thanks for the assistance and support of Sun Microsystems Labs,
  and everyone contributing, testing, and using this code.

  History:
  Date       Who            What
  30Jun1998  dl             Create public version
*/

package EDU.oswego.cs.dl.util.concurrent;
import java.lang.reflect.*;

// Comments have been stripped for brevity
```

```
public class FutureResult {
  protected Object value_ = null;

  protected boolean ready_ = false;
  protected InvocationTargetException exception_ = null;

  public FutureResult() { }

  public Runnable setter(final Callable function) {
    return new Runnable() {
      public void run() {
        try {
          set(function.call());
        }
        catch(Exception ex) {
          setException(ex);
        }
      }
    };
  }

  protected Object doGet() throws InvocationTargetException {
    if (exception_ != null)
      throw exception_;
    else
      return value_;
  }

  public synchronized Object get()
    throws InterruptedException, InvocationTargetException {
    while (!ready_) wait();
    return doGet();
  }

  public synchronized Object timedGet(long msecs)
    throws TimeoutException, InterruptedException,
      InvocationTargetException {
    long startTime = (msecs <= 0)? 0 : System.currentTimeMillis();
    long waitTime = msecs;
    if (ready_) return doGet();
    else if (waitTime <= 0) throw new TimeoutException(msecs);
    else {
      for (;;) {
        wait(waitTime);
        if (ready_) return doGet();
        else {
          waitTime = msecs - (System.currentTimeMillis() - startTime);
          if (waitTime <= 0)
            throw new TimeoutException(msecs);
        }
      }
    }
  }

  public synchronized void set(Object newValue) {
```

```
      value_ = newValue;
      ready_ = true;
      notifyAll();
    }

    public synchronized void setException(Throwable ex) {
      exception_ = new InvocationTargetException(ex);
      ready_ = true;
      notifyAll();
    }

    public synchronized InvocationTargetException getException() {
      return exception_;
    }

    public synchronized boolean isReady() {
      return ready_;
    }

    public synchronized Object peek() {
      return value_;
    }

    public synchronized void clear() {
      value_ = null;
      exception_ = null;
      ready_ = false;
    }
}
```

Lea's version allows us to peek at the returned value to see if the call has returned yet; my version didn't. Furthermore, FutureResult itself acts merely as a Factory, creating Runnable instances around the Callable instances passed in, allowing clients to either use the returned Runnable within its own Thread, if they choose to take control over the threading mechanism, or within his ThreadFactory system (as I choose to do). His approach is more componentized than the one I proposed, since FutureResult is now completely disconnected from, and not dependent on, the actual threading system used. My approach assumed that each Future would want its own thread, which may not always be the case.[5]

Once the Runnable instance has been returned, we pass it into ThreadedExecutor, which places the Runnable into its own Thread and executes it. This is no different than had it been written as:

```
new Thread(runnable).start();
```

[5] It may seem odd that I disparage my own code while extolling Lea's. I do this to show that any code, no matter how well-written, can usually be improved and that componentization can sometimes be a difficult thing to get right without tens, if not hundreds, of iterations and possible scenarios to draw from.

except that ThreadedExecutor implements the concurrent library's Executor interface, which all of Lea's thread factory classes implement. This allows clients to, if they choose, select a given Executor type at startup and use it generically:

```
// At startup, we write
ServerManager.setExecutor(new ThreadedExecutor());

// . . . Later . . .
ServerManager.getExecutor().execute(cmd);
```

Again, this may seem like splitting hairs. The consistent use of a single method of doing things, however, makes code simpler to maintain and easier to understand. It may require that adopters of this code need to spend a few days looking over and experimenting with Lea's concurrent library, but once that learning curve is applied, any code that uses the concurrent library will be easily understandable.

## 6.5   SUMMARY

As you can see, Threads offer impressive opportunities for successful partitioning of work and logic. By spinning off separate Threads to accomplish tasks in an asynchronous fashion, for example, we can isolate particular functionality of the application in well-encapsulated classes. For example, you might spin off a Thread to do some polling over an RDBMS table to keep watch on records being inserted into the database. Or you might spin off a Thread to handle a user request that the user may wish to cancel if the operation takes too long. And so on, and so on.

Threads also offer an opportunity to build some robustness into a system in which user-configured actions are taking place. Normally, it is unacceptable for a server-side process to hang due to external-resource delays; by placing the call or the access to the external resource in a separate Thread, we avoid the potential danger of a slow legacy-system call blocking the entire JVM.

## 6.6   ADDITIONAL READING

- Douglas Lea, *Concurrent Programming in Java: Design Principles and Patterns* (Addison-Wesley, 1997).

  Part of the JavaSoft "Java Series," this is the best reference on concurrent Java programming, bar none. If you work with threads in Java, you owe it to yourself to read this book at least twice. Martin Fowler, author of *Refactoring*, sums it up best: "The compiler ought to require that anyone who implements Runnable must read this book." (Note: the code examples for this chapter are from the first edition; as this book was going to press, a second edition became available.)

**CHAPTER 7**

# *Control*

Applications, unfortunately, are not autonomous entities—they very rarely contain enough intelligence to configure themselves (both initially and as circumstances change within the execution environment), monitor themselves, and know when to add or remove services within them. Asking an HTTP server, for example, to reread its configuration settings is a bit much—if it constantly rereads the settings, it will be taking adverse performance hits. But if it caches them, then it runs the chance that it may be out of sync with what the user has specified in the server's configuration file or, on Win32 machines, in the Registry.

As a result, humans must be able to control the applications we write. Note that I use the term humans and not system administrators or users. Who gets to control the application is, more often than not, a policy decision of the corporation or the departments within it. Far be it from me to lay down a blanket generalization about which group should get control. Instead, we'll simply leave it at "humans," or the more accurate term "application administrators" (or administrators, for brevity).

Despite this obvious requirement to allow administrators to control the application, many, if not all, custom server-side applications are analyzed, designed, implemented, and released without a thought or concern for how the application is to be controlled. Unfortunately, this leads to serious problems once the application is released. It doesn't take long for the lack of control facilities to become obvious, and developers are often bewildered by the subsequent requests for modification or outright rejection of the software.

This is, again, an area where a generic overserver helps. By designing a generic control and configuration interface for all Services running within the server, developers can focus more on the meat of the application, and less on the necessary trappings for controlling it. Less time spent on the tedious necessity of control interfaces means quicker turnaround time during development, but additionally, standardization of the control interface also means less learning curve for the administrators who must use the application.

One thing to understand before we begin: application *security* and application *control* are two very different subjects. Security is about who gets to control the application, in addition to who may use the application or administer the application. Control is about what an individual user or administrator can do to the application, such as reconfigure or restart or stop it. The two are somewhat intertwined, since security may be required to ensure that only authorized users are able to control the application, and control may in turn mean configuring who has what security rights to the application. No discussion of cryptography, secure sockets, or the Java cryptography extensions is presented here.

# 7.1    GJAS

The first several chapters have given us basic tools; now it's time to start putting them together into a coherent system. We know how to load classes from anywhere, we know how to ensure that when a class is loaded it always picks up the latest version of the code, and we know how to use multiple threads to ensure that the entire system isn't blocked waiting on one errant Service.

Recall from chapter 2, that we discussed the `IServerManager` interface and its static-method cousin, the ServerManager class. It's now time to provide a basic implementation of that class, functioning at the local JVM level. This LocalServerManager, in turn, will need an `IServer`-implementing class to control its Services, which we'll call LocalServer. Finally, we'll create some sample Services to demonstrate how well it all works.

Let's start with the LocalServerManager and LocalServer implementation.

## 7.1.1    Local implementation

The LocalServerManager.java code is long, but understanding LocalServerManager is crucial to understanding how the whole system is supposed to work together. This class, more than any other, is GJAS; everything else serves as an adjunct or assistant to the LocalServerManager.

```
/**
 * This class presents a local-to-this-JVM-only ServerManager.
 * It is useful for localized testing, and for loading/running
 * Services within their own JVM. Note that use of this
```

```
 * ServerManager does not inherently prevent object-sharing or
 * prevent inter-JVM communication of Services, since it does
 * nothing to block sockets or any other IPC communication. For
 * example, nothing prevents us from running a LocalServerManager
 * with a SocketControlService that allows us to remotely (through
 * the SocketControlService) start, stop, and otherwise control
 * the Services listed within this JVM.
 *
 * Note that LocalServerManager, by default, uses the local
 * (default) ClassLoader scheme to load and find its classes,
 * so any classes loaded will need to be found on the CLASSPATH
 * and/or as an extension.
 */
public class LocalServerManager
    implements IServerManager
{
    public LocalServerManager()
    {
        ServerManager.instance(this);

        // Set log & error streams
        try
        {
            m_logStream = new FileOutputStream("ServerManager.log");
            m_errStream = System.out;
            m_log = new PrintWriter(m_logStream);
            m_err = new PrintWriter(m_errStream);
        }
        catch (Exception ex)
        {
            ex.printStackTrace();
            System.exit(-1);
        }
    }
```

To start, the LocalServerManager constructor first registers itself as the `IServerManager`-implementing Singleton instance within this JVM; to do this, it calls the ServerManager `instance` method, passing in itself as the argument. At this point, we haven't seen the ServerManager class, but its implementation is straightforward, enough so that I won't present the code here, but refer you to the ServerManager.java code in the `com.javageeks.gjas` package for details. In summary, the key to ServerManager is in two parts: the Singleton methods, and the static helper methods that ease getting to the Singleton `IServerManager` instance. The Singleton methods, both named `instance`, one marked `public`, returning an `IServerManager`, the other made package-friendly (so that no one outside of `com.javageeks.gjas` can call on it) taking an `IServerManager` instance, provide the basic get/set behavior. The set `instance` method also performs a quick check to ensure that it hasn't been called before. If it has, that's a definite programmer error, and it throws a RuntimeException to that effect.

We've also added a few additional helper methods that provide commonly used functionality for ServerManagers—parseInputStream parses an InputStream for a class name and its associated arguments, and parseArg parses a String argument for the class name and any contained arguments within it. This allows us to fire off the ServerManager from the command line as

```
java com.javageeks.gjas.LocalServerManager "HelloAgainService 5 Hello!"
```

or by creating a servers.loader file, and placing the directives in there:

```
/*
 * servers.loader: Load a HelloAgainService instance
 */
HelloAgainService 5 "Hello, world, from GJAS!"
```

Supporting both approaches gives us additional flexibility, and since it's all refactored into ServerManager.java, it comes along for free for all IServerManager instances.

```
//=============================================
// IServerManager-inherited methods (implementations)
//

/**
 * Shut the entire system down, usually in preparation for terminating
 * this VM (or perhaps for doing a complete shutdown/restart cycling).
 * Effectively, this is the same as calling getServices to get all
 * Servers' instanceIDs, then calling removeService on each one.
 */
public void shutdown()
{
    log("Entering ServerManager.shutdown()");

    // Get a list of all the running instances, and try to
    // removeService on each one.
    //
    String[] svcs = getServices();
    for (int i=0; i<svcs.length; i++)
    {
        log("Shutting down " + svcs[i]);
        removeService(svcs[i]);
    }

    log("Exiting ServerManager.shutdown()");
}
```

The shutdown method iterates through every IServer in the m_servers dictionary, calling removeService on each one. Shutdown, in and of itself, does nothing to terminate the JVM in which LocalServerManager is running—the only way the LocalServerManager can completely exit is either by a call to System.exit, or by the last active non-daemon Thread terminating. If fired from LocalServerManager's main method, this is not an issue—stopping all Services will kill their associated Threads, and main's Thread will die as soon as the code that called shutdown quits.

```java
/**
 * Add the loaded Service to the list of Servers and start it
 */
public IServer addService(Service svc, String[] args)
{
    log("Entering ServerManager.addService()");

    try
    {
        log("Service " + svc.toString() + "(" +
            svc.getClass().getName() + " " +
            svc.getClass().getClassLoader().toString() +
            ") created");

        // Wrap our Service up in a LocalServer wrapper object
        IServer svr = new LocalServer(svc);

        // Drop it in our Dictionary of Servers....
        m_servers.put(svr.getInstanceID(), svr);

        // Start it; if the start fails, remove it
        if (svr.start(args))
        {
            log("Service started");
            return svr;
        }
        else
        {
            // Log the exception (if any) that caused the Service to fail
            PrintWriter pw = new PrintWriter(getLogStream());
            svr.getLastError().printStackTrace(pw);
            pw.flush();

            removeService(svr.getInstanceID());
            return null;
        }
    }
    catch (Throwable ex)
    {
        // Something "wrong" happened; in a production system, you
        // probably want to do something a bit more proactive here.
        PrintWriter pw = new PrintWriter(getLogStream());
        ex.printStackTrace(pw);
        pw.flush();
        return null;
    }
    finally
    {
        log("Exiting ServerManager.addService()");
    }
}
```

The addService method, when called, wraps the Service instance into an instance of IServer; in this case, LocalServer. We'll get to the LocalServer class later; for now, accept that it provides the standard IServer access to the Service instance it wraps. We then put the IServer instance into a dictionary of IServers (called m_servers), identified by the Service's getInstanceID return value. This is all that's necessary to hold the Service—we call the IServer's start method (which in turn passes directly into the Service's start method), passing in the array of Strings that was passed in to addService, and all should be well. In the event that the Service fails to start, we note it, and call removeService on it to get rid of it.

```
/**
 * Attempt to stop (if necessary) and remove an instance of a Server.
 * Because it's possible that multiple Servers of a given type can be
 * running simultaneously (for example, sockets-based Services listening
 * on multiple ports), we need to have the user identify which Server
 * they wish shut down by using the Server instance's instanceID.
 */
public void removeService(String instanceID)
{
    try
    {
        log("Entering ServerManager.removeService()");

        // Find the service given by 'instanceID'
        //
        IServer svr = getService(instanceID);
        if (svr != null)
        {
            // If it's still running, order it to stop
            //
            String svrState = svr.getState();
            if (svrState != Service.STOPPED && svrState !=
                Service.PAUSED)
                svr.stop();

            // Remove it from the Dictionary
            //
            log("Removing " + instanceID + " from system.");
            m_servers.remove(instanceID);
        }
    }
    finally
    {
        log("Exiting ServerManager.removeService()");
    }
}
```

The removeService method takes the String passed in, uses it to retrieve the IServer instance from the m_servers dictionary of IServers, and removes it from the dictionary. Before removing it, it calls stop on the IServer, giving the Service a chance to perform any shutdown processing necessary.

```
/**
 * Try to kill the Service--don't try to stop() it
 */
```

```
public void killService(String instanceID)
{
    m_servers.remove(instanceID);
    System.gc();
}
```

The killService method, however, is the mean-and-nasty version of removeService. Instead of calling stop on the Service, it removes it from the m_servers dictionary, and makes a call to the gc method of System, to force a garbage collection in an attempt to reclaim the now-garbage Service and IServer instances. While gc is not guaranteed to reclaim the Service on this pass (which means that Service-writers can't depend on this when building Services), there's a likely chance the Service will get finalized here and now, thus removing the Service for all time. The killService method is intended as a last-resort method, only. Terminating a Service like this, even with the presence of finalizer methods, can do serious damage to the JVM's ability to reclaim resources over time, and should always be viewed as an only-if-absolutely-necessary decision, in much the same manner as the Thread stop is.

```
/**
 * Obtain a list of every Server instance running in the system.
 */
public String[] getServices()
{
    log("Entering ServerManager.getServices()");

    String[] svrArray = new String[m_servers.size()];

    int ctr = 0; String list = new String("{\n");
    for (java.util.Enumeration e = m_servers.keys(); e.hasMoreElements(); )
    {
        svrArray[ctr] = (String)e.nextElement();
        list += "    " + svrArray[ctr++] + "\n";
    }
    list +="}";

    log("Exiting ServerManager.getServices(); list = " + list);
    return svrArray;
}
```

The getServices method, on the other hand, requires a bit more work. It uses an Enumeration returned from m_servers to build an array of Strings to be returned to the caller. Note that it also echoes this list of Services to the log, providing a convenient debugging aid. The array of Strings is then returned.

```
/**
 * Obtain a reference to a Server instance by ID. If it can't be found
 * (perhaps it's shut down since the user obtained the ID?), then return
 * a null instance.
 */
public IServer getService(String instanceID)
{
```

```
        return (IServer)m_servers.get(instanceID);
    }
```

The getService method, given what we saw in addService, is about as simple as they come—it takes the passed-in String, and asks the dictionary of IServers for the IServer instance answering to that title. The dictionary either returns null, indicating it's never heard of the IServer by that name, or it returns the IServer instance.

```
public void log(String msg)
{
    if (m_log != null)
    {
        StringBuffer m = new StringBuffer();
        m.append(new Date());
        m.append(" [" );
        m.append(Thread.currentThread().toString());
        m.append("]: ");
        m.append(msg);

        m_log.println(m);
        System.out.println(m);
        m_log.flush();
    }
}
public void log(Exception ex)
{
    if (m_log != null)
    {
        log("Exception raised: " + ex.toString());
        PrintWriter pw = new PrintWriter(getLogStream());
        pw.println(new Date() + " Exception raised: " + ex.toString());
        ex.printStackTrace(pw);
        pw.flush();
    }
}
public void error(String msg)
{
    if (m_err != null)
    {
        StringBuffer m = new StringBuffer();
        m.append(new Date());
        m.append(" [" );
        m.append(Thread.currentThread().toString());
        m.append("]: *** ERROR *** ");
        m.append(msg);

        m_err.println(m);
        m_err.flush();
    }
}
public void error(Exception ex)
```

```
{
    if (m_err != null)
    {
        error(": Exception raised: " + ex.toString());
        PrintWriter pw = new PrintWriter(getErrStream());
        pw.println(new Date() + " Exception raised: " + ex.toString());
        ex.printStackTrace(pw);
        pw.flush();
    }
}

//===========================================
// LocalServerManager-specific methods
//

/**
 * Return the OutputStream used for writing to the log.
 */
public OutputStream getLogStream()
{
    return m_logStream;
}
/**
 * Set the OutputStream used for writing to the log.
 */
public void setLogStream(OutputStream os)
{
    m_logStream = os;
    if (m_logStream != null)
        m_log = new PrintWriter(m_logStream);
    else
        m_log = null;
}
/**
 * Return the OutputStream used for writing errors.
 */
public OutputStream getErrStream()
{
    return m_errStream;
}
/**
 * Set the OutputStream used for writing errors. On your head
 * be the consequences if you set this to null!
 */
public void setErrStream(OutputStream os)
{
    m_errStream = os;
    if (m_errStream != null)
        m_err = new PrintWriter(m_errStream);
    else
        m_err = null;
}
```

The log and error methods write String and Exception objects to their respective OutputStreams. LocalServerManager also provides getLogStream, setLogStream, getErrorStream, and setErrorStream methods to get and set the log and error OutputStream objects, so that users within the JVM in which the LocalServerManager is running can redirect output where desired.

```
// main not shown here; see LocalServerManager.java for details
```

Finally, LocalServerManager provides a main method as a means of using LocalServerManager directly from the command line; however, we'll see later other (more effective and/or efficient) ways of kicking off the GJAS backplane.

```
    // Internal data
    //
    private Dictionary m_servers = new Hashtable();

    private OutputStream m_logStream = null;
    private OutputStream m_errStream = System.err;
    private PrintWriter m_log = null;
    private PrintWriter m_err = new PrintWriter(m_errStream);
}
```

There's nothing really earth-shattering about LocalServerManager.java; note that, as pointed out in the javadoc class comment block, this implementation uses the normal system ClassLoader to load all Services, so that the dynamic upgrade on-the-fly approach isn't possible, since we can't unload the system ClassLoader. We'll see how to make use of that later in this chapter.

To go along with the LocalServerManager, listing 7.1 shows LocalServer class, some of which we talked about in chapter 4:

**Listing 7.1   Code for LocalServer**

```
/**
 * Server wraps the Service instance, using Future calls to help preserve
 * the responsiveness and robustness of the ServerManager.
 */
public class LocalServer
    implements IServer
{
    // Prevent no-arg object instantiation
    //
    private LocalServer()
    {}

    /**
     * Construct a Server around a Service instance.
     */
    public LocalServer(Service svc)
    {
        m_service = svc;
    }
```

```java
/**
 * Start the wrapped Service instance. Services have 15 seconds in
 * which to either initialize, or else start a thread to perform the
 * necessary initialization and return. If a Service fails to respond
 * within 15 seconds of the start of its start call, the Server and/or
 * ServerManager are free to destroy it.
 */
public boolean start(final String[] args)
{
    // We want to fire off a Thread to make the start() call, and wait
    // up to 15 seconds to see if we return. If we don't by the time
    // the 15 seconds are up, we assume the Service has run off into
    // Limbo and needs to be killed. (Most Services of any complexity
    // will need to fire off their own Thread to do their work, so
    // their start() methods should come back pretty quickly.)
    //
    try
    {
        FutureResult futureResult = new FutureResult();
        Runnable cmd = futureResult.setter(new Callable()
        {
            public Object call()
            {
                try
                {
                    m_service.start(args);
                    ServerManager.instance().log(
                        m_service.getClass().getName() + ": started");
                }
                catch (Exception ex)
                {
                    m_exception = ex;
                    ServerManager.instance().log(ex);
                }
                return null;
            }
        });
        new ThreadedExecutor().execute(cmd);
        futureResult.timedGet(15*1000);
            // we want to wait 15 seconds, no more.

        return true;
    }
    catch (TimeoutException tEx)
    {
        m_exception = tEx;

        // The Service ran out of time starting up; kill it, note the
        // failure to start, and return
        //
        ServerManager.instance().log(tEx);
    }
    catch (InterruptedException iEx)
```

```java
        {
            m_exception = iEx;

            // For some reason, the thread doing the call failed; note the
            // failure to start, and return
            //
            ServerManager.instance().log(iEx);
        }
        catch (InvocationTargetException itEx)
        {
            m_exception = itEx;

            // Java Reflection failed; note the failure, and return
            //
            ServerManager.instance().log(itEx);
        }
        catch (Exception ex)
        {
            m_exception = ex;
            ServerManager.instance().log(ex);
        }
        return false;
    }

    // stop(), pause(), resume(), getState() and getInstanceID()
    // all are simple variations on start(), above, and are not
    // shown here

    public void kill()
    {
        m_service = null;
        System.gc();
    }

    public Exception getLastError()
    {
        return m_exception;
    }

    // Internal data
    //
    private Service m_service = null;
    private Exception m_exception = null;
}
```

If you look at the LocalServer.java code in the com.javageeks.gjas package, you'll notice that most of the length deals with using Threads (via Lea's FutureResult class from the Concurrent class library) to isolate the calls into the Service without blocking the entire system should the call hang or disappear. Everything else is either straightforward, or scaffolding to support the Service operations.

At this point, we've presented the basic skeleton for a running GJAS system, with one notable exception: we have no Services with which to test it!

### 7.1.2 Example: HelloService

We start with the GJAS-equivalent of the canonical first program written for any new system. HelloService simply writes "Hello, world!" to the console when it is started (listing 7.2).

**Listing 7.2   Code for HelloService**

```java
package com.javageeks.gjas.services.sample;

import com.javageeks.gjas.*;

public class HelloService
    implements Service
{
    public HelloService()
    { }

    public void start(String[] args)
        throws Exception
    {
        // We're starting
        //
        m_state = STARTING;

        // Print out "Hello, world!"
        //
        System.out.println("Hello, world! --From, HelloService");

        // We write the contents of args to the console, one line
        // per element in the array
        //
        for (int i=0; i<args.length; i++)
            System.out.println("\t" + args[i]);

        // We're running
        //
        m_state = RUNNING;
    }
    public void stop()
        throws Exception
    {
        // We're stopping
        //
        m_state = STOPPING;

        System.out.println("HelloService: stop()");

        // We've stopped
        //
        m_state = STOPPED;
    }
    public void pause()
        throws Exception
    {
```

*CHAPTER 7   CONTROL*

```
        // We're pausing
        //
        m_state = PAUSING;

        System.out.println("HelloService: pause()");

        // We've paused
        //
        m_state = PAUSED;
    }
    public void resume()
        throws Exception
    {
        // We're resuming
        //
        m_state = RESUMING;

        System.out.println("HelloService: resuming()");

        // We've started up again
        //
        m_state = RUNNING;
    }

    public String getState()
    {
        return m_state;
    }

    public String getInstanceID()
        throws Exception
    {
        return getClass() + ":" + "1.0";
    }

    private String m_state = STOPPED;
}
```

The code is fairly simple—the member m_state holds our current status, the method start iterates through the args array, writing each argument to the console, and stop, pause, and resume write out a message to the console, just so we know it's being called correctly, before returning. In fact, the majority of the code is spent shifting the various values of m_state to reflect the status of the HelloService instance.

Having written it, we need to test it.

## 7.2 TESTING THE LOCALSERVER IMPLEMENTATION

Testing LocalServer is as simple as executing the following from the command line:

```
C:\> java com.javageeks.gjas.LocalServer
    com.javageeks.gjas.services.samples.HelloService
```

```
Tue Jun 01 03:53:19 PDT 1999 [Thread[main,5,main]]:
    Entering LocalServerManager.main()
Tue Jun 01 03:53:20 PDT 1999 [Thread[main,5,main]]:
    Entering ServerManager.addService()
Tue Jun 01 03:53:20 PDT 1999 [Thread[main,5,main]]: Service
        com.javageeks.gjas.services.samples.HelloService@74ff6010(
        com.javageeks.gjas.services.samples.HelloService
        sun.misc.Launcher$AppClassLoader@85f606f) created
Hello, world! --From, HelloService
Tue Jun 01 03:53:20 PDT 1999 [Thread[Thread-1,5,main]]:
com.javageeks.gjas.services.samples.HelloService: started
Tue Jun 01 03:53:20 PDT 1999 [Thread[main,5,main]]: Service started
Tue Jun 01 03:53:20 PDT 1999 [Thread[main,5,main]]:
    Exiting ServerManager.addService()
Tue Jun 01 03:53:20 PDT 1999 [Thread[main,5,main]]:
    Exiting LocalServerManager.main()
```

There, right in between all the `ServerManager.log()` output, is the "Hello, world!" message from HelloService.

One concern is the ClassLoader report we get from the LocalServerManager when it adds the Service. In the example, the ClassLoader used to load the Service was a bootstrap (Launcher$sun.misc.AppClassLoader). If the system ClassLoader is used to load the Service, once the Class is defined within that ClassLoader, it will never get reloaded if the .class file changes on disk.

The reason for this is obvious, once you look into the ServerManager's `addServiceFromLocal` method:

```
public static IServer addServiceFromLocal(String svcName, String[] args)
{
    try
    {
        Service svc = (Service)Class.forName(svcName).newInstance();
        return addService(svc, args);
    }
    catch (Exception ex)
    {
        error(ex);
        return null;
    }
}
```

When the class name is finally determined, we use the `forName` method of Class to retrieve the compiled bytecode; as pointed out in chapter 2, if no other ClassLoader is used to load the Class, then `forName` uses the ClassLoader for the currently loaded class. In this case, the bootstrap ClassLoader was used to load LocalServerManager, so it is also used to load the HelloService class. This is bad, since it prevents the dynamic updates mechanism we discussed in chapter 2 from working.

For now, this oversight is acceptable, since we now know about it, but solving the problem is a bit trickier than you might first imagine. For those who can't wait, however, change the previous code to read instead:

```
String loaderDir = System.getProperty("gjas.loaderDir");
if (loaderDir == null)
    LoaderDir = System.getProperty("user.home");
ClassLoader cl = new FileSystemClassLoader(loaderDir);
Service svc = (Service)cl.loadClass(classname).newInstance();
ServerManager.addService(svc, argsArray);
```

This code creates a FileSystemClassLoader (from chapter 2) each time to load the requested class from disk, thereby placing each `Service` instance into its own Class-Loader. Make certain you add the appropriate `"import com.javageeks.class-loader.*"` statements, too, or the code won't compile.

Let's try one more sample service, then move on to more sophisticated Services involving the Threading techniques from the last chapter.

## 7.3 EXECSERVICE

At times, it will be useful to have a Service that merely fires off another application when the system is started. (Examples might include the RMI registry, a CORBA NamingService daemon, and so on.) ExecService will do just that—accept a single parameter as its argument, use the `Runtime.exec` facilities to create the process, and pipe its output to the console window (listing 7.3).

**Listing 7.3   Code for ExecService**

```
import java.io.*;

public class ExecService
    implements com.javageeks.gjas.Service
{
    // Internal data
    //
    private String m_state = STOPPED;
    private String m_cmdLine = null;

    public ExecService(String commandLine)
    {
        m_cmdLine = commandLine;
    }

    public void start()
        throws Exception
    {
        // We're starting
        //
        m_state = STARTING;

        // We expect at least one argument--the text of the command line
        // to fire off
```

```java
//
if (m_cmdLine == null)
{
    m_state = STOPPED;
    throw new IllegalArgumentException();
}

// Start the Process, and capture its output
//
Process p = Runtime.getRuntime().exec(m_cmdLine);
InputStream procOut = p.getInputStream();
InputStream procErr = p.getErrorStream();

while (true)
{
    try
    {
        int exitVal = p.exitValue();

        // If we didn't throw an exception on that call, then
        // the Process has terminated. Capture what remaining
        // output might be in stdout or stderr, display it,
        // and return
        //

        // Capture and display stderr output
        //
        int errAvail = procErr.available();
        byte[] errBytes = new byte[errAvail];
        int bytesRead = procErr.read(errBytes);
        if (bytesRead > 0)
        {
            String sb = new String(errBytes);
            System.out.print(sb);

            //err.print(sb);
            //err.flush();
        }

        // Capture and display stderr output
        //
        int outAvail = procOut.available();
        byte[] outBytes = new byte[outAvail];
        bytesRead = procOut.read(outBytes);
        if (bytesRead > 0)
        {
            String sb = new String(outBytes);
            System.out.print(sb);

            //err.print(sb);
            //err.flush();
        }

        break;
    }
```

```
            catch (IllegalThreadStateException ex)
            {
                // Not terminated yet, so display output
                //

                // Capture and display stderr output
                //
                int errAvail = procErr.available();
                byte[] errBytes = new byte[errAvail];
                int bytesRead = procErr.read(errBytes);
                if (bytesRead > 0)
                {
                    String sb = new String(errBytes);
                    System.out.print(sb);

                    //err.print(sb);
                    //err.flush();
                }

                // Capture and display stderr output
                //
                int outAvail = procOut.available();
                byte[] outBytes = new byte[outAvail];
                bytesRead = procOut.read(outBytes);
                if (bytesRead > 0)
                {
                    String sb = new String(outBytes);
                    System.out.print(sb);

                    //err.print(sb);
                    //err.flush();
                }
            }
        }

        // We're running
        //
        m_state = RUNNING;
    }
    public void stop()
        throws Exception
    {
        // We're stopping
        //
        m_state = STOPPING;

        // We've stopped
        //
        m_state = STOPPED;
    }
    public void pause()
        throws Exception
    {
        // We're pausing
```

```
            //
            m_state = PAUSING;

            // We've paused
            //
            m_state = PAUSED;
        }
    public void resume()
        throws Exception
    {
        // We're resuming
        //
        m_state = RESUMING;

        // We've started up again
        //
        m_state = RUNNING;
    }

    public String getState()
    {
        return m_state;
    }

    public String getInstanceID()
        throws Exception
    {
        return getClass() + ":1.0:" + System.currentTimeMillis();
    }
}
```

You can see that a majority of it looks like the HelloService we just wrote. In fact, except for the start method, the two Services are almost identical. This is somewhat to be expected, since both are essentially one-shot deals: do your thing when you start, and spend the rest of the time idling. One noticeable difference comes in ExecService's constructor, which expects the command line to execute on startup.[1]

ExecService's complexity comes in the start method. We create a Process object with the constructor-passed String as our command line to execute. We then capture the Process's stdout and stderr (standard output and standard error) streams into java.io.InputStream objects. Next, because we want to reroute the output from the Process to our console window, we have to poll the Process object for an exit value. If the Process object throws an IllegalThreadStateException, it means the Process is still running so we capture the output and echo it to our local console. If the Process object honors the exitValue call and returns normally, it means the Process ended. So we still have to capture the remaining output, echo it, then quit the loop. Note that while you could capture the Process's input stream and feed it keystrokes from our local

---

[1] This means that, in order to use ExecService, you have to subclass it; this is obviously not a feasible long-term solution.

console window, this system is intended to be running somewhere in a dark closet, with no user with whom to interact. That also means we should probably capture the output to someplace other than the console window, but this works for now. We can always change it later if we feel the need.

By the way, here's one additional note for users of ExecService on a Win32 (Win95/98/NT) system. If you want to fire off a series of shell commands (like COPY or DIR), place the commands in a batch file and fire off the batch file, instead of firing off the command shell with a /C argument and the command to run. Because the Sun JVM does not deal well with Runtime.exec calls with arguments of "COMMAND /C DIR", you'll effectively hang the system. If you absolutely had to have this behavior, you'd need to modify ExecService to expect the command in an array of Strings, with the command in the args[0] position, and any command-line arguments to the created process in args[1] and beyond. That, I leave as an exercise for the reader.

## 7.4    HelloAgainService

Threads can also be applied on an individual Service level. In fact, this is where most of the threading work will occur—Services will want their own thread in which to run, so as to be 100 percent available, instead of only when ServerManager calls into them. The basic pattern most Services will follow will be to fire off their own thread in start, kill the thread in stop, and have the thread pause itself when told to by pause and resume when told to by resume.

HelloAgainService (listing 7.4), like its ancestor, HelloService, simply serves to verify that we can, in fact, do these things within the framework given. The code is as follows:

**Listing 7.4    Code for HelloAgainService**

```
/**
 * HelloAgainService
 */
public class HelloAgainService
    implements Service, Runnable
{
    // Internal members
    //
    private int m_interval = 5; // in seconds
    private boolean m_paused = false;
    private Thread m_thread = null;
    private String m_message = "Hello, again!";

    private String m_state = STOPPED;
    private static int s_instanceCt = 0;

    public HelloAgainService()
    {
        m_thread = new Thread(this);
    }
```

```java
//
// Service interface methods
//
public void start()
    throws Exception
{
    // We're starting
    //
    m_state = STARTING;

    // Start our thread
    //
    m_thread.start();

    // We're running
    //
    m_state = RUNNING;
}
public void stop()
    throws Exception
{
    // We're stopping
    //
    m_state = STOPPING;

    // Stop our thread
    //
    m_thread.interrupt();
    m_thread.join();
        // Wait for thread to finish, which releases us

    // We've stopped
    //
    m_state = STOPPED;
}
public void pause()
    throws Exception
{
    // We're pausing
    //
    m_state = PAUSING;

    // Set the 'paused' member to true, which causes the run() loop
    // below to skip its message
    //
    m_paused = true;

    // We've paused
    //
    m_state = PAUSED;
}
public void resume()
    throws Exception
{
```

```java
        // We're resuming
        //
        m_state = RESUMING;

        // Set the 'paused' member to false, which causes the run()
        // loop below to display its message
        //
        m_paused = false;

        // We've started up again
        //
        m_state = RUNNING;
    }
    public String getState()
    {
        return m_state;
    }

    public String getInstanceID()
        throws Exception
    {
        return getClass() + ":1.0:" + System.currentTimeMillis();
    }
    //
    // Runnable interface methods
    //
    /**
     * Method called by Thread.start()
     */
    public void run()
    {
        try
        {
            while (!Thread.currentThread.isInterrupted())
            {
                Thread.sleep(m_interval * 1000);
                if (!m_paused)
                    System.out.println(m_message);
            }
        }
        catch (InterruptedException ex)
        {
            System.out.println("Going away now....");
        }
    }
}
```

Most of the HelloAgainService is scaffolding for the Service as a whole:

- the m_state member to store the Service's status (started, starting, stopped, stopping, and so on)
- the m_paused member to indicate the pause/resume status of the thread

- `start` to initialize and start the thread
- `stop` to interrupt and wait for the thread to die
- `pause` and `resume` to set the value of `m_paused` appropriately

and so forth. This is code that will need to be written for each and every Service that wants to make use of threads. Being the disciples of object-orientation that we are, this should raise an immediate red flag.

## 7.4.1    ThreadServer

Since this is all the code that any Service that wants to fire off its own worker threads will need to write, let's try to create a base class from which we can extend to do some of this drudgery (listing 7.5). As with any reuse-through-inheritance approach, however, there's only so much we can do in the base class with any degree of reliability.

**Listing 7.5    Code for ThreadServer**

```
/**
 * ThreadedServer
 */
public abstract class ThreadedServer
    implements Service
{
    // Internal data
    //
    private Thread m_thread = null;
    private Runnable m_runnable = null;
    private String m_state = STOPPED;
    protected boolean m_paused = false;
    protected boolean m_shouldStop = false;

    public void start()
        throws Exception
    {
        // We're starting
        //
        if (!getState().equals(STARTING))
            setState(STARTING);

        // Start our thread
        //
        if (m_thread == null)
            m_thread = new Thread(new ThreadGroup(this.toString()),
                m_runnable, getClass().getName());
        m_thread.start();

        // We're running
        //
        setState(RUNNING);
    }
    public void stop()
        throws Exception
```

```
{
    // We're stopping
    //
    if (!getState().equals(STOPPING))
        setState(STOPPING);

    // Sanity-check--did the Thread fail to initialize?
    //
    if (m_thread == null)
        return;

    // First we'll try the easy way
    //
    m_shouldStop = true;

    // Stop our thread; this assumes that the thread is written to be
    // sensitive to interrupts (that is, it checks isInterrupted() in
    // a timely fashion). If it doesn't respond within 10 seconds,
    // notify the system so a user can perhaps kill() it.
    //
    ServerManager.log(
        "Asking thread " + m_thread + " to stop.");
    m_thread.interrupt();
    m_thread.join(10 * 1000);
        // Wait for thread to finish for 10 seconds; if we're not back
        // by then, we'll move on

    if (m_thread.isAlive())
    {
        ServerManager.log(
            "ThreadedServer for " + getClass().getName() + ": " +
            "Thread refuses to stop within 10 seconds.");
        return;
    }

    // We've stopped
    //
    setState(STOPPED);
}
public void kill()
{
    // Sanity-check--did the Thread fail to initialize?
    //
    if (m_thread == null)
        return;

    // If we tried to stop, or thought we stopped, and the thread
    // is still alive, kill it. Note that this implementation WILL
    // generate deprecation warnings due to the call to stop(); if
    // this bothers you, comment this entire method out.
    if ((getState().equals(STOPPED) && m_thread.isAlive()) ||
        (getState().equals(STOPPING) && m_thread.isAlive()))
    {
        ServerManager.log(
```

```
                    "ThreadedServer for " + getClass().getName() + ":" +
                    "Calling stop() on Thread.");
                m_thread.stop();

                setState(STOPPED);
            }
    }
    public void pause()
        throws Exception
    {
        // We're pausing
        //
        if (!getState().equals(PAUSING))
            setState(PAUSING);

        // Sanity-check--did the Thread fail to initialize?
        //
        if (m_thread == null)
            return;

        // Set the 'paused' member to true
        //
        m_paused = true;

        // If you prefer a more decisive approach, and don't mind
        // deprecation warnings, then uncomment the following block
        /*
        m_thread.suspend();
         */

        // We've paused
        //
        setState(PAUSED);
    }
    public void resume()
        throws Exception
    {
        // We're resuming
        //
        if (!getState().equals(RESUMING))
            setState(RESUMING);

        // Sanity-check--did the Thread fail to initialize?
        //
        if (m_thread == null)
            return;

        // Set the 'paused' member to false
        //
        m_paused = false;

        // If you prefer a more decisive approach, and don't mind
        // deprecation warnings, then uncomment the following block
        /*
        m_thread.resume();
```

*CHAPTER 7  CONTROL*

```java
        */

        // We've started up again
        //
        setState(RESUMING);
    }

    public String getState()
    {
        return m_state;
    }
    public void setState(String val)
    {
        m_state = val;
    }

    public String getInstanceID()
        throws Exception
    {
        return getClass() + ":" + "1.0" + ":"
            + System.currentTimeMillis();
    }

    public boolean isPaused()
    {
        return m_paused;
    }
    public boolean shouldStop()
    {
        return m_shouldStop;
    }

    public void setRunnable(Runnable runnable)
        throws IllegalThreadStateException
    {
        if (m_thread != null && m_thread.isAlive())
            throw new IllegalThreadStateException();

        m_runnable = runnable;
    }
    public void setThread(Thread thread)
        throws IllegalThreadStateException
    {
        if (m_thread != null && m_thread.isAlive())
            throw new IllegalThreadStateException();

        m_thread = thread;
    }
    public Thread getThread()
    {
        return m_thread;
    }
}
```

A large amount of functionality has been factored back into this abstract base class, but it's not quite a cure-all. For example, if a client extends this class, overrides start, but fails to call up to the ThreadedServer implementation of it, then all bets are off regarding the state, the thread's status, and so forth. Additionally, extending this means that a class can no longer extend any other class, such as RemoteUnicastObject (for RMI servers).

ThreadedServer also provides a number of hooks to allow for customization of its threading policy. First, it takes a Runnable instance via its setRunnable method, meaning that a ThreadedServer could be used on its own (as opposed to being subclassed) to provide this separate-thread behavior. Additionally, the Thread itself can be specified by calling setThread on the ThreadedServer instance and firing that off, instead of allowing ThreadedServer to create its own Thread. This can be useful if a particular system wants to group all of its Threads under a ThreadGroup, for convenience.

To see how to use it, let's rewrite the HelloAgainService above using the ThreadedServer as a base class:

```java
import com.javageeks.gjas.services.ThreadedServer;

public class OneMoreHelloService extends ThreadedServer
{
    private String m_message = "Hello, once more!";
    private long m_interval = 5;

    public void start()
        throws Exception
    {
        setRunnable(new Runnable()
        {
            public void run()
            {
                try
                {
                    while (!Thread.currentThread().isInterrupted())
                    {
                        Thread.sleep(m_interval * 1000);
                        if (!OneMoreHelloService.this.isPaused())
                            System.out.println(m_message);
                    }
                }
                catch (InterruptedException ex)
                {
                    System.out.println("Going away now....");
                }
            }
        });

        super.start();
    }
}
```

Not bad. We've managed to cut the code down somewhat significantly. One problem we still have, however, is that the ServerManager is static and inflexible; we can't add new Services after the LocalServerManager has started. Let's fix that right away.

## 7.4.2 Example: ConsoleControlService

One thing we'd like to do is be able to control the ServerManager via some mechanism other than a file (listing 7.6). For example, we'd like to be able to bring the system down in some kind of ordered, controlled fashion and not via a break signal (CTRL-C/CTRL-D to the console window in NT or UNIX). Since we already have a console window running, why not use it?

**Listing 7.6   Code for ConsoleControlService**

```java
/**
 * ConsoleControlService:
 */
public class ConsoleControlService extends ThreadedServer
    implements Runnable
{
    public void start(String[] args)
        throws Exception
    {
        setRunnable(this);

        super.start(args);
    }

    public void run()
    {
        try
        {
            // Set up
            BufferedReader in =
                new BufferedReader(
                    new InputStreamReader(System.in));

            System.out.print("ServerManager >");
            for (String line = in.readLine();
                !line.equals("quit");
                line = in.readLine())
            {
                ServerManager.log(this.toString() +
                    ": '" + line + "'");
                if (line.trim().equals("shutdown"))
                {
                    ServerManager.shutdown();
                    //return;
                }
                else if (line.trim().startsWith("start "))
                {
                    // Extract classname
```

```java
            String currentLine =
                line.substring(6, line.length());

            if (currentLine.indexOf(" ") < 0)
            {
                // Classname appeared by itself, so there are
                // no additional args to parse
                String classname = currentLine;

                ServerManager.log(
                    "ConsoleControlService.run(): " +
                    "Calling ServerManager.addService(" +
                    classname + ", null)");
                ServerManager.addService(
                    classname, null);
            }
            else
            {
                ServerManager.log(
                    "ConsoleControlService.run: " +
                    "Any service started by the this service "+
                    "cannot have args; sorry.");
            }
        }
        else if (line.trim().startsWith("list"))
        {
            String[] svcs =
                ServerManager.getServices();

            System.out.println("Services: {");
            for (int i=0; i<svcs.length; i++)
                System.out.println("    " + svcs[i]);
            System.out.println("}");
        }
        else if (line.trim().startsWith("remove "))
        {
            // Parse argument, confirm removal,
            // call ServerManager.removeService()
        }
        else if (line.trim().startsWith("threads"))
        {
            // List all threads running in the JVM
            //

            // Find the ultimate ThreadGroup parent
            ThreadGroup ancestor =
                Thread.currentThread().getThreadGroup();
            while (ancestor.getParent() != null)
                ancestor = ancestor.getParent();

            // List all threads
            int ct = ancestor.activeCount();
            ct += ct/2;
            Thread[] array = new Thread[ct];
```

```
                    ancestor.enumerate(array, true);

                    for (int i=0; i<array.length; i++)
                    {
                        if (array[i] != null)
                        {
                            System.out.println(array[i].toString());
                        }
                    }
                }
                else
                {
                    System.out.println("Unrecognized command: " +
                        line);
                }

                System.out.print("ServerManager >");
            }
        }
        catch (java.io.IOException IOEx)
        { }
    }
}
```

Here we see a slightly different approach from the previous HelloAgainService; instead of creating an anonymous Runnable class and passing that into setRunnable, Console-ControlService implements Runnable and passes in this. Either way works equally well, but this approach seems more clear when run gets more complex, in my opinion.

Going over the code in detail, we find:

- start calls setRunnable(this), then calls up the chain to start the thread.
- run creates a BufferedReader around the InputStream System.in, then enters an infinite for loop, reading input from the console window. As each line is entered, run checks to see if it recognizes the first word, and if so, takes appropriate action. shutdown calls ServerManager.shutdown. "start" takes the class name to instantiate and feeds it to ServerManager.addService. "list" writes out a list of each Service currently executing within the system, and "threads" lists all the threads (including system threads) currently running

Why not have ServerManager itself read and write to the console window, instead of a Service? Principally, because it helps encourage modularization between the components in the system. ServerManager is responsible only for managing Servers, and not the console window. It also validates the idea (which we'll explore more fully, in subsequent chapters) that controlling the ServerManager can be done from outside the ServerManager itself.

One quirk of having this console control as a Service is that because ConsoleControlService is a user thread, calling ServerManager.shutdown doesn't bring the system down completely, because ConsoleControlService is still running.[2] In order to bring it down completely, you must first issue a `shutdown` command, followed by a quit to exit the ConsoleControlService `run` loop. This gives the administrator the opportunity to verify that the Services running have completely shut down (or not).

The easiest way to terminate ConsoleControlService during `shutdown` is to create a daemon thread to do the input, and have the ConsoleCreateService thread wait to be interrupted, or to have the daemon thread exit. Once either condition occurs, it can exit cleanly. You could set the ConsoleCreateService thread itself to be a daemon thread, without adding the second thread, but this means that the second the other user threads exit, the JVM terminates without even the kindness of a final message to the console screen.

The solution, of course, is to use two threads: the one spun off for us by ThreadedServer, and a daemon thread to do the actual work. (Listing 7.7).

**Listing 7.7    Code to terminate ConsoleControlService**

```
class ConsoleThread extends Thread
{
    public ConsoleThread()
    {
        setDaemon(true);
    }

    public void run()
    {
        try
        {
            // Set up
            BufferedReader in =
                new BufferedReader(
                    new InputStreamReader(System.in));

            System.out.print("ServerManager >");
            for (String line = in.readLine();
                !line.equals("quit");
                line = in.readLine())
            {
                ServerManager.log(this.toString() +
                    ": '" + line + "'");
                if (line.trim().equals("shutdown"))
                {
                    ServerManager.shutdown();
                    //return;
                }
                else if (line.trim().startsWith("start "))
                {
                    // Extract classname
```

---

[2] Calling `interrupt` on the thread doesn't break it out of the `readLine` call in the top of the loop.

```
        String currentLine =
            line.substring(6, line.length());

        if (currentLine.indexOf(" ") < 0)
        {
            // Classname appeared by itself, so there are
            // no additional args to parse
            String classname = currentLine;

            ServerManager.log(
                "ConsoleControlService.run(): " +
                "Calling ServerManager.addService(" +
                classname + ", null)");
            ServerManager.addService(
                classname, null);
        }
        else
        {
            ServerManager.log(
                "ConsoleControlService.run: " +
                "Any service started by the this service "+
                "cannot have args; sorry.");
        }
    }
    else if (line.trim().startsWith("list"))
    {
        String[] svcs =
            ServerManager.getServices();

        System.out.println("Services: {");
        for (int i=0; i<svcs.length; i++)
            System.out.println("    " + svcs[i]);
        System.out.println("}");
    }
    else if (line.trim().startsWith("remove "))
    {
        // Parse argument, confirm removal,
        // call ServerManager.removeService()
    }
    else if (line.trim().startsWith("threads"))
    {
        // List all threads running in the JVM
        //

        // Find the ultimate ThreadGroup parent
        ThreadGroup ancestor =
            Thread.currentThread().getThreadGroup();
        while (ancestor.getParent() != null)
            ancestor = ancestor.getParent();

        // List all threads
        int ct = ancestor.activeCount();
        ct += ct/2;
        Thread[] array = new Thread[ct];
        ancestor.enumerate(array, true);
```

```java
                    for (int i=0; i<array.length; i++)
                    {
                        if (array[i] != null)
                        {
                            System.out.println(array[i].toString());
                        }
                    }
                }
                else
                {
                    System.out.println("Unrecognized command: " +
                        line);
                }

                System.out.print("ServerManager >");
            }
        }
        catch (java.io.IOException IOEx)
        { }
    }
}

/**
 * ConsoleControlService:
 */
public class ConsoleControlService extends ThreadedServer
    implements Runnable
{
    public void start()
        throws Exception
    {
        setRunnable(this);

        super.start();
    }

    public void run()
    {
        ConsoleThread t = new ConsoleThread();
        t.start();

        try
        {
            // Block until the console is closed
            t.join();
        }
        catch (InterruptedException intEx)
        {
            // Do nothing but return
            return;
        }
    }
}
```

Not bad at all. We now have some black-box reusable code to do independently threaded Services, and we have a console by which we can control the ServerManager to load, unload, or list Services.

Now, however, let's move on from Service implementations, and look at a more interesting—and useful—`IServerManager` implementation.

C H A P T E R   8

# Remote control

Remember, one of our goals with all this was zero administration and/or zero deployment. One of the facets of zero administration is the ability to control the server from anyplace—not just sitting in front of the machine running the server, but from the administrator's cubicle, the administrator's house, even the administrator's PDA or laptop, using a cellular link. This sort of remote control normally isn't something that a developer would build into a custom server application, but since we're building a generic server backplane, and since all applications will inherit this functionality if it's there, it's worth the effort.

In this particular case, we can provide generic remote control functionality in a variety of ways. In the next chapter, we'll see a SocketControlService that will use a standard socket to present a text-based menu of options and allow an administrator to use a command line socket client to connect and drive the server remotely. However, we can get even more sophisticated than that, using Java's remote procedure call technology, RMI.

RMI, contrary to most peoples' beliefs, is not a distributed object technology. It doesn't really know anything about objects at all. Instead, RMI is about allowing one JVM to make remote method calls on an object living within another. The called object unpacks the arguments, performs the request, marshals up the result, and sends the result back over the socket. This is the same behavior provided by older RPC technologies, such as ONC RPC and Microsoft/DCE RPC.

Due to RMI's omnipresent nature within Java, however, it's an ideal means for "remote-izing" (for lack of a better word) the ServerManager. Essentially, we'll make the ServerManager system RMI-capable by creating a remote interface with a concrete implementation that in turn wraps an instance of LocalServerManager to do the real work. We'll also have to create a local proxy to the RMI-exported ServerManager instance. (Figure 8.1).

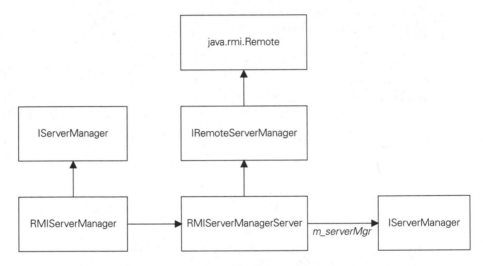

**Figure 8.1   RMIServerManager and RMIServerManagerServer**

As you can see, the RMIServerManagerServer instance is the actual RMI-server object to which instances of RMIServerManager will connect. Using the `IRemoteServerManager` interface, RMIServerManager clients can perform the same calls on the remote ServerManager as they could on a local one. What's more, because the actual IServerManager instance is buried beneath the ServerManager.java static methods, any Services or other code that reference the `IServerManager` Singleton do not even know they're talking to a remote instance.

## 8.1   RMI IMPLEMENTATION

RMIServerManager, the implementation of IServerManager that clients will use to call upon a remote IServerManager instance, is essentially an exercise in the Proxy design pattern.

The pattern's intent is to provide a surrogate or placeholder with which another object can control access to it. Things get tricky when we do this; we want the IServerManager-implementing instance to be in the client JVM, so the server version doesn't necessarily have to conform to the `IServerManager` interface. This is because the server version will provide its own Remote-extending interface that provides the same behavior as the `IServerManager` interface.

We start by examining the `IRemoteServerManager` interface (listing 8.1). It's more than just the `IServerManager` interface, since it also exposes the methods for `IServer`-implementing classes, as well; the reason for this will become clear a bit later in this section.

**Listing 8.1   Code for IRemoteServerManager interface**

```
public interface IRemoteServerManager
    extends java.rmi.Remote
{
    //=========================================================
    // These methods provide surrogate access for ServerManager
    // functionality
    public void remoteShutdown()
        throws RemoteException;

    public IServer remoteAddService(Service svc, String[] args)
        throws RemoteException;
    public void remoteRemoveService(String instanceID)
        throws RemoteException;
    public void remoteKillService(String instanceID)
        throws RemoteException;
    public String[] remoteGetServices()
        throws RemoteException;
    public IServer remoteGetService(String instanceID)
        throws RemoteException;

    public void remoteDeployService(String serviceName,
                              ClassLoaderStrategy strategy)
    public IServer remoteAddService(String svcName,
                              String[] args)
        throws RemoteException;

    public void remoteLog(String msg)
        throws RemoteException;
    public void remoteLog(Exception ex)
        throws RemoteException;
    public void remoteError(String msg)
        throws RemoteException;
    public void remoteError(Exception ex)
        throws RemoteException;

    //=========================================================
    // These methods provide access for IServer
    // functionality
    public boolean start(long ID, String[] args)
        throws RemoteException;
    public boolean stop(long ID)
        throws RemoteException;
    public boolean pause(long ID)
```

```
        throws RemoteException;
    public boolean resume(long ID)
        throws RemoteException;
    public void kill(long ID)
        throws RemoteException;

    public String getState(long ID)
        throws RemoteException;
    public String getInstanceID(long ID)
        throws RemoteException;
    public Exception getLastError(long ID)
        throws RemoteException;

    public static final String RMI_LOOKUPNAME =
        "javageeks.com/RMIServerManager:1.0.0";
}
```

Observant readers will notice that not only does IRemoteServerManager provide remote versions of all the IServerManager methods, but also the IServer methods with an added ID parameter. What gives?

One principal problem with many distributed object systems is that of scalability—as an object system grows, objects tend to call between each other in an indiscriminate fashion. This is fine within a local machine, but should a distributed object system attempt to mimic this behavior, the object system will quickly bog down due to the high overhead of network traffic and marshaling/unmarshaling of parameters on both sides of the call.

A naïve implementation of the RMIServer class would create and export an instance of an RMIServerServer object, to correspond directly with the RMIServer object handed back to the client from an addService call. Unfortunately, 99.9 percent of the IServer's lifetime is spent doing nothing. Most clients hold on to the IServer return value for potential use in the future, not constant use now. As a result, the server has now spent valuable resources[1] to provide an object that will spend most of its time doing nothing.

Instead, within the RMI ServerManager implementation we're building here, we have the server export only a single object—the RMIRemoteServerManagerServer (which we haven't seen yet), and that object provides both ServerManager and Server services. The RMIRemoteServerManagerServer maintains a collection of RMIServer instances, identified by numeric IDs, and they know about the RMIServerManagerServer instance and its specific ID number. Thus, an attempt by an RMIServer to stop its wrapped Service turns into a call into the RMIServerManagerServer's stop method with an ID parameter of 5, or whatever corresponds to the ID within the RMIServer instance on the client.

---

[1]  The most expensive of which is the memory for the object and the CPU cycles to listen on the active socket.

This is a clear violation of the object's know-how to perform its own behavior's principle, which object purists will argue, violates encapsulation. I won't argue any of these points, except to say that at times, object purism must be sacrificed on the altar of actual usability. It's a sad fact that what usually works out better for the user, is harder for the developer to do.

Within the RMIServerManagerServer code (which is far too long to be displayed here), we wrap an instance of the LocalServerManager to do the actual ServerManager work, and we wrap and "remote-ize" access to this LocalServerManager instance as appropriate. For example, the RMIServerManagerServer takes the IServer return value from the LocalServerManager's addService call, puts the IServer into the RMIServerManagerServer's HashMap of Server instances, and hands back an RMIServer instance (which is fully Serializable, and so doesn't need to be exported to the client according to the rules of RMI):

```
public class RMIServerManagerServer extends UnicastRemoteObject
    implements IRemoteServerManager
{
    // . . .

    /**
     * Add the loaded Service to the list of Servers and start it.
     * We throw away the return value from the LocalServerManager call
     * (the LocalServer instance) because we need to construct an
     * RMIServer instance to give back to the RMI caller.
     */
    public IServer remoteAddService(Service svc, String[] args)
        throws RemoteException
    {
        // Do the normal addService thing
        IServer svr = m_serverMgr.addService(svc, args);

        // Create our RMI Proxy
        long ID = m_serverCt++;
        RMIServer rmiSvr = new RMIServer(this, ID);
        m_serverMap.put(Long.toString(ID), svr);
            // Careful readers will note that this has an inherent design
            // flaw; when we get above the maximum count of a long, we will
            // wrap around, with the possibility that an existing Server
            // could be overwritten! However, my experience has led me to
            // believe that very rarely, if ever, will this actually occur.
            // Consider the mathematics--if a new Server were added every
            // second, it would take 2^64 seconds before overlap occurs,
            // and the human civilization hasn't been in existence that
            // long! Consider the mathematics: 2^32 seconds (4,234,967,296)
            // is 71582788 minutes, or 1193046 hours or 49,710 days, or 136
            // years! And Java uses 64-bit long types, which is 136 years,
            // squared, or roughly 18,500 years!

        return rmiSvr;
    }
```

```
// . . .

// Internal data
//
private LocalServerManager m_serverMgr;
private long m_serverCt = 0;
private HashMap m_serverMap = new HashMap();
}
```

Correspondingly, when a call comes in from a remote RMIServer, with the appropriate ID, we need to forward the call on to the appropriate local IServer instance stored within that map of Servers:

```
public class RMIServerManagerServer extends UnicastRemoteObject
    implements IRemoteServerManager
{
    // . . .

    /**
     *
     */
    public boolean start(long ID, String[] args)
        throws RemoteException
    {
        IServer svr = (IServer)m_serverMap.get(Long.toString(ID));
        return svr.start(args);
    }

    // . . .

}
```

Notice how we don't specify that we're using a LocalServer class within the start code, even though we know that we're using a LocalServerManager implementation as our ServerManager. We do this deliberately, because we never know when we may want RMIServerManagerServer to instead wrap an instance of another type of IServerManager. In fact, the entire RMIServerManagerServer class is built around this lack of knowledge of the actual IServerManager it is "remote-izing"; the RMIServerManagerServer constructor sets the IServerManager it wraps, and its main method passes in the LocalServerManager instance it will use by default:

```
public class RMIServerManagerServer extends UnicastRemoteObject
    implements IRemoteServerManager
{
    public RMIServerManagerServer(IServerManager svrMgr)
        throws RemoteException
    {
        m_serverMgr = svrMgr;
    }

    // . . .

    public static void main (String args[])
        throws Exception
```

```
    {
        // Create an instance of RMIServerManagerServer
        RMIServerManagerServer svr =
            new RMIServerManagerServer(new LocalServerManager());

        // Bind & export it
        Naming.bind(IRemoteServerManager.RMI_LOOKUPNAME, svr);
        svr.remoteLog("RMIServerManagerServer bound to registry");
    }
}
```

Because we maintain the encapsulation that IServerManager offers, RMIServerManagerServer can in turn wrap any other type IServerManager instance, even another RMIServerManager/RMIServerManagerServer pair.

It's somewhat anticlimactic by this point, but the RMIServerManager class provides the client-side shim code that forwards the request on to the RMIServerManagerServer instance exported on the server:

```
public class RMIServerManager
    implements IServerManager
{
    // Internal data
    //
    IRemoteServerManager m_rmiSvrMgr;

    public RMIServerManager(String host)
        throws Exception
    {
        // Set up ServerManager Singleton
        ServerManager.instance(this);

        // Connect to server; throw RuntimeException if that fails
      //System.out.println("In RMIServerManager--attempting lookup");
        IRemoteServerManager remoteSvrMgr =
            (IRemoteServerManager)Naming.lookup(
                "rmi://" + host + "/" + IRemoteServerManager.RMI_LOOKUPNAME);
      //System.out.println("In RMIServerManager--lookup complete");
        m_rmiSvrMgr = remoteSvrMgr;
    }
```

We do the classic RMI thing in the constructor by taking a String parameter of the host name to contact, and attempt to find it via the RMI lookup method of the Naming class, passing in the RMI URL. This particular sequence of steps may change in the very, very near future. JNDI is fast becoming the Java-approved way of providing exported-name services, such as that provided by the RMI Naming class. If the lookup call fails, we're in deep trouble as far as the RMIServerManager is concerned, so we make no pretense at hiding it. We throw the Exception back to the caller.

```
    public void shutdown()
    {
        try
        {
```

```
            m_rmiSvrMgr.remoteShutdown();
        }
        catch (java.rmi.RemoteException remoteEx)
        {
            throw new RuntimeException(remoteEx.toString());
        }
    }
    public IServer addService(Service svc, String[] args)
    {
        try
        {
            return m_rmiSvrMgr.remoteAddService(svc, args);
        }
        catch (java.rmi.RemoteException remoteEx)
        {
            throw new RuntimeException(remoteEx.toString());
        }
    }

    // . . . (Other methods omitted for brevity)
```

Notice how all the IServerManager-inherited methods (only one of which, addService, is listed here) simply forward the request on to the IRemoteServer-Manager instance we got back in the constructor. Notice, in particular, that if we catch a RemoteException from the client, we don't really do anything about it; instead, I package up the RemoteException's message into an instance of Runtime-Exception, and throw that back out.

This is another point of personal preference and coding style. Unfortunately, java.rmi.RemoteException extends the standard Java Exception class, instead of the RuntimeException class, which means that any method that wants to call an RMI method must either catch the RemoteException type, or declare it as part of its throws clause. Doing the latter, unfortunately, breaks the IServerManager interface, since Java (correctly) doesn't allow inherited methods to throw differing exception types. The first reaction might be, then, to simply add throws RemoteException to the methods declared in IServerManager; unfortunately, this would be flat-out wrong.

Remember, RMI is simply one method of making objects distributable across JVMs; in addition to RMI, we have the option of using JMS, CORBA, or even POS (Plain Ol' Sockets) as a middleware alternative. Declaring the IServerManager interface exposes the fact that we use RMI under the hood, and plainly breaks encapsulation. CORBA servers, for example, do not throw java.rmi.RemoteExceptions, but their own, unique, exception types. Should we declare IServerManager to throw those exception types, too?

Declaring the base interface (IServerManager) to throw any type of communi-cations-protocol exception forces clients to handle exceptions that they really don't care about. The client using IServerManager doesn't care, and needn't know, that the ServerManager in question is over a TCP/IP wire; all the client cares about is whether or not the request succeeded.

Let's continue looking at code.

```java
public static void main (String args[])
    throws Exception
{
    if (args.length < 1)
    {
        System.out.println("Usage: java RMIServerManager <hostname>");
        return;
    }

    // Create (and register) the RMIServerManager
    new RMIServerManager(args[0]);

    ServerManager.log("Entering RMIServerManager.main()");

    // Parse command-line arguments, if any
    //
    for (int argc=1; argc < args.length; argc++)
    {
        if (args[argc].startsWith("@"))
        {
            // The "@" argument indicates the file we should
            // parse for services to execute
            try
            {
                String arg = args[argc];
                String filename =
                    arg.substring(arg.indexOf("@")+1, arg.length());
                FileInputStream fis =
                    new FileInputStream(filename);
                ServerManager.parseInputStream(fis);
            }
            catch (Exception ex)
            {
                // Ignore it and move on

                ex.printStackTrace();
            }
        }
        else if ("TEST".equals(args[argc]))
        {
            // Deploy a Service, then try to add it.
            try
            {
                // Look for "TestService.class" in the current
                // directory
                String filename = "TestService.class";
                java.io.FileInputStream fis =
                    new java.io.FileInputStream(filename);

                byte[] bytes = new byte[fis.available()];
                fis.read(bytes);

                // Create a HashtableClassLoader
```

```
            com.javageeks.classloader.HashtableClassLoader
                hcl = new HashtableClassLoader();
            hcl.putClass("TestService", bytes);

            // Deploy it
            ServerManager.deployService("TestService", hcl);

            // Now add the Service
            IServer svr =
                ServerManager.addService("TestService",
                                            new String[0]);
            if (svr == null)
            {
                System.out.println("Test failed!");
            }
        }
        catch (Exception ex)
        {
            ex.printStackTrace();
        }
    }
    else
    {
        ServerManager.parseArg(args[argc]);
    }
}

    ServerManager.log("Exiting RMIServerManager.main()");
    }
}
```

The main method looks fairly straightforward—if "TEST" is not present as an argument, do much the same thing as we did in LocalServerManager: parse the file behind the "@" character, and load those services. If "TEST" is present, do a quick check to ensure that everything works the way it should, and exit.

### 8.1.1  Analysis

Let's talk more about the RMI-to-IServerManager adapter methods. Ideally, we should do something more intelligent with the error condition returned from the RMI call; however, knowing what to do is highly dependent on knowing what's wrong in the first place. Even then, having that knowledge doesn't immediately lead to the ability to affect the outcome. If, for example, the RemoteException was thrown because the server instance can't be found on the remote machine, it's a good indicator that either the machine isn't available, or the server process isn't up and running. In either case, there's nothing that a client can do about it except exit and try again.

For those developers who believe that the client can and should do something about the situation, one approach to solve this problem would be to create a NestedRuntimeException class that extends RuntimeException, and holds the actual Exception thrown as a parameter within the NestedRuntimeException. Then, within the `catch` block of these methods, instead of throwing a RuntimeException, the RMIServerManager can throw a NestedRuntimeException, with the RemoteException passed in. Then, on the client side, the client can catch NestedRuntimeExceptions, inspect the nested Exception, and decide what action to take from there.

In this case, more work needs to be done within the `try/catch` block of RMIServerManager. For example, in the current implementation, RMIServerManager assumes an optimisitic attitude, and attempts to call on the server instance regardless of what went on before. If the client catches the RuntimeException it threw because the server wasn't there a few seconds ago, it doesn't care—it will try again when called to do so.

This overly optimistic approach needs to be rethought when attempting to provide the client with more intelligence regarding remote operations—should the RMIServerManager zero out the IRemoteServerManager instance and attempt to reconnect via another call to `lookup`? Possibly, but this means more work within RMIServerManager's `try/catch` blocks, since now the RMIServerManager needs to test the IRemoteServerManager instance on each call and attempt the `lookup` if it's null, and set the instance to null in the event of a RemoteException being thrown.

All in all, it's been my experience that problems with remote connectivity are often not correctable by the client, and can only be communicated to the user, as opposed to being fixed within the client application. Usually this consists of the user either reattempting the connection, perhaps by firing up the client application again, or else contacting Tech Support to find out why the server is down.

What is of more importance to the enterprise developer is maintaining a consistent, location-transparent and protocol-independent interface for interacting with the IServerManager; for that reason, GJAS encapsulates away the knowledge of any RemoteException (or other protocol-specific error type) and keeps its interface pure. Other developers or development shops may disagree with this approach, especially those which have already standardized on their middleware protocol (sockets, CORBA, RMI, and so forth). This is fine, so long as the full import of that decision is realized, in that making that middleware protocol visible to the client in turn means that the code will require major reconstructive surgery if and when that middleware decision changes, as it is likely to do.

## 8.2   OTHER IMPLEMENTATIONS

RMI is not, by any stretch of the imagination, the only remote-method-call technology available to Java. For starters, there are CORBA, JMS, and straight Sockets-with-Serialization. Any of these could be adapted to "remote-ize" the ServerManager system in the same way. By creating an IServerManager-implementing subclass that acts as a proxy to the appropriate server object (as RMIServerManager serves as a proxy to the RMIServerManagerServer), you could easily create a CORBAServerManager, a JMSServerManager, a SocketServerManager, and so on.

Further, we don't have to stop with just those technologies available to Java. By using JNI, as shown in chapter 16, we can make C++-only middleware technologies available to us, as well—Microsoft named pipes, UNIX shared memory, even MacOS's AppleEvents. If it's a remote-capable technology, we can make it available to us as a means of controlling or participating in the ServerManager from anywhere.

## 8.3    NECESSARY IMPROVEMENTS

Unfortunately, making the ServerManager remote capable exposes the flaw we uncovered earlier, but in a worse way. Right now, when a Service is serialized and passed "over the wire" to the RMIServerManagerServer in the addService method, if the class isn't known on the other side, the RMIServerManagerServer will throw an exception and refuse to bring in the class. Normally, RMI downloads unfamiliar code through its annotated codebase URL property—a URL which is provided by the programmer as a URL to contact for .class files and the like if the RMI server's codebase doesn't already have the code. This is what provides RMI's thin-client capabilities—if it doesn't have the code locally, it'll connect to the URL, ask for the .class code it needs and use that. As soon as a developer or administrator updates the code on the server, the next time the client connects to the RMI server, it automatically retrieves the latest version of the code. Zero deployment has never been easier.

It might seem, at first, that we can simply make use of this approach ourselves—we provide the RMI system with an annotated codebase, and it should all work. There are a number of problems with this thinking. To start, RMI expects to use the appropriate protocol to contact the annotated codebase URL; that means if the URL is an http: protocol URL, then RMI will expect to have a web server on the other end waiting to receive HTTP requests. When we're in the standard client/server approach, where the client is requesting the new code of the server, this is trivial. Either a simple web server can rest on the RMI server machine to dispense the necessary code, or, if the RMI client is an applet, the applet's web host can act as the RMI class host, as well.

This would mean that, since in our case it's the client, not the server, providing the code, we'd need to have an HTTP server running on the client to provide the code desired. This isn't a major problem. In chapter 9, we'll see how we can create an HTTP server in about 400 lines of code, since we'd just open a socket on the client, listening for requests from the server on the usual port (80). The problem with this line of thinking, however, is that the client isn't going to remain alive forever, and the server will need that code in a completely nondeterministic way; we have no way of knowing precisely when or how often those code requests will come in. For example, consider a hypothetical Service we call AService. As part of its duties, AService uses the BUtilities class to do its work. When we send the AService class over the wire to the server, the server will immediately request the BUtilities code as part of its normal ClassLoading mechanism. This is all well and good.

But if the AService class doesn't directly refer to the BUtilities code, but instead loads the BUtilities class by name, we have a problem. When AService is serialized and sent over, BUtilities won't go with it; it's not directly referred to anywhere within AService. The only time BUtilities will be requested of the client is when AService actually executes the code that loads the BUtilities class by name, and that could conceivably be hours, days, weeks, or months after the client initially uploads the Service. By that time, the client that originally provided the Service will be long gone.

What we need is to provide a way for clients to either provide the code, in binary form, for the ServerManager to use when and how it needs it, or provide a mechanism by which the ServerManager can obtain the code it needs to finish the loading and executing of the Service. We can provide both in one mechanism.

To do this, we add two new methods to the IServerManager interface:

```
public interface IServerManager
{
    // . . . (as before)

    public void deployService(String serviceName,
                                ClassLoaderStrategy strategy);
    public IServer addService(String svcName, String[] args);
}
```

The first, `deployService`, takes a ClassLoaderStrategy instance from chapter 2 and a name of a Service to bind it to. This way, when the ServerManager is asked to load the Service whose name is the same as the serviceName parameter, IServerManager can use the ClassLoaderStrategy to load the Service instance, instead of the system ClassLoader. But since `addService` currently takes a Service instance as a parameter (implying that the class has already been loaded and resolved), we need to add an overloaded version of `addService` that takes the name of the Service to load, so that the ServerManager can do the loading instead of the client. This second version of `addService` will be the more popular method to use to add a new Service, since it requires less work on the part of the client.

Now that we've modified the base interface, of course, we need to modify the classes that implement it. In turn, we'll have to modify the classes that support the ServerManager system (thinking specifically of ServerManager.java), as well as any that act as Proxies to the ServerManager instance (such as IRemoteServerManager, RMIServerManager, and RMIServerManagerServer). We'll go over the details of the LocalServerManager implementation, but I'll leave it to the reader to follow up with the others to see how it's done there.

LocalServerManager only needs to add the two new methods to become completely compliant. Their implementation is as follows:

```
public class LocalServerManager
    implements IServerManager
{
    // . . . (As before)
```

```java
/**
 * Place a ClassLoaderStrategy into the service-loaders map,
 * so subsequent addService() calls can use the loader to
 * retrieve the necessary code.
 */
public void deployService(String serviceName,
                          ClassLoaderStrategy strategy)
{
    log("Entering ServerManager.deployService");

    m_serviceLoaders.put(serviceName, strategy);

    log("Exiting ServerManager.deployService");
}
/**
 * Add a Service by name; this presumes that the Service has
 * already been deployed to this ServerManager via the
 * deployService method.
 */
public IServer addService(String svcName, String[] args)
{
    try
    {
        log("Entering ServerManager.addService(String, String[])");

        // Get the ClassLoaderStrategy corresponding to the
        // service name
        ClassLoaderStrategy strat =
            (ClassLoaderStrategy)m_serviceLoaders.get(svcName);
        if (strat == null)
        {
            return null;
        }

        StrategyClassLoader scl =
            new StrategyClassLoader(strat);
        Service svc =
            (Service)scl.loadClass(svcName).newInstance();
        return addService(svc, args);
    }
    catch (Exception ex)
    {
        error(ex);
        return null;
    }
    finally
    {
        log("Exiting ServerManager.addService(String, String[])");
    }
}

// Internal data
//
// . . . (as before)
```

```
        private HashMap m_serviceLoaders = new HashMap();
}
```

Notice how the concepts from the ClassLoaders chapter are coming together here to give us an unparalleled amount of flexibility. For example, we can specify that the ServerManager is to load the Service from a relational database by using the JDBC-ClassLoader we'll write later:

```
ClassLoaderStrategy strat =
    new JDBCClassLoader(/* details omitted */);
ServerManager.deployService("MyService", strat);

// . . .

ServerManager.addService("MyService");
```

Now, when the ServerManager wants to load the MyService class, it will use the ClassLoaderStrategy instance `strat`, which happens to be our JDBCClassLoader.

Remember, our requirement was twofold: provide the code, in binary form, for the ServerManager to use when and how it needs it, or provide a mechanism by which the ServerManager can obtain the code it needs to finish the loading and executing of the Service. We've got the second part down cold. We can load the code from anywhere we choose, when we choose, and how we choose, by giving the ServerManager the ClassLoaderStrategy we want it to use.

We can achieve the first by loading all the code into a HashtableClassLoader and handing that to the ServerManager to use for our particular Service:

```
String filename = "TestService.class";
java.io.FileInputStream fis =
    new java.io.FileInputStream(filename);

byte[] bytes = new byte[fis.available()];
fis.read(bytes);

// Create a HashtableClassLoader
com.javageeks.classloader.HashtableClassLoader hcl =
    new HashtableClassLoader();
hcl.putClass("TestService", bytes);

// Deploy it
ServerManager.deployService("TestService", hcl);

// Now add the Service
IServer svr = ServerManager.addService("TestService", new String[0]);
```

In this particular case, we're only loading the TestService class into the Hashtable-ClassLoader. If it in turn requires other classes, we'd need to load them by hand into the HashtableClassLoader, too. This is a potential source of errors, since there's nothing programmatic preventing the developer from making this kind of "oops-I-forgot-to-load-a-class-into-the-Hashtable" mistake, but if it becomes a problem, create a `deployServiceJar` method on IServerManager that performs the recursive class-check necessary to ensure all the classes are in the .jar file or the normal CLASS-PATH/Extensions ClassLoader.

One final change is necessary to make all this work remotely: previously, Class-LoaderStrategy wasn't Serializable, which means sending the ClassLoaderStrategy across the wire won't work correctly. By marking the ClassLoaderStrategy as Serializable, we can send ClassLoaderStrategy instances from one JVM to the other, thus solving that problem without too much trouble.

With all this code behind us now, we need to test it to be sure it all works. In the sample code bundle, as a peer to the "Lib" directory, is a "Test" directory in which the TestService.java file sits. (See the source code on the publisher's website at www.manning.com/neward3.) Compile this file. We're going to test the RMIServerManager by giving it the special command-line parameter TEST. When the RMIServerManager finds this parameter, it tries to load the code for the TestService class from the current directory, places it into a HashtableClassLoader, deploys this HashtableClassLoader to the remote RMIServerManagerServer, and then tries to add the TestService service.

From the "Lib" directory, start the RMI registry:[2]

```
start rmiregistry
```

Then, once the RMI registry is started, from the same directory, start the RMIServer-ManagerServer:

```
java com.javageeks.gjas.RMIServerManagerServer
```

This will block the current console window; wait until the message "RMIServerMan-agerServer bound to registry" appears, then open a new console. The next point is critical: make certain that the "Lib" directory is in your CLASSPATH,[3] and move over to the "Test" directory. Fire up the RMIServerManager with the TEST parameter:

```
java com.javageeks.gjas.RMIServerManager localhost TEST
```

And, after a few moments, you should see a flurry of activity on the RMIServerMan-agerServer console, demonstrating that the RMIServerManagerServer is being called to deploy the HashtableClassLoader and add the TestService instance, and that it's all happening from within a unique ClassLoader.

Take a moment to consider what we've accomplished. By specifying the Class-LoaderStrategy to use when loading a particular Service, we've managed to completely remove all Deployment issues from moving code to the server. Now, we can force the ServerManager to pull code from anywhere, and the client who specified the Class-LoaderStrategy can be long gone when it actually happens. Zero deployment. What's more, administrators have complete control over the ServerManager from wherever they happen to sit. Zero administration.

---

[2]  The commands given are for Windows NT/9x systems; UNIX-heads will need to adjust accordingly.

[3]  Or the compiled .jar file with the GJAS code is in your Extensions directory.

Now that we've got Services running in the ServerManager, let's set up the ability to reconfigure them after they've started.

## 8.4 ADDITIONAL READING

- Andy Krumel, "Revolutionary RMI: Dynamic class loading and behavior objects." JavaWorld, (Dec. 1998). Available at http://www.javaworld.com/jw-12-1998/jw-12-enterprise.html.

  This article describes how RMI uses the annotated codebase to automatically download new classes, and demonstrates how this can be used to provide what the author calls behavior objects. He describes as "the capability to effortlessly pass true objects (data and code) between virtual machines without having to distribute the supporting class files." It's basically the same tenet as zero deployment, except he uses it within the context of a running application (his networked "scribble" example).

# C H A P T E R   9

# *Configuration*

Application configuration is typically an area that most developers do not consider during the design, implementation, and testing of an application; if any configuration is necessary, developers will typically lean toward tried-and-true mechanisms such as .INI, .properties files, or platform-specific methods such as the Win32 Registry. Rarely, if ever, will a developer stop to consider if this application will need configuration from a remote site, or whether configuration will need to be reinitialized without terminating the application, or even if it should be reread on the fly.

## 9.1   JAVA MODELS

Java models have two basic models for doing configuration of objects/applications: JavaBeans and Servlets. In a JavaBeans environment, each Bean exposes a method, `getPropertyDescriptors`, which returns an array of PropertyDescriptor instances, each of which carries information about a particular Property (exposed attribute) of that Bean type. A JavaBeans-enabled development environment can then Introspect the Bean, retrieving the Properties and, optionally, any PropertyDialogs necessary to display the Bean's properties.

This approach carries a couple of advantages. First, because the Property can be any actual Java object, the PropertyDialog allows Bean developers to create a customized Dialog for displaying and/or obtaining the value of the Property of the Bean instance. This, in turn, allows Beans to be of any complexity and any type, even if the

Bean's Property type is a custom object designed specifically for that Bean. Secondly, because all knowledge about the Bean is obtained at run time, no versioning or information dependency exists between the Bean and the environment. The environment discovers the Bean's Properties each time the Bean is hosted there. If a new version of the Bean is loaded, the new Properties are loaded without any regard to previous versions of that Bean; it's always a new Bean.

The other approach is the Servlet approach, in which each Servlet is handed a ContextInfo instance, where interesting information about the Servlet's host is passed to the Servlet for perusal. The Servlet can then pass certain information back to the server, for the server to examine as it sees fit.

This approach carries the advantage of location transparency—the Servlet doesn't have any guarantee that the ContextInfo is from a server in this JVM, or from some other. Even if in the current version, the server and the Servlet coreside in the same JVM, a future version of the server can add load balancing or clustering support without requiring modification to the Servlet's configuration mechanism.

A truly generic configuration mechanism wants to provide both options: location transparency (which will become even more important in distributed systems using RMI, CORBA or EJB), and property opacity (so that new types can be introduced as Property types without requiring recompilation or redesign of the property-gathering mechanism). The JavaBeans mechanism gives us the Property opacity we're looking for; the Servlet mechanism gives us the location transparency. What we need to do now is combine the two into a single mechanism, if that's possible.

### 9.1.1    Interface: ConfigProperty and ConfigProperties

To start with, we need to identify the things that make up a property for a GJAS service; the list I use is as follows:

- *Name*
  The property needs to have a name to identify it from the other properties the service uses; for example, port, message, and so on.

- *Type*
  The property needs to be able to describe the type of its value; some properties will be Strings, some will be Integers, and so on. This is so that any front end to the configuration mechanism (Swing applet, Servlet, etc.) knows how to sanity-check the value entered to ensure the user isn't specifying a bad value.

- *Compatible types*
  The property optionally should be able to specify a list of compatible types that are acceptable as values, as well; for example, an Integer value can be converted from Shorts, Longs, Floats and Doubles (with rounding), and even Strings (by parsing).

- *Value*
  The property needs to have a value tacked onto it.

- *Description*

  The property should have some sort of descriptive string to go with the property name, so that the configuration front end can provide an explanation about the property other than just its name. For example, a port property might have "TCP/IP socket port to use to listen for incoming requests."

- *Parser*

  Very often, configuration settings will be stored and/or sent as Strings; ideally, we'd like to have the configuration mechanism provide a way to convert the String value to its native (byte, Boolean, and so forth) value.

With that in mind, let's take a first swipe at the ConfigProperty class in listing 9.1.

### Listing 9.1   Code for ConfigProperty

```java
/**
 * Class to provide configuration information to interested parties
 */
public class ConfigProperty
    implements Serializable
{
    // Internal implementation
    //
    private String m_name = null;
    private String m_classType = null;
    private String[] m_compatibleTypes = new String[0];
    private Serializable m_value = null;
    private String m_desc = null;

    private transient Method m_parseMethod = null;
    private String m_parseMethodClass = null;
    private String m_parseMethodSig = null;

    public ConfigProperty()
    { }
    public ConfigProperty(String name, Object value, String desc)
    {
        setBaseInfo(name, value.getClass(), null, desc, null);
    }
    public ConfigProperty(String name, Class classType,
                          String[] compatibleTypes, String desc,
                          Method parser)
    {
        setBaseInfo(name, classType, compatibleTypes, desc, parser);
    }
    public ConfigProperty(String name, Class classType,
                          String[] compatibleTypes,
                          Serializable value, String desc,
                          Method parser)
    {
        setBaseInfo(name, classType, compatibleTypes, desc, parser);
        m_value = value;
    }
```

```java
public void setBaseInfo(String name, Class classType,
                        String[] compatibleTypes, String desc,
                        Method parser)
{
    m_name = name;
    m_classType = classType.toString();
    m_compatibleTypes = compatibleTypes;
    if (m_compatibleTypes == null)
    {
        m_compatibleTypes = new String[0];
    }
    m_desc = desc;

    if (parser)
    {
        m_parseMethod = parser;
        m_parseMethodClass = m_parseMethod.getDeclaringClass();
        m_parseMethodSig = m_parseMethod.toString();
    }
}

public String getName()
{
    return new String(m_name);
}
public String getClassType()
{
    return new String(m_classType);
}
public String[] getCompatibleTypes()
{
    String[] ret = new String[m_compatibleTypes.length];
    for (int i=0; i<ret.length; i++)
    {
        ret[i] = new String(m_compatibleTypes[i]);
    }

    return ret;
}
public String getDescription()
{
    return new String(m_desc);
}

public Serializable getValue()
{
    return m_value;
}
public String getValueClass()
{
    return m_value.getClass().toString();
}
public void setValue(Serializable value)
{
```

```java
        String valueClass = value.getClass().toString();

        // If it's the exact type, we're OK
        if (valueClass.equals(m_classType))
        {
            m_value = value;
            return;
        }

        // If the names match exactly, we're OK
        for (int i=0; i<m_compatibleTypes.length; i++)
        {
            if (m_compatibleTypes[i].equals(valueClass))
            {
                m_value = value;
                return;
            }
        }

        // If we're still here, the value failed to convert
        throw new RuntimeException("Value failed to convert");
    }
    public void setValue(String stringifiedValue)
    {
        // Test for parsers already in place (those types already
        // provided by Java; this will work for 95% of the time)

        // java.lang.* types
        if (m_classType.equals(String.class.toString()))
        {
            m_value = strigifiedValue;
        }
        else if (m_classType.equals(StringBuffer.class.toString()))
        {
            m_value = new StringBuffer(stringifiedValue);
        }
        else if (m_classType.equals(Boolean.class.toString()))
        {
            m_value = new Boolean(stringifiedValue);
        }
        else if (m_classType.equals(Byte.class.toString()))
        {
            m_value = new Byte(stringifiedValue);
        }
        else if (m_classType.equals(Character.class.toString()))
        {
            m_value = new Character(stringifiedValue);
        }
        else if (m_classType.equals(Double.class.toString()))
        {
            m_value = new Double(stringifiedValue);
        }
        else if (m_classType.equals(Float.class.toString()))
```

```
{
    m_value = new Float(stringifiedValue);
}
else if (m_classType.equals(Integer.class.toString()))
{
    m_value = new Integer(stringifiedValue);
}
else if (m_classType.equals(Long.class.toString()))
{
    m_value = new Long(stringifiedValue);
}
else if (m_classType.equals(Short.class.toString()))
{
    m_value = new Short(stringifiedValue);
}
// java.math.* types
else if (m_classType.equals(BigDecimal.class.toString()))
{
    m_value = new BigDecimal(stringifiedValue);
}
else if (m_classType.equals(BigInteger.class.toString()))
{
    m_value = new BigInteger(stringifiedValue);
}
// java.util.* types
else if (m_classType.equals(Date.class.toString()))
{
    m_value = new Date(df.parse(stringifiedValue));
}
// Well, it's not a "standard" type, so we've got to
// try and parse it
else
{
    try
    {
        // We have to parse the stringified value
        if (m_parseMethod == null &&
            m_parseMethodClass != null &&
            m_parseMethodSig != null)
        {
            Class c = Class.forName(m_parseMethodClass);
            Method[] methods =
                c.getDeclaredMethods();
            for (int i=0; i<methods.length; i++)
            {
                String methString = methods[i].toString();
                if (methString.equals(m_parseMethodSig))
                {
                    m_parseMethod = methods[i];
                    break;
                }
            }
```

```
        }

        if (m_parseMethod == null)
        {
            // We tried; nothing more to do
            return;
        }

            // Is it static, or virtual?
        int mods = m_parseMethod.getModifiers();

        Object instance = null;

        if (mods & Modifier.STATIC)
        {
            // We can call the Method directly; no instance
            // needed in order to do so
        }
        else
        {
            // We have to try and instantiate the Class type
            // in order to call on the Method
            Class c = Class.forName(m_parseMethodClass);
            instance = c.newInstance();
        }

        Object[] args = new Object[]
        {
            stringifiedValue
        };
        m_value = (Serializable)
            m_parseMethod.invoke(instance, args);
    }
    catch (Exception ex)
    {
        // We can't do anything with it; just give up
    }
    }
    }
}
```

As you can see, it's not a trivial implementation by any stretch of the imagination; ConfigProperty is intended to be as complex as necessary in order to make it as simple as possible for users.

The basic intent of the ConfigProperty interface is simple. Because we're separating the actual configuration mechanism from the thing being configured, we need to describe the configuration parameters (properties) in a generic way. That way, the mechanism can interpret the information and present it in a manner that best suits the configuration front end. Remember, the actual configuration mechanism hasn't been specified yet, and shouldn't be assumed to be via HTML, Applet, or any other form.

By doing this, we ensure that any configuration mechanism can adequately configure any running Service.

We want ConfigProperty to be a location-transparent class; that is, we shouldn't care from the calling side whether this ConfigProperty instance came to us from a Service locally to this JVM, or from across the wire. In order to best support that, we'll mark ConfigProperty as Serializable, so that instances of it can be sent to any other JVM in existence.

A couple of oddities may stand out from the code—to start with, notice how the m_parseMethod member is marked `transient`. The Method class, unfortunately, is not Serializable, so it's not going to move from one JVM to another.[1] As a result, the members m_parseMethodClass and m_parseMethodSig capture the Method instance's declaring Class and the method signature. Then, if this Config-Property is serialized and sent to another JVM, at least we have the information necessary to rebuild the Method instance when we need it. This, in turn, is the source of much of the complexity in the String form of the `setValue` method—if m_parseMethod is `null`, we attempt to rebuild the Method instance and `invoke` it.

At this point, we've established support for individual properties, but dealing with them as a group is more awkward. What we really want, in fact, is a single collection-class instance that we can pass back and forth, containing all the ConfigProperty instances for a given Service. Thus, we create the ConfigProperties class (refer to the web site for the code), also marked Serializable for easy transmission, to encapsulate the collection of ConfigProperty instances. ConfigProperties performs almost identically to the Properties class from the `java.lang` package, except no methods for reading or writing to file are provided. If a configuration mechanism wants to store a ConfigProperties instance to disk, for example, it can simply serialize the data to a File-OutputStream.

We've established the means by which we can get and set Properties; now let's establish precisely how Services make those properties (names and values) available to the configuration mechanisms that want to present or modify them. Doing so requires a modification to the GJAS system, the addition of two methods, getConfigInfo and setConfigInfo, to the Service interface:

```
public interface Service extends java.io.Serializable
{
    // . . .

    /**
     * Return the Properties configuration information
```

---

[1] Some may argue that, because Method represents a specific Java method (which in C++ could be a "function pointer"), it could mark the Class name and method signature as its Serializable data. Then, when deserialized, it could rebuild the Method instance, throwing an exception that the Method of that name and signature wasn't found. This way, if the recipient lacked the Class, or the Class itself was different from the source JVM, Method could signal the error without destroying the JVM.

```
    */
    public ConfigProperties getConfigInfo();
    /**
     * Set the Properties configuration information
     */
    public void setConfigInfo(ConfigProperties info);
}
```

The corresponding modifications must be made to IServer (to pass the instances in or out as necessary) and to any IServer-implementing classes, such as LocalServer or RMIServer. Notice how we've studiously managed to avoid actually specifying anything about that opaque configuration service. The configuration information could be coming from a text file on disk, with the configuration mechanism responding in recognition of a UNIX signal (the infamous "killall –HUP <process-name>" approach), or it could be a servlet-based HTML-driven approach. We could even be responding to a native Control Panel applet on WindowsNT, using JNI to interact with the ServerManager. We don't care how the information was configured, we only care that new configuration information is present and needs to be picked up.

It may strike readers as odd that we're making changes to code we just presented a few chapters ago. This is to demonstrate how most server development takes place—incrementally and in accordance with changing needs and/or requirements. Despite most book authors' professions that software must be allowed to evolve and take shape in incremental fashion, just about every book published presents its code in its finished form, without showing the steps along the way. It's my hope that showing the reader how this modification affects the rest of the system in turn heightens the reader's appreciation for the ripple effect that takes place when modification of an existing system takes place. This, in turn, should explain the need for the steps we'll take in later chapters to avoid this domino effect of change, in the GJAS system as well as in other systems we build.

### 9.1.2 Usage

Using the ConfigProperty system is fairly straightforward (listing 9.2). Services can store the ConfigProperty instances as individual members of the Service, and bundle them up into a ConfigProperties instance as necessary when sending them (getConfigInfo) and pick out the values when receiving them (setConfigInfo).

---

**Listing 9.2  Code for using ConfigProperty**

```
public class MyService
    implements Service
{
    // Internal data
    //
    private ConfigProperty myFirstProperty =
        new ConfigProperty("myFirstProperty", new String(""),
            "The first property to configure");
```

```
private ConfigProperty myNextProperty =
    new ConfigProperty("myNextProperty", new String(""),
        "The next property to configure");

// . . .

public ConfigProperties getConfigInfo()
{
    return new ConfigProperties(new ConfigProperty[]
    {
        myFirstProperty, myNextProperty
    });
}

public void setConfigInfo(ConfigProperties configInfo)
{
    ConfigProperty tmp;
    tmp = configInfo.get("myFirstProperty");
    if (tmp != null)
        myFirstProperty.setValue(tmp.getValue());
    tmp = configInfo.get("myNextProperty");
    if (tmp != null)
        myNextProperty.setValue(tmp.getValue());

    // Re-initialize service configuration, if necessary
}
}
```

Another approach is to use more standard value types and extract the values from the ConfigProperties sent in to the Service in setConfigInfo. Precisely how the Service uses these ConfigProperty instances is not important, so long as it understands two simple rules:

- *Do not assume the ConfigProperty passed out in getConfigInfo comes back to you in setConfigInfo.*
  Because the ConfigProperties instance may be Serialized and sent out, the exact instance of ConfigProperty that comes in via setConfigInfo may be an entirely separate instance, with the original unchanged. Services must assume that, inside of setConfigInfo, the ConfigProperty and ConfigProperties instances are entirely separate with no relationship to the one(s) passed out.

- *Do not assume that the ConfigProperties instance is entirely acceptable.*
  A variety of conditions exist, beyond the Service's control, that may prevent the ConfigProperties instance from containing all of the Services configuration information, or, more likely, containing more than just this Service's configuration information. For example, a developer may later subclass your Service instance and expect additional properties to be sent in, or the configuration front end may only send those values which were changed by the administrator to the

Service. Either way, don't throw away old values until you're sure you have new ones to replace them.

These are actually good rules-of-thumb for *any* interaction with a development framework. Always assume somebody will come in behind you and do something you hadn't expected, even in classes that you're sure will never get subclassed. Once the code is complete, you have no control over what happens to or around it after that.

Code defensively.

### 9.1.3 Configuration front ends

On the CD is a SwingControlPanel, an application that displays a Swing user interface about each of the Services loaded, and their corresponding ConfigProperties. The SwingControlPanel can connect to a GJAS instance through standard sockets, using the SocketControlService presented in chapter 10, by using RMI and an RMIControlService, or by using CORBA and a CORBAControlService. The means by which the SwingControlPanel communicates with the ServerManager instance is more or less irrelevant. So long as the communication mechanism understands sending raw bytes from sender to destination and back again, we can serialize and deserialize the configuration information without a problem.

Other front ends are certainly possible. One would be a ServletControlPanel, which uses an HTTP Servlet hosted within a web browser to connect to the ServerManager and configure/control the loaded Services. Another version would be a native Win32 ControlPanel application (applet), using JNI Invocation to create a JVM and communicate with the ServerManager on the other end. Doing this sort of integration reduces the system administrator's need for Java applications on the machine, thereby making use of an already established environment (the Win32 Control Panel) with which the administrator is already familiar. Less learning curve and greater centralization of administrative functions means a bigger shift towards zero administration.

Some readers may wonder why we don't simply store configuration settings to an RDBMS, or disk file, or any of the other commonly used configuration information repository systems. Nothing prevents us from doing so, and, in fact, it is quite a good idea because administrators won't want to spend time configuring an application, only to have to reconfigure the entire thing again when the application goes down. The point of this mechanism, however, is that a front end is free to store the configuration information anywhere it chooses; a ServletControlPanel may choose to save the settings in a local file (serializing all settings to disk) on command from the administrator, or a custom front end may read the ConfigProperties settings from all running Services, store them to an RDBMS, and provide them when requested to the Services loaded, typically on application start-up. This is all functionality that's easily possible from a front-end application, thus providing the administrator with the maximum flexibility in their setup. Security concerns, for starters, may dissuade system administrators from putting configuration information into an RDBMS where, presumably, database administrators have complete and total access. Correspondingly, a company may want to encrypt the configuration information with a particular private key before storing it to file or RDBMS; either way, the front end is responsible for this storage/retrieval, and can be customized as necessary. The configuration mechanism itself doesn't care, so long as the data is in ConfigProperties format when received by the recipient Service.

## 9.2  SUMMARY

This chapter presented the necessity of building control mechanisms for server-side applications. In addition to describing the basic framework and implementation of the GJAS system, we discussed how we can better achieve zero administration by developing a system in which control of the system can be maintained remotely (using RMI). Note that the RMIServerManager/RMIServerManagerServer partnership is different from a Service such as a RMIControlService/RMIControlServiceClient partnership. In the first case, we are creating a remote proxy to the ServerManager itself. In the second case (not discussed here), we are creating a standard Service that must be loaded within the ServerManager, thus providing the necessary control of the ServerManager instance in order for the Client to successfully connect and control the ServerManager. The distinction is a subtle one, but one which provides for future enhancements (such as fusing load-balancing/clustering support into the RMIServer-Manager system, by having each machine connecting to the RMIServerManager-Server become an available node in the cluster for executing Services).

Next, we built a generic configuration mechanism, ostensibly for use within GJAS, but in all practical cases, usable by any Java application. Note that, in and of itself, the configuration mechanism offers no real promises to its callers about when or how configuration information is parsed or read; that is up to the recipient application to decide. Services can either reread and reconfigure precisely when the setConfigInfo method is called, or reread the configuration values as necessary in code, picking up changes as they occur. This second approach carries a synchronization danger. If two configuration settings depend on one another (for example, working directory and file-name), the setConfigInfo and any other methods accessing those ConfigProperty instances must be synchronized to prevent reading one while the other is in process of being modified. If not, the potential exists that a system administrator might be configuring an application to use a new directory in which the filename originally given doesn't exist, and the application attempts to look for it before the changes are made.

# CHAPTER 10

# Sockets

Java's rich support for the Internet stems from its integral support for sockets programming. The core package `java.net` provides an easy way to allow a JVM to communicate with other machines (or with other JVMs on the same machine) in a scalable, robust fashion. The portable nature of sockets and their industrywide acceptance guarantee that heterogenous networks will be able to communicate seamlessly, and Java's built-in support for sockets makes it an ideal language for socket communications programming.

Just about every Java book written covers how to use Java's Socket and ServerSocket classes. For that reason, I'm assuming that you already know how to write Java code to use sockets. If you're unfamiliar with how to program with Java's Socket and Server-Socket classes, I recommend *Java Network Programming*. (See "Additional reading.")

## 10.1   SIMPLE SOCKET SERVICES

Some of the basic Internet services are present simply to provide some measure of diagnostic ability when setting up a TCP/IP network. Ping, for example, does nothing except provide a port where a ping client can attempt to connect, thereby verifying that the machine can be seen over a TCP/IP network. This helps TCP/IP network administrators when ensuring that a machine is configured correctly. Another service,

Echo, echoes back to the client any input it receives from the client. The Date service sends back the current date and time on the server and disconnects the connection.

All of these services share one common characteristic. They are trivial to write, and having them in GJAS serves the same purpose as they do for TCP/IP administrators: to verify that GJAS is, in fact, doing what it's supposed to do.

## 10.1.1 SocketClient

Before we dive into the server side of sockets, let's take a second and see how the client side of socket programming looks (listing 10.1). Because connecting to a server socket is universal, the socket client application we build here will be useful in testing any and all socket-based servers we build later in the chapter.

### Listing 10.1   Code for a SocketClient

```
import java.io.*;
import java.net.*;

/**
 * This thread reads from the socket and writes the bytes received to the
 * console window.
 */
class SocketToConsoleThread extends Thread
{
    public SocketToConsoleThread(Socket s)
    {
        m_socket = s;

        setDaemon(true);

        // Necessary to work around some platforms
        setPriority(Thread.currentThread().getPriority()+1);
    }

    public void run()
    {
        try
        {
            // Set up the necessary Reader from the Socket
            Reader fromSocket =
                new InputStreamReader(m_socket.getInputStream());
            // Set up the necessary Writer to the Console window
            Writer toUser =
                new PrintWriter(new OutputStreamWriter(System.out));

            int c;
            char[] buffer = new char[1024];
            while ((c = fromSocket.read(buffer)) != -1)
            {
                toUser.write(buffer, 0, c);
                toUser.flush();
            }
        }
    }
```

```java
        catch (java.io.IOException ioEx)
        {
            ioEx.printStackTrace();
            return;
        }
    }

    Socket m_socket;
}
/**
 * This thread reads from the console window and writes
 * the received keystrokes to the socket.
 */
class ConsoleToSocketThread extends Thread
{
    public ConsoleToSocketThread(Socket s)
    {
        m_socket = s;

        setDaemon(true);
    }

    public void run()
    {
        try
        {
            BufferedReader fromUser =
                new BufferedReader(new InputStreamReader(System.in));
            PrintWriter toSocket =
                new PrintWriter(new OutputStreamWriter(
                    m_socket.getOutputStream()));

            String line;
            while ((line = fromUser.readLine()) != null)
            {
                toSocket.println(line);
                toSocket.flush();
            }
        }
        catch (java.io.IOException ioEx)
        {
            ioEx.printStackTrace();
            return;
        }
    }

    Socket m_socket;
}
/**
 * Client: connect to <host> on port <port>
 */
public class Client
```

```
{
    public static void main(String[] args)
        throws Exception
    {
        if (args.length < 1)
        {
            System.out.println("Usage: java Client <hostname:port>");
            return;
        }

        // Parse out hostname and port
        String host = args[0].substring(0, args[0].indexOf(":"));
        Integer port =
            new Integer(args[0].substring(args[0].indexOf(":")+1,
                                        args[0].length()));

        System.out.println("Connecting to " + host + ":" + port);

        Socket socket = new Socket(host, port.intValue());

        SocketToConsoleThread s2c = new SocketToConsoleThread(socket);
        s2c.start();
        ConsoleToSocketThread c2s = new ConsoleToSocketThread(socket);
        c2s.start();

        s2c.join();
    }
}
```

■

The Client class is the central driver. The ConsoleToSocket class extends java. lang.Thread, [1] and provides a link from the console window's input stream to the connected socket. The SocketToConsole class, in similar fashion, reads from the socket and echoes to the console window's output stream. The SocketToConsole thread has its priority boosted by one due to problems with some JVM implementations that force all threads executing at the same priority level to block if one thread at that same level attempts to read from standard input.[2] Client starts both threads, and then calls join to block until the SocketToConsole thread returns, meaning we'll continue to interact until the Server disconnects from the client.

In fact, this "run-a-Thread-to-pull-from-an-InputStream-and-send-down-an-OutputStream" concept is common enough to merit the design of a specific class to do precisely that (listing 10.2); thus, we create the ThreadedPipeStream class.

---

[1] This would seem to contradict what I say in chapter 5, where I advocate implementing Runnable, instead of extending Thread, but bear with me. This is part of the refinement process.

[2] From *Java Examples in a Nutshell*, by David Flanagan, in the GenericClient.java implementation.

**Listing 10.2   Code for the ThreadedPipeStream Class**

```java
/**
 * ThreadedPipeStream: reads from an InputStream, sends the received
 * data down the given OutputStream.
 */
public class ThreadedPipeStream
    implements Runnable
{
    // Internal data
    private Thread m_thread;
    private InputStream m_from;
    private OutputStream m_to;
    private Exception m_lastException;

    public ThreadedPipeStream(InputStream in,
                              OutputStream out,
                              Thread thread)
    {
        m_thread = thread;
        m_from = in;
        m_to = out;
    }
    public ThreadedPipeStream(InputStream in,
                              OutputStream out)
    {
        m_from = in;
        m_to = out;

        // Create our Thread
        m_thread = new Thread(this);
        m_thread.setDaemon(true);
        m_thread.setName(toString());
        m_thread.setPriority(Thread.currentThread().getPriority()+1);
    }

    /**
     * Convenience method to save from having to reimplement all the
     * Thread methods: start(), stop(), resume(), interrupt(), and
     * so forth. Should probably put those methods in here at some
     * point.
     */
    public Thread getThread()
    {
        return m_thread;
    }

    public String toString()
    {
        return new String("ThreadedPipeStream:" +
                          m_from.toString() + ":" +
                          m_to.toString());
    }
```

```
        public void run()
        {
            try
            {
                // Set up the necessary Reader from the Socket
                Reader from =
                    new InputStreamReader(m_from);
                // Set up the necessary Writer to the Console window
                Writer to =
                    new PrintWriter(m_to);

                int c;
                char[] buffer = new char[1024];
                while ((c = from.read(buffer)) != -1)
                {
                    to.write(buffer, 0, c);
                    to.flush();
                }
            }
            catch (IOException ioEx)
            {
                m_lastException = ioEx;
                ioEx.printStackTrace();
            }
        }
    }
```

ThreadedPipeStream allows for a certain amount of flexibility in its implementation; by allowing users to specify the Thread to use, we can hook in to any custom Thread-processing scheme the client has going; if no explicit Thread is provided, Threaded-PipeStream creates its own. By using InputStream and OutputStream as the source and destination to use, we also make it possible to use any of the Java I/O types as source or sink, whether it be Socket, Console, or anything else. This, in turn, makes the Client implementation much simpler:

```
/**
 * Client: connect to <host> on port <port>
 *
 * Componentized implementation
 */
public class Client
{
    public static void main(String[] args)
        throws Exception
    {
        if (args.length < 1)
        {
            System.out.println("Usage: java Client <hostname:port>");
            return;
        }
```

```
            // Parse out hostname and port
            String host;
            Integer port;
            host = args[0].substring(0, args[0].indexOf(":"));
            port = new Integer(args[0].substring(args[0].indexOf(":")+1,
                                             args[0].length()));

            System.out.println("Connecting to " + host + ":" + port);

            Socket socket = new Socket(host, port.intValue());

            ThreadedPipeStream socketToConsole =
                new ThreadedPipeStream(socket.getInputStream(),
                                   System.out);
            socketToConsole.getThread().start();

            ThreadedPipeStream consoleToSocket =
                new ThreadedPipeStream(System.in,
                                   socket.getOutputStream());
            consoleToSocket.getThread().start();

            socketToConsole.getThread().join();
        }
    }
```

Once again, the act of creating a reusable component in turn leads to less development required later: zero development at its finest. We'll use this class (and this concept of feeding an OutputStream with the contents of an InputStream) again later.

To test, run the Client against a well-known web server on port 80, one such as this book's support web site (www.javageeks.com) or Manning's web site (www.manning.com). If you type in the HTTP header sent by the client (see later in this chapter), you should get back the full HTML file for that URL.

## 10.1.2 EchoService

Listing 10.3 demonstrates how an Echo-like service looks inside the GJAS system.

**Listing 10.3   Code for EchoService**

```
/**
 * EchoService simply echoes back the input it receives to the client.
 */
public class EchoService
    extends com.javageeks.gjas.services.ThreadedServer
    implements Runnable
{
    public void start()
        throws Exception
    {
        setRunnable(this);

        super.start();
    }
```

```java
    public void run()
    {
        try
        {
            ServerSocket svrSocket = new ServerSocket(7);

            Socket socket;
            while ((socket = svrSocket.accept()) != null)
            {
                ServerManager.instance().log("Socket accepted");

                Reader fromSocket =
                    new InputStreamReader(socket.getInputStream());
                Writer toSocket =
                    new OutputStreamWriter(socket.getOutputStream());

                try
                {
                    char[] buffer = new char[1024];
                    int c;
                    while ((c = fromSocket.read(buffer)) != -1)
                    {
                        toSocket.write(buffer, 0, c);
                        toSocket.flush();
                    }
                }
                catch (Exception ex)
                { }

                socket.close();

                ServerManager.instance().log("Socket closed");
            }
        }
        catch (java.io.IOException ioEx)
        {
            ioEx.printStackTrace();
            return;
        }
    }
}
```

The implementation of the EchoService is straightforward. In start, we simply call the ThreadedServer's setRunnable method with this as the parameter. Then, when the ThreadedServer calls the associated start method, control passes to our run method. In that, we create a ServerSocket on port 7 (the RFC-mandated port), we enter an infinite loop, blocking inside the ServerSocket's accept call until a new connection from a client comes in and we return with a new Socket instance. We set up a Writer to point to the OutputStream of the Socket, a Reader to pull from the InputStream of the Socket, then enter a new while loop to pull input from the client and write it back down the socket until the client terminates the connection. When that happens, we close the Socket and return.

This is not the world's most scalable implementation of the Echo service. Specifically, any requests for the Echo service that come in while the service is already occupied with a previous client will block until the first client terminates the connection. This means that we cannot service more than one Echo connection at a time, which is obviously not a scalable solution.

### 10.1.3 TimeService

TimeService is another easy service to implement:

```
/**
 * TimeService simply echoes back the input it receives to the client.
 */
public class TimeService extends ThreadedServer
    implements Runnable
{
    public void start()
        throws Exception
    {
        setRunnable(this);

        super.start();
    }

    public void run()
    {
        try
        {
            ServerSocket svrSocket = new ServerSocket(7002);

            Socket socket;
            while ((socket = svrSocket.accept()) != null)
            {
                ServerManager.instance().log("Socket accepted");

                Reader fromSocket =
                    new InputStreamReader(socket.getInputStream());
                PrintWriter toSocket =
                    new PrintWriter(
                        new OutputStreamWriter(
                            socket.getOutputStream()));

                toSocket.println(new Date());
                    // Date's default constructor constructs a Date
                    // with the current date/time; Date.toString()
                    // converts the date/time to readable format
                toSocket.flush();

                socket.close();

                ServerManager.instance().log("Socket closed");
            }
        }
        catch (java.io.IOException ioEx)
```

```
        {
            ioEx.printStackTrace();
            return;
        }
    }
}
```

TimeService is even less work than the EchoService, since we don't need to keep the Socket connection alive until the client quits. After the service sends the current date and time on the server, we close the Socket and wait for the next connection.

Here, as with EchoService, you can see that the TimeService is also inherently non-scalable. As with EchoService, we can only handle one concurrent connection, forcing any others to block until we're finished with the first. Unlike EchoService, however, chances are small (until we get into a large number of attempted concurrent connections) that we will actually have a performance problem, due to the speed with which we can deal with each connection—just get the date, send it down the Socket, and close.

### 10.1.4 Analysis

This also demonstrates an important difference between two approaches to sockets programming: dedicated and stateless. The EchoService is a dedicated service in that so long as the client remains connected to the Socket, we service one, and only one, client. More sophisticated dedicated services would maintain some form of state on behalf of the client, in a one-to-one fashion. This approach carries the advantage of being simple to understand, and offers the best performance on behalf of each connected client. No waiting necessary.

TimeService, on the other hand, simply services the client request and disconnects. If the client wishes the time on the server again, the client must reconnect to the TimeService on a new connection. One drawback to this approach is that if there is any context that must be maintained across requests, the client must track it and resend it on each new request. This is, in turn, offset by the fact that most stateless protocols are more scalable (they spend no time idling, waiting for additional client requests), as well as more efficient (a single TimeService instance can provide services for a large number of clients before requiring another TimeService instance to assist).

To see the difference, let's draw an analogy.[3] You are a business traveler planning a trip. In a dedicated service, you have a plane that is for your use only. You can command it to go anywhere, you can leave your bags on board, and you can have the pilot make the odd trip for you while you're meeting with clients. But the plane remains dedicated to your use only. As convenient as this is, it does not scale well when compared to stateless services—the use of commercial airlines or taxicabs. The first offers more direct control to the client (you), but it requires that the resource (the object

---

[3] Analogy loosely borrowed from Roger Sessions COM and DCOM: Microsoft's vision for *Distributed Objects* (John Wiley and Sons, 1997).

server, the limousine, the private plane) sit idle during those times when the client is not using it. To draw out the final comparison, the private plane will get you from A to B faster, since it doesn't make any additional stops along the way, but it requires one plane per customer. At that ratio, most commercial airlines would be bankrupt long before they were able to move 100 people across the country, the way they do now with jumbo jets and fixed routes.

One thing you might have noticed as we moved through these admittedly simple services is that much of the code for both looked alike. For example, the only real difference between EchoService and TimeService was this sequence of lines in the run methods:

```
// EchoService.run:
try
{
    char[] buffer = new char[1024];
    int c;
    while ((c = fromSocket.read(buffer)) != -1)
    {
        toSocket.write(buffer, 0, c);
        toSocket.flush();
    }
}
catch (Exception ex)
{ }

// TimeService.run:
toSocket.println(new Date());
toSocket.flush();
```

Any time this is apparent, it means there has to be some way of refactoring code out to a base class or a component.

## 10.2  ENCAPSULATION AND REFACTORING

As you probably guessed, we can elevate some common tasks into a base class. Lacking any real originality, I choose to call this base class SocketServer, not to be confused with the `java.net` class ServerSocket; the first is the ThreadedServer-derivative class that provides base functionality for sockets-based services; the second is a socket that receives client connections and hands back Socket instances for use.[4]

### 10.2.1  SocketServer

Realistically, SocketServer needs only one piece of information (the port number which with to initialize the ServerSocket) and requires only one customization of its clients (what to do once the client connects). We express this in two ways: for the first, we provide a constructor that takes the port as an argument as well as `get/set` methods to manipulate it, and for the second, we create an abstract method that derivatives

---

[4]  SocketServer encapsulates most of the need for clients or Service-writers to deal with ServerSockets.

must implement in order to compile. We extend ThreadedServer (from chapter 4) to allow the ServerSocket (listing 10.4) to block without concern for the main thread. Because the support and/or overhead for creating the thread can be encapsulated in the base class, derived classes have to focus only on the actual socket functionality.

---

**Listing 10.4   Code for SocketServer**

```
package com.javageeks.gjas.services;

import com.javageeks.gjas.ServerManager;
import com.javageeks.gjas.ConfigProperties;
import com.javageeks.gjas.ConfigProperty;
import java.io.*;
import java.net.*;
import java.util.*;

/**
 * SocketServer: abstract base class refactoring common behavior when
 * writing a service to handle clients via sockets. Derived Services
 * are expected to override serve and provide a port number
 * to use as our server socket either via the setPort
 * method or via a "port" property to setConfigInfo
 */
public abstract class SocketServer extends ThreadedServer
{
    // Nested Runnable class
    class SocketServerRunner
        implements Runnable
    {
        public void run()
        {
            Socket socket = null;

            // Start our (nearly) infinite loop waiting for connection
            // requests from clients
            //
            while (true) //(!Thread.currentThread().isInterrupted())
            {
                try
                {
                    socket = m_serverSocket.accept();

                    ServerManager.log(
                        getClass().getName() + ": Socket accepted");

                    // Calling getInetAddress() can cause machines
                    // not on a network to block for up to 15 minutes
                    // due to a "feature" within Microsoft's implementation
                    // of sockets. If your machine is on a TCP/IP network,
                    // comment out the following lines for a bit more
                    // information in the log regarding the connection.
                    //
                    //ServerManager.instance().log(
```

```java
//     getClass().getName() + ":" +
//     "Socket accepted from " +
//     socket.getInetAddress());

            // Pass it to the derived class
            serve(socket);

            // Derived class is responsible for closing it, since
            // if we close it, deriveds won't be able to deal with
            // the socket in a separate thread, if they so choose.
        }
        catch (InterruptedIOException ex)
        {
            if (shouldStop())
                return;
            else
                continue;
        }
        catch (Throwable t)
        {
            ServerManager.log(
                "Exception thrown from serve() on socket " +
                socket + ":");
            ServerManager.log(t.toString());
        }
    }
}

// Constants
//
protected static final String PORT_PROP = "port";
protected static final String TIMEOUT_PROP = "timeout";

// Internal data
//
protected ServerSocket m_serverSocket;

private ConfigProperty propPort =
    new ConfigProperty(PORT_PROP,
                    new Integer(0),
                    "TCP/IP socket to use");
private ConfigProperty propTimeout =
    new ConfigProperty(TIMEOUT_PROP,
                    new Integer(5 * 1000),
                    "Milliseconds before " +
                    "hanging up on client");

private ConfigProperties configInfo =
    new ConfigProperties(new ConfigProperty[]
    {
        propTimeout,
        propPort
    });
```

```java
/**
 * Constructor, taking no arguments. The port number on which to
 * listen must be specified (either through the args argument to
 * start or via setPort).
 */
public SocketServer()
{
    // Do nothing
}
/**
 * Constructor, taking the port number on which to listen as the
 * sole argument.
 */
public SocketServer(int port)
{
    setPort(port);
}

/**
 * Start the SocketServer
 */
public void start()
    throws Exception
{
    setState(STARTING);

    int port = ((Integer)propPort.getValue()).intValue();
    int timeout = ((Number)propTimeout.getValue()).intValue();

    // We've GOT to have a port # by now, or we can't create
    // the ServerSocket.
    if (port == 0)
        throw new java.net.ConnectException(
            "SocketServer must have a port argument!");

    ServerManager.log(
        getClass().getName() + ".start(): " +
        "Opening ServerSocket on port " + port);
    m_serverSocket = new ServerSocket(port);

    // Configure the ServerSocket so we don't block indefinitely
    // inside of accept()
    try
    {
        m_serverSocket.setSoTimeout(timeout);
            // Only wait for m_timeout milliseconds before coming back
    }
    catch(SocketException ex)
    {
        ServerManager.log(ex);
        return;
    }
    catch (IOException ex)
    {
```

```
                ServerManager.log(ex);
        }

        // Set the Runnable instance
        //
        setRunnable(new SocketServerRunner());

        // Call up to the base class (ThreadedServer) to let it do
        // its ancestor thing
        //
        super.start();
}
/**
 *
 */
public void stop()
    throws Exception
{

    // First call up the chain, to make the Thread (in which
    // we're listening to the ServerSocket) stop.
    super.stop();

    // Close the ServerSocket
    m_serverSocket.close();

}

// pause() and resume() are a little poorly defined here; if
// we have pause() and resume() close and reopen the socket,
// respectively, they have no differentiation from start()
// and stop(). On top of that, ThreadedServer already defines
// pause() and resume() to pause and resume the Thread, so
// additional redefinition would seem to be unnecessary
// here.

/**
 *
 */
public ConfigProperties getConfigInfo()
{
    return configInfo;
}
/**
 *
 */
public void setConfigInfo(ConfigProperties props)
{
    // We need to do a couple of things here; if the port or
    // the timeout values change, we need to shut down the
    // socket and open it again using the new values
    if (((Integer)configInfo.get(PORT_PROP).getValue()).intValue() !=
        ((Integer)props.get(PORT_PROP).getValue()).intValue() ||
        ((Number)configInfo.get(TIMEOUT_PROP).getValue()).intValue() !=
        ((Number)configInfo.get(TIMEOUT_PROP).getValue()).intValue())
    {
```

```
            try
            {
                ServerManager.log("Stopping Service: reconfigure");
                stop();

                // Read the new values
                ServerManager.log("Re-reading config values");
                configInfo.set(props);

                // Restart the Service
                ServerManager.log("Restarting Service");
                start();
            }
            catch (Exception ex)
            {
                ServerManager.error(ex);
            }
        }
    }

    /**
     * Return the port we accept clients on.
     */
    public int getPort()
    {
        return ((Integer)propPort.getValue()).intValue();
    }
    /**
     * Set the port number we plan to accept clients on; has no effect
     * after the service is started.
     */
    public void setPort(int newPort)
    {
        propPort.setValue(new Integer(newPort));
    }

    /**
     * Derived services must override this method. Once a client has
     * connected to us, this method is called to "do the work" of
     * handling the connection.
     */
    public abstract void serve(Socket socket)
        throws Exception;
}
```

SocketServer is a fairly straightforward implementation, but it's the most complex of the ones we've done so far, so a few moments to explain precisely what's going on within its various parts is necessary.

To start with, notice that SocketServer uses two ConfigProperty instances to represent the port on which we are to listen, as well as the timeout period before giving up on the client and closing the Socket. These are both specified as Integers, although any Number-extending class would work, since Number provides an `intValue` method.[5] Note also that within the SocketServer's `setConfigInfo` method, we stop the SocketServer, copy over the new values passed in, then re-start the Server. This is precisely what we intended to happen when we designed the whole Configuration system. The Service gets its new values, and can either reread them on the fly, or stop/reread/restart, as necessary for each Service.

SocketServer also specifies two constructors. One is the standard default constructor; the other is a constructor intended for subclasses to call within their own constructors, allowing for convenient setting of the port property. Nothing prevents a derived Service from calling SocketServer's base constructor and later either calling SocketServer's `setPort` method directly, or else modifying the value through `setConfigInfo`, but this provides a simple way to configure the port for listening.

SocketServer's `start` method, however, is by far the most interesting part of the class. It first extracts the port and timeout values from its configuration information. Should port be zero (which indicates it wasn't specified by either the Service class or the system administrator before starting), there's nothing SocketServer can do. We can't continue. We throw a `java.net.ConnectException` indicating why we threw it. In a more interactive system, we would probably make this its own type of Exception class, but I choose not to for a reason.

Normally, when an Exception is thrown, it falls into one of two categories: either the client can do something about it, or the client can't. Exceptions that can be handled include such as improper URL specifications, improper filenames, and so forth. In those situations, the client can reasonably catch the exception, and deduce from the type whether it can correct the problem. For example, with a FileNotFoundException, the code can pop up a dialog to the user asking if the filename is correct, and would the user like to create a new file. With a MalformedURLException, we can again query the user if the URL is correct.

With this, however, there's not much we can do—we can't expect ServerManager to be able to correct the action (it's not supposed to know anything about the Service), so the actual type of Exception thrown is fairly irrelevant. It's not going to try to undertake corrective action based on the type, as we would in client code. So we throw a type that's close enough, and continue.

Once the ServerSocket is created, we then call the `ThreadedServer.setRunnable` method with an instance of the inner Runnable class SocketServerRunner, whose `run` method spins in an infinite `while` loop blocking on `accept`. As each request comes in, it passes the local Socket off to an abstract method called `serve`. Note that we could pass in the InputStream and OutputStream from Socket instead

---

[5]  The semantics of the java.lang.Number class say that an `int` will be returned from `intValue`, and that so long as a class honors Number's interface, we're okay in using it for port values.

of the Socket itself, but Socket carries with it some information for which derived classes might have a use, and it's marginally simpler to pass in the Socket instead of the I/O streams.

We mark `serve` as abstract because I don't want to have a default implementation for it. The whole point of SocketServer is to serve as an implementation-inheritance base class; creating a SocketServer on its own would be pointless. We could create a Serveable interface, with the `serve` method as its own method, and take one of those in the SocketServer constructor, instead of using implementation-inheritance. Doing so would be more awkward, since specifying the name of the service to load (through the configuration information) would also have to have the name of the Serveable instance to create at the same time. Nevertheless, there are some definite advantages to this approach, and we'll do something just like this in the next section.

## 10.2.2     Example: Echo2Service

Let's see what EchoService looks like now that we've refactored some of the scaffolding code regarding sockets into the base SocketServer class:

```
import java.io.*;
import java.net.Socket;

public class Echo2Service
    extends com.javageeks.gjas.services.SocketServer
{
    public Echo2Service()
    {
        super(7);
    }

    /**
     * Handle a connection
     */
    public void serve(Socket socket)
        throws Exception
    {
        Reader fromSocket =
            new InputStreamReader(socket.getInputStream());
        Writer toSocket =
            new OutputStreamWriter(socket.getOutputStream());

        char[] buffer = new char[1024];
        int c;
        while ((c = fromSocket.read(buffer)) != -1)
        {
            toSocket.write(buffer, 0, c);
            toSocket.flush();
        }
    }
}
```

If you compare this version to the version a few pages back, we've added functionality—not only can we specify one via SocketServer's default configuration information handling, but we default to 7 if one isn't specified—while reducing the number of lines in the code. This is definitely moving in the right direction.

## 10.3  CONNECTION AND CONNECTIONMANAGER

SocketServer suffers from the same problem as its predecessors. Because it is executing within its own thread, each request is serialized. We must finish with the first request before we can move on the next. This is no good, especially when dealing with dedicated Services like EchoService. We've effectively undone all our hard work putting Threads into the system to go right back to a single-client system, at least at the Socket level.

Before we dive into the code, let me describe precisely what is being built. ConnectionManager (listing 10.5) will create Connection instances, just as ServerManager creates Service instances. The idea is that if a user creates a class that implements Connection, we can plug them into ConnectionManager just as we plug Service-implementing classes into ServerManager and it all just works. ConnectionManager will farm out each Connection to a separate Thread in order to achieve parallelization of client responses, up to a user-definable set number of Threads (in order to prevent denial-of-service attacks from crippling the entire JVM). ConnectionManager will also, therefore, be responsible for shutting down these Connections (if necessary) when the stop request comes through.[6]

Once ServerManager creates the ConnectionManager instance, ConnectionManager must now obtain three pieces of information in order to continue, two of which are vital to its ability to function. First, it needs to know the port number on which to listen (required), and it needs to know the name of the Class to instantiate in order to handle the client request (also required). Optionally, it also has a threads argument, which indicates the number of threads to create in the thread pool for Connections. If no argument is specified, then it is assumed that an infinite number of Threads can be created, which is dangerous in any but the most secure and trustworthy environments. In addition, because the loading of the Connection-implementing class is critical if ConnectionManager is to support the whole load-on-the-fly support from chapter 2, we also provide an optional loader property, which is a ClassLoaderStrategy instance to use to load the Connection class when starting.

---

[6]  In the source code available on the publisher's web site, this is actually not implemented, since most of these Services are stateless anyway, and will not require more than a second or two to complete. However, ConnectionManager is still responsible for the Connections it maintains. If you write a Connection that takes longer (and won't seriously muck things up if you kill it halfway through, which is the other reason I didn't implement it), then you need to have `ConnectionManager.stop` iterate across each Thread and call `stop` on it.

Got it? Let's take a look at the code, then:

**Listing 10.5 Code for ConnectionManager**

```
package com.javageeks.gjas.services;

import com.javageeks.gjas.*;
import com.javageeks.classloader.ClassLoaderStrategy;
import com.javageeks.classloader.StrategyClassLoader;
import EDU.oswego.cs.dl.util.concurrent.Callable;
import EDU.oswego.cs.dl.util.concurrent.Executor;
import EDU.oswego.cs.dl.util.concurrent.ThreadFactory;
import EDU.oswego.cs.dl.util.concurrent.ThreadFactoryUser;
import EDU.oswego.cs.dl.util.concurrent.PooledExecutor;
import EDU.oswego.cs.dl.util.concurrent.ThreadedExecutor;
import EDU.oswego.cs.dl.util.concurrent.DirectExecutor;
import java.io.InputStream;
import java.io.OutputStream;
import java.io.IOException;
import java.net.ServerSocket;
import java.net.Socket;
import java.util.Vector;

/**
 * ConnectionAdapter is an Adapter (see the GOF book) class that ties
 * together a Connection instance and a Thread to run it in. Java purists
 * will immediately cringe at the use of the non-private member fields in
 * this class, and claim that they should be initialized via a constructor
 * instead of by direct manipulation (see run() in ConnectionManager). I
 * won't argue that they could be initialized that way. However, because
 * ConnectionAdapter isn't intended as a reusable component, but as an
 * integral part of the ConnectionManager component (it began life as an
 * anonymous class inside of ConnectionManager, that's how tightly these
 * two are tied together), and therefore subject to some relaxation of the
 * "normal" rules regarding encapsulation.
 *
 * One interesting trick it makes use of is the "Runnable finish;" field.
 * ConnectionManager sets this field to an anonymous Runnable class instance
 * that ConnectionAdapter must call before it shuts down completely; this
 * is what helps ConnectionManager keep track of the Connections still
 * outstanding. I could have, certainly, simply exposed the m_connections
 * Vector in ConnectionManager through methods like "add(Connection c)" and
 * "remove(Connection c)", but even then there could be more than one
 * ConnectionManager running, so I would have had to have a ConnectionManager
 * reference in ConnectionAdapter, as well. This is more elegant, in my
 * opinion, and keeps the "cleanup" logic in the precise place where it
 * should be--in the ConnectionManager class code.
 */
class ConnectionAdapter
    implements Runnable
{
```

```
    public void run()
    {
        try
        {
            connection.serve(socket);

            socket.close();

            finish.run();
        }
        catch (InterruptedException intEx)
        {
            // Do nothing
        }
        catch (Exception ex)
        {
            ServerManager.instance().log(ex);
        }
        finally
        {
            // Close the Socket
            try { socket.close(); }
            catch(java.io.IOException ioEx) { }

            ServerManager.instance().log(
                getClass().getName() + ":" +
                "Socket closed");
        }
    }

    Connection connection;
    Socket socket;
    Runnable finish;
}

/**
 * ConnectionManager is a ThreadedServer that specifically manages a single
 * type of socket connection between this host and some anonymous client.
 */
public class ConnectionManager extends SocketServer
{
    // Internal members
    //
    private Executor m_executor = null;
    private Vector m_connections = new Vector();
    private Class m_connectionClass = null;
    private static int s_count = 0;

    private ConfigProperty propThreads =
        new ConfigProperty("threads", new Integer(1),
                           "Maximum number of threads to use");
    private ConfigProperty propType =
        new ConfigProperty("type", new String(""),
                           "Connection class to use");
    private ConfigProperty propLoader =
```

```
                new ConfigProperty("loader", ClassLoaderStrategy.class,
                            null, null,
                            "ClassLoaderStrategy instance to use " +
                            "to load Connection instances",
                            null);
    private ConfigProperties m_configInfo =
        new ConfigProperties(super.getConfigInfo(), new ConfigProperty[]
    {
        propThreads,
        propType,
        propLoader
    });

    /**
     * Start the Service.
     */
    public void start()
        throws Exception
    {
        setState(STARTING);

        ServerManager.log(
            "ConnectionManager: Loaded by " +
            getClass().getClassLoader().getClass().getName());

        // Determine which Executor to use; unless the "threads"
        // ConfigProperty has been modified, we default to using
        // a ThreadedExecutor
        switch (((Integer)propThreads.getValue()).intValue())
        {
            case 0:
                m_executor = new ThreadedExecutor();
                break;
            case 1:
                m_executor = new DirectExecutor();
                break;
            default:
                Integer numThreads =
                    (Integer)propThreads.getValue();
                m_executor =
                    new PooledExecutor(numThreads.intValue());
                ((PooledExecutor)m_executor).waitWhenBlocked();
                break;
        }
        ServerManager.log(getClass().getName() + ": " +
            "Executor: " + m_executor.toString());

        // Determine Connection Class to use
        String name = (String)propType.getValue();
        if (name.equals(""))
        {
            throw new Exception("You must specify a \"type\" " +
                "argument to ConnectionManager");
```

```
            }
            else
            {
                ServerManager.log(
                    getClass().getName() + ": Using " +
                    name + " as Connection type");

                // Determine if we've been given a specialized
                // ClassLoader instance to use; otherwise, just use
                // whatever ClassLoader loaded us
                ClassLoaderStrategy strat =
                    (ClassLoaderStrategy)propLoader.getValue();
                if (strat == null)
                {
                    ServerManager.log(
                        getClass().getName() + ": Using " +
                        getClass().getClassLoader().getClass().getName()
                        + " as ClassLoader for " + name);
                    m_connectionClass = Class.forName(name);
                }
                else
                {
                    ServerManager.log(
                        getClass().getName() + ": Using " +
                        strat.getClass().getName() + " as ClassLoader " +
                        "for " + name);

                    StrategyClassLoader scl =
                        new StrategyClassLoader(strat);
                    m_connectionClass = scl.loadClass(name);
                }
            }

        // Create a ThreadFactory that gives us a bit more
        // information in the Thread label; useful for tracing and
        // debugging. We only need to do this where we're using
        // Threads other than the 'main' Thread. (Both
        // ThreadedExecutor and PooledExecutor are ThreadFactoryUser-
        // implementing classes.)
        if (m_executor instanceof ThreadFactoryUser)
        {
            ((ThreadFactoryUser)m_executor).setThreadFactory(
                new ThreadFactory()
                {
                    public Thread newThread(Runnable cmd)
                    {
                        return new Thread(cmd,
                            m_connectionClass.getName() + s_count++);
                    }
                });
        }

        // Call up the chain so SocketServer can do its thing
        super.start();
```

```
        }
        /**
         *
         */
        public ConfigProperties getConfigInfo()
        {
            return m_configInfo;
        }
        /**
         *
         */
        public void setConfigInfo(ConfigProperties props)
        {
            m_configInfo.set(props);
        }

        /**
         *
         */
        public void serve(Socket socket)
            throws Exception
        {
            // Create the Connection instance, place it in our list
            final Connection connection =
                (Connection)m_connectionClass.newInstance();
            m_connections.addElement(connection);

            // On each connection, create a new Runnable to be
            // executed within the Executor to do the actual work
            ConnectionAdapter ca = new ConnectionAdapter();
            ca.connection = connection;
            ca.socket = socket;
            ca.finish = new Runnable()
            {
                public void run()
                {
                    m_connections.removeElement(connection);
                }
            };
                // The "finish" Runnable in ConnectionAdapter
                // provides a Java-acceptable way of performing
                // a callback into this object to remove the
                // Connection object without having to (a) expose
                // the m_connections Vector to outside use via
                // "add" and/or "remove" methods, or (b) make
                // the m_connections Vector package-available
                // by reducing the 'private' access specifier to
                // '' (nothing, which is package access).

            m_executor.execute(ca);
        }
    }
```

Again, as with SocketServer, this class is nontrivial in parts.

First, take a look at the initialization of the ConfigProperties instance for the ConnectionManager class. Because we want to preserve SocketServer's configuration information while at the same time adding our own, we use the ConfigProperties constructor that takes both a ConfigProperties instance and an array of ConfigProperty instances. This then gives ConnectionManager five properties: "port" and "time-out", which SocketServer will recognize and handle, and "threads", "type", and "loader", which ConnectionManager itself will handle. Also, because the "loader" property is a nonbasic type (that is, it's a ClassLoaderStrategy instance, not a String or an Integer), we use the longer form of the ConfigProperty constructor to specify the type independently of the value. We set the value of the "loader" property to be null; this means that the ClassLoader that loaded the ConnectionManager (most likely the Java App/Ext-ClassLoader pair, the bootstrap ClassLoader) will in turn load the Connection-implementing class specified in "type".

Because ConnectionManager is responsible for the threading policy of the connections, it uses Lea's Executor classes to manage its thread pools (or lack thereof). By default, the "threads" property is set to 0, indicating that ConnectionManager is free to fire off a Thread per connect. This is the easiest setting to use, and offers the best performance[7] of the three, but opens up the possibility of denial-of-service attacks by malicious clients; instead, in an untrusted environment, it's far safer to use a maximum number of Threads in a ThreadPool.

In order to better help track down the threads during execution, Connection-Manager has its Executor use a custom ThreadFactory (a simple interface that has only one responsibility—return new Thread objects when asked) in order to set the Thread names to something meaningful. Here, ConnectionManager sets the name of the thread to be that of the Connection type itself plus a static count (to keep the names unique).

On each connection, within the serve method, ConnectionManager creates a new instance of the Connection type, then creates a new ConnectionAdapter instance to go with it. ConnectionAdapter serves as the glue that ties the created Thread and the Connection instance together. It implements Runnable, allowing it to be placed as the target of a Thread, and calls the Connection instance's serve method (and catches any exceptions thrown from there, as well).

ConnectionManager stores each newly created Connection instance in a private Vector called m_connections. However, because ConnectionManager has no way of knowing when the Connection is finished, it cannot remove the Connection instance from the Vector. Instead, ConnectionManager creates an anonymous Runnable instance to call remove on the Vector, and hands this Runnable instance to the

---

[7] Using a fixed number requires some tuning, and using only one thread is certainly less performance-friendly.

ConnectionAdapter. Rather than place the Runnable instance (finish) within a Thread, however, ConnectionAdapter calls its run directly.

This approach may seem odd to some Java programmers. In fact, it's not a common idiom within Java to establish this kind of callback. Some would be tempted to provide addConnection and removeConnection methods to ConnectionManager and have the ConnectionAdapter call those. However, because multiple Connection-Manager instances can be running simultaneously, ConnectionAdapter would have to have a reference to the ConnectionManager that created it in order to call on the correct ConnectionManager. Moreover, it really isn't ConnectionAdapter's responsibility to know what sort of internal bookkeeping ConnectionManager is doing. If, for example, ConnectionManager later wants to track start and stop times for the Connection instances, that's ConnectionManager's business, and has nothing to do with Connection-Adapter. By using this anonymous Runnable instance built within ConnectionManager, the necessary cleanup measures required at the end of a Connection call remain encapsulated within ConnectionManager. Within two tightly coupled classes such as Connection-Manager and ConnectionAdapter, this is likely less of a concern than it would be with less-coupled classes, but it never hurts to still try to practice good encapsulation whenever possible.

That's it for ConnectionManager.

## 10.3.1    Example: EchoConnection

Once we've refactored all that code back into ConnectionManager, however, code in the corresponding service classes, like EchoConnection, should be much, much simpler:

```
public class EchoConnection
    implements Connection
{
    public void serve(Socket socket)
        throws Exception
    {
        Reader fromSocket =
            new InputStreamReader(socket.getInputStream());
        Writer toSocket =
            new OutputStreamWriter(socket.getOutputStream());

        char[] buffer = new char[1024];
        int c;
        while ((c = fromSocket.read(buffer)) != -1)
        {
            toSocket.write(buffer, 0, c);
            toSocket.flush();
        }
    }
}
```

In twenty lines, we now have a socket service that fully implements the Echo service, is scalable, and is trivial to maintain. What's more, we don't have to worry about opening the server port; we can open multiple Echo listeners on different ports,[8] and we can control the number of concurrent requests we can handle, all through parameters to the ConnectionManager's configuration information.

Consider the ramifications of what we've done. We've managed to create a server framework that requires all of twenty lines to implement a Thread-pooled, client-proof, scalable socket-based client/server architecture. What's more, as we'll soon see, it now becomes almost completely trivial to write sophisticated socket-based implementations.

## 10.3.2    Example: HTTPConnection

The true test of the ConnectionManager system comes when we try to implement a more complex protocol. Since everybody is going nuts over the Web and HTTP, let's see just how difficult it is to build an HTTP server. One caveat before we dive into this: We are not going to build a full-fledged, production-quality web server. In addition to being a topic that would require a book in itself, it would be heading in entirely the wrong direction. You can buy (or download for free) web servers if that's all you're looking for. This is simply a demonstration to show you how easily it can be done with the GJAS framework so far (listing 10.5); I'm not suggesting you finish it off, although you could without too much trouble. Given that, however, when we are finished, we will have a 100 percent HTTP 1.0-compliant HTTP server that you can easily extend (or incorporate) into your own projects.

The HTTP 1.0 protocol is a stateless protocol, consisting of client requests and server responses. A client sends a request consisting of a command, the URL, and the HTTP version it expects back, and waits while the server formulates the response. The response consists of a number of headers, followed by a blank line and the content of the resource requested.

Nowhere in this discussion do we ever mention HTML, which may surprise you. HTML and HTTP aren't as tightly integrated as one might suspect. An HTTP server can serve up all kinds of information beyond just HTML pages; XML is one commonly discussed option. The key is that it must be a format the client knows, recognizes, and understands how to present. HTML is perfect for this purpose, but it could easily be anything else, including PDF files, PostScript files, or even script command to be executed on the client.[9]

---

[8] This is another way to achieve scalability. By having the server listen on multiple ports, we reduce to almost nothing the chance of a client not being able to reach a server. Internet Relay Chat servers use this with great success.

[9] Now *there's* a switch. Asking the server to do things on the client? Fully possible, although obviously not from within your standard web browser. What's more, it can make copying files around and doing end-user configuration a snap—just ask users to point their "ScriptClient" to the company intranet and a particular URL, and let the client interpret and execute the returned script. Remember, HTTP is not intrinsically tied to HTML, and could, in fact, be used in a variety of situations for communication.

Once the returning content is identified and ready to send back, we first write a header indicating the HTTP version level we are sending back. In a more feature-filled server, we would examine the HTTP header sent by the client and determine if the client can support our highest-support HTTP version. Since there are only two versions of HTTP, 1.0 and 1.1, and we want to remain tightly focused on the framework, not the HTTP protocol, we only send back HTTP/1.0-compliant information.

After the "HTTP/1.0" string, we send back a return code that complies with the HTTP standard. Codes in the 200 range are generally "OK" codes, 300 range is for relocation or redirection codes, the 400 range is for client errors, and the 500 range is for server errors. In order to make them easily reusable (in case we have code outside of the HttpConnection class that wants to work with these constants), we make them part of the HttpConstants interface, and anybody who wants to use them can simply implement that interface. It's a blatant misuse of the interface concept (at least as it was originally intended, anyway), but it works.

Note that this web server is rudimentary—it offers no POST support (without which HTML forms are pretty useless), no URL parameter support (any parameters will be assumed to be part of the URL file path), no cookie support, just basic file-download and file-system-browsing capabilities. Even so, it provides these capabilities in less than 500 lines of commented Java code, including about 75 constants lines (listing 10.6).

---

**Listing 10.6    Code demonstrating building a web server**

```java
/**
 * A cheap way of doing #defines in Java; just implement this interface
 * (which costs you nothing), and you can refer to them directly
 */
interface HttpConnectionConstants
{
    // 2xx: "OK" response codes
    public static final int HTTP_OK = 200;
    public static final int HTTP_CREATED = 201;
    public static final int HTTP_ACCEPTED = 202;
    public static final int HTTP_NOT_AUTHORITATIVE = 203;
    public static final int HTTP_NO_CONTENT = 204;
    public static final int HTTP_RESET = 205;
    public static final int HTTP_PARTIAL = 206;

    // 3xx: relocation/redirect response codes
    public static final int HTTP_MULT_CHOICE = 300;
    public static final int HTTP_MOVED_PERM = 301;
    public static final int HTTP_MOVED_TEMP = 302;
    public static final int HTTP_SEE_OTHER = 303;
    public static final int HTTP_NOT_MODIFIED = 304;
    public static final int HTTP_USE_PROXY = 305;

    // 4xx: client error codes
    public static final int HTTP_BAD_REQUEST = 400;
    public static final int HTTP_UNAUTHORIZED = 401;
```

```java
        public static final int HTTP_PAYMENT_REQUIRED = 402;
        public static final int HTTP_FORBIDDEN = 403;
        public static final int HTTP_NOT_FOUND = 404;
        public static final int HTTP_BAD_METHOD = 405;
        public static final int HTTP_NOT_ACCEPTABLE = 406;
        public static final int HTTP_PROXY_AUTH = 407;
        public static final int HTTP_CLIENT_TIMEOUT = 408;
        public static final int HTTP_CONFLICT = 409;
        public static final int HTTP_GONE = 410;
        public static final int HTTP_LENGTH_REQUIRED = 411;
        public static final int HTTP_PRECON_FAILED = 412;
        public static final int HTTP_ENTITY_TOO_LARGE = 413;
        public static final int HTTP_REQ_TOO_LONG = 414;
        public static final int HTTP_UNSUPPORTED_TYPE = 415;

        // 5xx: server error codes
        public static final int HTTP_SERVER_ERROR = 500;
        public static final int HTTP_INTERNAL_ERROR = 501;
        public static final int HTTP_BAD_GATEWAY = 502;
        public static final int HTTP_UNAVAILABLE = 503;
        public static final int HTTP_GATEWAY_TIMEOUT = 504;
        public static final int HTTP_VERSION = 505;
}

/**
 * This class provides a simplistic HTTP/1.0 service; it uses only a single
 * root (as opposed to other Web servers, which allow for multiple "virtual
 * roots" in their setup), and offers only the most rudimentary of HTTP
 * protocol services. Because HttpConnection is a transient type (that is,
 * multiple HttpConnection instances will come and go without warning or
 * guarantee), we use static instances to carry expensive resources (like
 * the properties we use) from instance to instance without having to reload
 * them each time.
 *
 * Much of this code is cribbed from the WebServer.java example from the
 * JavaSoft site; however, if you're familiar with that code, you'll notice
 * that this version is much smaller, owing to the fact that GJAS factors out
 * much of the complexity unrelated to HTTP (like thread pools).
 */
public class HttpConnection
    implements Connection, HttpConnectionConstants
{
    static final String EOL = new String(new byte[] { (byte)'\r', (byte)'\n' });

    /**
     *
     */
    public void serve(Socket socket)
        throws Exception
    {
        // Before we even do anything, do we need to abort?
        if (s_exception != null)
            throw s_exception;
```

```java
        // Get streams from the Socket
        InputStream in = socket.getInputStream();
        OutputStream out = socket.getOutputStream();

        // Pick apart the URL sent; we only want the first line, really
        Properties headers = new Properties();  // HTTP headers we send back

        try
        {
            // Pick out the request, load the content and the headers
            parseRequest(in, headers);

            // Send back our HTTP/1.0 response
            sendResponse(out, headers);
        }
        catch (Exception ex)
        {
            // Send the server error back to the client
            sendError(HTTP_SERVER_ERROR, ex.toString(), headers);
            throw ex;
        }
        finally
        {
            // Send it back down the stream
            out.flush();
            in.close();
            out.close();
        }
    }

    /**
     *
     */
    public void parseRequest(InputStream in, Properties headers)
        throws IOException
    {
        headers.put("_HTTPVersion", "1.0");
        headers.put("Server", "GJAS-HttpConnection/1.0");
        headers.put("Date", new Date());

        // Pick out the command & URL in the incoming request
        BufferedReader reader =
            new BufferedReader(new InputStreamReader(in));
        String line;
        String clientCommand = null;
        while ((line = reader.readLine()) != null)
        {
            if (line.startsWith("GET"))
            {
                clientCommand = line;
                break;
            }
        }
        if (clientCommand == null)
```

```
{
    sendError(HTTP_BAD_METHOD, "Server only supports GET", headers);
    return;
}

// Pick out the command & URL
String URL = clientCommand.substring(4);
URL = URL.substring(0, URL.indexOf(" "));

// Turn the URL into a local filename
File target;
if (URL.equals("/"))
{
    target = new File(s_root.getCanonicalPath());
}
else
{
    String filename = new String(URL.replace('/', File.separatorChar));
    if (filename.startsWith(File.separator))
        filename = filename.substring(1);
    target = new File(s_root, filename);
}

// Find file/directory
if (!target.exists())
{
    sendError(HTTP_BAD_REQUEST, "URL '" + URL + "' not found", headers);
    return;
}
if (target.isDirectory())
{
    File targetIndex = new File(target, "index.html");

    if (targetIndex.exists())
    {
        // Send the file back
        target = targetIndex;

        headers.put("_ReturnCode", HTTP_OK + " OK");
        headers.put("_Content", new FileInputStream(target));
        headers.put("Last-modified", new Date(target.lastModified()));
        headers.put("Content-length", new Long(target.length()));
        headers.put("Content-type", "text/html");
    }
    else
    {
        // Send the contents of the directory back
        String html = listDirectory(URL, target);
        headers.put("_ReturnCode", HTTP_OK + " OK");
        headers.put("_Content",
            new ByteArrayInputStream(html.getBytes()));
        headers.put("Last-modified", new Date());
        headers.put("Content-length", new Long(html.length()));
        headers.put("Content-type", "text/html");
```

```
            }
        }
        else
        {
            // Send the file back
            headers.put("_ReturnCode", HTTP_OK + " OK");
            headers.put("_Content", new FileInputStream(target));
            headers.put("Last-modified", new Date(target.lastModified()));
            headers.put("Content-length", new Long(target.length()));
            String fname = target.getName();
            int ind = fname.lastIndexOf('.');
            if (ind > 0)
                headers.put("Content-type",
                            s_suffixMap.get(fname.substring(ind)));
            else
                headers.put("Content-type", "unknown/unknown");
        }
    }
    private void sendError(int errCode, String errText, Properties headers)
    {
        headers.put("_ReturnCode", errCode + " " + errText);
    }
    private String listDirectory(String URL, File dir)
        throws IOException
    {
        StringBuffer ret = new StringBuffer();

        // Header information
        ret.append("<TITLE>Directory of " + URL + "</TITLE>" + "\n<P>\n");

        if (!dir.getCanonicalPath().equals(s_root.getCanonicalPath()))
            ret.append("<A HREF=\"..\">Up one directory</A><BR>\n<P>\n\n");

        // Print list of files
        String[] list = dir.list();
        for (int i=0; list != null && i<list.length; i++)
        {
            File item = new File(dir, list[i]);
            if (item.isDirectory())
            {
                ret.append("<A HREF=\"" + URL + list[i] + "/\">" +
                    list[i] + "/</A><BR>\n");
            }
            else
            {
                ret.append("<A HREF=\"" + URL + list[i] + "\">" +
                    list[i] + "</A><BR>\n");
            }
        }

        // Print trailer
        ret.append("<P><HR><BR><I>" + new Date() + "</I><BR>");
        ret.append("<I>Generated by the Generic Java Application Server, " +
```

```
                getClass().getName() + " service</I>");

        return new String(ret);
    }

    /**
     *
     */
    public void sendResponse(OutputStream os, Properties headers)
        throws IOException
    {
        PrintWriter pw = new PrintWriter(os);

        // Send HTTP/1.0 <retCode> <text> line
        pw.print("HTTP/" + headers.get("_HTTPVersion") + " " +
            headers.get("_ReturnCode"));
        pw.write(EOL);

        // Send headers, one at a time
        for (Enumeration enum = headers.propertyNames();
            enum.hasMoreElements(); )
        {
            String key = (String)enum.nextElement();

            // Skip the lines starting with an underscore; those are for
            // HttpConnection internal use only
            if (key.startsWith("_"))
                continue;

            // Otherwise, print the key, a colon, the property, and an EOL
            pw.print(key + ": " + headers.get(key) + EOL);
        }

        // Write blank line after headers to mark end of headers section
        pw.write(EOL);
        pw.flush();

        // Read the content from the specified InputStream, and send it down
        InputStream content = (InputStream)headers.get("_Content");
        if (content != null)
        {
            byte[] buffer = new byte[1024];
            int nRead = 0;
            while ((nRead = content.read(buffer)) != -1)
                //pw.print(new String(buffer, 0, nRead));
                os.write(buffer, 0, nRead);

            // Write one more blank line, just for luck
            pw.write(EOL);
        }

        // Ba-whoosh!
        pw.flush();
    }

    // Internal members
```

```
    //
    private static Exception s_exception = null;
        // Reserved solely for exceptions generated from the static init block
    private static Properties s_properties = null;
    private static File s_root = null;
    private static Hashtable s_suffixMap = new Hashtable();

    // Internal methods
    //
    /**
     * Static initializer block--executed when this class is loaded into its
     * namespace.
     */
    static
    {
        // Load the s_properties instance with our http-properties file
        loadProperties();
        // Fill the suffix map with well-known file types
        fillMap();
    }

    /**
     *
     */
    private static void loadProperties()
    {
        try
        {
            // Load the properties from disk
            s_properties = new Properties();
            InputStream propFileStream;
            try
            {
                propFileStream = new FileInputStream(".http-properties");
                s_properties.load(propFileStream);
                s_properties.list(System.out);
                propFileStream.close();
            }
            catch (IOException ioEx)
            { }

            // Set up our instance data from the Properties read in
            String r = s_properties.getProperty("http-root");
            if (r != null)
            {
                s_root = new File(r);
                if (!s_root.exists())
                {
                    //s_exception =
                        new FileNotFoundException("Root doesn't exist!");
                    s_root = null;
                }
            }
```

```java
            // Use defaults
            if (s_root == null)
                s_root = new File(System.getProperty("user.dir"));

            ServerManager.instance().log(
                HttpConnection.class.getName() + ": http-root = " +
                s_root.getCanonicalPath());
        }
    catch (IOException ioEx)
    {
        // Nothing to do, so just move on
        s_exception = ioEx;
        ServerManager.instance().log(ioEx);
    }
}
/**
 *
 */
private static void fillMap()
{
    s_suffixMap.put("", "content/unknown");
    s_suffixMap.put(".uu", "application/octet-stream");
    s_suffixMap.put(".exe", "application/octet-stream");
    s_suffixMap.put(".ps", "application/postscript");
    s_suffixMap.put(".zip", "application/zip");
    s_suffixMap.put(".sh", "application/x-shar");
    s_suffixMap.put(".tar", "application/x-tar");
    s_suffixMap.put(".snd", "audio/basic");
    s_suffixMap.put(".au", "audio/basic");
    s_suffixMap.put(".wav", "audio/x-wav");
    s_suffixMap.put(".gif", "image/gif");
    s_suffixMap.put(".jpg", "image/jpeg");
    s_suffixMap.put(".jpeg", "image/jpeg");
    s_suffixMap.put(".htm", "text/html");
    s_suffixMap.put(".html", "text/html");
    s_suffixMap.put(".txt", "text/plain");
    s_suffixMap.put(".text", "text/plain");
    s_suffixMap.put(".c", "text/plain");
    s_suffixMap.put(".cc", "text/plain");
    s_suffixMap.put(".cpp", "text/plain");
    s_suffixMap.put(".c++", "text/plain");
    s_suffixMap.put(".h", "text/plain");
    s_suffixMap.put(".hh", "text/plain");
    s_suffixMap.put(".hpp", "text/plain");
    s_suffixMap.put(".h++", "text/plain");
    s_suffixMap.put(".pl", "text/plain");
    s_suffixMap.put(".java", "text/plain");
    }
}
```

It's a rather lengthy swath of code (it weighs in at just over 400 lines in a text editor), but think about what it represents—you now have complete control over how a web server can act. This offers powerful implications for your enterprise projects. Think about this. The web is one of the most powerful media by which to deliver information across the Internet. Web servers are scalable, adaptable, and flexible, and now they're a part of your programming arsenal.

### 10.3.3    Servlets

From the HttpConnection, it's a short jump into providing a full-fledged Servlet environment. As tempting as it would be, I'm not going to jump into Servlets, the Servlet API, or example Servlets here, principally because Servlets are well covered in other texts. Instead, I want to point out some interesting concepts underlying the Servlet concept:

- *Servlets can be a poor man's RMI.*
  Servlets are really all about communication—they're a simple marriage of CGI and HTTP, executing inside of a web server for best performance, although they don't have to be inside the server. This also means that Servlets, by serving up files other than HTML documents, can serve as a simple middleware layer on top of HTTP. For example, the RemoteStorageServer/RemoteStorageClient discussed in chapter 12: instead of using straight sockets, we could make the RemoteStorage-Server a servlet, and no specialized client would be required—just open a URL-Connection to the server, and deserialize the resulting stream coming back. (In fact, this is precisely the concept behind HTTP tunneling in RMI.)

- *Servlets can be a poor man's EJB.*
  Because many Web servers already provide some form of load-balancing, fault-tolerance and/or clustering support, servlets are sometimes called upon to perform in roles more appropriate to EJB servers, containers, and Beans. For example, consider the ubiquitous *n*-tier business system. The client communicates via a middleware layer to the database. In the J2EE model, the middleware layer is EJB layered on top of RMI/IIOP; in a lightweight version of this, however, the middleware layer is a collection of Servlets, layered on top of straight TCP/IP, sending and receiving Serialized objects. In this approach, the database can hide behind the firewall, so long as the web server has access to it.

- *A lightweight Servlet engine can provide easy monitoring/configuration.*
  If your enterprise application wants to be easily configurable and/or monitorable, embedding an instance of a Servlet engine—along with the Servlet to do the actual configuration or monitoring—allows administrators to remotely check on the progress or status of your enterprise application. If this sounds like a lot of work, it's not. New Atlanta, makers of the ServletExec servlet engine, makes freely available a lightweight servlet engine it calls "ServletDebugger." The intent is to allow Java developers to easily debug their servlets (by allowing you to execute the Servlet inside of an IDE or other debugger), but it would be just as

simple to embed the ServletDebugger into your enterprise application and kick off the Servlet to do the administrative work.

Servlets are capable of much, much more than this. The above examples should start you thinking about servlets in an entirely new light. Remember, servlets aren't just about HTML—servlets are a basic communications layer.

In fact, I've come to believe that most Java developers have a backward opinion of servlets: where they see Servlets as bringing Java into the web server, I see Servlets as bringing HTTP into the larger world of Java application servers. If you look carefully at a number of the Servlet implementations on the market (such as JRun, or even Sun's own reference implementation, JSWDK), you'll notice not only are they all implemented in Java, but even the basic Web-serving capabilities are done as a Servlet within the more generic server framework. This is partially why it's becoming so simple for Web server vendors to become EJB server vendors. Because the fundamental concepts behind the two are so similar, it's trivial to adapt their server framework to handle EJB containers and Beans. A web server is just a specialized form of the more generalized Application Server. Or, to put it in O-O parlance, "A web server IS-A application server."

## 10.4    ADVANCED SOCKET SERVICES

Having gone this far, let's now see how we can take sockets even farther.

### 10.4.1    SocketClassLoader and SocketClassService

In chapter 2, we talked about Java's ClassLoader facility giving developers the capability to retrieve bytecode from any resource; this extends to sockets as well. Given a bootstrap client on the user's local disk (to load the Java run time and a small bootstrap class that knows to use the customized ClassLoader to retrieve the next classes), a server can then provide the latest, up-to-date bytecode to a client when requested.

Doing so requires effort on the part of both the client and the server—the client must use the SocketClassLoader class, and the server must have an instance of the SocketClassConnection running to respond to the client's request. The client must know, at run time, the host name and port of the server, which is typically more of an administrative detail than a developmental one. The server must be informed of the full class name to retrieve, which is sent by the client in a plaintext string. The server can then either find the class (possibly from local disk, possibly through another ClassLoader), or simply close the port, indicating the class couldn't be found.

For more control, an HTTP-like protocol could be used to offer more verification (headers with content-length and possibly Java version expected are good candidates). For that matter, the HttpConnection code itself could be used, accepting URLs with .class extensions as a request to send back the actual bytecode. However, for an application of any size distributed in this way, the server will be hit a lot as users start and close the application; to add web-serving duties to the same server could bog both the web site and the SocketClassConnection service down to the point of impotence.

The SocketClassLoader (listing 10.7), as you might imagine, is pretty straight-forward, given what was presented in the chapter on ClassLoaders.

**Listing 10.7   Code for SocketClassLoader**

```
/**
 * SocketClassLoader retrieves bytecode for a given class via a
 * HTTP-like protocol.
 */
public class SocketClassLoader extends ClassLoader
    implements ClassLoaderStrategy
{
    /**
     * Constructor.
     *
     * @param host TCP/IP host name to contact
     * @param port TCP/IP port to contact host on
     */
    public SocketClassLoader(String host, int port)
    {
        this(SocketClassLoader.class.getClassLoader(), host, port);
    }
    /**
     * Constructor.
     *
     * @param host TCP/IP host name to contact
     * @param port TCP/IP port to contact host on
     */
    public SocketClassLoader(ClassLoader parent,
                             String host, int port)
    {
        // Establish the parent ClassLoader
        //
        super(parent);

        // Store off Socket settings
        //
        m_host = host;
        m_port = port;
    }

    /**
     * Return byte array (which will be turned into a Class instance
     * via ClassLoader.defineClass) for class
     */
    public byte[] findClassBytes(String className)
    {
        try
        {
            // Connect to the host on port
```

```java
            Socket socket = new Socket(m_host, m_port);

            BufferedReader reader =
                new BufferedReader(new InputStreamReader(
                    socket.getInputStream()));
            PrintWriter writer =
                new PrintWriter(socket.getOutputStream());

            // Send the class name
            writer.println("Classname:" + className);
            writer.flush();

            // Get back the resulting bytecode, or get nothing back (an error)
            String line = reader.readLine();
            if (line.equals("Error"))
                return null;
            else if (line.startsWith("Content-Length"))
            {
                // Find out how much we're expecting back
                int colonLoc = line.indexOf(":");
                Integer l =
                    new Integer(line.substring(colonLoc + 1, line.length()));
                byte[] classBytes = new byte[l.intValue()];

                // Throw away any data between
                // our current point in the stream
                // and the first magic number of the Java .class file ('CA')
                while (reader.read() != (int)0xCA)
                    ;

                // We already pulled back the first magic number of the class,
                // so manually insert it into the byte array. Read the rest
                // from the socket
                classBytes[0] = (byte)0xCA;
                for (int i=1; i<classBytes.length; i++)
                    classBytes[i] = (byte)reader.read();

                return classBytes;
            }
            else
                return null;
        }
        catch (UnknownHostException uhEx)
        {
            return null;
        }
        catch (IOException ioEx)
        {
            return null;
        }
    }

    /**
     * Return URL for resource given by resourceName
     */
```

```java
    public URL findResourceURL(String resourceName)
    {
        return null;
    }
    /**
     * Return Enumeration of resources corresponding to
     * resourceName.
     */
    public Enumeration findResourcesEnum(String resourceName)
    {
        return null;
    }

    /**
     * Return full path to native library given by the name
     * libraryName.
     */
    public String findLibraryPath(String libraryName)
    {
        return null;
    }

    /**
     * ClassLoader-overridden method to retrive the bytes
     */
    public Class findClass(String className)
        throws ClassNotFoundException
    {
        byte[] classBytes = findClassBytes(className);
        if (classBytes==null)
        {
            throw new ClassNotFoundException();
        }

        return defineClass(className, classBytes, 0, classBytes.length);
    }

// Internal members
//
String m_host;
int m_port;

// To test this effectively from the CD, copy
// SocketClassLoader.class to a directory elsewhere on your
// hard drive. Start GJAS in a separate directory,
// then run SocketClassLoader from the command-line.
public static void main(String[] args)
    throws Exception
{
    // If Hello.class exists in the current directory, the
    // bootstrap ClassLoader, which is always given first crack,
    // will pick it up and load the class, instead of the
    // SocketClassLoader.
    File file = new File("Hello.class");
```

```
            if (file.exists())
                System.out.println("Warning--Hello.class exists " +
                    "in the current directory.
                        SocketClassLoader will NOT be used " +
                    "to retrieve the file; the primordial ClassLoader will.");

            // Connect to the local host on port 8085 to see if Hello can be
            // loaded.
            SocketClassLoader scl = new SocketClassLoader("localhost", 8085);
            Class cls = scl.loadClass("Hello");
            Object h = cls.newInstance();
        }

}
```

The mechanics of SocketClassLoader should be apparent. Open a Socket to the given host on the given port, send a string with the class name requested, and look for either a "Content-Length" string followed by the class bytecode, or an "Error" string. Note that SocketClassLoader also implements the ClassLoaderStrategy interface, which in turn allows it to be used in all the ClassLoaderStrategy-related classes from chapter 2.

SocketClassLoader comes with a `main`, in order to allow for independent unit-testing and verification that the basic mechanism works. If you put the class Hello.class in the same directory as the SocketClassLoader class, and run it, Hello.class will be picked up by the bootstrap ClassLoader, and not by SocketClassLoader. Therefore, if you wish to run this test, copy the SocketClassLoader over to another point on your directory tree, and run it from there.

The SocketClassLoaderConnection is also fairly trivial, thanks in no small part to the scaffolding that GJAS and the SocketServer and ConnectionManager classes provide:

```
/**
 * SocketClassLoaderConnection
 */
public class SocketClassLoaderConnection
    implements Connection
{
    /**
     * Send class bytecode, if it can be found, back down the socket.
     */
    public void serve(Socket socket)
        throws Exception
    {
        ServerManager.instance().log(
            getClass().getName() + ".serve(): " +
            "Entered");

        InputStream in = socket.getInputStream();
        OutputStream out = socket.getOutputStream();

        BufferedReader br = new BufferedReader(new InputStreamReader(in));
```

```java
        PrintWriter pw = new PrintWriter(out);

        String classname = br.readLine();
        classname =
            classname.substring(classname.indexOf(":")+1,
                                classname.length());

        ServerManager.instance().log(
            getClass().getName() + ".serve(): " +
            "Request: " + classname);
        System.out.println("Request: " + classname);

        // Find the file on the disk
        try
        {
            FileInputStream inFile =
                new FileInputStream("./" + classname + ".class");

            // Tell SocketClassLoader how much data to expect
            pw.println("Content-Length:" + inFile.available());
            pw.flush();

            // We have to use OutputStream directly here, because Writer
            // and PrintWriter have no methods to write out bytes
            byte[] buffer = new byte[1024];
            int nRead = 0;
            while ((nRead = inFile.read(buffer)) != -1)
                out.write(buffer, 0, nRead);
            out.flush();

            // Write one more blank line, just for luck
            pw.write("\r\n");
        }
        catch (FileNotFoundException ex)
        {
            ServerManager.instance().log(
                getClass().getName() + ".serve(): " +
                "Error finding class file");
            ServerManager.instance().log(ex);

            pw.println("Error");
        }
        finally
        {
            pw.flush();
        }
    }
}
```

SocketClassLoaderConnection, again, shouldn't present any surprises. In this instance, we attempt to read the class as a file off of the local disk, and send the bytecode down the socket. Note that if the class is part of a package, then the filename must be a dot-separated filename on the disk; that is, if a request comes in for the class "mypackage.myclass", SocketClassLoaderConnection looks for a file called "mypackage.myclass.class" in the local directory. This is not, by any means, the only way classes could be resolved. SocketClassLoaderConnection could, in turn, use its own ClassLoader to load the classes (perhaps even the JDBCClassLoader mentioned in chapter 2 and explored in chapter 12). The actual mechanics of how SocketClassLoaderConnection resolves its requests is unimportant for the moment. Once it finds the bytecode, it sends it back down the socket to the client SocketClassLoader for use.

## 10.4.2    Concept: RedirectorService

One interesting application of sockets is the ability to accept the incoming request on a socket. Then, instead of providing the behavior requested, in turn, forward the request to a socket on another server. This is, in fact, the primary function of a firewall proxy server. It's a simple concept: when the Redirector receives a client-connect, it opens a new Socket connection to the host/port combination to which it is redirecting, and simply hooks up the Sockets' InputStreams and OutputStreams to one another via a custom class, ThreadedPipeStream, which is an abstraction of the spin-a-Thread-to-loop-over-input-and-fire-it-down-the-OutputStream concept used by Client.java a few pages back.

### Usage

One potential use for this is to place RedirectorService on a machine accessible to the public (in this case, referring to any clients using the system), having the Redirector-Service redirect to a machine with sensitive data on it within a firewall or special security zone. For companies with sensitive data, for example, it is imperative that the machine containing the sensitive data be hidden from public eye as much as possible. Using a Redirector, the development group can advertise machine "A" as the machine to connect to, and silently redirect all queries to machine "B," which contains the actual sensitive data. This protects "B" in two ways: first, malicious users will not know about "B," believing instead that the data is contained on "A." Secondly, "B" can be configured to ignore any and all requests from any machine other than "A."

We can also help reduce administrative costs by this same method; by advertising machine "A" as the front end to a particular socket-based service (such as a web server), and having it redirect to machine "B," we can vary the actual configuration, name, even IP address of machine "B," as necessary, so long as "A" knows where to redirect it. This provides a tremendous advantage during network rerouting or IP shuffling. It also begins to touch on the basic nature of fault-tolerance and/or clustering, since the redirector can now choose from machines "B," "C," "D," or "E," based on particular criteria (clustering) or availability (fault-tolerance). In fact, by using the RedirectorConnection, services which used to run on machine "A" can now silently be clustered, by having "A" run the RedirectorConnection (or its clustering cousin, ClusterRedirector-Connection, not implemented here) and choosing between the clustered machines without having to even notify the clients of the switch. As far as clients are concerned, they continue to access and use "A" just as they always have.

### 10.4.3　Concept: FilterService

A close cousin to RedirectorService is FilterService, which takes a FilterInputStream and/or a FilterOutputStream instance as a parameter, and passes all input and output through the filter before sending it on to its destination (the sender or the server).

#### *Usage*

FilterService can offer basic statistics-gathering support, such as number of client requests, length (in time) of each request, or even identification of clients making the requests.[10] Also, the filter allows for editing or translation of either input, output or both. For example, a corporation wants to give its managers the ability to query the database using English instead of SQL. A FilterService could be used, with appropriate FilterInputStream/FilterOutputStreams that translates the English request into an SQL statement, to pass on to any standard SQL engine.[11]

Alternative ideas are:

- *On-the-fly modification or generation of HTML.*
  For example, a FilterService could ping the URL of each HREF link it sees in a returned HTML document, to make sure each link exists; if the link doesn't exist, it could silently modify the HTML to put "(Broken Link)" in red text immediately after the HREF tag, or perhaps remove the link altogether. Alternatively, it could postprocess HTML, inserting corporate headers and footers onto the page, or adding advertising banners on Internet pages, and so forth. Finally, it could even generate HTML from non-HTML sources; for example, a FilterConnection could take Java or C++ files returned from an HTTP server and translate them into color-syntax-highlighted HTML files for easier reading.

- *On-the-fly compression or uncompression of data.*
  Data can be stored on the server in compressed form, to minimize storage requirements on the server, and uncompressed by a FilterService on its way back to the client.

- *On-the-fly encryption/decryption of data.*
  As with the compression/uncompression idea, input can be decrypted on the way in, and output can be encrypted on the way out, for the client to decipher upon receipt. By doing it this way, as opposed to encrypting it within the server itself, the server can be accessed in unencrypted form directly (perhaps for debugging, or because sources within a firewall are implicitly trusted). Also, the encryption formats can change simply by changing the FilterOutputStream instance placed within the FilterService.

---

[10] At least, as much as TCP/IP allows, sophisticated hackers can always "spoof" an IP address, so it can't be relied upon confidently or for security issues.

[11] This really isn't well-suited to the streaming nature of InputStream/OutputStream. It's easier by far to consider a sample implementation whereby we do byte-for-byte replacement, such as the compression/decompression of data, for example.

- *Censorship of sensitive data to untrusted clients.*
  The FilterService can also be used to monitor data being retrieved from the server. FilterService looks for particular keywords or tags to determine if the document is of a sensitive nature; if it is, and the client is untrusted, or the document is not permitted to be electronically transmitted, the FilterService can block the output from returning (sending a generic error message instead and perhaps noting the requestor's IP headers for administrative review). Alternatively, it could simply remove the sensitive portions and allow the remainder of the response to be sent.

### 10.4.4    Other types

Certainly, the above are not the only possibilities when considering Connection types. Any sockets-based communication protocol can be implemented and plugged into the ConnectionManager system by implementing the Connection interface.

It may seem odd that there is any separation whatsoever between Connection-Manager and SocketServer; if the features of ConnectionManager are so useful, why not roll them into SocketServer and call it done with that? Principally, the issue is one of design—have each class in the system provide one, and only one, specialization. SocketServer provides the basic socket functionality, ConnectionManager provides scalable socket functionality. This way, if a need arises where a particular socket-based system wouldn't want the multi-instanced nature of Connections (perhaps the code in turn uses non-thread-safe classes or legacy system code), it can choose to instead extend SocketServer.

## 10.5    SUMMARY

In this chapter, we extended our reach and availability outside of the local JVM. Now, through sockets, clients in other JVMs (either local or remote) can connect and interact with the server and its services. More importantly, the necessary scaffolding code to support scalable socket-based solutions was placed within reusable base classes, leaving service-writers to focus more tightly on the precise service being supported, instead of on how to write sockets code. Then we built Internet-standard-conformant services, including a basic HTTP-conformant web server. Even better, the design and implementation of these services are such that they could be used within applications outside of GJAS without modification.

We're not done with sockets, not by a long shot. In later chapters, we'll be using SocketServer and ConnectionManager over and over again as we expose additional services to clients via sockets. Java's ability to use sockets so effortlessly now offers servers the ability to reach out and touch the world. In fact, the ubiquitous socket is Java's best (and, in fact, only platform-portable) way of achieving interprocess and internetwork communications, and forms the foundation of every other Java network-aware system, such as Jini, JavaSpaces, or the Java Shared Data Toolkit.

## 10.6 ADDITIONAL READING

- Merlin Hughes, Michael Shoffner, and Derek Hamner, *Java Network Programming, 2nd Ed.* (Manning Publications Co. 1999).

  This book covers every aspect of Java network programming, and should be considered to be your first go-to book if the Socket and ServerSocket still confuse you.

# C H A P T E R   1 1

# Servlets

Servlets represent a particular place in the enterprise developer's bag of tricks. On the one hand, they represent an easy replacement for CGI scripts. They also serve as the fundamental heart of the JSP technology. Many people tie servlets irretrievably to the HTTP and HTML protocols; to do so, however, is to miss a huge part of their functionality. Servlets are more than Java CGIs. In fact, the Servlet specification served as the testing ground for a number of the features that would eventually come to define the Enterprise Java Beans specification.

We're not going to go over the basics of servlets or the Servlet API here. For detailed explanation of the Servlet API, and good examples of how to use servlets in general, see Alan Williamson's *Servlets By Example* (Manning), or Jason Hunter's *Java Servlet Programming* (O'Reilly).

## 11.1   RELATIONSHIP TO SOCKETS

A servlet, fundamentally, holds the same relationship as the Connection interface from chapter 10. The servlet is called to service a particular request, performs the service, and, in the case of an HttpServlet, returns the necessary HTML to the socket. Connection does the same thing. Interestingly enough, although the Servlet API does provide for the concept, servlets are rarely (if ever) seen outside of an HTTP context—the Servlet API is flexible enough to accommodate ideas such as FTP Servlets, Telnet Servlets, and so on.

From a practical perspective, this means that theoretically, we could create servlets—coding at the GenericServlet layer, instead of the HttpServlet layer, as most servlets do—that could be plugged into any generic application server, and be executed upon request. In fact, this is how the JSWDK itself performs—each web request, even if it is for a standard static HTML page, is handled by a servlet. In fact, this kind of pass-through servlet would probably be similar to the following:

```
import java.io.*;
import javax.servlet.*;
import javax.servlet.http.*;

public class PassthroughServlet extends HttpServlet
{
    private String docRoot;

    public void init(ServletConfig config)
    {
        docRoot = config.getInitParameter("docRoot");
        if (docRoot == null)
            docRoot = ".";
    }

    public void doGet(HttpServletRequest req,
                      HttpServletResponse res)
        throws ServletException, IOException
    {
        // Find file given on URL
        String filename = req.getServletPath();

        // Open it
        FileInputStream fis = new FileInputStream(docRoot + "/" + filename);

        // Send its contents back to the requester
        OutputStream out = res.getOutputStream();
        res.setContentType("text/html");
        int ch;
        while ((ch = fis.read()) != -1)
        {
            out.write(ch);
        }
    }
    public void doPost(HttpServletRequest req,
                       HttpServletResponse res)
        throws ServletException, IOException
    { doGet(req, res); }
}
```

As you can see, the servlet simply obtains the requested file (assuming this servlet is associated with the extension .html and/or .htm—see the Servlet API specification or the JSWDK 1.0.1 documentation for more details) and passes it directly through to the servlet's OutputStream instance. Notice how we use the `getServletPath()` method to retrieve the file path requested, and use that, plus the `docRoot` member, to find the file requested and present it.

In fact, this concept is strikingly familiar. In the previous chapter, we talked about some of the more interesting things to do with sockets; specifically, a FilterSocket and a RedirectorSocket. Both are easily portable to the servlet arena.

### 11.1.1 CodeServlet: A filtering servlet

Filter-style servlets are the easier to implement, because we can take the PassThrough-Servlet code base and tweak it just enough to do some manipulation of the text before we send it back down the pipe to the client. In this case, we'll create a CodeServlet (listing 11.1), which takes standard .java files and applies a simple series of rules to transform the returned stream into a color-highlighted HTML form:

**Listing 11.1    Code for CodeServlet**

```java
public class CodeServlet extends HttpServlet
{
    private static Map handlerMap;

    public interface FileHandler
    {
        public String handle(String file);
    }

    public static class JavaHandler
        implements FileHandler
    {
        public void handle(HttpServletRequest req,
                           HttpServletResponse res)
        {
            // code to transform java source into (for starters)
            // color-syntax-highlighted HTML markup
        }
    }

    public void doGet(HttpServletRequest req,
                      HttpServletResponse res)
        throws ServletException
    {
        // Find file given on URL
        String filename = req.getServletPath();
        for (Iterator iter = handlerMap.keySet().iterator(); iter.hasNext(); )
        {
            String key = (String)iter.next();
            if (filename.endsWith(key))
            {
                FileHandler fh = (FileHandler)handlerMap.get(key);
```

```
                fh.handle(req, res);
            }
        }
    }

    static
    {
        handlerMap = new HashMap();
        handlerMap.put("java", new JavaHandler());
    }

    // . . .
}
```

This isn't rocket science. We map the CodeServlet over to extensions of type .java in the servlet engine, and any URL (within the Servlet's zone) requesting a .java file will automatically be mapped onto the CodeServlet. In fact, CodeServlet could be extended to do any source file type simply by registering new FileHandlers with the CodeServlet in listing 11.1.

```
public class CodeServlet extends HttpServlet
{
    // . . . as before . . .

    /**
     *
     */
    public static class CPPHandler
        implements FileHandler
    {
        public void handle(HttpServletRequest req,
                        HttpServletResponse res)
        {
            // code to mark up C++ code to provide (for starters)
            // color syntax highlighting, for example
        }
    }

    static
    {
        handlerMap = new HashMap();

        // . . .

        handlerMap.put("cpp", new CPPHandler());
        handlerMap.put("cc", new CPPHandler());
        handlerMap.put("C", new CPPHandler());   // some UNIXes use
                                                 // uppercase ".C" as
                                                 // the C++ extension
        handlerMap.put("hpp", new CPPHandler());
        handlerMap.put("hh", new CPPHandler());
        handlerMap.put("H", new CPPHandler());   // ditto as ".C"
    }
}
```

We could even recode the PassthroughServlet to be another type of handler within the CodeServlet (which, by this point, is probably misnamed, since we're now dealing with types other than just programming source):

```
public class CodeServlet extends HttpServlet
{
    // . . . as before . . .
    /**
     *
     */
    public static class HTMLHandler
        implements FileHandler
    {
        public void handle(HttpServletRequest req,
                           HttpServletResponse res)
        {
            // Simply pipe back
        }
    }

    static
    {
        handlerMap = new HashMap();

        // . . .

        handlerMap.put("html", new HTMLHandler());
        handlerMap.put("htm", new HTMLHandler());
    }
}
```

By now, without a single change to the servlet engine supporting us, we have converted the servlet engine into a more-or-less functional web server, even if the servlet engine itself doesn't provide web-serving capabilities. It may seem strange to consider the idea of a servlet providing basic web-server functionality since most people see the servlet in terms of wanting to get away from what the web server provides. The point is that servlets aren't necessarily tied directly to a web server; it's possible to have a servlet executing inside of a generic application server (such as GJAS), providing web services for that application server on port 80 (or any other port).

### 11.1.2  HeaderFooter: a redirecting servlet

We can also create a redirector servlet. Under the servlet model, while redirecting is certainly an applicable concept, a better or more interesting idea is servlet chaining, which loosely follows the notion of redirection. Instead of redirecting the request to a new URL or socket, we redirect the flow of control to a new servlet within the same engine.

Under the Servlet 2.2 specification, however, servlet redirection takes on a different look. Under earlier versions of the servlet specification, a servlet simply had to call getServlet on the javax.servlet.ServletContext class (returned from the javax.servlet.GenericServlet's getServletContext method), and pass in the name of the servlet to obtain. Unfortunately, this had an inherent problem:

This means the servlet engine is no longer going to allow you *carte blanche* to obtain the servlet reference for another servlet in the system.

Does this mean servlet-chaining is dead? Absolutely not—it's too critical a concept to simply throw out. Instead, now a servlet that wishes to forward or chain its request to another servlet needs to go through the target's ServletContext's forward method, as shown in the following snippet:

```
public class ChainingServlet extends HttpServlet
{
    public void service(HttpServletRequest req,
                        HttpServletResponse res)
        throws ServletException
    {
        ServletContext cx = getServletContext();
        String otherServletDomain = "http://www.javageeks.com";
        String otherServletURL = "/servlet/otherServlet";
        RequestDispatcher servlet =
            cx.getRequestDispatcher(otherServletDomain +
                                otherServletURL);

        // Here we can do any other "pre-chain" work, like adding
        // new request parameters to the request parameters

        servlet.forward(req, res);
    }
}
```

When the forward method is called, it will effectively call into the otherServlet's service method, which, like all HttpServlet-extending classes, will get routed into either doGet or doPost (predominantly), and the other servlet is now in full control. Once the other servlet is finished, control returns to ChainingServlet.

This aspect of servlets allows for interesting behavior. For example, the Java Developer's Connection at the Javasoft web site (developer.javasoft.com) uses chained servlets to maintain its pages behind a login—each servlet request chains to a Login-Servlet, which determines whether or not you've logged in. If not, it will display a login page, and only if you authenticate correctly are you then directed to the original URL requested.

The same sort of behavior can be applied to your own servlets.. Suppose, for example, that you are building an Internet site for an e-commerce enterprise. In reality, you are building an application catering to a variety of clients, who in turn are telling their clients to use your Internet application on their behalf.

The problem is simple—you need to vary the decorations around the outside of the page on a per-client basis, so the customer (the end user) doesn't realize that he's on your web site and not your client's. One approach would be to have each client live on its own web page, with a web designer maintaining the graphics and HTML for each client. That's also a great way to see how quickly you can burn out your web designers. Can you imagine changing the clients' look and feel after about the third or fourth time, especially if the clients' site spans many pages?

Instead, you can create a servlet that builds on the filtering and the chaining concept and reduces the work your administrators have to do. Let's play it out step by step. Each client is going to require a hello page, welcoming the end user to the site and presenting a list of choices. These hello pages are all going to look similar—big banner graphic across the top, verbage and links in the middle, and a nice status bar with small-font copyright information across the bottom. Instead of embedding all that into a single welcome.html or WelcomeServlet, break it up into multiple servlets—one for the top banner graphics (which can be retrieved from a file or from an RDBMS based on either the incoming URL or on the URL request path), one to load that client's specific welcome page, and one for the bottom graphics.

What does this three-part chain get you? To begin with, chaining like this allows you to partition out certain aspects of the web application if they're conceptually different—the decorations around a page, for example, will typically remain constant, while the content of the page will vary. Instead of forcing the web designers to cut-and-paste the header/footer HTML onto each page, let a HeaderServlet and FooterServlet provide that. Then, chain to the HeaderServlet, load and redisplay the original HTML file requested, and chain to the FooterServlet before sending it on.

## 11.1.3    Server-side scripting capabilities

Servlet chaining is a useful aspect, but there will be situations where you will want to do more logic-driven execution than just simple inclusion of HTML content. In those situations, you have two choices:

- *Write a servlet for each logical sequence you wish to execute.*
  This will get real boring, real quickly, especially if the logic is of simple garden-variety if-this-show-this-page-else-show-that-page logic. What would be nice is to place some sort of logic within the page, so that your web designers could put some simple logic into the page.

- *Abandon servlets.*
  Servlets don't provide any sort of server-side scripting, so you're left with giving up on servlets and moving toward ASP.

In order to change any sort of logic within the servlet, you have to change the logic inside the servlet code, which requires a Java programmer (namely, you) to make the change. What's worse, many of these changes could be done by those less technical than you, because it's that simple logic described above. What would be nice would be to execute short snippets of some scripting language (such as ECMAScript, also known as JavaScript) within the servlet.

It just so happens we can do that; for example:

```
<HTML>
<HEAD>Scripted example</HEAD>
<BODY>
<SVRSCRIPT>
    (. . . script goes here . . .)
</SVRSCRIPT>
</BODY>
</HTML>
```

When the pass-through servlet is executed, it looks for the <SVRSCRIPT>...</SVR-SCRIPT> tags, and passes the contents to the appropriate scripting engine. This support could even be bundled inside its own servlet, and the pass-through servlet could chain to it (let's call it the ScriptingServlet) when it encounters the <SVRSCRIPT> tag. A certain amount of overhead within ScriptingServlet will be necessary (for example, establishing global objects within the scripting environment to send output to the end user's browser), and will be customized for each language. That's a manageable task, especially since it will sit once inside the ScriptingServlet and never be touched again.

This concept isn't new: Netscape introduced it as LiveWire in an early release of its Netscape Enterprise Server product, and Microsoft has enjoyed tremendous success with its version, ASP. In both cases, the ability to be able to execute actual code during the retrieval of the page offers interesting benefits, long before the page gets back to the client. Because this is happening within an industry-standard servlet, however, it can be plugged into any servlet 2.1-compliant servlet engine on any platform; by using this server-script, we're not limited to any one platform, web server, or environment.

With a bit of resourcefulness, various interpreters implemented in Java can be found and used to provide a rich variety of scripting languages within the pages. Mozilla makes available a freely distributable JavaScript engine called Rhino, at www.mozilla.org/rhino. Another JavaScript engine is FESI. In the January 2000 issue of *Dr. Dobb's Journal*, Kirby Angell describes how to build something similar to this using Python and the JPython engine available at www.python.org. John H. McCay describes the Pnuts thin procedural wrapper scripting language in the same issue, alongside the Mike McMillan article describing the PerlCOM component for embedding Perl as a COM component in Win32 applications.

## 11.1.4 Servlets: Not just about HTML anymore

Servlets aren't about web servers and HTML—they're about a means of delivery of arbitrary content.

Consider GJAS: thus far it is one of the weakest web servers ever concocted on this planet. It doesn't support any of the HTTP header commands except GET, and it certainly doesn't do that well, either. Assume for the moment, that I create a Servlet-ContainerService (or ServletContainerConnection) for GJAS that provides the basic servlet environment. Now it becomes possible to load servlets into the GJAS system, have them start listening on port 80 for incoming HTTP requests, and use the PassthroughServlet to start sending .html or .htm files back to the requester. In fact, we'd probably tie PassthroughServlet to all sorts of file extensions, such as .gif and .jpg, so as to be able to pass those files' contents directly back to the client, as well.

Let's take this concept one step farther. We've now provided HTTP services to GJAS; what about FTP? Or Gopher? Or Telnet? All of these are certainly feasible services for the GJAS system, and wouldn't be too terribly difficult to develop, assuming one has the appropriate RFC handy.

Here's a radical notion: A servlet isn't really code that's executed from within an HTTP server, but is really code that can be executed from within any generic application server (like GJAS). If that weren't enough to cause readers to rethink the whole servlet concept, Adam Smith, one of the reviewers of the early manuscript for this book, suggested the idea of creating servlets to other protocols, as well—FTP servlets, telnet servlets, mail servlets, and so on. In fact, just about any socket-oriented server can use the Sun servlet specification to create a servlet backplane for enhanced socket-to-socket serving. Look at the servlet interface:

```
public void init(ServletConfig config) throws ServletException;
public void service(ServletRequest request, ServletResponse response)
    throws ServletException, IOException;
public void destroy();
public ServletConfig getServletConfig();
public String getServletInfo();
```

This API is extremely generic and, says absolutely nothing about the underlying protocol the servlet is serving. ServletRequest and ServletResponse each have some methods that are somewhat HTTP-oriented (get/setContentLength, get/setContentType, etc.), but a servlet engine doesn't have to call these methods, and a non-HTTP servlet certainly doesn't have to do anything meaningful for them.

For example, consider a hypothetical FTP servlet, that acts as a virtual directory for uploading or downloading files; the servlet could take note of the FTP user's name and password, look up the user's privileges in a database or local file, and provide automatic masking of certain files to allow or prevent the upload/download of those files. Or, within that directory, it could provide virus-scanning behavior (perhaps using a JNI-to-native library connection, since no Java-based antiviral tools are available as yet). The FTP servlet has its service called when the user executes a command within the FTP/Servlet virtual directory, with the command coming in via the ServletRequest instance, and the appropriate output sent via the ServletResponse instance. A dir or ls command inside the hypothetical FTP VirtualDirectoryServlet would check the user's permissions against the files on the file system, and only display certain ones. The same would be true for get or mget commands.

Or consider a telnet servlet system, in which commands can be added to the telnet server to allow users to perform certain tasks from a telnet session without having to create shell scripts that sit on the server's file system. The telnet servlet would get the input from the user before handing it on to the command shell it wraps, perhaps filtering the commands before the command shell sees the input, or even performing a series of steps on behalf of the user, providing telnet with a certain amount of macro capability on the server side. Each telnet command gets checked against the list of running servlets in the system, and if the command matches a servlet name, the entire command line gets passed into the servlet's `service` method inside of a ServletRequest instance; the servlet sends the telnet output to the user via the ServletResponse instance.

Or consider a mail server servlet that performs the virus checking discussed previously before downloading the mail to the mail client, or even performs some sanity-checking on the incoming mail, perhaps doing a content scan in an attempt to filter out spam and other unwanted email. The mail server can load servlets on a user-by-user basis (users get to specify which servlets get run at certain points in the mail server's operations, such as when new mail comes in), or else on a global basis (only mail administrators get to specify the servlets run), and so on. A mail server servlet sends the mail message into the servlet's `service` method, and on incoming mail saves the ServletResponse-sent output as the mail message, or on outgoing mail sends the Servlet-Response-sent output as the actual mail message. The mail server servlet could even filter the messages before sending them out, to ensure that nothing of a confidential or proprietary nature is sent to someone outside the company address book.

In short, servlets aren't just for web servers. The ability to plug in and define custom behavior for a given service process is not new, nor is it particularly revolutionary. Some server programs (such as FTP or mail servers) already provide some of the behavior that an FTP servlet might provide; however, it would be nice to be able to mix and match that behavior as company policy or as the system administrator wishes. By providing a servlet engine within the FTP or mail-server's execution engine, the system administrator gets an unparalleled amount of control over what happens within the FTP or mail server.

## 11.2  SERVLETS AND THE N-TIER APPLICATION

One of the principal problems with server-side scripting, however, is that while it works well for programmers, it combines the presentation contents (the HTML) with logic for the display (the SQL to retrieve, for example). Considering that most web content designers have no eye for server-side logic, and that programmers have no eye for matching colors, this means that one of three scenarios will take place within an ASP (or other server-side scripting-based) shop:

- *First the content, then the logic*
  The web designers will lay out the page and align the text and the graphics, then turn the pages over to the programmers to put the logic behind it. Problems: Development is serialized, since programmers can't touch the pages until the web

designers are finished with them, and programmers can accidentally rearrange things on the page contrary to the web designers' intentions.

- *First the logic, then the content*
This approach seems to be the most popular. First the programmers embed the logic into the page and verify and test the functionality, then the web designers spruce it up. Problems: one, web designers can accidentally rearrange things on the page, breaking the code; work is inherently serialized, since the web designers can't touch the pages until the programmers are finished; the QA effort must be duplicated again after the web designers finish with the pages, since it's possible that the web designer introduced a bug.

- *Simultaneously*
This approach removes the serialized nature of the first two, but requires the web designers to be familiar with source-code control techniques or applications, or risk stomping over changes made by others, or even by the web designer.

The inherent problem is that the scripting-based web application is violating one of the principal rules in *n*-tier applications, by embedded business logic in the same layer as the presentation code (the HTML).

### 11.2.1    Separating logic from content

What really needs to happen is for the two groups to be able to work independently, without accidentally overwriting the other's work or creating more difficulties for the other side. One of the best ways to achieve this sort of parallelism is to separate the logic of the application (what to do) from the content of the application (what is seen by the user). Business objects, servlets, and their script-like cousin, JSP, build on the idea that the servlet/JSP page acts as the presentation layer, using Java to call into JavaBeans or EnterpriseJavaBeans while processing the page on the server.

There are a number of Open Source and freeware toolkits designed to provide this same separation. For example, WebMacro (http://www.webmacro.org) uses standard HTML mixed in with calls to retrieve objects out of its context (in which objects are also stored, for later retrieval) and places that data on the page dynamically. Other such systems use similar functionality, offering varying degrees of programmatic control over the page. This is, in fact, precisely what early web/database tools such as ColdFusion and NetDynamics were all about.

## 11.3    SERVLETS AS A POOR MAN'S RMI

There is a tremendous amount of possible crossover between your average servlet, and your average server application. Consider the average enterprise *n*-tier, database-backed, client-server system. When boiled down to its essence, any client/server system is simply a collection of request-response calls, similar in scope and style to what servlets provide. In fact, this has in turn led many developers and architects down an interesting road: using servlets not for HTML and thin-client applications, but as a middleware layer connecting client to server.

Stop and think about it: Within Java, opening a socket to communicate with a hypothetical setup like this is trivial:

```
URLConnection conn =
    new URLConnection("http://www.server.com/servlet/Custom?cmd=start");
InputStream in = conn.openContent();
```

Because URLConnection makes it trivial to open a connection to an arbitrary HTTP server, we can use HTTP as a simple, lightweight middleware protocol.

This approach offers a number of advantages:

- *Lightweight*
  The HTTP protocol is probably one of the lightest protocols available in the net-working tool chest. Its statelessness provides for tremendous scalability, and its simplicity allows it to be used within a variety of environments. To make things even simpler, it's all sent as straight ASCII text over a socket—you don't get much simpler than this.[1]

- *Content-neutral*
  HTTP doesn't care about the data it's sending back—that's what MIME is for, as far as it's concerned. All HTTP cares about is that it knows the length to send back (Content-Length), and a few clear-text headers the client must understand upon response. We can send back anything we wish, and let the client deal with it.

- *Security*
  Many, if not most, corporations have a firewall in place to keep their internal systems separated from the Internet. Trying to run an RMI, CORBA, or DCOM system from outside the firewall to inside the firewall is an exercise in frustration for all parties concerned. System administrators don't want to open additional holes in the firewall, developers don't want to lose the benefit of distributed objects, and customers are frustrated because all they know is that it just doesn't work. Running over HTTP, however, allows us to piggyback on top of the one port almost any corporation does allow through.

As with any technology or approach, however, running over HTTP has a couple of disadvantages, too:

---

[1] Compare this with a CORBA, RMI, or DCOM system, in which we have to have complex object mar-shaling, state management across the wire, and (for CORBA and DCOM, anyway) some measure of pointer-transferability between two separate processes. Granted, HTTP isn't an ORB, as are CORBA and DCOM, or even an RPC, like RMI, but is that really the point? HTTP facilitates quick, simple communication between two processes, which is often all we really need.

- *One way*

  The communication is entirely one way—the server cannot call back to the client. This means that the client, if it wishes to be notified of events occurring within the server, must poll the server to receive the updates. That, in turn, means higher bandwidth consumption. This could be mitigated by using keep-alive sockets from client to server, but this reduces the server's scalability by a significant factor.

- *Greater reliance on one component*

  If the web server is serving dual duty, both as the web server and as a messaging/communications server, more people are affected if and when the web server is down. As the old saying goes, if you place all your eggs in one basket....

- *Servlet abuse*

  It becomes tempting to overuse the servlet approach as a generic application server. In some servlet books, authors demonstrate how to create daemon servlets that spin off a thread to perform some sort of background processing. Unfortunately, this approach is nonportable; because the servlet engine always retains the right to shut down the servlet instance (for performance or scalability reasons, if nothing else), a daemon servlet may actually not run all the time, as it's supposed to. Equally unfortunately, this is a popular approach, due not only to the fact that many servlet engines support the notion of initially loaded servlets (i.e., servlets that are loaded, regardless of user requests) to facilitate this idea, but also to the inherent scalability support that web servers can provide.

It's very tempting to want to use the Servlet/HTTP layer as a middleware system, using applets as a front end, communicating through HTTP to a JDBC-driven servlet on the backend server. It's certainly possible to do, and works out quite well for passive server systems; it's when we want to develop active or polling servers that the ServletEngine-as-AppServer approach breaks down on us. A request-response protocol simply isn't ideologically prepared to deal with the kind of active objects we discussed in "Threading issues" (chapter 6).

### 11.3.1 Example: RemoteStorageServlet

In chapter 12, I show you a remote storage service, which accepts serialized objects over a socket, stores them, and retrieves them for requestors—a simple distributed database system. Within the code for this system, we had to deal with all the socket-layer communications ourselves, and the storage server class had to be run on its own in order to respond to requests. This means that system administrators must keep an eye on this process, as well as the other processes they would normally have to monitor—not a good way to make friends.

In fact, we could have leveraged the Servlet API to handle all of the communications-layer aspect of the remote storage server, making use of the HTTP protocol (listing 11.2) instead of the custom protocol I presented there. In the custom protocol form, we had GET, CHECKIN, CHECKOUT, and DIFF operations to support; we can support those commands directly within the HTTP protocol, as well.

**Listing 11.2   Code for the HTTP protocol**

```java
import java.io.*;
import java.util.*;
import javax.servlet.*;
import javax.servlet.http.*;

/**
 *
 */
public class RemoteStorageServlet
    extends HttpServlet
{
    private static final String GET = "GET";
    private static final String CHECKIN = "CHECKIN";
    private static final String CHECKOUT = "CHECKOUT";
    private static final String DIFF = "DIFF";

    protected void service(HttpServletRequest req,
                        HttpServletResponse res)
        throws ServletException, IOException
    {
        String method = req.getMethod();

        // Get the user's map--for now, keep one map per user
        // session; in a real robust system, we'd want to serialize
        // out the results when the session is destroyed, but
        // that's for a later date
        HttpSession session = req.getSession(true);
        Map userMap = session.getValue("MAP");
        if (userMap == null)
        {
            userMap = new HashMap();
            session.putValue("MAP");
        }

        if ("GET".equals(method))
        {
            String objName = req.getServletPath();

            Object obj = userMap.get(objName);
            if (obj == null)
            {
                String msg = "Object " + objName + " not found.";
                res.sendError(HttpServletResponse.SC_BAD_REQUEST, msg);
            }
            else
            {
                // Serialize the object
                ByteArrayOutputStream baos =
                    new ByteArrayOutputStream();
                ObjectOutputStream oos =
                    new ObjectOutputStream(baos);
```

```
            oos.writeObject(obj);
            oos.flush();

            byte[] serializedData = baos.getByteArray();
            res.setContentLength(serializedData.length);
            res.getOutputStream().write(serializedData);
        }
    }
    else if ("CHECKIN".equals(method))
    {
        // . . . details omitted
    }
    else if ("CHECKOUT".equals(method))
    {
        // . . . details omitted
    }
    else if ("DIFF".equals(method))
    {
        // . . . details omitted
    }
  }
}
```

Notice something interesting—we subvert the HTTP protocol itself in supporting CHECKIN, CHECKOUT, and DIFF as valid commands. The getMethod() call on ServletRequest tells us the actual command sent, which under most servlets will be one of GET, POST, OPTIONS, TRACE, and so on, as mandated by the HTTP/1.1 specification. However, if you're willing to accept the consequence that the RemoteStorage-Servlet is to be used only with a custom RemoteStorageServletClient, then writing the servlet to accept custom commands is perfectly acceptable.

### 11.3.2 Concept: poor man's RMI

RMI, as we'll see in chapter 15, is all about Java methods being able to call between JVM instances, even across the network. Unfortunately, RMI, like many other middleware solutions, suffers from one critical restriction—because requests can come in from clients on any port, it's devilishly difficult to keep a server system running an RMI server locked down. As a result, the use of distributed technologies like RMI has not seen much use outside of the corporate firewall.

Servlets can serve as a cheap, lightweight form of RPC, however, by using HTTP as the transport and serialized objects as the data communicated between client and server. Instead of allowing RMI to do the marshaling of parameters, the programmer opens a URLConnection, serializes the arguments into a ByteArrayOutputStream, and sends the resulting byte array down the socket as POST parameters to the HTTP request. On the server side, the poor man's RMI servlet deserializes the POSTed parameter, inspects the arguments, and makes the call given as part of the HTTP request; for example, an HTTP request such as "POST /myobjectinstance/mymethodcall HTTP/1.0" would call the `mymethodcall` method on the object instance referred to (within an object mapping table, such as a Hashtable) as `myobjectinstance`. Note that the hypothetical PMRMIServlet wouldn't even need precompiled stubs to be present; it can use reflection to look up the method name given as part of the HTTP request, unpack the arguments, and if the types don't match up, send a 404 or 500 error back to the client, who interprets those as fatal mismatch or something similar.

### 11.3.3 Concept: SOAP

In point of fact, such a poor man's RMI system already exists—it's called SOAP, the simple object access protocol, and it uses HTTP as the transport and XML (instead of serialized objects, since it's intended to be cross-language) as the RPC payload. SOAP, although still in the early stages of specification development at the time of this writing, promises to allow for an unprecedented amount of interconnectivity between the RPC mechanisms we'll talk about in chapter 16. Because Microsoft has committed to it, along with several leading CORBA vendors, it's entirely possible that by the time you read this, DCOM will be able to call into CORBA servants via SOAP.

## 11.4 SUMMARY

What has this bought us? Why bother changing the persistence examples from using straight sockets to using servlets and HTTP instead? What's the big deal about the poor man's RMI system, or SOAP?

Simply, we can now let the Servlet engine manage the necessary activation/passivation of the servlet as demand ebbs and flows. If the servlet engine sees that twenty-four hours (or less) has gone by without a request to the RemoteObjectServlet, the Servlet engine can `destroy()` the RemoteObjectServlet, then construct and `init()` a new instance of the Servlet when the next URL request comes in. This means less drain on resources on the server.

Secondly, because our service is now operating off of the web server, we don't have to punch a new hole through the firewall and yet our middleware mechanism is still available to Internet clients (if required). This makes the code firewall friendly, since we're not requiring additional work on the part of the firewall (except that it support HTTP requests through port 80, something most firewalls are already capable of doing).

## 11.5 ADDITIONAL READING

- Alan Williamson, *Java Servlets By Example* (Manning Publications Co., 1999).
  An impressive collection of sample code focusing exclusively on servlets. It's 500-plus pages of nothing but servlets, servlets, servlets.

- Jason Hunter, *Java Servlet Programming* (O'Reilly and Associates, 1998).
  This is fast becoming the must-have book for servlet programming. If you're working with servlets, this (or the Williamson book) is the place to start. Be

aware that the servlet specification has undergone several revisions (from 2.0 to 2.2, at the time of this writing) since his book became available, and certain methods in the servlet API have become deprecated.

- James Duncan Davidson, "Servlet 2.2 Specification," 1999, available at http://www.javasoft.com/products/servlets.

This is the fundamental definition of what is, and is not, available within the servlet API, and the classes which make up the `javax.servlet` package are available online from the same place. If you develop servlets, you need to read this, because vendors will be required to keep up with the spec, and you'll get burned someday if you don't.

# CHAPTER 12

# *Persistence*

Persistence refers, in our particular case, to the ability of objects to be able to *persist* themselves beyond the current application instance. Normally, most objects are transient, that is, they do not exist outside of the current application space. When the application quits, they disappear. Persistent objects live on, or at least appear to. In reality, while the actual object instance may be destroyed, the data that forms one half of the object (the other half being the code, which is reloaded each time the application is started) is saved off in some fashion, usually to disk. Then, when reloaded, an object of similar or compatible type is created, and the data from the previous instance is loaded. To all intents and purposes, that object has lived beyond the current application scope.

Persistence can take several forms of implementation. Java's Object Serialization specification is one. Using a relational database and JDBC is another. You can even use some customized approach to handle it on your own terms if you choose. Where the object's data resides between invocations doesn't matter, so long as the code using the persistent object knows how to recreate it when asked.

It's this latter requirement that typically provides the biggest headache. Saving an object off to disk or database usually isn't the problem; the problem comes when attempting to retrieve that particular object, out of the hundreds, or thousands or hundreds of thousands of objects available. In a relational database scheme, each object usually corresponds to one or more rows in one or more relational tables, whose uniqueness is given by a primary key. In classic JavaBeans Serialization, each object or collection of objects corresponding to a single entity is saved into its own filename.[1] For your custom approaches, you're on your own.

Note that persistent object systems and databases (be they relational or object-based) are not the same beast. The first merely describes the ability for an object to save and restore itself to some nonvolatile memory (disk, or some external device). The second describes a system not only in which objects can be stored and retrieved, but queried and examined in an ad hoc format. This marks an important difference; a persistent system may have no other way to access a given object other than retrieving the entire object tree. Consider a simple request to determine if a large entity (100-plus interconnected objects) exists; in a database system, I can fire off a simple query and examine the results without having to instantiate the objects themselves. A persistent system has no such ability; I must retrieve all 100-plus objects from disk or the persistent backing store and deserialize them (which in turn requires the construction of all 100-plus objects) before I get the chance to check if the object came back.

## 12.1  JAVA SERIALIZATION

Java's Serialization mechanism is, at heart, a simple one. Objects which implement the interface Serializable can be written directly to an ObjectOutputStream, in the following manner:

```
// Serialize today's date to a file
FileOutputStream f = new FileOutputStream("date");
ObjectOutputStream s = new ObjectOutputStream(f);
s.writeObject("Today");
s.writeObject(new Date());   // Date no-arg constructor
                             // uses current date/time
s.flush();
```

Reading from a Serialized stream is similarly simple:

```
// Deserialize file containing (we hope) today's date
FileInputStream f = new FileInputStream("date");
ObjectInputStream s = new ObjectInputStream(f);
String label = (String)s.readObject();
Date date = (Date)s.readObject();
```

In this case, we open a file and attempt to read in a String object, followed by a Date object. If it succeeds, label contains "Today", and date contains the date when the file "date" was written (since that was the value of the Date object at the time it was serialized).

---

[1] Note that there is no mention of files or filenames in the Object Serialization specification, a fact which will become more clear and lead to interesting tactics later in the chapter.

All of this should be old hat to you; if it's not, check out just about any text on JavaBeans. Most cover the basics of Serialization to some detail, since Serialization made its debut in JDK 1.1. Touted as a scheme by which JavaBeans could be customized within a Bean editor, stored off to disk (and presumably shipped with your application), and restored with all properties intact, Serialization never really got much press beyond that. RMI also uses this "basic" form of Serialization to ship objects across the wire from client to server or vice versa.

## 12.1.1 Serialization to other places

As RMI proves, we can Serialize objects to any place we can store and retrieve data streams. ObjectOutputStream, the default ObjectOutput-implementing byte container, wraps an OutputStream. This means that any class which extends Output-Stream can in turn be a sink for serialized objects. When you consider the wide variety of rich and well-defined stream classes Java has, this means that objects can, quite literally, be serialized anywhere:

```
ByteArrayOutputStream baos = new ByteArrayOutputStream();
ObjectOutputStream oos = new ObjectOutputStream(baos);
oos.writeObject(obj);
oos.flush();
byte[] serializedData = baos.toByteArray();

// ...

// Now reconstitute the object(s)
ByteArrayInputStream bais = new ByteArrayInputStream(serializedData);
ObjectInputStream ois = new ObjectInputStream(bais);
Object obj = ois.readObject();
```

This snippet[2] allows us to now send the serialized form of the object obj to any byte-centric data stream we choose: RDBMS binary object column, socket, XML format, wherever.

Furthermore, we can now manipulate the data in any way we see fit, even compress it:

```
import java.io.*;
import java.util.zip.*;

public class CompressedSerialization
{
    public static void main(String[] args)
        throws Exception
    {
        // Take a String, serialize it compressed to disk
        String data = "This is our test string";
```

---

[2] Effectively a longer-way-around replacement for Cloneable, although I strongly suggest that if you want to clone objects, you implement Cloneable and decide on shallow-copy or deep-copy semantics explicitly. ("Cloning-via-serialization" will always give you a deep copy, with new versions of each object.)

```
        FileOutputStream os =
            new FileOutputStream("data");
        GZIPOutputStream gzOS =
            new GZIPOutputStream(os);
        ObjectOutputStream oos =
            new ObjectOutputStream(gzOS);

        // Serialize the object
        oos.writeObject(data);
        oos.close();

        // Set up the input streams
        FileInputStream is =
            new FileInputStream("data");
        GZIPInputStream gzIS =
            new GZIPInputStream(is);
        ObjectInputStream ois =
            new ObjectInputStream(gzIS);

        String test = (String)ois.readObject();

        System.out.println("Compare: " + data + " vs. " + test);
        if (data.equals(test))
            System.out.println("Success!");
    }
}
```

Notice how Java's stream-chaining makes this a simple task. By placing the GZIP-OutputStream and GZIPInputStreams around the FileOutputStream or FileInput-Stream instances, and having the ObjectOutputStream and ObjectInputStreams talk to the GZIP streams, we now compress the serialized data on the way out, and decompress it on the way in. The act of performing the serialization or deserialization will take longer, granted, but this is to be expected of any compression task.

### 12.1.2   Security and Serialization

Serialization, in its basic form, for all its wonderful promise, leaves a very large security hole. If sensitive information is stored off to some serialized stream, then anyone who has access to the serialized data and the binary code for the class(es) which represent the serialized objects in that data stream can reconstitute the entire object with no security restrictions whatsoever. This means that if you serialize a record containing financial or other sensitive information off to disk, you need to make sure that unauthorized users can't access the disk files.

It would be nice if Java came with some cryptographic I/O streams that we could plug in to the Serialization process, as we did with compression, but none do. This means that in order to encrypt the data produced from a serialization stream, we either have to capture the entire byte array and encrypt it, or create an InputStream/Output-Stream pair that do the encryption on the fly as bytes are written in. Unfortunately, the more secure encryption algorithms don't handle on-the-fly encryption, but depending on your needs, simple on-the-fly encryption methods like listing 12.1 could work.

**Listing 12.1   Code for simple encryption**

```java
import java.io.*;
import java.util.zip.*;

class SimpleFilterInputStream extends FilterInputStream
{
    public SimpleFilterInputStream(InputStream in)
    { super(in); }

    /**
     * Offset the byte values by -1
     */
    public int read()
        throws IOException
    {
      int r = super.read();
      return r--;
    }

    /**
     * Offset the byte values by -1
     */
    public int read(byte b[])
        throws IOException
    {
      int ret = super.read(b, 0, b.length);

      for (int i=0; i<b.length; i++)
        b[i]--;

      return ret;
    }

    /**
     * Offset the byte values by -1
     */
    public int read(byte b[], int off, int len)
        throws IOException
    {
      int ret = in.read(b, off, len);

      for (int i=0; i<b.length; i++)
        b[i]--;

      return ret;
    }
}

class SimpleFilterOutputStream extends FilterOutputStream
{
    public SimpleFilterOutputStream(OutputStream out)
    { super(out); }

    /**
```

```java
      * Offset the bytes by +1
      */
     public void write(int b)
         throws IOException
     {
       out.write(b++);
     }

     /**
      * Offset the bytes by +1
      */
     public void write(byte b[])
         throws IOException
     {
       write(b, 0, b.length);
     }

     /**
      * Offset the bytes by +1
      */
     public void write(byte b[], int off, int len)
         throws IOException
     {
       for (int i = 0 ; i < len ; i++)
       {
         write((b[off + i])++);
       }
     }
}

/**
 *
 */
public class SecureSerialization
{
    public static void main(String[] args)
        throws Exception
    {
        // Take a String, serialize it compressed to disk
        String data = "This is our test string";

        FileOutputStream os =
            new FileOutputStream("data");
        SimpleFilterOutputStream fos =
            new SimpleFilterOutputStream(os);
        ObjectOutputStream oos =
            new ObjectOutputStream(fos);

        // Serialize the object
        oos.writeObject(data);
        oos.close();

        // Set up the input streams
        FileInputStream is =
```

```
        new FileInputStream("data");
    SimpleFilterInputStream fis =
        new SimpleFilterInputStream(is);
    ObjectInputStream ois =
        new ObjectInputStream(fis);

    String test = (String)ois.readObject();

    System.out.println("Compare: " + data + " vs. " + test);
    if (data.equals(test))
        System.out.println("Success!");
    }
}
```

Obviously, this sort of encryption would be simple for any serious encryption-breaking algorithm or hacker to tear apart. For added security (such as it is, anyway), we could slip a GZIP stream into the process, thus rendering the data offset by one, compressed and serialized, which would confuse any nonencryption-aware reader or application attempting to understand the data. Again, however, if your data is truly sensitive, if the data will be sent over insecure lines (such as anything outside your intranet), or if the data simply warrants added security, go with a more secure algorithm.

### 12.1.3 Customized Serialization

Serialization isn't limited to playing strictly by Sun's rules. The Object Serialization specification allows those classes that wish to control the manner in which they are serialized to do so.

As stated before, one way in which serialization is controlled comes via the seri-alizedPersistentFields member of a class; if one is present, Serialization will only persist those members specified in that array. Sometimes, however, that level of control isn't enough—the target system doesn't understand byte streams, or perhaps simply streaming off the bytes in Serialization's own format is inconvenient for further system development.

Under these circumstances, if a class provides readObject and writeObject methods (the access specifier on these methods must be marked as private, or Serialization will not find them), these methods will be called in addition to using default Serialization behavior to persist the object. This allows you to add optional data following the class when persisting it off which would otherwise not be stored (such as static fields, or references to objects that would normally sit outside the class, and so forth).

In listing 12.2, we replace the default Serialization mechanism with one of two different implementations. Both use the read and write methods of ObjectInput-Stream and ObjectOutputStream, respectively, and so aren't completely removed from Serialization, but alternate implementations are easy to imagine and see where and how they would plug in.

**Listing 12.2   Code for customizing Serialization**

```java
import java.io.*;
import java.util.*;

public class CustomSerialization
    implements Serializable
{
    public CustomSerialization()
    {
        m_int = 5;
        m_string = "This is a test";
        m_object = new Date();
    }

    private void writeObject(ObjectOutputStream oos)
        throws IOException
    {
        // One possible implementation
        /*
        oos.writeUTF("{BEGIN}");
        oos.writeInt(m_int);
        oos.writeUTF(m_string);
        oos.writeObject(m_object);
        oos.writeUTF("{END}");
        */

        // A second implementation
        Hashtable hash = new Hashtable();
        hash.put("m_int", new Integer(m_int));
        hash.put("m_string", m_string);
        hash.put("m_object", m_object);
        oos.writeObject(hash);
    }
    private void readObject(ObjectInputStream ois)
        throws IOException, ClassNotFoundException
    {
        // The deserialization to the implementation given first
        /*
        System.out.println((String)ois.readUTF());
        m_int = ois.readInt();
        m_string = ois.readUTF();
        m_object = ois.readObject();
        System.out.println((String)ois.readUTF());
        */

        // The deserialization to the second implementation
        Hashtable hash = (Hashtable)ois.readObject();
        m_int = ((Integer)hash.get("m_int")).intValue();
        m_string = (String)hash.get("m_string");
        m_object = hash.get("m_object");
    }
```

```java
    public int m_int;
    public String m_string;
    public Object m_object;

    public static void main(String[] args)
        throws Exception
    {
        CustomSerialization custom = new CustomSerialization();
        custom.m_int = 12;
        custom.m_string = "Test data";
        custom.m_object = new Vector();
        ((Vector)custom.m_object).addElement("One");
        ((Vector)custom.m_object).addElement("Two");
        ((Vector)custom.m_object).addElement("Three");

        // Serialize it off to disk
        FileOutputStream os =
            new FileOutputStream("data");
        ObjectOutputStream oos =
            new ObjectOutputStream(os);
        oos.writeObject(custom);
        oos.close();

        // Retrieve it from disk
        FileInputStream is =
            new FileInputStream("data");
        ObjectInputStream ois =
            new ObjectInputStream(is);
        CustomSerialization test =
            (CustomSerialization)ois.readObject();

        if (custom.m_int == test.m_int &&
            custom.m_string.equals(test.m_string))
        {
            System.out.println("It worked!");
        }
    }
}
```

The core of the example is in the writeObject and readObject methods of Custom-Serialization. In writeObject, the first implementation (which is currently commented out) uses ObjectOutputStream's methods to write a "begin" and "end" block around the serialized members, and readObject in turn uses these markers to ensure that the stream is synchronized correctly. The second implementation instead makes use of a standard Hashtable to contain the members in a name-value pair approach, and uses default Serialization to stream the Hashtable out to the data stream and back again. While neither of these approaches really gets away from using the default behavior of Serialization, (and neither approach warrants the need for custom Serialization) it highlights the necessary steps to implement customized Serialization.

## 12.1.4    Serialization and evolution

"The only thing constant in life is change." This is true of object systems, as well. Systems that remain constant aren't well-written, they're stagnant. Business changes, technology evolution, new ideas, even the simple act of administering the enterprise's corporate data center can introduce changes into an enterprise system and create additional requirements or changes to the system.

This introduces particular problems for the persistent object concept; how can objects change their internal representation and still be able to read (and potentially write) older versions of themselves? This is not a trivial task; the backward-compatibility target is one to which many systems aspire, yet few actually hit. It is difficult enough for developers to maintain a consistent set of methods and APIs at the object-model level so as not to require massive rework on the client side. Asking developers to also maintain the internal representation of objects, so as to remain compatible with the already Serialized versions of those objects, is downright impossible.

Fortunately, Serialization provides a certain amount of evolution-friendly capability. So long as developers do not violate one of the following rules,[3] the serialized versions of objects will be transparently read from disk without a problem:

- *Deleting fields*
  If a field is deleted in a class, the stream written will not contain its value. When the stream is read by an earlier class, the value of the field will be set to the default value because no value is available in the stream. However, this default value may adversely impair the ability of the earlier version to fulfill its contract.

- *Moving classes up or down the hierarchy*
  This cannot be allowed since the data in the stream appears in the wrong sequence.

- *Changing a nonstatic field to static or a nontransient field to transient*
  When relying on default serialization, this change is equivalent to deleting a field from the class. This version of the class will not write that data to the stream, so it will not be available to be read by earlier versions of the class. As when deleting a field, the field of the earlier version will be initialized to the default value, which can cause the class to fail in unexpected ways.

- *Changing the declared type of a primitive field*
  Each version of the class writes the data with its declared type. Earlier versions of the class attempting to read the field will fail because the type of the data in the stream does not match the type of the field.

- *Changing the* writeObject *or* readObject *method*
  Changing either method so that it no longer writes or reads the default field data or changing it so that it attempts to write it or read it when the previous version did not is a no-no. The default field data must consistently either appear or not appear in the stream.

---

[3] *Java Object Serialization Specification*, Section 5.6.1.

- *Changing a class from* `Serializable` *to* `Externalizable` *or vice-versa*
  This is an incompatible change since the stream will contain data that is incompatible with the implementation in the available class.

- *Removing either* `Serializable` *or* `Externalizable`
  When written it will no longer supply the fields needed by older versions of the class.

- *Adding the* `writeReplace` *or* `readResolve` *method to a class*
  This is incompatible if the behavior would produce an object that is incompatible with any older version of the class.

The following is a list of what is permitted to maintain compatibility:[4]

- *Adding fields*
  When the class being reconstituted has a field that does not occur in the stream, that field in the object will be initialized to the default value for its type. If class-specific initialization is needed, the class may provide a `readObject` method that can initialize the field to nondefault values.

- *Adding classes*
  The stream will contain the type hierarchy of each object in the stream. Comparing this hierarchy in the stream with the current class can detect additional classes. Since there is no information in the stream from which to initialize the object, the class's fields will be initialized to the default values.

- *Removing classes*
  Comparing the class hierarchy in the stream with that of the current class can detect that a class has been deleted. In this case, the fields and objects corresponding to that class are read from the stream. Primitive fields are discarded, but the objects referenced by the deleted class are created, since they may be referred to later in the stream. They will be garbage-collected when the stream is garbage-collected or reset.

- *Adding* `writeObject`/`readObject` *methods*
  If the version reading the stream has these methods then `readObject` is expected, as usual, to read the required data written to the stream by the default serialization. It should call `defaultReadObject` first before reading any optional data. The `writeObject` method is expected as usual to call `defaultWriteObject` to write the required data and then may write optional data.

- *Removing* `writeObject`/`readObject` *methods*
  If the class reading the stream does not have these methods, the required data will be read by default serialization, and the optional data will be discarded.

---

[4] *Java Object Serialization Specification*, Section 5.6.2.

- *Adding* `java.io.Serializable`
  This is equivalent to adding types. There will be no values in the stream for this class so its fields will be initialized to default values. The support for subclassing nonserializable classes requires that the class's supertype has a no-arg constructor and the class itself will be initialized to default values. If the no-arg constructor is not available, the InvalidClassException is thrown.
- *Changing the access to a field*
  The access modifiers `public`, `package`, `protected`, and `private` have no effect on the ability of serialization to assign values to the fields.
- *Changing a field from static to nonstatic or transient to nontransient*
  When relying on default serialization to compute the serializable fields, this change is equivalent to adding a field to the class. The new field will be written to the stream but earlier classes will ignore the value since serialization will not assign values to static or transient fields.

When evolving a class in a compatible form, allowing the evolved class to read and write the original class's serialized instances is a simple matter. Place the original's *serialver* (so named because it is obtained from the JDK utility "serialver") value as a static member of the evolved class, like so:

```
public class Evolved
{
    static final long serialVersionUID = -6756364686697947626L;
}
```

Now, when instances of the evolved class are deserialized from streams (which were serialized using the original class), the original instance will be read into the evolved instance. Those fields which weren't present in the original instance will be set according to the evolved instance's no-arg constructor (or to null, if a default constructor isn't defined for the class). Fortunately, when the evolved class is serialized, the serialVersionUID is ignored and the full evolved class is Serialized (as opposed to an original form of the evolved class).

To demonstrate, consider the following "original" class:

```
public class Evolution
    implements Serializable
{
    public static void main(String[] args)
        throws Exception
    {
        // Create an instance
        //
        Evolution e = new Evolution();
        e.printIt();

        // Serialize it out
        //
        FileOutputStream fo = new FileOutputStream("evolve.tmp");
```

```
        ObjectOutputStream so = new ObjectOutputStream(fo);
        so.writeObject(e);
        so.flush();
        fo.close();

        // Deserialize it back in, just to make sure
        //
        FileInputStream fi = new FileInputStream("evolve.tmp");
        ObjectInputStream si = new ObjectInputStream(fi);
        Evolution e2 = (Evolution)si.readObject();
        e2.printIt();
        fi.close();
    }

    public Evolution()
    {
        m_data = new String("This is a test");
    }

    public void printIt()
    {
        System.out.println("Data: " + m_data);
    }
    private String m_data = new String("Default value");
}
```

When the original is run, it first serializes an instance of itself, then deserializes it to verify that it is deserializable by the original. Next, look at the compatible evolution of the original class:

```
public class Evolution
    implements Serializable
{
    public static void main(String[] args)
        throws Exception
    {
        // Deserialize the old instance
        //
        FileInputStream fi = new FileInputStream("evolve.tmp");
        ObjectInputStream si = new ObjectInputStream(fi);
        Evolution e = (Evolution)si.readObject();
        e.printIt();
        fi.close();

        // Change the "new" data
        //
        e.changeData2();

        // Serialize it out to a new file
        //
        FileOutputStream fo = new FileOutputStream("evolve2.tmp");
        ObjectOutputStream so = new ObjectOutputStream(fo);
        so.writeObject(e);
        so.flush();
        fo.close();
```

```
        // Deserialize it back in, just to make sure
        //
        fi = new FileInputStream("evolve2.tmp");
        si = new ObjectInputStream(fi);
        Evolution e2 = (Evolution)si.readObject();
        e2.printIt();
        fi.close();
    }

    public Evolution()
    {
        m_data = new String("This is a test");
    }

    public void printIt()
    {
        System.out.println("Data: " + m_data);
        System.out.println("Data2: " + m_data2);
    }

    public void changeData2()
    {
        m_data2 = new String("This is different.");
    }
    private String m_data = new String("Default value");
    private String m_data2 = new String("Default data2 value");

    static final long serialVersionUID = -282360125859716471L;
}
```

When the evolved class is executed, it first deserializes the instance of the original, to ensure that it can, then serializes itself back to disk under a different filename. Finally, as a last check, it deserializes the new instance, to make sure that the new serialization format was used and not the old.

## 12.1.5 Replacement

In the event, however, that you must make changes that would make the class incompatible with its former serialized representation, Serialization allows a class to nominate its replacement type in the serialized stream, and to offer a replacement type when deserialized from the stream. This behavior is implemented with the `write-Replace` and `readResolve` methods, which are prototyped as follows:

```
<any access modifier> Object writeReplace()
    throws ObjectStreamException { . . . }
<any access modifier> Object readResolve()
    throws ObjectStreamException { . . . }
```

Note that the access specifier given to these methods (`public`, `private`, `protected`, or package-friendly) is irrelevant as far as Serialization is concerned. It will use Reflection to identify whether either method exists, and will ignore the access-specification when using them.

The problem with using these methods is that they are called after deserialization has taken place; that is, on the object that was deserialized from the data stream. Unfortunately, an incompatible change to the class means that deserialization will fail before `readResolve()` can be called to nominate a replacement object in its stead.

All is not completely lost; while it's not quite as seamless or as transparent as we might hope, we can use the `readResolve()` method to construct the new class using the old one as an argument to a new class constructor (what C++ referred to as a copy constructor):

```
public class NewClass
{
    // . . .

    public NewClass(OldClass source)
    {
        // Copy over data from 'source'
    }
}
```

The OldClass must then be written to nominate instances of NewClass when deserialized:

```
public class OldClass
{
    // . . .
    private Object readResolve()
        throws ObjectStreamException
    {
        return new NewClass(this);
    }
}
```

And, any place where an OldClass was expected from a deserialization operation, the code must be changed to expect a NewClass instead:

```
// code like this:
OldClass obj = (OldClass)objectInputStream.readObject();

// must be changed to:
NewClass obj = (NewClass)objectInputStream.readObject();
```

When the NewClass is serialized (listing 12.3), it will be serialized using its new format, and not the (incompatible) one written by OldClass. If, however, you desire to keep the old format in place, you can provide a `writeReplace()` method on NewClass that creates an OldClass for serialization.

### Listing 12.3    Code for NewClass (serialized)

```
import java.io.*;

/**
 * OldClass is the "old" serialized format we wish to maintain
 */
class OldClass
```

```java
    implements Serializable
{
    public OldClass(String data)
    {
        m_data = data;
    }

    public String getData()
    {
        return m_data;
    }

    public String toString()
    {
        return ("OldClass.m_data = " + m_data);
    }

    private String m_data;

    // Serialization Replacement method
    private Object readResolve()
        throws ObjectStreamException
    {
        return new NewClass(this);
    }
}

/**
 * NewClass is the "new" serialized format we wish to replace
 * OldClass with.
 */
class NewClass
    implements Serializable
{
    public NewClass(OldClass source)
    {
        System.out.println("Copy-constructing from " + source);
        m_ref = source;
        m_additionalData = null;
    }

    private Object m_additionalData;
    private OldClass m_ref;
        // This is counted as an incompatible change as far as
        // Serialization is concerned--we "removed" a serialized
        // field (m_data) from this new class type, we changed the
        // class name, and so forth.

    private Object writeReplace()
        throws ObjectStreamException
    {
        System.out.println("Nominating " + m_ref + " for " +
            "serialization instead of ourselves");
        return m_ref;
    }
}
```

```
/**
 *
 */
public class Replacement
{
    public static void main(String[] args)
        throws Exception
    {
        // Serialize out a version of OldClass to work with
        ByteArrayOutputStream out1 =
            new ByteArrayOutputStream();
        ObjectOutputStream objOut =
            new ObjectOutputStream(out1);
        OldClass data = new OldClass("Data value");
        objOut.writeObject(data);
        objOut.flush();

        // Deserialize written object into a NewClass instance
        ByteArrayInputStream in1 =
            new ByteArrayInputStream(out1.toByteArray());
        ObjectInputStream objIn =
            new ObjectInputStream(in1);
        NewClass newData = (NewClass)objIn.readObject();

        // Serialize NewClass instance back out to file
        ByteArrayOutputStream out2 =
            new ByteArrayOutputStream();
        ObjectOutputStream objOut2 =
            new ObjectOutputStream(out2);
        objOut2.writeObject(newData);
        objOut2.flush();

        // Ensure the two byte arrays (out1 and out2) are identical;
        // for this example, we'll just compare sizes
        if (out1.toByteArray().length == out2.toByteArray().length)
            System.out.println("Lengths are identical!");
    }
}
```

Note that NewClass has nothing to do with OldClass in any way so far as Serialization is concerned. We've made a number of incompatible changes to OldClass, not the least of which is the fact that we changed its name (to NewClass)! But, as you can see, Serialization still believes that the serialized versions of OldClass can be read and written by NewClass. Normally, being able to write out the new class as the old is less of an issue than being able to read in the new (notice that since NewClass does not have a readResolve() method, if the writeReplace() method in NewClass is removed, any serialized OldClass instances will be one-way transformed into NewClass instances), but being able to go from old to new back to old is possible, as demonstrated.

## 12.2   BEYOND THE SPECIFICATION

Having spent all this time discussing the mechanics of Serialization and Externaliza-tion, the curious reader may wonder what good this knowledge can serve when writ-ing server code. After all, Serialization is really just a JavaBeans thing, isn't it?

Not exactly. A good working knowledge of Serialization is not only necessary for usage in RMI (which, as mentioned before, uses Serialization for sending representa-tion of object instances across the wire), but can also have some direct capabilities in the server environment.

To start with, this inherent ability to gracefully (and silently) stream objects to data streams and back allows us some flexibility in the objects' actual location and environment. For example, nothing prevents us (assuming all objects are Serializable) from storing objects in a central server on the network. RMI also allows this, but con-current modification of objects can create problems in an RMI environment. Instead of adding complicated concurrency locking, we can instead allow clients to check out objects from this remote storage facility, and check in the objects when they are fin-ished with them. In addition to being as fast, if not faster, than RMI, this check-out/ check-in paradigm can, when combined with one of the distributed ClassLoaders pre-viously discussed, completely obviate the need for RMI for some purposes.

Secondly, now that we've seen the ability of Serialization to shuffle objects between JVMs, one begins to wonder if objects need to begin and end life within the same JVM. They don't, and the remote construction of objects offers a number of advantages that local construction of objects can't match without added complexity. Again, when combined with one (or more) of the distributed ClassLoaders from pre-vious chapters, we gain a measure of flexibility unparalleled by other languages or development environments.

### 12.2.1   Remote storage of objects

Much of the development work that goes on within an enterprise application centers around the idea of group-enabling access to data. For example, the employee applica-tion system developed in chapter 6 is precisely that—the ability for multiple clients to view and/or modify data from anywhere in the enterprise. Historically, centralized persistent forms of storage have been used for this role, regardless of their appropri-ateness toward that task. Specifically, relational databases are used to perform this role, forcing database administrators and developers into a relational frame of mind when storing off data. While the centralization of data is a worthwhile thing, for many systems and applications the use of a relational database is overkill.

Additionally, using a relational database forces the design team into making deci-sions based specifically on the basis that a relational database is being used. For exam-ple, implementing the kind of check-in/check-out system described earlier becomes painful under an RDBMS if the RDBMS itself does not provide some form of table or row locking. Also, for a number of applications, such as Internet applications or applets, the use of an RDBMS for any purpose is not only inconvenient, but inadvisable. (Most security experts recommend leaving the database behind the firewall to avoid hacking attempts.)

Remember one of object-oriented development's founding tenets: Encapsulation is good. There are a variety of persistent mechanisms already at use within the enterprise (not the least of which is the classic legacy system mainframe application suite), and access to these systems is not trivial by any standard.

Fortunately, we can avoid a number of these problems with the creation of a new GJAS service, the RemoteStorageService. This example code is certainly not ready for immediate production use (if the service shuts down for any reason, the data stored therein is lost), but provides a basic framework from which more robust implementations could easily be derived.

## 12.2.2    Example: RemoteStorageService and RemoteStorageClient

RemoteStorageService (listing 12.4) provides a check-in/check-out system of data storage on the GJAS server. It uses Serialization to stream the data from the client to the server, keeping track of check-outs solely by a client-provided identification string.

**Listing 12.4    Code for RemoteStorageService**

```
import java.io.*;
import java.net.*;
import java.util.*;

/**
 * RemoteStorageService
 */
public class RemoteStorageService extends SocketServer
{
    /**
     * Use this Socket to answer client requests for serialization
     * services. This service, in contrast to others, services only
     * one request/response pair, then shuts down. This is
     * deliberate, as ObjectOutputStream and ObjectInputStream do
     * some activity to the target stream (the socket) during
     * their construction; this means that after the client makes
     * its request and quits, the server will get an Exception
     * claiming the socket "unexpectedly" quit.
     *
     * Note also that order of construction of the streams (the
     * ObjectInput/ObjectOutput streams) is important;
     * because the client's ObjectInputStream is expecting to find
     * header information on the server's ObjectOutputStream, they
     * must be constructed in offsetting pairs. The server builds
     * them in Output-first-Input-second order, so the client must
     * build them in reverse (Input-first-Output-second) order. For
     * this reason, only use RemoteStorageRequest instances to
     * talk to the RemoteStorageService.
     */
```

```
public void serve(Socket socket)
    throws Exception
{
    // Set up
    ObjectOutputStream objOut =
        new ObjectOutputStream(socket.getOutputStream());
    ObjectInputStream objIn =
        new ObjectInputStream(socket.getInputStream());

    // Extract the command
    String cmd = objIn.readUTF();
    if (cmd.equals("GET"))
    {
        // Protocol: GET, obj name
        String objName = (String)objIn.readObject();

        Object objInTable = m_objectTable.get(objName);
        if (objInTable != null)
        {
            objOut.writeUTF("SUCCESS");
            objOut.writeObject(objInTable);
        }
        else
        {
            objOut.writeUTF("ERROR");
            objOut.writeObject(
                new Exception("Object not found"));
        }

        objOut.flush();
    } // GET
    else if (cmd.equals("CHECKIN"))
    {
        // Protocol: CHECKIN, client ID, obj name, obj
        String clientID = (String)objIn.readObject();
        String objName = (String)objIn.readObject();
        Object obj = objIn.readObject();

        // Is it there?
        Object objInTable = m_objectTable.get(objName);
        if (objInTable != null)
        {
            // It's there already; did we check it out?
            String ownerID = (String)m_checkOuts.get(objName);
            if (ownerID == null)
            {
                // It's not checked out at all
                objOut.writeUTF("ERROR");
                objOut.writeObject(
                    new Exception("Object not checked out"));
            }
            else if (ownerID.equals(clientID))
            {
```

```
                    // Yes, 'tis checked out, and client owns it

                    // Replace the old one; Hashtable allows dupes
                    m_objectTable.remove(objName);
                    m_objectTable.put(objName, obj);

                    // Remove the checkout
                    m_checkOuts.remove(objName);

                    // Send success
                    objOut.writeUTF("SUCCESS");
                    objOut.writeObject(obj);
                }
                else
                {
                    // Yes, 'tis checked out, but client doesn't
                    // own it, so they can't check it back in

                    objOut.writeUTF("ERROR");
                    objOut.writeObject(new Exception(
                        "Object checked out to " + ownerID));
                }
            }
            else
            {
                // It's not there; add it and return success
                m_objectTable.put(objName, obj);

                objOut.writeUTF("SUCCESS");
                objOut.writeObject(obj);
            }

            objOut.flush();
        } // CHECKIN
    else . . .
    // CHECKOUT and DIFF also supported; for full details, see
    // the full code listing

    // . . .

    // Internal members
    private Hashtable m_objectTable = new Hashtable();
    private Hashtable m_checkOuts = new Hashtable();
}
```

The client code, snipped somewhat, looks like this:

```
public class RemoteStorageClient
    implements Serializable
{
    // . . .

    public RemoteStorageClient(String ID, String host, int port)
    {
        m_clientID = ID;
        m_host = host;
```

```java
    m_port = port;
}

/**
 * Retrieves a "read-only" (that is, you don't own the lock on
 * this object) object by name.
 */
public Object get(String objName)
    throws Exception
{
    Socket socket = new Socket(m_host, m_port);
    ObjectInputStream fromSocket =
        new ObjectInputStream(socket.getInputStream());
    ObjectOutputStream toSocket =
        new ObjectOutputStream(socket.getOutputStream());

    // Send the request: "GET", name
    toSocket.writeUTF("GET");
    toSocket.writeObject(objName);
    toSocket.flush();

    // Check the response; if the response string is anything
    // other than "SUCCESS", throw the next object pulled from
    // the stream (which RemoteStorageService guarantees will be
    // an Exception type)
    String response = fromSocket.readUTF();
    if (response.equals("SUCCESS"))
    {
        return fromSocket.readObject();
    }
    else
    {
        throw (Exception)fromSocket.readObject();
    }
}

/**
 * Retrieves the object by name and locks it for exclusive
 * modification by this client.
 */
public Object checkOut(String objName)
    throws Exception
{
    Socket socket = new Socket(m_host, m_port);
    ObjectInputStream fromSocket =
        new ObjectInputStream(socket.getInputStream());
    ObjectOutputStream toSocket =
        new ObjectOutputStream(socket.getOutputStream());

    // Send the request: "CHECKOUT", client ID, obj name
    toSocket.writeUTF("CHECKOUT");
    toSocket.writeObject(m_clientID);
    toSocket.writeObject(objName);
    toSocket.flush();
```

```
        // Check the response; if the response string is anything
        // other than "SUCCESS", throw the next object pulled from
        // the stream (which RemoteStorageService guarantees will be
        // an Exception type)
        String response = fromSocket.readUTF();
        if (response.equals("SUCCESS"))
        {
            return fromSocket.readObject();
        }
        else
        {
            throw (Exception)fromSocket.readObject();
        }
    }

    // . . .

    // other methods supported—"checkin", "checkout", "diff", plus
    // a main() for testing.
}
```

The protocol between the client and the service is straightforward: clients send a UTF string down the socket consisting of one of four commands: GET, CHECKIN, CHECKOUT, and DIFF. When received, the service pulls the appropriate arguments after the command string. It responds to the client by sending a UTF string, either SUCCESS or ERROR. If the command is a success, it sends the object or return code as an object after the response string, whereas if the command is a failure, it will send an Exception back. For full details, check out the code associated with the book; all follow the same basic scheme used by get and checkout.

The system is not inherently flawless; because it uses Java Serialization, the RemoteStorageService must have the class bytecode for the actual object stored, either already loaded or somewhere on its CLASSPATH. If an object is sent whose class code is not available to the RemoteStorageService, the server will throw a ClassNotFoundException. If it becomes necessary to store arbitrary bytes without having the class bytecode on the server, simply write the bytecode into an Object-extending subclass that just stores the byte array:

```
public class ByteArray
    implements Serializable
{
    public ByteArray(byte[] array)
    { m_array = array; }

    public byte[] m_array;
}
```

Then, when storing the data, serialize the object to a ByteArrayOutputStream, save the bytes into a ByteArray, and store the ByteArray into the RemoteStorageService. Reverse the process when retrieving the object.

Notice what 200 lines of Java code on the server, and 170 lines on the client (which doesn't include the test driver), including comments, has now provided for us—a distributed storage system whose actual internals are irrelevant to the client's use. Because it uses Java Serialization, any Java application can make use of it, and because it uses sockets for its inter-JVM communication, even applets can use it to store objects on the server from which they came.

Because the actual storage details are encapsulated away from the client, the RemoteStorageService is free to do whatever it likes when retrieving or storing the object's data. From the client's perspective, these objects could be coming from a relational database, an object database, or a legacy mainframe application—the client's code never changes. In fact, the RemoteStorageService could be enhanced or rewritten to allow the server to defer the actual storage of the objects to another, dynamically loaded class instance.

Notice also what Serialization does for us regarding our client-service protocol. Instead of passing around clear-text strings which must be parsed and interpreted, as in HTTP, we can send entire objects over the wire, without having to worry about the details of how to represent those objects in text-based format.

In fact, for a more complex protocol, the request and response protocol could itself be wrapped in classes, all of which implement Serializable, and the entire request object serialized over the socket, deserialized on the server and picked apart there. The advantage in doing this is type-safety and protocol encapsulation—instead of having to remember when writing new extensions to the protocol to write the correct objects in the correct order, the Request class or derived class can take care of the details:

```
RemoteStorageClient client = . . .;

// . . .

Object obj = client.request(new RemoteStorageGetRequest("Test Data"));
```

This approach would also allow for code reuse when creating subtly different versions of various request types. One could almost imagine a Java-only HTML server that uses Serialization to send the various files across instead of HTTP.

Remote storage of objects doesn't have to be this check-in/check-out system; if desired, the service could implement more tradtional RDBMS insert/update/select/ delete operations. Doing this starts to move RemoteStorageService into the realm of an RDBMS server, however, and there are far better database implementations than anything I could ever produce.

### 12.2.3 Remote construction of objects

Java Serialization and sockets offer a new wrinkle to the classic Factory patterns. In a Distributed Factory system, clients send requests for new objects across a socket (or through other distribution channels, perhaps via RMI) to the Factory, which constructs the object and sends the constructed object back over the wire via Serialization. Advantages of this system are:

- *Security*

  System administrators may not want to make the means by which objects are constructed available on end-user machines. For example, RDBMS systems will typically be situated behind a firewall, where applets running on the client machine cannot get to them; instead, the applet must communicate with an agency running on the web server which in turn communicates with the database (or another proxy system, if the web server sits inside the firewall's DMZ).

- *Performance*

  Many back-end server systems are coming with JVM capabilities installed or as part of the system; examples include Oracle, DB2, and Lotus Notes. It will often be faster to construct business objects (or simple data objects containing only the data desired) on the local machine and send the constructed object over the wire, than it will be to negotiate the communication in a traditional client-server fashion. So, for example, when working with large query sets consisting of an abundant number of joins, create a query object that gathers the data on the server (where network bandwidth is not an issue). When the query is complete, the object is Serialized and sent back.

- *Availability*

  In some cases, data sources may be unavailable. Servers may go down once a week for routine maintenance, or users may demand the ability to be able to work remotely, without a constant connection to the back-end database. Under these circumstances, the Remote Object Factory can hold last-known representations of the data (if holding such information is convenient and/or not too heavyweight) and send these back to the clients. To make clients aware of such policies would be duplicative if this knowledge were coded into the client's code by hand each time the client requested a new object.

- *Centralization*

  JDBC-using systems require the presence of the JDBC driver on the JVM that wishes to execute the query, even if the database resides remotely. In a database-heterogenous environment, where more than one database vendor is in use, ensuring that potential clients have all the JDBC drivers they require can be a major chore, especially during version upgrades. (Even those shops that use only one database can find it a pain, especially if these clients are located geographically remote from the system administrators.) Having the data gathered on its own server and sent over the wire in constructed form eliminates the need for the JDBC driver on the client side, and thus reduces the administration headache.

- *Encapsulation*

  I repeat: Encapsulation is good. This is true even of the knowledge of how objects are constructed. The less knowledge the client system has regarding the internals of an object, the less code that will need to change on the client system if those internals ever change. Internals can be exposed, however, if object constructors

*CHAPTER 12  PERSISTENCE*

require particular parameters or knowledge in order to construct the objects.[5] This is the primary motivation for the Factory pattern in general, and carrying it over into a distributed arena simply makes the Factory now more widely available (and centralized on the server).

Constructing objects remotely will not be the answer for all problems. It certainly involves greater overhead—both in maintenance and execution—but having the details of how objects are constructed can lead to greater payoffs over time. When coupled with a SocketClassLoader (from chapter 4), objects can now be constructed on the server and deployed to the client in an on-the-fly basis, without requiring any additional support on the client machine.

## 12.2.4 Example: RemoteObjectFactory

The key to being able to create a generic object-creation service lies in Java's Reflection mechanism. If we know the name of the class we wish to instantiate, we can get a list of all the constructors it supports via the java.lang.Class method `getConstructors()`. Once we've found the Constructor we desire, we can call its `newInstance()` method, passing in an array of Objects as arguments to the constructor:

```
// Construct a String without calling "new String("Test value");"
Class c = Class.forName("java.lang.String");
Constructor ctor = null;
for (int i=0; i<c.getConstructors().length; I++)
{
    // Constructor.toString() returns a human-readable version of the
    // constructor with parameter list
    if (c.getConstructors()[i].toString().equals(
        "String(java.lang.String)"))
    {
        ctor = c.getConstructors[i];
        break;
    }
}
if (ctor == null)
    ; // What?!? String suddenly lost its copy-constructor?!?

String str = (String)ctor.newInstance(new Object[]
    {
        new String("Test value")
    });
System.out.println("str = " + str);
```

While this would be extremely awkward not to mention extremely type-unsafe— we've lost all ability for the compiler to catch any errors in which the wrong argument types are passed into the constructor—for use in normal code, for our purposes here

---

[5] JDBC Connection objects as constructor parameters to business objects are one particular example— you now know that the object must be coming out of a relational database.

it's precisely what we want. Keep in mind that using Reflection in this manner immediately removes any type-safety the compiler can provide us. We can pass bogus information into the constructor's arguments array and the compiler will happily comply, since it has no way of knowing that the argument types don't match the ones declared. This means that on the server side, we need to catch Exceptions thrown from the Constructor's `newInstance()` method and pass those back down to the client.

At this point, our only problem is that Constructor (nor Class, for that matter) is not Serializable. This means we can't just send the Constructor instance over the wire to the RemoteObjectFactory to use. Fortunately, this isn't a problem—we'll just send the Class name, string representation of the Constructor, and a Vector containing all the arguments to the Constructor down the wire. Once there, the RemoteObjectFactory can find the Class from the Class name, find the Constructor whose string representation matches the one we pulled off the wire, and unpack the Vector into an Object array to pass into the Constructor's `newInstance` method.

The server code looks like this:

```java
import java.io.*;
import java.lang.reflect.*;
import java.net.*;
import java.util.*;

/**
 * RemoteObjectFactoryService
 */
public class RemoteObjectFactoryService extends SocketServer
{
    /**
     * serve() takes a client request, sent via Serialization,
     * and extracts the class name, the constructor, and the
     * array of args to pass to the constructor, and proceeds
     * to attempt to construct an instance of that type. This
     * means that both the Service and the client must have the
     * bytecode of the exact Class returned available on the JVM's
     * CLASSPATH, or ClassNotFoundExceptions will result. (Note that
     * the client doesn't need to know exactly what type it's
     * getting back, it only needs to have it available via the
     * client's ClassLoader--a SocketClassLoader would effectively
     * make the entire mechanism load-on-the-fly.)
     */
    public void serve(Socket socket)
        throws Exception
    {
        // Set up
        ObjectOutputStream objOut =
            new ObjectOutputStream(socket.getOutputStream());
        ObjectInputStream objIn =
            new ObjectInputStream(socket.getInputStream());

        try
```

```
{
    // Protocol: class-name (UTF), ctor rep (UTF),
    // args (Vector)
    String className = objIn.readUTF();
    String ctorStringRep = objIn.readUTF();
    Vector args = (Vector)objIn.readObject();

    // First, get the Class object for className
    Class cls = Class.forName(className);

    // Next, find the Constructor corresponding to
    // ctorStringRep
    Constructor[] allCtors = cls.getConstructors();
    Constructor ctor = null;
    for (int i=0; i<allCtors.length; i++)
    {
        if (allCtors[i].toString().equals(ctorStringRep))
        {
            ctor = allCtors[i];
            break;
        }
    }
    if (ctor == null)
        throw new Exception("Constructor " + ctorStringRep +
            " not found on class " + cls.getName());

    // Unpack the args into an Object array
    Object[] argsArray = new Object[args.size()];
    for (int i=0; i<argsArray.length; i++)
        argsArray[i] = args.elementAt(i);

    // Construct the instance
    Object instance = ctor.newInstance(argsArray);

    // Make sure instance is Serializable
    boolean foundIt = false;
    for (int j=0; j<cls.getInterfaces().length; j++)
    {
        String interfaceName =
            cls.getInterfaces()[j].getName();
        if (interfaceName.equals("java.io.Serializable"))
        {
            foundIt = true;
            break;
        }
    }
    if (!foundIt)
        throw new NotSerializableException(className);
        // Caught in the catch() block a few lines down and
        // sent back over the wire to the client

    // Send it over the wire
    objOut.writeUTF("SUCCESS");
    objOut.writeObject(instance);
```

```
        }
        catch (Exception ex)
        {
            objOut.writeUTF("ERROR");
            objOut.writeObject(ex);
        }

        objOut.flush();
    }
}
```

The client code, complete with test driver, looks like this:

```
import java.io.*;
import java.lang.reflect.*;
import java.net.*;
import java.util.*;

/**
 * RemoteObjectFactoryClient
 */
public class RemoteObjectFactoryClient
{
    /**
     * RemoteObjectFactoryClient constructor
     */
    public RemoteObjectFactoryClient(String host, int port)
    {
        m_host = host;
        m_port = port;
    }

    /**
     *
     */
    public Object construct(Constructor ctor, Object[] ctorArgs)
        throws Exception
    {
        // Transform ctorArgs into a Vector for easier Serialization
        Vector args = new Vector();
        if (ctorArgs != null)
        {
            for (int i=0; i<ctorArgs.length; i++)
                args.addElement(ctorArgs[i]);
        }

        Socket socket = new Socket(m_host, m_port);
        ObjectInputStream objIn =
            new ObjectInputStream(socket.getInputStream());
        ObjectOutputStream objOut =
            new ObjectOutputStream(socket.getOutputStream());
            // Note that these streams must be constructed in
            // reverse order from how they are constructed in
            // the server class; see the code in RemoteObjectService
            // for more details
```

```java
        objOut.writeUTF(ctor.getDeclaringClass().getName());
        objOut.writeUTF(ctor.toString());
        objOut.writeObject(args);
        objOut.flush();

        // Read back the response string--SUCCESS or ERROR
        String response = objIn.readUTF();
        if (response.equals("SUCCESS"))
        {
            // Next object is our serialized object; deserialize
            // and return it
            Object obj = objIn.readObject();
            return obj;
        }
        else
        {
            // Next object is an Exception; deserialize and throw it
            Exception ex = (Exception)objIn.readObject();
            throw ex;
        }
    }

    // Internal members
    String m_host;
    int m_port;

    /**
     * Test driver
     */
    public static void main(String[] args)
        throws Exception
    {
        if (args.length < 1)
        {
            System.out.println(
                "Usage: java RemoteObjectFactoryClient <hostname:port>");
            return;
        }

        // Parse out hostname and port
        String host;
        Integer port;
        host = args[0].substring(0, args[0].indexOf(":"));
        port = new Integer(args[0].substring(
            args[0].indexOf(":")+1, args[0].length()));

        System.out.println("Connecting to " + host + ":" + port);

        RemoteObjectFactoryClient client =
            new RemoteObjectFactoryClient(host, port.intValue());

        // Try constructing a few well-known Java objects

        // new Date()
        Class dateClass = Class.forName("java.util.Date");
```

```
        Constructor dateDefaultCtor =
            dateClass.getConstructor(null);
        Date date = (Date)client.construct(dateDefaultCtor, null);
        System.out.println("new Date(): " + date);

        // new String(String)
        Class stringClass = Class.forName("java.lang.String");
        Constructor stringCtor =
            stringClass.getConstructor(new Class[]
            {
                Class.forName("java.lang.String")
            });
        String str =
            (String)client.construct(stringCtor, new Object[]
            {
                new String("Test value")
            });
        System.out.println("new String(String): " + str);
    }
}
```

A couple of caveats come with this code. To begin with, any objects passed in as arguments, as well as the return type itself, must be Serializable, because both the arguments and the return type have to be marshaled down the wire and back again. While this may seem overly restrictive, it's usually not. Java RMI has the same restriction, and that usually proves to be the least of an RMI developer's problems.

Secondly, as with the RemoteStorageService, both the client and the server must have the class bytecode available to the JVM in order to deserialize the exact type. The server needs it when attempting the newInstance() call, and the client will need it when the object is deserialized and returned from the construct() call. This doesn't mean the client needs to be aware of what the exact type returned is, only that the code for that type needs to be available (on the CLASSPATH, in an extension .JAR file, or loadable via the current ClassLoader). Again, as with the discussion of the RemoteStorageService, a SocketClassLoader can be used to provide both client and server with the class bytecode as required.

# 12.3   *JDBC*

The relational database forms the core of 90 percent of the enterprise's data. This isn't scientific fact, or even an informal poll, but simply anecdotal evidence, witnessed by the rise in influence and power of the relational database vendors, products, and advertising. Corporations scoff at products that don't have some way of storing data to the relational database. Want-ads and job postings for enterprise developers state "SQL experience a plus." When every development tool on the market comes with classes and objects to help ease the pain of obtaining data from a relational database, it becomes obvious that the relational database occupies a central place in the corporate enterprise.

One recent category added to the ranks of relational databases are 100 percent pure Java relational databases; these are databases implemented in Java, and are therefore inherently portable to any platform that can run Java. One such RDBMS system is the IDB RDBMS, which is the one used for the examples in this book. Another is the more widely known Cloudscape RDBMS. Because the Pure Java RDBMS is implemented in Java, there is no native code that requires porting between platforms, and allows any Java-compliant platform to run these examples. The 1.91 version of IDB is found on the publisher's web site, but be sure to check the IDB website (http://www.instantdb.co.uk) for later versions.

Because all the examples in this chapter are coded in pure JDBC, however, nothing prevents you from modifying the JDBC URLs and driver classnames to use your own database. For example, the following code creates the class_tbl table used by the JDBCClassLoader class later in the chapter:

```java
import java.io.*;
import java.sql.*;
import java.util.*;

/**
 * This code re-creates the schema for the examples used in this chapter.
 * Other JDBC-compliant databases could be used by substituting the
 * appropriate JDBC driver names and URLs in place of the IDB ones.
 */
public class CreateSchema
{
    public static void main(String[] args)
        throws Exception
    {
        // Load the IDB driver
        Class.forName("jdbc.idbDriver").newInstance();

        //
        Properties p = new Properties();
        Connection c =
            DriverManager.getConnection("jdbc:idb:sample.prp", p);

        // Drop & create the table in which we will store class bytecode
        //
        Statement s = c.createStatement();
        s.executeUpdate("DROP TABLE class_tbl");
        s.close();

        s = c.createStatement();
        s.executeUpdate("CREATE TABLE class_tbl " +
            "( " +
                "bytecode binary, " +
                "classname varchar(80) " +
            ")");
        s.close();
    }
}
```

Converting this to use an ODBC driver (with an appropriate ODBC data source named "ServerSideJava" already created) would mean changes only to the following lines:

```
// Load the JDBC-ODBC driver
Class.forName("sun.jdbc.odbc.JdbcOdbcDriver").newInstance();

//
Properties p = new Properties();
Connection c =
    DriverManager.getConnection("jdbc:odbc:ServerSideJava", p);
```

This ODBC data source could point to an SQL Server instance, an Oracle instance, or a Text file. (Note that if you modify the CreateSchema.java file, you should modify the LoadClass.java file in similar fashion, since it is this class that is used to populate the `class_tbl` table with bytecode.)

Most books on JDBC can talk about how to use the APIs provided by JDBC, both the 1.2 and the 2.0 specifications; what I want to do is discuss not only a useful JDBC-portable database utility, JDBCTerm (short for JDBC Terminal), but also some of the more interesting uses of JDBC, using the RDBMS as a repository for data that isn't data.

### 12.3.1 Transient data, state data, data that isn't data

Not all data within a database is business data. Specifically, not all data will be used to represent entities or objects that the business deals with. Although a significant percentage of the total will be tables and data to represent customers, addresses, sales orders, and inventory, not all applications are straightforward order-entry applications.

Some data will be workflow applications, in which data moves through a specific set of hands, stopping at virtual station after virtual station awaiting input, process, or approval before moving on. One example would be an order-tracking system. When an order is initially taken, the order sits on the sales desk until the customer indicates the order is complete. The order, once complete, is then sent to Finance to generate and mail an invoice. From there, the order moves to Shipping for processing, and once shipped, into the company's archives or data warehouse for storage and/or retrieval in the event of a customer call. Should Shipping discover that the inventory isn't on hand to support the order, the order can be bounced back to Sales, so that a customer service rep can call the customer and tell them the unhappy news. Because each of these steps in the process can span several days, the state of the order must persist across invocations of the client application. In fact, there would likely be several client applications: one for Sales, to take the order, one for Finance, to generate the invoice, one for Shipping, to view outstanding orders and mark orders as shipped, and so forth. It's simply impractical to expect that all these steps would be conveniently and cleanly supported in one application, or that all the users would be able to use the same running instance of the application, and that the application would remain open for the entire length of time the company is in business.

Toward that end, the database may maintain not only tables to support the logical objects but also tables to maintain the workflow state. (The actual workflow state table could itself be stored within the database, if it is complex enough or is subject to frequent change.) This holds two advantages for the enterprise: order status is now recorded within the database, and these tables can also be used to record a history of the order through the system. The first is useful from a reliability perspective—because most RDBMS vendors take great pains to ensure that data is not lost even in the event of a power failure, hence, it's far less likely that orders will get lost in the system. The second is important to all parties concerned for both accountability and tracking purposes. Quality control reps can make sure orders aren't lost on a regular basis, and if they are, determine who loses them. Managers can now implement targetable, quantifiable goals for their departments ("If we can push fifty orders out this week, I'll dress up in a chicken suit" or something similar).

In other cases, data may not be data at all, but simply a kind of marker. An application may, for example, write an entry into a table indicating the user name and time stamp the application was started. This would be one way to allow for easier tracking of current users of the system, or even to prevent the same user from using the client application more than once. When the user quits the application, the entry is removed. Other information within the database may be system data, such as user ID and password tables, or mostly static application data, such as lookup tables (cities, states or ZIP codes within the US, sales territories or regions for the company, or a list of the company's current campuses).

One such example of data that's not intended to be persistent or tracked is the idea of a message of the day. Many corporations need to distribute messages to every employee within a department, team, or even the entire company. This is especially true in companies that maintain call centers of customer support representatives or internal help desks. One way is to give each employee an email account. One drawback to this approach, however, is the administrative burden—these logins must be maintained, added, and deleted as employees within the call center fluctuate. With call centers of several hundred employees, this is no mean feat, and can represent up to thousands of man-hours per month. In addition, many corporations don't want these employees to have access to email, fearing wasted hours spent emailing other friends within the company (or outside the company, introducing the possibility of email-transmitted viruses in executable attachments). Coupled with this is the burden of knowing if the email were read. In an email system, the only way to verify that a message was seen is to ask that a return-receipt be generated. With a body of hundreds of employees receiving the message, this means hundreds of return-receipt emails, per day. Clearly this is an intolerable situation.

One solution, of course, is to store the message, and a table tracking those who have seen it (and the time stamp they were shown it) within the database itself. Users, when they log in to their client application, can be shown the message within a window, requiring them to click OK (indicating they have read the message) before being allowed to proceed. As each message is shown to the user, a time stamp is written to the message-viewed table. Supervisors can then run reports or queries against this table to see which users have not checked their messages recently, or precisely when a user did see a given message. The message itself can be stored in HTML or RTF format and displayed in a corresponding JFC/Swing JTextPane, to allow for more complex formatting or display.

## 12.3.2 Example: JDBCClassLoader

One such instance of data that isn't business data is class bytecode. Recall, from chapter 2, that one source for class bytecode can be a database column. The code to do this, presented then, is reproduced here.

**Listing 12.5   Code for JDBCClassLoader**

```java
import java.sql.*;

public class JDBCClassLoader extends ClassLoader
{
    /**
     * Constructor
     *
     * The SQL statement must return at least one row, the first column of
     * which will be a BINARY column, and must contain a ? where the name
     * of the fully qualified classname will appear. Example:
     * "SELECT bytecode FROM class_tbl WHERE class_tbl.name = ?"
     *
     * @param conn The JDBC Connection to use. Must be already connected.
     * @param sql The SQL statement to execute to retrieve the bytecode.
     */
    public JDBCClassLoader(Connection conn, String sql)
    {
        m_connection = conn;
        m_sql = new String(sql);
    }

    /**
     * Called by ClassLoader.loadClass when a classname is requested.
     */
    public Class findClass(String className)
        throws ClassNotFoundException
    {
        byte[] classBytes = retrieveClass(className);
        return defineClass(className, classBytes, 0, classBytes.length);
    }

    /**
     * Internal method to do the actual SQL-retrieval of the bytecode
     */
    private byte[] retrieveClass(String className)
    {
        try
        {
            // Create a SQL Statement
```

```java
        Statement stmt = null;
        stmt = m_connection.createStatement();

        // Build our SQL statement
        String pre = m_sql.substring(0, m_sql.indexOf("?"));
        String post = m_sql.substring(m_sql.indexOf("?")+1,
            m_sql.length());
        String sql = pre + className + post;

        // Do the query
        ResultSet rs = stmt.executeQuery(sql);
        if (rs.next())
        {
            byte[] bytes = rs.getBytes(1);
            return bytes;
        }
        else
            return null;
    }
    catch (Exception ex)
    {
        ex.printStackTrace();
        return null;
    }
}

// Internal members
//
private Connection m_connection;
private String m_sql;

/**
 * Test driver routine; assumes an IDB database with the following
 * schema:<BR>
 * CREATE TABLE class_tbl (
 *    bytecode binary,
 *    classname varchar(80) primary key
 * );
 */
public static void main(String[] args)
    throws Exception
{
    // Load the IDB driver
    Class.forName("jdbc.idbDriver").newInstance();

    //
    java.util.Properties p = new java.util.Properties();
    Connection c =
        DriverManager.getConnection("jdbc:idb:sample.prp", p);

    JDBCClassLoader jdbcClassLoader =
        new JDBCClassLoader(c,
            "SELECT bytecode FROM class_tbl WHERE classname = '?'");
```

```
        Class cls = jdbcClassLoader.loadClass("Hello");
        Object h = cls.newInstance();
            // Should print "Hello, world!"
    }
}
```

Given a basic knowledge of JDBC (JDBCClassLoader makes use of only JDBC 1.2 features) and the discussion of ClassLoaders given earlier, the code in listing 12.5 shouldn't present any problems or surprises. The constructor takes a String representing the SQL statement to execute (with the ? within it substituted for the actual fully qualified class name to look up) when a class is requested, and the Connection instance on which to make the SQL query. In the `findClass` method, a Statement is created from the Connection, the SQL string is modified to replace the ? with the class name requested, and the Statement is executed. If the Statement returns a ResultSet, the first column of the first row (assumed to be bytecode—if it's not, a SQLException will be thrown) is retrieved, stored into an array of `bytes`, then handed to `defineClass` for verification and initialization.

The code could be modified to overload the `findClass` method to take an SQL string each time to execute to find the bytecode, but the problem with this approach is that a ClassLoader can be called without your knowledge. In the following code, for example, the JDBCClassLoader will have its `findClass` method called twice, once for the class "TwoPartHello", and once for the class that "TwoPartHello" in turn references:

```
import java.sql.*;

public class TPHClient
{
    public static void main(String[] args)
        throws Exception
    {
        // Load the IDB driver
        Class.forName("jdbc.idbDriver").newInstance();

        // Make the connection
        java.util.Properties p = new java.util.Properties();
        Connection c =
            DriverManager.getConnection("jdbc:idb:sample.prp", p);

        // Set up the JDBCClassLoader to pull from class_tbl
        JDBCClassLoader jdbcClassLoader =
            new JDBCClassLoader(c,
                "SELECT bytecode FROM class_tbl WHERE classname = '?'");

        // Load the Class into the JVM
        Class cls = jdbcClassLoader.loadClass("TwoPartHello");
        Object obj = cls.newInstance();

        // Use Reflection to find its main() method
        // Reflect on the Class; find the method named "run" that takes
        // no arguments and returns no return value
        //
```

```
java.lang.reflect.Method[] methods = cls.getMethods();
for (int i=0; i<methods.length; i++)
{
    System.out.println("Checking name of " + cls.getName()
        + "." + methods[i].getName());
    if (methods[i].getName().equals("main"))
    {
        // methods[i] is the Method that corresponds to the
        // method "void run()". Call it.
        //
        Object[] mainArgs =
        {
            new String[] { }
        };
        Object ret = methods[i].invoke(obj, mainArgs);
        if (ret != null)
            System.out.println("??? main()'s not supposed to " +
                "return me something!");
        break;
    }
}
```

We have no control over the second call to `findClass`, because it's invoked on our behalf automatically by the JVM. Because of that, we have no way of specifying our custom argument to `findClass`.

As with the SocketClassLoader, use of this class allows for centralized control of code updates and revisions. Users no longer need to have the latest code on their local systems in order to receive the benefit of the latest changes—instead, a small bootstrap client is loaded, which then knows how to pull code from the database (via the JDBC-ClassLoader) when requested. Deployment is now centralized, users can remain blissfully unaware of the upgrade or patch, and system administrators and developers can back the changes out should unexpected problems arise with the latest deployment.

This distributed code approach carries with it some unique advantages and disadvantages. Because code no longer resides on the client side, security is improved—the code cannot fall into unfriendly hands where hacking can ensue. Code can also be customized to finer-grained levels than can usually be possible with standardized releases. As discussed in chapter 2, code can now be written customized for a given user, and deployed within the database without disturbing the other users. This allows for cleaner code (no more switching between dialog types or menu bar building code based on user role, for example), at the expense of some more complex file system layout on the developer's machine.[6]

---

[6] A Dialog class written for the CEO must be in a file called Dialog.java, and a Dialog class written for the administrator must also reside in a file called Dialog.java. This means the developer must have two distinct source trees.

The most serious drawback to this approach, however, is the fact that the code[7] will not reside on the local file system. This in turn implies that network bandwidth will be at a premium, since all the code must be carried across the wire. Within an intranet, where bandwidth is usually not an expensive or rare resource, and most users are physically connected by 10Mbps connections, this is a concern for the largest systems. However, over extranets or the Internet, this can be a much larger problem, even with the fastest dial-up connections. Under these circumstances, a hybrid approach (some GUI code, or likely-to-remain-constant utility classes, can be preloaded on the local file system and resolved from disk, since the bootstrap ClassLoader will always be given first crack at resolving a class) may serve best. With the advent of faster CPUs and higher throughput network connections, however, this may be less of a concern than you might think.

## 12.4  SUMMARY

The notion of persistent objects is not new to Java; in fact, persistent objects have been around almost as long as the concept of objects has been. The drive for easy persistent objects has produced a number of products from a number of vendors, and has in turn spawned a new standard, the ODMG standard for object databases, intended to make it easier to store objects to some persistent store.

In fact, if we go much further with this concept, we begin to enter the realm of mobile agents. If a full agent server (such as IBM's Aglet technology, or ObjectSpace's Voyager) is in place on the server, then these remote objects can, in fact, be full mobile agents, with the ability to migrate from server to client in seamless, transparent fashion. A data-request object becomes a data-request agent, which has the ability to move (or be moved, if the data can be retrieved faster on another system in the same cluster) to the server, gather its data, and return. A transaction request becomes a transaction agent, with the ability to migrate from server to server to server, executing its transactions as it goes, only committing them when all are complete.

In short, a standardized Serialization format now gives Java an ability to provide object storage and connectivity options that will guarantee to work across JVM implementations. This is, in fact, one of the central areas where C++ has fallen down; the lack of a standardized object storage/persistence system has made C++ code interconnectivity difficult, to say the least. With Serialization in place, I can Serialize any object in the system, store it to disk or other bytestream, and any other JVM can deserialize it (so long as it has the class definition for the Serialized class available) without any sort of ambiguity or portability problem.

---

[7]  Nor will any of the resources that go with the code, such as .GIF files that are displayed as part of the Swing GUI. Note that none of the ClassLoaders presented in this book implement the resource-loading methods to pull from their respective locations (sockets, database, and so forth), but it shouldn't be too difficult to see how this could be done.

The relational database system is a technology that's not going away any time soon; as a result, developers need to be able to best make use of the database, not just for data storage and categorization, but also as a centralized point of distribution and control. JDBC offers Java developers a feature-rich, yet remarkably uncomplicated interface for obtaining, manipulating, and creating data within the RDBMS.

More importantly, relational database doesn't have to mean a large-scale server-based system like Oracle or SQLServer. Instead, 100 percent Pure Java-implementations, like IDB or Cloudscape (www.cloudscape.com) can be deployed as part of the Java application to provide a platform-portable, zero-deployment data repository on end-user machines, if necessary. This can in turn make object- and/or data-storage requirements a virtual no-brainer: zero development.

## 12.5 ADDITIONAL READING

- "Java Object Serialization" specification (From serial-spec-JDK1.2.pdf on the Javasoft web site), Sun Microsystems, 1998.

- Jim Melton and Alan R. Simon, *Understanding the New SQL: A Complete Guide* (Morgan Kaufman Publishers, 1993).

  Published as a book about ANSI SQL-92's updates to SQL, this is nonetheless the best treatise on pure ANSI SQL I've ever run into, the publication date notwithstanding. If your RDBMS doesn't implement SQL the way Melton and Simon describe it, it's not ANSI SQL-92 compliant.

- "JDBC 2.0 Core API" specification, available online at http://java.sun.com/products/jdbc/download.html.

- "JDBC 2.0 Standard Extension API" specification, available online at http://java.sun.com/products/jdbc/download.html.

**C H A P T E R   1 3**

# Business objects

Building systems on the server is not just an exercise in mechanics—successful systems not only employ useful implementation tricks, but are intelligently and cleanly modeled to provide the enterprise with a consistent, logical object model, as well. Systems which aren't are usually late, over budget, and inherently weaker than systems that are. Cleanly designed systems pay off in other ways, for not only are they easier to maintain over time, but can often outlive the current goals to serve the needs of other projects.

For many years, designers have been talking about three-tier systems. As with most buzzwords, many developers are told to develop a system using the three-tier model without having a solid idea of what such a system is supposed to do, much less how it looks or behaves. While I refuse to hold myself up as an expert on all forms of three-tier, or *n*-tier, systems, in this chapter we will examine one way in which logic can be partitioned into logical, well-encapsulated layers. This is, in fact, the heart of the concept behind the tiered system: encapsulation. And, dare I say it yet again, Encapsulation is good.

## 13.1  MODELING DATA

It's about time to talk about data that is data, or, more specifically, data that's not transient, state, or system-related in nature; it's time to talk about data that's real data.

*340*

### 13.1.1    Two-tier systems vs. n-tier systems

You may hear the terms two-tier, three-tier and *n*-tier tossed about without having a real good idea of what the terms mean. As with most buzzwords, these have lost some of their definition, but the basic idea remains the same: partition the code up into logical layers, or tiers, and write the code within each layer such that it accesses only the layers immediately below it. Typically, the layers are divided into one of the following groupings:

- *Presentation*
  This is the code responsible for displaying the data and obtaining user input.

- *Business Rules or Business Objects*
  The code is responsible for applying business logic and/or rules to the data and/or input from the user. It is typically this layer that is responsible for verification and is typically the "meat" of an enterprise application.

- *Data Access or Data Storage*
  This is the code responsible for storing the data into some permanent nontransient storage system.

This is not, by any means, an exhaustive list of all the possible layers in a tiered system—the presentation layer, for example, could be broken out into multiple layers in and of itself. For example, one layer would be responsible for the actual GUI components (JLabel, JTable, and so on, in a Swing UI), and a second layer for the validation and/or formatting of the data coming in.[1] The Data Access layer is commonly separated, especially when dealing with centralized relational databases, into the layer that is the database itself, and a layer of code that encapsulates dealing with the database (be that JDBC, ODBC, or straight C/C++-level access).

### 13.1.2    One-tier systems

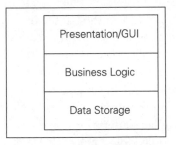

**Figure 13.1    A single-tier system**

A single-tier system (figure 13.1) is one in which all the code resides within the same codebase (executable file or system). This means that the UI elements can directly save to disk, read from disk, and so forth. However, as you might imagine, this makes the code itself extremely heavy (since all file-access code has to be stored within the codebase), as well as less reusable (because any attempt to reuse any part of this code can and usually will have dependencies on other parts of the system). Because

---

[1] Users familiar with Swing will recognize this as Swing's Model-View-Controller discussion—the first layer would be the code putting together the various Swing components into JFrames and JDialogs, and the second layer would be a layer of customized Swing Model classes.

most systems make use of a centralized relational database, however, one-tier systems are relatively rare. Most often, they will be stand-alone applications for single-user utilization, such as word processors, HTML editors, games, and so forth.

### 13.1.3 Two-tier systems

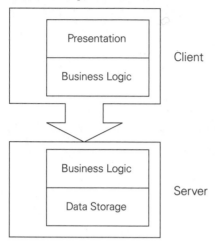

**Figure 13.2 Two-tier system**

In a two-tier system (figure 13.2), the application or system is broken out into two distinct tiers. Typically (although not always) the separation comes at the data-access level, with the data-storage system being (again, not always) a centralized relational database accessed through a JDBC (or ODBC, in traditional C/C++ code) driver. Many code-generation and visual-IDE tools build systems of this nature, using data-aware UI controls or compound controls that directly access database columns or tables so the developer doesn't have to write that code. Some tools can even go so far as to generate the entire UI for a given table just from the database schema, laying the controls out in a standard, if somewhat boring and uninspired, format. Most systems built using the last generation of Rapid Application Development (RAD) tools such as Visual Basic, Delphi, C++Builder, Visual J++, Café, JBuilder, and others end up in this model. This is by far the most popular form of model in the enterprise.

The unfortunate fact about this system is that it leaves the client-side extremely heavyweight. Because the only centralized portion of the system is the relational database server, the code that accesses and works with the data must reside on each and every single client's machine. In addition, any changes to the UI, the underlying business rules, logic or core process, or the database schema itself requires code change (and a new release to each and every client) to the application/system. As the application or system gets larger with more functionality, and as requests for new features come in, the codebase becomes exponentially more difficult to manage. There is no clear-cut method to accessing data, no clean separation of components, and so forth. Worse, most RAD tools cannot handle some commonplace enterprise scenarios; for example, the ability to handle data across not only multiple tables, but multiple databases.

### 13.1.4 *n*-tier systems

Where some would be tempted to build a three-tier architecture (with the three tiers being, as listed before, broken into presentation, business, and data-access codes), this may not, for some applications, be enough. Additional problems arise, as well, when working with the practical matter of what goes into what layer. For example, I stated the general rule that business logic should reside within the business logic layer, and presentation logic within the presentation layer. This is good rhetoric, but what about the situation raised earlier, regarding the validation of data within a UI field? For example, verifying that a Social Security Number entered by a user is, in fact, one contained within the database? If this verification code resides within the presentation layer, then it is a clear violation of the precept that "only presentation logic resides within the presentation layer." If, however, the presentation layer does no validation until the request is made of the business logic layer, we lose the opportunity to inform the user of the mistake the moment it is made. For simple query-by-some-attribute screens, this is less of an issue; for the example of a product order sheet, it is simply unacceptable to inform the user of a mistyped product number at the time the order is submitted.

This would seem to leave the three-tier model at a loss. If something so simple as single field validation in a timely manner cannot easily be answered by the three-tier model, it wouldn't seem that the three-tier model would be useful whatsoever.

This is where partitioning the model further can be beneficial. Recall, earlier, I suggested that the presentation layer could be further tiered into the actual composition of the UI elements into screens, and a layer created that knew how (or what) to display in the fields. In JFC/Swing terms, this would mean breaking the creation and layout of the JComponent-derived components in JFrames and JDialogs into the first layer (the topmost), and the various Model classes used by those UI components into the second layer. In practical terms, this would mean that, for example, the Product-ComboboxModel class would have the knowledge of how to retrieve the list of Products from the underlying Business tier. This means the developer coding the dialog containing the Product Order screen would only have to instantiate a ProductCombobox-Model as the model to the corresponding JComboBox instance, and not have to worry one iota about whether or not the Products displayed were legitimate. For the Social Security Number example, the same approach can be used. A JTextComponent (the base class for JTextField and JTextPane) has an associated Document class paired with it; this SSNDocument class can take the entered number and ask the underlying Business tier (which must, of course, have a method or class to provide this behavior) if the SSN exists within the database. Because most JFC/Swing components have an associated Model class tied to them, the Model classes can hold the knowledge of how to interact with the Business tier, and leave the UI manipulations up to the associated IDE or code-generating visual tool.

## 13.1.5    Benefits of an *n*-tier model

Going this route initially seems like a troublesome amount of work. Not having access to the database, for example, now means that any queries against the data—for example, to see if the Product ID or the Social Security Number exists—must now go through an API change to the Business tier. In addition to requiring more work on the part of more developers,[2] it would seem, quite correctly, that the added overhead would incur a performance penalty on the system. After all, wouldn't it be faster to execute the query directly, instead of having to go through one, two, or more, layers of intermediate code?

There's no arguing the point that it would, in fact, be faster to execute the SQL query directly. There's also no arguing that the code would execute faster if it were written in native CPU code, instead of in Java's portable bytecode format. In fact, there's no arguing that the code would execute much faster if it were written in assembly code for that CPU, instead of such wastefully high-level languages as C or C++. If all of these points hold true, why do programmers bother with languages like C or C++ or Java? We use these languages because speed of development often weighs in far more heavily than just speed of execution. If speed of execution is the primary focus of the application, you're in the wrong book.

More importantly, the tiered system offers some advantages that a nontiered system simply cannot. Specifically, tiering the system encapsulates the layers from one another, with the result that changes can be made within the system that won't affect the entire codebase. For example, assume that in the 1.0 release of the Product Order Entry system, Product IDs are ten-digit numeric numbers. During this time, however, the business acquires (or is acquired by) a competitor which uses fifteen-digit alphanumeric numbers. Were the Product ID-validating code written using direct SQL queries, every place within the UI code that executes that query now has to be rewritten to take into account the new Product ID type. Column sizes have changed, which in turn means field sizes must change. New types of characters are now accessible, which means the routines written to validate that the values entered were all numbers now have to be modified to accept the full range of alphanumerics, instead. In short, one relatively minor change to the business (the definition of a Product ID) results in a potentially catastrophic change to the code.

In a tiered system, however, Product (and, most likely, Product ID as well) would be its own class. The presentation layer wouldn't focus on the internals of what a Product ID is, but simply move them around in a more opaque fashion. The Business tier could even differentiate between an old-style Product ID and a new-style Product ID by creating two subclasses (or two sets of overloaded methods) to handle either type. Then, a few years later, after all new code has migrated over to using the new-style Product ID type, the old Product ID API support is deprecated and phased out.[3]

---

[2] Typically, different developers or teams of developers will maintain the various tiers. This makes requesting a change to a tier much more of a big deal than adding a method or class to the system.

[3] Java's support for the "@deprecated" javadoc tag in this regard is unparalleled. It is the only language I'm aware of that provides compile-time support of code evolution. The only other way to determine whether a method or class is in use within a system (in C++, for example) is to remove it and see what breaks. This way, the owners of an API can mark it as deprecated, leaving it up to clients when to change the code making use of that API. The clients will find out the next time they do a compile, without breaking their code.

This encapsulation works particularly well at the data-access layer. Design, development, and maintenance of a relational database system is a full-time job. Most corporations have individuals or teams specifically dedicated to that task, either as part of the development team, the system administrative group, or as its own department within the IT organization. Tuning and optimizing a relational database is something of a fine art. In short, most Java developers will not have the time, skills, or inclination to take on the (somewhat overwhelming) task of RDBMS maintenance. By encapsulating all of the details and knowledge about the RDBMS schema within its own code layer, hidden from any of the other Java developers on the project, the database can be developed in parallel by a separate team of DBAs and DBEs, who have free reign to design the table structure as best suits their needs or requirements.

Databases change over time. Users may report certain queries take too long, and must be optimized, or later data-driven requirements (such as that for ad hoc query support or reporting) may require a change to the schema. If the knowledge of this schema is required in the GUI code, then all that code must be revisited and modified when the schema changes.

It's also not uncommon for companies or departments to switch database vendors or products. Due to the differing specific functionality of database products, this may in turn require changes to the SQL used to access the data, which, again, can cause code changes. If the code to be changed is scattered throughout the system, tracking it down across the entire codebase can be tedious and error-prone. We, as object-oriented programmers, already know the virtues of encapsulation at the class and object level, and those before us who were procedural programmers knew about the virtues of encapsulation (they called it modularization). Why not apply it, in turn, to the basic architecture of the system?

Execution speed isn't everything, especially not in a system that's intended to be deployed within an enterprise. Scalability, reusability, and development time will often come much more highly requested than just speed of execution of the application. Moreover, developers quite often attempt to optimize code too early. Believing that users will spend 80 percent of their time in a particular query, a developer will spend weeks, even months, attempting to get it as fast as possible. Then, when the application is shipped, the query goes unused 95 percent of the time, because users realized that they didn't need that particular functionality after all. Scott Meyers said it best: "Get it right, *then* worry about making it fast." If performance is at the top of the users' requests, tell them that the first release will be a profiling release (or call it the beta release), so that you can identify which portions of the system need to be profiled. Most likely, the greatest performance-enhancing steps will be to tune the database, improve the network bandwidth, or boost the server hardware, all of which would have far more effect long before code enhancements would kick in.

### 13.1.6  Business objects, entity relationships

Database designers will already be familiar with *entity-relationship diagrams*, which may be a new concept to Java programmers. An entity-relationship diagram, in the classical sense, describes the entities within a business model. Historically, these diagrams were used as a starting point from which to build the logical database schema, but we can make use of them to identify the core business objects for our business object/rule/entity layer. In fact, the entity-relationship diagram is precisely what we're looking for in our business object model—a description of the data the business uses, tracks, and stores.

One warning goes with all of this: while your business object models should closely mimic the entity-relationship diagrams of a database-driven design, your physical object model may differ substantially from the corresponding physical database schema. There are a number of reasons for this, but the principal one is that Java code is a programmatic language, and the database schema is a description of how the data should be stored. Within the Java object model, it may make sense to have two related entities inherit from a common base class, whereas the database schema shows no such relationship. The database schema may, for reasons of tuning or better data warehouse support, break a given object's data representation into several tables, while the Java object model sees it as a logical unit. Or, in a straight reversal, the Java object model may implement a given entity as a collection of contained subobjects (in order to avoid having to execute huge queries to pull back a single object), where the database models the entity in a single, large, table. This is normal for a system. The key to remember is that the logical entities, the components, if you will, of the business object model should have corresponding logical entities modeled within the database.

### 13.1.7  Example: employee directory

Enough theory. Let's try putting some of this discussion into practice.

In the following example (which will become the running example for the next several chapters), the request has come down from on high that we build an employee database. As usual, the request is vague and full of ambiguities, but after careful questioning of potential users, repeated nagging for clarification from the higher-ups, and no small amount of sweat, tears, and agonized decision-making on the analysts' part, we've managed to nail down the basics of the system:

- An *employee* holds at least one, but possibly more, *positions* within the company.
- An *employee* has at least one, but possibly more, ways of being contacted: address, email, or by phone (which includes mobile phones, pagers, and/or fax).
- An *employee* works for a single *department* within the company.
- An *employee* reports to a single *manager* within the company.
- A *manager* is a specific type of *employee*, who manages one-and-only-one *department* within the company and has a number of *employees* that report to him/her.
- A *department* is in turn contained by a larger *department*.

Figure 13.3 illustrates primitive combination entity relationship/static-typing diagram (in UML notation) of this system.

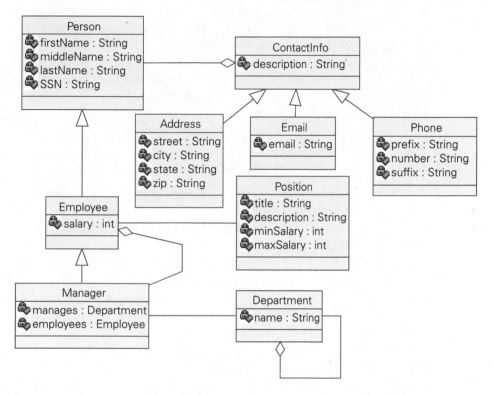

**Figure 13.3  Entity relationship/static-typing diagram of the Employee system**

Note that while it might seem that management is a specific type of Position, doing so makes modeling the manager-contains-employees relationship more awkward. For example, if managers were simply employees with particular positions, where then does the list of employees managed by this manager reside? Within the Position? Hardly—this would require a separate Position instance for each manager within the system. Within the Employee? Again, a bad design choice, since it implies that any Employee can have other Employees reporting to him/her.

The example is not intended as a right-way/wrong-way discussion of good design. In fact, this design violates one of the principal rules of current design thinking, in that roles (Employee, for example, is usually a role that a Person plays) shouldn't be modeled using inheritance, as we do in the model in figure 13.3. I do so here for a number of reasons: First, because the Employee model shown is one that's been used as an example in a number of discussions, thus it will be an easily recognizable example and requires less effort to understand and parse. Secondly, and more importantly, the Person-Employee-Manager relationship demonstrates how an inheritance relationship can function in the various implementations of the model we will be building.

There are plenty of books on the market that talk in far greater detail about how to model business objects, rules, and logic in a three- or *n*-tier system. This example is simply intended as a practical example of how business objects can in turn map into concrete Java classes and system tiers, with the focus intended on the various implementation approaches and details, rather than the object model itself. To put it bluntly, this is the way I designed it, and, as the saying goes, "Your mileage may vary." This is also not a full-fledged system—the presentation layer is minimal, and the database layer is purely functional and not at all intended as a paragon of good relational database design. The entire point of the example is the business objects layer, and the opportunities it offers for future development and maintenance.

## 13.1.8   Business objects layer interface layer

As we can see from the entity-relationship model, we have a number of entities[4] the system is attempting to track. Listing them, we have *Employee, Position, Department, Manager,* and *Contact Information.* I add the Person entity as an effort toward reusability—people that aren't employees may be modeled within this system at a later date (such as contractors, or perhaps the company would like to add employees' immediate family members within the system for benefits tracking). Remember, the business model for this could later be extended or merged with other systems, or even reused within an entirely different system. Always keep an eye out for potential reusability when modeling the business objects.

This code may be different than you expect. These are not abstract (or concrete) Java classes that know how to save themselves and restore themselves from storage. Instead, I build this layer as a series of interfaces, all of which know about each other and help to model the interaction of the business objects, yet offer no hints as to how the business objects are actually implemented. This approach, which I call *interface-based design*, is not new to Java. Microsoft's Component Object Model is built on this concept, and, to be quite honest, uses it quite well.

Let's take a second to examine the code:

Person has four get/set pairs, FirstName, MiddleName, LastName, and SSN. We encapsulate these using get/set methods, rather than as public members, to preserve the fact that the actual data may not even reside within this class, or even this JVM. That is an implementation detail, and will follow later. The code looks like this:

```
package Employee;

public interface IPerson
{
    public String getFirstName()
```

---

[4]  I use the term *entity* deliberately here, because we haven't yet given thought to whether this should be a single class or multiple related classes. We want to avoid the kind of premature pigeonholing that referring to it as a class might create.

```
        throws BusinessLayerException;
    public void setFirstName(String fName)
        throws BusinessLayerException;

    public String getMiddleName()
        throws BusinessLayerException;
    public void setMiddleName(String mName)
        throws BusinessLayerException;

    public String getLastName()
        throws BusinessLayerException;
    public void setLastName(String lName)
        throws BusinessLayerException;

    public String getSSN()
        throws BusinessLayerException;
    public void setSSN(String ssn)
        throws BusinessLayerException;

    public IContactInfo[] getContactInfo()
        throws BusinessLayerException;
    public void addContactInfo(IContactInfo contactInfo)
        throws BusinessLayerException;
    public void removeContactInfo(IContactInfo contactInfo)
        throws BusinessLayerException;
}
```

Note that because this is an interface, and not a full-fledged class, the class name is prefixed with "I". This is another COM holdover, but makes sense when working in an interface-based design paradigm. The "I", of course, stands for "interface." Notice also that each method throws the BusinessLayerException type; this provides us the ability to signal a variety of errors, from business rule or logic errors (i.e., SSN must have digits in the form *nnn-nn-nnnn*) to underlying implementation errors (i.e., RMIExceptions in the RMIModel, SQLExceptions in the RDBMSModel, or communications errors in a CORBA model).

The IEmployee interface extends the IPerson interface because, as we stated in our analysis discussion and in figure 13.3, an Employee is a specific type of Person. This means, of course, that IEmployee instances should have the same methods available on them as IPerson instances, and the only way to guarantee this in Java is to extend IEmployee from IPerson.

The code looks like this:

```
package Employee;

public interface IEmployee extends IPerson
{
    public IPosition getPosition()
        throws BusinessLayerException;
    public void setPosition(IPosition position)
        throws BusinessLayerException;

    public int getSalary()
```

```
        throws BusinessLayerException;
    public void setSalary(int salary)
        throws BusinessLayerException, IllegalSalaryException;

}
```

Note that setSalary not only throws a BusinessLayerException, but also an IllegalSalaryException. This is the means by which we enforce business rules. If an employee's salary is set to something that is defined to be illegal (in this case, we will decide that a salary above the employee's position's maximum salary is illegal), then we throw an IllegalSalaryException. These sorts of exceptions can be set on many more methods than just setSalary (IPerson's setSSN is a perfect example, where IllegalSSNException could also be thrown if a String consisting of something other than *nnn-nn-nnnn* is given). I choose not to in this example for simplicity. As an alternative, IllegalSalaryException could also be made a subclass of BusinessLayerException, so that the IllegalSalaryException wouldn't have to be explicitly named as part of the method's throws declaration. This makes the method more generic and maintainable, at the expense of the code-level documentation regarding the types of Exceptions it throws.[5]

Manager is, of course, a specialized Employee, one which in turn contains other Employees. The getEmployees method returns an array of Employee instances directly from the database, the addEmployee method screens the Employee passed in to make sure they're not already being managed by this Manager, and the removeEmployee method ensures that the Employee specified is one that this Manager actually manages before doing the database update. Pretty straightforward, but notice that the implementation of these methods defines our business logic—we have decided that more than one Manager may handle a given Employee (because we do not explicitly prevent it), and that Managers can have no Employees to manage (again, because we don't explicitly code against it). The business layer is the one layer whose implementation has ramifications throughout the entire system, so make certain that all cases are covered when coding.

The code appears as follows:

```
package Employee;

public interface IManager extends IEmployee
{
    public IEmployee[] getEmployees()
```

---

[5] There are a number of valid arguments in both directions on this issue. Specifying the exact Exception types thrown gives developers a type-safe means by which they can ascertain which Exceptions will be thrown from a method call. Because documentation is never guaranteed to be correct (or even present), this compiler-enforced type-safety is often the only documentation a developer gets. On the other hand, adding a new type to the method's throws declaration will cause every client call of that method to suddenly require modification (to deal with the new throws type), which is a maintenance nightmare and restricts change in the underlying implementation. As with most concepts of this type, make your own decisions, but be consistent.

```
        throws BusinessLayerException;
    public void addEmployee(IEmployee employee)
        throws BusinessLayerException;
    public void removeEmployee(IEmployee employee)
        throws BusinessLayerException;
}
```

Again, additional Exception types could be added here to enforce further business rules, such as having `addEmployee` throw `DuplicateEmployeeException`, or `removeEmployee` throw `UnknownEmployeeException`.

Position is a read-only entity within this system; users may not, using our object model, modify the values of any Position objects. We accomplish this by not providing any set methods for any of the attributes Position holds.

The code looks like this:

```
package Employee;

public interface IPosition
{
    public String getTitle()
        throws BusinessLayerException;

    public String getDescription()
        throws BusinessLayerException;

    public String getCategory()
        throws BusinessLayerException;

    public int getMinSalary()
        throws BusinessLayerException;

    public int getMaxSalary()
        throws BusinessLayerException;

}
```

Not much more to say about this, except to reiterate that Positions within this system are defined read-only, but later applications could change this by adding `setTitle`, `setDescription`, `setCategory`, `setMinSalary`, and/or `setMaxSalary` methods. The key point to make about this is if this change does occur, users of the old `IPosition` will not have to change any code.

As discussed earlier, Phone, Address, and Email are all specific types of Contact Information. As a result, `IPhone`, `IAddress`, and `IEMail` all extend `IContactInfo`. `IPhone` has three attributes, `prefix` (area code and/or country code), number, and `suffix` (extension, PIN number for pagers, and so on) with corresponding get/set methods. `IEMail` contains one attribute, `Email`, which is the textual representation of the user's SMTP email address. `IAddress` contains Street, City, State (or province), ZIP (or postal code) and Country.

The code (in multiple files) looks like this:

```
// IContactInfo.java
//
package Employee;
```

```java
public interface IContactInfo
{
    public String getDescription()
        throws BusinessLayerException;
    public void setDescription(String desc)
        throws BusinessLayerException;
}

// IAddress.java
//
package Employee;

public interface IAddress
{
    public String getStreet()
        throws BusinessLayerException;
    public void setStreet(String street)
        throws BusinessLayerException;

    public String getCity()
        throws BusinessLayerException;
    public void setCity(String city)
        throws BusinessLayerException;

    public String getState()
        throws BusinessLayerException;
    public void setState(String state)
        throws BusinessLayerException;

    public String getZip()
        throws BusinessLayerException;
    public void setZip(String zip)
        throws BusinessLayerException;

    public String getCountry()
        throws BusinessLayerException;
    public void setCountry(String country)
        throws BusinessLayerException;
}

// IEMail.java
//
package Employee;

public interface IEMail
{
    public String getEmail()
        throws BusinessLayerException;
    public void setEmail(String email)
        throws BusinessLayerException;
}

// IPhone.java
//
package Employee;
```

```
public interface IPhone
{
    public String getPrefix()
        throws BusinessLayerException;
    public void setPrefix(String prefix)
        throws BusinessLayerException;

    public String getNumber()
        throws BusinessLayerException;
    public void setNumber(String number)
        throws BusinessLayerException;

    public String getSuffix()
        throws BusinessLayerException;
    public void setSuffix(String suffix)
        throws BusinessLayerException;
}
```

Again, additional exception types could be added here in a production system. `IAddress`, especially, could use `InvalidZipException` on `setZip()`, and `IPhone` could use `InvalidNumberException` on `setNumber()`, or `Invalid-PrefixException` on `setPrefix()`.

`IDepartment`, of course, is the last interface in the Business Interface layer. The code appears as:

```
package Employee;

public interface IDepartment
{
    public String getTitle()
        throws BusinessLayerException;

    public String getDescription()
        throws BusinessLayerException;
    public void setDescription(String desc)
        throws BusinessLayerException;

    public IDepartment getParentDepartment()
        throws BusinessLayerException;

    public IDepartment[] getContainedDepartments()
        throws BusinessLayerException;

    public IManager getManager()
        throws BusinessLayerException;
    public void setManager(IManager mgr)
        throws BusinessLayerException;
}
```

Note, again, that additional checks would be desired in a production system; for example, if the enterprise decides that a Manager can run only one Department, then `setManager()` might throw `IllegalManagerException`.

That's our Business Objects Interface layer. At this point, it doesn't seem like much, but we already know enough to set up client code that can fully drive and exercise the Business Objects for this system without knowing a thing about the actual implementation. In fact, it's a good idea to do so, not only for regression and unit testing purposes, but to ensure that we have, in fact, given clients of this system the methods and behaviors they need to write the front ends to the system.

The code in listing 13.1 simply runs through various elements in the system, printing out information about each one:

**Listing 13.1   Code for the Business Objects Interface layer**

```
/**
 * Test driver
 */
public static void main(String[] args)
    throws Exception
{
    // Build the EmployeeModel; getEmployeeModel is a method that
    // (somehow) obtains the appropriate IEmployeeModel--it might
    // create an RDBMSModel with a JDBC Connection, or it might not;
    // the point is, we don't need to know the exact type of
    // IEmployeeModel we're using in order to use it.
    IEmployeeModel model = getEmployeeModel();

    // Get all Persons in the database
    System.out.println("\n\nAll Persons:");
    IPerson[] persons = model.findAllPersons();
    for (int i=0; i<persons.length; i++)
        printPerson(persons[i]);

    // Get all Departments in the database
    System.out.println("\n\nAll Departments:");
    IDepartment[] depts = model.findAllDepartments();
    for (int i=0; i<depts.length; i++)
        printDept(depts[i]);

    // Get all Positions in the database
    System.out.println("\n\nAll Positions:");
    IPosition[] positions = model.findAllPositions();
    for (int i=0; i<positions.length; i++)
        printPosition(positions[i]);

    // Get all Employees in the database
    System.out.println("\n\nAll Employees:");
    IEmployee[] employees = model.findAllEmployees();
    for (int i=0; i<employees.length; i++)
        printEmployee(employees[i]);

    // Get all Managers in the database
    System.out.println("\n\nAll Managers:");
    IManager[] mgrs = model.findAllManagers();
    for (int i=0; i<mgrs.length; i++)
```

```
                printManager(mgrs[i]);
        }

        private static void printPerson(IPerson person)
            throws Exception
        {
            System.out.println(person.getLastName() + ", " +
                person.getFirstName() + " " +
                person.getMiddleName() + " (" +
                person.getSSN() + ")");

            IContactInfo[] contactInfo = person.getContactInfo();
            for (int j=0; j<contactInfo.length; j++)
            {
                // Print ContactInfo
                System.out.println("      " +
                    contactInfo[j].getDescription() + ": " +
                    contactInfo[j].toString());
            }
        }
        private static void printEmployee(IEmployee employee)
            throws Exception
        {
            System.out.println(employee.getLastName() + ", " +
                employee.getFirstName() + " " +
                employee.getMiddleName() + " (" +
                employee.getSSN() + "): " +
                employee.getPosition().getTitle());

            IContactInfo[] contactInfo = employee.getContactInfo();
            for (int j=0; j<contactInfo.length; j++)
            {
                // Print ContactInfo
                System.out.println("      " +
                    contactInfo[j].getDescription() + ": " +
                    contactInfo[j].toString());
            }
        }
        private static void printDept(IDepartment dept)
            throws Exception
        {
            System.out.println(dept.getTitle() + ": " +
                dept.getDescription());
            System.out.println("    Run by " +
                dept.getManager().getLastName() + ", " +
                dept.getManager().getFirstName() + " " +
                dept.getManager().getMiddleName());
        }
        private static void printPosition(IPosition pos)
            throws Exception
        {
            System.out.println(pos.getTitle() + "(" +
                pos.getMinSalary() + " to " +
```

```
                        pos.getMaxSalary() + "): " +
                        pos.getDescription());
    }
    private static void printManager(IManager mgr)
        throws Exception
    {
        System.out.println(mgr.getLastName() + ", " +
            mgr.getFirstName() + " " +
            mgr.getMiddleName());
        IEmployee[] employees = mgr.getEmployees();
        for (int i=0; i<employees.length; i++)
        {
            System.out.println("    " +
                employees[i].getLastName() + ", " +
                employees[i].getFirstName() + " " +
                employees[i].getMiddleName());
        }
    }
}
```

This code can either be part of each `IEmployeeModel`-implementing class's interface, to allow for convenient testing, or a stand-alone class to exercise the system from outside the model.

One thing that should be obvious—and a bit confusing—is that none of these methods has any way of creating, obtaining, or removing objects from the system. In the example above, we presume that we already have objects in the database to view and display. This certainly won't be the case with an empty database, so how do we create a new Person?

Observant readers will have already spotted, in listing 13.1, the use of an interface not previously discussed. Listing 13.2 shows the `IEmployeeModel` interface, which is at the core of the interface layer.

**Listing 13.2    Code for IEmployeeModel**

```
package Employee;

/**
 * This class represents our business object layer
 * "model".
 */
public interface IEmployeeModel
{
    /**
     * Create IPerson object
     */
    public IPerson createPerson(
        String firstName, String middleName, String lastName,
        String ssn)
        throws BusinessLayerException, DuplicateObjectException;
```

*CHAPTER 13   BUSINESS OBJECTS*

```
/**
 * Create IEmployee object
 */
public IEmployee createEmployee(
    String firstName, String lastName, String middleName,
    String ssn, IPosition position, int salary)
    throws BusinessLayerException, DuplicateObjectException;

/**
 * Create IEmployee from IPerson
 */
public IEmployee createEmployee(IPerson person,
    IPosition position, int salary)
    throws BusinessLayerException, DuplicateObjectException;

/**
 * Create IManager object
 */
public IManager createManager(
    String firstName, String lastName, String middleName,
    String ssn, IPosition position, int salary)
    throws BusinessLayerException, DuplicateObjectException;

/**
 * Create IManager from IEmployee
 */
public IManager createManager(IEmployee employee)
    throws BusinessLayerException, DuplicateObjectException;

/**
 * Create IDepartment object
 */
public IDepartment createDepartment(
    String name, IDepartment parent)
    throws BusinessLayerException, DuplicateObjectException;

/**
 * Create IPosition object
 */
public IPosition createPosition(
    String title, String desc, int minSalary, int maxSalary)
    throws BusinessLayerException, DuplicateObjectException;

/**
 * Create IEMail object
 */
public IEMail createEMail(String email)
    throws BusinessLayerException, DuplicateObjectException;

/**
 * Create IPhone object
 */
public IPhone createPhone(
    String prefix, String number, String suffix)
    throws BusinessLayerException, DuplicateObjectException;
```

```
/**
 * Create IAddress object
 */
public IAddress createAddress(
    String street, String city, String state, String zip,
    String country)
    throws BusinessLayerException, DuplicateObjectException;

/**
 * Query for all Persons
 */
public IPerson[] findAllPersons()
    throws BusinessLayerException;

/**
 * Query for all Persons by last name
 */
public IPerson[] findPersonsByLastName(String lastName)
    throws BusinessLayerException;

/**
 * Query for all Persons by SSN
 */
public IPerson[] findPersonsBySSN(String ssn)
    throws BusinessLayerException;

/**
 * Query for all Employees
 */
public IEmployee[] findAllEmployees()
    throws BusinessLayerException;

/**
 * Query for all Managers
 */
public IManager[] findAllManagers()
    throws BusinessLayerException;

/**
 * Query for all Positions
 */
public IPosition[] findAllPositions()
    throws BusinessLayerException;

/**
 * Query for all Departments
 */
public IDepartment[] findAllDepartments()
    throws BusinessLayerException;

/**
 * Query for "root" Department
 */
public IDepartment findRootDepartment()
    throws BusinessLayerException;

/**
```

```
      * Remove a Person from the system
      */
    public void removePerson(IPerson person)
        throws BusinessLayerException, IntegrityConstraintException,
            UnknownObjectException;

    /**
      * Remove an Employee from the system
      */
    public void removeEmployee(IEmployee employee)
        throws BusinessLayerException, IntegrityConstraintException,
            UnknownObjectException;

    /**
      * Remove a Person from the system
      */
    public void removeManager(IManager manager)
        throws BusinessLayerException, IntegrityConstraintException,
            UnknownObjectException;

    /**
      * Remove a Department from the system
      */
    public void removeDepartment(IDepartment dept)
        throws BusinessLayerException, IntegrityConstraintException,
            UnknownObjectException;

    /**
      * Remove a Position from the system
      */
    public void removePosition(IPosition position)
        throws BusinessLayerException, IntegrityConstraintException,
            UnknownObjectException;

    /**
      * Remove an Address from the system
      */
    public void removeAddress(IAddress address)
        throws BusinessLayerException, IntegrityConstraintException,
            UnknownObjectException;

    /**
      * Remove a Phone from the system
      */
    public void removePhone(IPhone phone)
        throws BusinessLayerException, IntegrityConstraintException,
            UnknownObjectException;

    /**
      * Remove an EMail from the system
      */
    public void removeEMail(IEMail person)
        throws BusinessLayerException, IntegrityConstraintException,
            UnknownObjectException;
}
```

This class forms the starting point from which any use of the Business Layer originates. Users of the `Employee` package (which is the package holding all the Business Layer code) may not create, access, or otherwise know about Employee instances directly. They must go through this interface. Again, this is done deliberately, in order to encapsulate knowledge about the actual layout of the data away from those who want to use it.

Because this is an interface, users do not create an instance of `IEmployeeModel` directly. Instead, they create instances of a class that implements `IEmployeeModel`, such as the RDBMSModel class presented in chapter 14:

```
// Set up JDBC Connection
Connection conn = null;
try
{
    // Load the JDBC driver into the JVM
    Class.forName("jdbc.idbDriver");
    java.util.Properties p = new java.util.Properties();
    conn = DriverManager.getConnection("jdbc:idb:employee.prp", p);
}
catch (Exception ex)
{
    ex.printStackTrace();
    return;
}

// Build the EmployeeModel
IEmployeeModel model = new RDBMSModel(conn);
```

You may be curious why, after going to such great lengths to hide the fact that we're using a relational database, I then force users to make the JDBC Connection instance to pass in to RDBMSModel. For this particular example, it makes little difference whether this Connection takes place in the RDBMSModel constructor or the user's code. In a production system, however, usually users will not create the Model class directly, but receive it from someplace else (perhaps one of the custom ClassLoaders discussed in chapter 2), as in:

```
ClassLoader classLoader = . . .;
    // obtain the ClassLoader from someplace
IEmployeeModel model = (IEmployeeModel)
    ClassLoader.loadClass("Employee.EmployeeModel").newInstance();
```

Or the mechanics of using the ClassLoader itself could be buried within some routine inside the code that uses the Business Layer:

```
public IEmployeeModel getEmployeeModel()
{
    // Details unimportant to the user
}

IEmployeeModel model = getEmployeeModel();

IEmployee[] employees = model.findAllEmployees();
```

Note the simple power expressed in the foregoing snippet. Suddenly, as we've been talking about all along, the user doesn't know, nor does he care where the Employee objects are coming from, how they work, or how they store themselves off. The Employee Business Object Layer client simply uses them. The objects may be stored in a database, may be stored locally to disk via Serialization, or stored remotely via RMI, CORBA, or some other form of distribution. We could even change the location of these objects behind the scenes, and users would neither know nor care.

Some readers may, at this point, be curious to know how problems are handled. Normally, in a JDBC or RMI based system, exceptions of specific type are thrown to signal the caller that the request could not be completed, or was completed abnormally. "If I no longer know where the objects reside," they ask, "how can I know which exceptions to catch and handle? Or do I have to handle all of them?"

Unfortunately, there is no easy answer, because there are really two schools of thought on the issue. The first holds that any exception, regardless of cause or type, should be propagated upward to the caller, so they can display some type of informative screen to the user. The second holds that because the caller, due to encapsulation, has no real way of doing anything about the error, propagating the exception to them is simply a waste of time and effort. I hold more with the second approach than the first. Reasonably, what can I expect the user to be able to do about it if the database to which I am attempting to connect is down? For that reason, none of the interface classes presented here throw any kind of standard `Exception`. Instead, I have `BusinessLayerException`, a class which is thrown in case a transaction or request fails (for example, if a `setName` or similar method fails for some reason). This class in turn contains the actual `Exception` thrown from the lower layers, so that presentation-layer code can access it if desired. This way, clients of the Business Interface Layer need only catch one type of `Exception` from calls to that layer, and still do not have to know anything about the actual lower-object layer.

Querying for objects in the system is as easy as calling one of the `find()` methods on `IEmployeeModel`. Any place where client code would normally execute a `SELECT` statement on the database, or begin deserialization of a serialized object stream file, the client instead asks the `IEmployeeModel` instance it holds for an array of conformant types:

```
// Get all Persons in the database
System.out.println("\n\nAll Persons:");
IPerson[] persons = model.findAllPersons();
```

Above, the code asks the system for all Person objects in the database. If none were found, `findAllPersons()` returns `null`, and if the system couldn't comply, a `BusinessLayerException` is thrown. No further knowledge of how these objects are stored is necessary. The implementing `IEmployeeModel` takes care of all that.

Creating a new object within the system also requires the use of the `IEmployee-Model` instance:

```
// Create a new Person in the system
IPerson person =
    model.createPerson("Neward", "Charlotte", "Anne", "123-45-6789");
    // Add new ContactInfo instances to person as necessary
// Make the above Person an Employee
IEmployee employee =
    model.createEmployee(person, model.findPositionByName("CFO"));
// Now make her a Manager
IManager manager =
    model.createManager(person);
```

This would seem to be counterintuitive to good object-oriented design. In fact, it's not, because we have simply moved knowledge of how to create Business Objects to the one class that knows most about how to create them, the Model class.

Removing an object from the system again requires the `IEmployeeModel`:

```
// Remove given Manager from the system
model.removeManager(manager);
    // This recursively removes the manager-as-Employee and
    // the manager-as-Person, so explicitly calling those
    // methods is unnecessary
```

Should clients require an additional method of querying for, creating, or removing objects from the system, additional methods must be added to `IEmployeeModel`. While this approach may seem restrictive at first (and there's really no doubt about it, it is more restrictive), it offers some advantages in return:

- *Sanity-check*
  When clients request the additional query method, it offers the designers a chance to evaluate the legitimacy of the request and offer feedback to the clients. Some queries will be legitimate (such as `findEmployeesByLastName()` or `findManagersByLastName()`), while others can be handled given the existing API (instead of `findManagersByDepartment()`, use a new query, `findDepartmentByName()` and the returned `IDepartment` object's `getManager()`).

- *Knowledge of use*
  When designers are explicitly requested for new ways to access, create, or query for objects, they are (by definition) being told how clients are using the system. This knowledge in turn allows Business Object implementors better understanding of how the system is being used, and can optimize and tune accordingly. Some designers and coders will scoff at this, taking the position that "I know how they'll be using it, I don't need them to tell me." This is fantasy, pure and simple. Step onto any high school or college campus and take careful note of the sidewalks and surrounding grass; I have never been on a campus that didn't have at least one carefully worn dirt path through the grass. The moral? The architect who laid the sidewalks thought he knew, but didn't, which paths the students would take. Designers cannot know how others will use their system. You might know how you would use it, but that doesn't mean that others will.

- *Control over future implementation*

  Enterprise systems are constantly moving targets. Even as current phases are being implemented, future phases are on the drawing board. By forcing clients to go back to the Business Object architects with new requests, control over how the objects are being used remains firmly in the hands of the Business Objects team. This allows the Business Objects folks to prevent any uses or methods within the Business Objects layer that might, in turn, prevent future implementation from taking place. Don't believe you need this kind of control? Take a lesson from Microsoft—in *Undocumented Windows,*[6] Andrew Schulman describes Microsoft's woes in developing Windows 3.1 with full backward compatibility, caused in no small part because developers of applications for Windows (even within Microsoft) were decompiling and reverse-engineering functions and structures that Microsoft held as reserved for future implementation. As a result, those reserved fields had to be left as-is, and new schemes used. If you don't keep complete control over your API, you will lose it.

- *Ability to optimize*

  Because clients are removed from knowing the exact class to use, we can later add implementation optimization efforts, such as using stateless objects (*a la* Microsoft Transaction Server statelessness) or object pools to boost performance. Intelligent on-the-fly optimizations can be used; in a remote object Model system, if the client happens to be running on the same machine as the server, a lightweight RPC system might be used instead of the full remote proxy, thus reducing overhead. What's even better, because client code will usually request the `IEmployeeModel` instance to use from some sort of object-creational class or method, the decision regarding which optimized type to use (local or remote proxy) can be done at run time, based on whether the machine is local or remote; this sort of on-the-fly decisionmaking is only possible if the user's code is completely abstracted away from the details of the underlying model.

- *Easier enhancement*

  If all access to the objects is through a single class, adding features to the system as a whole becomes simpler. One common need is for security, or, more accurately, user roles within the system. Some users may be authorized to add, remove, or update objects within the system, while others are permitted read-only access. Some objects may be inaccessible to anyone other than system administrators, and so forth. Modifying `IEmployeeModel` to support this can be boiled down to adding an overloaded method for every method currently available, as in:

---

[6] *Undocumented Windows,* by Schulman, et al (Addison-Wesley)

```java
// IEmployeeModel with user roles added in
//
public interface IEmployeeModel
{
    /**
     * Query for all Persons, using default (guest) access
     */
    public IPerson[] findAllPersons();

    /**
     * Query for all Persons, using specified access
     */
    public IPerson[] findAllPersons(IUserRole role);

    /**
     * Query for all Persons by last name, using default
     * (guest) access
     */
    public IPerson[] findPersonsByLastName(String lastName);

    /**
     * Query for all Persons by last name, using specified access
     */
    public IPerson[] findPersonsByLastName(String lastName, IUserRole role);

    // And so forth, and so on . . .
}

// or, an alternative approach:
// IEmployeeModel with user roles added in
//
public interface IEmployeeModel
{
    /**
     * Specify caller user role
     */
    public void setUserRole(IUserRole role);

    /**
     * Query for all Persons
     *
     * @throws UserRoleException (subclass of
     *   BusinessLayerException) if the user's role is prevented
     *   from finding all Persons.
     */
    public IPerson[] findAllPersons()
        throws BusinessLayerException;

    /**
     * Query for all Persons by last name, using default
     * (guest) access
     *
     * @throws UserRoleException (subclass of
```

```
    *    BusinessLayerException) if the user's role is prevented
    *    from finding all Persons.
    */
   public IPerson[] findPersonsByLastName(String lastName);

   // And so forth, and so on . . .
}
```

Enhancing the system in this manner requires no code changes to clients that don't use user roles, but those clients may in turn be locked out of certain parts of the system, since they (by default, for security reasons) are given the lowest access available. The key is that what would otherwise be a major feature change is now manageable. Imagine what implementing security would have meant (in terms of man hours to implement) had clients been given direct access to the database or middleware system.

In short, just about every argument in favor of encapsulation of objects works as an argument in favor of encapsulation of the business object layer. In fact, those readers familiar with the GoF book of patterns will already recognize that the Business Object Interface layer is a Façade pattern.

Moreover, the entire idea of an *n*-tier logical model is an extension of the Façade concept. By encapsulating the complexity of the actual implementation away from the user, implementors gain an amount of flexibility in tailoring the implementation to specific needs, as well as responding to user requests or technology changes, without breaking client code. For example, if and when the enterprise decides to move to an EJB server architecture, the Business Object Interface implementation can be modified to use EJB concepts under the hood, without changing client code.[7] The same holds true for CORBA, or even Microsoft's Java/COM model.

If all this discussion of the Business Object Interface Layer and its associated Model class also reminds you of the old Model-View-Controller pattern, you're not too far off. The various interfaces of the Business Object Interface Layer are the View classes; the Model classes are buried away in the underlying layer (which we examine next chapter), and the Controller class is the `IEmployeeModel`-implementing class we keep referring to. Remember, patterns can nest—not only can patterns be used between subsystems, but within subsystems, as well. In this case, the Bridge pattern helps us cleanly divide the entire system into Presentation and Business Object layers, as well as divides code within the Business Object layer between interface and implementation. The Model class itself may (but doesn't have to be) a Singleton, and particular client code may select which `IEmployeeModel`-implementing class to use via a Factory Method or Abstract Factory.

---

[7] One possible exception to this is to add the `java.rmi.Remote` interface as a base class to the interfaces specified by the Business Object Interface layer, but we already have to do this to support RMI in a later chapter. Adding the `java.rmi.Remote`, much as adding java.io.Serializable, adds no additional methods that need to be implemented; it's just a placeholder and flag to the rmic RMI stub/skeleton compiler. Even the need to catch `java.rmi.RemoteExceptions` should be handled silently.

## 13.2   USING THE BUSINESS OBJECT LAYER

For all the wonder of our clean, encapsulated Business Object layer, in and of itself it pays no bills. True payoff comes when using the Business Object layer to view, manipulate, and otherwise use the data it models and represents. Despite how the data is used, either in a GUI application or in some kind of batch-driven background process, this is the Presentation layer. Again, the Presentation layer itself can have more than one layer within it (as the JFC GUI application does), but this should only be done where it is convenient and has concrete advantages. The UI code, for example, presented here uses another model-view design, while the import/export code does not.

### 13.2.1   Classic presentation code: GUIs

The Employee system example comes with two presentation-layer GUI applications for users to execute and use. The first, OrgTree, provides a tree-based hierarchy of the corporation's Department tree, in a split-view Explorer-like interface. The second, EmployeeView, provides a more address-book-like view of the Employees within the company, organized alphabetically and with each Employee's Contact Information listed in the data view.

In both applications, the UI code makes no assumptions about how the data arrived there. The data could be coming from a relational database, via RMI or CORBA, or even be an exported file of the data (discussed next). To stress this, each application, when started, presents the user with a dialog box indicating the IEmployeeModel choices (discussed in further detail in the next chapter) and allows you to choose which one to use. If further details are necessary to create the Model (such as JDBC URL, RMI, CORBA server location, XML, or Serialized filename), a subdialog containing the fields appears.

### 13.2.2   Example: OrgTree

OrgTree is a simple tree-based display of the company's Departmental organization. Each node in the tree to the left side of the main window is a Department within the company, and the panel to the right lists the Employees working for the Manager managing that Department. Note that the display is not recursive. Employees working for a Department contained by another Department will only show up once, not in each parent node all the way back to the root. Notice how, by creating our own customized TreeModel class (listing 13.3), we've almost trivialized the work necessary to build this Departmental tree, and the custom ListModel (for the right-hand panel) does the same for listing the Employees of the Department.

**Listing 13.3 Code for the DepartmentTreeModel**

```
/**
 * DepartmentTreeModel: Swing JTree model class for displaying
 * the organization chart, according to the IEmployeeModel.
 */
class DepartmentTreeModel
    implements TreeModel
{
    public DepartmentTreeModel(IEmployeeModel model)
    {
        m_model = model;
    }

    public void addTreeModelListener(TreeModelListener l)
    {
        m_listeners.addElement(l);
    }
    public Object getChild(Object parent, int index)
    {
        try
        {
            IDepartment dept = (IDepartment)parent;
            IDepartment[] children = dept.getContainedDepartments();
            if (children != null)
            {
                return children[index];
            }
            else
                return null;
        }
        catch (BusinessLayerException blEx)
        {
            blEx.printStackTrace();
            return null;
        }
    }
    public int getChildCount(Object parent)
    {
        try
        {
            IDepartment dept = (IDepartment)parent;
            IDepartment[] children = dept.getContainedDepartments();
            if (children != null)
                return children.length;
            else
                return 0;
        }
        catch (BusinessLayerException blEx)
        {
            blEx.printStackTrace();
            return 0;
```

```
            }
        }
        public int getIndexOfChild(Object parent, Object child)
        {
            return 0;
        }
        public Object getRoot()
        {
            try
            {
                return m_model.findRootDepartment();
            }
            catch (BusinessLayerException blEx)
            {
                blEx.printStackTrace();
                return null;
            }
        }
        public boolean isLeaf(Object node)
        {
            try
            {
                IDepartment dept = (IDepartment)node;
                if (dept.getContainedDepartments() != null)
                    return false;
                else
                    return true;
            }
            catch (BusinessLayerException blEx)
            {
                blEx.printStackTrace();
                return true;
            }
        }
        public void removeTreeModelListener(TreeModelListener l)
        {
            m_listeners.remove(l);
        }
        public void valueForPathChanged(TreePath path, Object newValue)
        {
            // unimplemented
        }

        // Internal members
        //
        IEmployeeModel m_model;
        Vector m_listeners = new Vector();
}
```

If you are unfamiliar with TreeModel's methods, I'd recommend you pick up a good Swing book before diving too deeply into the code. DepartmentTreeModel takes an `IEmployeeModel` in its constructor and stores it internally. If we chose to, we could extract the root `IDepartment` (which is all we need the `IEmployeeModel` instance for) in the constructor and not store the model instance, but it costs us nothing to hold it. Also, notice that because DepartmentTreeModel is stateless in its interactions with the containing JTree instance, getChild has to rely on the assumption that `IDepartment.getContainedDepartments` returns the array of contained `IDepartment` instances in exactly the same order every time it is called. If this assumption proves false, then DepartmentTreeModel needs to undertake other methods[8] to make certain the children can be found in order every time.

Now look at what's required to build a JTree that knows how to display, hierarchically, all of the Departments in the Employee system:

```
JTree tree = new JTree(
    new DepartmentTreeModel(getEmployeeModel(args)));
```

where `getEmployeeModel(args)` returns to us an `IEmployeeModel`.[9] If the simplicity of the above doesn't set your heart pounding and head spinning, then you never had to try to code one of these things the Hard Way, building the tree by hand. JFC's Model-View system makes the development of complex user-interfaces absurdly simple. What's more, because OrgTree uses the `IEmployeeModel` as its interface to the data, we can now use this application (or, more realistically, the classes developed during the development of this application) to view Employee system data from other sources. Had we written the DepartmentTreeModel to use JDBC or RMI instead of `IEmployeeModel`, it would be useless to us when we move the system from a JDBC-based system to an RMI-based approach.

Note that this is not the most efficient use of the `IEmployeeModel`; each time we need a new child, we requery the model:

```
public Object getChild(Object parent, int index)
{
    try
    {
        IDepartment dept = (IDepartment)parent;
        IDepartment[] children = dept.getContainedDepartments();
        if (children != null)
        {
            return children[index];
        }
}
```

---

[8]  Such as retrieving the array once, and storing it in a Hashtable or Dictionary, keyed to the `IDepartment` instance that produced it.

[9]  In typical systems, the Model being used will be obtained from a similar method or class, but here the `getEmployeeModel()` method allows users to choose which of the `IEmployeeModel`-implementing classes discussed in this book to use.

```
                else
                    return null;
            }
            catch (BusinessLayerException blEx)
            {
                blEx.printStackTrace();
                return null;
            }
        }
```

In a model that involves significant time delays or processing (such as using JDBC or RMI in the model), this can prove overly costly. These costly trips to the model could be optimized away by making the trip once, and caching the result locally. However, this sort of optimization is arguably more appropriately belonging in the IEmployee-Model and not in client code; the model knows better whether such optimization is necessary, and how best to optimize for it. Such optimization also carries with it an inherent danger if used in the client code—if the underlying model changes, and we keep using local cached results, we won't see the changes. This can in turn lead to significant problems downstream. Once again, however, it must be stated that because we abstracted away the details, we can silently make this optimization without changing a lick of user's code.

### 13.2.3   Feeling cheated?

You'll notice that the sample application doesn't make use of every business object method, nor is every business object exercised to its fullest; for example, I don't have a PositionEditor, or even an application that adds Employees to the system. This is deliberate, for two reasons. First, it's common for corporations to want to give limited access to all members of the corporation or outside the corporation (across the Internet, for example). Second, more practically, I wanted to keep this sample as simple as possible. Given how the model encapsulates away the details of the creation, manipulation, and removal of the actual data objects, it shouldn't be too difficult for readers to implement other editors, if desired.

## 13.3   *SUMMARY*

One of the principal goals of any enterprise development group is to produce systems that are maintainable, scalable, and reusable. An encapsulation layer between the actual storage mechanism and the code which presents or manipulates it aids in the reusability of the system as a whole. This layer, known as the Business Object layer, serves to protect the system from an inability to evolve because if we change this, all this code over here breaks. For example, we can start with a system that uses a simple Hashtable as its storage mechanism in order to expedite prototyping and rapid development in the early stages of project planning and architecture. Later, relational databases can be used, by simply modifying code beneath the Business Object layer to store to an RDBMS rather than a Hashtable. Additional legacy systems can be brought into the system by extending the Business Object layer to represent the new data types, and developing a Data Access layer that understands the different databases and where to retrieve data for which requests. (We implement both of the above-mentioned models in chapter 14.)

The Business Object layer also provides for the ability to add distribution capabilities into a system that lacks it; by virtue of the encapsulation provided by a Business Object layer, we can add a distributed capability without having to rewrite significant portions of user code; we talk about this in chapter 12, when we add RMI and other distributed technologies to the mix.

A Business Object layer provides developers with flexibility to meet the changing needs of the business. By providing, up front, the ability for a system to evolve, we run less risk of being caught off-guard by user requests. This inability to evolve is the principal reason many systems are started over from scratch. It's awkward to change and grow the system as users become more familiar with it. By providing layers of encapsulation wherever feasible, we protect ourselves (and our jobs) against unreasonable user requests. And as much as it might be exciting for us as developers to throw the current system away and start over, most clients are less than enthusiastic about accepting the kind of costs, both in time and in money, that a complete rewrite involves.

## 13.4  ADDITIONAL READING

- Desmond D'Souza and Alan Cameron Wills, *Object, Components, and Frameworks with UML* (Addison-Wesley, 1999).

  This is a great book for any developer involved at the design or analysis level, with clear focus on building shared business models, as well as providing a generalized approach to developing software that meets (or exceeds) client needs. It's not a lightweight book, by any means, weighing in at just under 700 pages (not counting appendices, index, or glossary), but it's possibly one of the best books any developer or architect will find.

- *Pattern Languages of Program Design*, ed. James O. Coplien, Douglas C. Schmidt, (Addison-Wesley, 1995).

- *Pattern Languages of Program Design 2*, ed. John Vlissides, James O. Coplien, and Norman L. Kerth, (Addison-Wesley, 1996).

- *Pattern Languages of Program Design 3*, ed. Robert Martin, Dirk Riehle and Frank Buschmann (Addison-Wesley, 1997).

**C H A P T E R   1 4**

# *Business object models*

In the previous chapter, we talked about building a business object model; in this chapter, we'll explore two potential implementations of it. The first, HashtableModel, is a simple implementation using a standard Java java.util.Hashtable instance as the storage mechanism for the business objects. The second, RDBMSModel, will be the more familiar relational-database-back end approach.

## 14.1   *EXAMPLE: HASHTABLEMODEL*

The HashtableModel is a simple model, the usefulness of which is limited to prototypes and those systems guaranteed to remain 24/7 for life. As its name implies, the HashtableModel stores all business objects in a simple Java Hashtable, giving it very fast response time at the expense of lacking any sort of persistent capability whatsoever. In other words, if the server goes down, all objects are lost. Despite its limitations, it serves as a useful starting point for both data-access models as well as a prototype model for working out the kinks in your Business Object Interface layer.

The HashtableModel is a prototyping and proof-of-concept model that stores any objects created in local Hashtable instances. Because of its lack of persistent capability, it will be useful only during prototyping, early development, and early testing. This doesn't mean you should dismiss it out of hand. Because of its characteristics (fast, temporary storage), a model that wishes to employ an optimization scheme could use the HashtableModel as a caching system. The HashtableModel could be a most recently used cache, moving the objects out of the cache down to persistent storage as time and/or the optimization strategy permits.

HashtableModel is also the easiest to understand, since there is no mapping of Java objects to persistent storage object representations. Because the Hashtable is the persistent layer, no translation to the persistent layer (as we will see with RDBMS-Model) is necessary. This in turn means that the HashtableModel can closely mimic the model for the Business Objects layer, which may or may not be true for other models requiring mapping or translation.

The code for HashtableModel can be found in HashtableModel.java.

### 14.1.1 Overview

The core of the HashtableModel comes from a collection of java.util.Hashtable objects stored as private members of the class:

```
public class HashtableModel
    implements IEmployeeModel
{
    // . . . Details omitted for the moment

    // Internal members
    private Hashtable m_persons = new Hashtable();
    private Hashtable m_employees = new Hashtable();
    private Hashtable m_managers = new Hashtable();
    private Hashtable m_positions = new Hashtable();
    private Hashtable m_departments = new Hashtable();
}
```

Observant readers will note a couple of curious points. First, there is no Hashtable for the contact information types—IContactInfo, IPhone, IAddress, and IEMail. This is because in the HashtableModel, the IPerson/Hashtable type (called HashtablePerson) itself can store these instances. Secondly, there are three Hashtable instances for persons, employees, and managers. This means that a given IManager type (called HashtableManager) must be stored in all three Hashtables—once as an IPerson, once as an IEmployee, and once as an IManager. If managers must be employees, and employees must be persons, couldn't the system save a bit in execution and omit some redundancy if only one Hashtable stored all three types?

The answer is complex. Yes, it would prevent a certain amount of redundancy. Yes, this in turn would save execution time. However, grouping all three types under one umbrella (as Persons) would make it more difficult to extract one as an Employee or Manager. Consider that an operation such as findAllManagers involves the code and would have to iterate over all Persons in m_persons, testing each one (via a successful cast to an IManager or some other HashtableModel-specific method) to see if it were an IManager type, and, if so, store it in the return array. What execution time is saved by storing such in one Hashtable is now lost.

Before we delve too deeply into the HashtableModel class, let's examine the actual Hashtable types that the HashtableModel will be handing back to callers.

## 14.1.2 HashtablePerson, HashtableEmployee, HashtableManager

In the HashtableModel, we create one class for each of these types. Because every employee is a person, and every manager is an employee, we use inheritance to help maintain that relationship:

```
class HashtablePerson
    implements IPerson
{
    // . . .
}
class HashtableEmployee extends HashtablePerson
    implements IEmployee
{
    // . . .
}
class HashtableManager extends HashtableEmployee
    implements IManager
{
    // . . .
}
```

HashtablePerson holds no real mysteries. It holds one String member for each of the four basic attributes of a Person—first name, middle name, last name, and SSN—as well as a Vector[1] for contact information. Remember, in the Hashtable model, all IContactInfo instances are stored directly within the Person instance itself, with no "external" storage involved. This means the methods addAddress, addPhone, and addEMail add the created HashtableAddress, HashtablePhone, and Hashtable-EMail instances directly to the HashtablePerson's m_contactInfo member.

Note that the HashtablePhone, HashtableEMail, and HashtableAddress classes do not have constructors other than the no-arg version that sets all members to null. HashtablePerson appears to have direct access to the members of these classes, and readers may wonder why, after all the work I've undertaken to preserve encapsulation, I would choose to break it here. The truth is that while encapsulation between layers is absolutely necessary, encapsulation within a layer, especially within such tightly coupled classes as those inside a data-access model, can be counterproductive. In truth, either method (encapsulated or not) can be used within the model. HashtablePerson, Hashtable-Employee, and HashtableManager all employ full encapsulation, while the rest of the classes within the HashtableModel do not. Within this model, it makes little difference, but inside of other models (most notably the RDBMSModel), this may change.

HashtableEmployee extends HashtablePerson, in order to reuse its implementation of the methods that IEmployee inherits from IPerson. This is an implementation

---

[1] Normally, in a Java2-centric system, I would use the new Collections classes and APIs to do the object storage and manipulation; however, because a large number of Java developers still seem somewhat uncomfortable with the Collections API, I've used the "old" collection classes and APIs (Vector and Enumeration, specifically) in the implementation.

decision only—if it made more sense to have HashtableEmployee define its own version of these methods, it could do so without clients' knowledge. So long as HashtableEmployee fully implements every method of `IEmployee`, clients' requirements are fully met.

HashtableEmployee stores a reference to the `IPosition` that this employee holds as the internal member `m_position`. We could have stored it as a HashtablePosition had we needed access to any special methods of HashtablePosition; because we don't, it makes no difference to store it as an `IPosition` or a HashtablePosition.

Also note a tiny bit of business logic inside the `setSalary` method of HashtableEmployee:

```
public void setSalary(int salary)
    throws BusinessLayerException, IllegalSalaryException
{
    if (salary > getPosition().getMaxSalary())
        throw new IllegalSalaryException("Max salary is " +
            getPosition().getMaxSalary());

    m_salary = salary;
}
```

If the proposed salary is greater than the employee's position allows, an `IllegalSalaryException` is thrown. This a bit dangerous, since it means that this business logic will need to be reimplemented in every model class we create. For only a few classes, and just a little logic, this is manageable, but without careful monitoring, keeping track of this across all classes could quickly spiral out of control. Should that happen, one potential alternative is to create an abstract base class, AbstractEmployeeModel, which contains no data-storage mechanism but simply implements just this business logic. Model classes would then extend this AbstractEmployeeModel, calling up to its methods wherever convenient. Another approach would be to make use of a Bridge pattern, with the business logic in the Abstraction or RefinedAbstraction class, and the actual implementation residing in the ConcreteImplementor. If your system plans to make use of multiple models, this is the better approach; it centralizes the business logic, yet still allows the implementation to vary from model to model.

HashtableDepartment, HashtablePosition, and the various Hashtable implementations of the contact information classes are similarly coded.

### 14.1.3 HashtableModel: Creating objects

Creating objects within the HashtableModel (listing 14.1) is conceptually as simple as calling new, storing the created object into the corresponding Hashtable within HashtableModel, and returning the newly created object to the caller.

**Listing 14.1 Code for creating object with HashtableModel**

```
/**
 * Create IPerson object
 */
```

```java
public IPerson createPerson(
    String firstName, String middleName, String lastName,
    String ssn)
    throws BusinessLayerException, DuplicateObjectException
{
    if (m_persons.get(ssn) == null)
    {
        HashtablePerson person =
            new HashtablePerson(firstName, middleName,
                lastName, ssn);
        m_persons.put(ssn, person);
        return person;
    }
    else
    {
        throw new DuplicateObjectException();
    }
}

/**
 * Create IEmployee object
 */
public IEmployee createEmployee(
    String firstName, String lastName, String middleName,
    String ssn, IPosition position, int salary)
    throws BusinessLayerException, DuplicateObjectException
{
    if (m_employees.get(ssn) == null &&
        m_persons.get(ssn) == null)
    {
        HashtableEmployee employee =
            new HashtableEmployee(firstName, lastName,
                middleName, ssn, position, salary);

        m_persons.put(ssn, employee);
        m_employees.put(ssn, employee);

        return employee;
    }
    else
    {
        throw new DuplicateObjectException();
    }
}

/**
 * Create IEmployee from IPerson
 */
public IEmployee createEmployee(IPerson person,
    IPosition position, int salary)
    throws BusinessLayerException, DuplicateObjectException
{
```

```
        if (m_employees.get(person.getSSN()) == null)
        {
            HashtableEmployee employee =
                new HashtableEmployee(person.getFirstName(),
                    person.getLastName(),
                    person.getMiddleName(),
                    person.getSSN(), position, salary);

            m_persons.remove(employee.getSSN());
            m_persons.put(employee.getSSN(), employee);
            m_employees.put(employee.getSSN(), employee);

            return employee;
        }
        else
        {
            throw new DuplicateObjectException();
        }
    }
```

Let's take these one at a time, although there's nothing complicated in what's going on here. The createPerson method first verifies that no object already exists within the m_persons Hashtable (to prevent duplication), then takes the first name, middle name, last name and SSN fields, creates a new HashtablePerson object, and stores it in m_persons before returning it.

The createEmployee method comes in two flavors, one taking an IPerson object (make an Employee out of this Person), the other taking all of the Person and Employee field data as parameters. In the version that takes all of the fields individually, if such an individual already exists in the m_persons array, it's considered a DuplicateObjectException. Why not simply take the Person in the m_persons array and "promote" them to an Employee?

My reasoning is simple: if the Person should be promoted to an Employee, then the client should be calling the second version of createEmployee (the one taking an IPerson object as a parameter). If we were to allow the first version to "promote" a Person found in the system already to an Employee, then there's no reason to have both versions of the method. Alternatively, if we were to strike the second method, there would be no way of explicitly promoting Person objects to Employee objects. In this particular system, nothing more than creating an Employee object where a Person object once stood is required. However, more sophisticated systems may require different processing (for example, removing the old Person object and replacing it with the new Employee object, and so on). The same argument goes for the createManager method.

The createDepartment and createPosition methods are straightforward. Merely create the appropriate HashtableModel object, place it within the appropriate Hashtable inside the HashtableModel, and return it to the caller.

### 14.1.4 HashtableModel: Finding objects

Once objects have been created, we need implementations that know how to find particular ones or retrieve the entire set of objects from the model. The Hashtable-Model will suffer most in this area, since the Hashtable implementation from Java doesn't allow for anything other than retrieval-by-key, or else iteration over the entire set. This means that retrieving a set of objects (finding all Persons by last name, for example) will require iteration over the entire set, returning only those which match the criteria.

```java
/**
 * Query for all Persons by last name
 */
public IPerson[] findPersonsByLastName(String lastName)
    throws BusinessLayerException
{
    // Filter out only those Persons with the given last
    // name
    Vector tmp = new Vector();
    for (Enumeration e = m_persons.elements();
         e.hasMoreElements(); )
    {
        IPerson person = (IPerson)e.nextElement();
        if (person.getLastName().equals(lastName))
            tmp.addElement(person);
    }

    // Return the collection as an array of IPerson
    IPerson[] retArray = null;
    if (tmp.size() > 0)
    {
        retArray = new IPerson[tmp.size()];

        for (int i=0; i<retArray.length; i++)
            retArray[i] = (IPerson)tmp.elementAt(i);

        return retArray;
    }
    else
        return null;
}
```

The queries themselves should, as with everything else in the HashtableModel, be straightforward and simple. For those methods looking to return all of some object, simple iteration over the contents of the corresponding Hashtable, copying the elements to an array to return is enough. For those methods looking to apply some filter, we apply the filter and add the current element only if the filter passes. The only method which breaks this model (slightly) is findRootDepartment(), which returns immediately as soon as it finds a Department object with no parent Department.

## 14.1.5    HashtableModel: Removing objects

And, as you would expect, removing objects from the HashtableModel is as straight-forward as it was to create them:

```
/**
 * Remove a Person from the system
 */
public void removePerson(IPerson person)
    throws BusinessLayerException,
        IntegrityConstraintException,
        UnknownObjectException
{
    m_persons.remove(person.getSSN());
}

/**
 * Remove an Employee from the system
 */
public void removeEmployee(IEmployee employee)
    throws BusinessLayerException,
        IntegrityConstraintException,
        UnknownObjectException
{
    m_employees.remove(employee.getSSN());
    m_persons.remove(employee.getSSN());
}
```

Because we're dealing with transient, in-memory storage systems only, removing an object is as simple as calling the `Hashtable.remove()` method with the object in question.

Notice that there are no methods for creating, finding, or removing the Hash-tableModel contact information classes; this is taken care of in the Person class (ContactInfo is associated directly with Person), so it is not necessary to create, find, or remove here. This does not, however, force us in this implementation to create/find/remove those objects in Person. In fact, thanks to the Business Object Interface layer, we could do all creation, location and removal of those objects from within the Hash-tableModel implementation itself.

## 14.1.6    Conclusion

As tempted as we might be to make use of the HashtableModel as a basic storage sys-tem, HashtableModel suffers from serious flaws that prevent its use without restric-tion. The key problem is its in-process design; because the Hashtable which stores all the objects exists nowhere outside this process, it is inherently unshareable. Coupled with the fact that HashtableModel lacks any form of communications capability, HashtableModel doesn't work well by itself.

If HashtableModel is intended as the central storage for a system, then it requires the ability to communicate with other processes (or rather, the ability to allow other processes to communicate with it). This implies the use of RMI, CORBA, or sockets to permit such communication. This is easily accomplished, but requires more effort; is it really worth it? Doing so would start to encroach on the basic aspects of a lightweight RDBMS, such as InstantDB, or a pure Java RDBMS, like Cloudscape.

HashtableModel works well in conjunction with other models, such as the RDBMSModel, as a cache or local object storage facility. For example, in a distributed system with noncontinuous connectivity (perhaps a local client which uses a dial-up connection to periodically update its local cache of data and send updates), local changes can be stored into a HashtableModel. Upon update, the objects are pulled from the HashtableModel and updated against the central model. Alternatively, when coupled with Serialization, the HashtableModel can provide a simplistic import/export facility. (Both ideas presume some sort of ability to shuffle objects from one Model instance to another.)

## 14.2 EXAMPLE: RDBMSMODEL

We'll now examine the RDBMSModel, the model likely to be in use most of the time. As its name implies, this model is the one used to manipulate data stored in a relational database, using JDBC to do the actual communication to the RDBMS driver, whatever that may be.

This approach will be the one most likely used for a variety of reasons:

- The data the application needs to use or have access to may already be stored, in its own schema, within a relational database. The company isn't interested in migrating its data to another data-storage system. So, whether the IT department likes it or not, it's stuck with using an RDBMS.

- Even if the data the proposed application uses isn't already stored within an RDBMS, the company may have standardized its data-storage systems on a specific RDBMS vendor/platform. Again, the decision where to store the data is no longer open to question—the data will be stored in the RDBMS selected.

- RDBMS systems have a wide variety of third-party tools available to ease in its development and administration. Reporting tools like Crystal Reports make creating ad hoc reports simple. Database wizards such as those that come with Microsoft Access make the prototyping and subsequent engineering of database schema easier. And ODBC-like single-interface engines provide a certain measure of portability across vendor systems to allow developers to learn one set of APIs and have their code port across all platforms.

- Data warehousing has become the latest hot buzzword in the data-storage industry. Building a data warehouse, a final repository for all of the company's data, is fast becoming an industrywide project. Because most data warehouses are built on top of the relational model, and because many in-house projects work with, around, or directly on top of the company's data warehouse, it is convenient to stick with the relational model for data storage.

Fortunately, due to the vendor-independent nature of JDBC, any database system can be used as the final storage system for the RDBMSModel, so long as we have a JDBC driver for it.

## 14.2.1 RDBMSModel: Storing Business Objects in an RDBMS

The RDBMSModel inherently faces a clash of opposing forces: it attempts to mix a relational-ordered view of the world and an object-ordered view. In effect, we are mapping classes to tables, objects to rows, and object members to columns. If only it were that easy.

This blending of the two, called an object-relational model, or an object-relational mapping layer or model, leads to problems at both the design and the implementational levels. Because the model is neither all object-based, nor all relational-based, trade-offs within each must be made with an eye toward the other. These compromises can, in turn, lead to lesser performance or more awkward manipulation than a pure model of either form would.

Numerous tools, both commercial and freeware, exist that attempt to automatically take care of this object-to-relational mapping. Unfortunately, automated tools cannot accommodate all necessary design forces in creating this object-relational mapping layer. For example, most automated tools assume that the database schema can be modified to fit the object model, which is untrue more often than not. Worse, many databases are deliberately denormalized for better performance, and asking an automated tool to recognize the relationship between two tables that have no explicit relationship is asking the impossible.

Instead, many of these object-relational layers must be created and coded by hand by system designers and architects. In fact, as might be expected, numerous pattern languages and papers talk directly about this topic: the "Crossing Chasms: A Pattern Language for Object-RDBMS Integration" paper by Kyle Brown and Bruce G. Whitenack,[2] or the "Accessing Relational Databases" paper by Wolfgang Keller and Jens Coldewey[3] are two examples.

Because designing and developing an object-relational layer is a subject that could comprise an entire book in and of itself, I'm not going to spend a lot of time rationalizing or justifying the decisions I've made in the RDBMSModel here. Instead, I will focus on the specific implementational needs of the model and leave the philosophical design decisions to be discussed in other forums. The implementation here is not intended as a one-size-fits-all design approach—no such silver bullet exists. Instead, examine this code critically, deciding for yourself which parts work, and which do not.

---

[2] *Pattern Languages of Program Design 2* (ed. by John Vlissides, James O. Coplien, and Norman L. Kerth (Addison-Wesley 1996), pp. 228–238

[3] *Pattern Languages of Program Design 3* (ed. by Robert Martin, Dirk Riehle, and Frank Buschmann (Addison-Wesley 1997), pp. 313–343

### 14.2.2 Overview

The basic SQL schema can be found as a `.SQL` file on the publisher's web site; it defines nine tables—person, employee, manager, manager_employees, dept., position, address, email, and phone. In this database, just about every class models into a stand-alone table, using integers for primary keys on each table. I deliberately attempted to keep the database as simple as possible. However, a few notes, about how the schema matches up against the class model, are in order:

- The manager_employees table is a link table to tie together manager and employee instances. We could have placed a foreign key in the employee table linking against the manager table, but it's possible that an employee could report to more than one manager (the dotted-line on the organization chart). By modeling this relationship as a separate table, we allow for many-to-many relationships between Managers and Employees.

- When I first began to work with this model, ContactInformation was a separate table, and each of the derived class tables (address, email, and phone) held a foreign key to the corresponding row in contact_info. However, it became apparent fairly quickly that this wasn't going to work well from the object perspective— the SQL to find all ContactInformation for a given Person started to get really ugly. I chose instead to denormalize the ContactInfo-Email/Address/Phone relationship, and propagate the description field to each individual table. Again, this is the power of the Façade; these decisions can be made and later changed without having to break any client code.

- Database designers may take issue with the fact that I've defined an arbitrary integer as my primary key, with no indexes or constraints using other columns to prevent logical duplication. For example, nothing prevents me from having two Person rows in the database with unique IDs, but identical SSNs. I'm not arguing that such indexes or constraints aren't necessary; in fact, they are, and will be, when using an object-relational layer in a system of even the smallest size or complexity. I leave them out here just for simplicity's sake.

- Good database performance tuners will immediately note the lack of any indexes on these tables. This is a database-implementation issue that, if used, will be well-shielded from the client; whether or not a column (or group of columns) is indexed will be completely opaque to the user of RDBMSModel. Again, remember, one of the advantages of encapsulating the database in this manner is to allow for parallel development—database gurus can work on database tuning and performance long after (or during) the development of the client code.

Part of supporting the object-relational approach is supporting the database overhead—things like establishing the database connection. Look briefly at some of the helper methods in RDBMSModel that weren't necessary in HashtableModel:

```
public RDBMSModel(Connection conn)
{
    s_connection = conn;
}

public static Connection getConnection()
{
    return s_connection;
}
private static Connection s_connection = null;
```

The RDBMSModel constructor expects a JDBC java.sql.Connection object to be passed in. This allows clients to decide precisely which database they wish to use for storage and retrieval of these objects. It might be marginally easier for clients to use if the knowledge of the database driver, username, and password were hard coded within the RDBMSModel code, but doing so would limit the functionality of the RDBMS-Model in a number of ways:

- *No vendor-independence*
  As it stands, RDBMSModel will work with any JDBC-compliant database, from Oracle to IDB. This allows RDBMSModel clients flexibility in determining which database to use for storage.

- *Single-instance restrictions*
  If RDBMSModel were to embed the database connection knowledge within itself, clients would be unable to open multiple connections. As it stands, nothing prevents a client from instantiating one RDBMSModel around a JDBC-ODBC connection to an Access database on a network sharepoint, another RDBMSModel around an Oracle JDBC driver to the corporate data warehouse, a third to a JDBC IDB driver pointing to the local machine, and using all three when storing/retrieving objects. This achieves a crude form of mirroring and fault-tolerance, assuming the client takes care to preserve transactional semantics (only update when all three can update, and so forth).

- *Home-grown security model*
  Most database vendors implement user-level security permissions at either the database-object or database-instance level. If database-connection semantics were embedded within the application, this would prevent us from using the database's own security model for user-validation and permissions, and force us to implement our own security/validation model. Why go to the extra effort, when we can let the DBAs define who gets to see what, and just let the database itself enforce it?

By requiring the java.sql.Connection object to be prebuilt, we force the client to perform a relatively trivial task—create the appropriate JDBC driver, obtain the user's login and password, and connect to the database. This removes from RDBMSModel the need to make these assumptions up front.

Critics will argue that this approach violates encapsulation. Clients need to know something about the RDBMS in order to be able to use it, instead of being able to just use IEmployeeModel methods without knowing or caring what it uses underneath. To a certain degree, that's true—at the time the RDBMSModel is constructed, a java.sql.Connection object needs to be ready and waiting. However, I maintain that whatever code (be it a Factory Method, Abstract Factory, or Singleton Pattern) already knows that it wants to create an RDBMSModel. If this knowledge is already present at that time, then obtaining a Connection object and passing it into the RDBMSModel constructor is not violating encapsulation any more than it already was.

Once inside the RDBMSModel constructor, we store it in a static member and create a public static method, getConnection, to retrieve it for use in the RDBMS classes. A few paragraphs ago, I stated that I wanted to be able to use multiple RDBMSModel instances. If I store the Connection instance in a static member, then I can't use multiple RDBMSModel instances, or the second constructor will over-write the contents in the static member, losing the first's Connection object. This is done deliberately, to contrast the approach in HashtableModel (where the HashtableDepartment contains a reference back to the HashtableModel with which it is associated) with the Model of our object. Again, in a production system, this reference to the RDBMSModel would need to be spread to each and every class in the RDBMSModel system (since all of the classes need to get at the Connection for this RDBMSModel).

This shared Connection object offers a few advantages as well as drawbacks. Because we're using one Connection over and over again, we should see better performance than if we were to open and close Connections each time we used one. This also allows us to share transactional semantics across object/tables and method calls, should we desire to do so.

RDBMSModel contains other helper methods that we will cover as we run across them as we go over the RDBMSModel Business Object Interface-implementing classes.

### 14.2.3  RDBMSPerson, RDBMSEmployee, RDBMSManager

We start, as we did with HashtableModel, by looking at the Person/Employee/Manager relationship. One of the preeminent drawbacks with a relational database system comes from the fact that relational databases do not model object inheritance relationships well. There have been a number of patterns written specifically to address this issue, mostly centering on the trade-off of purism versus performance. If we model the relational schema in a purist fashion, each class is its own table, and derived class tables hold foreign keys into base-class tables. However, this hurts performance—each table must be joined with any parent class tables when retrieving a derived type. The alternative is to model each derived class as its own table, but in that instance, we're losing the commonality a base class is supposed to give us. For example, unique constraints on one derived class table would not (without special database programming) apply to other derived class tables.

In this, admittedly simple, schema, each class receives its own table. I choose purism over performance because I can—I'm not concerned with performance of this application. As with any production system, part of the test cycle must include performance testing to determine if tuning or reengineering of the schema needs to happen. Because we've hidden the actual SQL from clients of this model, we can tune and reengineer the database as much as desired without breaking (or even modifying the semantics of) client code. Should this system suddenly have to support 100,000 concurrent users, modifications can be made to these classes (and others in this file), and any existing applications would run flawlessly with the new changes without requiring a line of code to be changed.

Now, let's dive into the code. We'll start with RDBMSPerson. There's a lot more to the RDBMSPerson class than there was to the HashtablePerson class. This is expected, since storing objects in relational databases requires much more work than storing the in-memory object to a Hashtable:

```
class RDBMSPerson
    implements IPerson
{
    RDBMSPerson(int personID)
        throws BusinessLayerException
    {
        try
        {
            // Retrieve Person info by ID
            Connection c = RDBMSModel.getConnection();
            Statement stmt = c.createStatement();
            ResultSet rs = stmt.executeQuery(
                "SELECT ID, f_name, m_name, l_name, ssn " +
                "FROM person WHERE person.id = " + personID);


            if (rs.next())
            {
                m_id = rs.getInt("ID");
                m_firstName = rs.getString("f_name");
                m_middleName = rs.getString("m_name");
                m_lastName = rs.getString("l_name");
                m_SSN = rs.getString("ssn");
            }
            else
                throw new BusinessLayerException("Person ID " +
                    personID + " not found");
        }
        catch (Exception ex)
        {
            ex.printStackTrace();
            throw new BusinessLayerException(ex);
        }
    }
```

Note that the constructor expects an integer representing the Person's primary key—the PersonID field—so as to be able to load the data from the person table in the RDBMS. We know that any constructor call that comes in on Person is a look-up, because if the system wanted to create a Person, it would use the creational methods on the RDBMS-Model implementation of the `IEmployeeModel` interface (covered later). In RDBMS-Person, the `m_id` field is made package-friendly, so that others (such as RDBMSEmployee and RDBMSManager, as well as RDBMSModel itself) can access, manipulate, and work with this value. This is also the principal predicate for almost every SQL statement in the class. Everywhere we want to retrieve, modify, or remote a Person from the relational database, we need to specify which one by the integer primary key.

```
public String getFirstName()
    throws BusinessLayerException
{
    return m_firstName;
}
public void setFirstName(String fName)
    throws BusinessLayerException
{
    m_firstName = fName;
    commit();
}
```

The `get/setLastName`, `get/setMiddleName`, and `get/setSSN` methods all look similar to the `get/setFirstName` methods, above. The `get` case is simple, but notice that the `set` version not only traps the changed value into the local class member of the same name, but calls the `commit` method:

```
public IContactInfo[] getContactInfo()
    throws BusinessLayerException
{
    Vector tempVector = new Vector();

    try
    {
        // First grab all Email instances
        //
        Connection c = RDBMSModel.getConnection();
        Statement stmt = c.createStatement();
        ResultSet rs = stmt.executeQuery(
            "SELECT ID " +
            "FROM email WHERE person_id_fk = " + m_id);

        while (rs.next())
        {
            int email_id = rs.getInt("ID");
            IEMail e = new RDBMSEMail(email_id);

            tempVector.addElement(e);
        }
        rs.close();
```

```java
        // Next grab all Phone instances
        //
        rs = stmt.executeQuery(
            "SELECT ID " +
            "FROM phone WHERE person_id_fk = " + m_id);

        while (rs.next())
        {
            int phone_id = rs.getInt("ID");
            IPhone p = new RDBMSPhone(phone_id);

            tempVector.addElement(p);
        }
        rs.close();

        // Next grab all Address instances
        //
        rs = stmt.executeQuery(
            "SELECT ID " +
            "FROM address WHERE person_id_fk = " + m_id);

        while (rs.next())
        {
            int addr_id = rs.getInt("ID");
            IAddress a = new RDBMSAddress(addr_id);

            tempVector.addElement(a);
        }
        rs.close();

        // Return the whole batch
        IContactInfo[] retArray = new IContactInfo[tempVector.size()];
        for (int i=0; i<retArray.length; i++)
            retArray[i] = (IContactInfo)tempVector.elementAt(i);

        return retArray;
    }
    catch (Exception x)
    {
        x.printStackTrace();
        throw new BusinessLayerException(x);
    }
}
```

Contact information becomes more complex with Person in the RDBMSModel, because the relationship between Person and contact information is more explicitly captured within the schema. Were this an object database, the contact information related to this Person would simply be retrieved along with the Person object (regardless of the efficiency of doing so). In an RDBMS, however, we must manage this ourselves. In the above case, the contact information isn't retrieved until it's asked for by the user—this is a lazy evaluation scheme, and may result in slower performance at the time contact information is requested. The alternative, of course, is to retrieve the information at the time the Person object is constructed, and store the results in a Vector or similar Collection within the Person class. Again, this is where user feedback can influence the implementation without changing dependents' code—because client code is written to the `IPerson` interface, and knows nothing about the actual RDBMS-Person class, we can freely vary the implementation used without blinking an eye.

```
public void addEMail(String desc, String email)
    throws BusinessLayerException
{
    // Create a new row in the email table
    try
    {
        int emailID =
            RDBMSModel.nextDatabaseID("email");

        Statement stmt =
            RDBMSModel.getConnection().createStatement();
        int result = stmt.executeUpdate(
            "INSERT INTO email " +
                "(ID, person_id_fk, description, email) " +
            "VALUES " +
                "(" + emailID + ", " +
                m_id + ", " +
                "'" + desc + "', " +
                "'" + email + "')");
        if (result < 1)
            throw new BusinessLayerException(
                "INSERT into database failed");
    }
    catch (Exception x)
    {
        x.printStackTrace();
        throw new BusinessLayerException(x);
    }
}
public void addAddress(String desc, String street, String city,
    String state, String zip, String country)
    throws BusinessLayerException
{
    // . . . snip . . .
}
public void addPhone(String desc, String prefix,
    String number, String suffix)
    throws BusinessLayerException
{
    // . . . snip . . .
}
```

Here, each of the `add` methods update the database immediately with the new `IContactInfo` object's data; alternatively, we might hang on to it until the user wishes to commit it somehow. Not committing it immediately, however, runs the risk of near-simultaneous modification of the same Person object, with each object unaware of the other's changes.

```java
public void removeContactInfo(IContactInfo contactInfo)
    throws BusinessLayerException
{
    try
    {
        // Need to determine which ContactInfo instance this is;
        // only way to do that is to cast (or getClass())
        String tableName = null;
        int infoID = 0;
        if (contactInfo instanceof RDBMSPhone)
        {
            RDBMSPhone phone = (RDBMSPhone)contactInfo;

            tableName = "phone";
            infoID = phone.m_id;
        }
        else if (contactInfo instanceof RDBMSEMail)
        {
            RDBMSEMail email = (RDBMSEMail)contactInfo;

            tableName = "email";
            infoID = email.m_id;
        }
        else if (contactInfo instanceof RDBMSAddress)
        {
            RDBMSAddress addr = (RDBMSAddress)contactInfo;

            tableName = "address";
            infoID = addr.m_id;
        }
        else
        {
            // We tried to remove an IContactInfo that doesn't
            // come from the RDBMSModel; throw an exception
            throw new BusinessLayerException("Not an RDBMSModel" +
                " ContactInfo instance: " + contactInfo.toString());
        }

        Statement stmt =
            RDBMSModel.getConnection().createStatement();
        int result = stmt.executeUpdate(
            "DELETE FROM " + tableName + " " +
            "WHERE ID = " + infoID);
        if (result < 1)
            throw new BusinessLayerException(
                "DELETE from database failed");
    }
    catch (Exception x)
    {
        x.printStackTrace();
        throw new BusinessLayerException(x);
    }
}
```

Removing contact information is a bit trickier, since we need to determine precisely what kind of IContactInfo object (Email, Address, or Phone) we need to remove from the RDBMS, but from there it's a simple "DELETE" statement in SQL.

```
// Internal methods
//
private void commit()
    throws BusinessLayerException
{
    try
    {
        Connection c = RDBMSModel.getConnection();
        Statement stmt = c.createStatement();
        int result = stmt.executeUpdate(
            "UPDATE person SET f_name='" + m_firstName + "', " +
                "m_name='" + m_middleName + "', " +
                "l_name='" + m_lastName + "', " +
                "ssn='" + m_SSN + "' " +
                "WHERE id = " + m_id);
    }
    catch (Exception ex)
    {
        ex.printStackTrace();
        throw new BusinessLayerException(ex);
    }
}
```

And commit, of course, takes the current values of the internal members (the locally cached values retrieved from the database) and stores them to the RDBMS using the usual SQL UPDATE statement.

```
    // Internal members
    int m_id;
    private String m_firstName;
    private String m_middleName;
    private String m_lastName;
    private String m_SSN;
} // RDBMSPerson
```

One last interesting tidbit about the RDBMSPerson class shows up in the add-Phone() method:

```
String toDBNumber = RDBMSModel.PhoneToDB(number);
```

One of the principal concerns regarding any data-storage effort is ensuring that the data is stored in a consistent format. Consider the standard U.S. phone number; typically we assume a ten-digit numeric field for number storage (area code, three digits, prefix, three digits, suffix, four digits). Unfortunately, this doesn't cover all possible U.S. phone numbers, as many companies use 1-800 numbers with alphanumeric symbols instead of purely numeric. Consider also the separator character used to set area code apart from the prefix and suffix—some databases use the dash (-) character, others use a slash (/). Still others use parentheses around the area code and a dash separating the prefix and suffix (as in (800) 555-1212). With so many different ways of representing a phone number, standardizing its database representation is crucial to allow for any sort of search-by-phone or search-within-area-code functionality.

In this system, we pass any input from the client to several RDBMSModel static methods to do the necessary formatting; in the addPhone() method of Person, we call RDBMSModel.PhoneToDB() to translate the String the client has handed us into the appropriate database representation before storing it. We reverse the process in the RDBMSPhone code, shown later.

We could, of course, embed this logic directly within the RDBMSPerson class, and the reverse logic within the RDBMSPhone, instead of within RDBMSModel. This approach suffers for two reasons.

First, if the database representation of the phone number needs to change (perhaps we're adding support for international numbers in a future release), then any code which retrieves, uses, or stores a phone number also needs to be updated. If the code that does this massaging is scattered across several places, then we need to ensure (usually through trial-and-error, testing it each time it's thought the update is finished) that each place gets updated appropriately. This is time-consuming and error-prone—if all of the code resides in a single place, programmers need only go to one place to find out what needs to be updated.

Secondly, having these sorts of business rules centralized makes it easier to understand all of the rules relating to how the data is stored within the database. This in turn makes migration to another database or, more likely, performance tuning within the database schema simpler. If clients are calling a central routine to format input into a common phone-number storage format, changing the code to use a database stored procedure instead of doing it in Java code requires no client changes.

This doesn't mean that this formatting code has to exist inside the RDBMSModel class; in fact, good arguments can be made that these sorts of rules should exist as a stand-alone class or interface (possibly RDBMSModelRules). For this example, however, these rules are simple enough to be wrapped in with the RDBMSModel itself.

RDBMSEmployee, RDBMSManager, RDBMSPosition, RDBMSDepartment, and the RDBMS contact information classes all follow a similar model; see the source code available on the publisher's web site for the EmployeeModel for the details.

## 14.2.4   RDBMSModel: Creating objects

Creating objects in the RDBMSModel is a two-step process—first, the appropriate row(s) in the appropriate table(s) are created within the database. If that succeeds (indicating that an object by that name or key doesn't already exist), then an appropriate in-memory Java object is created, assigned the ID used to create the row, and returned to the client. The following code shows the details involved in creating a new Position object:

```java
/**
 * Create IPosition object
 */
public IPosition createPosition(
    String title, String desc, int minSalary, int maxSalary)
    throws BusinessLayerException, DuplicateObjectException
{
    try
    {
        int posID = nextDatabaseID("position");

        Statement stmt = getConnection().createStatement();
        int result = stmt.executeUpdate(
            "INSERT INTO position " +
            "VALUES (" +
                posID + ", " +
                "'" + title + "', " +
                "'" + desc + "', " +
                minSalary + ", " +
                maxSalary + ", " +
                "')");

        if (result > 0)
            return new RDBMSPosition(posID);
        else
            throw new BusinessLayerException(
                "Invalid database state; can't insert");
    }
    catch (SQLException ex)
    {
        throw new BusinessLayerException(ex);
    }
}
```

Because this schema uses an integer-based primary key approach, we need to generate a sequential counter to produce unique IDs each time a new RDBMSPosition object wishes to be created. Under some database systems, this can be accomplished directly within SQL, such as Oracle's SEQUENCE types or Access's AutoIncrement columns. However, under other databases, this counter must be managed by hand on the part of the programmer.

Because of this inherent lack of portability, RDBMSModel provides the next-DatabaseID() method, which takes the name of the table and returns the next unique ID to use in creating a new row in the table. Again, this is to localize the RDBMS-management code within a single place. However, there is another danger that developers implementing a scheme such as this need to recognize. The basic format of the nextDatabaseID() method, as implemented within RDBMSModel, uses a SQL "SELECT" statement to retrieve the highest-numbered ID within the given table, increments it, and hands it back:

```
static int nextDatabaseID(String tableName)
    throws BusinessLayerException
{
    try
    {
        // Retrieve the ID
        int dbID = 0;

        Statement stmt = getConnection().createStatement();
        ResultSet rs = stmt.executeQuery(
            "SELECT MAX(id) FROM " + tableName);
        if (rs.next())
            dbID = rs.getInt("MAX(id)");
        else
            return 1;

        // Increment it and return it
        return ++dbID;
    }
    catch(SQLException ex)
    {
        throw new BusinessLayerException(ex);
    }
}
```

There is an inherent danger in this approach. In between the "SELECT" and the "INSERT" (which takes place in the appropriate create method of RDBMSModel), a new record may be inserted with that same ID before this object's insert can take place. This leads to a primary key violation and no small amount of confusion on the part of the user. In a single-user system, this is a nonissue, since a single user will find it almost impossible to insert the same type record simultaneously, but for a multiuser system, simultaneous inserts, updates, or removals are common.

At first, it might seem that the problem solves itself if the creation methods are marked synchronized, disallowing multiple threads to enter the method until the thread currently in the method exits. Unfortunately, this only carries through the current JVM—users on different machines or in different JVMs will be freely able to enter the creation method at the same time another user is doing the same. Under these circumstances, one of three options is available:

- Implement a cross-JVM synchronization system, either by making use of a socket-based synchronization construct or a native-code construct, that disallows multiple users from entering the "protected" method
- Use database facilities to prevent this sort of simultaneous access, such as table or row locking
- Create a table in the database to perform this sort of tracking and implement the locking mechanism by hand in the database

None of these is particularly attractive, but the second is by far the most preferable. Of course, if none of the three works for a given situation, it's always possible to move away completely from the integer primary key approach and move to a data-column primary key approach. (In this system, Persons would be uniquely identified by SSN, Departments by name, Positions by name, and so on.) Moving to a data-column primary key removes the need to generate unique IDs for each row, but makes foreign keys that much more difficult to use.

## 14.2.5 RDBMSModel: Finding objects

The power of a relational database lies in its ability to find objects stored therein. Because SQL specifies only what you're interested in, not how to find it, RDBMS vendors are free to take whatever steps are necessary to efficiently retrieve a single needle from the entire million row haystack.

Because the SQL involved in this model is relatively simple, I won't go over each and every find... method implemented in the RDBMSModel; all follow the same basic format:

```
class RDBMSModel
    implements IEmployeeModel
{
    // . . .

    /**
     * Query for all Managers
     */
    public IManager[] findAllManagers()
        throws BusinessLayerException
    {
        try
        {
            Statement stmt = getConnection().createStatement();
            ResultSet rs = stmt.executeQuery(
                "SELECT manager.ID FROM manager");

            Vector tempVector = new Vector();

            while (rs.next())
            {
                int mgrID = rs.getInt("manager.ID");

                IManager e = new RDBMSManager(mgrID);
                tempVector.addElement(e);
            }

            // Copy over from the Vector to the array to return
            IManager retArray[] = new RDBMSManager[tempVector.size()];
            for (int i=0; i<tempVector.size(); i++)
                retArray[i] = (IManager)tempVector.elementAt(i);

            return retArray;
        }
        catch (SQLException x)
```

```
            {
                x.printStackTrace();
                throw new BusinessLayerException(x);
            }
        }
    }
```

This is basic JDBC—issue a SELECT statement, walk through the ResultSet. Where this approach differs slightly from traditional JDBC code is in the creation of the RDBMSManager (in this case) instance, which in turn retrieves the appropriate data from the row given by the primary key integer in mgrID. Each RDBMSManager instance is added to a temporary Vector object, which is then transformed into an array of IManager references before being returned.

Implementors concerned about performance (and memory footprint, if these objects grow to be of hefty size) can optimize this without having to change the above code one bit. The RDBMSManager (or whatever) class constructor, instead of retrieving the data immediately, can use lazy evaluation and simply store the ID internally. Then, when actually asked for its data, it calls out to the database for the data requested (either all the data at once, or pieces thereof, whichever makes more sense).

### 14.2.6  RDBMSModel: Removing objects

Removing elements from a relational database is almost as easy as finding them, with one exception. Because most relational database systems enforce referential integrity (to some degree), rows must be removed from the table in leaf-first order. That means, in our system, that removing a Person instance from the system requires first removal of that Person instance's contact information rows:

```
class RDBMSPerson
    implements IPerson
{
    // . . .

    /**
     * Remove a Person from the system
     */
    public void removePerson(IPerson person)
        throws BusinessLayerException, IntegrityConstraintException,
            UnknownObjectException
    {
        try
        {
            // First remove all contact information associated with
            // this Person; if we don't delete these first,
            // referential integrity will prevent us from removing
            // their corresponding 'person' row
            Statement stmt = getConnection().createStatement();
            int result = stmt.executeUpdate(
                "DELETE FROM email " +
                "WHERE email.person_id_fk = " + person.m_ID);
```

```
            stmt.close();

            stmt = getConnection().createStatement();
            result = stmt.executeUpdate(
                "DELETE FROM phone " +
                "WHERE phone.person_id_fk = " + person.m_ID);
            stmt.close();

            stmt = getConnection().createStatement();
            result = stmt.executeUpdate(
                "DELETE FROM address " +
                "WHERE address.person_id_fk = " + person.m_ID);

            // Now we can remove the Person row itself
            stmt = getConnection().createStatement();
            result = stmt.executeUpdate(
                "DELETE FROM person " +
                "WHERE person.ID = " + person.m_ID);

            if (result < 1)
                throw new UnknownObjectException();
        }
        catch (SQLException x)
        {
            x.printStackTrace();
            throw new BusinessLayerException(x);
        }
    }
}
```

Notice that we don't particularly care how many email, address, or phone rows we remove. Persons can have 0 to *n* of any of these, so a DELETE statement that modifies 0 rows is nothing exceptional.

Employees and Managers have the same problem, due to their inheritance relationship with Person and Employee (respectively):

```
class RDBMSPerson
    implements IPerson
{
    // . . .

    /**
     * Remove an Employee from the system
     */
    public void removeEmployee(IEmployee employee)
        throws BusinessLayerException, IntegrityConstraintException,
            UnknownObjectException
    {
        try
        {
            Statement stmt = getConnection().createStatement();
            int result = stmt.executeUpdate(
                "DELETE FROM employee " +
                "WHERE employee.ID = " + employee.m_ID);
```

CHAPTER 14  BUSINESS OBJECT MODELS

```
            if (result < 1)
                throw new UnknownObjectException();

            removePerson(employee);
        }
        catch (SQLException x)
        {
            x.printStackTrace();
            throw new BusinessLayerException(x);
        }
    }

    /**
     * Remove a Manager from the system
     */
    public void removeManager(IManager manager)
        throws BusinessLayerException, IntegrityConstraintException,
            UnknownObjectException
    {
        try
        {
            Statement stmt = getConnection().createStatement();
            int result = stmt.executeUpdate(
                "DELETE FROM manager " +
                "WHERE manager.ID = " + manager.m_ID);

            if (result < 1)
                throw new UnknownObjectException();

            removeEmployee(manager);
        }
        catch (SQLException x)
        {
            x.printStackTrace();
            throw new BusinessLayerException(x);
        }
    }
}
```

Because the leaf, in the case of inheritance/foreign-key relationships, is the derived class, the derived class (the Employee or the Manager) is deleted first, then the corresponding base-class method (removePerson or removeEmployee) is called to remove the base-class row.

Other removal operations on RDBMSModel (removeDepartment and removePosition) are straightforward enough not to merit special discussion; see the code for details.

### 14.2.7   Conclusion

On the whole, the RDBMSModel above is useful precisely as intended—as an example of the object-relational mapping layer—and not much more. To begin with, numerous chances for data corruption abound throughout the code due to the lack of transaction support. For example, in the removeManager method, if the DELETE statement within removeManager succeeds but the removeEmployee call fails, the Manager row is still gone with no hope for retrieval. Transaction support within an RDBMS model is critical for robust data storage; fortunately, it is not difficult to add using JDBC:

```
class RDBMSPerson
    implements IPerson
{
    // . . .

    /**
     * Remove a Position from the system, with transaction support
     * (not found in sample code)
     */
    public void removePosition(IPosition position)
        throws BusinessLayerException, IntegrityConstraintException,
            UnknownObjectException
    {
        try
        {
            getConnection().setAutoCommit(false);

            Statement stmt = getConnection().createStatement();
            int result = stmt.executeUpdate(
                "DELETE FROM position " +
                "WHERE position.ID = " + position.m_ID);

            if (result < 1)
                throw new UnknownObjectException();

            getConnection().commit();
        }
        catch (SQLException x)
        {
            x.printStackTrace();
            getConnection().rollback();
            throw new BusinessLayerException(x);
        }
    }
}
```

Unfortunately, the JDBC Connection class doesn't inherently permit the notion of nested transactions, which would be required to fully support the manager-employee-person three-step removal process. In that case, transactions must be opened directly using SQL, or by providing special methods knowing when to call commit on the Connection object:

```
class RDBMSPerson
    implements IPerson
{
    // . . .
```

```
/**
 * Remove an Employee from the system
 */
public void removeEmployee(IEmployee employee)
    throws BusinessLayerException, IntegrityConstraintException,
        UnknownObjectException
{
    try
    {
        removeEmployeeNoCommit(employee);
        getConnection().commit();
    }
    catch (BusinessLayerException ex)
    {
        getConnection().rollback();
        throw ex;
    }
    catch (IntegrityConstraintsException ex2)
    {
        getConnection().rollback();
        throw ex2;
    }
    catch (UnknownObjectException ex3)
    {
        getConnection().rollback();
        throw ex3;
    }
}

private void removeEmployeeNoCommit(IEmployee employee)
    throws BusinessLayerException, IntegrityConstraintException,
        UnknownObjectException
{
    try
    {
        Statement stmt = getConnection().createStatement();
        int result = stmt.executeUpdate(
            "DELETE FROM employee " +
            "WHERE employee.ID = " + employee.m_ID);

        if (result < 1)
            throw new UnknownObjectException();

        removePersonNoCommit(employee);
    }
    catch (SQLException x)
    {
        x.printStackTrace();
        throw new BusinessLayerException(x);
    }
}
}
```

In the above sequence, if the user calls `removeEmployee`, it in turn calls into a `private` method, `removeEmployeeNoCommit`, which executes the actual `DELETE`. The `removeEmployeeNoCommit` method then calls into `removePersonNo-Commit`, which removes the Person (and all contact info) rows without calling `Connection.commit`. If everything returns successfully, `removeEmployee` calls commit on the shared Connection object, and the transaction is committed. Similarly, `removeManager` would call `removeEmployeeNoCommit`, which in turn calls `removePersonNoCommit`, and so on.

The other option would be to handle the commit logic directly within SQL, but that lies outside the JDBC API itself. Consult your local SQL guru and database vendor documentation for more details.

## 14.3 SUMMARY

Notice how the encapsulation of the actual storage mechanism behind the Business Object layer allows us to mix-and-match the actual implementation without modifying the client code—if you run the OrgTree example from the last chapter, for example, you can use either the HashtableModel or the RDBMSModel without changing a line of code.[4] This in turn means that underlying systems can be modified without requiring significant rewrite to existing applications. Should the enterprise decide to go with an OODBMS to replace the conventional RDBMS, for example, we only need pass in an OODBMSModel in place of the RDBMSModel currently in use.

This interface-based approach is not unique to business object models, however. Sun uses it extensively throughout most of the new Enterprise technologies within Java—JDBC and JNDI are just two of the more obvious examples. If you look carefully at the JDBC API, for example, the key classes (ResultSet, Statement, Connection, ResultSetMetaData) are all interfaces that the driver-developer must implement. Then, when your code calls `DriverManager.getConnection`, the driver returns its own class, which implements the Connection API. When your code calls `create-Statement` on that Connection, you get back a Statement-implementing object. Nothing prevents the driver-developer from handing back the same object in both situations—it may be a lightweight driver that only allows a single Statement at a time. Instead, you, as the user of the JDBC driver, only know that the object returned to you is guaranteed to implement the Connection or Statement or ResultSet APIs. Realistically, that's all you really care about.

There are drawbacks, however. Well-encapsulated systems also reduce visibility within them, leaving developers that use the systems out in the cold regarding their internal details. This can be viewed as both a positive and a negative force. Having

---

[4] Technically, that's not true—we need to get the actual `IEmployeeModel`-implementing instance from somewhere, and that usually means a special method or something similar to construct it. Beyond that, however, no other code requires modification.

well-encapsulated systems means outside developers can't use knowledge of the systems' internals to break future compatibility, but it also means debugging the system (or, more accurately, the outside developer's interaction with the system) is much more difficult. Systems which expose their internals are easier to abuse by outside developers, but also greatly reduce the future development-with-backward-compatibility of the system as a whole.

In a perfect world, where no software has bugs, complete encapsulation would be an out-and-out winner. Balancing the needs of developers to debug their products (in the face of potential bugs from vendors' products) against our needs to insulate developers from internal details is a fine art. Each organization will need to weigh in very carefully on where they draw the line.

## 14.4  ADDITIONAL READING

- Desmond D'Souza and Alan Cameron Wills, *Object, Components, and Frameworks with UML* (Addison-Wesley, 1999).

  This is a great book for any developer involved at the design or analysis level, with clear focus on building shared business models, as well as providing a generalized approach to developing software that meets (or exceeds) client needs. It's not a lightweight book, by any means, weighing in at just under 700 pages (not counting appendices, index, or glossary), but it's possibly one of the best books any developer or architect will find.

- James O. Coplien, Douglas C. Schmidt, *Pattern Languages of Program Design* (Addison-Wesley, 1995).

- John Vlissides, James O. Coplien, Norman L. Kerth, *Pattern Languages of Program Design 2* (Addison-Wesley, 1996).

- Robert Martin, Dirk Riehle, Frank Buschmann, *Pattern Languages of Program Design 3* (Addison-Wesley, 1997).

C H A P T E R   1 5

# Middleware

Like most buzzwords, middleware takes on different meanings depending upon the speaker, the audience, or the medium. Fundamentally, middleware, as I use the term, is the means by which two objects, functions, or processes communicate with one another. This includes such technologies as RMI, CORBA, JMS, even the ubiquitous BSD sockets. Some, like sockets, operate at a low level, providing the very basics of communication and nothing else; others, such as CORBA, carry significantly higher overhead but make the development of distributed object systems substantially easier. As with everything else in software development, making the right middleware choice means understanding the trade-offs.

## 15.1  WHY DISTRIBUTE?

It's a given that distributed object systems are somehow better than nondistributed versions. Ask any software developer about the advantages of a distributed system versus a nondistributed one; almost every one will say that the distributed version is better, but the exact reasons why may be a little fuzzy.

Principally, the decision to distribute an object system is made for one (or more) of four reasons: communication, performance, economics, reliability.

### 15.1.1 Communication

One of the most basic reasons to distribute an object system is that of simple communication: it's nearly a requirement of modern enterprise systems that they be able to communicate across a network with other systems in other rooms, buildings, or even continents. This means that, at a minimum, systems need to be able to share data, either in a traditional client/server mode, or in a more modern object-based approach.

Once we get beyond the need to share data, however, what more communication is really necessary? For about ten years, before the advent of Java and the parallel development of CORBA or COM/DCOM, developers quite happily pulled data across a network using database protocols such as ODBC or its ancestors (Oracle's OCI, for example). No object-complexity, just issue an SQL statement, bind the result columns to local variables, and pull the data back. If we needed communication with systems other than databases, we did what we've been doing on the Internet for about twenty years now—open a socket, send a request, get a response, continue until we're finished. Why the need for distributed object communication?

Partly, the reason stems from the gradual shift in system architecture and design, from procedural designs, to more object-centric ones.[1] For many years before the development of object-centric distributed systems, developers struggled to marry distributed systems like the OSF's Distributed Computing Environment (DCE) remote procedure call (RPC) system to object-centric languages and environments *a la* C++. Usually, it wasn't a happy marriage, with even the slightest change on one side causing major heartache and maintenance on the other. It was natural that developers would begin to look for object-centric solutions in their distribution technologies in order to minimize the marriage pains between the local object model and the distribution mechanics.

Partly, we want to be able to expose more and more aspects of the hardware systems across the network to any other system across the network. Consider the intranet/network most businesses have in place with regard to printing needs. Without a fundamental communications layer, being able to share printers would be impossible. To print a document, one would have to save the document to disk, walk the disk over to the machine to which the printer was connected, access the document using the program that created it, and print it. We ignore, for purposes of simplicity, the sticky situation one runs into in this sneakernet situation if the document in question is larger than the size of a floppy disk. Distributed object systems make it possible for clients all across the network to access resources on other systems without having to resort to physical means of access. If the print server is down the hall, it's a simple matter to walk the document to the print server; if it happens to be in Bangladesh, most Americans are just plain out of luck.

---

[1] Object-centric systems use objects as some part of their architecture. The difference is one of C++ versus Visual Basic.

Partly, however, the need to communicate across systems grows as we begin to rethink our fundamental distributed designs. Before, when communication was rudimentary and simple, communication needs were similarly simple and unsophisticated. Before long, however, business needs began to demand that we integrate a variety of databases together into a single, virtual database system. Sales data comes from the Sales database, Inventory comes from the Inventory database, but we still want to integrate the two into a unified whole. This requires more sophisticated communication than can be accomplished by simple sockets; more sophistication in turn means more chances to break things, if the complexity isn't buried inside of a communication/distribution technology layer.

## 15.1.2 Performance

Consider a hypothetical business system which requires the CPU to perform calculation of prime numbers. Where will these calculations be more quickly computed—on your Pentium-II/233 client workstation, or on a quad-processor 1GB-RAM 16GB RAID-array Pentium-III/450? It should be obvious that the higher computing power on the second machine would lead to faster computation, but there's a huge monetary cost to putting Pentium-III high-end servers on each individual's desk.

Now, consider the classic client/server model applied to the calculation of prime numbers; if a client wants a particular prime number, instead of calculating it locally, it instead passes the necessary parameter information over a socket to the server, which processes the request and returns the result. The advantages of this approach are:

- *CPU power*
  The server is likely to be several times more powerful than the client making the request, meaning that the result will likely be computed that much faster.

- *Caching*
  Because the server is a single entity, and requests coming to it may be duplicates from previous clients, the server can spend the necessary resources to keep a cache of most-recently used prime numbers. (For a prime number server, it may even precalculate all prime numbers up to some reasonable number, and only calculate primes for any that fall outside of that range.) For a client that may only request three or four numbers per run, this sort of cache would be intolerable. For a server, answering up to hundreds of client requests per hour/minute/second/ whatever, the cache is far more justifiable.

- *Centralized scalability*
  If the demands on the system grow (say each client now needs to calculate a hundred prime numbers per run, instead of the three or four initially required), the centralized server can be upgraded to more powerful hardware, with no loss of performance to the clients. This is a far simpler task than upgrading every computer system across the client's userbase.

On top of this, what begins to happen if we introduce a clustered environment into the local network? If you're sitting in the office, stand up for a moment and walk around; notice how many CPUs are currently sitting idle. If you think that the Sales department is even making use of 5 percent of the total CPU power during the day, you're in for a rude shock. The fact is, billions upon billions of CPU clock cycles are wasted every day, just idling, waiting for user input.

What if we could harness all that idle power? The concept isn't new, nor is it a particularly foreign one. Symantec, for example, introduced a distributed make system in its Symantec C++ product several years ago. More recently, as part of the movement to break the most recent 128-bit security key, several developers created a Windows screen saver that, when the screen saver kicked in, would download a snippet of the key to attempt a brute-force crack. Because screen savers only kick in during the CPU's idle moments, the impact of the idle-time processing is minimized to the user, and the idle CPU cycles aren't lost.

Consider what an enterprisewide version of that could accomplish. Imagine we create a distributed job system, using some of the dynamic ClassLoading techniques described in chapter 2, to farm work out to the various idle CPUs in the company. Since most business systems also have a common file-sharing area, we could create a distributed make system, with each CPU building a separate file, or we could automate the distribution of files to client systems by farming out a copy-file-to-here job to each machine. In short, if we have 100 machines, each running at 200 MHz, we can create a 20,000 MHz supercomputer by placing a simple clustering server on each one.

### 15.1.3 Economics (clustering/fault-tolerance)

Since we're talking about the notion of clustering a number of systems, let's examine the economics of doing so. Presuming we have the 100 machines at 200 MHz in the previous section, what would be the cost of purchasing a single 20,000 MHz super-computer, assuming such a machine could even be bought? Easily far more than the cost of a hundred machines at approximately $1,500 apiece ($150,000).

Furthermore, consider the cost of maintenance and parts for the above machine. Something that high-powered has to be backed by service agreements and specialized parts (not to mention the liquid-oxygen-cooled room it has to sit in, lest it spontaneously combust from all the heat generated). Finding qualified personnel to administer it and service it can also be an expensive proposition. Compare this with the costs of finding a PC-qualified technician and buying off-the-shelf PC parts. In some cases, if a part goes bad, the corporation can simply throw it away and spend $50 on a new one.

This, of course, assumes that the two approaches (the single-server and the distributed-cluster) produce equal performance, and that's not always a safe assumption. In many cases, a well-designed distributed object system can outperform an equivalently powered single-server system, since it can more effectively "parallelize" portions of the client's request. The one area where the single-server system will constantly outperform the distributed version will be in I/O-tight operations, where the overhead of sending data across the network will outweigh the gains of a distributed approach.

### 15.1.4 Reliability (clustering/load-balancing)

Going back to our distributed-cluster versus single-server comparison, consider the necessary downtime in both environments. Assuming that a given system has a 1 percent downtime, which is actually quite reasonable for many systems, it means that users will experience complete shutdown 1 percent of the time. For a data center looking to achieve five-nines (99.999%) uptime, this is obviously not an acceptable situation. Even if the machine has a 0.1 percent downtime, we're still not reaching 99.999 percent uptime.

Assume, in contrast, that a standard PC has a 5 percent downtime. This means that in a 100-machine cluster, five machines will be down at all times. The difference? Users won't experience any complete shutdown—instead of the single server's all-or-nothing approach, the distributed-cluster system simply adjusts by moving the load out to the other machines. If the administrators notice that they're experiencing unacceptable loads on the 100-machine cluster because five machines are constantly down, they can add five more machines to pick up the slack without major expense, in either time or money.

## 15.2 DISTRIBUTED OBJECT DESIGN VS. CLASSIC OBJECT DESIGN

Adding distribution into an object system is not as simple as making objects able to communicate with another process or object within another process. Any time communication takes place between two processes, a certain amount of overhead is required. If this overhead is negligently ignored during the design phase, the resulting system will fail to scale as more and more users are added.

This danger becomes particularly pronounced with RMI and/or CORBA distributed object systems; the ease with which RMI and/or CORBA make it possible to call other objects across the software bus can lead developers down a dark and dangerous path, where hundreds, if not thousands, of objects are exported for client calls. This in turn bogs the server down; more and more objects are created, exported, and sit idle while clients mull over their options in front of their own local displays, and developers are called to the carpet to explain why the system runs so painfully slow. Unfortunately, developers don't understand—it ran fine when they tested it....

### 15.2.1 Stateful vs. stateless

The core problem with distributed object designs is that objects, by nature, tend to be stateful beasts. For example, look at an instance of the JDBC Connection class. At any given moment, it has an inherent state that affects whether it can or cannot complete certain operations. For example, if the Connection is already connected to a given database, calling `close` closes the connection; under the condition where it isn't connected, close should do nothing. Attempting to obtain a Statement instance when the Connection is closed yields an error or a null Statement, whereas attempting the same thing with an open Connection yields a good Statement handle. In short, the Connection instance maintains a state that can be affected by client actions, and can in turn affect its behavior during client requests.

As an opposite example, consider the classic HTTP connection—the client makes a request, the server fulfills it, sends the response, and the client disconnects. The server maintains no state on behalf of the client, and the client maintains no state on behalf of the server.[2] The principal benefit of this approach is that the HTTP server is now free to dedicate the socket resource, just recently used on behalf of the old client, toward answering the request of a new client.

Think of it this way.[3] Years ago, when visiting the local bank, each bank teller station would have its own line, and as a bank patron, you would have to pick a line to stand in. If you happened to know the tellers, you might know that the one on the right was an experienced, efficient teller, as opposed to the one on the left. You might then choose to stand in the line of the one on the right, even though her line was longer, because you knew she'd be able to handle more people faster than the one on the left. If you didn't know that, you would see the line on the left, with only one person, and take it. You'd then be forced to wait and watch, as the efficient teller on the right handled the four people who would have been in front of you had you stood there, along with the three or four that came in after you.

In this particular case, each teller is a stateful entity—the teller can deal with one, and only one, client at a time. The client has the use of the teller for as long as he/she wishes, until the bank closes, regardless of what the clients behind them think or want. If the bank officers were particularly customer-friendly, they might open a new teller line to relieve some of the pressure behind the client taking so long, but it's not guaranteed that the next client might not do the same thing. In fact, the only way to guarantee timely access to each and every client is to have one teller for each and every client who walks through the bank door, an obvious waste of human resources. What are all those bank tellers going to do when there's only one person in the bank?

From a software perspective, we have a few advantages the bank lacks; for example, we can create and destroy tellers as the need demands without concern, but we're still left with basic inefficiency. In the average client-server transaction, 95 percent of the server's time is spent idling, waiting for a client request. Even if the server isn't actively tying up a socket connection to the client, the server object is using resources (core memory, if nothing else) that are yielding no productivity. Put another way, the teller

---

[2] Web gurus will disagree, citing cookies or JSP/ASP Session variables as examples, but this isn't a valid argument. Cookies are always sent as part of each HTTP request, and JSP/ASP Session-tracking support is usually tied to having cookie support on the client. Most JSP/ASP scripts are inherently stateless in and of themselves, especially if the ASP code uses MTS COM objects (which are also stateless).

[3] This analogy originally came from Roger Sessions' *COM and DCOM*.

is simply standing there, waiting, while you balance your checkbook to see if you need to look up any additional checks.

A stateless protocol, on the other hand, requires that the client bundle up each request and send that to the server. Going back to the HTTP protocol, for example, the client must send the entire HTTP request to the server, not just part of it. A client can't, for example, send a relative (to the page it was just on) URL to the server; it must send the complete and full URL for the resource it wants. It needs to do this because the server may have handled a dozen requests since the client last sent a request.

Typically, a stateless protocol will be simpler to implement but more difficult for clients to use. Because the server is now inherently stateless, it can't track the various stateful information that's necessary to complete a client request. Consider the ubiquitous e-commerce shopping cart. Without tracking the existing things the user has placed within the cart, the cart as a server is pointless. Unfortunately, a shopping cart is a poor choice for a stateless protocol; since the server won't track the cart's items, the client has to.

We can simplify the client-side process by providing an opaque handle/object for the client to pass in on every call; it's tedious, but it works, and so long as the client doesn't see the details:

```
// Fictitious RMI Shopping Cart example
IShoppingCartServer svr = (IShoppingCartServer)
    Naming.lookup("rmi://host/ShoppingCart");

// Create opaque token
Serializable clientToken = svr.createToken();

// Add an item to our cart
String itemName = get_item_from_user();
clientToken = svr.addItem(clientToken, itemName);

// Add another item to the cart
itemName = get_item_from_user();
clientToken = svr.addItem(clientToken, itemName);

// Conclude the shopping trip
svr.purchase(clientToken);
```

As you can see, this is a stateless protocol system using RMI, but any other sort of middleware (CORBA, JMS, even straightforward sockets-and-Serialization) would work equally well. The key point is that all state information is maintained inside the opaque clientToken Serializable object that gets returned on each RMI call. The RMI server maintains all state information for the ShoppingCart inside this Serializable object—which can be anything the server wants it to be, so encapsulation is preserved, and the client's only responsibility is to hand it back on each and every RMI request to the server. Because the client doesn't know the precise type of this object, encapsulation is preserved.

This seems directly contrary to the entire notion of distributed objects; if stateless protocols are so great, why did the world clamor for distributed objects? It's definitely more awkward to use this kind of system; there's no disputing it. The payoff in this approach comes on the server side—now that the client is maintaining all state information, the server is free to provide only one RMI server that can support up to hundreds of clients simultaneously. The RMI protocol will provide necessary synchronization inside of the RMI protocol; any further synchronization required within the body of the RMI server implementation can be provided by the RMI server, and this server object can answer dozens of simultaneous requests without further concern for per-client separation. This is almost directly akin to the idea from chapter 4, in talking about Threads and thread synchronization, where it was suggested that per-Thread information be stored within the Runnable or Thread instance itself.

Stateless protocols also suffer from the fact that long-term resource requirements will need to be opened and closed on each client request. In the ShoppingCart example assume the server wants to store the information about the cart's contents inside an RDBMS. If each client is accessing a different RDBMS, then each time a client makes an "addItem" call on the server, it needs to reconnect to the appropriate database. This act of opening a Connection, performing its operations and closing the Connection again would seem to be wasteful.

It *is* wasteful. Because Connection instances aren't Serializable (and so aren't capable of being sent back to the client inside the Serializable token), the server needs to store the Connection information in the client's token, and reopen the Connection each time the client makes a call to the server. At the conclusion of the RMI call, the server then has to close the Connection it just opened, since it can't hold an infinite number of Connections open forever.

Alternatively, JDBC 2.0 specifies Connection-pooling at the JDBC driver level, which "allows for a single connection cache that spans the different JDBC drivers that may be in use. Since creating and destroying database connections is expensive, connection pooling is important for achieving good performance, especially for server applications."[4] This in turn means that the server can open and close Connections with impunity, relying on the JDBC driver underneath to maintain a cache of Connections to frequently used databases to prevent the actual cost of opening and/or closing the Connection. If a particular database is used frequently, the Connection to that database won't leave the cache, so opening a new Connection to that database doesn't cost a thing. Or, if a particular client generates a lot of traffic to a particular database, that Connection will be opened the usual way the first time the database is hit, but each successive hit will require no time to open, since the Connection will already be in the cache. Either way, high-volume Connections get reused, which is functionally equivalent to maintaining a separate object per client with its own Connection object.

---

[4] Section 3.6 in docs/guide/jdbc/spec2/jdbc2.0.frame3.html, from the JDK 1.2 documentation set.

JDBC isn't the only high connection cost resource a server will need, so we can't brush aside all concerns by just waving JDBC Connection Pooling and calling it done. The server may require access to CORBA object servers, RMI object servers, even standard socket connections to other servers, none of which (currently) provide any connection pooling. In this case, the server can do as HTTP/WebServer-based application servers have done for two years now, which is to establish a session ID for each client, and send that session ID back to the client. The server then stores the session ID as a key in a HashTable to the Connection itself, and the next time the client calls in, the server can retrieve the Connection based on the client's session ID in the token. If the resource limits the number of Connections, then the server will most likely want to open one Connection and share that among all clients, something it probably had to do anyway, since it can't just provide an individual Connection per client in a stateful system.

Not all distributed object designs will be able to take advantage of the stateless protocol approach. As the object system gets more complex and more intricate, it will become increasingly difficult to maintain a stateless system. As the number of distributed objects grows, so goes the number of dependencies on other distributed objects. More dependencies on other distributed objects mean greater need for per-client state, which in turn makes it more difficult (especially when trying to pass distributed object references from one machine to another) to keep the stateless approach. Still, for all that, in a standard client/server distributed object approach, a stateless system is usually a practical and efficient way to keep server object-implementation requirements to a minimum.

## 15.3  TECHNOLOGIES

Distributed technologies mainly fall into four camps:

- *Raw access*
  Accessing and using the communications protocol directly; this includes native implementations *a la* Microsoft's Named Pipes, Mailslots, and the standard IP (TCP/IP and/or UDP/IP) sockets communication stacks. While good for those situations requiring low-level access, typically the lower the level one goes, the more work needs to be done in endpoint (client or server) code to maintain and access the low-level communications' protocol. In Java, the typical choice at this layer is the Sockets protocol, since it comes pre-implemented in the java.net package.

- *Remote procedure calls*
  RPCs operate on the concept of making calls to servers (functions in old-style RPCs, or object methods in new-style RPCs, like RMI) without having to realize that the call is actually made to a remote process or machine. RPC technology includes OSF/DCE RPC, Microsoft's RPC, and Java's RMI technology; of these, RMI is by far the preferred method of RPC in Java, since it comes as part of the standard Java distribution. As a subset of the RPC category, however, messaging

systems (like JMS) and publish/subscribe systems offer a means by which communications can be decoupled from both client and server. Some messaging systems, like IBM's MQSeries, come with a long history and pedigree, others, such as Microsoft's MSMQ, are brand-new to the Message-Oriented Middleware (or MOM) game. Others are Java-specific such as iBus, from Soft-wired Inc.

- *Object request brokers*
  These are really RPC systems on steroids. Object request brokers, also known as ORBs, usually are spoken of in the same breath as CORBA, but can include other systems such as HORB or DCOM. Among Sun Java programmers, the favored ORB to use is a CORBA-compliant ORB, although a number of Microsoft-centric developers are achieving good results using Microsoft's Java implementation packages and DCOM.

- *Objects across the wire*
  This category stretches from the concept of mobile objects, which live within a single process but can migrate from process to process across the network, to shared objects, which are shared across the entire network and connected processes. Just as static members can be modified by any instance of that class, a shared object can be modified by any process subscribed to it. The main advantage of this object-across-the-wire approach is its neat integration with the rest of the object paradigm; it's an object, you just use it that way. The main disadvantage of these approaches is the fact that they're very new, and require some new thinking in distributed object design and implementation. Mobile object implementations are available from ObjectSpace (Voyager toolkit) and IBM (Aglets toolkit); shared object implementations are available from Javasoft (Java Shared Data Toolkit and/or JavaSpaces, part of Jini) and ObjectSpace (Subspace system within the Voyager product).

All of these are viable technologies for achieving the same goal of making objects live across the network instead of on just one node within it. We'll discuss some of these in turn.

### 15.3.1   Raw access: Sockets

We've already examined sockets within Java, so it's not too difficult to imagine how a socket-based middleware service would behave. By marking objects Serializable and sending them over a socket via the `ObjectOutputStream` and `ObjectInputStream` methods, we already have a primitive, if low-level, form of distributed communication. Look back at the RemoteStorageService, for example. We could easily store an instance of the HashtableModel there, and have clients check out the HashtableModel, send it over the wire to the client, modify it, and send it back and check it in. This would provide the necessary object-sharing semantics we're desiring for an enterprise system.

What's more, it's easy to imagine how we could build either a stateful or a stateless system. In a stateful system, the client simply holds the socket open for as long as it wishes, sending requests and receiving replies until it chooses to close the socket. For a stateless system, the client can open the socket, send the request, get the response, and close the socket, or the server can even close the socket itself after sending the request, to prevent abuse by the client. In fact, the server could even do some performance monitoring, and keep connections alive when it sees that it has the available resources to do so, and close connections when it doesn't. This would seem to be a good foundation for a middleware system.

Unfortunately, it also carries with it a number of drawbacks. For starters, all the communications have to be handled by hand within developer code. Some of this impact can be minimized by placing all necessary communications code within a reusable library or component, but it doesn't duck the fact that a developer still must create that initial library. Second, this form of middleware will be unique to each shop, department, or corporation that uses it, which minimizes the chance of using off-the-shelf components or systems with the home-grown middleware. Third, any such protocol would always be pass-by-value, since Serialization doesn't support the sending of references; the entire object is Serialized. Thus, any pass-by-reference functionality would need to be handled by developers passing Proxy objects to the recipient, and the Proxy objects in turn sending modifications to the server (which, in turn, brings up the nasty subject of how to keep the Proxies up-to-date with changes made to the server by other clients). Last, any features desired beyond just basic communication—such as RMI's Activation or CORBA's Event or Trading Services—have to be coded by hand. That in turn opens up greater chance of bugs, which in turn requires more testing time and personnel, and so on.

Still, despite all that, the Sockets-based approach has a number of positive aspects to it, not the least of which is its simplicity—just open a Socket, and send the Serializable object down the ObjectOutputStream—and its lack of overhead. For simple or light-use scenarios, it serves admirably, as we've already seen in chapter 7. What's more, the cross-linguistic nature of sockets opens the possibility of cross-language communication, so long as the other side understands Java's Serialization specification (or else the Java side limits itself to text-only representations; XML is a wonderful alternative in this case). As the distributed object system grows more complex, however, maintaining a Sockets-based system becomes an additional drain on developer resources, and extending it or expanding its featureset becomes more and more convoluted.

## 15.3.2   Java RPC: remote method invocation

Java RMI is Java's version of remote procedure calls. As with most RPC-based technologies, the hard part isn't contacting the host, or even specifying the method to call. The hard part is getting the parameters to the call across the wire accurately and correctly, and getting the return value back again. This process, known as *marshaling* when packing the parameters for transport, and *unmarshaling* when unpacking them upon receipt, is typically by far the hardest part of distributed object development.

RMI uses rmic, a tool provided by the Sun JDK, to produce stubs and skeletons that encapsulate the details of marshaling and unmarshaling the parameters from client to server and back again. When used as directed by most RMI books and articles, rmic can appear to be a mysterious, opaque beast that magically generates Stub and Skel `.class` files from your RMI-interface-implementing class. As we'll see, however, there's nothing truly mysterious about RMI.

One advantage of RMI is its Java roots: because RMI grew out of Java, with no other agenda or considerations, RMI feels very natural to the average Java programmer. To create an RMI interface, just create a standard Java interface class that extends java.rmi.Remote. To make an RMI remote call, just obtain a proxy to the server via the Naming class's `lookup` method, and call methods on it as if it were a local object. RMI objects are garbage-collected just as other Java objects are, so no lifetime management of the distributed object (or its local proxy) is necessary, as is the case with CORBA.

Unfortunately, RMI isn't quite as nonintrusive as all that. To start with, all remote methods must be declared as throwing `java.rmi.RemoteException`, which means that clients have to catch this Exception or pass it up the chain. This means that clients, in direct contrast with the goals of encapsulation, now have to worry about the details of the middleware. It may mean that clients do nothing more than rethrow the `RemoteException` out of the catch handler, but it's still code that has to be written (and executed) each time the remote call is made.

Despite RMI's insistence on the specification of a remote interface, RMI is not an interface-based tool. In fact, if you write an RMI interface and attempt to call rmic on it, rmic will complain that the interface isn't a remote class and do nothing. RMI, instead, wants to build stubs and skeletons only for implementation classes. This in turn yields a problem: RMI can connect only to an *implementation*, not an interface.

Consider our notion of zero deployment. We want to be able to modify classes at a whim on the server, without having to make a modification to the client environment. RMI promises this capability, but I'll let you in on a secret—RMI cheats. It relies on the client making an HTTP connection to a URL specified in the client's annotated codebase to retrieve RMI stubs that the client doesn't have locally. No HTTP connection, no annotated codebase, and no zero deployment.

Given, however, that RMI can download the necessary implementation stubs, is this really an issue? To be honest, it's probably not something most RMI developers will worry about. Because RMI can use the HTTP connection to do the stub downloading (which most, if not all, Java shops will be able to provide), the fact that RMI depends on the implementation class is less critical. Contrast this with CORBA, in which no code downloading can take place; there, the idea of connecting to an interface, as opposed to an actual implementation, is critical, because the client can't just download the necessary _Stub class as it needs it.

Additionally, if the _Stub classes are available, via CLASSPATH or Extension, to the RMI registry when the registry is started, then the HTTP server isn't even necessary—the RMI registry will send the _Stub down to the client of its own accord. For the most part, however, this isn't something to rely on, as most systems will run multiple RMI servers, but only one RMI registry; thus, each system can't count on the registry having access to its _Stub classes. Worse, if the _Stub changes, unless the RMI registry is recycled (taken down and restarted), the change never gets propagated into the environment. Remember, as long as the ClassLoader that loaded a Class exists, the Class is never reloaded.

From a theoretical perspective, however, this is ducking the issue. The fact is that an RMI client still needs the exact implementation-class's _Stub in order to properly function. Currently, RMI makes that _Stub available via two methods, HTTP-serving (that is, via the annotated codebase property, `java.rmi.server.codebase`, which will usually be an HTTP URL reference) and/or downloading it from the RMI registry. This, to be quite technical and ultraprecise, is not zero deployment although deployment is still taking place, albeit in an automated (and administrative-dependent[5]) fashion.

Instead, in order to achieve true zero deployment, we need to make RMI connect on an interface level instead of an implementation level.[6] Because RMI can build only stubs and skeletons around a class (that is, a concrete class type, instead of a Java interface type), let's give RMI a class to chew on. Instead of placing the actual implementation within this class, however, we make the class abstract and do nothing:

```
// INameServer.java: Generate random names
public interface INameServer extends java.rmi.Remote
{
    public String generateName()
        throws java.rmi.RemoteException;

    public static String RMI_BINDING_NAME =
        "NameServer_1.0.0";
}
```

This is a standard RMI remote interface. Normally, we would create a concrete class extending the java.rmi.server class UnicastRemoteObject, and run rmic on that. What we'll do instead, in order to be able to vary the implementation of the server object transparently, is this:

```
// NameServer.java:
import java.rmi.server.*;

public abstract class NameServer extends UnicastRemoteObject
    implements INameServer
{
```

---

[5] Somebody needs to make sure the HTTP server is running, for example, and that port 80 (or whatever port on which the RMI-HTTP class server is running) on the RMI server machine isn't currently occupied.

[6] Thanks to Owen Tallman, of DevelopMentor, for our discussion on this topic and this trick.

CHAPTER 15  MIDDLEWARE

```
    public NameServer()
        throws RemoteException
    { }
}
```

Notice how we have to specify a default constructor that throws `RemoteException`; because UnicastRemoteObject, this class's direct ancestor, specifies a default constructor that throws this exception. Thus, we have to match the signature exactly if we want to override the constructor. Normally, we wouldn't need to override the default constructor if we don't have any particular default behavior we want; instead, we let the compiler build one for us behind the scenes. Unfortunately, the compiler can't synthesize a default constructor for us if the base class version throws an exception, so we have to do it by hand.

Next we build an implementation of the NameServer:

```
public class NameServerImpl1 extends NameServer
{
    public String generateName()
        throws java.rmi.RemoteException
    {
        return "Fred";
    }

    public NameServerImpl1()
        throws java.rmi.RemoteException
    { }

    public static void main (String args[])
        throws Exception
    {
        // Create an instance of NameServerImpl1 and
        // export it
        //
        NameServer ns = new NameServerImpl1();
        Naming.bind(INameServer.RMI_BINDING_NAME, ns);
        System.out.println("NameServerImpl1 bound as '" +
                    INameServer.RMI_BINDING_NAME + "'");
    }
}
```

As you can see, NameServerImpl1 isn't really any different from any other RMI class, except that instead of implementing the remote interface directly, it gets it from its abstract parent, NameServer.

Connecting to and using this `INameServer`-implementing class is the same as any other RMI server:

```
public class NameClient
{
    public static void main (String args[])
        throws Exception
    {
```

```
    // Lookup host
    //
    String lookupName = "rmi://" + args[0] + "/" +
                        INameServer.RMI_BINDING_NAME;
    INameServer nameSvr =
        (INameServer)Naming.lookup(lookupName);

    // Make remote call
    //
    String name = nameSvr.generateName();
    System.out.println("Generated name: " + name);
    }
}
```

NameClient isn't doing anything fancy; just connect to the server given in the first command-line arg, and call its generateName method.

Notice something very important when we build this; if you look at the makefile in the Middleware directory of the source code, notice that rmic is only being run on NameServer, not NameServerImpl1. This is key—RMI needs to know only how to marshal the parameters and return value for the method call; it doesn't care specifically which class it's for. Once that marshaling/unmarshaling logic is in place, the implementation of the method is resolved as any other Java method call is—virtually.

The payoff of all this comes in the client-side deployment. To simulate separate environments (and ClassLoaders), the client.jar file is built in a temp directory under the Middleware directory. Within this .jar file are only the INameServer, NameServer, NameServer_Stub, and _Skel class files. Run the .jar file from the java interpreter (it has the appropriate Main-Class directive in its manifest), and NameClient successfully connects to and generates a name from the NameServerImpl1 instance.

Next, let's create a new Server implementation, called NameServerImpl2 (not listed here for brevity—only the generateName changes substantively, to return "Barney" instead of "Fred"). Shut down the NameServerImpl1 instance and RMI-Registry, restart the RMIRegistry and bring up a NameServerImpl2 instance. Run the NameClient, unchanged, from the temp directory. Once again, NameClient has successfully managed to obtain the name, from a different RMI server implementation, without having to use the annotated codebase to obtain the new class code.

One last test—let's switch the server implementations around without the client knowing. Look at NameServerImpl3:

```
public class NameServerImpl3 extends NameServer
{
    public String generateName()
        throws java.rmi.RemoteException
    {
        String returnName = "Wilma";

        try
        {
```

```
        Naming.rebind(INameServer.RMI_BINDING_NAME,
                    new NameServerImpl1());
        System.out.println("NameServerImpl1 rebound");
    }
    catch (Exception ex)
    {
        returnName = ex.toString();
    }

    return returnName;
}

public NameServerImpl3()
    throws java.rmi.RemoteException
{ }

public static void main (String args[])
    throws Exception
{
    // Create an instance of NameServerImpl3 and
    // export it
    //
    Naming.bind(INameServer.RMI_BINDING_NAME,
                new NameServerImpl3());
    System.out.println("NameServerImpl3 bound as '" +
                    INameServer.RMI_BINDING_NAME + "'");
    }
}
```

This should look a little different. After the first call to generateName, NameServerImpl3 replaces itself with an instance of NameServerImpl1. Run it, then drop into the temp directory and try NameClient twice in a row—the first connects to the NameServerImpl3 instance, gets "Wilma" back, then when it is run again, it gets the NameServerImpl1 instance and "Fred". We've effectively changed our server implementation without having to deploy new stubs or skeletons to the client.

### 15.3.3  Analysis

It may not be obvious what we've just done; by contrast, change NameServerImpl3 to be a normal RMI server object by extending UnicastRemoteObject and implementing the INameServer interface. Compile it, and try to run the server—the RMIRegistry will complain that the Stub/Skel classes can't be found. Run rmic to generate the Stub/Skel classes, start the server, and try to run the client. The client will throw a java.rmi.UnmarshalException for the same reason as the RMIRegistry— the Stub/Skel classes can't be found. This is because RMI uses the class name of the implementation object (NameServer in the previous approach, but now NameServerImpl3) as the name of the appropriate Stub or Skel class to load. RMI normally gets away with this by having the client contact an HTTP server for the new class to load via the annotated codebase property; since we gave it none, it can't download the new code, so it complains and gives up. When we used NameServer as the abstract base, instead, and built the Stub/Skel classes from that, we effectively introduced an implementation interface to satisfy RMI's Stub/Skel requirements while still giving us the ability to vary the actual implementation class used on the server.

By doing this, we gain flexibility in the actual implementation of the server object. We can continue to update and/or modify the actual implementation class used to satisfy client requests without having to worry about making sure the Web server can see the new code. For example, consider a classic use of RMI, to build a business objects layer. Business objects, of course, must be sensitive to user roles and security. Instead of building one large business object class that contains all the necessary logic for each and every user role, have users pass their credentials to a factory class instance. This factory object then returns an instance of a class which extends the BusinessObject abstract base class (which in turn implements the `IBusinessObject` remote interface). Because the BusinessObject Stub/Skel classes reside on both client and server, the user won't know whether it's an AdministratorBusinessObject, a NormalUser-BusinessObject, or a ReallyLowPeonBusinessObject. RMI could do all this before but now you can do it without the use of an HTTP server. This also means that the actual code is hidden from the clients, a security enhancement.[7] In addition, you don't need to have an HTTP server running where one normally wouldn't be.

The problem with this basic approach is that it inherently uses the precious implementation inheritance slot for the abstract base class. Given that Java allows us to extend only one class, and that there will be times when we need or want to extend from some other base class, this doesn't help much. Another approach to achieve this same effect is to use a Decorator pattern approach, and create a shim class that forwards all requests to another object:

```
public class NameServerDelegator extends NameServer
{
    INameServer delegate;

    public NameServerDelegator(INameServer delegate)
    {
        this.delegate = delegate;
    }

    public String generateName()
        throws RemoteException
    {
        return delegate.generateName();
    }
}
```

---

[7] If the code has to be downloaded to the client, there is a possibility that the client can open, decompile, and examine the code, and use that knowledge to compromise the system as a whole.

As you can see, we pass in the instance of the `INameServer`-implementing object in the NameServerDelegator constructor, store it within the NameServerDelegator instance, and make calls on that instance any time a remote call comes in.

The remote call comes in to the NameServerDelegator, which then passes the call to the delegated instance. The client never sees the actual implementation, which allows us to preserve encapsulation, and the results from the class are passed back to the client in normal fashion.

Remember, this is only necessary because RMI binds to implementations of a Remote interface, instead of to the interface itself. Had rmic chosen to use the interface as its template for building the marshaling/unmarshaling code, instead of the implementing class, we wouldn't have to go through this. It's important to remember that having rmic build the proxy/stubs off of the implementation of the Remote interface allows us to cast the proxy and/or stub in normal Java fashion, instead of using a helper method as CORBA does. It's a trade-off, once again.

### 15.3.4  RMI/JRMP

One aspect that will surprise a number of Java developers is that RMI itself specifies nothing about the wire protocol—if you read through the RMI specification, you'll not find one line, one section, or one word on how the data is to be passed across the wire to the other side. This in turn allows RMI implementors to use whatever protocol they wish—to a point.

When RMI was first released by Sun, it was released using a wire protocol called Java Remote Method Protocol (JRMP). This was the only option for doing RMI in JDK 1.1, and remained that way for a long time. With the release of JDK 1.2, however, Sun also released an Early Access version of RMI/IIOP (RMI using the CORBA Internet InterOperability Protocol). This, in theory, allows Java developers to use RMI to communicate with CORBA objects.

RMI/JRMP is the default form of RMI, and unless you go the extra distance to download the RMI/IIOP implementation from Sun, this will be the form you use in your own RMI development. Most discussions of RMI over the past two years have implicitly used JRMP as the wire protocol, and the RMI Specification discusses the JRMP protocol in detail. JRMP offers two advantages: established use and distributed garbage collection.

The first advantage of RMI/JRMP is its historical nature—JRMP was the first wire protocol specified for RMI, and, up until the recent release of RMI/IIOP, was the only wire protocol available for RMI. This means that unless your RMI code was written within the first half of 1999 using the Early Access or beta versions of RMI/IIOP, all the RMI code written to date uses JRMP. Therefore, for any existing RMI systems, JRMP is likely (on the order of 99 percent likely) to be the protocol of choice for communications.

The problem with this is that JRMP is itself completely and totally incompatible with anything else in the world. No other languages can communicate with Java objects using JRMP, no other communication protocols or middleware systems can access RMI/JRMP-exported objects, and this, in turn, means that any distributed objects done using RMI/JRMP are invisible outside of the Java world. This may seem like a small problem to those Java developers who rarely leave the Java world. Unfortunately, as many Java developers are discovering, this state of affairs is a poor one at best. Java wasn't the first system to develop the concept of distributed objects, and Java developers are increasingly called upon to integrate with existing distributed object systems.

Secondly, JRMP offers distributed garbage collection (what I call DGC) in order to continue to offer Java-like concepts to the distributed object model. This means that, as when working within single-JVM systems, Java developers no longer have to worry about distributed object lifetimes, instead relying upon Java's internal garbage collection to recycle the local proxies to the remote objects. In turn, the local proxy will notify the remote skeleton of the decrease in the number of client proxy/stub objects, and the remote VM will recycle (or not) as necessary the actual remote object.

The problem with DGC is simple—bandwidth. Even if no user-specified communication is taking place between an RMI Stub and its exported skeleton, the Stub and the associated Skeleton are chewing up bandwidth by keeping the distributed reference count alive. They need to do this, because the server object (as CORBA systems quickly learned) has no ability to tell client idleness from a client crash. When a client connects to the remote object, it takes out a short-term lease on the object, which the server guarantees will remain alive as long as the lease indicates. Thereafter, the client has to ping the server every so often to keep the lease alive. If the client fails to ping frequently enough, the server assumes the client has died and removes its lease on the exported object, thus possibly recycling the exported object.

This has serious implications on scalability, since RMI system designers can't simply assume that "if we don't call the remote objects very often, we won't have a bandwidth problem." Remember, each and every exported object has to go through this negotiated lease rigamarole, so as the number of exported objects increases, so does the total bandwidth consumed across the system. And this is on a per-client basis: if five clients hold proxies to the same exported object, we've still got five sets of negotiations going on across the wire.

RMI/JRMP offers dynamic code download, a feature missing in CORBA and COM/DCOM. As we discussed earlier, RMI can automatically download the necessary _Stub classes for the client's use, as necessary, assuming the server has an annotated codebase properly set up.

Despite whatever happens regarding it and its possible successor, RMI/IIOP, RMI/JRMP will remain a viable and useful choice for distributed object systems in 100 percent pure Java environments. DGC is a natural extension of Java to across-the-wire systems, and although it doesn't give us the same scalability as other distributed implementations offer, for many shops, it will be just good enough, which is sometimes the best we can hope for.

## RMI/IIOP

RMI/IIOP is a new technology from Sun that uses the IIOP protocol from the CORBA 2.x standard to implement the same kind of RPC capability as RMI/JRMP provides. As of this writing, RMI/IIOP stands as a fringe technology that looks to gain significant steam as Sun makes its transition from JRMP to IIOP as the default wire protocol for RMI.

Using RMI/IIOP is fundamentally similar to RMI/JRMP, except for a few niggling details. To start with, RMI/IIOP uses JNDI to bind and export RMI/IIOP objects, which is the direction RMI/JRMP is heading as well. Unfortunately, this means a new set of APIs to learn and start using. This isn't as much work as it might at first imply, for two reasons: one, the basic concepts are still the same so the basic methods and usage haven't changed much, and two, JavaSoft has done what it can to keep the two as close as possible. Further, JNDI is Java's future for all naming needs; EJB uses it, some Java-based CORBA ORBs use it, and the new JDBC 2.0 specification uses it. Taking the time to learn the basics of JNDI has benefits beyond just RMI/IIOP.

We'll start by examining the RMI/IIOP implementation of the name server, which is found in the file IIOPNameServer.java. The remote interface, `IName-Server`, remains identical to the RMI/JRMP version—methods must still throw `java.rmi.RemoteException`, must be interfaces, and so on. The IIOPName-Server class extends the RMI/IIOP base class PortableRemoteObject instead of UnicastRemoteObject, and uses JNDI to bind itself to the IIOP Naming Service plug-in inside of JNDI:

```
import java.rmi.*;
import javax.naming.*;
import javax.rmi.PortableRemoteObject;

/**
 * NameServer class ported to use RMI/IIOP instead of RMI/JRMP
 */
public class IIOPNameServer extends PortableRemoteObject
    implements INameServer
{
    public IIOPNameServer()
        throws java.rmi.RemoteException
    { }

    public String generateName()
        throws java.rmi.RemoteException
    {
        return "Fred";
    }

    public static void main (String args[])
        throws Exception
    {
        // Set up the InitialContext factory for JNDI
        //
```

```
            System.setProperty("java.naming.factory.initial",
                            "com.sun.jndi.cosnaming.CNCtxFactory");

            // Set up the JNDI Naming provider URL
            //
            System.setProperty("java.naming.provider.url",
                            "iiop://localhost:900");

            // Create an instance of IIOPNameServer and
            // export it
            //
            Context ctx = new InitialContext();
            INameServer ns = new IIOPNameServer();
            ctx.rebind(INameServer.RMI_BINDING_NAME, ns);

            System.out.println("IIOPNameServer bound as '" +
                            INameServer.RMI_BINDING_NAME + "'");
    }
}
```

The constructor and `generateName` methods are identical to the versions in the RMI/JRMP implementation. Only the `main` implementation changes, and this only so that IIOP is used instead of normal JRMP. Since this scaffolding in an RMI server object only needs be done once, at the server object's startup, most RMI implementations will be identical between both IIOP and JRMP, which is precisely what they should be. Remember, IIOP is simply the wire protocol that RMI uses to communicate between client and server; the server and/or client implementation that uses RMI shouldn't change in the slightest.

The client implementation similarly has to use JNDI to obtain the initial server object:

```
import java.rmi.*;
import java.util.*;
import javax.naming.*;
import javax.rmi.PortableRemoteObject;

public class IIOPNameClient
{
    public static void main (String args[])
        throws Exception
    {
        // Set InitialContext properties
        Hashtable env = new Hashtable();
        env.put("java.naming.factory.initial",
                "com.sun.jndi.cosnaming.CNCtxFactory");
        env.put("java.naming.provider.url",
                "iiop://localhost:900");

        // Obtain JNDI InitialContext
        Context ic = new InitialContext(env);

        INameServer nameSvr =
            (INameServer)PortableRemoteObject.narrow(
```

```
                    ic.lookup(INameServer.RMI_BINDING_NAME),
                    INameServer.class);

        // Make remote call
        //
        String name = nameSvr.generateName();
        System.out.println("Generated name: " + name);
    }
}
```

Notice in both the client and the server, the JNDI InitialContext instance is created either with a Hashtable passed in, or using the System properties to identify two key elements: `java.naming.factory.initial` and `java.naming.provider.url`. These are JNDI properties that need to be set, either in code or on the command line, to tell the JNDI implementation which InitialContext implementation to use. Here, we use the CosNaming[8] JNDI implementation to identify the server object's name, and to obtain the remote interface from the server for the client. Once the `INameServer` instance has been bound and/or retrieved, however, the RMI/IIOP overhead is finished, and we call on the `INameServer` `generateName` method as we do in the RMI/JRMP implementation.

Compiling the stubs and skeletons ("_Stub.class" and "_Tie.class", respectively) uses rmic:

```
rmic -iiop INameServer
rmic -iiop IIOPNameServer
```

The first command generates INameServer_Stub.class, the second IIOPName-Server_Tie.class. Once again, notice how IIOP generates the Stub based on the interface, not the actual implementation. As with the RMI/JRMP example, if we put the IIOPNameClient.class, INameServer.class, and INameServer_Stub.class files into a JAR file, and drop that into the Temp directory, start the tnameserv[9] application from the RMI/IIOP bundle, start the IIOPNameServer class and run it, it executes flawlessly.

The main advantage to using RMI/IIOP is its compatibility with CORBA objects, which gives it the ability to call on CORBA objects, and be called upon in turn. This offers Java a significant integration and cross-system capability that it lacked before (without going to full CORBA integration). Java programmers retain the familiar RMI interface; implementation details aren't largely different, and Java clients can now

---

[8]  The Corba Object Service: Naming service, and is a CORBA-mandated universal service for providing string representations of objects. It serves essentially the same purpose as the RMI Registry, except for CORBA systems.

[9]  The CosNaming implementation that comes with the RMI/IIOP bundle; in theory, any CosNaming implementation would work as well. By default, tnameserv uses port 900 to receive requests from clients; under some UNIX-like operating systems, this port is reserved for use only by "root" users. In this event, start tnameserv with the parameter "-ORBInitialPort 1050", and make sure to modify the "java.naming.provider.url" appropriately ("iiop://<hostname>:1050").

make use of CORBA objects written three years ago using C++ or Smalltalk—if you don't have to rewrite the server, that's zero development.

This interoperability works both ways—Java servers can now be called upon by non-Java, IIOP-compatible ORBs of other languages, such as C++. For example, in the same directory is a C++ client that calls on the IIOPNameServer to obtain a name, just as the Java IIOPNameClient example does. The trick to making this work, however, is the generation of the necessary CORBA IDL files that represent the Java RMI interface (in this case, `INameServer`). This is accomplished by using a new switch on the rmic compiler, -idl:

```
rmic -idl INameServer
```

This in turn generates the INameServer.idl file:

```
/**
 * INameServer.idl
 * Generated by rmic -idl. Do not edit
 * Wednesday, June 23, 1999 5:52:23 PM PDT
 */

#ifndef __INameServer__
#define __INameServer__

#include "orb.idl"

    interface INameServer {

        const wstring RMI_BINDING_NAME = "NameServer_1.0.0";
        ::CORBA::WStringValue generateName( );

    };

#endif
```

If it appears to be a mystery, don't worry; if you're using another language to access the INameServer server instance written in Java, then you will already recognize most of the above. If you're not using anything other than Java to access the INameServer server, then you probably will never generate the IDL file and never have to worry about its syntax. The key thing to recognize is that we were able to generate CORBA-compliant IDL from the standard Java RMI interface `INameServer`.

The obscurity of the above IDL file raises a drawback to using RMI/IIOP in general, however. Because IIOP was birthed from CORBA, it is well-steeped in CORBA rules, syntax, and context. RMI/IIOP is brand-new to Java developers and the Java software world as a whole, and to say that we really don't have a good idea as to the implications of using it would be a gross understatement. Is IIOP faster or slower than JRMP? Will it scale better or worse than JRMP? Will it scale better or worse than using full-blown CORBA objects? Nobody knows at this point.

Using CORBA in Java isn't all that much more difficult than the above—once the IDL files are written, the IDL is passed through an IDL-to-Java compiler, and the Java developer now has a set of interfaces that needs to be implemented in a server implementation object. This is precisely the same sequence of steps that takes place in an RMI system—define the interface, develop the implementations. Because RMI/IIOP can generate the IDL from the RMI Remote interface, no handwritten IDL is necessary, and if basic IIOP communications are all that are required, most Java-friendly ORBs are already easier to use, in many respects, than standard RMI/JRMP itself. If interoperability with CORBA objects is necessary, why not go that tiny extra distance and use a full-fledged CORBA ORB?

### Using both JRMP and IIOP

At this point, the Java-RMI developer is likely to believe that it's an all-or-nothing prospect—either you support JRMP or you support IIOP. This is a difficult decision to make. Forsake historical compatibility for future flexibility, or vice versa? These are the kinds of decisions that keep technical leads and architects up at night wrestling with which way to go and knowing they'll get burned, regardless.

Alternatively, the architect is fully behind the notion of using RMI-IIOP, and wants to begin the transition from RMI/JRMP to RMI/IIOP, but must still maintain complete service for all of the clients across the enterprise still using RMI/JRMP. (We're presuming the clients were originally coded without zero deployment in mind, and releasing a new client would require the physical install of the software on new machines.) How can we transition from JRMP to IIOP if we have to choose one protocol or the other? Maintaining two functionally equivalent, yet developmentally separate, systems is certainly not an attractive option, by any means.

Or, the architect of the Java-only project is suddenly required to integrate with a CORBA system beyond his/her control—he/she can't arbitrarily require these CORBA clients to be redeveloped to use RMI/JRMP, and he/she can't re-code the existing RMI/JRMP clients to use RMI/IIOP. Again, the architect is faced with an uncomfortable prospect—developing a shim layer to sit between the CORBA objects and the RMI/JRMP objects.

Fortunately, it's possible to create an RMI server object (listing 15.1) that uses both JRMP and IIOP, simultaneously.

**Listing 15.1  Code to create an RMI server object**

```
import java.rmi.Naming;
import java.rmi.RemoteException;
import java.rmi.server.UnicastRemoteObject;
import java.util.Properties;
import javax.naming.Context;
import javax.naming.InitialContext;
import javax.rmi.PortableRemoteObject;

/**
 * Class which exports as both a UnicastRemoteObject
 * and a PortableRemoteObject
 */
```

```java
public class CombinedNameServer
    implements INameServer
{
    public CombinedNameServer()
        throws RemoteException
    {
        // Export as an IIOP object
        //
        PortableRemoteObject.exportObject(this);

        // Export as a JRMP object
        //
        UnicastRemoteObject.exportObject(this);
    }

    public boolean bindIIOP()
        throws Exception
    {
        // Set up the InitialContext factory for JNDI
        //
        Properties iiopProps = new Properties();
        iiopProps.setProperty("java.naming.factory.initial",
                            "com.sun.jndi.cosnaming.CNCtxFactory");

        // Set up the JNDI Naming provider URL
        //
        iiopProps.setProperty("java.naming.provider.url",
                            "iiop://localhost:900");

        // Obtain the Context and bind us into the IIOP
        // COSNaming Provider
        //
        Context ctx = new InitialContext(iiopProps);
        INameServer ns = this;
        ctx.rebind(INameServer.RMI_BINDING_NAME, ns);

        System.out.println("CombinedNameServer bound (IIOP) as '" +
                        INameServer.RMI_BINDING_NAME + "'");

        return true;
    }
    public boolean bindJRMP()
        throws Exception
    {
        // Our to-be-exported instance
        //
        INameServer ns = this;

        // Use standard RMI-Registry/Naming code to bind the
        // server object
        //
        Naming.bind(INameServer.RMI_BINDING_NAME, ns);
        System.out.println("CombinedNameServer bound (JRMP) as '" +
                        INameServer.RMI_BINDING_NAME + "'");
```

```
    // Could also use JNDI-JRMP using this code:
    //
    /*
    Properties jrmpProps = new Properties();
    jrmpProps.setProperty("java.naming.factory.initial",
        "com.sun.jndi.rmi.registry.RegistryContextFactory");

    Context ctx = new InitialContext(jrmpProps);
    ctx.rebind(INameServer.RMI_BINDING_NAME, ns);
    System.out.println("CombinedNameServer bound (JRMP) as '" +
                        INameServer.RMI_BINDING_NAME + "'");
    */

    return true;
}

public String generateName()
    throws RemoteException
{
    return "Fred";
}

public static void main (String args[])
    throws Exception
{
    CombinedNameServer cns = new CombinedNameServer();

    if (cns.bindIIOP() && cns.bindJRMP())
    {
        System.out.println("Ready for both IIOP and JRMP");
    }
}
}
```

If you run this class, it can now answer requests from either the IIOPNameClient or the standard JRMP NameClient class. In either case, CombinedNameServer provides the responses.

The key here is the use of the static exportObject methods of both Unicast-RemoteObject and PortableRemoteObject. Instead of inheriting from either of these classes to receive the auto-exporting behavior offered by their constructors, we simply implement the NameServer interface (which in turn, remember, extends Remote), and pass this into the parameter for the exportObject method. This trick works equally well for those classes which are forced, for various reasons, to extend from some other base class.

Several advantages come out of this approach. To start with, it's easy to see that existing RMI/JRMP systems are going to require time to migrate to RMI/IIOP; not so much because of the recoding necessary to convert an RMI/JRMP system over to using IIOP, but because the Java 2 platform doesn't (yet) support IIOP straight out of the box, and deploying clients (or web browsers) with the necessary classes to support RMI/IIOP. Until that changes, all existing client applications will need to have the IIOP support implementation patched in by hand, which represents something of an administrative nightmare, and can be effectively considered impossible for Internet clients.

It also offers a crude way of allowing CORBA objects to interoperate with RMI objects, thus getting around RMI/JRMP's isolation from the rest of the world of distributed objects. It's not an entirely transparent situation, since CORBA clients will need to know the IDL of the RMI/IIOP system before they can be coded to connect with it,[10] and the IDL generated from rmic is not only a bit awkward (from a CORBA implementor's point of view), but also conforms to CORBA 2.3 semantics, which, as of this writing, has only limited commercial support.

Beyond these points, however, there really is no compelling reason to support both protocols. Ideally, a given enterprise would simply pick one (RMI/JRMP, RMI/IIOP, or CORBA) as the backbone of the enterprise, and use that across the entire system. Once the decision has been made, all systems would be converted or adapted to use the new backbone, and this hybrid approach wouldn't be necessary. It doesn't always happen ideally, however, and being able to use both protocols concurrently can go a long way toward easing the transition from one to the other.

### 15.3.5   Object Request Brokers: CORBA

CORBA is not a single technology, but a group of standards among vendors for intercommunication between a variety of products. The CORBA core specification, for example, is simply a listing of those operations (names, parameters, and expected results) that each vendor must provide in its ORB implementation before the product can be called CORBA-compliant. The official language of CORBA is IDL, which is not a programming language, but one which specifically declares interfaces. The Object Management Group (the vendor council that defines the CORBA standard, among others) also defines a number of IDL-to-language bindings that specify how a given IDL file maps into a particular language; as of this writing, IDL bindings exist for C, C++, Smalltalk, and Java, and numerous others are on the table undergoing review.

Assuming that we get the IIOP implementation working correctly, we should be able to call it from any IIOP-compliant client, such as Java's JavaIDL or a C++ ORB such as Object Oriented Concepts' (www.ooc.com) ORBacus. To demonstrate CORBA's interlanguage interoperability, let's build a pair of CORBA clients and servers, one using Java and Java's JavaIDL ORB, the other using the ORBacus ORB in C++.

We start with some IDL, which provides the basic definition of the exported objects' behavior:

---

[10] CORBA also rules out completely the notion of downloading the code to the client—all client-side stubs have to be in place before the communication takes place, since the CORBA ORB may be a C++ or Ada95 ORB; downloaded Java stubs would be meaningless in such a situation.

```
#ifndef __INameServer__
#define __INameServer__

module SSJ_Chapter12
{
    interface INameServer
    {
        const string RMI_BINDING_NAME = "NameServer_1.0.0";

        string generateName( );
    };
};

#endif
```

Notice it's the same IDL generated by the rmic compiler from a few paragraphs back, with two major changes. First, the wide-string types (wstring and ::CORBA::WStringValue) have been replaced by standard CORBA 2.2 "string" types, and secondly, the interface INameServer is now wrapped within the module name "SSJ_Chapter12". This is necessary for this demonstration because CORBA 2.3-compliant ORBs aren't yet available; once they are, we can simply reuse the clients and servers from the RMI/IIOP examples above.

Using the JavaIDL ORB is relatively straightforward; as with all CORBA clients, first we need to compile the IDL file into a form we can use in code. Each ORB uses its own IDL compiler to transform the IDL into native code. In the case of the JavaIDL ORB, the IDL-to-Java compiler comes as part of the RMI-IIOP download bundle. Running idlj[11] on the INameServer.idl file generated from the RMI-IIOP rmic compiler generates the INameServer.java, INameServerHelper,java, INameServer-Holder.java, INameServerOperations.java and _INameServerStub.java files. These are just the client-side CORBA implementation assistants. (Generating too many files is part of the reason that CORBA is cited as more complex than RMI.)

The JavaIDL client code, however, doesn't look too terribly different from what we do in RMI. The client code first has to obtain (from the ORB) a reference to the CORBA Naming Service (a direct parallel to the RMI Registry, or JNDI), then use the NamingService to obtain the exported reference to the INameServer instance. From there, it's a simple matter to make the call on the returned INameServer instance:

```
import org.omg.CosNaming.*;   // IDLNameClient will use the naming service.
import org.omg.CORBA.*;       // All CORBA applications need these classes.

import SSJ_Chapter12.*;       // Created by "idltojava" tool from JavaIDL

public class IDLNameClient
{
    public static void main(String args[])
```

---

[11] A batch file under Win95/98/NT, or a script under Solaris. It should have been installed into the RMI-IIOP bin directory when RMI-IIOP was installed. Alternatively, use the older idltojava utility that comes as part of the JavaIDL download.

```
    throws Exception
{

    // Create and initialize the ORB
    ORB orb = ORB.init(args, null);

    // Get the root naming context
    org.omg.CORBA.Object objRef =
        orb.resolve_initial_references("NameService");
    NamingContext ncRef = NamingContextHelper.narrow(objRef);

    // Resolve the object reference in naming
    NameComponent nc =
        new NameComponent("INameServer", "");
    NameComponent path[] = {nc};
    INameServer ns =
        INameServerHelper.narrow(ncRef.resolve(path));

    // Call the RemoteHello server object and print results
    String name = ns.generateName();
    System.out.println(name);
}
}
```

The client first initializes the Java2 ORB via the `init` call; other ORB clients will have slightly different ways of doing the same. Once the ORB is in place, the client calls the CORBA-standard `resolve_initial_references` method to obtain the instance to the CORBA NameService running. Notice that a simple cast from the CORBA.Object to the NamingContext isn't used here, as one might expect in Java; instead, we need to use the CORBA-standard `narrow` method exposed from the <Class>Helper class, in this case the NamingContextHelper class.

This offers an opportunity to point out the central benefit of JNDI; notice how we have to use CORBA-specific naming/lookup APIs to retrieve the exported CORBA object. Assuming that we have the CosNaming plug in for JNDI available (and the RMI-IIOP bundle already provides it), we could use JNDI, instead of the CORBA-specific code, to access the INameServer-implementing object. The advantage is simple: if we use JNDI, we only have to learn the JNDI API, and not the RMI API, the CORBA API, the JMS API, and so on.

Once we've obtained the NamingContext instance, we use NamingContext methods to build the path to the CORBA service we're looking for. In this case, we're looking for the `INameServer` directly off the root of the Naming system, by the name of `INameServer`. The `resolve` method of the NamingContext returns the instance it finds there, and we use the INameServerHelper `narrow` method to cast to an INameServer instance. From there, it's trivial to call the `generateName` method.

We'll not demonstrate the Java IDL implementation of the INameServer server implementation, nor the C++ clients or servers; this isn't a book on CORBA, per se. Instead, you'll find them in the source code available for download on the publisher's web site, in the CORBA directory under the Middleware directory.

Is this any simpler than using RMI-IIOP directly? Markedly not. CORBA introduces a level of complexity into the system that RMI doesn't have. Where RMI seeks to emulate as much of the Java way within distributed systems, CORBA deliberately approaches things from a language-neutral standpoint. What's more, at least for the immediate term, the RMI-IIOP rmic compiler generates IDL that is CORBA 2.3 compliant. As I said earlier, no freely available ORB (and few, if any, commercially available ones) are CORBA 2.3-compliant. This in turn means that RMI-IIOP-generated IDL is inherently unportable, at least until CORBA 2.3 is standardized and vendors begin to implement it.

The nonlanguage-specific nature of IDL means that a CORBA ORB is inherently cross-linguistic. For example, under the CORBA/IDL umbrella, once the IDL interfaces for a given system are defined, developers can choose just about any language they wish to implement the client or server sides, so long as a corresponding ORB and IDL binding are available. For example, object servers that require access to legacy C API components can be developed in C; the C++ developer who refuses to give up his favorite language can develop his objects in C++, the CORBA objects that access a JDBC-driver-accessible relational database can be written in Java, and the entire front end might be coded in Visual Basic or Python. All of the objects developed, regardless of the language, are first-class citizens in the world of CORBA.

In addition, CORBA has grown to include not only a base definition of interconnectivity, but to define a rich set of services that a variety of vendors may implement and sell as plug-in objects. For example, CORBA specifies a Security service, a Persistence service, a Trading service, a Collections service, a Transaction service, and so on. Any vendor's CORBA-compliant Security service is guaranteed, by way of the basic CORBA interoperability, to work with any vendor's Persistence service. In turn, any CosSecurity-compliant vendor's capabilities are completely known and well-defined, and clients don't have to scramble to adjust their security-usage code to a new vendor if vendors need to change. As a result, developers and system architects can now build a complete best-of-breed system without having to worry about compatibility and/or interoperability.

This rich set of services isn't limited to broad-base specifications such as Transactions or Lifecycle, either; CORBA facilities are being developed that are specific to particular industries—Bioscience, Telecommunications, and so on. Before 1996, this was one of the weakest areas of CORBA, but CORBA's growing interest has sparked a tremendous amount of growth in this area. This, in turn, offers tremendous potential for standardization and reuse within vertical industries.

The immediate drawback to CORBA is its overwhelming size and scope—it is huge. With over 800 participating vendors, and that number climbing every day, CORBA consists of a tremendous number of interfaces, products, vendors, and meetings. What's more, because CORBA is, quite literally, a design by committee, it doesn't move as fast as technologies developed by single vendors, such as Microsoft DCOM/MTS or Sun RMI and EJB technologies. Worse, parts of CORBA will be vendor-specific, and one particular vendor's ORB may have features that another vendor's, on a different platform, may not. This in turn makes it difficult for new CORBA developers to determine precisely which features of the ORB are CORBA, and which aren't (and need to be avoided in the name of portability).

Despite these drawbacks, I believe CORBA to be a critical technology to the ultimate success of Java; Java is built upon the concepts of cross-platform compatibility and binary interoperability, concepts which CORBA has espoused almost since its inception. In addition, freeware ORBs such as MICO, ORBacus, and omniORB (from the UK arm of AT&T Research) give Java developers no reason not to, at the very least, investigate this technology.

### 15.3.6   Object Request Brokers: Distributed Component Object Model

Microsoft Distributed Component Object Model, as maligned as it is within the Java community, is another option as an ORB; unlike other ORBs, however, DCOM is not an ORB that has its roots in CORBA, but in its localized immediate ancestor, COM.

COM originally grew out of Microsoft's quest to improve interapplication communication and coordination. COM was born on the backs of such technologies as DDE (dynamic data exchange) and OLE (object linking and embedding), both of which in turn were carried on the weight of Microsoft Windows' Clipboard. Despite this rather unglorified beginning, COM quickly became the de facto standard for object interoperability on a machine. By 1995, Microsoft had publicly stated its intention to move all of its development and technologies over to a common COM backplane, and by 1998, that goal was largely realized; only the basic Windows API calls (`CreateWindow`, `ShowWindow`, `CreateProcess`, and so forth) are still written with C/C++-centric interfaces.

Like Java, COM relies heavily on the separation of interface from implementation. In COM and DCOM, a developer creates an interface class that describes the behavior an object type promises to provide; for example, all COM objects must implement the `IUnknown` interface, which provides just three methods: `AddRef`, `Release`, and `QueryInterface`. The first two deal with COM's reference-counting architecture, the last provides the basic mechanism by which the other interfaces supported on this object can be obtained. Some COM object implementations will simply provide implementation for a variety of interfaces, while others will create custom interfaces for custom application use. ActiveX controls, for example, are nothing more than COM components that implement a prescribed set of interfaces that ActiveX containers call on at various times.

It may be heretical and sacrilegious to say this among Java developers, but COM/DCOM isn't that bad an architecture. Granted, it is principally limited to the Win32 platforms (Windows 95/98 and NT), but within the Windows world it truly reigns supreme. Any sort of interapplication or interobject access to any existing product almost certainly provides a COM interface, and Microsoft's Java/COM integration as part of its JVM implementation, while certainly nonstandard and nonportable across platforms, is still by far the best way to access COM components. What's more, COM's tight integration with the Windows platform offers COM components a much greater degree of flexibility and accessibility to the underlying system than Java alone can provide.

I am not advocating the use of COM/DCOM on all projects; far from it. COM and DCOM are not the be-all and end-all technology any more than EJB or CORBA are. COM/DCOM are, however, sometimes the most practical solution for working with code and systems on the Windows platform. Given that the Windows platform commands an overwhelming presence on the desktop market, Java developers as a whole simply cannot ignore the presence of this technology as an option.

### 15.3.7    Message-Oriented Middleware: JMS

One of the problems with traditional call-based synchronous systems such as CORBA, RMI, or COM/DCOM is that they're notoriously unforgiving. If the server is down, the call fails. If the network connection happens to lose a few of the packets in the call, the call fails. If there is any version or marshaling discrepancy between the caller and the server, the call fails. A traditional call-synchronous system is so inflexible it's a wonder it works at all.

In addition, a traditional call-based system requires a recipient object on the other side. It becomes more difficult and awkward to implement a clustered system when a specific target has to be known before the call is made. In many cases, life would be much simpler if we could simply dump the call into a queue for any available object to pull, answer, and send a response. In a lot of ways, we'd like to be able to make software calls in the same manner in which we send email, instead of the current request-respond system, which more closely imitates a phone conversation.

This analogy is actually a very accurate one. With a phone call, the exact recipient must be known, and the recipient must be available in order for the phone conversation to take place. The call is intrusive, in that the recipient must spend time immediately to be a part of the conversation; sometimes the recipient can do other things while participating, but this is recipient-specific and not always guaranteed. If the phone lines are noisy or bad, the conversation may not be able to take place, or worse, the content of the conversation may be garbled or misunderstood. Sometimes the recipient is busy and can't answer the phone, and the caller has to abandon the attempt at some point and either try the call again or figure out how to cope without the benefit of the call.

In an email conversation, however, many of these requirements are relaxed. The recipient only has to be known insofar as the email account to which the email is sent needs to be known; any individual (or group of individuals) can access the account and read the sent message. Email is inherently nonintrusive, in that the message is simply (and silently) deposited into the email account, and the recipient, when he/she has the time, can access the message and take appropriate action whenever it best fits in with the current schedule. If a more pressing concern is at hand, the recipient can simply ignore the request until a more convenient time. If the recipient can do multiple things simultaneously, he/she can answer multiple messages at once; if not, they are handled in serial fashion. The recipient is thus permitted greater latitude in optimizing their behavior.

If the network drops a packet or two, the email system can either request the packet over again, or send a message back to the sender that the message could not be delivered. The sender can then decide whether or not to retry. At the same time, the email system may decide to let the recipient make that decision, and inform the recipient of the message and its garbled nature. The recipient can then decide how best to handle the situation, either by attempting to ungarble the message, or simply request a retransmission of the request.

Enter MOM.

A message-oriented system, as its name implies, is one that uses discrete messages between client and server (although these terms aren't exactly correct in this situation) to communicate, much as individuals in a corporation use email to communicate and corroborate. The sender creates a message, and sends it to the recipient's input sink, which accepts the message. At this point, the first phase of the conversation is complete, with no expectations left on either side. The recipient can respond, or not, depending on what it chooses to do.

Although a number of MOM systems exist, including IBM's MQSeries or Microsoft's MSMQ, Java presents Java Message Service (JMS), which presents a common interface and API for using any messaging system. In effect, JMS provides a Façade interface over any and all messaging systems. A messaging system that provides a JMS API is called a JMS *provider*.

In this manner, JMS allows the maximum amount of vendor flexibility:

> "Some systems are capable of broadcasting a message to many destinations. Others only support sending a message to a single destination. Some systems provide facilities for asynchronous receipt of messages (messages delivered to a client as they arrive). Others support only synchronous receipt (a client must request each message). Each messaging system typically provides a range of service that can be selected on a per message basis. One important attribute is the lengths to which the system will go to insure delivery. This varies from simple best effort to guaranteed, only once delivery. Other important attributes are message time-to-live, priority and whether a response is required."
>
> Java Message Service Specification 1.01a p. 13

One of the principal advantages this offers is the notion of disconnected clients: a client can physically disconnect from the server or network, and send requests to a persistent queue of messages for later transmission and receipt. This means that the software using the middleware no longer has to worry about the connectedness of the client; the client simply sends the message.

The drawback, of course, is that if the request is one requiring an immediate response, the client needs to be written in such a way as to tie the response to the request. This means that an inventory system, for example, can be built with JMS, and the salesman running the client-side application doesn't have to be connected to the Internet to process an order. Instead, the JMS system queues up the message, and as soon as the JMS provider is able to make the send, it passes the message on to the server, which processes the request and sends a reply (or not). Try this sort of disconnected operation with RMI, CORBA, or DCOM, and you'll have to manage this "am-I-connected?" differentiation yourself.

### 15.3.8    Objects across the wire: Mobile objects

As its name implies, a mobile object is free to move from its current process or implementation space into another one with few, if any, restrictions on its ability to do so.

One key aspect to understand is the difference between mobile objects and mobile agents. A mobile object is an object, both executable code and its accompanying data, that can migrate from one process space to another, either on another machine or in a separate process on the same machine. A mobile agent is a specialized form of mobile object, one that contains the necessary intelligence to understand and direct its own course. For example, a mobile agent might be dispatched to an auction or classifieds site with orders to find Sacramento Kings playoff tickets for under $100; the agent would also contain the necessary data to complete the transaction once a satisfactory result is found, perhaps the user's credit card number or a phone number to call to allow humans to complete the transaction. This is an "intelligent" agent, and doesn't necessarily imply mobility. The same agent, for example, might be able to conduct its search entirely from a remote client/server approach instead of physically picking itself up and moving to the server site.

Mobile objects take the concept of the distributed object to one extreme, where an object is completely location-independent, but location-specific. By that, we mean that the object lives in one and only one JVM, but that exact JVM can change from one moment to the next. The mobile object cannot be seen from any other JVM other than the one in which it currently lives, but may move (either when called or when told to) to that same JVM as necessary to complete its business.

Mobile objects offer a number of advantages over remote procedure call or object request broker systems. Because the object is always local to its clients (remember, it can't be seen outside of its current living space), no stub or skeleton code is required. When the object moves, the code to execute the object moves with it. Because the code always moves with the object, no deployment issues are at stake—no stubs and no skeletons means no need to make sure that code exists on both client and/or server environments. Encapsulation can be preserved, because the object can be identified through a well-known interface and nothing more specific. And, even more important in high-traffic distributed object systems, network bandwidth can be reduced to the minimum necessary to transmit the object itself and nothing more.

Consider, for example, a mobile transaction object in a database system. Instead of opening a transaction space on the server, the client creates a mobile transaction object on the client. It loads up the transaction object with the requested changes to the database entities by making the changes to the transaction object itself. Then, when the client wants to commit the entire transaction, the mobile transaction object picks itself up, moves to the server, and executes each of the database requests directly on the server. If one of the requests fails, the transaction object can move back to the client with the reason for the failure; if it succeeds, the transaction object returns with the success indicator. If the client needs to cancel the transaction for any reason, it simply throws away the transaction object before it is sent, and no server activity was wasted on a transaction that wasn't ever going to be committed in the first place.

The mobile object paradigm works well for object-oriented developers because it is inherently object-based. Both RPC and ORB systems are functionally based—a call to a remote object involves sending the parameters to the call across the wire to be executed over there, and retrieving the return value back over here. The RPC-based or ORB-based object, despite the appearance it tries to present of being colocated with the client, consists of two parts: a local Proxy object, and the remote Server object that does the actual work. A mobile object, on the other hand, has no such dual personality; it is either local or not there.

The mobile object paradigm also fits in well with the encapsulated thread-object concept discussed in chapter 4 and other Java Threading discussions. Just as objects can now be active, with a Thread tied specifically to the object to execute the object's code, now the object can use that Thread to move from process to process. Now the object can not only execute independently of other objects in the process, but it can operate independently of process boundaries as a whole.

One big disadvantage to the mobile object concept, however, is the increased overhead of transmitting the object overhead from one process to another as opposed to making a standard distributed call. This sounds contradictory with the reduced bandwidth discussion, but it depends on the context of the discussion. For example, for a one-shot request-response protocol such as HTTP, moving the object to the server and back again for that one request is horribly inefficient. Remember, not only does the object's data need to be moved, but if the object has never been there before, so may the object's code. The payoff comes in two forms: when the object remains on the server to conduct a number of requests one-after-the-other, and when the object can conduct filtering or other processing on the server instead of having to bring it all back to the client.

Consider the mobile-object database system discussed earlier—instead of sending the ResultSet back to the client for the client to filter, the mobile-object database request can instead filter it on the server. Then, after the appropriate data has been found, the mobile object moves back to the client with its reduced data set. (SQL experts will scoff at this simplified example, since well-written SQL can do precisely the same sort of filtering, which accomplishes the same result: filtering the data on the server. Typically, however, database systems can't apply a filter across multiple databases, where a mobile-object system could—load a result set from one database, check it against the results from another database, and bring the reduced result set back to the client. A better example might be a POP3 mobile object system, where the mobile object journeys to the server, applies its filter rules to filter out spam messages, then returns only those messages not filtered out.)

Another particularly sensitive disadvantage is the very notion of a mobile object—obtaining code from another source to be executed on this machine. This, if used maliciously, is a huge security hole, and one which mobile object vendors have to answer before they can be taken seriously for anything outside of a well-protected intranet. Because the mobile object server cannot necessarily discern good code from bad (code that starts deleting files across the hard drive could either be a mobile-object virus, or a periodic sweep-the-garbage daemon), extreme care is necessary when working with mobile objects in anything but the most trusted of environments.

Mobile object systems have tremendous possibilities completely outside of the mobile agent arena. Mobile objects can be used for transactioning, as described above. A mobile object can contain the necessary data to apply a variety of requests or demands on a variety of different servers—for example, a mobile object that contains a single email template request. The mobile object first moves to a database server, to execute a set of SQL statements to obtain a list of customers to whom the email template will be sent. After storing the results set into the mobile object, the object then moves to the email system, generating a single email whose contents may vary based on the data retrieved from the result set. Once the emails have been sent, the mobile object can remain on the server until a response is received from each email recipient, or until delivery has been guaranteed, and returns to the client with a list of those customers whose emails failed, or whose responses were received by a certain date.

Mobile object systems also offer some load-balancing opportunities. A collection of servers is set up, each with a mobile object server running on it, and a single server is designated as the gateway server. Mobile Request objects are forwarded to the gateway mobile object server, which then takes note of the CPU loads on each of the servers in this primitive cluster, and dispatches the incoming mobile object to the one with the lowest CPU load. The same approach can be taken to provide a limited form of failover support—an object, upon receipt, is first dispatched to the primary mobile object server. If it fails to respond, or the mobile object fails to return after a certain period of time, the incoming mobile object can be redispatched to a secondary or tertiary server.

This collection of mobile object servers also provides the ability to hide servers from public access. Incoming mobile objects are dispatched to a single point-of-access mobile object server, which then examines the actual incoming mobile object's type and redirects the object to another server. In this manner, the database server, the mail server, and other machines with sensitive data (including distributed object servers) can be hidden from public view.

Lastly, the mobile object concept offers disconnected operations, a capability that no RPC or ORB system can match. Because the mobile object's network bandwidth comes in one whole shot, and requires no further connection back to its sender, should the network go down between the sender and the recipient, the mobile object isn't adversely affected. In fact, it will continue to operate just as it normally would up until the point it needs to return. Then, rather than being forced to abandon the entire operation, as might be necessary with an RPC or ORB system, the mobile object can sleep for a few minutes, hours, or days, periodically trying to move until it succeeds. In an unreliable or unguaranteed network, this can mean the crucial difference between 99.9 percent reliability and 50 percent reliability. By doing this, we've reduced the vulnerability of the system to the network. Instead of being vulnerable to outages the entire time the client is attempting to communicate with the server, we're now only vulnerable during the object's dispatch. Should the object fail to successfully transfer, the object (and its inherent state, which is the far more critical concern) remains alive and well in its original process space. The object can then attempt to retry right away, with no loss of service except a bit of time.

### Java's suitability for mobile objects

Mobile objects have been around in research circles for years, but not until the widespread acceptance of Java as a real development language did mobile objects begin to gain credibility as an enterprise production system option. Java's inherent portability allows for mobile object systems to transcend machine/operating system boundaries. Java's Serialization support allows for easy transference of objects across the wire. And, to top it all off, Java's ClassLoading mechanism offers a strong model by which Java can bring new code into the system and unload it again when necessary or desired.

In fact, if you stop to think about it, by combining Object Serialization over a Socket with the SocketClassLoader system discussed in chapter 6, you already have the basic makings of a mobile object system. The object, when it wishes to move from one JVM to another, opens a connection to the recipient JVM on a given Socket, and sends its class name and a Serialized representation of itself across the wire. On the recipient end, the mobile object server tries to instantiate an instance of the class given by the class name sent using a SocketClassLoader that points back to the sender's JVM. If the recipient has the code for the mobile object, the rules of Java 2 say that it will be loaded before asking the sending JVM; if not, the sending JVM will send the bytecode representation. The recipient then deserializes the object representation into the newly created object, and the object has suddenly moved from one JVM to the other. The only tricky part at this point is getting the newly transferred object to restart execution within the method which caused the object to move; this can be achieved through a variety of ways, including having the sender include a method name to execute once the object is transferred, and leaving it to the object to deal with its sudden transfer.

### Mobile object basics

Currently, two mobile object implementations are in wide use: the Voyager system from ObjectSpace, and the Aglets toolkit from IBM. The Voyager toolkit enjoys better name recognition and has better commercial recognizability, owing principally to its position as the product of the only widely known vendor (perhaps the only vendor, period) of a mobile object system, but the Aglets toolkit also enjoys a wide following, and IBM's work in (and support of) Java is certainly nothing to ignore.

Implementing a mobile object in the Aglets toolkit looks something like the following:[12]

```
public class CreationChild extends com.ibm.aglet.Aglet
{
    public CreationChild()
    {
        // Print to the console...
    }
    public void onCreation(Object init)
    {
        // Print to the console...
    }
    public void run()
    {
        // Print to the console...
    }
}
```

In the Aglets toolkit, a mobile object must extend the Aglet class; this gives it the basic functionality to move from one JVM to another. To actually create and move the Aglet, use something like the following:

```
public class CreationExample extends Aglet
{
    public void run()
    {
        try
        {
            getAgletContext().createAglent(
                getCodeBase(), "CreationChild", null);
            dispatch(new URL("atp://some.host.com/context"));
        }
        catch (Exception e)
        { System.out.println(e.getMessage()); }
    }
}
```

In this code, the CreationExample needs to extend Aglet in order to obtain the Aglet-Context (the host for all Aglets running in this process) in order to create the Aglet.

---

[12] *Programming and Deploying Java Mobile Agents with Aglets*, pp. 43, 54

The `createAglet` method expects an array of Objects in the third parameter, which it then directly passes on as the parameter to the created·Aglet's `onCreation` method. After the Aglets' `onCreation` is called, it's given its own Thread to operate within, and the Aglet's `run` method is called. The `dispatch` method then does the actual move of the object to the remote machine, in this case using the Aglets Transport Protocol (ATP) to move the Aglet from the current host to the remote host.

Implementing a mobile object in Voyager[13] is as simple as calling the mobile object's `moveTo` method with the URL of the host-and-port to send the object to, and optionally the name of the method on the class to call when the object is successfully transferred. The code below[14] creates a StockMarket object on the Voyager server running on port 8000 on the machine named "dallas", and moves it to the Voyager server running on port 9000 on the machine named "tokyo":

```
IStockmarket market =
    (IStockmarket)Factory.create("Stockmarket", "//dallas:8000");
// . . .
IMobility mobility = Mobility.of(market);
mobility.moveTo("//tokyo:9000");
```

In essence, it's that simple. The `IStockmarket` interface is written by the user and the Stockmarket class is a custom class that implements the `IStockmarket` and `Serializable` interfaces. Note how Voyager, in comparison to the Agelts toolkit, requires no other hooks or base classes in your class implementations. None are necessary—Voyager will synthesize the necessary code where required to enable remote communications, as we discussed in chapter 2.

Clients (or the objects themselves) can also receive notifications on mobility events by implementing Voyager's `IMobile` interface, which in turn provides the `preDeparture`, `preArrival`, `postArrival`, and `postDeparture` methods for Voyager to call as each event takes place. This capability gives the object awareness of the environment into which it has been moved, which can be useful in giving the object some self-awareness or self-direction capability (in short, moving the object closer to becoming a mobile agent instead of just a mobile object).

### Mobile object design

One of the issues that immediately confronts the mobile object developer is that designs must accommodate this shift in thinking. Server objects in a distributed system are hung out off the server system for anyone to find them; a mobile object, on the other hand, lives in one and only one process. Where a client in an RPC or ORB system creates a connection to the single server object and obtains its own proxy, the client in a mobile object system fires his own object at the mobile object server on the

---

[13] These examples are using Voyager 2.0; as of this writing, ObjectSpace had released Voyager 3.0

[14] *ObjectSpace Voyager Core Technology 2.0 User Guide*, p. 40

server machine, and waits for the object to return with the completed request. Or the client sends some sort of lightweight message to a server object (by using a messaging call, in Voyager, or perhaps by dispatching a lightweight mobile object) and obtains his own mobile object server back. Regardless, this is now completely different from what RPC/ORB developers are accustomed to.

This isn't to say that it's any more difficult to work with a mobile-object-based distributed system; it's only to say that it's different, and requires a new approach and new way of thinking. Instead of thinking in terms of opening connections to the server, think in terms of sending an object to make a request, and receiving an object containing the reply in return.

## 15.3.9 Objects across the wire: shared objects

Shared objects, such as mobile objects, take the object-oriented paradigm to the very edges of the distributed world, but in the opposite direction. Instead of making objects move across the network one node at a time, a shared object is visible to every node across the network, simultaneously and asynchronously. If one process on the network modifies the shared object, every process sees that modification. If a new object is placed into the shared space by one process, every node on the network immediately knows about it and has access to it. In short, where the mobile object paradigm told developers to ignore the limitations of machine and/or process boundaries by granting the object mobility, the shared object paradigm tells developers to ignore the limitations of machine and/or process boundaries by simply paying no attention to the middleware in between. It's an exciting concept, and one that fits in even more nicely with the general notion of object-oriented development.

### Shared object basics

While a number of shared object implementations are available, all basically center around the same concept: in order to share an object across the wire, space needs to be created into which these objects can be placed. Clients (peers, actually) then join that particular space, and request objects from the space to obtain a local copy of the shared object. Once retrieved, clients can modify the shared copy by setting the object's value via its accessor/mutator (get/set) methods, and the underlying shared object system takes care of the details from there. The next time a client accesses the shared object, its new values are presented, without having to worry about polling for its new values or making a call to the remote server object.

Some systems also carry the more primitive/basic notion of information channels, to which clients can subscribe for messages sent down the channel. As opposed to creating a shared canvas on which each client is free to make its own modifications, a channel creates a public chat room to which clients can make comments of any form. The difference is subtle.

Any time an object can be modified by more than one entity in a single moment, synchronization issues arise. Until now, synchronization/concurrency issues have all been within a multithreaded context—multiple threads attempting to access and/or modify a single instance at the same time. Within Java, this is corrected by using the `synchronized` keyword, and by using the Object methods `wait` and `notify` or `notifyAll` to guard against sensitive areas of code being accessed by more than one Thread at a time.

Unfortunately, Java monitors are entirely intraprocess; this means that if a particular Thread has a lock on an instance, that lock is good for that JVM only. Threads running in separate JVMs have no idea the lock—or even the instance—exists. This raises a distinct problem when data is being shared across multiple JVMs, as shared objects are. A shared-object system must provide for some kind of cross-JVM concurrency synchronization, or the same thing will happen within the shared-object system as happens in unsynchronized multithreaded JVM applications—chaos. Typically, this answer is to provide, explicitly or implicitly, the ability for a client to obtain a lock on a given shared object, to which no other client will be given until the currently holding client releases it.

Four implementations of the shared object approach are currently freely available: IBM's SDO (Shared Data Objects) from the AlphaWorks IBM site (www.alpha-works.ibm.com), ObjectSpaces's Subspace mechanism within its Voyager product (www.objectspace.com), Sun's JavaSpaces implementation that comes as part of the Jini toolkit (www.javasoft.com), and Sun's independent Java Shared Data Toolkit. (http://java.sun.com/products/java-media/jsdt/index.htm).

### IBM Shared Data Objects

In the IBM SDO toolkit, shared objects must be registered within a SharingContext, which runs on a particular server. Because an SDO server must be running in order to permit the SharingContext to be found and connection established, SDO is not a clustered object-sharing approach as much as a client/server object-sharing approach. Because of that, SDO will not offer clustering-reliability benefits—if the server goes down, all the shared objects within the SharingContexts held by that server go down with it.

The starting point of the SDO toolkit is the ObjectFactory class, which contains a number of static methods to retrieve various SDO objects; for example, the Object-Factory class must be used to create the SharingContext for this particular client. In fact, the ObjectFactory doesn't create the SharingContext on the server (unless this is the first client to attempt a connection with the given SharingContext), but creates a Proxy to the SharingContext within this client's JVM. Once the SharingContext is retrieved, objects implementing the SDO SharableObject interface can be shared (placed into or copied from) the SharingContext.

To connect to a particular server and retrieve an object "Foo" from the Sharing-Context "Bar", for example, the following code would be used:

```
String userName = "Joe";
SharingContext ctx = ObjectFactory.createSharingContext();
```

```
ctx.join("server", "Bar", userName, userName, null);
SharableObject obj = ctx.share("Foo");
```

The `join` call has several forms; the above call uses "server" as the server to connect to, "Bar" as the name of the SharingContext to join, "Joe" (inside userName) as the user's authentication name and nickname, and `null` as the user's credentials (for security purposes). To create an object to be shared within the SharingContext, the various forms of the `create<objectType>` methods may be used to create the Sharable instance; the instance still has to be registered within the SharableContext, however, before its state is copied to all clients that will look to register with it:

```
SharableString stringObj = ctx.createSharableString();
stringObj.setValue("This is a shared String");
stringObj.share(ctx, "Foo");
```

Each SharingContext has a limited lifetime—it exists only so long as it has clients connected to it. Once the last client leaves the SharingContext, it is destroyed, and any shared objects within it are lost. If the shared objects need to remain alive even while no clients are connected, a PersistentSharingContext can be used instead, by calling ObjectFactory's `createPersistentSharingContext`. The principal difference between this and the nonpersistent version is that any shared objects within the SharingContext will never die—instead, clients will be individually responsible for destroying the shared instances within the SharingContext. Failure to do so will result in bloated SharingContexts, but no other detrimental effects.

### Java Shared Data Toolkit

JSDT's notion of shared space is a Session object, and peers access (or create) a Session by using a specialized form of URL to identify a unique Session by host name, port, connection type, and name. JSDT, unlike the other shared object implementations, explicitly allows for varied communication wire protocols. JSDT provides four different implementations for the communications layer: TCP/IP sockets, using HTTP commands, using an external lightweight reliable multicast package (LRMP), or RMI calls. Note that a Session using one of these communications layers is not accessible via another communications implementation; so, for example, a socket Session would not be accessible to a Client wishing to use the RMI protocol to communicate with it.

JSDT shared objects also have to have a centralized point by which created Sessions can be found by those wishing to connect to the host, just as RPC and/or ORB systems have. (This means JSDT is similar to IBM's SDO, in that it is a client-server object-sharing system.) Correspondingly, JSDT requires that an instance of the appropriate communications layer's Registry be running when attempting to create a Session on that host. Multiple Registries for different communications layers are permitted, but multiple Registries for a single communications layer are not. Clients can either rely on the appropriate Registry instance to be run outside of the current JVM, or can create an instance of the Registry within the local JVM. Running the Registry outside the current JVM requires that it be fired up as a separate process, a la the RMI Registry; running the Registry instance inside the current JVM means that the lifetime of the Registry is tied to that of the current Java process, and since only one Registry can be running on a given host at a given time for a given protocol, all shared objects living in that Registry die when the Registry goes down. For a system on which only a single JSDT application is running, this is not a problem, since the Registry won't be necessary once the application quits. Should other JSDT applications join that first one, however, it becomes less feasible to run the Registry instance within the process, since other applications may depend on that Registry; when it goes down, they all go down.

Objects which wish to participate in JSDT are required to implement the Client interface if they wish to create or access shared objects. The Client interface consists of two methods, getName and authenticate. The first identifies the Client uniquely within the Session, while the second gives the shared object a chance to control which Clients are permitted to join the Session (or objects therein).

The following code demonstrates a Client accessing the Session "TestSession" running on the host "localhost" on the port 4567, using the socket protocol, and accessing the ByteArray called "Test":

```
import com.sun.media.jsdt.*;
import com.sun.media.jsdt.event.*;

public class ClientMain
    implements Client
{
    private Session m_session;
    private String m_name;

    public ClientMain()
    {
        m_name = "TestClient" + System.currentTimeMillis();
    }

    public static void main(String[] args)
    {
        //
        ClientMain m = new ClientMain();

        // Create the JSDT URL
        URLString url =
            URLString.createSessionURL("localhsot", 4567, "socket",
                                "TestSession");

        // Connect to the Session; if the Session isn't there yet,
        // spin in a loop, sleeping every 5 seconds, until it is
        boolean created = false;
        try
        {
            // Connect
            while (created==false)
            {
```

```
            if (SessionFactory.sessionExists(url))
            {
                m_session =
                    SessionFactory.createSession(m,
                                                 url,
                                                 true);
                created = true;
            }
            else
            {
                try
                {
                    Thread.sleep(5 * 1000);
                }
                catch (InterruptedException intEx)
                { }
            }
        }

        // Get the ByteArray object
        ByteArray byteArray =
            m_session.createByteArray(m, "TestBA", true);

        Object obj = byteArray.getValueAsObject();
    }
    catch (JSDTException jsdtEx)
    {
        jsdtEx.printStackTrace();
    }
    catch (Exception ex)
    {
        ex.printStackTrace();
    }
}

//=======================================================
// Client methods
public Object authenticate(AuthenticationInfo info)
{
    return null;
}
public String getName()
{
    return name;
}
}
```

In the preceding code, main, after creating the ClientMain object instance we'll use to access the shared objects, first creates a JSDT URL that references the host "localhost", on port 4567, using sockets, and the Session "TestSession". URLString is an assistant class that provides several static convenience methods for building correct JSDT URLs; the above URL, when written out as a String, appears as:

```
jsdt://localhost:4567/socket/Session/TestSession
```

The URLString method `createURLString` simply builds them with less chance of a typo introducing a bug.

Next, the `main` method attempts to connect to the Session given by the above URLString. It uses the `sessionExists` method of the class SessionFactory to determine whether the Session given by that URLString is actually available; if not, it sleeps for five seconds before trying again. Note that this isn't required; the method could simply call `createSession` without checking to see if it exists already. If the Session didn't exist, `createSession` would go ahead and create it. Remember, this is collaborative computing: any Clients in the Session are peers, not simply clients requesting actions of a server.

Once the Session exists, ClientMain connects to it by calling `createSession` on the SessionFactory class. The `createSession` call takes the Client that wishes to join/find/create the Session, the URLString of the Session, and a `boolean` parameter indicating whether the Client wishes to immediately join the Session. Clients need not join it right away; they may have good reason not to just yet.

Once the Client has joined the Session, it can participate in Channels, look up or create ByteArrays, attempt to obtain Tokens, or listen to events fired by any of these objects. Creating or joining a Channel is as simple as calling the Session's `create-Channel` method, and listening for data sent down the Channel means implementing the `ChannelConsumer` interface and providing an implementation to the `data-Received` method. Note that because `dataReceived` can be called from any Thread in the system, `dataReceived` must be thread-safe and/or marked synchronized.

In the ClientMain sample, after joining the TestSession Session, `main` attempts to obtain the ByteArray named "Test", and store its value to the local Object instance `obj`. ByteArrays can store either raw arrays of Java byte data, or store Serializable Object data.

Interested parties can also implement one of the Listener interfaces in JSDT— `SessionListener`, `ChannelListener`, `ByteArrayListener`, `TokenListener`, or `ClientListener`, and register themselves with the appropriate object type:

```
public class MyListener
    implements ByteArrayListener
{
    // . . . implement the ByteArrayListener methods here
}
ByteArray ba = session.createByteArray(client, "Test", true);
ba.addListener(new MyListener());
```

Now, whenever the ByteArray named "Test" is joined by a Client, or is changed, or a Client leaves, is expelled from, or is invited to join the ByteArray, the MyListener object will be notified. (Clients wishing to be notified on the construction or destruction of a ByteArray will need to implement the `SessionListener` interface and register themselves with the Session itself.)

## Shared object design

As with the mobile object approach, shared object design requires a bit of forethought on the part of the system architect in order to create a successful software system. In some ways, shared objects make the architect's life easier, by allowing the design to focus on the object model, and not on the middleware technology underneath. No more focusing on client or server arrangements, no more time spent building Factory objects that in turn created the objects in which clients are interested. Simply create the object to be shared in a shared object space, and let every node on the network see it.

Unfortunately, this carries with it its own set of drawbacks, as well. Consider a classic three-tier system consisting of the usual database, business object and presentation layer. Simply placing all of the database objects into a shared space has serious ramifications regarding scalability—if the database grows to hold a million rows (that is, a million separate entities, each of which will probably translate into an individual object), a million objects in the shared object space will easily kill most servers. Yet a traditional RPC/ORB system can deal with such a large-sized database easily, because it is understood that not all of these objects will be needed at the same time—some can be safely removed from working space and cached off to disk. If a shared-object system attempts to do the same sort of caching, then the act of moving the objects to and from disk is exposed to clients.

Worse yet, because any peer can modify the objects in the shared space, a specific listener must be established to listen to changes to *any* of these objects, and mirror those changes back to permanent storage (database, file, OODBMS, and so forth). If no permanent storage system is in place, the system runs a risk of a power outage across all the machines bringing down the system's data. Interestingly enough, the outage must affect all of the machines participating in the shared space; if even one remains up, all of the data will be preserved, since that machine will have localized copies of all the data stored in the shared space. This has some interesting ramifications for fault-tolerance and failover, but equally disturbing ramifications about the amount of core memory that must be available on each system participating in the shared-object session.

Additionally, one of the problems faced by several shared-object implementations is the assumption that code for the shared object is already present within the peer/client's name space. For example, if I try to put a custom object up into a JSDT Session (using the socket type), and the code for the object isn't present in another connected Client's JVM, that Client, when it attempts to reference the object, will generate a `ClassNotFoundException`. One approach to working around this is to create a specialized ClassLoader Session that in turn is shared across all peers, as well, so that any object type placed up into a Session can also have the code for that object type placed up in the corresponding ClassLoader Session, as well. Then, any Client looking to obtain the object can ask the ClassLoader Session for the code for that object, and everybody is back on the same page. (Because JavaSpaces is based on Jini, which in turn uses RMI as its communications layer, JavaSpaces lacks this problem.)

Just as mobile object systems required some special attention to particular aspects of the design, so do shared object systems. In the past, using RPC/ORB systems, we were able to get away with a certain amount of laziness and sloth regarding encapsulation of the data-access layer because the RPC/ORB system hid the actual implementation from clients by nature. A shared object system, however, doesn't offer us that implicit shield, and so the design will need to do so instead, if necessary.

## 15.4 EMPLOYEE MIDDLEWARE MODELS

Going back to our Employee system, we're still looking for a solution that permits us to access the IEmployeeModel instance from any JVM, from any machine. We'd like to take advantage of the opportunities offered by the various middleware technologies, but which technology we finally use depends in large part on what, precisely, our goals are in distributing the system. Our options include:

- *Sockets*
  The old Internet standby. We use the Serialization techniques from chapter 7 to create objects in a RemoteObjectStorage instance, and simply pass them back and forth. What this approach offers in simplicity (at first), it lacks in scalability and really lacks in connectivity—because all the objects are being passed around by value, it means that any changes made locally will not take effect until they are checked back into the server, and all clients immediately obtain the new instance. It's clumsy, awkward, and highly inefficient, but sometimes, it's all you have to work with.

- *RMI*
  The old Java Client/Server RPC standby. We can build a standard client/server RMI (either RMI/JRMP or RMI/IIOP, it won't matter much to the actual implementation) server that in turn wraps an IEmployeeModel (either Hashtable or RDBMS) instance for the actual storage. This is the most popular (at least when counting example implementations in books, magazines and conference papers) approach.

- *CORBA*
  Another version of the Client/Server-RPC system, using CORBA instead of RMI.

- *DCOM*
  Probably not an option in a heterogenous system, but on an all-Microsoft network, given DCOM's integration into the Windows OS layers, this offers opportunities that CORBA or RMI can't. DCOM will really fall down in an Internet-distributed system, whereas RMI or CORBA will shine.

- *CORBA/RMI/DCOM Hybrid*
  This offers excellent options. Using a commercial COM-CORBA bridge, such as that offered by Iona (www.iona.com), Jintegra (www.linar.com) or VisualEdge (www.visualedge.com), we can "glue" COM and CORBA objects together to call transparently from one to the other. This offers us a best-of-both-worlds approach:

use RMI or CORBA to reach across heterogenous systems, and COM/DCOM to integrate more tightly into a Windows environment.

- *RmiJdbc 2-tier RDBMSModel*
  By placing the RDBMSModel on each client, and using the RmiJdbc JDBC driver to reach across the network to the server, we can gain very quick connectivity without requiring any additional development. Unfortunately, this isn't a true *n*-tier model, but since all the details of the actual model used are hidden behind the `IEmployeeModel` interface, clients neither know nor care.

- *Shared-object model*
  Despite the inherent scalability restrictions, it's certainly possible to build a JSDTModel or SDOModel that places all the business objects (IPerson, IEmployee, and so forth) into a shared space for any and all clients (peers, actually) to find and modify. A designated listener peer can then listen for changes to each of the business objects and store them back to some permanent storage, such as the RDBMSModel.

- *JMS*
  Using JMS, we can define a message-based system—clients would send updates/ change messages to the JMS Server, which would then apply the changes/updates to the centralized storage system. Optionally, JMS could then broadcast an event to registered parties, allowing those clients interested in up-to-the-moment data to be aware of the change.

- *Mobile-object model*
  A mobile-object system could be used in a couple of ways. First, a client could fire off to the server a mobile object request for a copy of the object in question, which would populate it with the data requested and send the object back. It incurs an additional amount of overhead, since mobile-objects incur higher bandwidth costs to move around. Worse, this sort of request-reply functionality is more a client/server approach, and won't suit mobile objects well. We either decide that each business object is its own mobile object (What happens when two clients want the same business object?), or we decide that we can have any number of mobile objects representing a business object (we have to come up with some way to keep them all synchronized regarding their contents). For this type system, the mobile-object model may not be the best choice.

- *Client/Server-to-Shared-object/Federated-system model*
  This approach actually comes dazzlingly close to a clustered server system. Clients use a traditional client/server approach to make calls on a server, which in turn is part of a cluster of machines (a Federation, according to Nelson[15]) that hosts a shared-object space containing all of the objects. It offers exciting possibilities in a number of ways: the actual cluster can be distributed across entire continents, and the chances of all of the machines going down simultaneously grow

---

[15] *Programming Mobile Objects in Java*, p. 581.

exponentially more remote as each new machine is added to the Federation. Permanent storage may even be unnecessary, since the only advantage of permanent storage is the retention of data after power is removed from the system; with a Federation of machines, chances are likely that power will never be removed from all machines at any time. Because each machine in turn carries a complete copy of the entire shared space, so long as one machine remains alive, all machines can connect back and restore the complete collection of objects to their local memory. In addition, because these machines can be scattered across a variety of locations, if a communications breakdown occurs, shattering the cluster, the individual members of the cluster can continue to support their local clients' requests, and merge the changes back together once the communications breakdown is restored.

- *Client/Server-JMS Hybrid model*
  Under this model, we use standard client/server technology to make our requests of the server, but then register listeners on event channels published via JMS to receive notifications of modification to the objects we're currently holding. This prevents the polling inherently required of a traditional client/server technology, and allows us to publish objects by value, while still being able to receive the up-to-the-second modifications on that object. This in turn reduces the load on the server: each business object no longer has to be exported as a remote object; instead, we pass it by value to the client, then the client is responsible for registering an interest in that object's modifications. This also allows clients to choose how synchronized they wish to be; for example, a client that simply displays all of the Persons in the system doesn't need to register an interest in each one—it doesn't care about any changes to any of them. This reduces bandwidth and processing necessary on both the client and the server. Further, if we use a UDP/IP broadcast system such as iBus, the actual cost of sending the updates is precisely one per object update, instead of the $n$, where $n$ is the number of clients listening on a TCP/IP socket. This reduces the total amount of consumed bandwidth on the network channel, and in turn reduces the necessary overhead of maintaining these broadcast updates.

As you can see we have a variety of options. In this section, we'll examine two such approaches. In the first, we'll do the standard old Java thing: using RMI to make remote method calls on the server's RMIModelServer. This is intended mostly as a point of reference rather than a recommendation. In the second approach, we'll be using JSDT to hang the Employee objects off the server for shared communication all around. This may not be the most scalable approach regarding peer memory and bandwidth requirements, but it is an intriguing model, nonetheless. While it may not be suitable for large databases consisting of millions of objects, those systems which need to share only a few objects (distributed games, for example, typically would like to share the same GameBoard and GamePieces objects) will find this approach very attractive.

### 15.4.1 RMI implementation

The RMI model is, by far, the most popular choice for Java middleware models—it is natural Java syntax, it is well-supported by the Java community, and its approach is one that's relatively well understood by Java developers. For many development shops, this would be the natural approach to take. For reasons of space, we'll go over the basic concepts of building an RMI implementation, and leave it at that.

To start with, the design of our hypothetical RMI model is split into two parts: RMIModel, which is the client-side proxy to the other side, the RMIModelServer. RMIModelServer wraps an instance of IEmployeeModel to do the real work; this Decorator pattern approach allows us to use any sort of IEmployeeModel instance for actual storage. For now, the only choices are between HashtableModel or RDBMSModel (the far more likely choice), but an OODBMSModel or FileSystemModel are easily possible and shouldn't be excluded from being able to be accessed remotely.

RMIModelServer, in turn, exports a variety of RMI objects for use by the RMIModel clients. This means that, unlike the RMI example from chapter 5, the RMIModelServer is not a stateless machine, and instead exports a number of objects for clients to connect to individually. We do this because the business objects that RMIModelServer wants to export need to be constant and always up-to-date. The best way to accomplish this, while realizing that this is going to tie up network bandwidth, is to export the business objects, and have the local proxies to the remote instances call back to the remote objects on each get/set method. It's not as scalable as a stateless design would be, but the bandwidth requirements in a stateless design would be even worse.

Assume, for the moment, that every object changes its internal values (first name, last name, SSN, etc.) every second; not an unreasonable assumption in a large-scale distributed system. This means that for all practical purposes, clients must reconnect back to the server each and every time they request any of the object's data, which in a stateless system means just as many calls back to the server. By not using a stateless protocol, we avoid having to send the entire object back on each call.

We can get away with the stateless approach in the GJAS RMIServerManager system (from chapter 5) for two reasons. First, because Services aren't stateful objects in the same manner as are business objects, the ServerManager system fits a stateless protocol approach more easily. Secondly, because attempting to wrap a stateless server around a business objects layer is usually an exercise in complete frustration—unlike the GJAS model, a business objects layer is usually fraught with change as the business adapts and modifies its product line, its customer base, and so on. That is, after all, the reason we build a business objects layer, so development speed of the layer, as well as its maintainability, will in many cases outweigh the need for scalability.

With these points in mind, let's get back to our hypothetical RMIModelServer. Since we want to create individually exported RMI objects, it's relatively easy to imagine RMIModelServer's logic. Upon each create request, it issues a similar request to the wrapped IEmployeeModel instance. If the request fails, the exception is wrapped inside a RemoteException and thrown back to the client. If the request succeeds, the resulting business object instance is wrapped inside of an RMI equivalent, exported, and handed back to the client for use from there. Upon a find request, the entire array returned is similarly wrapped and exported. Upon a remove request, the RMIModelServer first unbinds the object, then makes the similar call to the wrapped instance.

By itself, this approach would be fine except once exported, an RMI object will remain exported until the server explicitly unbinds it. This means that once any client has called for the list of all Persons, Employees, Managers, and so on, all of those objects remain bound and exported. Because that client could then require some (or all) of the objects thus returned, we need to export every object returned to that client. This means that, in a system containing 1,000 Persons, 1,000 RMIPerson objects would be exported upon the findAllPersons call. This is obviously wasteful, and needs to be addressed.

Fortunately, RMI provides a useful answer. If a remote object implements the java.rmi.server.Unreferenced interface, RMI guarantees that it will call the Unreferenced interface's unreferenced method when all clients have disconnected (that is, are garbage-collected on the client-side) from the remote object. This in turn allows us to register the object with a low-priority Thread, running within the RMIModelServer, to unbind and clean up the remote object, thus removing the resource-drain that object was creating.

### RMI/IIOP implementation

Thanks to the RMI/IIOP implementation from Java, we can make our RMIModel-Server an IIOP-communicating object, thereby giving us access to the system from CORBA clients. To do so, as described, we need make the few cosmetic changes to RMIModelServer, and call it RMIIIOPModelServer.

One drawback, however, to using IIOP is the fact that RMI/IIOP lacks the sort of Unreferenced capability that RMI/JRMP has; this is because IIOP in turn specifies that no sort of garbage collection takes place across the wire, as does JRMP. We could provide a release() or finished() method on the exported Remote interface to allow clients to explicitly release their reference, but this in turn means that should the client crash while holding a reference to the server object, that server will always have a reference count of one more than it should. Even if every other client disconnects successfully, the crashed client's reference can never be released, which leads to unnecessary server objects on the server machine.

### 15.4.2 JSDTModel: Shared-object implementation

The JSDTModel offers an entirely different approach to sharing data from the RMI model. As discussed earlier, shared-object systems typically offer less in the way of scalability since all objects in the system have to reside in the shared-object space, rather than on disk until called for. As a result, the code presented here is not recommended for a production system, at least not without some form of listener to catch modifications to each object and in turn capture the modifications to disk in some fashion.

With that in mind, let's look at how we're going to make this work. In many respects, what we're really looking to do is to take the various objects, store them into the session space, and then let anybody make modifications on them. We don't need to worry about persistence, disk storage, or any other concerns—just capture the data. This is precisely what we did two chapters ago, when we built the HashtableModel, so we'll use that as our starting point.

JSDTModel is, as always, our IEmployeeModel-implementing class. Like HashtableModel, it defines several Vectors which form the core data storage for the various business objects stored within the system. Notice, however, that JSDTModel (listing 15.2) contains several constructors.

### Listing 15.2    Code for JSDTModel

```
public class JSDTModel
    implements IEmployeeModel, java.io.Serializable,
        Client, SessionManager, SessionListener
{
    // Package-friendly data
    //
    Session m_jsdtSession = null;

    // Internal data
    //
    private String m_clientName = "";
    private URLString m_jsdtURL = null;
    private ByteArray m_byteArray = null;

    private Hashtable m_persons = new Hashtable();
    private Hashtable m_employees = new Hashtable();
    private Hashtable m_managers = new Hashtable();
    private Hashtable m_addresses = new Hashtable();
    private Hashtable m_emails = new Hashtable();
    private Hashtable m_phones = new Hashtable();
    private Hashtable m_positions = new Hashtable();
    private Hashtable m_departments = new Hashtable();

    public JSDTModel(String name, String host)
    {
        this(name, host, 4567, "socket", "JSDTModelSession");
    }
    public JSDTModel(String name, String host, int port,
                     String type, String session)
    {
        m_clientName = name;

        URLString url =
            URLString.createSessionURL(host, port, type, session);

        boolean created = false;
        try
```

```
        {
            // Create the Registry if it doesn't exist yet; this
            // should probably be in a separate process
            if (RegistryFactory.registryExists(type) == false)
            {
                RegistryFactory.startRegistry(type);
            }

            // Create the Session if it doesn't exist yet
            m_jsdtSession =
                SessionFactory.createSession(this, url, true);

            // Put up or get the HashtableModel
            if (m_jsdtSession.byteArrayExists("HashtableModel"))
            {
                // Retrieve it
                m_byteArray = m_jsdtSession.createByteArray(this,
                    "HashtableModel", true);

                retrieve();
            }
            else
            {
                // Put it up
                m_byteArray = m_jsdtSession.createByteArray(this,
                    "HashtableModel", true);

                submit();
            }

            // Add a listener to track changes to the shared object
            m_byteArray.addByteArrayListener(new ByteArrayAdaptor()
            {
                public void byteArrayValueChanged(ByteArrayEvent e)
                {
                    System.out.println(e.toString());
                    retrieve();
                }
            });
        }
        catch (JSDTException jsdtEx)
        {
            jsdtEx.printStackTrace();
        }
    }

    // . . .
}
```

The first is a shorthand form of the second, using some predefined defaults (using port 4567, over standard sockets, using the name "JSDTModelSession" as the name for the Session). Notice that there is no differentiation between client and server;

remember, in a shared-object scenario, everybody is a peer. As a result, the only differentiation within the second constructor to mark the server from any connecting clients is the check to determine if the ByteArray holding the Vectors holds any data yet. If not, then this is the first JSDTModel to connect on this host, so it establishes the (empty) Vectors into the session space.

There are a couple of JSDT-specific points to notice before we move on into the core implementation. First, notice that JSDTModel, in addition to implementing IEmployeeModel, also implements JSDT's Client, SessionManager, and SessionListener interfaces. The Client interface is obvious—any object that wishes to participate in a JSDT Session must have a Client to identify and authenticate it, and it makes sense to have the JSDTModel be its own Client. JSDTModel also wants to identify and screen out unauthorized Clients, so JSDTModel implements SessionManager to force authentication on any Clients joining the JSDTModel Session. For this model, no real authentication takes place, but having it in place makes it simple to provide it later, perhaps using PGP or other challenge-response security measures. It also has to implement Serializable in order to be stored up into the Session space.

First, notice that our Client implementation is very straightforward:

```
public class JSDTModel
    implements IEmployeeModel, java.io.Serializable,
        Client, SessionManager, SessionListener
{
    // . . .

    //=========================================================
    // Client methods
    public Object authenticate(AuthenticationInfo info)
    {
        return null;
    }
    public String getName()
    {
        return m_clientName;
    }

    // . . .
}
```

The member m_name is set within the JSDTModel constructor, and we've already discussed the fact that we use no authentication scheme. It means that any JSDT Client is free to connect and access our JSDTModel Session, but the same holds true of our RMIModel, as well.

This authentication policy is expressed in the sessionRequest method of the SessionManager interface JSDTModel implements:

```
public class JSDTModel
    implements IEmployeeModel, java.io.Serializable,
        Client, SessionManager, SessionListener
{
    // . . .

    //=========================================================
    // SessionManager methods
    public boolean sessionRequest(Session session,
                                    AuthenticationInfo info,
                                    Client client)
    {
        String challenge = "<challenge>";
        String expectedResponse = "<response>";
        String reply = null;

        info.setChallenge(challenge);
        reply = (String)client.authenticate(info);
        return (reply == null);
            // For the moment, they *all* return null (no security)
    }

    // . . .
}
```

In the event we wanted to add a security policy to the JSDTModel, it would be here that the modifications would take place. A simple authentication model might be to send a blank challenge String and receive a username and password separated by some delimiter, which the JSDTModel could check against a user database of some form.

Toward the very end of the second constructor, notice that we build an anonymous ByteArrayAdapter to listen for changes on the ByteArray instance containing the JSDTModel stored in Session space. We have to do this in order to know about any changes to the shared object, and to retrieve it. We could avoid this if we retrieved the data from the ByteArray on every call within JSDTModel, but that's simply too much work to manage all over the place; instead, by pulling it only when it changes, we minimize the amount of work we have to do. Should it come to pass that the JSDTModel is spending too much time tracking changes, we can switch to a more demand-driven pull-type model for retrieving changes. In that event, any time a user makes a get-style call on any of the objects, the entire JSDTModel needs to be retrieved. The actual retrieval of the JSDTModel occurs within the package-friendly method `retrieve`:

```
public class JSDTModel
    implements IEmployeeModel, java.io.Serializable,
        Client, SessionManager, SessionListener
{
    // . . .

    void retrieve()
    {
        try
        {
```

```
                byte[] bytes = m_byteArray.getValueAsBytes();
                ByteArrayInputStream bais =
                    new ByteArrayInputStream(bytes);
                ObjectInputStream ois =
                    new ObjectInputStream(bais);

                m_persons = (Hashtable)ois.readObject();
                m_employees = (Hashtable)ois.readObject();
                m_managers = (Hashtable)ois.readObject();
                m_positions = (Hashtable)ois.readObject();
                m_departments = (Hashtable)ois.readObject();
                m_contactInfo = (Vector)ois.readObject();
            }
        catch (ClassNotFoundException cnfEx)
        {
            cnfEx.printStackTrace();
        }
        catch (java.io.IOException ioEx)
        {
            ioEx.printStackTrace();
        }
        catch (JSDTException jsdtEx)
        {
            jsdtEx.printStackTrace();
        }
    }

    // . . .
}
```

As you can see, it's a simple exercise in Serialization, reading each collection from the ObjectInputStream.

The reverse is true for any modification of the data within this JVM; if a user adds an EMail instance, creates a Person, or removes a Department, the other peers in the system need to know about it. As a result, within each of the various business object implementation classes (JSDTPerson, for example), after the modification has taken place, we call the package-friendly method submit on JSDTModel:

```
public class JSDTModel
    implements IEmployeeModel, java.io.Serializable,
        Client, SessionManager, SessionListener
{
    // . . .

    void submit()
    {
        try
        {
            ByteArrayOutputStream baos =
                new ByteArrayOutputStream();
            ObjectOutputStream oos =
                new ObjectOutputStream(baos);
```

```
        oos.writeObject(m_persons);
        oos.writeObject(m_employees);
        oos.writeObject(m_managers);
        oos.writeObject(m_positions);
        oos.writeObject(m_departments);
        oos.writeObject(m_contactInfo);

        byte[] bytes = baos.toByteArray();

        m_byteArray.setValue(this, bytes);
      }
      catch (java.io.IOException ioEx)
      {
        ioEx.printStackTrace();
      }
      catch (JSDTException jsdtEx)
      {
        jsdtEx.printStackTrace();
      }
    }

    // . . .
}
```

Again, this is nothing more than a simple exercise in Serialization to transform the various collections into a single array of bytes, then set those bytes into the ByteArray instance. Because each JSDTModel is listening to ByteArray changes, all JVMs connected to the JSDTModel Session on this host will receive the change and update themselves accordingly.

We set up the "hook" between a JSDT-business object and the JSDTModel in the appropriate `create` method, by setting a package-friendly JSDTModel reference to point to `this`; for example, here's the implementation for `createPerson`:

```
public class JSDTModel
    implements IEmployeeModel, java.io.Serializable,
      Client, SessionManager, SessionListener
{
    // . . .

    public IPerson createPerson(
        String firstName, String middleName, String lastName,
        String ssn)
        throws BusinessLayerException, DuplicateObjectException
    {
        if (m_persons.get(ssn) == null)
        {
            JSDTPerson person =
                new JSDTPerson(firstName, middleName,
                    lastName, ssn);

            // Hook the JSDTPerson to the JSDTModel
            person.m_model = this;
```

```
        m_persons.put(ssn, person);

        submit();
        return person;
    }
    else
    {
        throw new DuplicateObjectException();
    }
}

// . . .

}
```

The code is precisely the same as what occurs within HashtableModel, except for the statement setting the JSDTPerson member m_model to this. This reference is in turn used to tell the JSDTModel to update itself each time the JSDTPerson instance is modified by a user:

```
class JSDTPerson
    implements IPerson, java.io.Serializable
{
    // Internal members
    //
    private String m_firstName;
    private String m_middleName;
    private String m_lastName;
    private String m_ssn;
    private Vector m_contactInfo = new Vector();

    JSDTModel m_model;

    public void setFirstName(String fName)
        throws BusinessLayerException
    {
        m_firstName = fName;
        m_model.submit();
    }

    // . . .

}
```

This approach has some bad implications if the JSDTModel is used in a system where frequent modification of objects takes place. Because we're asking the JSDTModel to serialize itself on each and every modification of any business object, that means that a sequence of calls such as

```
JSDTModel model = new JSDTModel(...);
IPerson p = model.createPerson(...);
p.setFirstName("Joe");
p.setMiddleName("Bob");
p.setLastName("Smith");
```

will in turn generate one deserialization and four serialization efforts. Given that Serialization is not the fastest process, this is a large burden to bear just to modify the Person's name.

### 15.4.3   Analysis

We've built two middleware systems for providing access to and distribution of our fictitious Employee system: an RMI-based model and a JSDT-based model. Each one offers its own unique strengths and weaknesses, but reality usually dictates that actual production software will not be this simple or straightforward.

For example, several times during the development of these models, I turned a blind eye to issues that might complicate the example code. One such issue is that of security—we usually don't want just anybody in the company or outsiders, for that matter, to have access to the company's personnel records. Providing a security layer is usually a mandatory item for an enterprise system, but the implementation thereof is another matter.

One approach is to create a generic security doorway through which any client must pass before even allowing access to any resources. This doorway can be a small URLClassLoader-loaded dialog that obtains username and password, and in turn validates that the client can access the application, or something so sophisticated as to provide access roles and privileges, tying into Java's SecurityManager.

Another issue has been that of performance and scalability. The JSDTModel, for example, is an inherently nonscalable approach. However, if it turns out that, using the RMIModel, enough clients are using the system such that every business object is being exported anyway, it may be a resource savings to use the JSDTModel approach. That way, instead of making calls across the network each time an attribute is requested, the calls go across the network only when the attributes change. Note that we could build an RMI-based system that performs the same sequence of steps—create a local Proxy that uses RMI to obtain the object's initial state, then registers itself in a callback chain when the server receives a change to that object. Of course, we've also demonstrated that we could also build an RPC-style system like RMI using just plain sockets and Serialization; in fact, we could drop out of Java completely and build the entire system using 80x86 assembly language, too. There comes a trade-off point, however, where complexity of the resulting application source code far outweighs the benefits of doing it all from scratch. That's where the art of our particular industry comes into play.

This, however, demonstrates the power (and necessity) of encapsulation: because both the RMI approach and the JSDT approach implement IEmployeeModel, we don't have to change our client code to use the new approach. It's been said before, but it deserves repeating: by burying the details of how the IEmployeeModel implementation handles the details underneath the IEmployeeModel interface, we provide flexibility and allow for the evolution of the system. Allowing for that evolution, in turn, reduces the necessary development cost when moving from one middleware approach to another, or (more likely) integrating one or more together to solve bandwidth or resource bottlenecks.

## 15.5 ADDITIONAL READING

- "Java Object Serialization" specification, Sun Microsystems. Available from http://www.javasoft.com.

  This is the definitive work on Java's Serialization mechanism; because Serialization is so key to RMI/JRMP, developers working with RMI/JRMP need to have a good feel for what gets serialized and when.

- "Java RMI" specification, Sun Microsystems. Available from http://www.javasoft.com.

  The RMI Specification covers JRMP (chapter 10), the RMI Distributed Garbage Collection scheme (chapter 9), and RMI's use of dynamic class loading (chapter 3), among other points. Any developer wishing to move beyond basic "Hello, world!" RMI applications needs to have this next to the workstation.

- "Java RMI-IIOP Programmer's Guide," Sun Microsystems. Available from http://www.javasoft.com.

  At the moment, this is the sole source of documentation on RMI/IIOP, aside from the OMG documents on the IIOP protocol itself. It assumes you are already familiar with RMI programming.

- "JavaIDL," Sun Microsystems. Available from http://www.javasoft.com.

- Michi Henning and Steve Vinoski, *Advanced CORBA Programming with C++* (Addison-Wesley, 1999).

  CORBA isn't just about Java, and it helps to get a good, hard look at what CORBA implementations look like in other languages. This book is by far the best C++/CORBA book on the market. Remember, one of CORBA's advantages is its cross-linguistic capabilities, so if your distributed object system has no reason to communicate with other languages, CORBA may not be the best approach for your system; if it does, C++ is likely to be one of those languages, and this book is invaluable in that realm.

- Dirk Slama, Jason Garbis and Perry Russell, *Enterprise CORBA* (Prentice Hall, 1999). Messaging, security, fault-tolerance, load-balancing, failover, all using CORBA; for CORBA lovers, it doesn't get much better than this.

- Don Box, *Essential COM* (Addison-Wesley, 1998).

  If you use Java on Microsoft operating systems, in either client or server fashion, you will almost inevitably run into COM in some fashion. In that event, you will want this book to teach you precisely what COM is—and isn't.

- Don Box, Keith Brown, Timothy Ewald, and Chris Sells, *Effective COM* (Addison-Wesley, 1998).

  As with *Essential COM*, this book is a must-have for anybody looking to use COM/DCOM, regardless of source language—although much of the example code is given using C++, the basic concepts hold for Java/DCOM implementations as well.

- Mark Hapner, Rich Burridge, and Rahul Sharma, "Java Message Service" specification 1.01a Sun Microsystems. Available from http://www.javasoft.com.

  This is the basic bible on JMS, and until more discussion and experience is had with JMS as a middleware system, it is likely to be the best source of information on JMS for a long time.

- Jeff Nelson, *Programming Mobile Objects with Java* (Wiley Computer Publishing, 1999).

  An excellent book that was one of the first to make clear the key difference between mobile *agents* and mobile *objects*, Nelson's book also contains 13 software design patterns specifically adapted or mined for mobile objects.

- Danny B. Lange and Mitsuru Oshima, *Programming and Deploying Java Mobile Agents with Aglets* (Addison-Wesley, 1998).

  One of the first books out on mobile objects (mobile agents, they were called then), Lange now works at General Magic Inc, one of the other commercial mobile object/agent vendors. As with Nelson's book, Lange/Oshima presents the basic sketches of ten more mobile object/agent patterns, two of which (Master-Slave and Itinerary) they explore in detail. If the Aglets toolkit is your preferred platform for mobile object development, this book is indispensable.

## C H A P T E R   1 6

# *Java Native Interface*

From its conception, Java gave programmers the ability to interact with code written specifically for the operating system or hardware underneath the executing JVM. Even since the days of the Java 1.0, Java has specified the word native as a Java keyword, not to be used anywhere else within a Java source file. And although it received little fanfare (and still does), this ability of Java's to interact with natively compiled code (such as that written in C or C++) is quite possibly the most powerful of all of Java's features.

Without this capacity to go native, Java becomes a closed system, much as other languages are. Most of the RAD tools and systems on the market contain the ability to interact with an RDBMS; in fact, most are optimized for that particular task. Consider, however, that you are a programmer working for a large corporation whose data already resides within a system (mainframe, RDBMS, OODBMS) that cannot be accessed except through a closed API set. None of these RAD systems work for you. They can't, because they are closed systems, lacking the ability to call any of these APIs. Java, without this ability to interact with native code, would be just as closed and just as useless for real work.

# 16.1 JAVA NATIVE INTERFACE

Java's official mechanism for native code interaction is the Java Native Interface. JNI is, in fact, Java's only mechanism for interacting with the platform underneath the JVM. Any method in the Java packages which requires access to native resources or behavior (such as filesystem access, sockets, or the ability to launch and monitor other processes) in turn goes through JNI code to accomplish it. The JVM itself contains no knowledge of how to do any of these things. It relies on the native methods developed for the particular platform on which it is running to carry out these requests.

By exposing the method by which Java interacts with native libraries to the public, Sun allows anyone to do the same. This means that you can use Java, and still continue to use that legacy system that permits access only through its C-language API set. This ability offers a tremendous amount of power to the Java programmer willing to endure the complexity it presents.

However, using JNI comes with its share of costs:

- *Administrative*
  Utilizing a native library in your Java code means that the native library must be installed, in whatever form is necessary for that particular platform (DLLs Win32 platforms, shared libraries for UNIX platforms, and so forth). This means that wherever that code is to be run, its corresponding native library must be written, compiled, tested, and installed on that machine. We move away from zero deployment and zero development when we do this.

- *Security*
  Native libraries have the freedom to do anything they choose. It's native code, so it exists outside of the Java Security model. This is the reason applets aren't allowed to load native code when downloaded to the client's Web browser.

- *Robustness*
  Remember all the bad things that happen with pointers when they're deleted twice, or accessed after they're released? The Java language made pointers safe and handled all the issues regarding ownership. In C++, you're back to handling these things on your own, if you're not delegating them to a third-party garbage-collecting library.

- *Development*
  Developers working with native libraries now have two environments to which they must acclimate themselves, Java and C/C++. This implies two compilers, two debuggers, two sets of naming conventions, and two languages. Of all of those, the worst adjustment is the complete lack of a C++-and-Java debugger—debugging the JNI code means using a native C++ debugging environment to trap the JNI calls, and flipping back and forth between the two as calls cross the barrier between the two. Quite frankly, it's usually easier to use the old printf or System.out.println debugging trick when faced with this prospect.

- *Portability*

  Native code isn't portable. A DLL compiled for Win32 won't run under Solaris. In some cases, the C/C++ code won't even compile when ported to other platforms. "Write Once, Run Anywhere" becomes impossible the moment a Java developer adds the native keyword to any part of his/her code, and Sun 100 percent Pure Java certification becomes a distant, unattainable, goal.

Why bother with native code if the costs are so high? Java's portability, for example, has been one of the paramount reasons for its existence. Writing native code reduces that portability. Why would any logical, sane, Java-loving developer deliberately break one of Java's greatest strengths?

## 16.1.1  Native code on the server

Let's stop to consider precisely where we are. The code in question is code that will be executing on a server. By strict definition of the term, this means that the machine on which this code will be executing will be well-known and unlikely to change. This in turn means that Java's portability is of lesser concern to us. In fact, Java's portability is of little to no use in server-side development, except in those situations where the server environment is heterogenous. Even then, the systems involved are well-known to the developers, and those situations where the same code needs to execute on multiple machines can have the necessary native methods developed specifically for those machines.

More importantly, there is a performance gain from using native code. That Java has made significant performance improvements is not being debated—Just-In-Time compilers inside the JVM, optimizing bytecode compilers, and faster JVMs make execution of Java code that much faster. However, for all the improvements Java makes to its ability to interpret bytecodes, it cannot get beyond the basic fact that it is an interpreter. It will always be at least marginally (and in some cases substantially) slower than natively compiled executable code. Using native code for highly used routines within your Java code can result in a substantive improvement in execution speed, in much the same way that using assembly code in C++ systems can do the same. However, before you start coding common Java routines in C or C++, remember the painful lessons learned by C++ programmers who did the same thing, and found that well-written, well-designed C++ code could often outperform poorly written or poorly designed C++/assembly code.

This chapter presumes that the reader is at least passingly familiar with JNI; if not, at least glance over the Sun JNI specification document or a JNI tutorial before moving on. This chapter also presumes that the reader understands C/C++ at an intermediate (one year or so of experience) level.

As a crude benchmark, consider this code, which generates prime numbers in both Java and C++:

```
// JPrimes.java: Java front-end to calculating prime numbers
//
import java.awt.*;

public class JPrimes extends Frame
    implements java.awt.event.ActionListener
{
    public static void main(String[] args)
    {
        // Build the GUI frame
        //
        JPrimes f = new JPrimes();
        f.show();
    }

    // GUI-related public interface
    //
    JPrimes()
    {
        /*
         * Local initialization
         */
        super("Java vs. C++ Primes calculation sample");

        // Turn off layout manager--we'll do it ourselves
        setLayout(null);
        reshape(100, 100, 310, 200);

        // Set height & width

        /*
         * Insert controls
         */
        // Close button
        m_btnClose = new Button("Close");
        m_btnClose.reshape(5, 25, 100, 25);
        m_btnClose.setActionCommand("Close");
        m_btnClose.addActionListener(this);
        this.add(m_btnClose);

        // "Java" button
        m_btnJava = new Button("Java");
        m_btnJava.reshape(105, 25, 100, 25);
        m_btnJava.setActionCommand("Java");
        m_btnJava.addActionListener(this);
        this.add(m_btnJava);

        // "Native" button
        m_btnNative = new Button("Native");
        m_btnNative.reshape(205, 25, 100, 25);
        m_btnNative.setActionCommand("Native");
        m_btnNative.addActionListener(this);
        this.add(m_btnNative);
```

```
// Labels for calculation times
Label l = new Label("Time started:");
l.reshape(5, 55, 100, 20);
this.add(l);
l = new Label("Time ended:");
l.reshape(5, 75, 100, 20);
this.add(l);

// Calculation time labels
m_lblTimeStarted = new Label("");
m_lblTimeStarted.reshape(105, 55, 100, 20);
this.add(m_lblTimeStarted);

m_lblTimeStopped = new Label("");
m_lblTimeStopped.reshape(105, 75, 100, 20);
this.add(m_lblTimeStopped);

m_lblPrimes = new Label("");
m_lblPrimes.reshape(5, 100, 300, 20);
this.add(m_lblPrimes);
}
```

The code, up until this point, is a straightforward exercise in Swing—we create a Frame with a couple of buttons ("Close," "Native" and "Java") and a couple of Labels.

```
// ActionListener
//
public void actionPerformed(java.awt.event.ActionEvent e)
{
    if (e.getActionCommand() == "Close")
    {
        dispose();
        System.exit(0);
    }
```

The actionPerformed method is, of course, called when any of the buttons are clicked. (We implement ActionListener, and register this with all three buttons, above. Normally, I'd use an anonymous class to be the Listener, since it will tend to clutter this class if the UI is nontrivial, but this is a simple example, and not necessary here.) If "Close" is clicked, exit the application. Plain and simple.

```
    else if (e.getActionCommand() == "Java")
    {
        m_lblPrimes.setText("");

        // Note starting time
        java.util.Date start = new java.util.Date();

        String result = calculatePrimes(50000);

        // Note ending time
        java.util.Date end = new java.util.Date();

        m_lblTimeStarted.setText(start.getHours() + ":" +
            start.getMinutes() + ":" + start.getSeconds());
```

```
        m_lblTimeStopped.setText(end.getHours() + ":" +
            end.getMinutes() + ":" + end.getSeconds());
        m_lblPrimes.setText(result);
    }
    else if (e.getActionCommand() == "Native")
    {
        m_lblPrimes.setText("");

        // Note starting time
        java.util.Date start = new java.util.Date();

        String result = nativeCalculatePrimes(50000);

        // Note ending time
        java.util.Date end = new java.util.Date();

        m_lblTimeStarted.setText(start.getHours() + ":" +
            start.getMinutes() + ":" + start.getSeconds());
        m_lblTimeStopped.setText(end.getHours() + ":" +
            end.getMinutes() + ":" + end.getSeconds());
        m_lblPrimes.setText(result);
    }
}
```

Otherwise, if the "Java" or "Native" buttons were clicked, note the current date/time
(by constructing a new Date object), calculate the Primes up to 50,000 using either
the `calculatePrimes` or `nativeCalculatePrimes` methods, note the current
date/time after the call, and display the difference.

```
// Internal implementation
//
public String calculatePrimes(int stop)
{
    String primes = new String();

    // Algorithm cribbed from Sedgewick's "Algorithms in C++"
    int i;
    int j;
    int a[] = new int[stop + 1];

    for (a[1]=0, i=2; i<= stop; i++)
    a[i] = 1;

    for (i=2; i<stop/2; i++)
    for (j=2; j<=stop/i; j++)
    a[i*j] = 0;

    for (i=1; i<=stop; i++)
    if (a[i] != 0)
    primes += i + " ";

    return primes;
}
```

The `calculatePrimes` method is

```
    public native String nativeCalculatePrimes(int stop);
    static
    {
        System.loadLibrary("JPrimes");
    }
```

The `nativeCalculatePrimes` method isn't defined here—the native implementation of `nativeCalculatePrimes` lives in the file JPrimes.cpp. As we'll see, this file implements two methods, only one of which is directly related to JNI. The `DllEntryPoint` function is required by Win32 DLLs and can be ignored for the moment. (Non-Win32 platforms won't need this function.) The other function,

```
JNIEXPORT jstring JNICALL Java_JPrimes_nativeCalculatePrimes
(JNIEnv* env, jobject, jint stop)
```

is the actual routine the JVM will call when Java code indicates a call to the JPrimes `nativeCalculatePrimes` method. We'll go over the first two parameters later, but the `stop` parameter is the upper end of the number range for which we're calculating prime numbers. (For a description of the algorithm used, see *Algorithms in C++*, by Robert Sedgewick.)

```
    // Internal data
    //
    private Button m_btnClose;
    private Button m_btnJava;
    private Button m_btnNative;
    private Label m_lblTimeStarted;
    private Label m_lblTimeStopped;
    private Label m_lblPrimes;
}
```

That's the .java side of the JNI approach. Next, we'll look at the C++ side.

```
#include "JPrimes.h"

#include <windows.h>
#include <stdlib.h>
#include <sstream>
using namespace std;

// Basic scaffolding that must be in place for every Win32 DLL
//
DWORD WINAPI DllEntryPoint(HINSTANCE, DWORD, LPVOID)
{
    return TRUE;
}
```

Again, `DllEntryPoint` is a Win32-specific function dealing solely with the loading of the DLL into a process's address space; it, in itself, has nothing to do with JNI except provide a useful place for doing per-DLL initialization.

```
// Prototypes/stubs taken from javah-generated JPrimes.h
//
/*
 * Class:     JPrimes
 * Method:    nativeCalculatePrimes
 * Signature: (I)Ljava/lang/String;
 */
JNIEXPORT jstring JNICALL Java_JPrimes_nativeCalculatePrimes
(JNIEnv* env, jobject, jint stop)
{
    char* tmpbuffer = new char[stop];
    ::memset(tmpbuffer, 0, stop);

    // Algorithm cribbed from Sedgewick's "Algorithms in C++"
    int i, j;
    int* a = new int[stop + 1];

    for (a[1]=0, i=2; i<= stop; i++)
        a[i] = 1;
    for (i=2; i<stop/2; i++)
        for (j=2; j<=stop/i; j++)
            a[i*j] = 0;
    for (i=1; i<=stop; i++)
        if (a[i])
        {
            char stringifiedI[10];
            itoa(i, stringifiedI, 10);
            strcat(tmpbuffer, stringifiedI);
            strcat(tmpbuffer, " ");
        }

    delete [] a;

    // Convert to Java java.lang.String object
    jstring primes = env->NewStringUTF(tmpbuffer);
    return primes;
}
```

This code must be compiled with a Win32 C++ compiler into a DLL named JPRIMES.DLL. (In this case, the code was written assuming Microsoft Visual C++ 5.0.)

Lastly, notice that the JPrimes.java file contains a static initializer block with just one statement:

```
static
{
    System.loadLibrary("JPrimes");
}
```

This loads the native library "JPRIMES" into the JVM, performing all run-time linking. (Because it needs to do this linking at run time, the native library must be a shared library appropriate to that platform—DLLs for Win32, shared libs for Unix, and so on.) The actual filename the JVM looks for will vary according to the platform. Under the Sun Win32 JDK, it will look for "JPRIMES.DLL", while the Sun Solaris JDK looks for "libJPRIMES.so". Other platforms may look for other names—check the documentation of the JVM you are using. Where the JVM expects to find this shared library is, again, platform-specific. Under Win32, for example, the Sun JVM expects to find the native libraries in the same manner the Win32 engine expects to find any DLL—in the current directory, along the PATH, or in the "Windows"[1] or "System32" directory. Again, check the JVM documentation to find out the details for your particular JVM implementation. Placing the DLL in the same directory as the JPrimes.class file allows the JVM to find it when required.

This is a crude and unscientific benchmark. It is unoptimized Java code, and attempts to take no code shortcuts to speed things up. For example, the string concatenation within calculatePrimes uses Java's += syntax, as opposed to the faster method of calling StringBuffer's append method directly, whereas the C/C++ version uses the much-quicker stdio function strcat. Still, in spite of all that, it does offer some insight into the relative speedup offered by natively compiled code: on one particular run, the "Java" option took five seconds, while the "Native" option took only one. (This run took place on a Pentium-II/266 laptop, under the JDK 1.2 environment with JIT active.)

This is not a fair comparison. The calculation of prime numbers is highly CPU-intensive, and will be biased, by its very nature, in favor of the native code for that reason. Benchmarks of a more realistic nature, such as tests involving file or socket I/O, will even out somewhat, and the Java code can be written in a more optimized fashion. This is not intended to start a debate or discussion about the relative merits of using Java as opposed to C++ or C for fast execution. This example intends solely to prove the point that JNI code offers a speed increase over (mostly) equivalent Java code. Does this imply that all of your Java code should immediately be converted to C++, on the grounds that it will be faster? Absolutely not. Execution speed, as we've stated before, is not the sole benchmark in an enterprise application—there is also speed of development, which can be particularly crucial in fast-moving enterprise systems.

By far, the most important virtue of JNI comes in the fact that it allows Java code to interact with your legacy code. By legacy code, I mean that body of code written in C (or C++) which must continue to be used for reasons outside our control. It could be a library, framework, or set of in-house routines used in applications throughout the enterprise for any reason—security, data-access, or even I/O. Under certain cases, this legacy code will actually be facilities of the operating system itself to which Java has no default access, such as native GUI controls or special device drivers. Having the ability to lean on this already-written body of native code means less work for us as Java developers, and that's a direct move towards zero development.

---

[1] This name can vary, which is why I use quotes; under a standard NT installation, the path will be C:\WINNT and C:\WINNT\SYSTEM32, whereas on a standard Win95/98 system will be C:\WINDOWS and C:\WINDOWS\SYSTEM32.

As we'll see, Java's ability to call C routines allows for tremendous code reuse opportunities within the Java environment. At the same time, JNI's ability to allow native C/C++ applications to in turn create a JVM within the native process space offers some powerful integration opportunities.

## 16.2  *JNI* ESSENTIALS

JNI is substantially more than can be explained in one chapter. As a result, this will not be an exhaustive discussion of JNI, but enough to get you past the basics and able to recognize what's going on within the code. For detailed discussion of JNI, refer to one of the books mentioned in the "Additional reading" section at the end of this chapter.

JNI breaks down into three categories, arranged in order from least complex to most:

- *Java calling native code*
  This is the easiest to work with—the Java code calls into the native code implementation, which executes and returns when it is finished. If you are profiling your Java code, looking for places to drop native code in order to gain a performance improvement, this will likely be the only form of JNI you write.

- *Native calling Java code*
  Not all native code interactions will be one-way. Circumstances will often dictate that the native code be able to call into Java routines or the JVM itself in order to obtain more data or manipulate objects. This area of JNI is conceptually easy to understand, but occupies the most amount of space in any JNI discussion.

- *Native applications creating and using a JVM*
  This is probably the trickiest, and most powerful, option within the JNI API set. Using the Invocation API, as it's called, a native C/C++ application can create a JVM within its process space, load Java classes, execute them, and so forth, just as if the Java code had been launched from the command line. This feature makes Java unique among every other programming language—while others have some facility for calling out to native code, no other language allows native code to create its execution environment within a different process space. This feature is a powerful one, allowing us to use Java in ways other languages can't touch.

Let's go over these three options to give you an idea of what JNI can do for us on the server.

### 16.2.1  Java calling native

The JPrimes sample examined earlier demonstrates this sort of usage. In this case, the interaction of Java to native code goes entirely one-way; the Java code calls a native method, the native method executes, perhaps calling other native methods in turn, then returns. Because the native code never calls back into the JVM, this is probably the simplest of the JNI styles, and the easiest introduction into JNI/native-method development. Most of the complexity involved here is not in the programming, but in understanding what tools to use, when to use them, what Java expects of the native code, and what the native code in turn can expect from Java. Typically, this style will be used to access a native API or optimize/hand tune a frequently called Java routine.

Be very conservative when optimizing or hand tuning a frequently called Java routine, and make certain you undertake it as a last resort; rewriting or restructuring the flow of the Java code quite often provides enough of a speedup to avoid native coding. Still, for CPU-intensive operations called often, this can provide a substantial boost.

In both cases, the interaction between the JVM and the native code is from-Java-to-native-and-back-again.

Usually, the native calls will be wrapped privately within an API wrapper class, thereby hiding from clients the fact that the method call is, in fact, native:

```
public SomeObject
{
    // . . .

    public void doSomething()
    {
        nativeDoSomething();
    }

    private native void nativeDoSomething();
}
```

By encapsulating the actual implementation of the call, implementors have the ability to provide next-best-thing behavior on those platforms that lack the native call. For example, it will be faster for Java applications running in a JVM on the same Win32 machine to use memory-mapped files to share memory, instead of using a more portable Jini/JavaSpaces or Java Shared Data Toolkit approach. However, this implementation will only work on a Win32 platform:

```
public class Foo
{
    public void writeData(int offset, byte[] data)
    {
        if (s_useNative)
            nativeWriteData(offset, data);
        else
            portableWriteData(offset, data);
    }
    public byte[] readData(int offset, int length)
    {
        if (s_useNative)
            nativeWriteData(offset, data);
        else
            portableWriteData(offset, data);
    }
    private native void nativeWriteData(int offset, byte[] data);
    private native byte[] nativeReadData(int offset, int length);
    private void portableWriteData(int offset, byte[] data)
    {
        // details omitted
```

```
        }
        private byte[] portableReadData(int offset, int length)
        {
            // details omitted
        }
        static
        {
            try
            {
                System.loadLibrary("foo");
                s_useNative = true;
            }
            catch (Exception ex)
            {
                s_useNative = false;
            }
        }
        static boolean s_useNative;
}
```

The magic of the above occurs during the static initializer block. If the `System.load-Library()` call succeeds, it means the JVM found a shared library implementing the native methods expected, and the static member `s_useNative` is set to `true`. If the call fails, the JVM couldn't link the library, and the code should use the portable (but slower or less feature-rich) code.

Practitioners of design patterns will recognize an opportunity for the use of a Bridge pattern here, instead of the above approach. In the following code, the JPrimes example from above is rewritten to make use of a native library if one is available, or the portable Java implementation if not. Again, because the actual implementation is shielded from the client, the client need not make any decisions or require any knowledge of the switch:

```
interface PrimeCalculator
{
    public String calculatePrimes(int stop);
}

class NativePrimeCalculator
    implements PrimeCalculator
{
    NativePrimeCalculator()
        throws Throwable
    {
        System.loadLibrary("JPrimes");
    }
    public String calculatePrimes(int stop)
    {
        return nativeCalculatePrimes(stop);
    }
```

```
        private native String nativeCalculatePrimes(int stop);
}

class PortablePrimeCalculator
{
    public String calculatePrimes(int stop)
    {
        // Details omitted
    }
}

public class JPrimes extends Frame implements java.awt.event.ActionListener
{
    // GUI-related public interface
    //
    JPrimes()
    {
        // Details omitted (initialize the GUI)

        // Which calculator should we use?
        try
        {
            m_calculator = new NativePrimeCalculator();
        }
        catch (Throwable t)
        {
            m_calculator = new PortablePrimeCalculator();
        }
    }

    public void actionPerformed(java.awt.event.ActionEvent e)
    {
        if (e.getActionCommand() == "Calculate")
        {
            m_lblPrimes.setText("");

            // Note starting time
            java.util.Date start = new java.util.Date();

            String result = m_calculator.calculatePrimes(50000);

            // Note ending time
            java.util.Date end = new java.util.Date();

            m_lblTimeStarted.setText(start.getHours() + ":" +
                start.getMinutes() + ":" + start.getSeconds());
          m_lblTimeStopped.setText(end.getHours() + ":" + end.getMinutes() +
                ":" + end.getSeconds());
            m_lblPrimes.setText(result);
        }
    }

    // Internal data
    //
    private PrimeCalculator m_calculator;

    // ...
}
```

Notice how, by moving the logic into separate stand-alone classes, JPrimes now has no knowledge (and, therefore, no dependency) on whether the implementation is done in a native or portable fashion. This is in keeping with the Bridge pattern's Intent: "Decouple an abstraction from its implementation so that the two can vary independently."[2] This discussion applies equally well to the Strategy pattern: "Define a family of algorithms, encapsulate each one, and make them interchangeable. Strategy lets the algorithm vary independently from clients that use it."[3] As with most things pattern-related, the intent of the code (the "forces") defines which is more applicable.

To be true to the Bridge and Strategy patterns, as defined by *Design Patterns*, the actual implementation (NativePrimeCalculator or PortablePrimeCalculator) should be encapsulated. In the previous example, our client, JPrimes, has to make the decision regarding which implementation to use, which breaks the very encapsulation sought. True encapsulation requires either a wrapper class that contains the knowledge, or a Factory object that performs the construction step and hands back an instance of PrimeCalculator:

```
public class PrimeCalculatorFactory
{
    public static PrimeCalculator manufacture()
    {
        try
        {
            return new NativePrimeCalculator();
        }
        catch (Throwable t)
        {
            return new PortablePrimeCalculator();
        }
    }
}
```

Another approach would be to have PrimeCalculator be an abstract class with a static method by which instances can be obtained, a variation of the above Factory-based approach:

```
public abstract class PrimeCalculator
{
    /**
     * Derived classes must implement this
     */
    public abstract String calculatePrimes(int stop);

    /**
     * Same as PrimeCalculatorFactory.manufacture(), above,
     * but now the code's all in one place.
     */
```

---

[2] *Design Patterns*, p. 151

[3] *Design Patterns*, p. 315

```
public static PrimeCalculator manufacture()
{
    try
    {
        return new NativePrimeCalculator();
    }
    catch (Throwable t)
    {
        return new PortablePrimeCalculator();
    }
}
}
```

The expense of this approach, of course, is that PrimeCalculator is now a class, which must be extended, instead of an interface. This implies that implementing RMI, CORBA, or other PrimeCalculator classes that must extend some other base class will be more difficult.[4]

A large number of native API calls can be wrapped using this approach, offering Java the ability to interact with the operating system directly, or even other, native, applications. Some examples include:

- *Accessing Win32 Inter-Process Communication mechanisms*
  A number of applications on the NT/Win9x platform use Win32 IPC mechanisms (mailslots, named pipes, memory-mapped files, and so forth) to communicate. By wrapping Java classes around these API calls, Java applications executing on the Win32 platform can also participate in this communication.

- *Accessing UNIX signals*
  A significant percentage of C/C++ code written for UNIX-based systems use signals for fast forms of simple IPC communication. By wrapping the UNIX system call into a Java class with JNI implementations, Java applications can now send those same signals to native UNIX processes.

- *Access the Registry*
  Under the Win32 platform, a well-behaved Win32 application stores all configuration and/or user-preferences information in a central hierarchical database called the Registry. While it's not recommended that a pure Java application do this, a Java application that interacts with native Win32 applications may want or need to access the Registry to extract necessary configuration information (such as user name, ODBC names, or settings for accessing ODBC databases using the JDBC/ODBC bridge, and so on). This holds especially true if a Java application needs to know which application is associated with a particular file extension on the user's system.

---

[4] Remember, in Java extension (*implementation inheritance*, as opposed to "implements," or *interface inheritance*) is a precious resource—you can only extend one-and-only-one class, whereas you can implement any number of interfaces. This means that where there's a choice, choose to implement instead of extend.

- *Use Microsoft RPC*

  Microsoft remote procedure calls, a derivative of DCE RPC, are used at the C level to allow two processes, executing either locally on the same machine, or across the network, to execute methods remotely within the other. The same can be said of ONC RPC (Sun's standard RPC mechanism) on Solaris platforms. Java code wrappers the calls to the RPC server, and thereby extends the life of RPC-based servers without having to convert to RMI or CORBA.

Readers will, no doubt, come up with other ideas. The nature of making these API calls makes this approach to JNI extremely easy to implement.

## 16.2.2 Native calling Java

Most of the JNI specification's API listings deal with allowing native code to call back into the JVM for any purpose. Just about anything that can be done within the JVM can also be done via the JVM's JNI calls—load classes, instantiate objects, throw exceptions, catch exceptions, enter synchronization blocks, and so on. This leads to some very interesting possibilities for native code to control the JVM.

When talking about Java calling native code, the situation and context was easy to understand. The JVM would only call into the native code when the native code was there, and when a native-marked Java method was called. Under the native calling Java situation, the context isn't quite so simple. This is particularly true when dealing with many asynchronous native mechanisms, such as signal handlers (under either UNIX or Win32).

For those unfamiliar with signal handlers, the C/C++ standard allows user code to establish a series of callback routines to be called when particular signals (early forms of exceptions) are raised, either by the OS or another process. For example, pressing CTRL-C in the console window of the following C application spits out a message instead of immediately quitting:

```
// if using MSVC++ 5, use "cl signal.cpp";
//
#include <signal.h>

#include <iostream>
using namespace std;

extern "C" void sig_handler(int sig);

void sig_handler(int sig)
{
    cout << "Signal " << sig << " received" << endl;
    //exit(-1);
}

int main(int argc, char* argv[])
{
    if (argc <= 1)
    {
        // Register sig_handler
```

```
        cout << "Registering signal handler" << endl;
        for (int i=0; i<63; i++)
            signal(i, sig_handler);

        // loop forever, waiting for signal
        cout << "Looping forever" << endl;
        while(1)
            ;

    }
}
```

Signal handlers can be established for a variety of conditions, not the least of which are segmentation faults, or access violation exceptions, as they are called under Win32. (Experienced Win32 developers will immediately recognize the similarities between signal handlers and structured exception handling.) This offers us as Java developers some interesting possibilities. Consider the following Java/C++ class:

```
/**
 * Signal.java
 */
import java.io.*;

public class Signal
{
    public static void main(String[] args)
        throws Exception
    {
        Signal s = new Signal();

        System.out.println("Setup complete");

        while (true)
            Thread.yield();
    }
    public Signal()
    {
        setSignalHandler();
    }
    private static void signalSent()
    {
        System.out.println("Signal handler called");
    }
    private native void setSignalHandler();
    static
    {
        System.loadLibrary("signal");
    }
}
// Signal.cpp (Win32/MSVC++ 5.0)
//
#include "Signal.h"

#include <iostream>
using namespace std;
```

```cpp
#include <signal.h>

// Internal signal handler
void signalHandler(int sig)
{
    cout << "signalHandler called with value " << sig << endl;

    // We have to attach this thread to the JVM
    JavaVM** vmBuff = new JavaVM*[1];
    jsize bufLen = 1;
    jsize numVMs;
    jint i = JNI_GetCreatedJavaVMs(vmBuff, bufLen, &numVMs);

    if (numVMs > 0)
    {
        JNIEnv* envPtr;
        vmBuff[0]->AttachCurrentThread((void**)&envPtr, 0);
        jclass cls = envPtr->FindClass("Signal");
        jmethodID methodID =
            envPtr->GetStaticMethodID(cls, "signalSent", "()V");
        envPtr->CallStaticVoidMethod(cls, methodID);
    }
    else
        cout << "No JavaVMs created?!?" << endl;

    cout << "ready to return " << endl;
}

/*
 * Class:      Signal
 * Method:     setSignalHandler
 * Signature: ()V
 */
JNIEXPORT void JNICALL Java_Signal_setSignalHandler
    (JNIEnv* env, jobject thisPtr)
{
    // Set signal handler for all signals 0 through 63
    for (int i=0; i<63; i++)
        signal(i, signalHandler);
}
```

In this code, we call a native method to set up the signal handler, then enter an infinite spin/yield loop inside of Signal.main(). If you press CTRL-C at the console, the signalHandler() function in the C/C++ code is called with the signal value 2 (SIGINT, as defined by Visual C++'s signal.h file), then calls the static method Signal.signalSent(). Notice the rigamarole we have to go through before we can call the Java method, however. Because Win32/VisualC++ uses multiple threads to handle signal callbacks, we have to attach the thread to the JVM established by java.exe. This also has the desired side-effect of giving us a local JNIEnv pointer to call through; without that, we'd have to store it off in the Java_Signal_setSignalHandler implementation. Notice also that I'm completely ignoring synchronization issues in the above code. Any method that the signal handler calls back into must be completely re-entrant (as it is in the above example) or guarded with synchronization mechanisms to prevent concurrent-access problems.

All details aside, this short snippet of code offers some powerful capabilities; if you're not shivering at the thought of all the potential lying under the surface, you should be. Here are two possibilities:

- *Diagnostic controls*
  Remember all those diagnostic messages GJAS sends to the console as it's executing? It's too much information for anyone other than a developer trying to trace a problem. Use signal handlers (and the UNIX `kill` command, which sends signals to a process) to raise and lower the diagnostic output accordingly.

- *Crash protection*
  Because signal handlers can catch a variety of different signals, you can establish a signal handler to catch segmentation faults at the start of your Java application. In the event that the JVM has a bug in it which causes a crash, or (more likely) a native library routine called has a bug in it which causes a crash, the signal handler gets an opportunity to handle the exception. This in turn gives it the chance to either correct for it or exit in a more graceful manner.

The ideas aren't limited to only signal-handlers; they just provide a UNIX/ Win32-portable way of providing such behavior. This kind of power, especially on a server application, goes a long way toward making your Java code more robust.

When calling back into the JVM from native code, the native-code programmer has to take extra steps to make certain Java's semantics are preserved. Specifically, Java's support for exception handling and synchronization needs to be coded by hand, since Java implements both of these within the JVM, rather than using native (and nonportable) mechanisms. Moreover, the reverse is true—the native code must also guarantee that none of its mechanisms escape back into the JVM.

Native methods are not constrained by Java exceptions the way Java methods are. Normally, in standard Java code, calling a method with a `throws` clause means the calling method must either catch the exception type(s), or pass them back to its caller:

```
public class Example
{
    private void doSomething()
        throws Exception
    {
        // . . .
    }

    private void callingMethod()
    {
        doSomething();
            // will not compile; callingMethod() must either catch Exception
            // or declare a "throws Exception" clause of its own
    }
}
```

Native methods, however, are under no such restriction. This offers a serious loophole in the Java exception-checking semantics:

```
public class Example
{
    private void doSomething()
        throws Exception
    {
        throw new Exception();
    }

    private native void doSomethingNative();
        // Assume that the native implementation simply calls doSomething()

    private void callingMethod()
    {
        doSomethingNative();
            // will compile; because doSomethingNative() doesn't declare
            // a "throws" clause, this method is not in violation of the
            // exception rules
    }
}
```

Practically speaking, this implies that any native methods that raise exceptions in JNI code should be declared with a throws clause. These are solely for the Java compiler's benefit, however—the JNI stub generated by javah does nothing with the clause whatsoever. This raises a dangerous possibility—the native code could throw a Java exception within it that isn't declared in its throws declaration on the Java side:

```
public class Example
{
    // . . .
    private native void doSomething();
        // Notice--no way of knowing on the Java side that
        // this method throws Exception
}

/*
 * Class:     Example
 * Method:    doSomething
 * Signature: ()V
 */
JNIEXPORT void JNICALL Java_Example_doSomething
    (JNIEnv* env, jobject thisPtr)
{
    // Throw an Exception
    env->ThrowNew(env->FindClass("java.lang.Exception"),
                "This is an exception from doSomething()");
    return;
}
```

Because Java programmers are so dependent on javadoc-generated documentation or the source code itself, there is absolutely no way for the Java programmer calling this native method to know that he/she needs to catch this exception type.

The other half of the exception-handling problem comes when implementing native code using C++. Sure enough, C++ exceptions and Java exceptions mean absolutely nothing to one another. This means that if a C++ exception propagates out of a native method called from within the JVM, the C++ exception will immediately bypass the rest of the JVM and terminate the application (unless the JVM is wrappered within a C++ `try` block; see the next section). This in turn means that if native code has even the smallest possibility of seeing a C++ exception, the entire native block must be wrapped within a C++ `try`/`catch` block that disallows any exception to filter out of it:

```
/*
 * Class:     Example
 * Method:    doSomething
 * Signature: ()V
 */
JNIEXPORT void JNICALL Java_Example_doSomething
    (JNIEnv* env, jobject thisPtr)
{
    // Wrap all C/C++ code in a try/catch block
    try
    {
        // Do something
    }
    catch (MyExceptionType& ex1)
    {
        // Throw corresponding Java exception type
    }
    catch (YourExceptionType& ex2)
    {
        // Throw corresponding Java exception type
    }
    catch (...)   // catch all exception types
    {
        // Signal to the JVM that a C++ exception was thrown
        env->ThrowNew(env->FindClass("java.lang.Throwable"),
                    "Unknown C++ exception thrown");
        return;
    }
}
```

Make it a standard habit to do this with any of your native code implementations. Because C++'s exception-checking mechanism is a fair bit looser than Java's, it's relatively simple for a C++ exception (especially those dealing with RTTI-casting or heap-allocation) to be thrown and not caught within the code you call. That means if your native code implementation doesn't catch it, nobody will. What's more, even those native-code programmers who believe they have nothing to worry about—are not writing C++ code, after all, just straight C—and still have to worry about this. Many C++ compilers use the same run-time library implementation for both C and C++ code, and may have C++ semantics turned on by default. Check your compiler documentation to be certain.

The same sorts of considerations go for Java synchronization monitors—if you need to hold one from within native code, make sure you release it through every possible control path. Otherwise, deadlock results, and it will be fiendishly difficult to track down. For the most part, if you need to hold onto a Java monitor, create a Java method (or class) to do the synchronized call, and have the native method call into that. This way, all of Java's standard synchronization mechanics are satisfied.

The reverse is true, as well, if you create any native-code synchronization mechanisms within your native code (under Win32, this includes events, semaphores, mutexes and/or critical sections). Make sure that they aren't held when the native code returns the JVM, or subsequent native calls (using that synchronization object in its implementation) will fail. These are standard rules in concurrent programming, but need to be reiterated here; remember, you're not in Java-land anymore, and you definitely need to obey the local customs.

### 16.2.3 JNI invocation

The last form of JNI, called JNI invocation, by far outstrips the rest of JNI in potential, in my opinion. The ability for native code to create, call into, and control a JVM offers so much in the way of flexibility and integration that it's surprising more hasn't been written on the subject. This holds doubly true on the server, where we have intimate knowledge (and concrete needs to access the nonportable features) of the underlying operating system.

For example, Java would make a wonderful tool-building language, if only it weren't so clumsy to use from the command line. By this, I mean that Java's string-handling mechanism and high-level syntax make it nearly trivial to create tools for system administrators and environment-maintenance developers to ease their tasks. Scripts and batch files only go so far; for example, it would be nice to have a command-line utility that converted DOS line-terminator (newline-linefeed) pairs into UNIX (linefeed) line-terminators. Java is perfect for this, except that the JVM-interpreter is the executable to be launched, and we'd much rather be able to refer to the tool as if it were an executable.

The code in listing 16.1 does precisely as the Sun "java" tool does—creates a JVM, loads a class given on the command line, and calls its main() method. While not particularly interesting by itself, once we have this code created, we can actually create a tool-building tool—code that in turn creates code.

**Listing 16.1    Code for JNItest.cpp**

```cpp
#include <jni.h>

// StdC++ headers
#include <iostream>
#include <fstream>
#include <string>
#include <vector>

// Namespaces in use
using namespace std;

int main(int argc, char* argv[])
{
    vector<string> jvm_argv;
    string classname;
    string classpath;
    bool verbose = false;

    // We must have reached the classfile
    classname = argv[1];

    // The remainder of the arguments are assumed to be command-line
    // parameters to the Java class
    int j;
    for (j=2;j<argc;j++)
        jvm_argv.push_back(argv[j]);

    JavaVMInitArgs vm_args;
    JavaVMOption options[4]; int n=0;

    options[n++].optionString = "-Djava.compiler=NONE";
        /* disable JIT */
    options[n++].optionString = "-Djava.class.path=.";
        /* user classes */
    //options[n++].optionString = "-Djava.library.path=c:\mylibs";
        /* set native library path */
    //options[n++].optionString = "-verbose:jni";
        /* print JNI-related messages */

    vm_args.version = JNI_VERSION_1_2;
    vm_args.options = options;
    vm_args.nOptions = n;
    vm_args.ignoreUnrecognized = true;

    /* Note that in JDK 1.2, there is no longer any need to call
     * JNI_GetDefaultJavaVMInitArgs.
     */
    JavaVM* vm;
    JNIEnv* env;
    jint res = JNI_CreateJavaVM(&vm, (void **)&env, &vm_args);

    // argv[1] is the Java class to load
    jclass cls = env->FindClass(argv[1]);
    if (!cls)
```

```cpp
    {
        cout << argv[1] << ".class not found" << endl;
        return -1;
    }
    jmethodID cls_main =
        env->GetStaticMethodID(cls, "main", "([Ljava/lang/String;)V");
    if (!cls_main)
    {
        cout << "main(String[]) not found" << endl;
        return -1;
    }

    // Build args to main()
    jvalue call_args[1];

    jclass cls_java_lang_String = env->FindClass("java/lang/String");
    jobject defaultValue = env->NewStringUTF("");
    jobjectArray args =
        env->NewObjectArray(argc-1, cls_java_lang_String, defaultValue);

    // Populate "args"
    int i=0;
    for (vector<string>::iterator iter = jvm_argv.begin();
        iter != jvm_argv.end();
        iter++)
    {
        jstring str = env->NewStringUTF((*iter).c_str());
        env->SetObjectArrayElement(args, i++, str);
    }
    call_args[0].l = args;

    //
    // Call "main"
    //
    env->CallStaticVoidMethodA(cls, cls_main, call_args);

    //
    // Report any uncaught Java exceptions thrown from within the JVM
    //
    jthrowable ex;
    if ((ex = env->ExceptionOccurred()) != NULL)
    {
        env->ExceptionDescribe();
    }

    //
    // Clean up
    //
    vm->DestroyJavaVM();

    return 0;
}
```

As stated earlier, JNITest.cpp isn't particularly interesting by itself. Simply duplicating the behavior of the JDK java interpreter isn't exactly exciting. However, if we were to replace the `argv[1]` argument with a hard-coded class name, we would have a native executable whose implementation was actually Java code.

Using Invocation to create the JVM within C/C++ code will seem like gross over-kill to many. Why not just build a script or batch file to launch java.exe and the class name? As awkward and unwieldly (compared to just writing a simple batch or script file), JNI Invocation offers some very credible reasons for using it:

- *The Invocation-related C++ code needn't be treated as a black box.*
  C++ developers can use it as a basic starting point, adding other features (new options to the Java compiler, perhaps establishing the signal handlers discussed in the previous section, and so forth) to the C++ code.

- *Precedent.*
  This is precisely what the JDK itself does—javac.exe builds a JVM and calls `sun.tools.javac.Main()`, rmic.exe builds a JVM and calls `sun.rmi.rmic.Main`, and so on. The JDK does it because forcing developers to type "java sun.tools.javac.Main MyCode.java" is, let's face it, awkward.

- *Encapsulation of implementation.*
  There will be times we, as developers, don't want clients or customers to know that the code is written in Java. By wrapping the invocation of the JVM in a native executable in a native-code shell, we keep the Java portion of it hidden from casual prying.

Not all enterprise systems will want or need to make use of this. For those that do, though, there's real potential for superscripting here; I've used JNIGen to create shells around a number of Java applications that comprise tools in my development environment to automate makefile-generation and maintenance, configuration management, and so forth.

## Drawbacks and caveats

Unfortunately, Invocation isn't as simple as this. As always, there are complications.

To begin with, some of the featureset given in the Java executable isn't automatically supported by the JVM created by Invocation. For example, the ability to execute a JAR file (as described in chapter 3) is a function of the native C/C++ code in java.exe, not part of Invocation itself. Passing "-jar <jar-file-name>" in as one of the JVM options (through the use of the JavaVMOptions array) will have no effect. If your JVM created by Invocation is to support this ability, you need to code it in yourself.

Secondly, Sun changed (in the Win32 JDK, at least) how the native-side support for Java was loaded and executed by the OS. Under JDK 1.1, you made these JNI calls (with slightly different syntax for the options to the VM), included the JNI headers, and linked in the JNI libs. The native process would create the JVM, find classes, call methods, and so on. So long as the necessary DLLs were someplace the OS could find them when it was asked to load them, everything ran precisely as expected.

With the advent of JDK 1.2, however, Sun threw something of a monkey wrench into the works. With 1.1, all that was necessary to run the JVM from native code was to be sure that the JDK or JRE bin directory was somewhere along the system PATH, for both Windows and Solaris. In Java 2 (JDK 1.2), this changed; now, the JDK saves a path to the installed JRE in the Windows Registry, and uses that, and not paths relative to the bin directory in which the appropriate DLL was found, to locate where the installed Java execution engine resides.

To complicate matters further, it's not sufficient to just put the JDK or JRE bin directory on the path. In an effort to support drop-in JIT support (for its Hotspot JIT compiler), Sun uses Win32 C/C++ run-time linking to dynamically determine if the Hotspot compiler is present, and if so, to load it instead of the classic JVM engine. The idea is quite cool—we don't need to add any more support or code to install Hotspot— just drop the native-side files into a hotspot directory under the bin directory of the JDK/JRE, and Hotspot comes along for free.

What this means, however, is that not all of the files necessary to execute the JVM reside in the bin directory anymore. Some reside in bin, and others will reside in either classic or hotspot, depending on whether the normal or the JIT execution engine is to be used. What this means to us, as Java developers, is that using JNI Invocation is no longer simple. Where before we could simply call `JNI_CreateVM` and expect everything to work flawlessly, now we have to worry about obtaining the path to the installed JDK out of the Registry, run time loading the appropriate DLLs, and so on.

Fortunately, Sun helps out immeasurably with this; in the src.jar file that ships with the Win32 or Solaris JDK download bundle are four files, under src/launcher. This is the native code that Sun uses in its own native-code development, such as the java.exe (and other) execution engines; specifically, this is the code for java.exe. By providing this code under the standard download license (as opposed to Sun's more restrictive Source Community License), you are able to either cut and paste the code into your own native development, or compile and link in the relevant routines.

The four files, java.c, java.h, java_md.c, and java_md.h, contain the following C API[5] functions:

- `main (java.c)`:
  This is the standard entry point in C/C++, and performs the same function here. The `main` function will create a JVM (either Hotspot or classic, as defined by a command-line argument), find the class passed on the command line, and invoke it with the command-line arguments following the class. Unfortunately, `main` will also be unusable in its current form, since a C/C++ application can

---

[5]  The code is presented in C, so as to be accessible from either C or C++ (or any other language that understands the Win32 C API, such as Delphi, VB or even PowerBuilder).

only have one `main`, and that (usually) will be the `main` defined in your own native code. Still, looking at the `main` implementation gives a good idea of how to load the JVM and start it, and nothing prevents us from changing the name from `main` to `java_main`, to allow it to be loaded and linked as a library from other native apps.

- `LoadJavaVM (java_md.c)`: This is a general-purpose routine that, while not quite as detailed or feature-ridden as the `main` implementation in `java.c`, does go through all the necessary rigamarole required to load and run the JVM either as the classic or the JIT/Hotspot JVM. In fact, it will check for a JRE first in the same directory as the native application (looking for a bin directory underneath the current application directory). If not found there, it then checks to see if the application shipped a private JRE (in a jre subdirectory underneath the application's home directory). Note that the launcher assumes that the application is being launched from a bin directory underneath the application's actual home directory; for example, it assumes a directory layout similar to that of the JDK download itself. The home directory may be `C:\JDK1.2`, but the directory in which the executable resides is `C:\JDK1.2\bin`. If no jre subdirectory is found (in `C:\JDK1.2\jre`, for example), it checks the Win32 Registry to attempt to find (what it calls) a public JRE installation. If you look carefully at the JDK 1.2 installation, this precise hierarchy is established—when java.exe is created, it will find that it has a jre subdirectory under its home directory, and will use the JVM support files found there.

This three-step approach to finding the JRE to use as the JVM for Invocation provides a tremendous amount of flexibility—now we can ship native C/C++ applications that use a colocated or private JRE implementation to provide Java capabilities. This is a tremendous step toward zero administration. Instead of making system administrators responsible for installing the appropriate version of the JRE onto a user's machine, with all the versioning problems thus incurred, we can drop a JRE installation in the same directory as our native application. The C/C++ launcher code will pick it up automatically, and, more importantly, it won't interfere with a standard Java installation on the user's machine.

In fact, this offers an interesting solution to an oft-cited complaint of Java. System administrators, particularly, have often complained about Sun's release of a new version of the JDK every two to four months. As we've discussed before, every time a new release of software is made that is in use by a corporation, the system administrators are the ones who have to go around to all the users' machines and install it. This is not a good way to make friends with the system administrators, especially if your user base is scattered across multiple buildings, cities, states, or even countries.

We've already discussed ways to create a zero deployment environment for our Java code, but the JVM/JRE itself is another matter. It would be awkward to have executing Java code try to download a new version of the JRE and install it, since the files being replaced are currently being executed. Not only does this present a potential sharing violation, but now the Java code has to somehow shut itself down and restart the application, so as to take advantage of the new code.

JNI offers an interesting solution to this issue. Instead of asking Java code to do this sort of upgrade-the-JDK-on-the-fly, run a custom java.exe launcher that, upon first invocation, uses native C/C++ code to contact a central deployment server for the latest version of the JRE in use. The JNI code can even go so far as to construct the JVM, make a `System.getProperties("java.version")` call to obtain the version of the JVM in use and compare it against the version on the remote server. If the version on the remote server is greater, download the new JRE (most likely in .zip or .tar.gz format), explode it on top of the user's current working directory, and then start the JVM.

Your system administrators are happy because they don't have to walk around to every user's machine, they don't have to ask the users to do the install themselves, and they're still able to support your development efforts and not seem as a stumbling block to continued progress. You, meanwhile, bask in the glory of their praise for your system even as you upgrade the JDK to the latest and greatest, as needed.

One final problem with using Invocation is that because we're so deeply into native code, we need to pay very close attention to the context when calling into the JVM. Any exceptions thrown need to be handled, any synchronization monitors need to be carefully tracked, and global and local references (to prevent garbage-collection of Java objects) need to be held where necessary. When working within multiple native-thread code, special care must be taken in order to prevent a crash from the JVM native code—each thread that wishes to access or call on the JVM must attach itself to the JVM before making a single call on it.

Still, JNI Invocation is by far the most underrated API of the Java API sets. One idea offering interesting possibilities is to embed a JVM within your user front-end application, and use Java as your application's user macro language; this is precisely what Java Server Pages do.

### Debugging tip

Interestingly, reading the launcher code also yields a very practical benefit:

```
/*
 * Entry point.
 */
int
main(int argc, char **argv)
{
    /* . . . */
    if (getenv("_JAVA_LAUNCHER_DEBUG") != 0) {
        debug = JNI_TRUE;
        printf("----_JAVA_LAUNCHER_DEBUG----\n");
    }
    /* . . . */
}
```

For non-C/C++ developers, the foregoing code checks for the presence of an environment variable _JAVA_LAUNCHER_DEBUG, and if found, turns on a debug flag that causes all sorts of interesting information to be displayed when the executable is running:

```
C:\Projects\Books\SSJ\cd\Src\Chap13>java Hello
Hello, world!

C:\Projects\Books\SSJ\cd\Src\Chap13>set _JAVA_LAUNCHER_DEBUG=1

C:\Projects\Books\SSJ\cd\Src\Chap13>java Hello
----_JAVA_LAUNCHER_DEBUG----
Path to JVM is C:\PRG\JDK1.2\jre\bin\classic\jvm.dll
JavaVM args:
    version 0x00010002, ignoreUnrecognized is JNI_FALSE, nOptions is 1
    option[ 0] = '-
Djava.class.path=.;C:\JRE\1.2\lib\rt.jar;C:\PRG\JDK1.2\lib\to
ols.jar;C:\PRG\JDK1.2\lib\dt.jar'
678724 micro seconds to InitializeJVM
Main-Class is 'Hello'
Apps' argc is 0
224188 micro seconds to load main class
----_JAVA_LAUNCHER_DEBUG----
Hello, world!

C:\Projects\Books\SSJ\cd\Src\Chap13>
```

As you can see, we get quite a collection of information that comes back—the path to the JVM, the arguments to the JVM (including the value of the CLASSPATH environment variable), the Main-Class loaded, which will be either the class specified on the command line, or the Main-Class directive in the JAR's Manifest file, and some profiling information.

Just for curiosity's sake, this is what we get when we run "javac" with the _JAVA_LAUNCHER_DEBUG turned on:

```
C:\Projects\Books\SSJ\cd\Src\Chap13>set CLASSPATH=

C:\Projects\Books\SSJ\cd\Src\Chap13>javac Hello.java
----_JAVA_LAUNCHER_DEBUG----
Path to JVM is C:\PRG\JDK1.2\jre\bin\classic\jvm.dll
JavaVM args:
    version 0x00010002, ignoreUnrecognized is JNI_FALSE, nOptions is 3
    option[ 0] = '-Dapplication.home=C:\PRG\JDK1.2'
    option[ 1] = '-
Djava.class.path=C:\PRG\JDK1.2\lib\tools.jar;C:\PRG\JDK1.2\cl
asses'
    option[ 2] = '-Xms8m'
625375 micro seconds to InitializeJVM
Main-Class is 'sun.tools.javac.Main'
Apps' argc is 1
    argv[ 0] = 'Hello.java'
450462 micro seconds to load main class
----_JAVA_LAUNCHER_DEBUG----

C:\Projects\Books\SSJ\cd\Src\Chap13>
```

Interesting. In this snippet, we first set the CLASSPATH to be empty, to demonstrate what the launcher code does with the CLASSPATH if none is found. As you can see, it builds its own classpath, consisting of the application home path with lib\tools.jar and classes appended. (This is the CLASSPATH used for the execution of the sun.tools.javac.Main class, not the CLASSPATH used by the compiler to find classes defined in your own code.)

This is useful information to have when debugging Java, and it's all there for us to see just by turning on this undocumented feature of the launcher code. In fact, this is a handy trick for development in general; one of the keys to zero administration is the ability to turn on debugging information without having to redeploy or recompile the application. In this case, simply define an environment variable and rerun the application, and debug information begins to pour across the screen. It may not be as interactive as using a Java debugger, but it's a quick-trick that the system administrators can do themselves. Then, if the problem persists, the output can be captured to file and given to the developers for examination.

## 16.2.4    JNI changes in JDK 1.2

With the release of JDK 1.2 came some changes in the nature of native libraries. Unfortunately, no corresponding JNI 1.2 specification has come with those changes. As of this writing, the JNI 1.2 specification consists of reading the JNI 1.1 specification and the JNI 1.2 enhancements document that comes as part of the JDK 1.2 download. While the changes made to JNI for 1.2 aren't profound or significant, a few new features added offer additional flexibility you may welcome:

- *Native library startup/shutdown routines*
  When the JVM loads the native library via the `loadLibrary` method, it will attempt to look for a function in the library with the signature

  ```
  jint JNI_OnLoad(JavaVM* vm, void* reserved);
  ```

  The `JNI_OnLoad` function must return the JVM version it requires to run; this means that if any native-code implementations use JNI 1.2 features, this function must return `JNI_VERSION_1_2`. Conversely, when the native library is unloaded from the JVM, it will call

  ```
  void JNI_OnUnload(JavaVM* vm, void* reserved);
  ```

  This behavior was introduced to allow native libraries the opportunity to perform on-load or on-unload initialization (for example, to establish/close connections to a database, or perform initialize/uninitialize calls to a third-party library, and so forth). Under the Win32 platform, DLLs have the ability to use a DLL entry-point function (DllMain under Visual C++, DllEntryPoint under BorlandC++) to do the same thing. Other platforms may do so, as well. Because Java now provides a mechanism to do this, however, any new native-library code written should use the `JNI_OnLoad`/`JNI_OnUnload` functions.

- *Reflection support*

  One discrepancy in JNI 1.1 was the fact that JNI `jmethodID`s and `jfieldID`s had no relationship to Reflection, other than twice looking up the same field or method by name (once in Reflection and once in JNI). This meant that within a native library, if the native-code implementation needed to find the `jmethodID` of a java.lang.reflect.Method instance, it had to get the Class instance from the Method, turn the Class into a jclass, get the name from the Method, call `Get-MethodID` on the jclass using the Method's name, and finally call through the `jmethodID`, all of which took an extraordinary amount of time. In JNI 1.2, it boils down to a single call:

  ```
  // Convert "methodObj" (a jobject) into a jmethodID
  jmethodID methodJNI_ID = envPtr->FromReflectedMethod(methodObj);
      // Note that methodObj must be a jobject referencing a
      // java.lang.reflect.Constructor or java.lang.reflect.Method
      // object instance, or Bad Things will occur
  ```

  This gives JNI code the ability to conveniently use Java's Reflection mechanism. This can also go both ways—the JNI methods `ToReflectedMethod`/`ToRe-flectedField` convert a JNI `jmethodID` or `jfieldID` to a java.lang.reflect.Method/java.lang. reflect.Constructor or java.lang.reflect.Field instance.

- *Changes in the Invocation mechanism*

  Because of the way the JNI 1.1 JDK1_1InitArgs structure was written, introducing features to the JVM via Invocation was impossible. In JNI 1.2, a new structure was introduced, JavaVMInitArgs, which in turn contains an array of 0 to *n* JavaVMOption structures; the JNITest.cpp file demonstrated this:

  ```
  JavaVMInitArgs vm_args;
  JavaVMOption options[4];

  options[0].optionString = "-Djava.compiler=NONE";
              /* disable JIT */
  options[1].optionString = "-Djava.class.path=c:\myclasses";
              /* user classes */
  options[2].optionString = "-Djava.library.path=c:\mylibs";
              /* set native library path */
  options[3].optionString = "-verbose:jni";
              /* print JNI-related messages */

  vm_args.version = JNI_VERSION_1_2;
  vm_args.options = options;
  vm_args.nOptions = 4;
  vm_args.ignoreUnrecognized = TRUE;

  /* Note that in JDK 1.2, there is no longer any need to call
   * JNI_GetDefaultJavaVMInitArgs. */
  res = JNI_CreateJavaVM(&vm, (void **)&env, &vm_args);
  ```

A few other items came in as well; see the JDK documentation for further details.

## 16.3 OTHER METHODS OF JAVA-TO-NATIVE INTERACTION

JNI isn't the only way by which Java can communicate with native code.

### 16.3.1 Sockets

One of the easiest ways to get Java code to communicate with non-Java code is to use TCP/IP sockets to facilitate the communication. Because of their ubiquitous nature and the popularity of the Internet, just about every language commonly available has the capacity to open and communicate over a socket. In fact, this sort of communication occurs almost constantly, as web browsers written in C or C++ use sockets to communicate with web (and other) servers that may or may not be written in Java, C/C++, Python, or Visual Basic. Because the HTTP protocol is a completely text-based protocol, no big-endian/little-endian concerns apply; the same is true of any text-based protocol, which explains its popularity among Internet standards.

This in turn implies that if you require your Java application to communicate with a C++ server, simply specify a text-based socket protocol for both sides, write the necessary code to read and write from those sockets, then ensure that clear TCP/IP communication exists between the two processes. Sockets also possess a measure of location transparency. They can be used for either a local IPC mechanism, in which two processes on the same machine communicate, or as remote IPC across multiple machines. Either way, the sockets neither know nor care.

There are, however, drawbacks to the sockets alternative. Sockets are slow and carry a fairly hefty amount of overhead in establishing connections. In a high-performance application, this could easily become a sizable bottleneck. Additionally, binary representations of objects cannot be shared, but must instead be sent entirely across the socket. If your non-Java environment understands the Java Object Serialization specification, the entire object tree can be Serialized and sent over, but without this, some other form of representation must be used. XML is a good candidate for this, but requires an XML parser for both sides.

Consequently, unless the separation between the two systems is clean and well-defined, sockets as an interface mechanism between Java and non-Java code can quickly become more trouble than they are worth. This can especially be true if the desire to move to non-Java code is one of performance. In those cases where a textual-based system and/or well-known binary data exchange is possible (the classic case being a web server), sockets provide an easily understood mechanism for the exchange of data between Java and external code.

### 16.3.2 CORBA

CORBA also, because of its multilinguistic nature, also allows Java code to access non-Java code. This is entirely by intent. CORBA has been, from its very beginning, targeted as a cross-language, cross-platform solution that brings together all languages into a unified whole. The cost of this software bus, as the OMG calls it, is a measure of complexity not found in pure Java code, coupled with the overhead of the CORBA

ORB and related code on each side. The overhead of IIOP will certainly defeat most attempts to use CORBA as a native-code performance-tuning mechanism.

In some ways, using CORBA to access code written in C/C++ (or any of the other languages for which CORBA has bindings, including Ada and COM/DCOM Automation) doesn't quite qualify as native interaction, since the Java code isn't accessing the native code directly (as it is with JNI). Instead, the Java code calls into the CORBA ORB, which in turn passes the request on to the recipient CORBA object in its own, native, form. Still, regardless of the technical discrepancies, CORBA allows our Java code to communicate directly with C/C++ code, which is precisely the goal.

## 16.4  *INTEGRATING THE SERVER: GJAS GOES NATIVE*

Despite Java's incredible flexibility as a server-side tool, sometimes it's simply easier to use and administer an application if it is a native executable, rather than an interpreted bytecode (or script) file. For example, Java would make a strong scripting language, to replace complex UNIX shell scripts, except that a Java application must be fired off as the Java interpreter, with the class name to execute as part of the command line. This requirement makes using Java as an integral part of the operating system suite of tools an awkward and clumsy process. We might be able to work around it by using batch or script files to hide the Java interpreter, but that's still clumsy, and won't work in many cases.

### 16.4.1  Making GJAS an NT service

One such area where Java's interpreted nature can trip itself up is in the arena of daemon processes. Daemons, for those unfamiliar with the UNIX terminology, is an application that runs irrespective of user presence. For example, most HTTP and FTP server processes are run as daemons, so that even if no user is currently logged into the system, the process will still run and execute as soon as the system comes up. Under NT, daemons are called Services, and are started as soon as the NT machine boots, just like daemons.

Unfortunately, where a daemon process can be any Unix executable with any command-line (daemons are specified in plain text files specific to each Unix operating system, so firing off a Java app is as simple as specifying "java MyClass param1 param2"), NT has a very specific mechanism. Services in NT must follow a very strict form, and cannot be simply any executable—it must be an executable that takes very specific steps, registering itself with the NT Service Control Manager, and receiving callbacks from the SCM as the load process proceeds.

Because of this, a Java application cannot, by itself, be a Service. Some may wonder why this is even an issue—after all, we just log in, start the Java application, and leave it running, correct? Those familiar with NT know this is not the case—NT refuses to log out so long as a user-created process (like a Java process) remains running. This means that the only way, other than to create a Service, to have a process running on NT is to leave it logged in. This is, as any NT administrator will tell you, a huge security hole, as it means that anyone with physical access to the server can now (deliberately or accidentally) alter or shut down the Java process.

Instead, we need to create a native NT Service to create a JVM, load a class specified in the Service's command-line parameters, and execute it. Unlike a normal Java application, however, we're not going to try and filter everything through `main`; instead, we're going to make use of JNI's ability to call any method on the class and create a pseudo-protocol for allowing any arbitrary Java class to behave as an NT service.

This isn't a book on NT Services, so I'm not going to go through the necessary steps to build an NT Service.[6] The key point to draw away from this is that because of JNI, we can create a custom-OS-specific application that in turn wrappers our JVM. This lets us poke Java into just about any place on the platform that we want.

## 16.4.2 Using NT IPC mechanisms: Named pipe

The Win32 API also has a rich set of interprocess communication mechanisms: named and anonymous pipes, atoms, the Windows clipboard, DDE, system hooks, memory-mapped files, mailslots, standard sockets, even the WM_COPYDATA message in the windowing layer. As a result, native Win32 applications can communicate in a wide variety of ways. Because of this, we may want our Java code to be able to communicate with these native Win32 applications using their mode of communication. Again, this is precisely what JNI is for—to allow us to call down to the underlying platform.

We'll use the basic design that Java uses for Sockets. The NamedPipe class (listing 16.2) will parallel the Socket class, a basic encapsulation of the details of connecting to a given NamedPipe. From that NamedPipe instance, we'll obtain an Output-Stream and InputStream for writing to and reading from the named pipe, respectively. These will be the NamedPipeOutputStream and NamedPipeInputStream classes, although they shouldn't be visible to users of the NamedPipe, just as the Socket's specific OutputStream and InputStream classes aren't visible.

---

**Listing 16.2   Code for NamedPipe.java**

```
/**
 * This class serves the same purpose as the Java Socket class;
 * a simple abstraction of connecting to and using a named pipe.
 */
public class NamedPipe
{
    static
    {
        System.loadLibrary("NamedPipe");
    }

    // Constants
    //
```

---

[6] *Essential JNI*, mentioned in the "Additional reading" section, does precisely this.

```java
public static final int DUPLEX = 3;
public static final int WRITE = 2;
public static final int READ = 1;

// Internal members
//
/*package-friendly*/ int m_hPipe;
private int m_openMode;

public NamedPipe()
{ }
public NamedPipe(String pipeName, int openMode, int timeout)
    throws IOException
{
    m_openMode = openMode;

    open(pipeName, openMode, timeout);
}
public void finalize()
{
    close();
}

public void open(String pipeName, int openMode, int timeout)
    throws IOException
{
    m_hPipe = nativeOpen(pipeName, openMode, timeout);
    if (m_hPipe == 0xFFFFFFFF)
    {
        throw new IOException("NT NamedPipe error");
    }
}
public void close()
{
    nativeClose(m_hPipe);
}

public OutputStream getOutputStream()
    throws IOException
{
    if ( (m_openMode == DUPLEX) ||
         (m_openMode == WRITE))
    {
        return new NamedPipeOutputStream(this);
    }
    else
        throw new IOException("Named-Pipe is inbound only");
}
public InputStream getInputStream()
    throws IOException
{
    if ( (m_openMode == DUPLEX) ||
         (m_openMode == READ))
    {
```

```
            return new NamedPipeInputStream(this);
        }
        else
            throw new IOException("Named-Pipe is outbound only");
    }

    // Native methods
    //
    static private native
        int nativeOpen(String name, int mode, int timeOut);
    static private native
        boolean nativeClose(int pipeHandle);
}
```

The NamedPipe class, like the Socket class, offers two constructors: a default that simply creates the instance and performs no initialization, and one that takes the Win32 UNC name of the named pipe to connect to. This name will be one of a variety of forms:

- "\\.\pipe\pipename": Tells the Win32 API to connect to the pipe named "pipename" on the local machine; using "." is the named pipe equivalent of "localhost" as the host name to a Socket.
- "\\*\pipe\pipename": Tells the Win32 API to connect to the pipe named "pipename" anywhere on the network; this means that only one "pipename" will exist across the entire NT domain or workgroup.
- "\\machinename\pipe\pipename": Tells the Win32 API to connect to the pipe "pipename" on the machine "machinename". Only one "pipename" can exist on "machinename", but "pipename" could exist on other machines without a problem.
- "\\domain\pipe\pipename": Tells the Win32 API to connect to the pipe "pipename" on the domain "domain"; only one "pipename" will exist for the domain, but will not conflict with "pipename" on individual machines.

The NamedPipe class itself does no validation or sanity-checking of the UNC name; it just passes it directly on to the JNI methods to give to the Win32 call.

NamedPipe has three native methods, which are implemented in a separate tree on the CD (in the "Src/native/win32" subdirectory), and look like this:

```
#include "com_javageeks_net_NamedPipe.h"

#include <windows.h>

#include <iostream>
using namespace std;

/*
 * Class:     com_javageeks_net_NamedPipe
 * Method:    nativeOpen
 * Signature: (Ljava/lang/String;II)I
 */
JNIEXPORT jint JNICALL Java_com_javageeks_net_NamedPipe_nativeOpen
```

```
(JNIEnv* env, jclass, jstring pipeName, jint mode, jint timeOut)
{
    int debug = (getenv("_JAVAGEEKS_DEBUG") != 0);

    // Convert from Java to UTF-8; we're in trouble if we ever use
    // Unicode as a pipeName, but I don't want to deal with
    // Unicode-to-ASCII conversions right now
    const char* c_pipeName = env->GetStringUTFChars(pipeName, NULL);
    if (debug)
    {
        cout << "Java_com_javageeks_net_NamedPipe_nativeConstruct: "
             << "c_pipeName = " << c_pipeName << endl;
    }

    DWORD fileMode;
    if (mode==com_javageeks_net_NamedPipe_DUPLEX)
    {
        fileMode = GENERIC_READ | GENERIC_WRITE;
    }
    else if (mode==com_javageeks_net_NamedPipe_READ)
    {
        fileMode = GENERIC_READ;
    }
    else if (mode==com_javageeks_net_NamedPipe_WRITE)
    {
        fileMode = GENERIC_WRITE;
    }
    else
    {
        // Uh-oh; we didn't expect this
        if (debug)
        {
            cout << "What is mode " << mode << "???" << endl;
        }
    }

    // Make the call
    HANDLE hPipe = ::CreateFile(c_pipeName, fileMode,
                                0, NULL, OPEN_EXISTING, 0, NULL);
    // Check for busy
    if (hPipe == INVALID_HANDLE_VALUE)
    {
        if (::GetLastError() == ERROR_PIPE_BUSY)
        {
            // Wait up to the timeout parameter; after that, it's
            // a failed connect and return
            if (::WaitNamedPipe(c_pipeName, timeOut))
            {
                hPipe = ::CreateFile(c_pipeName, fileMode, 0, NULL,
                                     OPEN_EXISTING, 0, NULL);
            }
        }
    }
```

```
    if (hPipe == INVALID_HANDLE_VALUE)
    {
        DWORD error = ::GetLastError();

        if (debug)
        {
            cout << "hndl == INVALID_HANDLE_VALUE; "
                 << "ErrNo: " << ::GetLastError() << endl;
        }

        hPipe = (void*)-1;
    }

    // Release
    env->ReleaseStringUTFChars(pipeName, c_pipeName);

    return (jint)hPipe;
}

/*
 * Class:     com_javageeks_net_NamedPipe
 * Method:    nativeClose
 * Signature: (I)Z
 */
JNIEXPORT jboolean JNICALL Java_com_javageeks_net_NamedPipe_nativeClose
    (JNIEnv* env, jclass cls, jint namedPipe)
{
    int debug = (getenv("_JAVAGEEKS_DEBUG") != 0);

    HANDLE hPipe = (HANDLE)namedPipe;

    if (::CloseHandle(hPipe))
    {
        return JNI_TRUE;
    }
    else
    {
        if (debug)
        {
            cout << "ConnectNamedPipe failed; error "
                 << ::GetLastError() << endl;
        }

        return JNI_FALSE;
    }
}
```

For those who aren't C++ gurus, this is a fairly basic exercise in both JNI and Win32 API calls. The `nativeOpen` call decodes the jstring argument into a native C/C++ char* string, and passes that into the `CreateFile` call. Note that because this is a client (and not a server), if the named pipe doesn't exist, an error will result. Another danger: remember that in Java, all Strings are Unicode, but most C/C++ code still works with the ASCII character set. When decoding Strings from Java, if the String is entirely ASCII, it can be safely used as an ASCII string when retrieved/converted as a

UTF-8 String; should somebody pass in a Unicode name as the choice of the named pipe, however, the JNI code mentioned is going to blow up—big time. I'm not including any code to convert Unicode to ASCII for the simple reason that it clutters the example; if this code is intended for an international market, such conversion would probably be necessary before deployment to production.

Note how we make use of the "_JAVA_LAUNCHER_DEBUG" environment-variable trick in the JNI code; if the environment variable "_JAVAGEEKS_DEBUG" is defined, we spit out some interesting debugging information along the way. We could even make this more sophisticated by setting the environment variable to various levels (1 and up), corresponding to more and more output, but this works, for now.

Notice that the getOutputStream and getInputStream methods of NamedPipe return new instances of NamedPipeOutputStream and NamedPipeInput-Stream, respectively:

```
/**
 * Receive input from an NT named pipe (presumably with INBOUND
 * mode set on it). Can only be obtained from a NamedPipe instance;
 * cannot be instantiated on its own.
 */
public class NamedPipeInputStream extends InputStream
{
    // Internal members
    //
    private NamedPipe m_pipe;

    /**
     * Package-friendly constructor. Used solely by NamedPipe.
     */
    /*package-friendly*/ NamedPipeInputStream(NamedPipe pipe)
    {
        m_pipe = pipe;
    }

    public int available()
    {
        return 0;
    }
    public void close()
    {
        // Do nothing--the named pipe may still be open in outbound
        // mode, so we don't want to close it
    }
    public boolean markSupported()
    {
        return false;
    }
    public int read(byte[] b)
    {
        return nativeRead(m_pipe.m_hPipe, b);
    }
```

```
    public int read()
    {
        return nativeRead(m_pipe.m_hPipe);
    }

    // Native methods
    //
    private static native void nativeAvailable(int hPipe);
    private static native int nativeRead(int hPipe, byte[] b);
    private static native int nativeRead(int hPipe);
}
```

The JNI implementation looks like:

```
#include "com_javageeks_net_NamedPipeInputStream.h"

#include <windows.h>

#include <iostream>
using namespace std;

/*
 * Class:     com_javageeks_net_NamedPipeInputStream
 * Method:    nativeAvailable
 * Signature: (I)V
 */
JNIEXPORT void JNICALL
Java_com_javageeks_net_NamedPipeInputStream_nativeAvailable
    (JNIEnv* env, jclass, jint namedPipe)
{
    int debug = (getenv("_JAVAGEEKS_DEBUG") != 0);

    HANDLE hPipe = (HANDLE)namedPipe;

    // Not sure what to do here....
}

/*
 * Java_com_javageeks_net_NamedPipeInputStream_nativeRead__I not
 * shown here for brevity
 */

/*
 * Class:     com_javageeks_net_NamedPipeInputStream
 * Method:    nativeRead
 * Signature: (I[B)I
 */
JNIEXPORT jint JNICALL
Java_com_javageeks_net_NamedPipeInputStream_nativeRead__I_3B
    (JNIEnv* env, jclass, jint namedPipe, jbyteArray bytes)
{
    int debug = (getenv("_JAVAGEEKS_DEBUG") != 0);

    HANDLE hPipe = (HANDLE)namedPipe;

    // Read bytes.length characters
    DWORD arrayLength = env->GetArrayLength(bytes);
    DWORD nRead;
```

```
      CHAR* recvArray = new CHAR[arrayLength];

      if (!::ReadFile(hPipe, recvArray, arrayLength, &nRead, NULL))
      {
          if (debug)
          {
              cout << "ERROR: Unable to read from named pipe" << endl;
          }
      }

      // recvArray now holds the named pipe data; transfer it to
      // the 'bytes' array
      env->SetByteArrayRegion(bytes, 0, nRead, (jbyte*)recvArray);

      return nRead;
}
```

Note that InputStream provides `available`, a method for determining how many
bytes can be read before blocking, but that the JNI code does nothing with this. In
fact, the Java code in NamedPipeInputStream simply returns 0. This is the normal
response to use when working with a stream that offers no buffering. We could add
buffering of the named pipe to the input stream without much difficulty, but, again,
would make the JNI code much more complex.[7]

NamedPipeOutputStream.java and its corresponding JNI code look very similar:

```
package com.javageeks.net;

import java.io.*;

public class NamedPipeOutputStream extends OutputStream
{
    // Internal members
    //
    private NamedPipe m_pipe;

    /*package-friendly*/ NamedPipeOutputStream(NamedPipe pipe)
    {
        m_pipe = pipe;
    }

    public void close()
    {
        // Do nothing--the named pipe may still be open in incoming
        // mode, so we don't want to close it
    }
    public void flush()
    {
        nativeFlush(m_pipe.m_hPipe);
    }
```

---

[7] In addition, attempting to support this functionality in its purest form (lookahead support) under
Win32 could be somewhat problematic or inefficient, since it would require making a separate API call
to determine how many characters are left to read on the named pipe.

```
    public void write(byte[] b)
    {
        nativeWrite(m_pipe.m_hPipe, b);
    }
    public void write(int ch)
    {
        nativeWrite(m_pipe.m_hPipe, ch);
    }

    // Native methods
    //
    private static native void nativeFlush(int hPipe);
    private static native void nativeWrite(int hPipe, byte[] bytes);
    private static native void nativeWrite(int hPipe, int ch);
}
```

Notice that we provide an implementation for flush, even though the current JNI implementation always sends the data down the named pipe in the write call; this is (again) to support buffering later, if we choose to do so.

The JNI implementation is as follows:

```
#include "com_javageeks_net_NamedPipeOutputStream.h"

#include <windows.h>

#include <iostream>
using namespace std;

/*
 * Class:     com_javageeks_net_NamedPipeOutputStream
 * Method:    nativeFlush
 * Signature: (I)V
 */
JNIEXPORT void JNICALL
Java_com_javageeks_net_NamedPipeOutputStream_nativeFlush
    (JNIEnv* env, jclass, jint pipe)
{
    int debug = (getenv("_JAVAGEEKS_DEBUG") != 0);

    HANDLE hPipe = (HANDLE)pipe;
}

/*
 * Java_com_javageeks_net_NamedPipeOutputStream_nativeWrite__II not
 * shown here for brevity
 */

/*
 * Class:     com_javageeks_net_NamedPipeOutputStream
 * Method:    nativeWrite
 * Signature: (I[B)V
 */
JNIEXPORT void JNICALL
Java_com_javageeks_net_NamedPipeOutputStream_nativeWrite__I_3B
    (JNIEnv* env, jclass, jint pipe, jbyteArray bytes)
```

```
{
    int debug = (getenv("_JAVAGEEKS_DEBUG") != 0);
    if (debug)
    {
        cout << "Entering NamedPipeOutputStream_nativeWrite__I_3B" << endl;
    }

    HANDLE hPipe = (HANDLE)pipe;

    // Convert jbyteArray to char*
    DWORD arrayLength = env->GetArrayLength(bytes);
    CHAR* sendArray = new CHAR[arrayLength];
    env->GetByteArrayRegion(bytes, 0, arrayLength, (jbyte*)sendArray);

    if (debug)
    {
        cout << "Sending: '" << sendArray << "'" << endl;
    }

    DWORD cbWritten;

    // Do the Write
    BOOL success = ::WriteFile(hPipe, sendArray, arrayLength + 1,
                               &cbWritten, NULL);

    if (!success)
    {
        if (debug)
        {
            cout << "ERROR: WriteFile failed: " << ::GetLastError()
                 << endl;
        }
    }
}
```

We do nothing inside of nativeFlush, since we're sending the messages down the named pipe as soon as the write call is made. Note also that the write(int ch) method, under a nonbuffered implementation, is going to be an expensive call, sending a single character down the named pipe on each call. This is why the NamedPipe-OutputStream class provides an implementation of the write(byte[] b) method, instead of using the default: simply looping across the array and calling write(int ch) would be horribly inefficient.[8]

A couple of other notes about the NamedPipe implementation:

- *"Close" support*
  Neither the NamedPipeInputStream nor the NamedPipeOutputStream call CloseHandle on the named pipe handle, instead leaving it to the NamedPipe

---

[8] This is also why the sample code in NamedPipe's main uses the write method to send the data down the pipe, instead of the more Java-familiar wrap-a-PrintWriter-around-the-OutputStream-and-use-println. Because PrintWriter writes each character using the write(int) method of OutputStream, to send a collection of bytes it's more efficient to use write directly, even if it is more awkward.

to do this during its garbage-collection step (or when its `close` method is called directly). This is because a given InputStream and OutputStream could both be attached to the same handle, and having one close it would deny it to the other. Instead of trying to build a complex reference-counting scheme, we let Java do the work for us. When NamedPipe gets recycled (which it never will, until any NamedPipeInputStream or NamedPipeOutputStream instances are also recycled), it closes the named pipe itself.

- *No named-pipe "byte" versus "message" differentiation.*
Under Win32, named pipes can be in one of two modes, either "byte" or "message" mode. In "byte" mode, bytes are simply written and sent, with no inherent break between one send and the next. Contrary to this, in "message" mode, when one message is sent down the named pipe, the entire message is retrieved at once, making transaction-based communications easier. Adding support to the NamedPipe class would be a simple exercise in additional JNI/Win32 C/C++ calls. Unfortunately, it would complicate the NamedPipeInputStream/NamedPipeOutputStream classes, because they would need to know in which mode the named pipe was operating, and make translations as necessary.

As a test, the Microsoft Visual C++ compiler comes with a number of samples, one of which is a multithreaded named-pipe server.[9] Compile and start it, then use the `main` method of NamedPipe (not shown in the previous listing) to connect to the Microsoft named pipe server, and exchange data between clients.

## 16.5 OTHER JNI USES

There is more to JNI than being able to call down the OS or create an opaque JVM to use. JNI also offers the opportunity for API control of the JVM itself.

### 16.5.1 Debugging support

I have lamented the loss of Java's placement of environment variables into the System "properties" Properties instance. Given that we have the source available for the Java interpreter for both the Win32 and Solaris platforms, it would be relatively trivial to use native C/C++ code to walk through the environment variables and place them into the System's properties. This would, in turn, give us the debugging support from environment variables that Java itself uses, but would require the use of this specialized interpreter.

This, by itself, may not be all bad—it means that production code can use the standard Java interpreter, and use our customized debugging interpreter only when

---

[9] Use the documentation that comes with MSVC, or an MSDN subscription, to look up "Pipes" under the "PlatformSDK" heading, and use the "Multithreaded Named Pipe Server" example. Note that because the Java implementation uses byte-oriented named pipes, the MSVC sample will need to be modified to use byte-oriented (instead of message-oriented) named pipes.

the debugging or problem-tracking needs to take place. It probably wouldn't qualify as 100 percent pure Java, however, and other Java-based products that control the JVM, such as EJB Application Servers or Servlet-compliant HTTP servers, wouldn't have this support. Still, for developers, this may be a useful trick to have for debugging or administration support.

## 16.5.2 JVMDI

The Java Virtual Machine Debugger Interface (JVMDI) is a native-code API that allows native libraries to have special control with the JVM. JVMDI was introduced with the release of JDK 1.2, and while Sun claims it to be part of the standard Java platform, it is (so far) only implemented within the Sun JDK 1.2 release.

Some would believe that knowing this API would only interest those creating a debugger for Java; in fact, JVMDI (and its partner, JVMPI) offers interesting capabilities, especially in the area of JVM events. For example, we can implement a code-unintrusive, line-by-line method trace by using JVMDI to attach to the JVM, set up frame-entry and frame-exit event handlers. Within the event-handler callback, use JNI to extract the class and method name, and the parameters to the call, if necessary, as well as the thread on which the call was made, and display all of this to the screen (or file, or wherever the trace information is destined). While it reduces the JVM's execution speed to a crawl (especially since JVMDI, at least in its current form, requires any JIT compiler to be turned off), only running the code in a debugger would produce a more detailed report of what happened within the JVM.

Additionally, because this technique occurs within the JVM itself, it applies equally well to any Java code, whether it was developed in-house, by a third-party, or even parts of the JDK run-time library itself. This reduces the need for trace code to be written within the Java code and offers the ability to trace any code we could possibly execute. Having the ability to act as a debugger gives server applications an extra measure of robustness—we can use the JVMDI API to not only report on any unexpected conditions, but to handle the problem in a manner that would be unavailable to us within standard Java code.

For example, we can use JVMDI to trap events relating to class loading, in order to preempt the standard class-loading mechanism, by obtaining the bytecode the JVM wants to load from some other source. Recall the discussion regarding on-the-fly compilation of Java code; instead of routing the compilation through a Java class, we can use native code to execute a native-code Java compiler (such as IBM's Jikes compiler) in a separate process. Or, in order to determine the smallest number of Java classes that need to be distributed when an application is shipped, we can use the JVMDI API call `GetClasses` to list all the classes loaded in the JVM at the time the JVM shuts down.

A JVMDI shared library must be loaded with some special, nonstandard flags to the Sun JDK interpreter:

```
java -Xdebug -Xnoagent -Djava.compiler=NONE -Xrunjvmdi YourClass
```

The "-X..." options are nonstandard JDK options that may or may not be the same for non-Sun Java distributions. More details on each are in the JVMDI documentation. Again, because JVMDI is so new, it is likely that non-Sun implementations of Java 2 will not have JVMDI.

### 16.5.3  JVMPI

The Java Virtual Machine Profiler Interface (JVMPI) is another JNI API, not yet standardized, specifically geared for creating Java code profilers. Because of its profiling emphasis, the JVMPI API set contains far more in the way of event-notifications (for example, notifications when garbage-collection begins and ends), but less in the way of ability to control the JVM itself (such as the ability to set breakpoints within the loaded code). In any event, until the JVMPI API is standardized by Sun, any usage within your own code must be classified as experimental and completely nonportable to other JVMs.

## 16.6  SUMMARY

Getting Java code to talk to non-Java code presents some best of both worlds opportunities on the server. Thanks to JNI, we can combine the speed and capability of C/C++ code with the high-level constructs and developmental ease of Java. This comes with a cost, however. Coupling with native code, in any form, forces some restrictions on Java code that may or may not be acceptable to you.

Native code offers too many advantages to ignore, however. The ability to call down to the underlying platform, the ability to provide hooks for the underlying platform to call into the JVM, and the ability to integrate with the native platform's capabilities are simply too tempting to ignore or pass by. What's more, Java's portability loses some of its necessity when dealing with server-side applications, since the target system will already be known when the application is deployed, making it simpler to use JNI and native code.

## 16.7  ADDITIONAL READING

- Rob Gordon, *JNI By Example* (Addison-Wesley, 1998).

  The only book of its kind available, *JNI By Example* focuses specifically and exclusively on JNI. If you are a beginner to the JNI, or plan to do extensive work with it, this is a good place to go for an exhaustive discussion of JNI. This book also discusses another approach to making Java/NT-Service combinations.

- "Java Native Interface" specification, Sun Microsystems Inc. Available in the JDK 1.2 documentation set at jdk1.2\docs\guide\jni\spec\jniTOC.doc.html.

  Written for the JNI 1.1 release, this specification details the nuts and bolts of working with JNI. While terse in some places, and vague in others, this is the best reference work for JNI.

- "JNI Enhancements in JDK 1.2," Sun Microsystems Inc. Available in the JDK 1.2 documentation set at jdk1.2\docs\guide\jni\jni-12.html.

  This is the official Sun document detailing the enhancements made to JNI for the JDK 1.2 release, at least until the JNI Specification document is updated to reflect these changes.

C H A P T E R    1 7

# Monitoring

Processes fail. Exceptions are thrown. Threads die. Applications crash. It's a fact of a developer's life that bugs creep into a project, regardless of the amount of effort spent to find them. Unfortunately, this translates into a fact of life for the system administrator as well. Therein lies the cause for a significant amount of tension between developers and support staff that needs to be addressed.

Developers typically don't see the work necessary in managing, configuring, and monitoring an application. Developers are also usually under a tremendous amount of pressure to deliver the application. Because many (if not most) software development projects run longer than expected and cost more than predicted, the usual remedy is to cut features not seen as critical to the application's functionality.

Unfortunately, this arrangement usually comes back to haunt developers and administrators, because system administrators are responsible for ensuring the application is running at all times. System administrators constantly have to check the application's up status, either by physically looking on the monitor of the machine on which it is running, or by using the NT TaskManager (or by using "ps" under UNIX) to check the process's status.

## 17.1    IMPORTANCE GROWS

As the application's size and featureset grows, so does its importance to the enterprise. Usually by the time issues of configuration, control, and monitoring begin to arise in corporate meetings, it's too late to introduce them without requiring major recoding

510

or redesign. This in turn makes the developers balk at doing it, which makes administrators frustrated, which can in turn create further havoc later. All of this can be avoided if developers acknowledge that administrators need to be able to monitor the application, and code accordingly. If we can develop a generic system by which this monitoring can take place, so much the better: zero development along with zero administration.

Applications need monitoring at several levels. To start, administrators need to know when an application fails. Remember, unlike most consumer or user-interactive software, most server applications run in the background with no immediate pop-up access; in some cases, they run on machines without a monitor. Server applications simply cannot fail silently without notification. Silent failure means hours of headaches trying to trace back to the location of the failure, not to mention the reason for the failure and how it can be prevented in the future.

### 17.1.1 Liveness

One of the first basic questions any system administrator needs to be able to answer at any time is, "Are the servers still up and running?" An inability to answer this most basic query indicates the system administrators have no real control over the system. In a well-run server environment, administrators should be able to call up an application or tool and see some visible evidence the application is still running; unfortunately, few custom-developed applications give administrators that ability.

To developers, this may seem unnecessary. After all, if we check the process list, and the process is still there, it's still running, right? As reasonable as it may seem to a developer, this is usually not acceptable to the system administration group, for a simple reason: to check the system, the administrator must regularly poll the system to see if the process is still running. Just as polling in distributed objects is inefficient and a waste of network bandwidth, so too is polling to query the system every hour a waste of the system administrators' time and energy.

The HeartbeatService is a simple publish/subscribe service in much the same way as AWT/Swing components accept EventListeners and make callbacks. The HeartbeatService listens on a given socket port, accepting connections and storing them into a Vector. When the service is started, it creates its own PeriodicThread to send a String down each Socket connection when fired.

Note that this is only one implementation of this type service. The HeartbeatService (listing 17.1) could be written to use RMI, CORBA, COM/DCOM, or any other technology allowing for objects across processes to communicate with one another. An RMI or CORBA (or COM/DCOM) HeartbeatService could accept remote objects that implement an `IHeartbeatServiceListener` interface, and make periodic callbacks onto the Listener to reassure the object on the other side that all is well. A JMS-based HeartbeatService could periodically send a message to a waiting Queue for consumption by anybody subscribed to the Queue. Or, a mobile object

HeartbeatService could send a mobile object out with instructions to reach forth and touch any servers/mobile object clients to offer the same reassurance.

**Listing 17.1   Coding for HeartbeatService**

```java
package com.javageeks.gjas.services;

import java.io.IOException;
import java.io.OutputStreamWriter;
import java.io.PrintWriter;
import java.net.Socket;
import java.util.Enumeration;
import java.util.Vector;
import com.javageeks.thread.PeriodicThread;
import com.javageeks.gjas.ConfigProperties;
import com.javageeks.gjas.ConfigProperty;
import com.javageeks.gjas.ServerManager;

/**
 * HeartbeatService sends a message to any listening clients every
 * n milliseconds. Put basically, this is the same publish-
 * subscribe behavior found in a variety of other places, such as
 * AWT/Swing's Event-EventListener system.
 *
 * This concept isn't necessarily limited solely to socket-based
 * communication--this could easily be adapted to other forms of
 * communicative technology, like RMI, CORBA, JMS, Mobile Objects,
 * and so on.
 */
public class HeartbeatService
    extends SocketServer
{
    // Internal members
    private Vector m_listeners = new Vector();
    private PeriodicThread m_pingThread;
    private ConfigProperty propInterval =
        new ConfigProperty("interval", new Integer(5 * 1000),
                           "Milliseconds between heartbeats");
    private ConfigProperty propMessage =
        new ConfigProperty("message", new String("PING"),
                           "Message to send on heartbeat");

    private ConfigProperties configInfo =
        new ConfigProperties(super.getConfigInfo(),
                             new ConfigProperty[]
    {
        propInterval,
        propMessage
    });

    /**
     * Inner class to store the Socket and associated streams
     */
```

```
class Listener
{
    public Listener(Socket socket)
        throws IOException
    {
        m_socket = socket;
        toSocket = new PrintWriter(
            new OutputStreamWriter(m_socket.getOutputStream()));
    }

    public Socket m_socket;
    public PrintWriter toSocket;
}

/**
 * Inner class to do the actual work of sending out the
 * "ping" messages
 */
class Heartbeat
    implements Runnable
{
    public void run()
    {
        // Synchronize on m_listeners to prevent anyone
        // from modifying the Vector while we're iterating
        // through it sending ping messages; it probably
        // wouldn't cause a major problem if it *did* happen,
        // since Vector protects against corruption within
        // itself, but
        synchronized (m_listeners)
        {
            for (Enumeration enum = m_listeners.elements();
                 enum.hasMoreElements(); )
            {
                // Get next element
                Listener l = (Listener)enum.nextElement();

                // Send the ping message
                l.toSocket.println(
                    (String)propMessage.getValue());
                l.toSocket.flush();
            }
        }
    }
}

/**
 *
 */
public HeartbeatService(int port, int interval, String pingMsg)
{
    super(port);
```

```
        propInterval.setValue(new Integer(interval));
        propMessage.setValue(new String(pingMsg == null ? "PING" : pingMsg));
}
/**
 *
 */
public HeartbeatService()
{ }

/**
 *
 */
public void start()
    throws Exception
{

    // Call up to our base to allow SocketServer to do all its
    // work on our behalf
    super.start();

    // Start our ping thread
    m_pingThread =
        new PeriodicThread(new Heartbeat(),
                        ((Integer)propInterval.getValue()).intValue());
    m_pingThread.start();
}
/**
 *
 */
public void stop()
    throws Exception
{

    m_pingThread.interrupt();
    super.stop();
}

/**
 *
 */
public ConfigProperties getConfigInfo()
{
    return configInfo;
}
/**
 *
 */
public void setConfigInfo(ConfigProperties props)
{

    configInfo.set(props);

    // Check and reset interval value if different
    if (m_pingThread != null &&
        m_pingThread.getInterval() !=
        ((Integer)propInterval.getValue()).intValue())
```

```
        {
            m_pingThread.setInterval(((
                Integer)propInterval.getValue()).intValue());
        }
    }

    /**
     * Derived services must override this method. Once a client has
     * connected to us, this method is called to "do the work" of
     * handling the connection.
     */
    public void serve(Socket socket)
        throws Exception
    {
        // Add this Socket to the list of Sockets we must broadcast
        // the "ping" message down
        m_listeners.addElement(new Listener(socket));
    }
}
```

Notice how using several of the components developed earlier makes the development of this service almost trivial. To start, HeartbeatService extends SocketServer, which provides the basic GJAS socket capabilities. HeartbeatService uses a Periodic-Thread to do the every-*n*-milliseconds broadcast of the ping message, and extends the SocketServer's `start` and `stop` methods to manage the thread's lifetime. The HeartbeatService also establishes two new properties to the Service, `"interval"`, to know how often (in milliseconds) to send the message, and `"message"`, to know what text to send down the socket.

In its current implementation, HeartbeatService assumes that any client connecting up to its associated port will be interested in one and only one heartbeat signal; each HeartbeatService will send one and only one signal at a time, given by the `"message"` property (defaulting to `"PING"`). However, it wouldn't be too difficult to make this a multicast service. This would imply that multiple heartbeats (messages) would be managed by this service. One option would be to simply broadcast multiple messages to all clients, in true multicast fashion; clients would then have to examine the text of the message received to determine if it was the heartbeat in which it was interested. This has the advantage of being easier to code, but requires more work on the part of the heartbeat client. A second approach would be to have the client, upon connection, send some kind of identifying message to the HeartbeatService, telling the server in which heartbeat(s) the client was interested, and have the server track listeners separately for each heartbeat signal. More work for the server, less for the client.

HeartbeatService stores its connections to clients in an inner class, Listener, which contains both the Socket instance it received from the HeartbeatService's `serve()` method, and the PrintWriter instance it constructs using the Socket's output stream. These Listener instances are stored inside the Vector m_listeners. A second inner class,

Heartbeat, implements the Runnable interface needed by the PeriodicThread, and does the actual work of broadcasting the message down the sockets. The run method in Heartbeat is the only place where explicit synchronization is used throughout the HeartbeatService. Remember, Vector provides its own synchronization, which guards against data corruption should multiple threads attempt to access the Vector at the same time. This in turn protects HeartbeatService against being corrupted should multiple threads connect to the port simultaneously. The only reason Heartbeat explicitly locks out others from modifying the m_listeners Vector during broadcast is to prevent some potentially awkward situations; for example, it's entirely possible a client connecting to the HeartbeatService could receive a ping message before it even finishes the connection steps on its end, if it happens to connect (and be added to the m_listeners Vector) just as the broadcast is going out. It's an unlikely scenario, and performance-minded implementors could remove the synchronization block without introducing corruption.

HeartbeatService can be used in one of two fashions—as a JVM-wide monitor and as a Service-specific monitor. In the first case, the ServerManager, when started, loads an instance of HeartbeatService and starts broadcasting. So long as the Server-Manager JVM remains alive, the HeartbeatService continues to beat. In the second case, a Service can create an instance of the HeartbeatService, and add it to the Server-Manager. Assuming that the Service provides the HeartbeatService with the Thread to use, which we presume in turn comes from the Service's own ThreadGroup, the HeartbeatService will give a relatively good idea of when the Service itself dies or is hung. Granted, it's not a perfect monitor, since one Thread in a JVM can be completely blocked without blocking others, so the HeartbeatService could keep beating while the application blocked indefinitely. However, if more accurate monitoring were desired, the Service could subclass HeartbeatService to check against some vital statistic within the parent Service to ensure it was still running; if that statistic hasn't changed, then it doesn't send out the signal, thus generating some concern on the recipients' end.

To prove the mechanism, start up an instance of the ServerManager with a HeartbeatService instance running within it on port 8090 with an interval of five seconds. Once the ServerManager finishes initialization, fire up a console window and run the standard Client, connecting to port 8090. From that point, no further typing is necessary—every five seconds, a ping message shows up on the console. Create additional Clients on the same port, disconnect some, and the message still goes out to anyone listening, every five seconds.

### Heartbeat listening

Broadcasting the Heartbeat is only half the solution, however. In order for the heartbeat to have any meaning, there has to be something at the other end, listening for it and detecting when it fails. The key problem here is the fact that a single missed heartbeat ping can't be immediately assumed to be a failure on the part of the server;

networks can commonly lose network packets and require a resend. The following code demonstrates how to listen on a Socket for up to five seconds for a "ping" message, and to give up listening after three missed ping messages:

```java
public class HeartbeatClient
{
    public static void main(String[] args)
        throws Exception
    {
        if (args.length < 1)
        {
            System.out.println("Usage: java Client <hostname:port>");
            return;
        }

        // Parse out hostname and port
        String host;
        Integer port;
        host = args[0].substring(0, args[0].indexOf(":"));
        port = new Integer(args[0].substring(args[0].indexOf(":")+1,
                                            args[0].length()));

        System.out.println("Connecting to " + host + ":" + port);

        Socket socket = new Socket(host, port.intValue());
        BufferedReader fromSocket =
            new BufferedReader(new InputStreamReader(socket.getInputStream()));

        // We want to block for only 5 seconds waiting for input
        // (this would be programmatically controlled in other
        // more flexible systems)
        socket.setSoTimeout(5000);

        // Wait for up to three missed pings before giving up
        int giveUpCount = 0;
        while (giveUpCount < 3)
        {
            try
            {
                String line = fromSocket.readLine();
                if (line == null)
                    giveUpCount++;
                else if (line.equals("PING"))
                    giveUpCount = 0;
            }
            catch (java.io.InterruptedIOException ex)
            {
                giveUpCount++;
            }
        }

        System.out.println("Giving up--the heartbeat's not there anymore");
    }
}
```

The key to the client comes in two parts. The first is the Socket's `setSoTimeout` method, which dictates how long the InputStream attached to the Socket will block waiting for input. Without this, the InputStream (and any Readers or InputStreams wrapped around it) will block forever waiting for input from the server. While it would be possible (through use of Threads and timeouts and the like) to achieve the same behavior without using Socket timeouts, it's far simpler to set the timeout and let Java throw an exception (`java.io.InterruptedIOException`) if a timeout occurs. Note that we also have to test the returned line for a null value before testing its contents. This is because if the server process (GJAS) terminates, the fromSocket's `readLine` call will generate an infinte number of null results.

The second part is the `giveUpCount` variable. For a variety of reasons, a single ping might be lost without cause for alarm—normal network packet loss, for example. Because we don't want to abandon hope right away, we wait up to three missed pings before assuming the HeartbeatService died or is no longer in contact with the recipient. If we could be guaranteed that delivery of messages across the network (intranet or Internet), then this would be unnecessary. The other alternative to this approach would be to wait up to fifteen seconds (instead of the five hardcoded into the above client) for a signal before surrendering.

## HeartbeatListenerClient and HeartbeatListener

Because coding something like the foregoing could get repetitive and awkward after the second or third time recoding it, let's work to make it into a single reusable component.

The key to a successful reusable component will be its ability to operate in either an asynchronous or synchronous fashion. Under most circumstances, clients will want the HeartbeatListenerClient component to handle the details of listening for the heartbeat signals without blocking, but occasionally a client will want to block. The easiest way to accomplish this sort of dual-sided behavior is to have the client object implement the `Runnable` interface—that way, clients can either pass the Client object into a Thread for asynchronous execution, or call its `run` method directly for synchronous behavior.

The second part to the asynchronous nature of the HeartbeatListenerClient is to establish a method by which the HeartbeatListenerClient (listing 17.2) can notify its owner/client of the pings. It does this by creating an "event" interface, which interested parties must implement in order to receive Heartbeat events, just as interested parties must implement an AWT/Swing EventListener to receive Java's GUI messages. The HeartbeatListener event interface is simple:

```
public interface HeartbeatListener
{
    public void onHeartbeatPing(String msg);
    public void onHeartbeatFail(String msg);
}
```

The first method, onPing, is called with the ping message each time a ping comes in from the HeartbeatService; normally, clients solely watching for heartbeat failure will simply ignore this call. Clients listening to more than one heartbeat will need to examine the String parameter in onPing to determine which HeartbeatService sent it, while clients listening on multicast HeartbeatServices will need to examine it as well to determine which heartbeat the ping is for.

In the event the Heartbeat is determined to have failed (that is, interval seconds went by retryCount times without a signal from the source), the Listener's onHeart-beatFail method is called. Note that the Heartbeat message that should have arrived is passed in as the msg parameter to onHeartbeatFail, again so as to give implementations a chance to differentiate one heartbeat failure from another (listing 17.2).

**Listing 17.2   Coding for HeartbeatListenerClient**

```
public class HeartbeatListenerClient
    implements Runnable
{
    // Internal members
    //
    private String m_host;
    private int m_port;
    private String m_pingMsg;
    private int m_interval;
    private int m_giveUpCount;
    private Thread m_thread = null;
    private Vector m_listeners = new Vector();

    /**
     * "Complete" constructor--initialize with all given values
     */
    public HeartbeatListenerClient(String host, int port,
                                   String msg, int interval,
                                   int giveUpCount, Thread thread)
    {
        m_host = host;
        m_port = port;
        m_pingMsg = msg;
        m_interval = interval;
        m_giveUpCount = giveUpCount;
        m_thread = thread;
    }
    /**
     * Convenience constructor--assumes defaults of "PING", 15
     * seconds, and 3 attempts
     */
    public HeartbeatListenerClient(String host, int port)
    {
        this(host, port, "PING", 15 * 1000, 3, null);
    }
```

```java
/**
 * Add a HeartbeatListener to the list of interested parties
 */
public void addListener(HeartbeatListener listener)
{
    m_listeners.addElement(listener);
}
/**
 * Remove a HeartbeatListener from the list of notification
 * targets on heartbeat pings or failures
 */
public void removeListener(HeartbeatListener listener)
{
    m_listeners.remove(listener);
}

/**
 * Start listening for heartbeat messages
 */
public void startListening()
{
    if (m_thread == null)
    {
        m_thread = new Thread(this);
    }

    m_thread.start();
}
/**
 * Cease listening for heartbeat messages
 */
public void stopListening()
{
    m_thread.interrupt();
}

/**
 *
 */
public void run()
{
    Socket socket = null;
    try
    {
        socket = new Socket(m_host, m_port);
        BufferedReader fromSocket = new BufferedReader(
            new InputStreamReader(socket.getInputStream()));

        // We want to block for only 5 seconds waiting for input
        // (this would be programmatically controlled in other
        // more flexible systems)
        socket.setSoTimeout(m_interval);

        // Wait for up to three missed pings before giving up
```

```java
            int giveUpCount = 0;
            while (giveUpCount < m_giveUpCount)
            {
                try
                {
                    String line = fromSocket.readLine();
                    if (line == null)
                        giveUpCount++;
                    else if (line.equals(m_pingMsg))
                    {
                        // Reset giveUpCount; we got a message
                        giveUpCount = 0;

                        // Broadcast the message on to our listeners
                        for (Enumeration enum =
                                m_listeners.elements();
                                enum.hasMoreElements(); )
                        {
                            HeartbeatListener l =
                                (HeartbeatListener)enum.nextElement();

                            l.onHeartbeatPing(line);
                        }
                    }
                }
                catch (java.io.InterruptedIOException ex)
                {
                    giveUpCount++;
                }
            }

            // If we got here, it's because we gave up
            for (Enumeration enum = m_listeners.elements();
                    enum.hasMoreElements(); )
            {
                HeartbeatListener l =
                    (HeartbeatListener)enum.nextElement();

                l.onHeartbeatFail();
            }
        }
        catch (Exception ex)
        {
            // Not a very reusable option, but the only way to know
            // when an Exception is thrown, since we can't throw it
            // out of run (Runnable.run has no "throws" clause)
            ex.printStackTrace();
        }
    }

    /**
     * Test driver; for testing purposes only.
     */
    public static void main(String[] args)
```

```
        {
            if (args.length < 1)
            {
                System.out.println("Usage: java HeartbeatListenerClient"
                                + " <hostname:port>");
                return;
            }

            // Parse out hostname and port
            String host = args[0].substring(0, args[0].indexOf(":"));
            Integer port =
                new Integer(args[0].substring(args[0].indexOf(":")+1,
                                            args[0].length()));

            System.out.println("Connecting to " + host + ":" + port);

            HeartbeatListenerClient client =
                new HeartbeatListenerClient(host, port.intValue(),
                                        "PING", 15 * 1000, 3, null);

            client.addListener(new HeartbeatListener()
            {
                public void onHeartbeatPing(String pingMsg)
                {
                    System.out.println("PING!: " + pingMsg);
                }
                public void onHeartbeatFail()
                {
                    System.out.println("Heartbeat's stopped!");
                }
            });

            client.startListening();
        }
    }
```

There are a couple of items to note in this implementation.

First, HeartbeatListenerClient is Thread friendly. Because it implements Runnable as an interface, users can place the HeartbeatListenerClient instance into their own Thread instance, let HeartbeatListenerClient create its own Thread to use, or call the run method directly. This flexibility means that users can control the circumstances in which the component does its work.

Secondly, HeartbeatListenerClient provides two methods, startListening and stopListening, to encapsulate the start and termination of the listening Thread. We use the Thread interrupt method to break the infinite loop in HeartbeatListenerClient's run method, instead of the deprecated stop method, as discussed in chapter 4. Take care when using HeartbeatListenerClient for repeated start-stop cycles; although the Win32 and Solaris implementations of the JVM permit this, other JVMs may not be so forgiving. Since an application usually wishes to listen for a Heartbeat source for the duration of the client's lifetime, this normally won't be a problem.

Thirdly, HeartbeatListenerClient is inherently unicast—a single Heartbeat-ListenerClient can only listen for heartbeats from a single source. This could be modified, allowing HeartbeatListenerClient to listen for multiple heartbeats, by having multiple Threads, each one listening to a single heartbeat. (One Thread couldn't listen to more than one heartbeat, since the interval times may be different, and the Thread will block the entire time listening for a message, thus serializing the heartbeat-listening process. This means that if Thread One is listening to Heartbeats A and B, while listening for A, it can't simultaneously be listening for B—it can only listen for B once it has received the message from A, or A has timed out.) Implementing this properly would likely require the use of one of Lea's ThreadFactory implementations from chapter 4, so as to give users better control over how the HeartbeatListenerClient creates and manages the Threads.

Lastly, HeartbeatListenerClient, on a heartbeat failure, does not stop listening. Instead, it will continue to listen, for up to the full interval period, for further heartbeat messages. Should a HeartbeatListener wish to avoid this, it needs to remove itself from the HeartbeatListenerClient's listener list. Correspondingly, HeartbeatListenerClient also continues to listen for heartbeat messages even if it has no listeners registered with it. This is a waste of CPU cycles and network bandwidth, but can be modified easily enough for those who wish to.

## 17.1.2 Notification

Now that it's been established that we can monitor the liveness of an application via the HeartbeatService, we have to decide what to do in the event the Heartbeat fails. The natural answer is simple: Tell somebody. The problem is, how? What provides the best, asynchronous way by which to notify a human or other process (which will in turn notify a human, presumably) that there is an issue that needs to be addressed and/or resolved?

A variety of methods are available; the following list is just a partial collection of ideas:

- *Event log*
  The heartbeat failure is simply logged to file (or perhaps, using JNI, NT's Event-Log or the UNIX syslog daemon), and left there for an administrator to find later when perusing the logs. While this is a good second-line option, since it can provide as much detail as the log can handle, it's not an ideal candidate as the only notification option, since it requires the administrator to proactively look in the logs every x minutes/hours/days. System administrators are just like developers—usually too much to do with not enough time to do it in. Asking them to faithfully check a logfile at a regular interval is usually a recipe for disaster, either for the administrators, the developers, or, more often, both.

- *File, database, etc.*
  This is a cheaper version of the Event log approach. Instead of writing the failure to the system event log, the notification is written to a standard text file, or a database row, or some other form of permanent storage. This, like the Event log

approach, results in a passive system—administrators must actively poll the storage system (look at the file, query the database for new rows, etc.) for any notifications posted. Where it has an advantage over the Event log approach is in its ability to use the same storage system the software system is using for other purposes. For example, an RDBMS-centralized application may want to store notifications to the RDBMS in order to keep all system-related information, both data and these notification (and other administrative) messages, in a single place.

- *Email*
Sending an email to a system administrator is probably one of the most effective ways of getting attention. The SMTP protocol for sending email is relatively simple to use, and Java's recent JavaMail extension makes it even simpler. The email can contain as much information as the notification client can handle, and system administrators can react immediately or not, depending on their priority schedule at the time. The problem with email, however, is that it's not a guaranteed service—email is never guaranteed to arrive at its destination (owing to lost packets or down mail gateways in between), so it's possible that a system administrator would never receive a critical warning. Further, unless a generic account is set up, the target email account must be kept updated as personnel enter and leave the IT group, change responsibilities, or even change names due to marriage or legal proceedings. All of this means a bit more administrative work to keep everything running smoothly.

- *Alphanumeric pager*
With many pager systems having online access for sending messages to the pager, it becomes relatively feasible to access the online pager-send system from within Java code, building a short message, and firing it off to the pager. This has the advantage of being somewhat more reliable, but it's still not an absolute guarantee that the message will be received by the individual wearing the pager. What's more, most pagers are somewhat limited in the information they can receive, so full details of the problem can't be sent. Still, in conjunction with an email, this can be a very effective, yet not-so-intrusive, solution.

- *Phone call*
With the advent of the Java Sound API, and the forthcoming Java Telephony API, this isn't as farfetched as it might first sound. The JTAPI would be used to open a phone circuit to the system administrator's mobile, work, or home phone, and the Java Sound API could play a prerecorded message describing the problem. This has the advantage of being almost completely reliable, since the phone call is, for the most part, a guaranteed service, and the system will know when the call has been successfully received, either by a human or phone-mail recording system. Depending on the sophistication of JTAPI and the phone system, it might actually demand a code response entered by touch-tone keypad, to ensure a human received the message.

- *Screen pop*

  The phone call option might be technically interesting, but of more practical use is the screen pop technique. In a nutshell, when a heartbeat listener realizes the heartbeat it's been listening for has faltered, it can simply pop up a dialog box or other window, perhaps playing a sound at the same time, describing the problem. Novell's Netware is by far the best example of this approach, slapping up a dialog box on every machine attached to the network in the event that an attached volume runs low on disk space. The recipients of the message can choose to take whatever action is feasible for them, from simply clicking OK to make the dialog go away, to acknowledging the dialog and then fixing the problem. It's more intrusive than the email approach (since the dialog pops up on top of whatever applications are currently running, demanding a bit more attention than just email), but still less intrusive than a page or a phone call.

These certainly aren't the sum total of ideas, but they give us a good place from which to start working.

All of the following example demonstrated Services use the standard socket-based HeartbeatService; it would therefore be relatively simple to adapt these to use RMI, CORBA, or DCOM, as necessary.

### LogListener

This is a simple HeartbeatListener that writes the failure messages to a text file, and optionally writes out the date/time of each heartbeat message received (listing 17.3). Most clients won't want the heartbeat written to file; if the heartbeat interval is every five seconds, over the period of a single day the log file will be filled with 17,280 messages! Having to wade through all of these every day (or, more likely, 720 every hour) is error-prone as eyes glaze over seeing only what they expect to see. More likely, however, the log file will never be looked at until a failure, at which point administrators can consult it to determine the time (approximate, to the nearest "interval" seconds) the heartbeat failed.

**Listing 17.3   Code for LogListener**

```
public class LogListener
    implements HeartbeatListener
{
    // Internal members
    //
    private PrintWriter m_writer;
    private boolean m_verbose = false;

    /**
     * Constructor
     */
    public LogListener(String filename, boolean verbose)
        throws java.io.IOException
    {
```

```java
        m_writer =
            new PrintWriter(
                new FileOutputStream(filename));
        m_verbose = verbose;
    }
    /**
     * Return the verbosity of the Listener; if set to true, the
     * LogListener will write out onHeartbeatPing messages to the log
     */
    public boolean getVerbose()
    {
        return m_verbose;
    }
    /**
     * Set the verbosity of the Listener; if set to true, the
     * LogListener will write out onHeartbeatPing messages to the log
     */
    public void setVerbose(boolean verbose)
    {
        m_verbose = verbose;
    }

    /**
     * HeartbeatListener method. Received each time a 'ping' is
     * received from the HeartbeatService
     */
    public void onHeartbeatPing(String msg)
    {
        if (m_verbose)
        {
            m_writer.println(new Date() + ": " + msg + " received.");
            m_writer.flush();
        }
    }
    /**
     * HeartbeatListener method. Called when the
     * HeartbeatListenerClient determines the heartbeat has failed
     */
    public void onHeartbeatFail(String msg)
    {
        m_writer.println(new Date() + ": ***Heartbeat failure: " +
                         msg);
        m_writer.flush();
    }
}
```

As you can see, the implementation is fairly simple: open a FileOutputStream on construction (creating the file if necessary), create the HeartbeatListenerClient, and register itself with the HeartbeatListenerClient. If the HeartbeatListenerClient is provided in the constructor, then it doesn't create a HeartbeatListenerClient instance, but instead uses the one passed in.

We can also create a LogListenerService (listing 17.4), which is a GJAS Service-implementing class that simply creates a LogListener, using the properties given to the LogListenerService, creates a HeartbeatListenerClient private to itself on `start`, and starts listening for messages.

**Listing 17.4   Code for LogListenerService**

```java
public class LogListenerService
    implements com.javageeks.gjas.Service
{
    // Internal members
    //
    private HeartbeatListenerClient m_hcl;
    private String m_state = STOPPED;
    private ConfigProperty m_file =
        new ConfigProperty("file", "",
                            "Filename to write messages to");
    private ConfigProperty m_verbose =
        new ConfigProperty("verbose", new Boolean(false),
                            "Write all messages, or just failures?");
    private ConfigProperty m_host =
        new ConfigProperty("host", "",
                            "Host to listen to");
    private ConfigProperty m_port =
        new ConfigProperty("port", new Integer(0),
                            "Port on host to connect to");
    private ConfigProperties m_configInfo =
        new ConfigProperties(new ConfigProperty[]
        {
            m_file, m_verbose, m_host, m_port
        });

    /**
     * Start the Service.
     */
    public void start()
        throws Exception
    {
        m_state = STARTING;

        if (m_hcl == null)
        {
            // Get ConfigProperty values
            String file = (String)m_file.getValue();
            boolean verbose =
                ((Boolean)m_verbose.getValue()).booleanValue();
            String host = (String)m_host.getValue();
            int port = ((Integer)m_port.getValue()).intValue();

            m_hcl = new HeartbeatListenerClient(host, port);
```

```
            m_hcl.addListener(new LogListener(file, verbose));
        }

        m_hcl.startListening();

        m_state = RUNNING;
    }
    /**
     * Stop the Service.
     */
    public void stop()
        throws Exception
    {
        m_state = STOPPING;

        m_hcl.stopListening();

        m_hcl = null;

        m_state = STOPPED;
    }
    /**
     * Pause the Service.
     */
    public void pause()
        throws Exception
    { }
    /**
     * Resume the Service.
     */
    public void resume()
        throws Exception
    { }
    /**
     * Get the current state of the Service; must be one of the
     * following types: STOPPED, STARTING, RUNNING, STOPPING,
     * PAUSING, PAUSED, or RESUMING.
     */
    public String getState()
    {
        return m_state;
    }
    /**
     * Return a String uniquely identifying this instance of the
     * Service; this String must be unique not just to the Service
     * class, but to the Service instance itself. Suggested return
     * format is something like:
     *
     * String instanceID = this.getClass().getName() + ":" +
     * getClassVersion() + ":" + System.currentTimeMillis();
     *
     * Note that maintaining an "instance count" of the number of
     * instances of this class will fail, since all instances will
     * be maintained within their own ClassLoader, and static
```

```
        * members are stored on a per-ClassLoader basis.
        */
    public String getInstanceID()
        throws Exception
    {
        return "LogListenerService:1.0.0:" +
            System.currentTimeMillis();
    }

    /**
     *
     */
    public ConfigProperties getConfigInfo()
    {
        return m_configInfo;
    }
    /**
     *
     */
    public void setConfigInfo(ConfigProperties props)
    {
        // Read the settings if they've changed
        if ( !((String)m_configInfo.get("host").getValue()).equals(
                ((String)props.get("host").getValue())) ||
            ((Integer)m_configInfo.get("port").getValue()).intValue() !=
                ((Integer)props.get("port").getValue()).intValue() ||
            !((String)m_configInfo.get("file").getValue()).equals(
                ((String)props.get("file").getValue())) ||
            ((Boolean)m_configInfo.get(
                "verbose").getValue()).booleanValue() !=
            ((Boolean)props.get("verbose").getValue()).booleanValue())
        {
            try
            {
                // Stop the Service
                ServerManager.log("Stopping Service: reconfigure");
                stop();

                // Read the new values
                ServerManager.log("Re-reading config values");
                m_configInfo.set(props);

                // Restart the Service
                ServerManager.log("Restarting Service");
                start();
            }
            catch (Exception ex)
            {
                ServerManager.error(ex);
            }
        }
    }
}
```

The Service itself is very simple: create a HeartbeatListenerClient, register a LogListener with it, and start listening on start, stop listening on stop. It is not overly complex as Services go, and it provides us with persistent storage of the heartbeat's liveness.

### OutputStreamListener

In truth, LogListener is really a specific form of listener—one that listens for heartbeats and writes the results to a file. Since a file is a specific form of OutputStream (remember, FileOutputStream extends OutputStream), we can create a more generic form of LogListener by taking in an OutputStream instance instead of a filename to open. This then allows OutputStreamListener (listing 17.5) to write its output messages to any output sink to which Java can write, including the console.

**Listing 17.5    Code for OutputStreamListener**

```java
public class OutputStreamListener
    implements HeartbeatListener
{
    // Internal members
    //
    private PrintWriter m_writer;
    private boolean m_verbose = false;

    /**
     * Constructor
     */
    public OutputStreamListener(OutputStream out, boolean verbose)
        throws java.io.IOException
    {
        m_writer = new PrintWriter(out);
        m_verbose = verbose;
    }
    /**
     * Constructor
     */
    public OutputStreamListener(PrintStream outStream, boolean verbose)
        throws java.io.IOException
    {
        m_writer = new PrintWriter(outStream);
        m_verbose = verbose;
    }
    /**
     * Constructor
     */
    public OutputStreamListener(PrintWriter writer, boolean verbose)
        throws java.io.IOException
    {
        m_writer = writer;
        m_verbose = verbose;
    }
```

```
/**
 * Return the verbosity of the Listener; if set to true, the
 * listener will write out onHeartbeatPing messages to the log
 */
public boolean getVerbose()
{
    return m_verbose;
}
/**
 * Set the verbosity of the Listener; if set to true, the
 * listener will write out onHeartbeatPing messages to the log
 */
public void setVerbose(boolean verbose)
{
    m_verbose = verbose;
}

/**
 * HeartbeatListener method. Received each time a 'ping' is
 * received from the HeartbeatService
 */
public void onHeartbeatPing(String msg)
{
    if (m_verbose)
    {
        m_writer.println(new Date() + ": " + msg + " received.");
        m_writer.flush();
    }
}
/**
 * HeartbeatListener method. Called when the
 * HeartbeatListenerClient determines the heartbeat has failed
 */
public void onHeartbeatFail(String msg)
{
    m_writer.println(new Date() + ": ***Heartbeat failure: " +
                        msg);
    m_writer.flush();
}
}
```

Note how OutputStreamListener takes three forms: one constructor taking an Ouput-Stream instance, one taking a PrintStream instance, and one taking a PrintWriter instance. This is to permit the maximum flexibility in the OutputStream addressed.

We could probably drop LogListener in favor of this more generic class, or at least make LogListener extend this one and provide file-specific behaviors and/or methods. This is an implementation detail, however, and has no real bearing on its usage by clients.

The real advantage in this class is that because it deals with OutputStream instances, we can do the standard Java Stream-chaining approach to provide additional functionality—for example, we could use a TeeOutputStream (in com.javageeks.io) to send the output to multiple sinks, or a FilterOutputStream to add additional output to the written message, and so on.[1] For example, using the OutputStreamListener to write to console would be as simple as:

```
HeartbeatListenerClient hcl = ...;
hcl.addListener(new OutputStreamListener(System.out, false));
hcl.startListening();
```

OutputStreamListenerService is given, since the complexities of constructing an OutputStream to set into the OutputStreamListener are too complex for the configuration-management system; any such construction has to come from within Java code.

### NTEventLogListener

This is the native version of the Event log option from above. When the onHeartbeatPing and onHeartbeatFail messages are received, we use JNI code to write to the NT Event Log. The code is remarkably similar (at least at the Java layers) to the above LogListener or OutputStreamListener classes, so it's not shown here; in the same vein, the code for NTEventLogListenerService is also not displayed here. Both classes are given in the source code available on the publisher's website: www.manning.com/neward3.

### MailNotificationService

Another approach is to send an SMTP mail message to a system administrator (or other designated support email account) when a Heartbeat fails. Sending an email via SMTP is actually a straightforward application of sending text over a socket to an SMTP server, but, again, the JavaMail API, is by far the better way to go. Email target address, subject line, and body of the message can all be specified as parameters to the Service, or the Service might be developed with the appropriate properties hard-coded. The first approach allows for greater reuse of the MailNotificationService, the second permits greater customization of the message.

Using JavaMail is beyond the scope of this book; using straight sockets is simpler, but numerous Java classes and components (including the undocumented[2] sun.net.smtp.SmtpClient class) abound for simplifying this task. Unless the emails being sent include MIME attachments, it's about equal between using a home-grown

---

[1] For example, wrap an HTMLFilterOutputStream (one that translates each line of text into an HTML paragraph by placing <P> and </P> before and after each line/carriage-return) around a FileOutputStream, and point the FileOutputStream to write to a file in a Web-server's HTML repository, and you have a crude but effective form of Web-browser-based monitoring.

[2] Elliott Rusty Harold covers its use in his book *Java Secrets*, from IDG Press.

SMTP client class, and using JavaMail. But if there's a choice, go with JavaMail—it's the new Java standard for doing any form of electronic messaging from within Java, and spending the time to learn it will pay off later.

### Concluding thoughts

All of the above listeners use a standard socket approach; each one could also, in turn, be written to use RMI, CORBA, or DCOM as the transport mechanism by which the heartbeat message is broadcast to the listeners. There will be times, in fact, especially as regards CORBA or DCOM, when this sort of multiplicity of transport will be useful— for example, we may want a notification client to be written in Visual Basic, or in C++.

Writing a parallel group of Listeners and ListenerServices, however, can be extremely tiring and error-prone. If a bug is found in one and fixed, then that same fix needs to be applied to its peer using a different protocol. In fact, the only difference between a LogListener and a LogRMIListener or LogCORBAListener or LogDCOM-Listener is the actual transport mechanism used to receive the ping from the Heartbeat producer; alternatively, the listener itself could be distributed, meaning the transport mechanism is what is used to make the onHeartbeatPing or onHeartbeatFail call. In fact, these two could be combined, so a given HeartbeatListenerClient could receive the pings via RMI and inform its registered HeartbeatListeners via CORBA. Typically, variation in both the ping transport and the listener transport will be unnecessary, but not inconceivable.

Should this be the case, the actual protocols involved should be broken out into separate class hierarchies, with the actual protocol used passed in at run time:

```
HeartbeatListenerClient hcl =
    new HeartbeatListenerClient(
        new HeartbeatSocketTransport("localhost", 8080),
        new HeartbeatListenerRMITransport());
```

In the above snippet, for example, we create a HeartbeatListenerClient that would attempt to receive pings from a socket-based server listening on port 8080, and would send notifications out to listeners via RMI.

## 17.2  SUMMARY

The need to monitor applications, both for their liveness and their current statistical numbers, is a necessary part of most server-side applications. With a client-side application, liveness is easy to detect—if the application is running, the client can see it and interact with it. The server-side is a different story—the server typically runs in stand-alone fashion, with no human feedback to indicate failure or death.

Developing a system that provides this information in as generic a fashion as possible serves two aims: zero administration and zero development. By reducing the amount of work required to administer the application by providing mechanisms by which administrators can check the liveness of the application, we make it easier to check, as well as somewhat proactive in notifying necessary personnel in the event of a failure.

By no means are the discussed techniques the only, or even the best, available for monitoring of your application. In some cases, simple "is it alive?" questions are not sufficient—statistical numbers must be generated and tracked to allow for a measurement of the application's performance. This is where embedding an HTTP/servlet engine into your application pays off. Your server application simply opens a Server-Socket, receives the HTTP requests from across the system, gathers the statistics, and reports them. (Ideally, the report format would be in XML, with an XSL stylesheet to transform the XML to HTML for human consumption, so that automated processes could also gather the data.) Nevertheless, in many cases, a simple heartbeat ping will go a long way toward making your system administrators like you—and as a result, is something that should rank high on your list of extras to deliver.

# epilogue

Whew! It's been a long ride, one which I hope you enjoyed as much as I did in the writer's seat. Java as an enterprise development tool is an exciting concept, one which offers us, as developers, incredible opportunities. Just take a look at the laundry list of Java Enterprise APIs available at the end of 1999 (the items not explained here are covered thoroughly in this book):

- *Enterprise Java Beans*
  The EJB specification is, if we measure by the amount of material written on it, the most interesting one within the J2EE system. Offering the ability to factor all of our business logic into a common area, EJB also was the first to differentiate between the roles people play during the development of a project: component designer, application assembler, and so on. In many ways, however, EJB was simply an outgrowth of the Servlet specification, as people began to realize ways of using servlets (and the accompanying load-balancing features offered by some servlet engines) to encapsulate business logic away from the client tier.

- *Java Transaction API* and *Java Transaction Service*
  We're not dealing with relational databases anymore. Object databases, CORBA object systems, RMI object systems, even the odd COM component all find their way into the heterogeneous system found in many environments today. Unfortunately, the need for guaranteed transactions within the system has grown with the numbers of storage and logic systems within the enterprise. It's not enough to guarantee that the transaction will either entirely succeed or entirely fail within just the RDBMS portion. Now, systems are requiring that the transactions to both the CORBA and the RMI system, as well as the RDBMS, be either entirely successful or entirely rolled back. JTA and JTS work to provide that. JTA/JTS, for example, would make it possible for the business objects layer to store/update changes to both the HashtableModel and RDBMSModel instances, or throw those changes away, without requiring extensive coding on the part of the developer.

- *CORBA* (through JavaIDL)
- *RMI*
- *JDBC*
- *Servlets* and *Java Server Pages (JSP)*

  In many ways, this is where people really began to consider Java as a server-side enterprise development tool. RMI, JDBC, and the other APIs from 1.1 were all slanted toward using applets as the working environment, until Servlets became available as part of the Sun Jeeves web server. Once people began to realize the capability of the thin-client model, Servlets became more and more popular. It is safe to say that servlets reinvented the entire client/server model.

- *JavaMail*

  JavaMail provides messaging access—email, basically, both sending and receiving—to Java. Now your enterprise systems can send and receive email, opening up entirely new options in the handling and routing of information. Client application in the enterprise system crashes? Have a `try`/`catch` block around all the code in `main`, and mail the developers the stack trace from the Exception object. Users (internal or external) want to be notified as their request is handled each step of the way? Fire an email. The options are endless.

- *JavaHelp*

  Having a good help system is even more important in an enterprise system than in a commercial off-the-shelf package. Because of the close proximity of developers to the customers for whom this system is intended, training and user documentation tend to be shelved, in favor of contacting the developers directly when a problem occurs. By providing a well-written, well-machined help system, enterprise developers can avoid phone calls from "stupid" users and get back to doing what they do best—writing code.

- *Java Activation Framework*
- *Java Naming and Directory Interface (JNDI)*
- *Java Messaging Service (JMS)*
- *Java2 Enterprise Edition (J2EE) specification*

  This is, of course, the document that tries to tie all of the above into a single, unified whole. Whether or not it will succeed is still the subject of some debate, and will be for some time, but to ignore it entirely would be the same as writing off the Internet as a passing fad.

And all this is on top of the list of functionality found within the Java2 Standard Edition environment, such as CORBA, Reflection, Threads, and so on.

The point of all this is simple—even before the J2EE specification, even before the EJB specification, Java was a useful server-side application platform. As we've proved ithin these pages, it's possible to build fully functional, highly componentized applications without J2EE or EJB. Does that imply that all applications will not want to use EJB? Absolutely not. EJB is a highly useful technology, and to dismiss it out-of-hand would be as much of a crime as to blindly utilize it everywhere.

Remember, my four goals for readers of this book:

- *Understand some of the basic concepts that go into an application server*
  By demonstrating how Threads and ClassLoaders can work together to provide a dynamic Service-loading/executing capability, you can now understand how the core parts of an EJB or J2EE Application Server works. It's also easy to see now how Servlet Engines can do dynamic updating of servlets—by maintaining a separate ClassLoader per servlet, per web application, per virtual host, or whatever. It's also easy to see how you could roll that functionality into a system which doesn't currently have it—by having the servlet in turn create a new Class-Loader to load the actual servlet class, and reload if the date/time of the .class file on disk is newer than what it was when you loaded it.

- *Be able to incorporate some of those concepts into your own code*
  As an enterprise developer, I get called on to do all sorts of things that don't fit in with the traditional client/server model. I've coded clients that acted more like servers and servers that acted more like clients. I've coded peer-to-peer systems, where everyone is both a client and a server. I've coded servers that had no clients, and clients that had no servers. All of these would break under the traditional J2EE model, but I'm not ready to give up the functionality offered by those systems, such as remote configuration and/or control. By building those concepts into a lightweight application server framework (think GJAS), I can have those features, and still be different.

- *Use the code that comes with the book in your own systems*
  Much of this code grew out of my own experience, and I fully expect that it will continue to change and develop as time goes by. I encourage you to do the same. Use it where appropriate, change it to fit your needs, and discard it when something else works more appropriately. It's just code. There's nothing mysterious or mystical about it.

- *Prepare you for the coming changes in server development*
  You're now in a position to solidly evaluate forthcoming J2EE Application Server products, and better understand precisely what they offer, and what they don't. The application server you're using doesn't support JNI–dependent classes? Use a socket to communicate to another Java process that performs the JNI work for you. Having problems accessing classes loaded from your database inside of the application server? It's probably a ClassLoader-parentage problem. You're now better equipped to understand what the forces are, and how to deal with them.

It may still come as a surprise, however, that this book wasn't more about J2EE and/or more of the buzzword technologies such as EJB, or servlets or JSP. Looking back at what was covered, let's examine the relevance of each of the topics to the J2EE platform and how it all relates:

- *ClassLoaders*

  ClassLoaders still play a fundamental part of any application server, and J2EE will be no different. As programmers, we need to know about separate ClassLoaders and the name spaces they define, so that we understand why the Servlet 2.2 specification prevents us from directly calling methods on another servlet. It represents a security hole, because servlet engines would be extremely hard-pressed to support on-the-fly servlet upgrades if all servlets had to be loaded through a single ClassLoader (in order to support the calling of servlet methods across servlet instances). Furthermore, now that we have a thorough grounding in how the parent-child ClassLoader relationship works, it's easy to see where we could get into namespace troubles if our code is loaded from one ClassLoader, but third-party code used in our application is loaded by a different (peer) ClassLoader.

- *Extensions*

  The Java2 Extension mechanism and the Java Archive (.jar) mechanism define the basis for Java componentry in the J2EE system—servlet applications are now called web applications, and are to be deployed in .war files that contain all of the web application's code and resources. Having examined this in chapter 3, it's fairly easy to see how this is (or could be) simply a .jar file with some extra tags defining particular behavior.

- *Threads*

  Again, knowledge of how the Java Threading mechanism works provides some useful insight into how application servers may help to prevent rogue servlets or EJBs from taking over the CPU and hanging the system. Furthermore, it's also somewhat easier to see why the EJB specification itself prohibits the creation of Threads from within an EJB Bean—if the EJB server/container wants to provide some kind of ThreadPool architecture, to best balance responsiveness with scalability (too few threads, and we have bottlenecks; too many threads, and the overhead of switching between the threads will leave us with no real work time), it needs to make sure that any Threads being created are under its control. The same can be said for servlet engines—if a servlet spins off its own Thread within its code, then when the servlet is unloaded, what do we do with the Thread it created? This also impacts clustering and machine-independence in a big way. If the servlet is unloaded on one machine (in a cluster), and then later reloaded on a different machine, will it start the Thread all over again? What should happen to the old Thread on the original machine? By preventing client code (namely, servlets and/or EJBs) from creating Threads, these issues never arise.

- *Control*

  In the current specification, J2EE says very little about how applications are controlled and/or configured by system administrators; this is more or less left up to the vendors or developers to provide. J2EE does provide for a *deployment descriptor*, an XML file that describes the Enterprise ARchive (.ear) file's type (ejb, java or web), along with other deployment information, but this is primarily baseline-level information necessary, and not in any way able to configure the server application's context-specific configuration properties. For that, the application needs to either configure itself, or provide an interface allowing system administrators to configure it. By creating a single generic system for configuration and/or control, we can make the system adminstrator's life much, much easier as we roll out application after application.

- *Sockets*
  The fundamental backbone of J2EE, Java, even the Internet itself, is the TCP/IP socket. Just about everything ultimately travels over either TCP/IP or UDP/IP sockets from client to server and back again. As we discussed in chapter 6, not all protocols are so complex as to require RMI or CORBA as the underlying protocol. In many cases, a simple text-based protocol can be used to allow clients written in all sorts of languages to communicate with our Java server. More importantly, many legacy systems don't understand RMI or CORBA, but speak just Plain Old Socket; to communicate with them, we need to have our system speak the same.

- *Persistence*
  J2EE doesn't address persistence, except to provide JDBC as an API for developers to use. As of late 1999 Sun was working to provide the Java Data Object specification, which will provide a default object-relational mapping, but JDO will only address storing objects to an RDBMS; not all persistence needs to be to an RDBMS, but can instead be Serialized to disk, across a socket, or even to a column within the RDBMS.

- *Business Objects*
  As mentioned before, Sun is working to provide a default object-relational mapping, but until it becomes available (and standardized), developers will continue to need to provide their own mapping between the object model and the underlying storage model, be it an RDBMS, object-database, or a shared-object system. More importantly, by building the business object model, developers are able to switch between underlying storage models when necessary, and perform optimizations within the storage layer that wouldn't be possible if the layer of encapsulation provided by the Business Object layer weren't present.

- *Middleware*
  Communicating across processes is, and will be for some time to come, a key component in enterprise systems. We're no longer dealing with stand-alone PCs that can share data only via the floppy drive. Everything is interconnected, and the enterprise is all about getting data to the farthest corners of the universe in the shortest amount of time.

- *JNI*

  As much as Sun might like to daydream, Java is not the answer to everything. Believing that every software system should be rewritten in Java is as ludicrous as believing that every building should be torn down just so we can rebuild it using modern power tools. More importantly, Java's emphasis on "Write once, run anywhere" means that there will always be specific features of the underlying operating system or environment that are unique to one particular platform that Java won't natively support. Providing that access—and access to legacy systems outside of Java—through JNI is a win-win situation for all.

As you can see, all of these concepts map directly back into the J2EE specification and technology base in direct fashion. Granted, one can use J2EE (or any of its individual technologies) without having a clear understanding of its underpinnings. Without that knowledge of the fundamentals developers will be, at best, left in the dark when trying to develop an application that doesn't fit the J2EE model perfectly.

More importantly, there will be applications and systems that won't fit the J2EE model, either because they challenge the traditional notion of enterprise systems, or because the developers will simply be unable to use the technologies offered by the J2EE system. In those situations, a knowledge of what the J2EE system does behind the scenes, and why, will provide an invaluable aid in building these home-grown systems.

Sometimes, however, developers and corporations will choose to build a home-grown system instead of making use of an existing application server. Reasons for doing this include:

- *Control*

  Vendors come, vendors go. It's a fact of life in the enterprise computing field that the vendor on which you standardize today may not be in business tomorrow. Or that vendor will have been bought out by a competitor or partner and have their technology deprecated in favor of the purchaser's. Or will simply not have the featureset you require, when you require it, and so on. Vendor failure is a major risk in software development that must be assessed when determining the buy versus build decision. If you build the system from scratch, you have control, and so long as your business remains afloat, so does the software on which you rely.

- *Technical capability*

  If you use an OpenSource or home-grown system, you can tailor the technical capability of the system to your specific needs. For example, if security is of high concern or priority, EJB will fall down completely; it still lacks good security controls. Or, if you need to develop active server implementations that poll on a database or perform scheduled tasks, EJB will fail you—all of its Beans are passive, requiring activation by another process or client to function. By developing a server-side framework and generic server, you retain the ability to add whatever technical capability you require.

- *Technical flexibility*

  Despite the rush to OpenSource solutions, most server-side systems are still closed-source systems, meaning you don't have the ability to access or modify the source to suit your needs. Sometimes a full-fledged server system isn't what you require, but a lighter version of one that can be embedded inside a larger application or system. For example, in order to determine how well computers are working across the enterprise, the IT staff may want to place a lightweight GJAS instance on each machine, running a HeartbeatService to monitor the machine's up- and down-time. From there, a more sophisticated diagnostic service might be feasible, using JNI to call down to OS-specific routines and offer the IT staff some proactive ability in dealing with help-desk requests.

- *EJB immaturity*

  Let's face it: EJB, despite its tremendous hype and enormous market backing, is still an immature technology. This is not to say it's not useful, but that it still has a number of warts to work out before it begins to settle down. For example, the EJB 1.1 draft specification was released less than six months after the 1.0 specification was finalized, and the 1.1 draft already defers a number of points, including JMS support, to the forthcoming 2.0 specification. This means that vendors will be scrambling to catch up on the new features required by the new specifications. What's more, EJB 1.1 made a significant change to the 1.0 specification, requiring that Deployment Descriptors now be specified in XML, where 1.0 left those details up to the vendor. This is a major change, requiring porting time on the part of any clients accustomed to using the vendors' 1.0 approach, and now must adjust to using the 1.1 approach.

  Certainly, most vendors will seek to provide necessary backward compatibility, but that delays the inevitable; it doesn't solve the porting problem. CORBA addresses some of this immaturity problem, but it also suffers from some of the same problems. For example, the CORBA Persistence Service, defined a few years ago, has recently been completely tossed and started over on a 2.0 Persistence Service. The reason? "It was based on a two-level storage model and was extremely complex. In addition, it was not integrated with other services that deal with persistence-related topics like transactions and concurrency."[1] The point? If a group of the finest minds on object persistence can get it wrong the first time around, then it can happen to anybody, any technology, at any time. Rushing out to embrace a technology during its hype period can sometimes lead to fatal results, as the technology moves and shifts to better accommodate its users' needs.

- *Strategic Acceptance*

  Many companies, for some or all of the reasons cited above, are still leery of EJB and other new-fangled technologies; getting approval to use EJB or CORBA may be more

---

[1] *Enterprise CORBA*, p. 36

difficult than getting approval to build something from scratch. In turn, building the system from scratch can incorporate ideas and concepts from EJB and/or CORBA, which can in turn lead into use of EJB and/or CORBA technologies directly.

## WHERE TO GO FROM HERE?

By no means have we exhausted every possible topic in this area; in fact, this has been merely an introduction to the wide possibilities available to Java developers when writing server code. GJAS itself has a long way to go before it begins to offer the kind of functionality that a viable commercial product would or should offer. Examples include:

- *Better location transparency*
  Right now, Services are buried underneath the `IServer` interface, and if a Service provides specialized methods, they are inaccessible outside of the JVM in which they were instantiated. Ideally, we'd be able to access those methods, regardless of the JVM we're in. This is possible by dynamically generating the Server instance when the Service is loaded into the JVM, building shim methods that simply pass the information on to the encapsulated Service target transparently. With RMI this would be a bit trickier, but not impossible. The RMI Server could provide a "`generic_call`" method that takes a String for the name of the method, and an array of Serializable objects that would represent the individual arguments. This would limit the Service to Serializable-only calls, but that would still make it better than what's currently there.[2] Alternatively, we could build the complete RMI stub and skeleton code on the fly, perhaps invoking rmic from within the GJAS code, in something of the same manner as we did for the CompilerClassLoader.

- *Better services*
  It would be relatively trivial to implement the more common TCP/IP socket services in GJAS using SocketServer or ConnectionManager—FTP, TFTP, Telnet, and so on. Once GJAS is Servlet-compliant, it can then run Java Server Pages, as well.

- *EJB server/container support*
  We could build EJB support into GJAS by creating an EJBService, or even breaking it out into an EJBEntityService, an EJBStatefulSessionService, and an EJBStateless-SessionService. It would certainly be a project of some magnitude, but would definitely be easier to attempt within the GJAS framework than by building everything from scratch. Doing so would offer the benefits provided by the standardization EJB promises, as well as the functionality discussed above that EJB lacks.

- *JNDI integration*
  GJAS is a natural candidate as a JNDI service provider—each GJAS instance becomes a Context, and the individual Services running within it are entries

---

[2] In fact, any argument passed into the RMIServerManager to be passed on to the RMIServerManager-Server needs to be Serializable anyway, so no functionality from the current system is lost.

therein. Because JNDI is protocol-independent, we'd need to decide upon a particular protocol to use to communicate from the client to the GJAS server, but that could easily be specified via a property in the JNDI InitialContext constructor, much as JSDT uses its type field.

- *CORBA integration*
  Although it's possible to fire off CORBA server implementations from within a Service, it would be gratifying if GJAS had some slightly better integration with CORBA, perhaps by using the CORBA Naming Service or Trading Service to provide services to other CORBA applications, or use them in turn.

- *Clustering support*
  GJAS, as with any application server, is a natural candidate for basic clustering support, even something as basic as designating a group of JVMs as available nodes for work, and farming out GJAS Services to the JVMs as each new Service comes in. Alternatively, we could also introduce a clustering at the Service level; a Service could spin off multiple instances of itself into other JVMs as its load increased; for example the HttpConnectionManager could, if its Thread pool were exhausted, forward the request on to an HttpConnectionManager instance running on a separate machine, *a la* RedirectorConnection.

- *Activation support*
  A number of these Services will simply sit idle, waiting for clients to connect and use them; for rarely used Services, such as the ControlServices, we could provide an ActivationService, which would listen on a number of ports, and when a request came in, create the Service instance to handle the request. Once the Service is activated the ActivationService would then bow out, until the Service determined that no further requests were coming in and notified the ActivationService of its imminent shutdown. This permits optimal CPU usage when Services aren't being used, while still providing complete availability of a Service.

- *Load balancing support*
  Once the clustering support is present within GJAS, the system could use JNI methods to obtain real-time or near-real-time statistics on the individual CPUs on each node, and make better decisions about where to farm out the next request, rather than doing so in a blind round-robin fashion.

- *Better administrative front-ends*
  Right now, GJAS has only the single front-end to administer and run the GJAS instance. Certainly, more sophisticated and feature-rich implementations are imaginable and feasible.

This is just a partial list; more ideas are certainly possible.

## PARTING ADVICE

Don Box, "COM Guy Extraordinaire" and one of the co-authors of *Effective COM*, offers at the back of that book, some of the best parting advice I've ever heard. Paraphrased to be more appropriate to our Java-centric word, they read like this:

### Be a skeptic

Like it or not, our industry is filled with wild marketing hype, erroneous technical summaries, and thinly-veiled propaganda in the form of "factual reports." Don't believe a thing you hear, see, or read, until you can prove it to yourself. Vendor A's AppServer is ten times faster than Vendor B's, according to Vendor A's marketing material? Ask for an eval CD of both and the code they ran to generate the benchmarks. Read an article that claims Enterprise JavaBeans can't scale? Create a simple test and run it for a week; compare the statistics against a similarly-structured test in some other technology. Be skeptical even when reading this book, or any other—authors, like most people, are human, too, and we'll generally be the first to admit it. We make mistakes. Technology changes. If something you read doesn't jibe with what you've seen or experienced firsthand, don't simply assume you were wrong and I'm right, or vice versa—*prove* it to yourself. Then drop me an email and show me; I don't want to be wrong any more than you do.

### Read all about COM, DCOM, and MTS

COM/DCOM is another object broker. Understanding COM/DCOM will help you to better understand the Java object broker you end up using, EJB or CORBA (or both). MTS is another scalable-application-server technology; understanding MTS will give you insights into EJB.

### Read all about EJB

Enterprise Java Beans are the future direction of enterprise applications. Understanding EJB (and by that, I mean reading the EJB specification itself) will give you insights into when and where EJB technology will be applicable or relevant to your project.

### Read all about CORBA

Java has been hailed as CORBA's saving grace within the realm of distributed object development. Java needs CORBA almost as much as CORBA needs Java. CORBA provides Java with an easy gate to the software bus of CORBA objects, and Java's similar syntax to C++ means that CORBA (which drew much of its inspiration from C++) maps well into Java with only a few stumbles. More importantly, CORBA provides a number of defined services—such as the CosEvent service, the CosTrader service, the CosNaming service, and so on—that Java applications can now make use of, without having to recode them. More importantly, CORBA developers have much richer controls and understanding over distributed object concepts than most Java-RMI developers. RMI tries to provide some of that with Activation, but falls short of some of the functionality provided by CORBA ORBs; in fact, much of the EJB activation/passivation logic is already incorporated into the ORB 2.3 portable object adapter.

### Participate

Join a mailing list. Post to the list, both questions *and* answers, even if you're not sure you're correct. Nothing will drive a point home more forcefully than to post to a mailing list with a possible answer, only to have somebody else correct you with documented fact. Just as participating in a group discussion on a hot topic, such as politics or economics, will expose you to new ideas and perspectives, so will being a part of a mailing list.

## SUMMARY

You came, you read, you conquered. You know how to integrate ClassLoaders, Threads, Sockets, JNI, and middleware into a unified whole. You have a fundamental grounding in the construction of business object models. You are ready to go forth, code like crazy and reap the rewards of a successful project.

And one more element from the parting advice.

Have fun.

# index

# New Java Titles from Manning

# New Java Titles from Manning

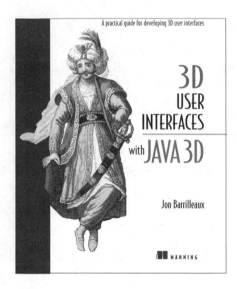